A Treasury of Mahāyāna Sūtras

The Buddhist Association of the United States

Chief Translator:	Fayen Koo
Translators:	Shu-Lien Miao
	Yang-chu Hsu
	Yi-tze Liu
	Kuang-mo Ho
Editors:	V.S. Brown
	Walter Hsieh
	Janet Gyatso
	T.C. Tsao

A Treasury of Mahāyāna Sūtras

Selections from the Mahāratnakūṭa Sūtra

大寶積經

Translated from the Chinese by
The Buddhist Association of the United States

Garma C. C. Chang, General Editor

The Pennsylvania State University Press
University Park and London

Published in cooperation with
The Institute for Advanced Studies of World Religions
New York, N.Y.

Titles in the IASWR Series

Buddhist Monastic Discipline: The Sanskrit Prātimokṣa Sūtras of the Mahāsāṃghikas and Mūlasarvāstivādins, by Charles S. Prebish.

The Holy Teaching of Vimalakīrti: A Mahāyāna Scripture, translated by Robert A. F. Thurman.

Hua-yen Buddhism: The Jewel Net of Indra, by Francis H. Cook.

Sūtra of the Past Vows of Earth Store Bodhisattva: The Collected Lectures of Tripitaka Master Hsüan Hua, translated by Heng Ching.

Avatāra: The Humanization of Philosophy Through the Bhagavad Gītā, by Antonio T. de Nicolás.

Scripture of the Lotus Blossom of the Fine Dharma, translated by Leon Hurvitz.

Library of Congress Cataloging in Publication Data

Tripiṭaka. Sūtrapiṭaka. Ratnakūṭa. English.
Selections.
A treasury of Mahāyāna sūtras.

I. Chang, Chen-chi, 1920– . II. Buddhist
Association of the United States. III. Title.
BQ1752.E5 1983 294.3′85 82-42776
ISBN 0-271-00341-3

Designed by Dolly Carr

Printed in the United States of America

Contents

Acknowledgements

Mr. Kuang-Mo Ho and Ms. Tze-Ming Yang both participated in the translation work for some time. We acknowledge our gratitude to them.

The work of the U.S. team is greatly appreciated. The team members are: Dr. T. Cleary, Mr. D. Fox, Rev. L. Jamspal, Ms. N. A. Larke, Dr. N. Maxwell, Prof. R. Thurman, and Ms. L. Zahler.

Out of his kindness and enthusiasm, Dr. C.T. Shen invited various Buddhist scholars to review certain chapters at the beginning of the translation work. These reviewers are: Dr. T.W. Berry, Prof. R.S.Y. Chi, Rev. Jen Ching, Prof. D. Daye, Dr. C.S. George, Dr. Charles Luk, Prof. W. Pachow, Dr. J. Penley, Dr. W. Stablein, Prof. C.N. Tay, Prof. R. Thurman, Prof. T.C. Tsao, Prof. S.H. Wan, Ms. C. Wu Whang, Dr. T.T. Yi, and in particular, the members of the Sino-American Buddhist Association. In its final stages the work was also reviewed by Dr. J. Gyatso. We are grateful to all for their valuable comments.

Mr. P.C. Ko provided administrative assistance for the Institute, and Ven. Je Hui offered us valuable research assistance. We appreciate their kindness.

We also thank Drs. W.W. Hsu and H.Y. Li for their inspiration in the formation of the Institute.

Ven. Yin Shun, the renown Buddhist scholar, graciously allowed the Institute to use the facilities of Fu Yen Temple in Hsinchu. We thank him for his generosity and for his kind help in interpreting certain passages for the translators.

Prologue

Origin and History of This Work

Many important scriptures of Theravāda Buddhism have been translated into English in the past few decades. However, translations of Mahāyāna sūtras remain scarce, though interest seems to have grown rapidly in recent years. To make the major texts of Mahāyāna Buddhism available to readers of English, Mr. C.T. Shen of the Buddhist Association of the United States launched a project to translate the Chinese Tripiṭaka into English. His aim was to introduce to the West hitherto unavailable Mahāyāna scriptures for general readers, Dharma-seekers, and scholars alike. A team of Chinese scholars in Taiwan was formed to undertake the translation task.

Among the major Mahāyāna sūtra groups, the *Mahāratnakūṭa Sūtra*, the Great Jewel-Heap Sūtra, here rendered *A Treasury of Mahāyāna Sūtras*, is one of the most voluminous. It is actually not one sūtra, but a prodigious collection of forty-nine different sūtras which cover a manifold range of topics. In order to provide a broad perspective of Mahāyāna doctrine, Mr. Shen chose this work as the first to be translated.

Under the leadership of Mr. Shen and Mr. Fayen Koo, the translation of the entire *Mahāratnakūṭa Sūtra*, totalling more than a million words, was completed in the fall of 1976. We, the translators and editors, then faced a very difficult problem: Should we publish the sūtra group in its entirety, or select those sūtras which are most useful to general readers? After much consideration, we decided upon the latter course and selected twenty-two sūtras for publication.

The Role of Mahāyāna Sūtras

Despite the vastness of Mahāyāna literature and its subtle and complex doctrines, the central tenets of the Mahāyāna can be generally summarized under the topics of the perfection and infinity of Buddhahood, and the aspiration for and the path leading to that state. Although the infinity of Buddhahood is usually described by negative terms such as "inconceivable," "unutterable," "beyond the reach of thought," and the like, it can also be described positively, as in the following statement:

> The infinity of Buddhahood is the two-in-one of great wisdom and great compassion; the way that leads to its realization is the practice of those virtues which are in consonance with this wisdom/compassion whole.

The bulk of Mahāyāna sūtras, including the *Mahāratnakūṭa*, present wisdom and compassion as their two cardinal themes. Compassion is perhaps easier to understand, for we have all experienced it at one time or another. However, that which is totally transcendent—the "wisdom that goes beyond," or *prajñāpāramitā*—is almost impossible to explain. How can one understand that which is simultaneously existent and nonexistent, transcendental and mundane, a state often described as totally beyond words and thought?

To express the inexpressible and to enable man to "catch" that which is totally transcendent or empty, Buddhism in the course of history has developed a great variety of methods. As an example, for the intellectually inclined, Mādhyamika philosophy wipes out the limited intellect by rejecting and refuting all philosophical views; when views are abandoned, the door to the understanding of emptiness will eventually open. For those who revolt against Buddhist cliches and prefer a direct approach, Zen Buddhism provides koan exercises, "shock treatment" (in the form of kicks, blows, or enigmatic remarks), and serene reflective meditation. One will thus see penetratingly into one's own mind and thereby awaken to various degrees of Wu or Satori experience.

The problem is that not everyone is inclined to Mādhyamika or Zen, and both these approaches can be misleading and dangerous without proper guidance. The greatest danger of Mādhyamika study is that one may fall into the extreme view of nihilism, or, with one's head stuffed with hair-splitting polemics, become cynical towards everything, including the basic teachings of Buddhism. Eventually this can lead to confusion and a total collapse of faith. The method of Nāgārjuna and his eminent followers was effective in some cases, but there also have been many Dharma-seekers who became pedants and at their death-beds found their entire lives wasted by excessive study of academic Buddhism. By its proliferating pedantry, Mādhyamika had long ceased to be a direct means of liberation; it had become an out-of-date academic discipline with questionable religious and pragmatic values.

Concerning Zen Buddhism, no one can deny its great contribution in bringing thousands to direct realization. Zen is emptiness in action, the living prajñāpāramitā. It is hard to find words to praise Zen adequately. The more one studies and practices Dharma, the more one appreciates and admires Zen. However, without proper guidance and sufficient preparation, Zen can also be dangerous and futile. By misconstruing a pseudo-experience as true enlightenment, one may develop an unwarranted self-conceit. Zen can also induce a devil-may-care attitude and one may eventually lose all ground in one's Dharmic efforts.

The pitfalls of these and other Buddhist schools, however, are not unavoidable; they can easily be eschewed by frequently seeking guidance in the sūtras. Buddhist sūtras are rather plain and evident; they contain straightforward Dharma teaching, often in the form of dialogues, with an occasional insertion of an allegory to illustrate a specific point. Therefore, they are least likely to be misunderstood. Although we cannot claim that Mahāyāna sūtras are simple enough to be easily understood by everyone, it is quite obvious that they are relatively easier to understand than the literature of Mādhyamika and Zen. Furthermore, sūtras are the source of all Buddha-Dharmas; all Buddhist schools (including Mādhyamika and Zen) look upon the sūtras as their guide and final arbiter. This is why we have given first priority to the translation of the sūtras.

Special Characteristics of the *Mahāratnakūṭa Sūtra*

In working with the *Mahāratnakūṭa*, we observed the following points:

1. We have found this work to contain a broad coverage of various subjects. The topics discussed range from the monastic precepts (Vinaya) to intuitive wisdom (*prajñā*), from good deportment to the manifestation of the Tathāgata's light, from illusion (*māyā*) and ingenuity (*upāya*) to the nature of consciousness and the Pure Land practice. It can perhaps be called a small encyclopedia of Mahāyāna Buddhism, which should be useful to general readers as well as to scholars.

2. Emptiness, or *śūnyatā*, is the outstanding, if not unique teaching of Buddhism. It is the central pillar of the Mahāyāna edifice, and every Buddhist school has its own way of dealing with this doctrine. Here in the *Mahāratnakūṭa*, we find elaborate discussions on emptiness in different settings, from different angles, and with different interpretations. It is perhaps one of the most elaborate documents on emptiness in Buddhist literature. Through the introduction of Prajñāpāramitā, Mādhyamika, and Zen literature, the doctrine of emptiness is already familiar in the West; nevertheless, we believe that this book will enhance the understanding of the teaching of emptiness and its far-reaching significance.

3. The modern reader will most likely find fault with the *Mahāratnakūṭa*

Sūtra for its repetitiousness, stereotyped formulas, and excessive numerical lists of maxims. As far as literary style is concerned, we are sympathetic to these criticisms. On the other hand, it should be noted that many of these shortcomings in literary style are not without value for religious practice, because through repeated reading and mindfulness, new religious insight can come forth. It is common Buddhist experience that realization can be engendered through long years of frequent recitation of sūtras. Therefore, the purpose of reading a Buddhist sūtra is not only to grasp its meaning, but also to acquire religious insight and experience. To achieve this one should not just read the sūtra once and digest the information therein, but should read it again and again, even out loud, so that the words of the sūtra become totally absorbed into one's subconscious mind. This is tantamount to letting the sūtra take over the mind and run its course to reach the beyond. It is for this reason that the intentional repetition in Buddhist scriptures should not be treated entirely as a defect, but rather as a constructive and beneficial method for Dharma practice.

Nevertheless, to avail the modern readers who may not be able to appreciate the volume of repetition in this sūtra, we have adopted two ways of handling the text:

a. The texts which we felt are significant and readable were left intact.

b. We made some deletions in those sūtras which have portions that are extremely prolix, repetitious, or insignificant in our view. Most of the deletions involve only a few sentences; in a few cases a page or two were left out. All deletions have been indicated by the insertion of three ellipsis points in the appropriate hiatus.

4. In our translation of the *Mahāratnakūṭa* we have attempted consistently to offer the closest English rendering of the original text. However, in those cases where a technical term has too broad a meaning to be adequately represented by an equivalent English term, we have retained the Sanskrit word. The reader is urged to consult the glossary at the end of this volume for all Sanskrit terms, as well as for a variety of English phrases which have a special meaning in Buddhism. A numerical glossary has also been provided for the standard lists of items of Buddhist doctrine.

A Brief Introduction to the Selected Texts

The *Mahāratnakūṭa Sūtra* in its present form as found in the Chinese Tripiṭaka consists of forty-nine sūtras.[1] They are not grouped together in different sections

1. For a summary of the history of the *Mahāratnakūṭa* texts, see K. Priscilla Pedersen, "Notes on the *Ratnakūṭa* Collection", *Journal of the International Association of Buddhist Studies*, Vol. 3, No. 2 (1980):60–66. For an analysis of the various translations of the collection, see Richard A. Gard, ed., *Buddhist Text Information,* No. 20 (June 1979):1–11; No. 22 (December 1979):5–8; No. 28 (June 1980):5–11; and following issues.

according to their contents, nor to a chronological order. Why these sūtras are arranged in their present sequence and form remains a puzzle to us. We have consulted many scholars but failed to find a satisfactory answer. Our guess is that the forty-nine sūtras were collected haphazardly throughout the ages without a premeditated plan or scheme. Therefore, to facilitate comprehension we have taken the liberty to re-group the selected twenty-two sūtras into eight sections according to their contents, and a new table of contents has been provided to substitute for the traditional Chinese arrangement. A few words of introduction to these sūtras are given below.

Section I: On Māyā and Miracles

This topic is elucidated by the story of the magician Bhadra's contest of magic power with the Buddha. The emphasis here is that the Buddha's superior power is not attained through spells, magic formulas, deity worship, or even meditation power. It is attained, rather, through the full realization of illusion (*māyā*) and the cultivation of virtues and altruistic deeds. The central theme of Mahāyāna Buddhism, the cultivation and perfection of wisdom and compassion, is stressed here.

Section II: On Emptiness

Nine sūtras were selected to cover this teaching. Emptiness can be illustrated by one word, e.g., the vowel *Ā*; by one stanza, e.g., the first gāthā of the *Mādhyamikakārikā*; by one sheet of paper, e.g., the *Heart Sūtra*, or through the innumerable volumes of Prajñāpāramitā literature. The contents and depth of emptiness are regarded by Buddhists as all-embracing and inexhaustible, and its teaching is the basis of Mādhyamika, Zen, and most other schools of Mahāyāna. It is our hope that the nine sūtras included herein may further understanding and appreciation of this all-important subject.

Section III: On the Light of the Tathāgata

Among the twenty-two sūtras presented in this volume, *The Manifestation of Lights* is perhaps the most difficult one to comprehend. The central question is: What is this so-called "light"? Is it simply a certain kind of luminous entity such as rays or beams of light, or is it the spiritual illumination, the so-called "mystical light" testified to by many mystics? To give an exact answer is difficult. Noticeably, the lights treated in this sūtra seem to denote all the dynamic aspects of Buddhahood, i.e., the Saṁbhogakāya and Nirmāṇakāya, and all merits and functions of Tathāgatahood are expressed in terms of light. One even has the impression that all essential principles of Mahāyāna Buddhism are given in terms of this light.

In general, religious experience and achievement are often linked with light. Words such as 'illumination,' 'enlightenment,' 'revelation,' and so forth all imply that these experiences are somehow or other related to light. The Old Testament states that God is spirit and God is light. Buddha Amitābha means 'Infinite Light.'

We can even go so far as to say that in Buddhism, all achievements in meditation and intuitive-cognition practice (*śamatha-vipaśyanā*) can be appraised by the realization of different kinds or degrees of light. The exact meaning, implication and significance of the various lights reported in this sūtra are perhaps beyond our ken at present, but we believe that the material here will be of importance to students of religious studies in the years to come.

Section IV: On Consciousness

The reader will find that the consciousness discussed in this sūtra is in many ways similar to the Yogācāra idea of the store consciousness (*ālayavijñāna*). It is our belief that this sūtra is one of the forerunners or germinal sources of the Mind-Only philosophy of the Yogācāra school. As is stated here, "The consciousness is devoid of form and substance, yet it manifests itself by feelings and conception, . . . it upholds all the dharmadhātu, . . . it is fully endowed with the power of wisdom and can even know events of past lives. . . . Consciousness is the seed which can bring forth the sprout of various bodily forms as a result of karma. Perception, awareness, conception, and memory are all comprised in the consciousness. . . ." Here, we clearly see the precursor of the store consciousness theory. For those who are interested in the Buddhist view on consciousness, this sūtra should be a useful reference.

Section V: On Virtue and Discipline

Two short sūtras were selected to introduce the basic moral codes of Buddhism; both texts are simple and routine. The *Definitive Vinaya* is a very significant sūtra; it expounds upon the fundamental principle and spirit of the Bodhisattva-path and spells out the differences between the Bodhisattva's Vinaya and that of the Śrāvaka. The moral principles of the Mahāyāna are also set forth here. *Abiding in Good and Noble Deportment Sūtra* attempts to define the true śramaṇa; it also gives detailed descriptions of various kinds of monks. To most people, the required standard for the perfect monk as set forth here may be too rigorous, even frightening, but to those who are seriously interested in leading a monk's life, or in studying monasticism, this sūtra may serve as a valuable reference.

Section VI: On Pure Land

In the *Mahāratnakūṭa*, there are two sūtras concerning Buddha's Pure Land; both are included here in our selection. Since the majority of people cannot successfully perform the meditation and intuitive observation practice, nor lead an ascetic monastic life, the alternative path of Pure Land practice is provided. By the power of the original vows of Buddha, such a practitioner is assured rebirth in a Pure Land, which is not considered to be a heaven or celestial paradise, but rather an ideal training ground for furthering one's journey toward enlightenment. According to

Buddhist tradition, there are innumerable Buddha's Pure Lands in the infinite universes. Two samples are described in the *Mahāratnakūṭa*; one sūtra contains a discussion of Buddha Amitābha's Pure Land in the western direction, and the other that of Buddha Akṣobhya in the east.

Section VII: On General Mahāyāna Doctrines

The True Lion's Roar of Queen Śrīmālā Sūtra is a short but quintessential text covering many important teachings of Mahāyāna Buddhism. There are already several translations of it in English. Some passages in this sūtra are extremely obscure. We hope that our translation and notes will facilitate further studies of this text.

The Sūtra of Assembled Treasures is the original *Ratnakūṭa Sūtra*. It gives various admonishments to the followers of Mahāyāna, expounds on the right observation of the Middle Way, and discusses the various kinds of śramaṇas.

Dialogue with Bodhisattva Infinite Wisdom. This sūtra defines the transcendental bodhicitta, deliberates on the merits and achievement of the ten stages, and describes the various visions acquired by the Bodhisattvas in the ten successive stages.

Section VIII: On the Pāramitā of Ingenuity

Upāya (方便) is difficult to translate into English properly. It has been rendered as skillfulness, ingenuity, expediency, and so forth, but none of these translations can cover the broad implications of the word. In this sūtra, the basic meaning and specific implications of upāya are discussed. Since the advanced Bodhisattvas have all perfected their upāya, how can they ever make any mistakes or blunders? A meaningless or accidental act by an enlightened Bodhisattva is unthinkable. Hence, the author of this sūtra is compelled to explain every deed of Gautama Buddha teleologically. When a religious leader is deified, new problems ensue. This is perhaps universal. We believe that this sūtra will be highly interesting to those who are interested in the comparative study of religions and in the history of the development of Buddhist thought.

Garma C.C. Chang
University Park, Pennsylvania

I

On Māyā and Miracles

1 授幻師跋陀羅記會

The Prophecy of the Magician Bhadra's Attainment of Buddhahood

Thus have I heard. Once the Buddha was dwelling on Mount Gṛdhrakūṭa near Rājagṛha, accompanied by twelve hundred fifty great monks who were Arhats known to all, and five thousand Bodhisattva-Mahāsattvas who had achieved great, miraculous powers to perform magical feats at will; had achieved the Realization of the Nonarising of Dharmas; and had acquired dhāraṇīs. They were led by Bodhisattva Lion, Bodhisattva Lion Wisdom, Bodhisattva Wonderful Sandalwood, Bodhisattva Subduer, Bodhisattva Great Subduer, Bodhisattva Superior Light, Bodhisattva Revealing Light, Bodhisattva Dignified Light, Bodhisattva Adorned with Light, Bodhisattva Bright Enlightenment, Bodhisattva Assembly Leader, Bodhisattva Subduer of Sentient Beings, all the Bodhisattvas of the Worthy Kalpa, Bodhisattva-Mahāsattva Maitreya, the Dharma Prince Mañjuśrī, and others. They were surrounded by the Four Great Deva Kings; Śakra; Brahmā, master of the Sahā World; and incalculable numbers of gods, dragons, yakṣas, asuras, gandharvas, kinnaras, mahoragas, and so forth.[1]

The Tathāgata, the World-Honored One, was renowned throughout the world as the Tathāgata, the Worthy One, the Supremely Enlightened One, the One Perfect in Learning and Conduct, the Well-Gone One, the World-Knower, the Unexcelled One, the Great Tamer, the Teacher of Gods and Humans, the Buddha, the World-Honored One, the All-Knowing One, the All-Seeing One. He had achieved the ten powers, the four fearlessnesses, the four kinds of unimpeded understanding, and the eighteen unique qualities of a Buddha. He had great kindness and great compassion, possessed all the five kinds of eyes, and was perfect in

Sūtra 21, Taishō shinshū daizōkyō 310, pp. 486–492; translated into Chinese by Bodhiruci.

the miraculous ability to admonish people, to teach them the Dharma, and to wield magical powers.[2]

He could set on a hair's tip a billion-world universe, with all its earths, cities, meadows, trees, forests, Mount Sumerus, oceans, rivers, and celestial palaces; he also could make the universe remain uplifted in space without tilting or moving at all for one kalpa, more than one kalpa, or as long as he wished.

At that time, the king, ministers, brāhmins, lay devotees, and subjects in the city of Rājagṛha all held the Tathāgata in great esteem and respectfully offered him the best beverages, food, clothing, bedding, and medicine.

In that city lived a magician named Bhadra, who was well versed in heterodox doctrines, skilled at using spells, and was the foremost magician in the city. Everyone in the kingdom of Magadha was bewitched by him and believed in him, except those who had realized the truth, and the laymen and laywomen of right faith.

Learning of the merits and reputation of the Tathāgata, the magician thought, "Now, all the people in this city revere me, except Śramaṇa Gautama,[3] who has not yet been converted to my way. I should go challenge him to a contest. If he yields to me, I will be even more respected by the people in the kingdom of Magadha."

At that time, the good seeds the magician had sown in his previous lives were maturing, and by the blessing of the Buddha's awesome, virtuous power, Bhadra left the city of Rājagṛha for Gṛdhrakūṭa. There he saw the light of the Buddha, which surpassed hundreds of thousands of suns; the handsome face of the Buddha, which was like a full moon; the perfect body of the Buddha, which was as well proportioned as a banyan tree; the white hair between the Buddha's eyebrows, which was as pure as a brilliant pearl; and the Buddha's eyes, which were deep blue, like a blue lotus flower. The top of the Buddha's head could not be seen even by those in the Brahmā Heaven. With his pure voice of sixty qualities,[4] he was preaching the Dharma to the multitude.

Although the magician saw the extraordinary, awe-inspiring majesty of the Tathāgata, he remained arrogant. He thought to himself, "I should test him now. If he is the All-Knowing One and the All-Seeing One, he will know my intention."

With this thought in mind, he approached the Buddha, prostrated himself with his head at the Buddha's feet, and said, "May the Tathāgata accept my meager offering tomorrow."

Seeing that the time had come for the good roots of the magician and the other sentient beings in the city of Rājagṛha to mature, the World-Honored One accepted the invitation in silence for the purpose of bringing those good roots to maturity.

When the magician saw that the World-Honored One had accepted his invitation, he thought, "Gautama does not know my intention; he is definitely not an All-Knowing One." Then he bowed and took his leave.

The Venerable Maudgalyāyana[5] was in the assembly at that time and saw what had happened. He approached the Buddha and said to him, "Bhadra intends to deceive the Tathāgata and the monks. May the World-Honored One decline his invitation!"

The Buddha told Maudgalyāyana, "Do not think in this way. Only those who have desire, hatred, and ignorance can be deceived, but I eradicated those defilements long ago, for I realized that not a single dharma ever arises. I have been firmly abiding in right action for many kalpas. How can anyone deceive me?

"Now, you should know that the magician does not perform real magic, but the Tathāgata does. Why? Because the Tathāgata realizes here and now that all dharmas are illusory. Even if all sentient beings were as skilled in magic as Bhadra, all their magical powers combined could not compare with those of the Tathāgata, even if their powers were multiplied by a hundred, a thousand, or any amount, numerical or figurative."

The Buddha asked Maudgalyāyana, "What do you think? Can the magician magically produce a billion-world universe and magnificently adorn all of it?"

Maudgalyāyana answered, "No."

The Buddha said, "Maudgalyāyana, you should know that I can magically produce magnificently adorned worlds, as numerous as the sands of the Ganges, inside a hair's tip, and even this does not exhaust the Tathāgata's miraculous powers.

"Maudgalyāyana, you should know that there is a great wind wheel[6] called Breaker that can break a billion-world universe to pieces.

"There is another wind wheel called Great Hurricane that can ruin worlds and then rebuild them.

"There is another wind wheel called Propeller that can revolve worlds.

"There is another wind wheel called Secure Abiding that can blow as high as the Akaniṣṭha Heaven.

"There is another wind wheel called Scatterer that can whirl away and scatter Mount Sumeru, the Black Mountain, and other mountains.

"There is another wind wheel called Fierce Flame that can blow fierce flames up to the Brahmā Heaven during the raging conflagration at the end of a kalpa.

"There is another wind wheel called Quencher that can quench the raging conflagration at the end of a kalpa.

"There is another wind wheel called Cool that can cause a cloud to cover a billion-world universe.

"There is another wind wheel called Universal Downpour that can pour down heavy rains on the worlds during the raging conflagration at the end of a kalpa.

"Moreover, there is a wind wheel called Drying Up that can dry up the spreading flood at the end of a kalpa. There are so many wind wheels that I could not finish enumerating them even if I spoke until the end of this kalpa. All this, Maudgalyāyana, you should know.

"What do you think? Can the magician dwell securely in any of these wind wheels for a moment?"

Maudgalyāyana answered, "No."

The Buddha told Maudgalyāyana, "The Tathāgata can walk, stand, sit, and lie undisturbed in the wind wheels. The Tathāgata can also put those wind wheels into a mustard seed and display their motions without the mustard seed either expanding or contracting, and without the wind wheels in the seed obstructing each other. Maudgalyāyana, you should know that the feats of magic accomplished by the Tathāgata have no limit."

When the Venerable Mahāmaudgalyāyana and the assembly heard the Tathāgata's words, they were all overwhelmed by wonder and awe. They all bowed down before the Buddha and exclaimed in unison, "Because we have now met the great Teacher who has these awe-inspiring miraculous powers, we are greatly blessed. One who has an opportunity to hear of the wonderful miraculous powers of the Tathāgata, the World-Honored One, and generates profound faith and understanding will certainly gain great blessings and bring forth a vow to attain supreme enlightenment."

That evening, the magician Bhadra went to the lowliest and dirtiest place in the city of Rājagṛha and conjured up a very spacious, level, square site for teaching the Dharma, adorned with banners and canopies of colored silk, permeated with the fragrance of flowers, and covered by a jewelled tent. He also magically produced eight thousand rows of jewelled trees. Under each jewelled tree was a lion-throne. There were also numerous splendid cushioned seats. As offerings to the monks, he further produced by magic hundreds of courses of the most delicious food and drink, and five hundred servants dressed in white, ornamented clothing.

When these magical feats had been performed, the Four Deva Kings came to the site and told the magician, "In order to make offerings to the Tathāgata tomorrow, you have magically produced these innumerable, beautiful things. Because of this, you have achieved great merit. Now, in order to help you make offerings to the Tathāgata, we wish to produce by magic a second site for teaching the Dharma. Will you allow us to do so?"

Hearing this, the magician felt curious, and he gave them permission at once. Thereupon, the Four Deva Kings magically produced myriads of wonderful ornaments, twice as many as the magician had produced.

Then Śakra, king of gods, together with thirty thousand of his celestial subjects, came to the site and told the magician, "I, too, wish to adorn the site, because you are making offerings to the Tathāgata." Astounded, the magician gave him permission, too. Thereupon Śakra, for the sake of the Tathāgata, magically produced a hall as splendid as the palace in the Heaven of the Thirty-Three. He also magically produced pārijāta trees, kovidāra trees,[7] and other beautiful, celestial trees, arranged in orderly rows.

Seeing all these, the magician exclaimed in wonder and felt remorse. He wished to withdraw the things he had conjured up, but they remained as they were, in spite of all his spells. "This is very strange," he thought. "In the past I could at will make my magical productions appear or disappear. But now I cannot make these go away! This is surely because they are offerings for the Tathāgata."

Reading the magician's thoughts, Śakra told him, "Yes, indeed. It is because of the Tathāgata that you cannot make your magnificent teaching site disappear. Therefore, you should know that if one brings forth even a single thought of the Tathāgata, that good root will eventually act as a cause for that person's attainment of parinirvāṇa."

When he heard Śakra say this, the magician was very glad. The next morning, he went to the Tathāgata and said, "World-Honored One, now I have finished making all the preparations. Please be so kind as to come."

Thus, on that morning, the World-Honored One put on his robe, took up his bowl, and went into the city of Rājagṛha to the magician's teaching site, together with the assembly that respectfully surrounded him.

The heterodox, the brāhmins, and others in the kingdom of Magadha who wanted the Tathāgata to be deceived by the magician all came to the site hoping to see that occur. At the same time, many monks, nuns, laymen, and laywomen also came, because they all wanted to see the miraculous feats of the Tathāgata and to hear him preach in a lion's roar.

Then the Tathāgata, by his miraculous powers, caused the magician, Śakra, and the Four Deva Kings to see the World-Honored One simultaneously at each of the places they had adorned.

Seeing this, the magician cast away his arrogance and pride. He approached the Buddha, prostrated himself at his feet, and said, "World-Honored One, now I repent and confess my wrongdoing in the presence of the Tathāgata. Blinded by ignorance, I have tried to deceive the Buddha by conjuring up various magnificent adornments. Although I now feel remorseful, I cannot make my magical creations disappear."

The World-Honored One told the magician, "All sentient beings and material objects are illusory, like magic, conjured up by karma; all the monks are also illusory, like magic, conjured up by the Dharma; my body is also illusory, like magic, conjured up by wisdom; a billion-world universe is also illusory, like magic, conjured up by all sentient beings as a whole; all dharmas are illusory, like magic, conjured up by combinations of causes and conditions.

"Now you should offer to these people one by one the beverages and food you have produced by your magic."

Thereupon, the magician, the Four Deva Kings, Śakra, their retinues, and their magically produced servants offered the beverages and food to the Buddha and the Saṃgha. They provided fully for everyone in the assembly.

Then Mahākāśyapa spoke in verse:

"Food is illusory:
Recipients, too, are illusions.
When a giver comprehends their equality,
His giving may be called pure."

Mahāmaudgalyāyana spoke in verse:

"Seats are illusory:
Those seated upon them, too, are illusions.
When a giver comprehends their equality,
His giving may be called pure."

Śāriputra spoke in verse:

"Servants are illusory:
The minds of those served, too, are illusions.
When a giver comprehends this truth,
His giving may be called pure."

Subhūti spoke in verse:

"Do not see giving as giving,
Nor regard receiving as receiving.
If a giver can do this,
His giving may be called pure."

Ānanda spoke in verse:

"Gifts are empty, like space,
And no recipient can be found.
When a giver is detached from body and mind,
His giving is purest."

Bodhisattva Banner of Light spoke in verse:

"All dharmas are illusory,
Like the adornments
Conjured up by the magician,
But this is beyond the awareness of fools."

Bodhisattva Adorned with Light spoke in verse:

"Seats and trees are all produced
By an illusory mind.
What difference can there be
Between an illusory mind and empty space?"

Bodhisattva Lion spoke in verse:

"A jackal is fearless
Before it hears the lion's roar,
And growls and howls among the trees.
But once it hears the lion's roar,
It will be at a loss to hide or run.

It is just so with the magician:
Before he met the Tathāgata,
He boasted to the heretics
Of his superiority over the Buddha.

Though the magician can conjure up objects,
His magical power is limited.
Not so with the magical power of the Buddha,
Which can never be exhausted;
No god or demon
Can know its bounds."

Bodhisattva Lion Wisdom spoke in verse:

"To know that food, drink,
Servants, and those who partake
Are all illusory, like magic,
Is the best offering of all."

Bodhisattva Maitreya spoke in verse:

"Just as a fire is intensified
When oil is poured upon it,
So the World-Honored One's magic
Is magnified by comparison with the magician's."

Bodhisattva Mañjuśrī spoke in verse:

"All virtuous deeds done in this assembly
Have never come into being;
So it is with all dharmas:
Empty, and passed into nought
In the forever unobtainable past."[8]

At that time, the World-Honored One, in order to bring Bhadra the magician to maturity, magically produced an elder approaching the assembly. The man asked Bhadra, "What are you doing here?"

The magician answered, "I am making offerings of food and beverages to Śramaṇa Gautama."

The elder told him, "Do not say that. Right now, the Tathāgata and the monks are taking the food offered to them in the palace of King Ajātaśatru." Thereupon, by the miraculous power of the Buddha, the magician was able to see the Tathāgata and the monks feasting there.

Then the World-Honored One magically created a second elder, who also asked the magician, "What are you doing here?"

The magician answered, "I am making offerings to Śramaṇa Gautama."

The second elder said, "Do not say that. Right now, the Tathāgata and the monks are begging for food in the streets where the heterodox believers live." By the miraculous power of the Buddha, the magician was able to see the Tathāgata and his venerable followers making the rounds of the streets begging for food.

Then the World-Honored One produced magically a third elder, who told the magician, "Right now, the Tathāgata is teaching the wonderful Dharma to the four kinds of devotees in the garden of Jīva, the most prominent physician." Thereupon, by the miraculous power of the Buddha, the magician was able to see the Tathāgata there.

Then the World-Honored One created by magic a śakra, who came to the magician and said, "Right now, the Tathāgata is teaching the Dharma to the assembly in the Heaven of the Thirty-Three." The magician again saw the Tathāgata, this time teaching the essence of the Dharma to a host of gods.

He also beheld the Tathāgata, endowed with the thirty-two auspicious signs and the eighty minor ones, simultaneously present among the trees, flowers, and foliage; upon countless lion-thrones; amid the walled streets in the city of Rājagṛha; and in houses, halls, and other superior places. He also saw himself, in all the places where the Tathāgata was, repenting and confessing his wrongdoings.

Then the magician saw nothing except the Buddha everywhere. He was overwhelmed with joy, whereupon he attained the Samādhi of the Recollection of the Buddha.[9]

Coming out of samādhi, he joined his palms toward the Buddha and spoke in verse:

"In the past, my conjurations
Were thought to be unexcelled in the world,
But now I see they cannot compare
With even a tiny part
Of the miraculous powers of the Buddha.

Now I know how inconceivable
Are the Buddha's miraculous powers.
He can at will produce
Manifested Buddhas as innumerable
As the sands of the Ganges.

All the Tathāgatas that I see
Have the same auspicious signs.

May the World-Honored One show me
Which one is the real Buddha.

I wish to make offerings
To [one of] these Tathāgatas.
May the World-Honored One tell me
Which will lead me to reap the supreme fruit.

Ordinary people who do not esteem the Buddha
Will forfeit peace and happiness.
Now, in the presence of the World-Honored One,
I confess I have committed
The sin of foolishly testing the Tathāgata.
I hope this misdeed will be forever annulled.

May Brahmā, Śakra, and the assembly
All bear witness for me:
In order to deliver sentient beings,
I now make a solemn vow to strive for bodhi.

I shall enlighten all beings
With the light of wisdom;
I shall give them the nectar of Dharma,
And fill the entire world with it.

How can a sensible person not aspire to bodhi
When he sees the Buddha perform
Such miraculous feats,
Hears his pleasant words, and witnesses
His wonderful deeds and unimpeded wisdom?

May the World-Honored One show me
The way to bodhi and all pure deeds.

Pray show me the [superior] devotion
Which is beyond Śrāvakas and Pratyekabuddhas.

In what should one abide when practicing the Dharma?
How can one always win respect and offerings?
How can one be dignified in demeanor?
How should one remove doubts and regrets,
Seek wide learning tirelessly,
And firmly establish oneself in it?

How can one teach others the true Dharma
And cause them to delight in it?
How can one teach without
Expecting material rewards?

How can one be grateful and return favors?
How can one always be
A permanent friend of sentient beings?
How can one avoid bad company
And associate with good friends?

How can one meet Buddhas
And make offerings without weariness?

What are the right subjects of study
And how can one esteem and sanctify them?
What are the essential elements to produce samādhi?

How can one achieve a mind
In harmony with the truth,
And cast away the mind
In discord with the truth?
How can one acquire right thought?
How can one be free of timidity and weakness
And become invulnerable to demons?

How should one contemplate the meaning of the Dharma?
How can one never forsake sentient beings?
What is to be preserved?
What should be embraced without clinging?

How can one practice right action
And be endowed with ingenuity?

How can one cultivate kindness and compassion,
Achieve miraculous powers,
Realize unimpeded eloquence,
And acquire dhāraṇīs?

How can one attain the realization of the Dharma truth[10]
And obtain pure eloquence?
How should one abandon what must be abandoned?
How can one penetrate the profound doctrines?
How can one fulfill vows and aspirations,
And gain nonregression from the pāramitās?

I am willing to practice
All Dharmas with diligence.
May the Honored One of great compassion
Explain them for me."

The World-Honored One answered in verse:

"If one knows that all dharmas
Are like magic and illusions,
He is able to produce magically
The bodies of ten billion Buddhas
And deliver beings in millions of lands,
Just as by magic Bhadra can conjure up
Various things out of nothing.

Things do not arise or cease;
Nor do they abide, come, or go.
The same is true of the monks
And the transformation bodies[11] of Buddhas;
They neither come into being nor perish,
Nor attain nirvāṇa.
All these are the Tathāgata's
Inconceivable miracles.

Troops mounted on elephants or horses
Conjured up by a magician
Are mistaken for real
By confused sentient beings.
In truth, these mounted troops
Have no entity and do not arise.
Similarly, Buddhas have no real appearance;
They neither go nor come.

Those who hold a view of a self
Wrongly conceive an idea of the Buddha.
One cannot contemplate the Tathāgata
According to appearance, caste,
Birthplace, or pure voice;
Nor can one discriminate Buddhas
By the mind or consciousness.

The Dharma-body of the Buddhas
Transcends all time.
It is by nature free of all forms
And beyond all categories of dharmas.

Magically produced Tathāgatas
By nature do not arise;
Nor have they aggregates, entrances, or elements.[12]
They do not depend on anything.
Similarly, the Dharma-body of the Buddhas
Cannot be seen with the five kinds of eyes.

If you claim you see a Buddha,
You see no Buddha at all.
See the Buddha as you see the unseeable;
See him like the trace of a bird flying in the sky.

The Buddhas you see
And the others you do not
Are equal and like empty space.
They are identical,
Utterly indistinguishable.

All Tathāgatas are undifferentiated
In their merits of discipline,
meditation, wisdom, liberation,
And the knowledge and views
Derived from liberation.[13]
They all abide in emptiness
And are detached from all dharmas.
They are illusory, like magic,
Without a nature, and do not arise.

To make offerings to one Tathāgata
Is to make offerings to countless Buddhas,
For the Dharma-body of all Buddhas
Is everywhere equal and undifferentiated.

Therefore, all Buddhas can confer
Great blessings and benefits.
Making offerings to any Tathāgata,
[Real or magically produced,]
Will yield great fruit.

Since all Tathāgatas have realized
The equal, pure Dharma-nature,
They are one, without any difference.

You asked which is the true Buddha;
Cast aside your distracted mind
And heed my words.

Abide in the wisdom of right mindfulness
And observe all dharmas:
Nothing arises at all,
But dharmas are mistaken for real.

If form arose, then it would cease.
Tathāgatas do not arise in any way,

And have never in the past arisen;
Therefore, they will not cease to be.

Contemplate the Tathāgata in this way;
See him as you do the unseeable;
Then will you find that the Buddhas you see
Abide nowhere.

Upon the five aggregates
Do all ordinary men depend.
Contemplate the aggregates
As you do the Buddhas!

Then will you find
That Buddhas, dharmas, and sentient beings
Have as their form the absence of form;
They depend upon nought.

If you take such a view,
You will soon realize enlightenment.

No dharmas in truth exist;
They arise from false discrimination.
Causes and conditions are empty in essence,
For they lack a self which acts.
One who comprehends this
Will comprehend the unsullied, pure Dharma,
And see Tathāgatas with the clear Dharma-eye."

When the magician had heard this, he achieved the Realization of Compliance with the Dharma Truth. Also, five thousand sentient beings brought forth supreme bodhicitta,[14] and two hundred Bodhisattvas reached the Realization of the Nonarising of Dharmas.

After the World-Honored One had taken his meal, he again spoke in verse in order to fulfill the magician's wish:

"Giving without discriminating
A thing given, a giver, or a recipient[15]
Is perfect giving."

Then Ānanda said to the Buddha, "World-Honored One, we hope that the Tathāgata, with his miraculous powers, will help the magician to make the magnificent things he has magically produced remain for seven days."

At the request of the assembly, the Tathāgata caused that teaching site to remain well adorned for a full seven days.

Then the Tathāgata, surrounded respectfully by the monks, great Bodhisattvas, gods, dragons, yakṣas, gandharvas, and so forth, returned to Mount Gṛdhrakūṭa to teach the Dharma to the assembly.

Later, the magician came to the Buddha again. He prostrated himself with his head at the Buddha's feet, circumambulated him three times to the right, withdrew to one side, and said, "World-Honored One, please explain the Bodhisattva-path so that those who study and practice industriously may rapidly arrive at the bodhi-site."

The Buddha said, "Listen attentively and think well about this. I will explain it to you."

The magician said, "Yes, World-Honored One, I will listen with joy."

The Buddha said, "Good man, there are four things that constitute the path of a Bodhisattva. By practicing them, a Bodhisattva will rapidly arrive at the bodhi-site. What are the four?

(1) Never to retreat from or lose bodhicitta;
(2) never to forsake sentient beings;
(3) to seek all good roots without becoming weary or satiated; and
(4) most vigorously to protect and uphold the true Dharma. . . .

"Furthermore, there are four things which only Bodhisattvas can practice, and which Śrāvakas and Pratyekabuddhas cannot practice. What are the four?

(1) To cultivate dhyāna[16] without hoping to be reborn in the dhyāna heavens;[17]
(2) to be able to recognize the profound doctrines;
(3) to have great compassion for sentient beings; and
(4) to teach the Dharma without hindrance by using various kinds of eloquence. . . .

"Furthermore, there are four things that can cause a Bodhisattva to become a permanent friend of sentient beings. What are the four?

(1) To wear the great armor of patience;
(2) to benefit sentient beings without expecting any reward;
(3) never to regress from great compassion; and
(4) never to forsake even those who often annoy and hurt him.

"Moreover, there are four things that can cause a Bodhisattva to meet Buddhas. What are the four?

(1) To be mindful of Buddhas constantly and single-mindedly;
(2) to praise the merits of the Tathāgatas;
(3) to be completely flawless in observing the precepts that have been taken; and
(4) to make great vows with supreme aspiration. . . .

"Furthermore, there are four things that are the essential elements to produce samādhi. What are the four?

(1) To stay away from noisy crowds;
(2) to delight in quietude and peace;
(3) to be mentally undistracted; and
(4) to increase one's good roots.

"Moreover, there are four things that a Bodhisattva should cultivate well in order to have right thought. What are the four?

(1) To suffer willingly the pain of saṁsāra for innumerable kalpas, even for the sake of only one sentient being;
(2) to know the different natures and characters of the sentient beings before teaching them the Dharma to rid them of afflictions;
(3) to eradicate all evil, cultivate all virtues, subdue the army of demons, and realize supreme enlightenment; and
(4) to teach, with one pure voice, the essence of the Dharma to the countless sentient beings in a billion-world universe.

"Furthermore, there are four things that can free a Bodhisattva from cowardice and weakness, and make him invulnerable to demons. What are the four?

(1) To view all dharmas as illusory, like magic;
(2) always to be in harmony with the true, right wisdom;
(3) to make no distinctions among dharmas; and
(4) to be detached from all forms. . . .

"Moreover, there are four things that can cause a Bodhisattva to have ingenuity. What are the four?

(1) To place before all other vows the vow to attain enlightenment, and to cause even defiled persons to advance toward supreme enlightenment, let alone those with virtuous minds;
(2) to view all sentient beings, even those who hold wrong views, as worthy to receive the Dharma;
(3) to understand that no dharma has a self-nature; and
(4) to cultivate liberation without being attached to samādhi. . . .

"Furthermore, there are four things that can cause a Bodhisattva to obtain unimpeded eloquence. What are the four?

(1) To follow the meaning of the doctrine, not the letter;
(2) to conform to the Dharma, not to any person;
(3) to realize that all dharmas are beyond words; and
(4) to teach untiringly, using the words that convey the ultimate truth. . . .

"Furthermore, there are four things that can cause a Bodhisattva not to regress from the pāramitās. What are the four?

(1) By ingenuity, to master all pāramitās by mastering one pāramitā;
(2) by ingenuity, to know all sentient beings by knowing one sentient being;

(3) by ingenuity, to realize the purity of all dharmas by realizing the purity of one dharma; and
(4) by ingenuity, to understand all Buddhas by understanding one Buddha. Why? Because things are not different in nature."

When the Buddha taught these fourfold doctrines of a Bodhisattva, Bhadra the magician gained the Realization of the Nonarising of Dharmas. In ecstasy, he rose up in midair to a height of seven palm trees.

Then the World-Honored One smiled graciously, emitting from his face innumerable lights, which illuminated all Buddha-lands and then returned and entered the top of his head.

Seeing this, Venerable Ānanda thought to himself, "There must be a reason for the smile of the Buddha, the Worthy One, the Supremely Enlightened One." Thereupon, he rose from his seat, bared his right shoulder, knelt on his right knee, joined his palms toward the Buddha, and asked him in verse:

"Omniscient, Honored One,
You are renowned throughout the three realms.
Your awe-inspiring virtue and wisdom
Are inconceivable.
You have already reached
The meritorious shore of enlightenment.
What is the reason for your smile just now?

The sentient beings of the five planes of existence
In the ten directions
Differ in their mental activities
And in their inclinations,
But the Tathāgata fully knows them all.
Why did you smile just now?

The many wonderful voices uttered
By humans and all eight divisions of divinities
Cannot compare in excellence
With the slightest sound
Of the pure voice of the Tathāgata.

The lights of the World-Honored One
Illuminate all the countless Buddha-lands
Throughout the ten directions.
The brilliance of the sun, the moon,
Bright pearls, and Brahmā
Cannot bear comparison
With the brilliance of the Tathāgata.

You understand the profound doctrine of emptiness
So that you hold no view of a self,
A personal identity, or a sentient being.
You abandon the extreme views
Of existence and nonexistence.
You know well that past, present, and future
Are like the moon mirrored in water.

Now, who moves toward the supreme vehicle,
Inherits the Dharma, extends the Buddha's lineage,
And is reborn in the vastness of the Three Jewels?
Please explain the reason for your smile.

The lights of the Tathāgata's smile
Move differently
According to which vehicle they concern.
If they vanish into the knee or shoulder,
They concern Śrāvakas or Pratyekabuddhas.
Just now you emitted immeasurable lights,
All of which entered the top of the Tathāgata's head.
Whose attainment of enlightenment
Will the Supreme One among gods prophesy?"

The World-Honored One asked Ānanda, "Do you see Bhadra?"

Ānanda answered, "Yes, I do."

The Buddha told Ānanda, "This good man will become a Buddha, called Tathāgata King of Miraculous Feats, the Worthy One, the Supremely Enlightened One. He will dwell in the Land of Great Adornment after ninety-two thousand kalpas have passed, during the Kalpa of Skillful Reforming.

"The people of his Buddha-land will be prosperous, peaceful, secure, rich, and happy. The land there will be level, and as soft as cotton, with flowering trees and fruit trees growing in orderly rows. Banners and precious canopies will adorn that land, and musical instruments of all kinds will sound spontaneously. Everywhere a wonderful fragrance will permeate the air. Food and drink will appear as soon as the need of them comes to a person's mind. All the enjoyments and necessities of life will be exactly the same as those used in the Heaven of the Thirty-Three. Because of the many magnificent adornments in that Buddha-land, it will be called the Land of Great Adornment. The people there will all abide in the Mahāyāna with deep, firm faith.

"Tathāgata King of Miraculous Feats will live for ten thousand years, and his true Dharma will last in that world for ten billion years. At the point of entering parinirvāṇa,[18] he will prophesy Bodhisattva Renowned's attainment of supreme enlightenment, saying: 'You will be the next Buddha [of this land] in your future life, and you will be called Tathāgata Surpassing All, the Worthy One, the Supremely Enlightened One.'"

Having heard the Tathāgata thus prophesy, Bhadra descended from midair, prostrated himself with his head at the Buddha's feet, and said, "Now I take refuge in the Tathāgata, the Worthy One, the Supremely Enlightened One; and also in the Dharma and the monks." This he repeated earnestly again and again.[19] Then he said, "The Buddha, the World-Honored One, sees that suchness allows of no distinctions, and says that all dharmas are identical with suchness—undifferentiated, perfect, indistinguishable, nonarising, and inactive. I say the same about my present taking of refuge."

Thereupon Venerable Ānanda said to Bhadra, "If your taking refuge is identical with suchness, as the Buddha has taught, then you must have obtained something from the Dharma-nature of the Buddha. Have you not done so?"

The magician answered, "I myself am the Dharma-nature of the Tathāgata. Why? The Tathāgata and I are not two, not different, because all dharmas are suchness. Suchness means that all dharmas are in nature undifferentiated. So is it with sentient beings. Venerable sir, you should know this: when we speak of nonduality, we mean that nondiscrimination is nonduality. Why? Because it is the wisdom of the Buddha to know that all dharmas are names only."

Venerable Ānanda approached the Buddha and said, "How strange it is, World-Honored One, that Bhadra has such wisdom and eloquence! Previously, he deluded and confused the world with his magic, but now he is doing so with his wisdom."

The Buddha asked Bhadra, "Good man, are you really doing that?"

Bhadra said, "I delude and confuse others just as the Buddha does. Why do I say so? Because the Buddha, the World-Honored One, says that there are sentient beings and life, though actually no self exists. This is most deluding and confusing to the world. Also, the Tathāgata speaks of coming, going, and saṁsāra, though he has known ever since he realized supreme enlightenment that there are no such dharmas as coming, going, or saṁsāra. In my opinion, the Tathāgata is the only one who greatly deludes and confuses the world."[20]

The Buddha said, "Good man, well said, well said! Just as you have said, the Buddhas, Tathāgatas, say that there are sentient beings and so forth, in order to conform to conventions, even though they know that there is actually no self, saṁsāra, going, or coming. There is no dharma that can be called nirvāṇa, either. However, in order to [cause others to] realize the Dharma leading to nirvāṇa, they discourse on nirvāṇa."

Having heard this, Bhadra approached the Buddha and said, "I wish to leave the household life to become a monk."

Then the World-Honored One told Bodhisattva-Mahāsattva Maitreya, "You should shave off this good man's beard and hair and confer upon him the full ordination."

In accordance with the Buddha's instructions, Bodhisattva Maitreya allowed Bhadra to leave the household life and fully ordained him.

After becoming a monk, Bhadra said to the Buddha, "World-Honored one, this renunciation of the household life is only so in appearance; it is not true renunciation of the household life. Only the Bodhisattvas who detach themselves from all appearances and remain in the three realms to bring sentient beings to maturity can be said to have truly renounced the household life."[21]

When this was spoken, five thousand sentient beings brought forth supreme bodhicitta, and their minds were liberated from all defilements.

Then Ānanda said to the Buddha, "World-Honored One, what shall we call this sūtra? How shall we accept and uphold it?"

The Buddha told Ānanda, "This sūtra will be called 'The Prophecy of the Magician Bhadra's Attainment of Buddhahood,' or 'The Doctrine of the Gradual Realization of Bodhi.'[22] Sentient beings who desire to see the Tathāgata and to do the Buddha's work for others in the future should accept, read, and recite this sūtra and explain it extensively to others. Why? Because to do so is to see the Tathāgata and do the Buddha's work for others. Therefore, Ānanda, to uphold, read, recite, and circulate this sūtra is to pity, benefit, and gladden sentient beings. Those who aspire to advance toward supreme enlightenment should also study and practice this sūtra diligently. This sūtra can cause [the seed of] supreme enlightenment to germinate and to grow. Therefore, it can also be called 'The Discourse on the Germination and Growth of [the Seed of] Bodhi.' It should be known that Buddhas abide within those who accept and uphold this sūtra, let alone within those who study and practice it properly."

Then Bhadra said to the Buddha, "World-Honored One, this sūtra is also called 'The Revelation of Good Roots.' Why? Because now that I have heard this sūtra from the Buddha, all good roots are revealed to me."[23]

When the Buddha had taught this sūtra, the entire assembly of Venerable Ānanda, Bhadra, gods, humans, asuras, gandharvas, and so forth were jubilant over what the Buddha had taught, accepted it with faith, and began to practice it with veneration.

NOTES

1. For explanations of names, Sanskrit words, technical terms, and types of beings, see Glossary. For numbered groups, see Numerical Glossary.

2. Anything in the universe can be regarded as a miraculous feat. Here, besides the wielding of magical powers, the other two deeds of the Buddha—admonishing people and

teaching the Dharma—are also said to be miraculous abilities. These three deeds are called the three kinds of miraculous feats of the Buddha.

3. A name of Śākyamuni Buddha.

4. The Buddha's voice is said to have sixty-four attributes. They are listed in full in the *Inconceivable Esoteric Mahāyāna Sūtra* (不思議秘密大乘經), and include liquid, soft, agreeable, pleasant, clear, like a lion's roar, like a peal of thunder, etc.

5. Listed in the Glossary as Mahāmaudgalyāyana ('Great' Maudgalyāyana). Kāśyapa, too, is sometimes called Mahākāśyapa, and is so listed in the Glossary.

6. A wind wheel, in mythological Buddhist cosmology, is a vast circle of air or "wind" upon which each world rests.

7. Pārijāta is a flowering tree which blooms in Śakra's garden. Kovidāra is another kind of flowering tree.

8. Literally, "Always equal to the past."

9. This samādhi involves three kinds of devotion: to contemplate single-mindedly the auspicious physical form of the Buddha, to contemplate reality (the Dharma-body) single-mindedly, and to invoke the Buddha's name single-mindedly. The achievement of this samādhi leads to a mental state wherein all the Buddha's bodies are revealed as one reality.

10. Dharma truth: the suchness or emptiness of all dharmas.

11. Transformation body (or, 'incarnated body'; Skt. *Nirmāṇakāya*): one of the three bodies of the Buddha, not a magically produced Buddha. See Numerical Glossary, "three bodies of the Buddha."

12. See Numerical Glossary, "five aggregates," "twelve entrances," and "eighteen elements." See also Glossary, "aggregate."

13. Sometimes these are called "the five factors of the Dharma-body," which here does not refer to the Dharmakāya of the Mahāyāna.

14. See Glossary, "bodhicitta."

15. See Numerical Glossary, "three wheels."

16. We render 定 as 'dhyāna' not 'samādhi', here and elsewhere. For 三昧 and 三摩地 we use 'samādhi'. The reasons are as follows:

a. Although 定 and 三昧 are almost interchangeable in Mahāyāna sūtras, they are not so in every case. No translator renders 四色界定 (the four dhyānas of form) as 'the four samādhis of form', or 四無色定 (the four formless dhyānas) as 'the four samādhis without form'. Therefore, for the sake of convention and uniformity, we distinguish the two terms. Although in some sūtras the same "trance" may be referred to as 定 and 三昧 in different places, we leave the responsibility to such sūtras themselves, and we do not assume the liberty of changing our rendering at will.

b. If we compare the eight Hīnayāna dhyānas with the mystical, dynamic Mahāyāna samādhis, we find a vast difference between the two. To point up this distinction, we use dhyāna for 定 and samādhi for 三昧.

c. From the etymological viewpoint, there is also a difference. Dhyāna is derived from the Sanskrit root *dhyā*, which means 'to muse', 'to contemplate', or 'to meditate'. Therefore, the eight Hīnayāna "trances" should be translated as dhyānas, not samādhis. The dhyānas denote specific meditational states, while the samādhis of Mahāyāna have various dynamic functions.

d. The fifth of the Bodhisattvas' six pāramitās (Skt. *dhyāna-pāramitā*, Ch. 禪定波羅密多), is translated as 'the pāramitā of meditation', or simply 'the pāramitā of dhyāna'. No translator so far has translated this as 'the pāramitā of samādhi'. Since 定 is an abbreviation of

禪定, it is obvious that we should follow the established rule in rendering all 定 as 'dhyāna', not 'samādhi'.

e. The fifth pāramitā, *dhyāna-pāramitā*, is translated in Tibetan as *bsam-gtan* (= dhyāna) *gyi pha-rol-tu phyin-pa,* not as *tiṅ-ṅe-'dzin* (=samādhi) *gyi pha-rol-tu phyin-pa*. This is another reason to translate 禪定 or 定 as 'dhyāna' but not as 'samādhi'.

To avoid later complications and possible misunderstandings, we translate these two terms on the basis of this principle.

Mr. Miao is fully aware of this principle, but disagrees with its application in Chapter 12. See "A Discourse on Ready Eloquence" below, note 2. (G.C.)

17. According to Buddhist tradition, attachment to the bliss of meditation can lead a meditator to rebirth in the dhyāna heavens. Birth in the heavens is not to be sought for several reasons. One cannot gain supreme enlightenment if one is a god in heaven. Furthermore, the rewards of good karma and the power of meditation will someday be exhausted, and the god must then suffer the agony of death and possible rebirth in miserable states. Finally, a wish for birth in the dhyāna heavens is contrary to the selfless ideals of the Mahāyāna. (V.S.B.)

18. Literally "nirvāṇa."

19. The original reads, "incalculable hundreds of thousands of millions of times."

20. Employing speech as skillful means, the Buddha spoke many sūtras, which should only be taken as "the finger that points to the moon," not the moon itself. The Buddha said, "I have not taught a single word during the forty-nine years of my Dharma preaching." The sūtras often admonish us to rely on meaning rather than on mere words. (See Numerical Glossary, "four reliances.") Readers should bear in mind that it is not the words themselves but the attachment to words that is dangerous. The crucial function of the sūtras as a finger pointing to the moon should be upheld. (W.H.)

21. In the Mahāyāna, a layman may be said to have "really left the household life" if he does what is taught in this passage. Vimalakīrti, the layman with great wisdom and ingenuity, is an illustrious example.

22. Bhadra the magician first attained the Samādhi of the Recollection of the Buddha, then the Realization of Compliance with the Dharma Truth, and finally the Realization of the Nonarising of Dharmas, whereupon he received the Buddha's prophecy of his attainment of Buddhahood. (W.H.)

This passage suggests the gradual realization approach. It is my opinion that the reader should not regard the so-called "instantaneous" realization as superior to the gradual. We should bear in mind that many Zen Buddhists strive for instantaneous realization all their lives and get nowhere. Thus, the gradual approach is perhaps more solid, steady, and practical. With regard to the *view of prajñā*, instantaneous realization (頓悟) may be more thorough and "superior" to the gradual approach; but from the pragmatic viewpoint, the gradual approach seems to be preferable. Furthermore, the three realizations Bhadra attained are of a very advanced stage. In particular, the Realization of the Nonarising of Dharmas is supposed to be attained only by Bodhisattvas of the eighth stage. (G.C.)

23. In an earlier part of the sūtra (p. 4) we find: "The time had come for the good roots of the magician. . . . to mature."

II

On Emptiness

2 善德天子會

The Demonstration of the Inconceivable State of Buddhahood

Thus have I heard. Once the Buddha was dwelling in the garden of Anāthapiṇḍada, in the Jeta Grove near Śrāvastī, accompanied by one thousand monks, ten thousand Bodhisattva-Mahāsattvas, and many gods of the Realm of Desire and the Realm of Form.

At that time, Bodhisattva-Mahāsattva Mañjuśrī and the god Suguṇa were both present among the assembly. The World-Honored One told Mañjuśrī, "You should explain the profound state of Buddhahood for the celestial beings and the Bodhisattvas of this assembly."

Mañjuśrī said to the Buddha, "So be it, World-Honored One. If good men and good women wish to know the state of Buddhahood, they should know that it is not a state of the eye, the ear, the nose, the tongue, the body, or the mind; nor is it a state of forms, sounds, scents, tastes, textures, or mental objects. World-Honored One, the nonstate is the state of Buddhahood. This being the case, what is the state of supreme enlightenment as attained by the Buddha?"

The Buddha said, "It is the state of emptiness, because all views are equal. It is the state of signlessness, because all signs are equal. It is the state of wishlessness, because the three realms are equal. It is the state of nonaction, because all actions are equal. It is the state of the unconditioned, because all conditioned things are equal."

Mañjuśrī asked, "World-Honored One, what is the state of the unconditioned?"

The Buddha said, "The absence of thought is the state of the unconditioned."

Sūtra 35, Taishō 310, pp. 566–571; translated into Chinese by Bodhiruci.

Mañjuśrī said, "World-Honored One, if the states of the unconditioned and so forth are the state of Buddhahood, and the state of the unconditioned is the absence of thought, then on what basis is the state of Buddhahood expressed? If there is no such basis, then there is nothing to be said; and since there is nothing to be said, nothing can be expressed. Therefore, World-Honored One, the state of Buddhahood is inexpressible in words."

The Buddha asked, "Mañjuśrī, where should the state of Buddhahood be sought?"

Mañjuśrī answered, "It should be sought right in the defilements of sentient beings. Why? Because by nature the defilements of sentient beings are inapprehensible. [Realization of] this is beyond the comprehension of Śrāvakas and Pratyekabuddhas; therefore, it is called the state of Buddhahood."

The Buddha asked Mañjuśrī, "Does the state of Buddhahood increase or decrease?"

"It neither increases nor decreases."

The Buddha asked, "How can one comprehend the basic nature of the defilements of all sentient beings?"

"Just as the state of Buddhahood neither increases nor decreases, so by their nature the defilements neither increase nor decrease."

The Buddha asked, "What is the basic nature of the defilements?"

"The basic nature of the defilements is the basic nature of the state of Buddhahood. World-Honored One, if the nature of the defilements were different from the nature of the state of Buddhahood, then it could not be said that the Buddha abides in the equality of all things. It is because the nature of the defilements is the very nature of the state of Buddhahood that the Tathāgata is said to abide in equality."

The Buddha asked further, "In what equality do you think the Tathāgata abides?"

"As I understand it, the Tathāgata abides in exactly the same equality in which those sentient beings who act with desire, hatred, and ignorance abide."

The Buddha asked, "In what equality do those sentient beings who act with the three poisons abide?"

"They abide in the equality of emptiness, signlessness, and wishlessness."

The Buddha asked, "Mañjuśrī, in emptiness, how could there be desire, hatred, and ignorance?"

Mañjuśrī answered, "Right in that which exists there is emptiness, wherein desire, hatred, and ignorance are also found."

The Buddha asked, "In what existence is there emptiness?"

"Emptiness is said to exist [only] in words and language. Because there is emptiness, there are desire, hatred, and ignorance. The Buddha has said, 'Monks! Nonarising, nonconditioning, nonaction, and nonorigination all exist. If these did not exist, then one could not speak of arising, conditioning, action, and origination. Therefore, monks, because there are nonarising, nonconditioning, nonaction, and nonorigination, one can speak of the existence of arising, conditioning, action, and origination.' Similarly, World-Honored One, if there were no emptiness, signlessness, or wishlessness, one could not speak of desire, hatred, ignorance, or other ideas."

The Buddha said, "Mañjuśrī, if this is the case, then it must be, as you said, that one who abides in the defilements abides in emptiness."

Mañjuśrī said, "World-Honored One, if a meditator seeks emptiness apart from the defilements, his search will be in vain. How could there be an emptiness that differs from the defilements? If he contemplates the defilements as emptiness, he is said to be engaged in right practice."

The Buddha asked, "Mañjuśrī, do you detach yourself from the defilements or abide in them?"

Mañjuśrī said, "All defilements are equal [in reality]. I have realized that equality through right practice. Therefore, I neither detach myself from the defilements nor abide in them. If a śramaṇa or brāhmin claims that he has overcome passions and sees other beings as defiled, he has fallen into the two extreme views. What are the two? One is the view of eternalism, maintaining that defilements exist; the other is the view of nihilism, maintaining that defilements do not exist. World-Honored One, he who practices rightly sees no such things as self or other, existence or nonexistence. Why? Because he clearly comprehends all dharmas."

The Buddha asked, "Mañjuśrī, what should one rely upon for right practice?"

"He who practices rightly relies upon nothing."

The Buddha asked, "Does he not practice according to the path?"

"If he practices in accordance with anything, his practice will be conditioned. A conditioned practice is not one of equality. Why? Because it is not exempt from arising, abiding, and perishing."

The Buddha asked Mañjuśrī, "Are there any categories in the unconditioned?"

Mañjuśrī answered, "World-Honored One, if there were categories in the unconditioned, then the unconditioned would be conditioned and would no longer be the unconditioned."

The Buddha said, "If the unconditioned can be realized by saints, then there is such a thing as the unconditioned; how can you say there are no categories in it?"

"Things have no categories, and the saints have transcended categories. That is why I say there are no categories."

The Buddha asked, "Mañjuśrī, would you not say you have attained sainthood?"

Mañjuśrī asked in turn, "World-Honored One, suppose one asks a magically produced person, 'Would you not say you have attained sainthood?' What will be his reply?"

The Buddha answered Mañjuśrī, "One cannot speak of the attainment or nonattainment of a magically produced person."

Mañjuśrī asked, "Has the Buddha not said that all things are like illusions?"

The Buddha answered, "So I have, so I have."

"If all things are like illusions, why do you ask me whether or not I have attained sainthood?"

The Buddha asked, "Mañjuśrī, what equality in the three vehicles have you realized?"

"I have realized the equality of the state of Buddhahood."

The Buddha asked, "Have you attained the state of Buddhahood?"

"If the World-Honored One has attained it, then I have also attained it."

Thereupon, Venerable Subhūti asked Mañjuśrī, "Has not the Tathāgata attained the state of Buddhahood?"

Mañjuśrī asked in turn, "Have you attained anything in the state of Śrāvakahood?"

Subhūti answered, "The liberation of a saint is neither an attainment nor a nonattainment."

"So it is, so it is. Likewise, the liberation of the Tathāgata is neither a state nor a nonstate."

Subhūti said, "Mañjuśrī, you are not taking care of the novice Bodhisattvas in teaching the Dharma this way."

Mañjuśrī asked, "Subhūti, what do you think? Suppose a physician, in taking care of his patients, does not give them acrid, sour, bitter, or astringent medicines. Is he helping them to recover or causing them to die?"

Subhūti answered, "He is causing them to suffer and die instead of giving them peace and happiness."

Mañjuśrī said, "Such is the case with a teacher of the Dharma. If, in taking care of others, he fears that they might be frightened, and so hides from them the profound meanings of the Dharma and instead speaks to them in irrelevant words and fancy phrases, then he is causing sentient beings to suffer [birth,] old age, disease, and death, instead of giving them health, peace, bliss, and nirvāṇa."

When this Dharma was explained, five hundred monks were freed of attachment to any dharma, were cleansed of defilements, and were liberated in mind; eight thousand devas left the taints of the mundane world far behind and attained the pure Dharma-eye that sees through all dharmas; seven hundred gods resolved to attain supreme enlightenment and vowed: "In the future, we shall attain an eloquence like that of Mañjuśrī."

Then Elder Subhūti asked Mañjuśrī, "Do you not explain the Dharma of the Śrāvaka-vehicle to the Śrāvakas?"

"I follow the Dharmas of all the vehicles."

Subhūti asked, "Are you a Śrāvaka, a Pratyekabuddha, or a Worthy One, a Supremely Enlightened One?"

"I am a Śrāvaka, but my understanding does not come through the speech of others. I am a Pratyekabuddha, but I do not abandon great compassion or fear anything. I am a Worthy One, a Supremely Enlightened One, but I still do not give up my original vows."

Subhūti asked, "Why are you a Śrāvaka?"

"Because I cause sentient beings to hear the Dharma they have not heard."

"Why are you a Pratyekabuddha?"

"Because I thoroughly comprehend the dependent origination of all dharmas."[1]

"Why are you a Worthy One, a Supremely Enlightened One?"

"Because I realize that all things are equal in the dharmadhātu."

Subhūti asked, "Mañjuśrī, in what stage do you really abide?"

"I abide in every stage."

Subhūti asked, "Could it be that you also abide in the stage of ordinary people?"

Mañjuśrī said, "I definitely abide in the stage of ordinary people."

Subhūti asked, "With what esoteric implication do you say so?"

"I say so because all dharmas are equal by nature."

Subhūti asked, "If all dharmas are equal, where are such dharmas as the stages of Śrāvakas, Pratyekabuddhas, Bodhisattvas, and Buddhas established?"

Mañjuśrī answered, "As an illustration, consider the empty space in the ten directions. People speak of the eastern space, the southern space, the western space, the northern space, the four intermediate spaces, the space above, the space below, and so forth. Such distinctions are spoken of, although the empty space itself is devoid of distinctions. In like manner, virtuous one, the various stages are established in the ultimate emptiness of all things, although the emptiness itself is devoid of distinctions."

Subhūti asked, "Have you entered the realization of sainthood and been forever separated from saṁsāra?"

"I have entered it and emerged from it."

Subhūti asked, "Why did you emerge from it after you entered it?"

Mañjuśrī answered, "Virtuous one, you should know that this is a manifestation of the wisdom and ingenuity of a Bodhisattva. He truly enters the realization of sainthood and becomes separated from saṁsāra; then, as a method to save sentient beings, he emerges from that realization. Subhūti, suppose an expert archer plans to harm a bitter enemy, but, mistaking his beloved son in the wilderness for the enemy, he shoots an arrow at him. The son shouts, 'I have done nothing wrong. Why do you wish to harm me?' At once, the archer, who is swift-footed, dashes toward his son and catches the arrow before it does any harm. A Bodhisattva is like this: in order to train and subdue Śrāvakas and Pratyekabuddhas, he attains nirvāṇa; however, he emerges from it and does not fall into the stages of Śrāvakas and Pratyekabuddhas. That is why his stage is called the Buddha-stage."

Subhūti asked, "How can a Bodhisattva attain this stage?"

Mañjuśrī answered, "If Bodhisattvas dwell in all stages and yet dwell nowhere, they can attain this stage.

"If they can discourse on all the stages but do not abide in the lower stages, they can attain this Buddha-stage.

"If they practice with the purpose of ending the afflictions of all sentient beings, but [realize] there is no ending in the dharmadhātu; if they abide in the unconditioned, yet perform conditioned actions; if they remain in saṁsāra, but regard it as a garden and do not seek nirvāṇa before all their vows are fulfilled—then they can attain this stage.

"If they realize egolessness, yet bring sentient beings to maturity, they can attain this stage.[2]

"If they achieve the Buddha-wisdom yet do not generate anger or hatred toward those who lack wisdom, they can attain this stage.

"If they practice by turning the Dharma-wheel for those who seek the Dharma but make no distinctions among things, they can attain this stage.

"Furthermore, if Bodhisattvas vanquish demons yet assume the appearance of the four demons, they can attain this stage."

Subhūti said, "Mañjuśrī, such practices of a Bodhisattva are very difficult for any worldly being to believe."

Mañjuśrī said, "So it is, so it is, as you say. Bodhisattvas perform deeds in the mundane world but transcend worldly dharmas."

Subhūti said, "Mañjuśrī, please tell me how they transcend the mundane world."

Mañjuśrī said, "The five aggregates constitute what we call the mundane world. Of these, the aggregate of form has the nature of accumulated foam, the aggregate of feeling has the nature of a bubble, the aggregate of conception has the nature of a mirage, the aggregate of impulse has the nature of a hollow plantain, and the aggregate of consciousness has the nature of an illusion. Thus, one should know that the essential nature of the mundane world is none other than that of foam, bubbles, mirages, plantains, and illusions; in it there are neither aggregates nor the names of aggregates, neither sentient beings nor the names of sentient beings, neither the mundane world nor the supramundane world. Such a right understanding of the five aggregates is called the supreme understanding. If one attains this supreme understanding, then he is liberated, as he [actually] always has been.[3] If he is so liberated, he is not attached to mundane things. If he is not attached to mundane things, he transcends the mundane world.

"Furthermore, Subhūti, the basic nature of the five aggregates is emptiness. If that nature is emptiness, there is neither 'I' nor 'mine.' If there is neither 'I' nor 'mine,' there is no duality. If there is no duality, there is neither grasping nor abandoning. If there is neither grasping nor abandoning, there is no attachment. Thus, free of attachment, one transcends the mundane world.

"Furthermore, Subhūti, the five aggregates belong to causes and conditions. If they belong to causes and conditions, they do not belong to oneself or to others. If they do not belong to oneself or to others, they have no owner. If they have no owner, there is no one who grasps them. If there is no grasping, there is no contention, and noncontention is the practice of religious devotees. Just as a hand moving in empty space touches no object and meets no obstacle, so the Bodhisattvas who practice the equality of emptiness transcend the mundane world.

"Moreover, Subhūti, because all the elements of the five aggregates merge in the dharmadhātu, there are no realms. If there are no realms, there are no elements of earth, water, fire, or air; there is no ego, sentient being, or life; no Realm of Desire, Realm of Form, or Realm of Formlessness; no realm of the conditioned or realm of the unconditioned; no realm of saṁsāra or realm of nirvāṇa. When Bodhisattvas enter such a domain [free of distinctions], they do not abide in anything, though they remain in the midst of worldly beings. If they do not abide in anything, they transcend the mundane world."

When this Dharma of transcending the world was explained, two hundred monks became detached from all dharmas, ended all their defilements, and became liberated in mind. One by one they took off their upper garments to offer to Mañjuśrī, saying, "Any person who does not have faith in or understand this doctrine will achieve nothing and realize nothing."

Then Subhūti asked these monks, "Elders, have you ever achieved or realized anything?"

The monks replied, "Only presumptuous persons will claim they have achieved and realized something. To a humble religious devotee, nothing is achieved or realized. How, then, would such a person think of saying to himself, 'This I have achieved; this I have realized'? If such an idea occurs to him, then it is a demon's deed."

Subhūti asked, "Elders, according to your understanding, what achievement and realization cause you to say so?"

The monks replied, "Only the Buddha, the World-Honored One, and Mañjuśrī know our achievement and realization. Most virtuous one, our understanding is: those who do not fully know the nature of suffering yet claim that suffering should be comprehended are presumptuous. Likewise, if they claim that the cause of suffering should be eradicated, that the cessation of suffering should be realized, and that the path leading to the cessation of suffering should be followed, they are presumptuous. Presumptuous also are those who do not really know the nature of suffering, its cause, its cessation, or the path leading to its cessation, but claim that they know suffering, have eradicated the cause of suffering, have realized the cessation of suffering, and have followed the path leading to the cessation of suffering.

"What is the nature of suffering? It is the very nature of nonarising. The same is true concerning the characteristic of the cause of suffering, the cessation of suffering, and the path leading to the cessation of suffering. The nature of nonarising is signless and unattainable. In it, there is no suffering to be known, no cause of suffering to be eradicated, no cessation of suffering to be realized, and no path leading to the cessation of suffering to be followed. Those who are not frightened, terrified, or awestricken upon hearing these Noble Truths are not presumptuous. Those who are frightened and terrified are the presumptuous ones."

Thereupon, the World-Honored One praised the monks, saying, "Well said, well said!" He told Subhūti, "These monks heard Mañjuśrī explain this profound

Dharma during the era of Kāśyapa Buddha. Because they have practiced this profound Dharma before, they are now able to follow it and understand it immediately. Similarly, all those who hear, believe, and understand this profound teaching in my era will be among the assembly of Maitreya Buddha in the future."

Then the god Suguṇa said to Mañjuśrī, "Virtuous one, you have repeatedly taught the Dharma in this world. Now we beg you to go to the Tuṣita Heaven. For a long time, the gods there have also been planting many good roots. They will be able to understand the Dharma if they hear it. However, because they are attached to the pleasures [of their heaven], they cannot [leave their heaven and] come to the Buddha to hear the Dharma, and consequently they suffer a great loss."

Mañjuśrī immediately performed a miraculous feat that caused the god Suguṇa and all others in the assembly to believe that they had arrived at the palace of the Tuṣita Heaven. There they saw gardens, woods, magnificent palaces and mansions with sumptuous tiers of railings and windows, high and spacious twenty-storied towers with jewelled nets and curtains, celestial flowers covering the ground, various wonderful birds hovering in flocks and warbling, and celestial maidens in the air scattering flowers of the coral tree, singing verses in chorus, and playing merrily.

Seeing all this, the god Suguṇa said to Mañjuśrī, "This is extraordinary, Mañjuśrī! How have we arrived so quickly at the palace of the Tuṣita Heaven to see the gardens and the gods here? Mañjuśrī, will you please teach us the Dharma?"

Elder Subhūti told Suguṇa, "Son of heaven, you did not leave the assembly or go anywhere. It is Mañjuśrī's miraculous feat that causes you to see yourself in the palace of the Tuṣita Heaven."

The god Suguṇa said to the Buddha, "How rare, World-Honored One! Mañjuśrī has such a command of samādhi and of miraculous power that in an instant he has caused this entire assembly to appear to be in the palace of the Tuṣita Heaven."

The Buddha said, "Son of heaven, is this your understanding of Mañjuśrī's miraculous power? As I understand it, if Mañjuśrī wishes, he can gather all the merits and magnificent attributes of Buddha-lands as numerous as the sands of the Ganges and cause them to appear in one Buddha-land. He can with one fingertip lift up the Buddha-lands below ours, which are as numerous as the sands of the Ganges, and put them in the empty space on top of the Buddha-lands above ours, which are also as numerous as the sands of the Ganges. He can put all the water of the four great oceans of all the Buddha-lands into a single pore without making the aquatic beings in it feel crowded or removing them from the seas. He can put all the Mount Sumerus of all the worlds into a mustard seed, yet the gods on these mountains will feel that they are still living in their own palaces. He can place all sentient beings of the five planes of existence of all the Buddha-lands on his palm, and cause them to see all kinds of exquisite material objects such as those available in delightful, magnificent countries. He can gather all the fires of all the worlds into a piece of cotton. He can use a spot as small as a pore to eclipse completely every sun and moon in every Buddha-land. In short, he can accomplish whatever he wishes to do."[4]

At that time, Pāpīyān, the Evil One, transformed himself into a monk and said to the Buddha, "World-Honored One, we wish to see Mañjuśrī perform such miraculous feats right now. What is the use of saying such absurd things, which nobody in the world can believe?"

The World-Honored One told Mañjuśrī, "You should manifest your miraculous power right before this assembly." Thereupon, without rising from his seat, Mañjuśrī entered the Samādhi of Perfect Mental Freedom in Glorifying All Dharmas, and demonstrated all the miraculous feats described by the Buddha.

Seeing this, the Evil One, the members of the assembly, and the god Suguṇa all applauded these unprecedented deeds, saying, "Wonderful, wonderful! Because of the appearance of the Buddha in this world, we now have this Bodhisattva who can perform such miraculous feats and open a door to the Dharma for the world."

Thereupon, the Evil One, inspired by Mañjuśrī's awesome power, said, "World-Honored One, how wonderful it is that Mañjuśrī possesses such great, miraculous power! And the members of this assembly, who now understand and have faith in the Dharma through his demonstration of miraculous feats, are also marvelous. World-Honored One, even if there were as many demons as the sands of the Ganges, they would not be able to hinder these good men and good women, who understand and believe in the Dharma.

"I, Pāpīyān the Evil One, have always sought opportunities to oppose the Buddha and to create turmoil among sentient beings. Now I vow that, from this day on, I will never go nearer than one hundred leagues away from the place where this doctrine prevails, or where people have faith in, understand, cherish, receive, read, recite, and teach it.

"However, World-Honored One, some of my kindred are determined to distract the devotees' minds so as to destroy the Dharma of the Tathāgata. I will chant the following dhāraṇī so that devotees can vanquish these demons. If good men or good women read, write, and recite this incantation, or teach it to others, the celestial demons will benefit and will, in return, cause the teachers of this Dharma to feel joyful in body and mind, to practice vigorously, to possess unimpeded eloquence and dhāraṇīs, and not to lack services, food and drink, clothing, bedding, or medicine."

Then he uttered the incantation:

> "TADYATHĀ AMALA VIMALE STHITATVE AKALAVANIRJITAŚATRU JAYE JAYAVATI BHŪTAMATIŚAME ŚVANATI APHUME BUSUME ADHIRE AGEMAKHE KHAKHEYISILE AGAMEPHULELA PHULAPHULE PHAŚUME ŚUŚUMA DHID-

HIRE ANAVANATE STHITATE KRITĀRATE KRITABHIDHYE PIROCATĀNA SADDHARMABHANAKOSYA SŪTRATRASYADHARIKA ABHRABUGATA IVASŪŪRYASVĀHĀ."[5]

Then, Pāpīyān said, "World-Honored One, if good men or good women accept this dhāraṇī wholeheartedly and chant it with concentration, they will be protected by gods, dragons, yakṣas, gandharvas, asuras, garuḍas, kinnaras and mahoragas, and no evil demons will be able to take advantage of them."

When Pāpīyān the Evil One spoke this incantation, quakes of six kinds occurred in the billion-world universe.

The World-Honored One then told Pāpīyān the Evil One, "Wonderful, wonderful! You should know that your eloquence is a manifestation of Mañjuśrī's miraculous power."

When Mañjuśrī was revealing his miraculous power and Pāpīyān the demon was chanting the dhāraṇī, thirty-two thousand gods resolved to attain supreme enlightenment. . . .

When the Buddha finished teaching this sūtra, the god Suguṇa, Elder Ānanda, and all the humans, gods, dragons, gandharvas, asuras, and so forth, were jubilant upon hearing what the Buddha had taught.

NOTES

1. Our text reads, "Because I cause sentient beings to believe in and awaken to the dharmadhātu." However, this is irrelevant to the above question. We have adopted another version here (Taishō 340, p. 109), also translated by a Bodhiruci (who may have lived more than 100 years before this Bodhiruci, or perhaps is the same person).

2. This rendering is based on Taishō 340, p. 110.

3. This refers to the doctrine of original or inherent Buddha-nature which states that we are all in an enlightened state—saṁsāra *is* nirvāṇa—but that our enlightenment is obscured by veils of passions and ignorance, so we are not aware of it.

When one first becomes enlightened, he is usually astonished at the fact that he has not realized anything new. He has been in the enlightened state all the time. That is why certain Mahāyāna sūtras and Zen texts say that at the time of Buddha's enlightenment, he exclaimed, "How strange this is! All sentient beings are already enlightened, yet are not aware of it."

4. These incredible feats are the consequences of Mañjuśrī's realization of the nonobstructing aspect of emptiness (*śūnyatā*). One who has reached this stage is free of the bondage of time and space; therefore, he is able to perform miraculous feats.

5. This *mantra* is transliterated from the Tibetan text, Peking edition, which the editor finds is clearer for transliteration than the Chinese. The Chinese rendering of the Sanskrit *mantra* is not based upon a transliteration system or alphabet, but upon the pronunciation of Chinese characters. It is extremely difficult, if not well-nigh impossible, to accurately reconstruct the Sanskrit from the Chinese. (G.C.)

3 恆河上優婆夷會

Flawless Purity: A Dialogue with the Laywoman Gaṅgottarā

Thus have I heard. Once the Buddha was dwelling in the garden of Anāthapiṇḍada, in the Jeta Grove near Śrāvastī. At that time, a laywoman named Gaṅgottarā came from her dwelling in Śrāvastī to see the Buddha. She prostrated herself with her head at the Buddha's feet, withdrew to one side, and sat down.

The World-Honored One asked Gaṅgottarā, "Where do you come from?"

The laywoman asked the Buddha, "World-Honored One, if someone were to ask a magically produced being where he came from, how should the question be answered?"

The World-Honored One told her, "A magically produced being neither comes nor goes, neither is born nor perishes; how can one speak of a place from which he comes?"

Then the laywoman asked, "Is it not true that all things are illusory, like magic?"

The Buddha said, "Yes, indeed. What you say is true."

Gaṅgottarā asked, "If all things are illusory, like magic, why did you ask me where I came from?"

The World-Honored One told her, "A magically produced being does not go to the miserable planes of existence, nor to heaven; nor does he attain nirvāṇa. Gaṅgottarā, is that also true of you?"

The laywoman replied, "As I see it, if my own body were different from a magically produced one, then I could speak of going to the good or miserable planes of existence, or of attaining nirvāṇa. I see no difference, though, between

Sūtra 31, Taishō 310 pp. 549–550; translated into Chinese by Bodhiruci.

my body and a magically produced one, so how can I speak of going to the good or miserable planes, or of attaining nirvāṇa?

"Furthermore, World-Honored One, nirvāṇa's very nature is such that it is not reborn in the good or miserable planes, nor does it experience parinirvāṇa. I perceive that the same is true of my own nature."

The Buddha asked, "Do you not seek the state of nirvāṇa?"

Gaṅgottarā asked in turn, "If this question were put to one who had never come into being, how should it be answered?"

The Buddha replied, "That which has never come into being is nirvāṇa itself."

Gaṅgottarā asked, "Are not all things identical with nirvāṇa?"

The Buddha replied, "So they are, so they are."

"World-Honored One, if all things are identical with nirvāṇa, why did you ask me, 'Do you not seek the state of nirvāṇa?'

"Furthermore, World-Honored One, if a magically produced being asked another magically produced being, 'Do you not seek the state of nirvāṇa?' what would the answer be?"

The World-Honored One told her, "A magically produced being has no mental attachments [and thus seeks nothing]."

Gaṅgottarā inquired, "Does the Tathāgata's very question stem from some mental attachment?"

The World-Honored One told her, "I raised the question because there are in this assembly good men and good women who can be brought to maturity. I am free of mental attachments. Why? Because the Tathāgata knows that even the names of things are inapprehensible, let alone the things themselves or those who seek nirvāṇa."

Gaṅgottarā said, "If so, why all the accumulation of good roots for the attainment of enlightenment?"

[The Buddha replied,] "Neither Bodhisattvas nor their good roots can be apprehended, because in the Bodhisattvas' minds there is no discriminative thought as to whether they are accumulating good roots or not."

Gaṅgottarā asked, "What do you mean by 'no discriminative thought'?"

The World-Honored One answered, "The absence of discriminative thought cannot be understood or grasped by means of thinking. Why? Because in the state [of no discriminative thought], even the mind is inapprehensible, let alone the mental functions. This state, in which the mind is inapprehensible, is called inconceivable. It cannot be grasped or realized; it is neither pure nor impure. Why so? Because, as the Tathāgata always teaches, all things are as empty and unimpeded as space."

Gaṅgottarā inquired, "If all things are like empty space, why does the World-Honored One speak of form, feeling, conception, impulse, and consciousness; the [eighteen] elements; the [twelve] entrances; the twelve links of dependent origination; the defiled and the undefiled; the pure and the impure; saṁsāra and nirvāṇa?"

The Buddha told Gaṅgottarā, "When I speak of a 'self,' for example, although I express the concept by a word, actually the nature of a 'self' is inapprehensible. I speak of form, but in reality the nature[1] of form is also inapprehensible, and so it is with the other [dharmas], up to nirvāṇa. Just as we cannot find water in mirages, so we cannot find a nature in form, and so it is with the others, up to nirvāṇa.

"Gaṅgottarā, only a person who cultivates pure conduct in accordance with the Dharma, perceiving that nothing can be apprehended, deserves to be called a real cultivator of pure conduct. Since the arrogant say that they have apprehended something, they cannot be said to be firmly established in genuine pure conduct. Such arrogant people will be terrified and doubtful when they hear this profound Dharma. They will be unable to liberate themselves from birth, old age, sickness, death, worry, sorrow, suffering, and distress.

"Gaṅgottarā, after my parinirvāṇa, there will be some people able to spread this profound Dharma, which can stop the rounds of saṁsāra. However, some fools, because of their evil views, will hate those Dharma-masters, and will contrive to harm them. Such fools will fall to the hells for that."

Gaṅgottarā asked, "You speak of 'this profound Dharma which can stop the rounds of saṁsāra.' What do you mean by 'stop the rounds of saṁsāra'?"

The World-Honored One replied, "To stop the rounds of saṁsāra is [to penetrate] reality, the realm of the inconceivable. Such a Dharma cannot be damaged or destroyed. Hence, it is called the Dharma that can stop the rounds of saṁsāra."

Then the World-Honored One smiled graciously and emitted from his forehead blue, yellow, red, white, and crystalline lights. The lights illuminated all the numerous lands, reaching as high as the Brahmā Heaven, then returned and entered the top of the Buddha's head.

Seeing this, the Venerable Ānanda thought to himself, "The Tathāgata, the Worthy One, the Supremely Enlightened One, does not smile without a reason." He rose from his seat, uncovered his right shoulder, knelt on his right knee, and joined his palms toward the Buddha, inquiring, "Why did the Buddha smile?"

The Buddha replied, "I recall that, in the past, a thousand Tathāgatas also taught this Dharma here, and each of those assemblies was also led by a laywoman named Gaṅgottarā. After hearing this Dharma preached, the laywoman and all the assembly left the household life. [In time,] they entered the nirvāṇa without residue."[2]

Ānanda asked the Buddha, "What name should be given to this sūtra and how should we accept and uphold it?"

The Buddha said, "This sūtra is called 'Flawless Purity,' and you should accept and uphold it by that name."

During the preaching of this sūtra, seven hundred monks and four hundred nuns were liberated from defilements forever and their minds were set free.

At that time, the gods of the Realm of Desire magically produced various kinds of wonderful celestial flowers and scattered them upon the Buddha, saying, "Rare indeed is this laywoman, who can converse fearlessly with the Tathāgata on equal terms. She must have served and made offerings to countless Buddhas, and planted good roots of every kind in their presence."

After the Buddha had finished speaking this sūtra, the laywoman Gaṅgottarā and all the gods, humans, asuras, gandharvas, and so forth were jubilant over the Buddha's teaching. They accepted it with faith, and began to follow it with veneration.

NOTES

1. The word 'nature' here is a translation of the Chinese character 相, which is more often rendered as 'sign', 'attribute', 'characteristic', 'appearance', 'form', etc. However, in certain sūtras, 相 is sometimes also used to mean 性, which is properly translated as 'nature'.

2. Whether the Gaṅgottarā referred to here is the same individual as the Gaṅgottarā present during the preaching of this sūtra is not clear from the text. Though she could be another person with the same name and similar karma, it is likely that she is the same person. The question may arise, "If Gaṅgottarā left the household life and entered nirvāṇa without residue long ago, how is it that she appears here as a lay questioner?"

According to the Hīnayāna doctrine, this question is almost impossible to answer, since that tradition asserts that if one enters nirvāṇa without residue, one never returns to the world. In Mahāyāna, however, the occasion of a Dharma preaching is looked upon as a drama which may be replayed again and again, and a person who has entered nirvāṇa may reappear in a body to benefit sentient beings.

The Mahāyāna description of nirvāṇa, called "non-abiding nirvāṇa," states that it is possible to achieve liberation and yet remain in the world for universal salvation. Such a person abides neither in saṁsāra nor in nirvāṇa. However, the nonabiding nirvāṇa of Mahāyāna is not contradictory to the Hīnayāna understanding of nirvāṇa. This is clearly demonstrated by the famous story of the "Buddha's silence" (see *Aggi-Vacchagottasutta*, in I.B. Horner, trans., *The Middle Length Sayings* (London: Luzac & Co., 1957), vol.2, pp. 162–167) when he refused to answer the question whether after parinirvāṇa there exists a being which is conscious of that state. Thus, even according to the Buddha's teaching in the Pāli traditions, one cannot say nirvāṇa is annihilation, or that he who enters nirvāṇa will never return to the world. The Buddha gave neither an affirmative nor a negative answer to this problem. (G.C.)

4 善住意天子會

How to Kill with the Sword of Wisdom

I

Thus have I heard. Once the World-Honored One was dwelling on Mount Gṛdhrakūṭa near the city of Rājagṛha, accompanied by sixty-two thousand great monks, all of whom possessed great virtue and were endowed with miraculous powers. The monks were led by certain great Śrāvakas.

Also in the assembly were forty-two thousand Bodhisattva-Mahāsattvas, led by Bodhisattva Mañjuśrī, Bodhisattva Lion Banner, Bodhisattva Maitreya, Bodhisattva Avalokiteśvara, Bodhisattva Mahāsthāmaprāpta, Bodhisattva King of Great Eloquence, . . . and others.

Also in the assembly at that time were sixty thousand devas, led by the Four Deva Kings; the deva kings of the Heaven of the Thirty-Three; and Brahmā, master of the Sahā World. Present, too, were the devas Well-Abiding Mind, Virtue, and Great Ease, leaders of thirty thousand devas who had long been abiding in the Bodhisattva-path; twenty thousand asura kings; . . . and sixty thousand great dragon kings, . . . all of whom had also been abiding in the Bodhisattva Path. In addition, innumerable gods, dragons, yakṣas, . . . monks, nuns, laymen, and laywomen joined the assembly.

When the World-Honored One, surrounded by the assembly of countless hundreds of thousands, was teaching the Dharma, Bodhisattva-Mahāsattva Mañjuśrī, in his dwelling place, had entered the Samādhi Devoid of Contention and Mind, remaining quiet and motionless. Then Mañjuśrī rose from the samādhi with a calm mind, and at once six quakes occurred in innumerable Buddha-lands in the ten directions.

Sūtra 36, Taishō 310, pp. 571–592; translated into Chinese by Dharmagupta.

Rising from the samādhi, Mañjuśrī thought, "In [each of] those infinite, innumerable worlds, only one Buddha, a Tathāgata, a Worthy One, a Perfectly Enlightened One, appears, and such a one appears as rarely as the blossoming of an uḍumbara flower. Therefore, the Tathāgatas, the Worthy Ones, the Perfectly Enlightened Ones, are most extraordinary in the worlds and their appearance is very unusual. The Dharma they teach can end rebirth and [saṁsāric] existence and lead to the ultimate quiescence of nirvāṇa; this is inconceivable, apart from discrimination, very profound, incomparable, and difficult to comprehend or fathom. If Buddhas did not come into the worlds, sentient beings would be unable to hear the Dharma explained, and their sufferings would be interminable. Therefore, now I should go to see the Tathāgata, the Perfectly Enlightened One, and ask him about the Dharma, so that sentient beings may achieve good roots, and so that all those who tread the Bodhisattva [-path] may have no doubt about the very profound, inconceivable Buddha-Dharmas and may attain the enlightenment of the Buddha. Since the sentient beings in the Sahā World are full of desire, hatred, and ignorance; do not perform white dharmas; are obtuse, deceitful, insensitive to shame, arrogant, and conceited; keep Buddhas at a distance; and disobey the Dharma and the Saṁgha, I should cause them to hear the very profound, wonderful Dharma explained so that they may acquire the clear wisdom-eye."[1]

Mañjuśrī thought further, "Now I should call together a host of Bodhisattvas from the ten directions, so that all of them may hear the wonderful Dharma-door explained by the Tathāgata and attain the realization of profound Dharma."

With this thought, Mañjuśrī entered the Samādhi of Adorning all with Undefiled Illumination. While in this samādhi, he emitted a great light which illuminated Buddha-lands in the east as numerous as the sands of the Ganges, so that all those lands became mild, lustrous, clean, clear, spotless, and inexpressibly wonderful. The light also illuminated worlds in the other nine directions: in the south, the west, the north, the four intermediate directions, the zenith, and the nadir. As a result, all the dark, secluded places, cliffs, forests, great and small mountains . . . became bright, limpid, and transparent.

At that time, all the Buddhas teaching the Dharma in the worlds in the ten directions as numerous as the sands of the Ganges were asked by their respective disciples, "World-Honored One, why does this great, auspicious light appear in the world? World-Honored One, we have never heard of or seen such a pure, subtle light. World-Honored One, what light is this, which causes us to be overwhelmed by great joy and to be pure in mind? What is this light which also frees sentient beings from desire, hatred, ignorance, and other defilements, so that they stop doing evil? World-Honored One, who emits this light and by whose power does it appear here?" When the disciples[2] asked these questions, their World-Honored Ones kept silent and gave no answer.

At that time, in the worlds in the ten directions, all kinds of sounds, such as the sounds of devas, dragons, yakṣas, gandharvas, asuras; . . . of humans and nonhumans; of elephants, horses, and other animals were hushed. The sounds of wind, fire, water, sea waves, music, and the singing of hymns were also hushed by the power of the Buddha. All was in silence.

Then, the disciples of the Buddhas in the worlds in the ten directions asked their respective Buddhas again, "World-Honored One of great kindness, may you, in order to show pity for and give peace, happiness, and benefit to all devas and humans, explain to us the origin of this light and why it can illuminate all Buddha-lands!"

The Buddhas in [the worlds of] the ten directions gave the same answer, in the same pure voice which is possessed by all the Tathāgatas, as numerous as the sands of the Ganges, of the worlds in the ten directions. They all answered as if only one Tathāgata spoke. When the Buddhas answered their respective disciples in this wonderful voice, all Buddha-lands quaked; hundreds of thousands of musical instruments of devas, humans, and asuras sounded simultaneously and spontaneously. . . .

At that time, the Buddhas, the World-Honored Ones in the ten directions, told their respective attendants and disciples, "Good men, you should not ask about these things. Why? Because the occurrence of this light is beyond the comprehension of all Śrāvakas and Pratyekabuddhas; if I speak of it, all humans, devas, and asuras will become confused and lost. Therefore, you should not ask about it. If Buddhas, the Tathāgatas, account for this light, they will say, 'This light can cause and fulfill inconceivable, superior good roots [of sentient beings]. Also, from these inconceivable, superior good roots can arise such practices as the pāramitās of giving, discipline, patience, vigor, meditation, and wisdom.' All such practices [as the pāramitās] are caused by this light and are also accomplished by it. Therefore, even if we Buddhas, Tathāgatas, praise the merits of this light for less than a kalpa or for an entire kalpa, we cannot praise them all. Moreover, since this light is cultivated through such good roots as kindness, compassion, joy, and equanimity, it can cause bliss."

Then, the disciples of the Buddhas [of the innumerable worlds] in the ten directions made the same earnest request again and again, saying, "May the World-Honored One explain to us the occurrence of this light in order to comfort, benefit and show sympathy for all devas and humans, as well as to bring to maturity the good roots of Bodhisattvas!"

When those Bodhisattvas had made this request, all the Buddhas, the World-Honored Ones in the ten directions, told their respective attendant disciples, "Good men, you should listen attentively. I am going to explain it to you."

The disciples said, "Yes, World-Honored One, we shall listen with pleasure."

Thereupon, the Buddhas told them, "Good men, there is a world named Sahā. In that world, there is a Buddha named Śākyamuni Tathāgata, the Worthy One, . . . the World-Honored One. He has appeared in a world of the five depravities. The sentient beings there are afflicted with desire, hatred, ignorance, and other defilements; they feel no respect and know no shame or remorse, and most of their deeds are evil. However, Śākyamuni Buddha was able to attain supreme enlightenment in such a depraved world. Now he is teaching the Dharma to the people around him.

"Good men, in that world, there is a Bodhisattva-Mahāsattva named Mañjuśrī, who is a great disciple of Śākyamuni Tathāgata. He has great virtue; he is fully endowed with wisdom; he strives with vigor and courage; he possesses awesome miraculous powers; he can cause other Bodhisattvas to acquire joy, to complete their Dharma practices, to increase their power, and to strive courageously and diligently; he understands well all expressions of the Dharma; he has reached the other shore[3] of unhindered wisdom; he has completely achieved unhindered eloquence; he has a free command of dhāraṇīs; and he has already achieved all the inconceivable merits of a Bodhisattva. Now he is going to ask Śākyamuni Tathāgata, the Worthy One, the Perfectly Enlightened One, about a very profound Dharma-door, in order to cause other Bodhisattvas to achieve good roots and to cause those who follow the Bodhisattva-vehicle to secure all the inconceivable Buddha-Dharmas. Now, good men, Mañjuśrī emits this light to call countless Bodhisattvas together from [the innum rable worlds] in the ten directions, so that they may acquire the superior Dharma. For this reason, Mañjuśrī emits this great light to illuminate all Buddha-lands."

The disciples of the Buddhas in the worlds of the ten directions asked their respective Buddhas again, "World-Honored One, in what samādhi does Mañjuśrī abide so that he can emit this light?"

The Buddhas in the ten directions told their respective attendant disciples, "Good men, Mañjuśrī has entered the Samādhi of Adorning All with Undefiled Illumination to give forth this light."

The attendant Bodhisattvas said to their respective Buddhas further, "World-Honored One, we have never before seen a light so pure, a light that can make body and mind so joyful."

The Buddhas said to the Bodhisattvas, "Is he not going to call together a host of Bodhisattvas to teach them how to practice the Dharma? Is he not going to summon a host of Bodhisattvas and explain a subtle sūtra to them?". . .

The Bodhisattvas said to their respective Buddhas, "World-Honored One, now we wish to go to the Sahā World to visit Śākyamuni Tathāgata; we will pay homage and make offerings to him and attend him; and we will ask him about the meaning of the truth. We wish to see Mañjuśrī and the other Bodhisattva-Mahāsattvas as well."

Thereupon, the World-Honored Ones said to the Bodhisattvas, "Good men, you may go, as you wish. You should know it is the time."

After bowing down with their heads at their Buddhas' feet, countless hundreds of thousands of [millions of] billions of trillions of inconceivable, incalculable, immeasurable myriads of Bodhisattva-Mahāsattvas [in the worlds] in the ten directions disappeared from their respective lands and reappeared in the Sahā World as quickly as an able-bodied man stretches and bends his arm. All of them came to the World-Honored One, Śākyamuni Tathāgata, the Worthy One, the Perfectly Enlightened One; some came scattering various kinds of fragrant things, such as perfumed ointment, powdered incense, and fragrant garlands; some came strewing flowers, such as blue lotus flowers, red lotus flowers, white lotus flowers, . . . and so forth; some came uttering hundreds of thousands of the most wonderful sounds; some came extolling the merits of the Buddhas in one voice heard all over the billion-world universe. With so many kinds of magnificent [offerings], they came to the World-Honored One, Śākyamuni Tathāgata, the Worthy One, the Perfectly Enlightened One.

When those Bodhisattva-Mahāsattvas arriving from [the worlds in] the ten directions gathered in the Sahā World, all the sentient beings in this billion-world universe, including the beings in the planes of hell-dwellers, animals, hungry ghosts, and the domain of Yama, became tranquil, physically and mentally peaceful and happy, and free from desire, hatred, ignorance, and other poisonous mentalities, such as jealousy, deceit, arrogance, and ill temper. All those sentient beings became kind and extremely joyful. Why? Because of the awesome, miraculous [blessing] power of the great Bodhisattvas from [the worlds in] the ten directions.

When the infinite . . . Bodhisattva-Mahāsattvas from the ten directions arrived at the dwelling-place of the World-Honored One, . . . they bowed down with their heads at the Buddha's feet and circumambulated him three times to the right. Then, they ascended in midair and entered the Samādhi of Invisibility. When they were in the samādhi, sitting cross-legged on hundreds of thousands of various wonderfully colored large lotus flowers, . . . they hid themselves from view and did not appear again. . . .

Then the Venerable Mahākāśyapa asked the Buddha, "World-Honored One of great virtue, why is there such a subtle, wonderful light in the world? Why do such clear, unprecedented auspicious signs suddenly appear?"

The World-Honored One answered Mahākāśyapa, "Kāśyapa, you should not ask these questions. Why? Because this realm is beyond the comprehension of Śrāvakas and Pratyekabuddhas. If I speak of the meaning of this light, all the humans, devas, and asuras will be afraid, doubtful, and confused. Therefore, you should not ask."

Mahākāśyapa entreated the Buddha further, "May the World-Honored One of great kindness explain the profound occurrence of this light to benefit and comfort all devas and humans.". . .

Thereupon, the Buddha told Mahākāśyapa, "Kāśyapa, now Mañjuśrī is in the Samādhi of Adorning All with Undefiled Illumination, and, because of the power of the samādhi, he is emitting this light to illuminate Buddha-lands more numerous than the sands of the Ganges in the ten directions, calling countless Bodhisattva-Mahāsattvas to the Sahā World. They have already arrived here, bowed down with their heads at my feet, and made three circumambulations to my right. Now they have ascended in midair to the height of a palm tree, sitting cross-legged on thrones of lotus flowers. . . .

"Kāśyapa, because all those Bodhisattva-Mahāsattvas are in the Samādhi of Invisibility, no Śrāvaka or Pratyekabuddha can see them; only Buddhas and great Bodhisattvas who abide in that realm can do so. . . ."

Mahākāśyapa asked the Buddha further, "World-Honored One, what achievements should a Bodhisattva-Mahāsattva attain, what good roots should he cultivate, and what merits should he acquire in order to enter the Samādhi of Invisibility?"

The Buddha answered Kāśyapa, "If a Bodhisattva-Mahāsattva achieves ten things, he can acquire the Samādhi of Invisibility. What are the ten?

(1) To be gentle, peaceful, and to abide deeply in right faith;
(2) never to forsake any sentient being;
(3) to achieve a mind of great kindness and great compassion;
(4) to understand all dharmas while remaining unattached to their forms;
(5) never to grasp delusively for any Buddha-Dharmas, in spite of his aspiration to seek them all;
(6) not to aspire for the wisdom of Śrāvakas or Pratyekabuddhas;
(7) to be capable of renouncing ungrudgingly all mundane possessions, even body and life, let alone other things;
(8) not to be contaminated by or attached to conditioned dharmas, although he may undergo countless afflictions in saṁsāra;
(9) to cultivate the immeasurable pāramitās of giving, discipline, patience, vigor, meditation, and wisdom without making distinctions among them; and
(10) always to think, 'I will establish all sentient beings in the pursuit of Buddha's enlightenment . . . and yet without conceiving any notion of enlightenment or sentient beings.'

Kāśyapa, the fulfilment of these ten things enables a Bodhisattva-Mahāsattva to obtain the Samādhi of Invisibility.". . .

Then the Venerable Mahākāśyapa said to the Buddha again, "World-Honored One, now we are very eager to see those Bodhisattva-Mahāsattvas. Why? Because it is a rare opportunity to encounter them."

The Buddha said to Kāśyapa, "You should wait until Mañjuśrī arrives. Those Bodhisattvas will rise from the samādhi, and after that, you may see them. Kāśyapa, now that you have acquired countless hundreds of thousands of samādhi doors,[4] you should concentrate your mind to discover where those Bodhisattva-Mahāsattvas abide, how they behave, and what they are doing."

As soon as he received the instruction of the Buddha, Mahākāśyapa entered twenty thousand different samādhi-doors by the awesome miraculous powers vested in him by the Buddha and by his own miraculous powers, trying to discover where those Bodhisattvas were and how they behaved. [He thought,] "Are they walking? I cannot see them walking. Are they standing? I cannot see them standing. Are they lying down? I cannot see them lying down. Are they sitting? I cannot see them sitting. What is more, I do not know what they are saying, what activities they are engaged in, where they come from, or where they are going."

He then rose from the samādhis and approached the Buddha, saying, "It is strange, World-Honored one! It is strange, World-Honored One! I entered twenty thousand samādhi-doors to seek those Bodhisattvas, but I did not see any of them. World-Honored One, even those Bodhisattvas, who have not yet realized all-knowing wisdom, have obtained such a wonderful samādhi. What could be said of those who have attained supreme enlightenment! World-Honored One, it is absolutely impossible for the good men and good women who have witnessed this miraculous feat not to bring forth supreme bodhicitta promptly. World-Honored One, even the Samādhi of Invisibility is so powerful that it is beyond my comprehension, let alone other, [superior] samādhis."[5]

The Buddha told Kāśyapa, "It is so, it is so, just as you say. Even Śrāvakas[6] and Pratyekabuddhas cannot comprehend this realm, let alone other sentient beings." . . .

II

At that time, certain leading devas in the assembly, such as Well-Abiding Mind, Wonderfully Tranquil, and Humility, accompanied by nine billion six hundred million devas, all of whom followed the Bodhisattva-path, went together to Mañjuśrī's dwelling place. When they arrived at his door, they made seven circumambulations to the right, and then caused celestial flowers of the coral tree to rain down. The flowers raining down spread out in space to form a floral net, [and then accumulated, forming a floral] platform ten leagues[7] high, shaped like a precious stūpa.

Mañjuśrī picked up the floral platform and offered it to the World-Honored One, and then, by his miraculous powers, he caused the space over all the lands in the billion-world universe to be spread with floral nets. The radiance of the flowers illuminated the whole billion-world universe, making it become clear and bright throughout. There also rained down celestial flowers of the coral tree.

Then Bodhisattva-Mahāsattva Mañjuśrī, graceful and serene, emerged from his dwelling. By his miraculous powers, he further caused a wonderful throne made of the seven treasures to appear spontaneously in that place, a throne most majestic and beautiful. After adjusting his robe, Mañjuśrī took his seat on the precious throne with a solemn look. As soon as he saw that Mañjuśrī had been seated on the precious throne, the deva Well-Abiding Mind bowed down with his head at Mañjuśrī's feet, and then stood to one side. The other devas all did the same.

At that time, Mañjuśrī thought, "Today, who can discuss the profound Dharma with me in the presence of the World-Honored One? Who can be the Dharma-vessel to take in statements that are inconceivable; statements that are most difficult to realize; statements without a location,[8] beyond attachment, and beyond play-words; statements which are inapprehensible, inexpressible, very profound, true, unhindered, and indestructible; statements concerning emptiness, signlessness, and wishlessness; statements concerning suchness, reality, and the dharmadhātu; statements that are intangible, and cannot be grasped or abandoned; statements concerning the Buddha, the Dharma, and the Saṁgha; statements concerning the fullness of wisdom, the equality of the three realms, the unattainability of all dharmas, and the nonarising of all dharmas; statements of the lion;[9] statements of valor; statements which are no statements at all? Who can hear these statements?"

Mañjuśrī continued thinking, "Now, among the devas here, only Well-Abiding Mind has made offerings to many Buddhas, attained the realization of the profound Dharma, and fully acquired eloquence; he alone can discuss the meaning of reality with me in the presence of the World-Honored One."

With this thought, Mañjuśrī said to Well-Abiding Mind, "Son of heaven, you have already attained the realization of the profound Dharma and fully acquired unhindered eloquence. Shall we now go to see the World-Honored One to discuss the profound, subtle doctrines?"

Well-Abiding mind answered Mañjuśrī, "Great sage, I would only discuss [these doctrines] with a person who does not speak to me, nor give me any discourse, question me, or answer me; or else with a person who says that there is no Buddha, Dharma, or Saṁgha, that the three vehicles should be put to an end, that there is neither saṁsāra nor nirvāṇa, that dharmas neither combine nor scatter, that nothing is revealed or generated, that no sound is uttered, and that all words should be put aside."

Mañjuśrī said to Well-Abiding Mind, "Son of heaven, I would speak to one who can take in my [discourse] without hearing, without reading, without reciting, without accepting, without upholding, without thinking, without remembering, without grasping, without abandoning, without perceiving, without knowing, and without listening to my words or explaining them to others.[10] Why? Because the bodhi of all Buddhas is originally beyond all letters, without mind and apart from the mind, and devoid of enlightenment. Though enlightenment is spoken of with arbitrary names, the names are also empty."

Well-Abiding Mind continued, "Great sage, now please discourse to these devas. They are willing and happy to hear whatever you say."

Mañjuśrī said, "Son of heaven, I will not discourse to those who like to listen, nor to those who accept what they have heard. Why? Because those who like to listen and those who accept a discourse are attached. To what are they attached? They are attached to a self, a personal identity, a sentient being, a life, and a person. Being attached, they accept what they have heard. It should be known that those who accept what they have heard abide in three kinds of bonds. What are the three? The view of a self, the view of a sentient being, and the view of dharmas. Son of heaven, you should know that those who hear the Dharma explained without being bound by these three views abide in three kinds of purity. What are the three? Not to see, distinguish, think of, or perceive oneself [as a hearer]; not to see, distinguish, think of, or perceive someone as a teacher; and not to see, distinguish, think of, or perceive something as being taught. These are the three kinds of purity. Son of heaven, if a person is able to hear in this way, he hears with equality, not with inequality."

Well-Abiding Mind praised Mañjuśrī, saying, "Well said, well said! How wonderfully you have spoken! Great sage, those who can speak thusly will certainly not regress."

Mañjuśrī said, "Stop, son of heaven! You should not think delusively and discriminatively of the regression of a Bodhisattva. Why? Because if a Bodhisattva ever regresses, he will never be able to attain supreme enlightenment. Why? Because in bodhi there is no such thing as regression."

At this, Well-Abiding Mind asked, "Great sage, if so, from what does regression arise?"

Mañjuśrī answered, "Son of heaven, regression arises from desire, hatred, and ignorance; from craving for existence; from ignorance up to birth and death—the twelve links of dependent origination; from causes, views, names, and forms; from the Realm of Desire, the Realm of Form, and the Realm of Formlessness; from the deeds of a Śrāvaka and the deeds of a Pratyekabuddha; from discrimination, attachment, signs, and clinging to signs; from the view of nihilism and the view of eternalism; from grasping and abandoning; from the thought of a self, the thought of a sentient being, the thought of a life, the thought of a person, and the thought of a personal identity; from thinking, bondage, and perversion; from the view of a self and the sixty-two views based on the view of a self; from the [five] covers; from the [five] aggregates, the [twelve] entrances, and the [eighteen] elements; from the thought of the Buddha, the thought of the Dharma, and the thought of the Saṁgha; and from such thoughts as: 'I shall become a Buddha,' 'I shall teach the Dharma,' 'I shall deliver sentient beings from saṁsāra,' 'I shall defeat demons,' and 'I shall acquire wisdom!' Therefore, son of heaven, if one does not discriminate the Tathāgata's ten powers, four fearlessnesses, and eighteen unique qualities; his roots, powers, enlightenment, and path;[11] . . . and does not discriminate those who discriminate and regress—then he is said to be nonregressing."

Well-Abiding Mind asked Mañjuśrī further, "Great sage, if so, how can a Bodhisattva achieve nonregression?"

Mañjuśrī answered, "Son of heaven, you should know that nonregression can be achieved from being conversant with the Buddha-wisdom, with emptiness, with signlessness, with wishlessness, with suchness, with the Dharma-nature, with reality, and with equality."

Well-Abiding Mind said, "Great sage, according to what you say, discrimination and nondiscrimination are not different. Why? Because they both arise from thinking and discrimination. In this sense, regression may be spoken of."

Then he asked further, "Is regression existent or nonexistent?"

Mañjuśrī answered, "Regression is neither existent nor nonexistent."

Well-Abiding Mind asked, "Great sage, if so, how can one regress?"

Mañjuśrī answered, "To regard regression as existent and to regard it as nonexistent are both delusory grasping, perverted grasping, and devious grasping. I refer to regression in such a sense that I do not grasp for [its existence or nonexistence,] nor do I not grasp. The so-called regression cannot be said to be existent or nonexistent. Why not? Because whether you say that regression is existent or say it is nonexistent, in both cases you fall into error. Why? Because to say that regression exists is to err on the extreme of eternalism, while to say that regression does not exist is to err on the extreme of nihilism. The World-Honored One says that one should abide neither in eternalism nor in nihilism; that things should be regarded neither nihilistically nor eternalistically.

"Son of heaven, if, in the way I have described, one considers [regression] as unreal, then his view is neither nihilistic nor eternalistic. Son of heaven, this is the Dharma-door of a Bodhisattva's [non-] regression."

When this doctrine was spoken, ten thousand devas achieved the Realization of the Nonarising of Dharmas.

III

Well-Abiding Mind said to Mañjuśrī, "Great sage, now we may go together to see the Tathāgata, prostrate ourselves with our heads at his feet, hear from him doctrines we have not yet heard, and raise our questions in accordance with the Dharma."

Mañjuśrī said, "Son of heaven, do not attach yourself discriminatively to the Tathāgata!"

Well-Abiding Mind asked, "Great sage, where is there any Tathāgata to be attached to?"

Mañjuśrī answered, "He is here now."

Well-Abiding Mind asked, "If so, why do I not see him?"

Mañjuśrī answered, "Son of heaven, if you can see nothing now, you really see the Tathāgata."

Well-Abiding Mind asked, "If the Tathāgata is here now, why do you warn me not to be attached to him?"

Mañjuśrī asked, "Son of heaven, what is here now?"

Well-Abiding Mind answered, "The realm of voidness."[12]

Mañjuśrī said, "It is so. Son of heaven, the Tathāgata is no other than the realm of voidness. Why? Because all dharmas are equal, like voidness. Voidness is the Tathāgata and the Tathāgata is voidness. Voidness and the Tathāgata are not two; they are not different. Son of heaven, he who wishes to see the Tathāgata should contemplate in this way. If he comprehends Reality as it is, he will find that nothing in it can be discriminated."

Then, by his miraculous powers, Bodhisattva-Mahāsattva Mañjuśrī produced from nothing thirty-two square, multistoried, jeweled halls furnished with imperial carriages. . . . In the halls, there were wonderful precious couches covered with exquisite garments. On each couch sat a magically produced Bodhisattva possessing the thirty-two auspicious signs of a great man.[13]

Having manifested these magnificent things, Mañjuśrī left to see the Buddha, together with the magically produced Buddhas and Bodhisattvas sitting on their lotus seats . . . in jeweled halls furnished with imperial carriages. Having made seven circumambulations to the right of the Buddha and his monks, they all leapt into midair and illuminated the assembly at the Dharma-site[14] with their lights. Then they stood to the four sides.

Though Mañjuśrī had set out later than Well-Abiding Mind, he had suddenly arrived at the Buddha's dwelling-place earlier than the deva.

Well-Abiding Mind asked, you take to arrive here so quickly?"

Mañjuśrī answered, "Son of heaven, even those who make offerings and pay homage to Tathāgatas as numerous as the sands of the Ganges cannot see my going and coming, advancing and stopping." . . .

IV

The Venerable Śāriputra asked the Buddha, "World-Honored One, who has caused this auspice? Who can cause . . . the magically produced Bodhisattvas sitting on the lotus seats, and also those in the jeweled halls furnished with imperial carriages, to emit great lights illuminating the assembly, . . . and cause such incalculable billions of devas and innumerable Bodhisattvas to come to join us?"

The Buddha answered Śāriputra, "The awesome miraculous powers of Mañjuśrī cause these wonderful, magnificent things to appear and the multitudinous Bodhisattvas and devas to gather together. Why? Śāriputra, because Mañjuśrī and the deva Well-Abiding Mind have led a great assembly here in order to ask me about the Dharma-door called the Samādhi of Defeating Demons, and how the inconceivable, profound Buddha-Dharma can be fully achieved."

Then Śāriputra asked the Buddha, "World-Honored One, if so, why do I not see Mañjuśrī in the assembly?"

The Buddha answered Śāriputra, "Wait a moment. Mañjuśrī has gone to cause all the demon kings and their subjects and palaces to undergo great ruin and deterioration. His miraculous feats are awesome and magnificent. He is about to come back, and you will see him yourself."

Meanwhile, Mañjuśrī had entered the Samādhi of Defeating Demons. Because of the power of this samādhi, ten billion demon palaces in the billion-world universe immediately became dilapidated, old, and dark, and seemed about to fall to ruin. After undergoing these changes, the demons' palaces lost their splendor and were no longer liked by the demons. The demons saw their bodies become dull, decrepit, weak, and emaciated, and they had to walk with staffs; and the celestial maidens[15] were transformed into old hags. Seeing these [changes], all the demons felt very distressed, and the hair on their bodies stood on end. They each thought fearfully to themselves, "What bizarre events and inauspicious signs are these occurring inside and outside of my body? Has the hour of death come and my karmic reward been spent? Are these the catastrophes heralding the destruction of the world at the end of the kalpa?"

When the demons were thinking in this way, Mañjuśrī again used his miraculous powers to magically produce ten billion devas who appeared before the demons and told them, "Don't be worried and afraid! These are not misfortunes befalling you, nor do they signify the end of the kalpa. Why? There is a nonregressing, great Bodhisattva named Mañjuśrī, who has great, awesome miraculous powers and excels worldly beings in virtue. Now he is entering the Dharma-door called the Samādhi of Defeating Demons. It is because of the awesome power of that Bodhisattva's samādhi that all these things take place, not for other reasons."

When the magically produced devas said this, all the demon kings and their subjects became more fearful on hearing . . . the name of Bodhisattva Mañjuśrī; all of them trembled and felt insecure, and all of their palaces shook violently.

Thereupon, the demon kings begged the magically produced devas, "May you be so kind as to save us from danger!"

The magically produced devas said to the demons, "Do not be afraid! Do not be afraid! Now you had better go quickly to see Śākyamuni Buddha, the World-Honored One. Why? Because that Buddha, the Tathāgata, is very kind and compassionate; sentient beings will be eased of their worries and sufferings and be given peace and happiness if they go to take refuge in him when they are afflicted with melancholy and fear."

Having uttered these words, the magically produced devas disappeared suddenly. At that time, all the demon kings and their subjects were overjoyed at what the magically produced devas had told them. Although so emaciated and weak that they had to walk with staffs, they all wished to go. Instantaneously, they arrived at the place where Śākyamuni Buddha was and said in unison, "World-Honored One with great virtue, may you protect and save us from the pain and peril of this bizarre catastrophe! May you protect and save us! We would rather accept the names of hundreds of thousands of millions of billions of Buddhas than hear Bodhisattva Mañjuśrī's name alone. Why? Because as soon as we hear the name of Bodhisattva Mañjuśrī mentioned, we feel greatly terrified, as if we were going to die."

At this, the World-Honored One said to the demons, "Pāpīyāns,[16] why do you say this? Whatever Bodhisattva Mañjuśrī teaches is beneficial to sentient beings. Hundreds of thousands of [millions of] billions of Buddhas never accomplished this in the past, nor are they doing it at present, nor will they do so in the future. It is Mañjuśrī alone who has done, is doing, and will do this great feat for sentient beings.[17] After he has brought sentient beings to maturity, he leads them to liberation. Why do you, who are not distressed or terrified even when hearing the names of hundreds of thousands of Buddhas, say 'We are horrified when we suddenly hear the name of Mañjuśrī'?"

The demons replied, "World-Honored One, we utter these words because we are ashamed and afraid to become old and weak. World-Honored One, from now on we take refuge in you, the Perfectly Enlightened One. May you be so kind as to restore us to our original appearance!"

The Buddha told them, "Wait a moment. When Mañjuśrī returns, he will rid you of your shame."

Having risen from his samādhi, Mañjuśrī returned to the Buddha together with incalculable hundreds of thousands of devas, Bodhisattva-Mahāsattvas, dragons, yakṣas, gandharvas, asuras, . . . and so forth. . . . On arrival, they bowed down with their heads at the Buddha's feet, made three circumambulations to his right, and then stood to one side.

The World-Honored One asked Mañjuśrī, "Mañjuśrī, did you enter the Samādhi of Defeating Demons?"

Mañjuśrī answered, "Yes, World-Honored One, I did so for some time."

The Buddha asked, "Mañjuśrī, from what Buddha did you hear this samādhi? How long did it take you to cultivate and achieve it?"

Mañjuśrī answered, "World-Honored One, before I brought forth bodhicitta, I had heard this samādhi from a Buddha."

The Buddha asked, "Mañjuśrī, what was the name of that Buddha, that World-Honored One, who explained this samādhi to you?"

Mañjuśrī answered, "World-Honored One, I remember that countless, inconceivable, incalculable numbers of kalpas ago, there was a Buddha named Tathāgata Fragrance of the Coral Tree Flower, the Worthy One. . . . He explained the Samādhi of Defeating Demons when he appeared in the world. I heard it then for the first time."

The Buddha asked Mañjuśrī, "How can one cultivate and achieve this samādhi?"

Mañjuśrī answered, "World-Honored One, if a Bodhisattva-Mahāsattva performs twenty things to perfection, he can achieve this Samādhi of Defeating Demons. What are the twenty?

(1) To denounce desire and destroy the mind of desire;
(2) to denounce hatred and destroy the mind of hatred;
(3) to denounce ignorance and destroy the mind of ignorance;
(4) to denounce jealousy and destroy the mind of jealousy;
(5) to denounce arrogance and destroy the mind of arrogance;

(6) to denounce the [five] covers and destroy the mind blocked by the five covers;
(7) to denounce burning passions and destroy the mind afflicted with burning passions;
(8) to denounce thoughts and destroy the thinking mind;
(9) to denounce views and destroy the mind holding to views;
(10) to denounce discrimination and destroy the discriminating mind;
(11) to denounce grasping and destroy the grasping mind;
(12) to denounce attachment and destroy the attached mind;
(13) to denounce forms and destroy the mind attached to forms;
(14) to denounce the existence of dharmas and destroy the mind that believes in the existence of dharmas;
(15) to denounce the [view that] dharmas are permanent and destroy the mind that believes in the permanence of dharmas;
(16) to denounce the [view of the] annihilation of dharmas and destroy the mind that believes in the annihilation of dharmas;
(17) to denounce the [five] aggregates and destroy the mind attached to the [five] aggregates;
(18) to denounce the [twelve] entrances and destroy the mind attached to the [twelve] entrances;
(19) to denounce the [eighteen] elements and destroy the mind attached to the [eighteen] elements; and
(20) to denounce the three realms and destroy the mind attached to the three realms.

World-Honored One, a Bodhisattva-Mahāsattva who fulfils these twenty deeds will achieve this samādhi.

"Furthermore, World-Honored One, a Bodhisattva-Mahāsattva who cultivates four things to perfection can achieve this samādhi. What are the four?

(1) To be pure and gentle in mind and deed;
(2) to be simple, honest, and straightforward;
(3) to be mentally attached to nothing and to penetrate into the realization of the profound Dharma; and
(4) to be able to give everything, internal and external.[18]

"Furthermore, World-Honored One, a Bodhisattva-Mahāsattva who accomplishes four things can achieve this samādhi. What are the four?

(1) To have a perfectly deep mind;[19]
(2) to speak honestly;
(3) to enjoy living constantly in a secluded place; and
(4) to be unattached to forms.

"Furthermore, if a Bodhisattva accomplishes four things, he can achieve this samādhi. What are the four?

(1) To associate closely with virtuous friends;
(2) to be content always;
(3) to sit alone in meditation; and
(4) not to take pleasure in noisy crowds. . . .

"Furthermore, if a Bodhisattva accomplishes four things, he can achieve this samādhi. What are the four?

(1) To cultivate emptiness and give up ego;
(2) to cultivate signlessness and be detached from all signs;
(3) to cultivate wishlessness and get rid of all wishes; and
(4) to abandon all possessions. . . ."

At this, the Venerable Śāriputra said to the Buddha, "How extraordinary it is, World-Honored One, that Mañjuśrī could achieve the Samādhi of Defeating Demons long, long ago and, by the power of this samādhi, can cause Pāpīyāns [demon-kings] and their demon subjects to become so decrepit, grayhaired, and weak in appearance and will."

The Buddha said to Śāriputra, "What do you think? Do you say that Mañjuśrī has made only the demons of this billion-world universe so decrepit? Śāriputra, you should not think in this way. Why? Because, Śāriputra, now all the other demons in the Buddha-lands as numerous as the sands of the Ganges in the ten directions are debilitated, too. This is completely due to Mañjuśrī's awesome powers."

Then the World-Honored One told Mañjuśrī, "Mañjuśrī, now withdraw your miraculous powers and restore the demons to their original appearance."

When he received the instruction of the Buddha, Mañjuśrī asked the demons, "Kind sirs, do you really detest this appearance of yours?"

The demons answered, "Yes, great sage."

Mañjuśrī said to the demons, "If so, now you should detest desire and not attach yourselves to the three realms."

The demons said, "Yes, great sage. After we hear your good teachings, how dare we disobey? May you use a little of your awesome miraculous powers to free us from this shame and pain!"

Thereupon, Mañjuśrī withdrew his miraculous powers and restored the demons to their original appearance, so that they became as magnificent as before.

Then, Mañjuśrī said to the demons, "Pāpīyāns, take your eyes for example. What is the eye? What is the thought of the eye? Where is the attachment of the eye, the form of the eye, the entanglement of the eye, the hindrance of the eye, the notion of the eye, the ego of the eye, the reliance of the eye, the joy of the eye, the play-words of the eye, the ego-objects of the eye, the protection of the eye, the impression of the eye, the grasping of the eye, the abandoning of the eye, the discrimination of the eye, the contemplation of the eye, the achievement of the eye, the arising of the eye, the cessation of the eye, and so on, including the coming and going of the eye? All these notions cherished in your minds become demonic deeds and obstructions of your realm. So it is with the ear, nose, tongue, body, and mind; forms, sounds, odors, tastes, textures, and dharmas. All these notions cherished in your mind become demonic deeds and obstructions of your realm. You should know them as they really are.

"Furthermore, Pāpīyāns, all your eyes are not eyes; they are no eyes. There is no thought of the eye, no attachment of the eye, no form of the eye . . . [and so on]. These dharmas are beyond your realm. You cannot be master of them; you have no method and no power to cope with them freely; they are beyond your grasping. So it is with the ear, nose, tongue, body, and mind; forms, sounds, odors, tastes, textures, and dharmas—all these you should know as they really are."

When Mañjuśrī had explained this doctrine in the assembly, ten thousand demon kings engendered supreme bodhicitta and eighty-four thousand demon subjects were freed from defilements and acquired the clear Dharma-eye.

V

Then the Venerable Mahākāśyapa said to the Buddha, "World-Honored One, we will ask Mañjuśrī to allow us to see those Bodhisattva-Mahāsattvas. Why? Because, World-Honored One, it is a rare opportunity to encounter such great sages."

The World-Honored One told Mañjuśrī at once, "You should know that everyone in this assembly is now yearning to see the physical forms of the Bodhisattva-Mahāsattvas who have come here from the ten directions. Now it is time for you to show them to us."

Having received the instruction of the Buddha, Mañjuśrī told Bodhisattva Dharma Wheel, Bodhisattva Moonlight, Bodhisattva Exorcising Demons, Bodhisattva Wonderful Voice, Bodhisattva Undefiled, Bodhisattva Ultimate Quiescence, Bodhisattva Choice, Bodhisattva Roaring of the Dharma King, and countless other Bodhisattva-Mahāsattvas, "Great sages, now you should reveal yourselves in your respective palaces and manifest the forms and shapes you have in your own lands."

After Mañjuśrī had said this, the Bodhisattvas rose from their samādhi and revealed their physical forms for the whole assembly to see. Some of the Bodhisattvas' physical forms were as big as Mount Sumeru. Some were eighty-four thousand leagues tall. Some were one hundred thousand leagues tall; some, ninety thousand, eighty thousand, seventy thousand, and so on down to ten thousand leagues. Some were . . . one thousand leagues . . . one hundred leagues . . . ten leagues . . . and so on down to one league. Some of the Bodhisattvas' physical forms were the height and size of the people in the Sahā World.

At that time, the billion-world universe was so fully occupied by the great crowd that [it appeared to have] no vacant space, not even the size of the head of a stick. All the Bodhisattva-Mahāsattvas in the universe were endowed with sublime merits, profound wisdom, and awe-inspiring power. By their miraculous powers, they emitted great lights to illuminate countless hundreds of thousands of Buddha-lands in the ten directions. . . .

Then Mañjuśrī rose from his seat, adjusted his robe, bared his right shoulder, knelt on his right knee, joined his palms toward the Buddha, and said, "World-Honored One, now I wish to ask the Tathāgata, the Worthy One, the Perfectly Enlightened One, some questions. Will the World-Honored One permit me to do so?"

The Buddha told Mañjuśrī, "The Tathāgata, the Worthy One, the Perfectly Enlightened One, permits you to ask your questions. He will explain the answers to you to resolve your doubts and give you joy.". . .

Mañjuśrī then asked, "World-Honored One, what is a Bodhisattva-Mahāsattva? What is the meaning of 'Bodhisattva'?"

The Buddha replied to Mañjuśrī, "You ask what is a Bodhisattva [-Mahāsattva] and what is the meaning of 'Bodhisattva.' A Bodhisattva-Mahāsattva is one who can understand and realize all dharmas. Mañjuśrī, the dharmas, all of which are realized by a Bodhisattva, are spoken of by mere words. . . . Mañjuśrī, the Bodhisattva realizes that the eye is by nature empty and, in spite of this realization, he never harbors any such thought as: 'I can realize [the eye].' Likewise, he realizes that the ear, nose, tongue, body, and mind are empty by nature, and in spite of this realization, he never harbors any such thought as: 'I can realize them.' He also realizes that form is by nature empty, and in spite of the realization, he never thinks discriminatively: 'I can realize [form].' Likewise, he realized that sounds, odors, tastes, textures, and dharmas are by nature empty, and in spite of this realization, he never thinks discriminatively: 'I can realize them.' These are the ways in which a Bodhisattva realizes all dharmas. . . .

"Furthermore, Mañjuśrī, how does a Bodhisattva-Mahāsattva realize desire, hatred, and ignorance? He realizes that desire is caused by discrimination; that hatred is caused by discrimination, and that ignorance is caused by discrimination. He also realizes that discrimination itself is empty, nonexistent, devoid of anything, beyond play-words, inexpressible, and unrealizable. These are the ways in which a Bodhisattva realizes all dharmas.

"Mañjuśrī, how does a Bodhisattva-Mahāsattva realize the three realms? He realizes that the Realm of Desire is without a self and a personal identity, that the Realm of Form is without action, that the Realm of Formlessness is empty and nonexistent, and that the three realms are remote and far away [from him].[20] These are the ways in which a Bodhisattva realizes all dharmas.

"Furthermore, Mañjuśrī, how does a Bodhisattva-Mahāsattva understand the deeds of sentient beings? He understands that some sentient beings act from desire; some from hatred; some from ignorance; and some equally from desire, hatred, and ignorance. After he understands and realizes this, he reveals his knowledge to sentient beings, then teaches and converts them, causing them to achieve liberation. These are the ways in which a Bodhisattva realizes all dharmas.

"Moreover, Mañjuśrī, how does a Bodhisattva-Mahāsattva understand all sentient beings? He understands all sentient beings by knowing that they are only names; that, apart from the names, there is no sentient being; that, therefore, all sentient beings are no other than one sentient being and one sentient being is no other than all sentient beings; and that, therefore, sentient beings are not sentient beings. If he can practice nondiscrimination in this way, the Bodhisattva-Mahāsattva realizes all dharmas.

"Furthermore, how does a Bodhisattva realize all dharmas? If a Bodhisattva-Mahāsattva can realize the path of enlightenment, he realizes all dharmas." . . .

VI

Mañjuśrī asked the Buddha, "World-Honored One, the Buddha has spoken of the Bodhisattva-Mahāsattva's initial generation of bodhicitta.[21] What do you mean by the initial generation of bodhicitta?"

The Buddha answered, "If a Bodhisattva views the three realms as equal and gives rise to all thoughts, he is said to be initially generating bodhicitta. Mañjuśrī, this is called the Bodhisattva's initial generation of bodhicitta."

Mañjuśrī said to the Buddha further, "World-Honored One, as I understand the doctrine taught by the Buddha, for a Bodhisattva, the generation of desire in his mind is the initial generation of bodhicitta; the generation of hatred in his mind is the initial generation of bodhicitta; the generation of ignorance in his mind is the initial generation of bodhicitta. World-Honored One, are these not the initial generation of bodhicitta?"

Then, the deva Well-Abiding Mind said to Mañjuśrī, "Great sage, if a Bodhisattva's generation of desire, hatred, and ignorance is called the initial generation of bodhicitta, then all the ordinary people in bondage are to be called Bodhisattvas who have generated bodhicitta. Why? Because ordinary people have always been generating the three poisons—desire, hatred, and ignorance—in their minds, from the [beginningless] past until now."

Mañjuśrī said to Well-Abiding Mind, "Son of heaven, you say that ordinary people have always been generating the three poisons in their minds, from the past until now. That is not true. Why not? Because, their minds being weak and inferior, ordinary people cannot generate desire, hatred, or ignorance. Only Buddhas, World-Honored Ones, Arhats, Pratyekabuddhas, and Bodhisattvas who have attained the stage of nonregression can generate desire, hatred, and ignorance; ordinary people cannot do so."[22]

Well-Abiding Mind said, "Great sage, why do you now say such things, which may cause the assembly to feel ignorant and to fall into a terrible maze?"

Then, Mañjuśrī asked Well-Abiding Mind, "Son of heaven, what do you think? When a bird flying about in the sky leaves no trace in empty space, is it generating movement or not?"

Well-Abiding Mind answered, "We cannot say that it is not generating movement."

Mañjuśrī said, "It is so, it is so. Son of heaven, in this sense, I say that only Buddhas, Śrāvakas, Pratyekabuddhas, and nonregressing Bodhisattvas can generate desire, hatred, and ignorance.[23] Son of heaven, you should know that to rely on nothing is generation and that to be attached to nothing is generation. 'To rely on nothing and to be attached to nothing' is an expression of nothingness, which is called generation. It is an expression of nondiscrimination,[24] which is called generation. It is an expression of nonproduction, which is called generation. It is an expression of insubstantiality, which is called generation. It is an expression of nonentity, which is called generation. It is an expression of no coming, which is called generation. It is an expression of no going, which is called generation. It is an expression of nonarising, which is called generation. It is an expression of no entanglement, which is called generation. It is an expression of no realization, which is called generation. It is an expression of no contention, which is called generation. It is an expression of no thinking, which is called generation. It is an expression of indistructability, which is called generation. It is an expression of inexpressibility, which is called generation. It is an expression of unbreakability, which is called generation. It is an expression of wordlessness, which is called generation. It is an expression of no clinging, which is called generation. It is an expression of no abiding, which is called generation. It is an expression of no grasping, which is called generation. It is an expression of no abandoning, which is called generation. It is an expression of no eradication, which is called generation. Son of heaven, you should know that this is the Bodhisattva's initial generation of bodhicitta.

"Son of heaven, if a Bodhisattva who brings forth bodhicitta does not attach himself to, nor think about, nor see, nor know, nor hear, nor recognize, nor grasp, nor abandon, nor engender, nor eliminate any dharma, he has truly brought forth bodhicitta.

"Son of heaven, if a Bodhisattva-Mahāsattva can thus rely on the dharmadhātu, equality, reality, and ingenuity, he will generate desire, hatred, and ignorance. If he can definitely rely on these, he will generate the eye, ear, nose, tongue, body, and mind; and will generate the attachment to form, feeling, conception, impulse, and consciousness. In this way, he will generate all views; he will generate ignorance and craving for existence; he will generate the twelve links of dependent origination; he will generate the five sensuous desires; he will generate attachment to the three realms; he will generate the view of 'I'; he will generate the view of 'mine'; he will generate the sixty-two views based on the view of 'I'; he will generate the thoughts of the Buddha, the Dharma, and the Saṅgha; self and others; earth, water, fire, air, space, and consciousness; he will generate the four wrong views; he will generate the four abodes of consciousness;[25] he will generate the five covers; he will generate the eight errors,[26] the nine afflictions,[27] and the ten evil deeds.

"Son of heaven, I say briefly that Bodhisattvas should generate all discriminations, all objects of discrimination, all modes of expression, all forms, all pursuits, all aspirations, all attachments, all thoughts, all ideas, and all hindrances. You should know them as they really are. Son of heaven, because of this, if you are able not to attach yourself to or think of these dharmas, you truly generate them."[28]

The World-Honored One praised Mañjuśrī, saying, "Well said, well said, Mañjuśrī! It is excellent that you have fully explained for these Bodhisattvas the meaning of the initial generation of bodhicitta.[29] Mañjuśrī, it is because in the past you made offerings to innumerable Buddhas, World-Honored Ones, more numerous than the sands of the Ganges, that you can do this now."

The Venerable Śāriputra asked the Buddha, "World-Honored One, is the Bodhisattva's initial generation of bodhicitta, as explained by Mañjuśrī, equal to and not different from the Bodhisattva's [later] attainment of the Realization of the Nonarising of Dharmas?"[30]

The Buddha answered, "It is so, it is so, just as you say. Śāriputra, in the past, Dīpaṁkara, the World-Honored One, predicted, 'Māṇavaka, you will become a Buddha named Śākyamuni Tathāgata, the Worthy One, the Perfectly Enlightened One, after incalculable numbers of kalpas in the future.' Śāriputra, at that time, I achieved the Realization of the Nonarising of Dharmas without parting from [such a state of] mind. Therefore, Śāriputra, you should know that the Bodhisattva's initial generation of bodhicitta is exactly what Mañjuśrī has said it is, and not something else."

Mañjuśrī said to the Buddha, "World-Honored One, as I understand the doctrine taught by the Buddha, all [generations of bodhicitta] are the initial generation of bodhicitta. Why? Because, according to what the World-Honored One has said, the initial generation is no generation, and no generation is the Bodhisattva's initial generation of bodhicitta."

When this doctrine was spoken, twenty-three thousand Bodhisattvas attained the Realization of the Nonarising of Dharmas; five thousand monks ended their defilements and achieved liberation; and six billion devas were freed from filth and acquired the clear Dharma-eye.

Then Mahākāśyapa said to the Buddha, "World-Honored One, Mañjuśrī can do such a difficult deed as explaining this very profound Dharma-door for the great benefit of many sentient beings."

Mañjuśrī said to Kāśyapa, "Virtuous Kāśyapa, actually I have never done anything that was difficult to do. Why? Because no deed[31] is done; nothing was, is, or will be done. For this reason, Mahākāśyapa, I do not perform any deeds, nor leave any deeds undone. Kāśyapa, I do not deliver sentient beings from saṁsāra, nor do I let them remain in bondage. Why? Because all dharmas are nonexistent.

Kāśyapa, why do you say in the presence of the World-Honored One that I can do what is difficult to do? Mahākāśyapa, I do nothing; therefore, be careful not to say that I can do what is difficult to do. Mahākāśyapa, I really do not do anything. Not only do I do nothing, but Tathāgatas, Pratyekabuddhas, and Arhats also do nothing. Mahākāśyapa, who can do what is difficult to do? Correctly speaking, only children and ordinary persons can do what is difficult to do, and one who says so is called an able speaker. Why? Because no Tathāgata acquires, has acquired, or will acquire anything. Śrāvakas and Pratyekabuddhas do not acquire anything, either. Only ordinary people acquire all things."

At this, Mahākāśyapa asked Mañjuśrī, "Great sage, what do Buddhas not acquire?"

Mañjuśrī answered, "Buddhas do not acquire a self, nor a personal identity, nor a sentient being, nor a life, nor a person, nor a view of nihilism or eternalism, nor the [five] aggregates, nor the [twelve] entrances, nor the [eighteen] elements, nor name and form; [they do not acquire] the Realm of Desire, Form, or Formlessness; [they do not acquire] discrimination, nor contemplation, nor mindfulness, nor anything arising from causes, nor perversion; [they do not acquire] desire, hatred, or ignorance; [they do not acquire] this era or any other era, nor the 'I' or 'mine.' In short, they do not acquire any dharma whatsoever. Virtuous Kāśyapa, not a single one of all the dharmas can be acquired or lost. There is no bondage and no liberation; no attachment and no relinquishment; no approaching and no departure. Thus, Kāśyapa, should you understand this Dharma-door. Buddhas, the World-Honored Ones, attain nothing, while ordinary people, who act against the Dharma and lack learning, attain everything. Therefore, ordinary people can do what is difficult to do, not Buddhas, Pratyekabuddhas, or Arhats. This is called the action of ordinary people."

Kāśyapa asked further, "What do ordinary people do?"

Mañjuśrī answered, "They hold the view of nihilism and the view of eternalism; become contaminated and attached; rely upon someone or something; remember and think of the past; grasp and abandon things; wield all play-words; and discriminate things as superior or inferior and act accordingly. Therefore, Virtuous Kāśyapa, the Buddhas, the World-Honored Ones, do not do anything. They have not done, do not do, and will not do anything. Only ordinary people can do what is difficult to do."

Then Mañjuśrī asked the Buddha, "World-Honored one, what is the so-called Realization of Nonarising? World-Honored One, why is it also called the Realization of the Nonarising of Dharmas? How can a Bodhisattva achieve this realization?"

The Buddha replied to Mañjuśrī, "Actually, not a single person achieves the Realization of the Nonarising [of Dharmas] amid the dharmas which arise. To say that one has achieved it is nothing but words. Why? Because the dharmas that do not arise are unattainable and beyond perception, so that the Realization [of the

Nonarising] of Dharmas is unattainable. To attain is not to attain; there is nothing to attain or to lose—this is called the attainment of the Realization of the Nonarising of Dharmas.

"Furthermore, Mañjuśrī, the Realization of the Nonarising of Dharmas is to realize in this way: no dharma arises; no dharma comes; no dharma goes; no dharma has a self; no dharma has a master; no dharma is grasped; no dharma is abandoned; no dharma can be found; no dharma is real; all dharmas are supreme; all dharmas are equal to the supreme; all dharmas are incomparable; all dharmas are uncontaminated, like space; all dharmas are free from destruction, apart from nihilism, undefiled, beyond purity, empty, signless, and unsought; all dharmas are apart from desire, hatred, and ignorance; all dharmas are no other than suchness, the Dharma-nature, and reality. Thus should one realize that all dharmas are beyond discrimination, response, memory, play-words, contemplation, action, and power, and that all dharmas are fragile, false, and deceptive, just like illusions, dreams, echoes, shadows, reflections in a mirror, [hollow] plantains, foam, and bubbles on water. In that which is realized, there is nothing to be realized. The realization is neither a dharma nor a nondharma; it is only by words that the realization is spoken of, yet these words are also inapprehensible, being devoid of basic nature.

"If, concerning the realization thus explained, a Bodhisattva-Mahāsattva has faith, understanding, and aspiration; is free of doubt, bewilderment, fear, horror, vacillation, and depression; normally feels all kinds of sensations through contact without conceiving that there is a body or an abiding place; then, Mañjuśrī, he attains the Realization of the Nonarising of All Dharmas. He attains it also because there is no thought whatsoever acting [in his mind]."

Then Mañjuśrī asked the Buddha, "World-Honored One, what is the so-called realization? Is not that which cannot be damaged by external objects called realization?"

At this, Well-Abiding Mind asked Mañjuśrī, "Great sage, what is that which cannot be damaged by external objects?"

Mañjuśrī answered, "Son of heaven, what damages the eye? Good forms and bad forms damage the eye. Just as forms damage the eye, so sounds damage the ear; [odors, the nose; tastes, the tongue; textures, the body;] dharmas, the mind. Son of heaven, if a Bodhisattva sees forms with his eyes, he will not be attached to, indulge in, discriminate, conceptualize, crave, or abhor the forms, because he knows that they are empty by nature. He has no thought of forms, so he is not hurt by them. The same is true with the other sense-objects, including objects of the mind.

"Son of heaven, if a Bodhisattva is neither bound to nor hurt by his six senses, he abides in the Realization of the Dharma. Abiding in the Realization of the Dharma, he will do away with discrimination of all dharmas; he does not discriminate or think of them as arising or nonarising, defiled or undefiled, wholesome or unwholesome, conditioned or unconditioned, mundane or supramundane. This is called the Realization of the Nonarising of Dharmas."

When this doctrine was explained, sixty-three thousand sentient beings engendered supreme bodhicitta and twelve thousand Bodhisattvas acquired the Realization of the Nonarising of Dharmas. . . .

VII

Well-Abiding Mind asked Mañjuśrī further, "Great sage, if people come to you and ask to be fully ordained as śramaṇas, how do you answer them? How do you teach them the way to lead a monastic life? How do you confer the precepts upon them and teach them to keep the precepts?"

Mañjuśrī answered, "Son of heaven, if people come to me to renounce the household life, I teach them by saying, 'Good men, now you should not vow to leave the household life. If you do not vow to leave the household life, then I shall teach you the true ways to lead a monastic life.' Why? Because, son of heaven, one who seeks to leave the household life is [unwittingly] attached to[32] the Realms of Desire, Form, and Formlessness. He is also attached to the five sensuous pleasures of the world, to karmic rewards in the future, and so forth. If good people seek something, they will not realize the Dharma-truth, and as a result they will apprehend the mind. On the other hand, son of heaven, if people grasp nothing, they will realize the Dharma-truth, and as a result they will not apprehend the mind. Not perceiving the mind, they will not need to leave the household life; having no need to leave the household life, their intention to leave the household life will not arise; having no intention to leave the household life, they will not vow [to leave the household life]; not vowing [to leave the household life], they will give rise to nothing; giving rise to nothing, they will put an end to suffering; putting an end to suffering, they will achieve ultimate exhaustion; achieving ultimate exhaustion, they will achieve nonexhaustion; achieving nonexhaustion, they will be beyond exhaustion. What is beyond exhaustion is empty space.[33] Son of heaven, this is what I teach those good men.

"Furthermore, son of heaven, if people come to me and ask to leave the household life, I teach them, saying, 'Good men, do not vow to leave the household life. Why not? Because the vow does not arise and cannot be made. Do not think otherwise and still intend to make such a vow.'

"Furthermore, son of heaven, if people come to me and ask to leave the household life, I teach them, saying, 'Good men, if you do not shave your beard and hair[34] now, you have truly left the household life.'"

At this, Well-Abiding Mind asked Mañjuśrī, "Great sage, why do you say this?"

Mañjuśrī answered, "Son of heaven, the World-Honored One has said that there are no dharmas to be severed and renounced."

Well-Abiding Mind asked further, "What is not to be severed and renounced?"

Mañjuśrī answered, "Son of heaven, forms are not to be severed and renounced, nor are feelings, conceptions, impulses, or consciousness.

"Son of heaven, if someone thinks, 'Only after I shave my beard and hair am I a śramaṇa,' you should know that he abides in the notion of a self. Because he abides in the notion of a self, he does not perceive equality. Also, because he perceives a self, he perceives a sentient being. Because he perceives a sentient being, he perceives beard and hair. Because he perceives beard and hair, he engenders the thought of shaving.

"Son of heaven, if one does not perceive the form of self, he does not perceive the form of other. As a result, he is not arrogant. Because he is not arrogant, he does not hold the view of a self. Because he does not hold the view of a self, he does not discriminate. Because he does not discriminate, he does not waver. Because he does not waver, he does away with play-words. Because he does away with play-words, he grasps nothing and abandons nothing. Because he grasps nothing and abandons nothing, he is free of action and inaction, severance and nonseverance, separation and combination, decrease and increase, gathering and scattering, thought and mindfulness, speeches and words. Thus, he abides securely in the truth."

Well-Abiding Mind asked, "Great sage, what is the meaning of the truth?"

Mañjuśrī answered, "Son of heaven, the truth is no other than voidness.[35] Thus, voidness may be called the truth. Voidness is said to be the truth because it is without beginning and end, without decrease and increase. That [dharmas are] empty by nature is the truth. Suchness is the truth. The dharmadhātu is the truth. Reality is the truth. Thus, such a truth is no truth [at all]. Why? In the truth there is nothing to be obtained; therefore, it is said to be no truth [at all]."

Then Mañjuśrī said to Well-Abiding Mind, "Son of heaven, if people come to me and ask to leave the household life, I teach them, saying, 'Good men, if you can be unattached to a monastic robe now, I shall say that you have truly left the household life.'"

Well-Abiding Mind asked, "Great sage, why do you say this?"

Mañjuśrī answered, "Son of heaven, Buddhas, the World-Honored Ones, are attached to nothing. One should not grasp or be attached to anything they teach." . . .

At that time, Well-Abiding Mind asked Mañjuśrī, "Great sage, who is a monk who practices meditation?"

Mañjuśrī answered, "Son of heaven, if a monk selects one practice from all Dharma-teachings, that is, the doctrine of nonarising, and thoroughly complies with it, he is said to truly practice meditation. Moreover, [if he knows that] there is not a single dharma that can be grasped, he is said to practice meditation. What does he not grasp? He does not grasp this era or that era, the three realms, and so on, including all dharmas. [Abiding in] such equality, he is said to practice meditation. Son of heaven, if one who practices meditation does not respond to any dharma, neither unifying himself with it nor separating himself from it, he is said to [truly] practice meditation." . . .

VIII

Well-Abiding Mind asked Mañjuśrī, "Great sage, will you allow me to cultivate pure conduct [together with you]?"

Mañjuśrī answered, "Son of heaven, I shall give you permission to do so if you do not set your mind on practicing, seeking, or pursuing."

Well-Abiding Mind asked, "Great sage, why do you say this?"

Mañjuśrī answered, "Son of heaven, if there is action, pure conduct can be spoken of; if there is no action whatsoever, how can there be anything called pure conduct? Furthermore, son of heaven, if there is something apprehensible, pure conduct can be spoken of; if there is nothing apprehensible, how can there be anything called pure conduct?"

Well-Abiding Mind asked, "Great sage, are you not cultivating pure conduct now?"

Mañjuśrī answered, "No, son of heaven, I am not cultivating any pure conduct. Why not? Because the so-called pure conduct is not pure conduct; because it is not pure conduct, I call it pure conduct.". . .

Mañjuśrī continued, "Son of heaven, now, if you can take the lives of all sentient beings without using a knife, a cudgel, a large stick, or a stone, I will cultivate pure conduct with you."

Well-Abiding Mind asked, "Great sage, why do you say this?"

Mañjuśrī answered, "Son of heaven, regarding sentient beings, what do you think of them?"

Well-Abiding Mind answered, "I think that sentient beings and all other dharmas are nothing but names and are all concocted by thoughts."

Mañjuśrī said, "Son of heaven, I therefore say that now you should kill the thoughts of a self, of a personal identity, of a sentient being, and of a life, eliminating the thoughts even of these names. You should kill in this way."

Well-Abiding Mind asked, "Great sage, what instrument should one use to kill [in this way]?"

Mañjuśrī answered, "Son of heaven, I always kill with the sharp knife of wisdom. In the act of killing, one should hold the sharp knife of wisdom and kill in such a manner as to have no thought of holding the knife or of killing. Son of heaven, in this way, you should know well that to kill the thoughts of a self and a sentient being is to kill all sentient beings truly. [If you can do that,] I will give you permission to cultivate pure conduct [with me]." . . .

IX

At that time, in the assembly there were five hundred Bodhisattvas who had achieved the four dhyānas and the five miraculous powers. These Bodhisattvas were immersed in dhyāna, whether sitting or standing. They did not slander the Dharma, though they had not yet acquired the realization of the Dharma-truth. Possessing the miraculous power of knowing their past lives, these Bodhisattvas perceived their past evil karma—killing their fathers, mothers, or Arhats; destroying Buddhist temples or stūpas; or disrupting the Saṁgha. Because they clearly perceived their past evil karma, they were always obsessed by profound misgivings and remorse, so that they could not realize or penetrate the profound Dharma. It was because they discriminated a self and were unable to forget their past transgressions that they could not achieve the realization of the profound Dharma.

At that time, in order to rid those five hundred Bodhisattvas of mental discrimination, the World-Honored One inspired Mañjuśrī with his miraculous power; as a result, Mañjuśrī rose from his seat, adjusted his robe, bared his right shoulder, and holding a sharp sword in hand, advanced straight toward the World-Honored One to kill him.

Hurriedly, the Buddha said to Mañjuśrī, "Stop, stop! Do not do the wrong thing. Do not kill me in this way. If you must kill me, you should first know the best way to do so. Why? Because, Mañjuśrī, from the beginning there is no self, no others, no person; as soon as one perceives in his mind the existence of an ego and a personal identity, he has killed me; and this is called killing."

Having heard the Buddha say this, the [five hundred] Bodhisattvas thought, "All dharmas are illusory, like magic. In them there is no self, no personal identity, no sentient being, no life, no person, no human being, no youth, no father, no mother, no Arhat, no Buddha, no Dharma, no Saṁgha. There is neither killing nor killer; how can there be falling [to the miserable planes of existence] because of killing? Why is this so? Now, Mañjuśrī is wise and intelligent, and his unrivaled wisdom is praised by the Buddhas, the World-Honored Ones. He has already achieved the unhindered realization of the profound Dharma, made offerings to countless . . . billions of myriads of Buddhas . . . comprehended well and in detail all Buddha-Dharmas, and can discourse on those true doctrines. He [used to] have equal respect for all Tathāgatas. But now, he suddenly came to kill the Tathāgata with a sword, and the World-Honored One told him hurriedly, 'Stop, stop! Mañjuśrī, do not kill me! If you must, you should know the best way to kill me.' Why? Because if there were any real dharma that could come into existence through the combination of various elements, so that it could be called Buddha, Dharma, Saṁgha, father, mother . . . , and if these dharmas could definitely be grasped, then they could never be demolished. Actually, all dharmas are without substance or entity; they are nonexistent, unreal, delusive, perceived through wrong views, and empty, like magic productions. Therefore, there is no sinner and no sin. Where is the killer to be punished?"

Having contemplated and understood this, the [five hundred] Bodhisattvas immediately achieved the Realization of the Nonarising of Dharmas. Overwhelmed with joy, they ascended in midair to the height of seven palm trees one upon another, and spoke in verse:

"All dharmas are like magic;
They arise from discrimination.
None of them can be found;
All of them are empty.

Because of our perverted, delusive thoughts
And our ignorant, ego-grasping minds,
We brooded over the most wicked
Among our past karmas.
We committed great offenses
By killing fields of blessings—
Parents, Arhats, and monks
These are vile transgressions.
For these evil karmas,
We should undergo great pain.

Sentient beings caught in the net of doubt
Will be rid of their remorse and bewilderment
When they hear the Dharma explained.
The One with Great Renown[36]
Has extracted poison from us
And resolved all our doubts.

We have been enlightened to the dharmadhātu
And know that no evils can be found.
The Buddha possesses ingenuity
And understands well our thoughts.
He skillfully ferries sentient beings over saṁsāra,
And frees them from the bondage of doubts.

Where are the Buddhas?
Where are the Dharma and the Saṁgha?
Nowhere can they be found!
From the beginning,
There are no father and mother,
And Arhats are also empty and quiescent.
Since there is no killing of them,
How can there be retribution for that deed?

All dharmas by nature do not arise,
Like magical productions.

Mañjuśrī is a person of great wisdom,
Who has penetrated to the dharmas' source.
Wielding a sharp sword,
He rushed to kill the Tathāgata.
The sword and the Buddha
Are of one nature, not two;
Both are devoid of form and do not arise.
How can there be killing?"

When this subtle Dharma-door of wielding the sword was spoken, six quakes occured in Buddha-lands in the ten directions, as numerous as the sands of the Ganges. Meanwhile, in the Buddha-lands in the ten directions, all the Buddhas were teaching the Dharma before their assemblies. The Buddhas' attendant disciples rose from their seats and asked their respective Buddhas, "World-Honored One, who performed the miraculous feat that caused the great earths to quake?"

The Buddha in the ten directions answered their respective disciples, "Good men, there is a world named Sahā. In that land, there is a Buddha named Śākyamuni Tathāgata, the Worthy One, the Perfectly Enlightened One, who is now teaching the Dharma. In that world, there is an eminent Bodhisattva-Mahāsattva named Mañjuśrī, who has not regressed from supreme enlightenment since the remote past. In order to dispel the mental attachment of some novice Bodhisattvas, he himself, with a sharp sword in hand, rushed to kill Śākyamuni Tathāgata as a means of revealing the profound Dharma. It is for this reason that the great earths quaked. Because of this sword of Wisdom, that Buddha, the World-Honored One, explained the profound Dharma to cause incalculable myriads of sentient beings to acquire the clear Dharma-eye, to achieve mental liberation, or to attain the realization of the profound Dharma, so that they all abide securely in [the pursuit of] bodhi."

When performing this great miraculous feat, the World-Honored One, by the power of ingenuity, caused all the novice Bodhisattvas in the assembly who had few good roots, as well as the sentient beings who had not parted with discrimination and who were attached to forms, not to see Mañjuśrī wielding the sword, nor to hear the doctrine explained.[37]

At that time, the Venerable Śāriputra asked Mañjuśrī, "Great sage, now you have performed the most wicked karma. You attempted to kill the great Teacher of gods and humans. When this karma comes to maturity, what retribution will you receive?"

Mañjuśrī answered Śāriputra, "It is so, virtuous one, just as you say; I have performed such a wicked karma. However, I really do not know how I shall receive any retribution. Śāriputra, in my opinion, I shall undergo it just as a magically produced being does when his illusory karma ripens. Why? Because the magically produced being makes no discrimination and has no thoughts, and all dharmas are illusory, like magic. Furthermore, Śāriputra, let me ask you something, and you may answer as you like. What do you think? Do you think that you have really seen the sword?"

Śāriputra answered, "No."

Mañjuśrī asked, "Are you sure that the evil karma definitely exists?"

Śāriputra answered, "No."

Mañjuśrī asked, "Do you definitely perceive a retribution for that evil karma?"

Śāriputra answered, "No."

Mañjuśrī said, "Thus, Śāriputra, since there is no sword and no karma or retribution, who performs that karma and who will undergo the karmic retribution? Yet you now ask me what retribution I will receive."

Śāriputra asked, "Great sage, why do you say so?"

Mañjuśrī answered, "In my opinion, there is no such thing as the ripening of a karmic result. Why? Because all dharmas are devoid of karma, karmic results, and the ripening of karmic results." . . .

X

The World-Honored One said to Mañjuśrī, "Mañjuśrī, one who hears the explanation of this sūtra, this profound Dharma-door, is not different from one who lives at the time when a Buddha appears in the world. Mañjuśrī, one who hears this sūtra explained is not different from one who realizes the fruit of a Stream-enterer, of a Once-returner, of a Nonreturner, or of an Arhat. Why? Because this sūtra is not different from suchness.

"Mañjuśrī, one who believes and understands this sūtra after having heard it explained is not different from a Bodhisattva in his last existence, who will without fail attain supreme enlightenment sitting on the bodhi-site under the bodhi-tree. Why? Because this Dharma-door is the essential path of the Buddhas, the World-Honored Ones, in the past, present, and future."

At this, Mañjuśrī said to the Buddha, "World-Honored One, it is so, it is so, just as the Buddha says. This sūtra is not different from emptiness, signlessness, wishlessness, suchness, the dharmadhātu, reality, equality, liberation, and freedom from passions."

Then, Mañjuśrī continued, "World-Honored One, may the Tathāgata protect and maintain this profound Dharma-door so as to cause this sūtra to prevail in the world for five hundred years in the [coming] Last Era, so that all the good men and good women then will be able to hear it!"

When Mañjuśrī made this request, countless musical instruments sounded spontaneously in the billion-world universe, all the trees burgeoned spontaneously, and all the flowers bloomed. Also, six quakes occurred in the billion-world universe. Great lights were emitted to illuminate the whole billion-world universe so brightly that sunlight and moonlight were outshone and seen no more. . . .

Then, Mañjuśrī asked the Buddha, "World-Honored One, does this unusual auspice portend that this Dharma-door will last forever and prevail all over the world in the future?"

The Buddha replied, "It is so, it is so. This good omen is manifested solely to show that this sūtra will last forever and prevail all over the world.". . .

After the World-Honored One had finished teaching this sūtra, Mañjuśrī, Well-Abiding Mind, the Bodhisattvas from the ten directions, all the devas, the Venerable Śāriputra, the Venerable Mahākāśyapa, the monks, all the gods, humans, asuras, dragons, ghosts, spirits, and so forth were overjoyed at hearing what the Buddha had taught. They accepted it with faith and began to practice it with veneration.

NOTES

1. See Numerical Glossary, "five kinds of eyes." A Stream-enterer acquires the clear Dharma-eye, the enlightened vision which clearly *sees* the Dharma-truth—the emptiness of all dharmas. An Arhat or a Pratyekabuddha acquires the clear wisdom-eye, which enables him to *realize* or *penetrate* the Dharma-truth. The difference between the two is in their degree of profundity, not in their nature.

2. 'Disciples' here is not a translation of 'Śrāvakas'. As indicated below, many of the disciples are Bodhisattvas.

In this and many of the following passages, the Chinese text alternately reads 'disciples', 'attendants', or 'attendant disciples'. We have not adopted the term 'attendants', however.

3. See also "six pāramitās" in the Numerical Glossary.

4. Such samādhis are called samādhi-doors because they lead to the countless samādhis of Buddhas. (See *Ta Chih Tu Lun*, Chap. 22)

5. The original text reads: "World-Honored One, the Bodhisattva-Mahāsattvas who can achieve the Samādhi of Invisibility are never apart from this wonderful samādhi in spite of the fact that they wear the armor of vigor in order to save all sentient beings." Another rendering is: "World-Honored One, Bodhisattva-Mahāsattvas who can acquire the Samādhi of Invisibility, although they intend to be vigorous and save all sentient beings, should never be apart from this wonderful samādhi." Both translations do not fit the context. Thus we have here adopted Bodhiruci's version (Taishō 341, p. 119).

6. Mahākāśyapa is a Śrāvaka.

7. We translate the Skt. *yojana* as 'leagues', because we cannot find an exact equivalent. A *yojana* is said to be the distance of a day's march for the royal army.

8. I.e., inapprehensible.

9. In the Chinese tradition, Mañjuśrī is symbolically associated with the lion. He is

usually portrayed as riding a lion in Chinese art. The lion symbolizes intrepidity, which arises from wisdom. In Part IX below, Mañjuśrī, who is the embodiment of the wisdom of all Buddhas, dauntlessly wields the sword of wisdom.

10. Originally this sentence was translated: "Son of heaven, I would speak to one who can take in my [discourse] without hearing, reading, reciting, accepting, upholding, thinking, remembering, grasping, abandoning, perceiving, knowing. . . ." From the viewpoint of literary translation, this is preferable and less clumsy. However, from a religious or yogic viewpoint it is better to repeat each negation, so that a devoted reader can meditate on emptiness while he reads the sūtra. Thus our original translation would serve well as a conceptual negation of the actions listed; however, it falls short of being a meditative device to practice emptiness. (G.C.)

11. Namely, the five roots, the five powers, the seven factors of enlightenment, and the eightfold noble path.

12. Or, "the realm of space,"

13. That is, the thirty-two auspicious signs of a Buddha or a universal monarch.

14. The place where the Dharma is taught.

15. Refers to the female demons who live in the Sixth Heaven, which is the dwelling place of celestial demons.

16. Pāpīyān is the name of the demon king who rules the Sixth Heaven, the highest heaven in the Realm of Desire of a small world. Here the plural form refers to all demon kings in the billion-world universe.

17. This statement is an example of how, in my opinion, the sūtras are symbolic and pedagogical, and should not be interpreted literally. Mañjuśrī, who embodies the wisdom of all Buddhas, is shown here as being of more benefit to sentient beings than is the Buddha. The reason for this seeming overstatement is to stress the fact that only the transcendental wisdom of *prajñāpāramitā*, which Mañjuśrī embodies, can conquer demons, and not magical formulas, spells, or other thaumaturgical techniques. (G.C.)

Mañjuśrī has been referred to as the "mother" of the Enlightened Ones in the three periods of time. In a sūtra called "放缽經" the Buddha says, "I owe it to Mañjuśrī that I now become a Buddha. Innumerable Buddhas in the past had been Mañjuśrī's disciples, and those who will become Buddhas in the future also owe their enlightenment to his awesome power. Just as children in the world have their own parents, so Mañjuśrī assumes parenthood on the Buddha-path."

18. Following each list of four is the statement, "Fulfillment of these four things enables a Bodhisattva-Mahāsattva to achieve this samādhi." We omit this repetition for brevity's sake.

19. 'Deep mind' seems to imply the deep aspiration for the Dharma, the aspiration for profound, supreme Buddhahood.

20. The two Chinese characters 遠離 may be translated as 'far apart.' They are translated as 'detached' in other places. In this context, however, it seems to be more appropriate to render them as 'remote and far away'; taken in this sense, they imply that the three realms are something forever inapprehensible.

21. Here, the "initial generation of bodhicitta" probably refers to the transcendental bodhicitta (勝義菩提心), shared by Bodhisattvas in the ten stages. It differs from the generation of bodhicitta by a beginner Bodhisattva.

22. Desire, hatred, and ignorance are utterly empty of any self-entity. For this reason, as Mañjuśrī explains below, only those who have true realization of emptiness can "generate"

or experience the three poisons (or any other dharmas) *as they are*—as empty of self-nature. Ordinary people view and experience the three poisons only in the *illusory* aspect of those dharmas, as apparently self-existent entities. But when a complete identification of desire, hatred, and ignorance with emptiness has been made, one can at that moment experience the three poisons in their basic nature. (V.S.B.)

23. Those who have realized emptiness do indeed encounter the poisons (here compared to the movement of a bird in the sky), but they do so while dwelling in emptiness (compared to "leaving no trace in empty space").

24. Nothingness, nondiscrimination, and so forth are all approximate characteristics of emptiness, the dynamic function of which "generates" all dharmas.

25. The abodes of consciousness are the objects which the consciousness abides in, relies on, and clings to. The other four aggregates—form, feeling, conception, and impulse—are the four abodes of consciousness.

26. The opposites of the eight items of the eightfold noble path: wrong view, wrong thought, and so forth.

27. The nine activities (sometimes given as ten) which the Buddha suffered in this world, for example, practicing asceticism for six years, returning with an empty bowl after begging for food in a village, etc. For details, see "On the Pāramitā of Ingenuity" (Chap. 22).

28. Mañjuśrī's remark here appears to nullify all good and evil, right and wrong, Dharma and non-Dharma, and so forth, and thus to invalidate all the usual Buddhist teachings; however, from a higher viewpoint of thorough emptiness and thorough equality, i.e., the totalistic at-one-ment of all in one and one in all, the remark is an ineluctable corollary of the emptiness doctrine. If one can truly understand the principle of "form is emptiness and emptiness is form," he should also be able to understand that all passion-desires are bodhi itself, and that the virtuous and the evil, the good and the bad, etc., are ultimately equal and at-one. Here, we may witness how Tantric philosophy is a natural outcome of the emptiness doctrine. (G.C.)

29. This, we believe, refers to the initial generation of the transcendental bodhicitta of the first stage.

30. There are different opinions as to at what stage (*bhūmi*) a Bodhisattva achieves the Realization of the Nonarising of Dharmas; some texts say the first, but most texts say the eighth. The passage here obviously implies the eighth stage. One begins to abide in the first stage when he initially generates the true or transcendental bodhicitta.

31. Literally, "dharmas."

32. Based on Bodhiruci's version (Taishō 341, p. 127). The original reads "seeks."

33. For more explanation, see "The Manifestation of Lights" (Chap. 11).

34. Literally, "sever and renounce."

35. Literally, "empty space."

36. That is, the Buddha.

37. In order to protect profound doctrines from being distorted, and to protect certain sentient beings from grave misunderstanding, the Buddha sometimes does not reveal particular teachings to those sentient beings who are not yet able to understand them. Such doctrines are called "esoteric."

5 無垢施菩薩應辯會

A Discourse on Ready Eloquence

I

Thus have I heard. Once the Buddha was dwelling in the garden of Anāthapiṇḍada in the Jeta Grove near Śrāvastī, accompanied by the thousand great monks. Except for Ānanda, those monks were all Arhats. Having ended all their defilements, they no longer suffered any afflictions. They were at ease with everything. They had done what they had set out to do, laid down the heavy burden [of saṁsāra], acquired benefit for themselves, and broken the ties of existence. Through right knowledge, they had achieved liberation, both from passions and from ignorance. They were mentally free; their minds, like great elephant kings, were subdued. They had reached the other shore and had entered the eightfold liberation.

Also in the assembly were twelve thousand Bodhisattva-Mahāsattvas, all adorned [with merits] and known to all, who had attained nonregression and would achieve Buddhahood in their next lives. Among them were Bodhisattva Precious Hand, Bodhisattva Treasury of Virtue, Bodhisattva Adorned with Wisdom, Bodhisattva Wish-Fulfiller, Bodhisattva Avalokiteśvara, Dharma Prince Mañjuśrī, Dharma Prince Pleasant Voice, Dharma Prince Inconceivable Liberative Deeds, Dharma Prince Unobstructed Contemplation of All Dharmas, Bodhisattva Maitreya, Bodhisattva Giver of Lightheartedness, Bodhisattva No Deluded Views, Bodhisattva Exempt from Miserable Realms, Bodhisattva No Deluded Deeds, Bodhisattva Free of Darkness, Bodhisattva Free from All Covers,[1] Bodhisattva Adorned with Eloquence, Bodhisattva Awesome Wisdom and Precious Merit, Bodhisattva Golden Flower of Brilliant Virtue, and Bodhisattva Unobstructed Thought.

Sūtra 33, Taishō 310 pp. 556–564; translated into Chinese by Nieh Tao-chen.

One morning, eight great Śrāvakas and eight great Bodhisattvas, wearing monastic robes and holding bowls, entered Śrāvastī to beg for food. They were: the Virtuous Śāriputra, the Virtuous Maudgalyāyana, the Virtuous Mahākāśyapa, the Virtuous Subhūti, the Virtuous Pūrṇamaitrāyaṇīputra, the Virtuous Revata, the Virtuous Aniruddha, the Virtuous Ānanda, Dharma Prince Mañjuśrī, Bodhisattva No Deluded Views, Bodhisattva Precious Form, Bodhisattva Exempt from Miserable Realms, Bodhisattva Free from All Covers, Bodhisattva Avalokiteśvara, Bodhisattva Adorned with Eloquence, and Bodhisattva No Deluded Deeds. On the way, each of them had one thought in his mind and discussed it with the others.

The Virtuous Śāriputra said, "When I reach Śrāvastī to beg for food, I will enter a dhyāna[2] that will cause all the sentient beings in the city to hear the four noble truths."

The Virtuous Maudgalyāyana said, "When I reach Śrāvastī to beg for food, I will enter a dhyāna that will cause all the sentient beings in the city to be free from demons' influence."

The Virtuous Mahākāśyapa said, "When I reach Śrāvastī to beg for food, I will enter a dhyāna that will cause all the sentient beings in the city who give me food to receive endless rewards until they achieve nirvāṇa."

The Virtuous Subhūti said, "When I reach Śrāvastī to beg for food, I will enter a dhyāna that will cause the sentient beings in the city who see me to be reborn in heaven or as humans, to enjoy all pleasures, and to suffer no more."

The Virtuous Pūrṇamaitrāyaṇīputra said, "When I reach Śrāvastī to beg for food, I will enter a dhyāna that will cause all those in the city who follow wrong paths, such as brahmacārins and naked ascetics, to acquire right view."

The Virtuous Revata said, "When I reach Śrāvastī to beg for food, I will enter a dhyāna that will cause all the sentient beings in the city to enjoy the pleasure of nondisputation."

The Virtuous Aniruddha said, "When I reach Śrāvastī to beg for food, I will enter a dhyāna that will cause all the sentient beings in the city to recognize the retributions for karmas committed in past lives."

The Virtuous Ānanda said, "When I reach Śrāvastī to beg for food, I will enter a dhyāna that will cause all the sentient beings in the city to remember all the Dharma they have learned."

Dharma Prince Mañjuśrī said, "I will cause all the doors, windows, walls, implements, trees, branches, leaves, flowers, fruits, clothes, and necklaces in the city of Śrāvastī to make sounds [teaching] emptiness, signlessness, wishlessness, egolessness, nothingness, avoidance of play-words, and the absence of self-entity."

Bodhisattva No Deluded Views said, "I will cause everything seen by the sentient beings in Śrāvastī who deserve supreme enlightenment to become a Buddha-image, and in this way I will cause them to attain supreme enlightenment without fail."

Bodhisattva Precious Form said, "I will cause prodigious quantities of the seven treasures to appear in the houses of all the people in Śrāvastī, regardless of caste."

Bodhisattva Exempt from Miserable Realms said, "I will cause the sentient beings in Śrāvastī who are destined to fall to the miserable planes of existence [after death] to undergo slight sufferings in their present lives [instead] and to be liberated quickly."

Bodhisattva Free from All Covers said, "I will cause the sentient beings in Śrāvastī to completely rid themselves of the five covers."

Bodhisattva Avalokiteśvara said, "I will cause the imprisoned sentient beings in Śrāvastī to be freed quickly, those who are about to be killed to be saved, and those who are frightened to become fearless."

Bodhisattva Adorned with Eloquence said, "I will cause all the sentient beings in Śrāvastī who see me to obtain eloquence, so that they can exchange questions and answers in wonderful verse."

Bodhisattva No Deluded Deeds said, "I will cause the sentient beings in Śrāvastī who see me to have no delusive views and to attain supreme enlightenment without fail."

Discussing their thoughts in this manner, the eight Śrāvakas and the eight Bodhisattvas arrived at the gate of Śrāvastī.

At that time, King Prasenajit's daughter, named Pure Giving, was living in the city. She was extraordinarily beautiful, though only eight years old. It was the eighth day of the second month, the day on which the star Puṣya[3] appeared. Carrying a bottle of water in her hand, she went out of the city together with five hundred brāhmins to bathe the deva-image. When the five hundred brāhmins saw the monks standing outside the city gate, they all considered the sight inauspicious. Then the oldest of the five hundred brāhmins, a man named Brahmā who was one hundred twenty years old, told Pure Giving, "These monks are standing outside the gate. This is inauspicious; we had better go back to the city and not meet[4] them. If we meet them, it is not good for our sacrificial rites."

Thereupon Pure Giving spoke in verse to the brāhmin;

"These men are all passionless,
And most worthy of praise.
They can wash away all evils
From vast numbers of sentient beings.

These men are pure and immaculate,
For they thoroughly know the four noble truths;
But followers of wrong paths are impure,
Shrouded in delusion and ignorance.

Innumerable rewards will accrue
To those who make offerings to
The Honored One among gods and men,
The field of blessings.
Whatever is planted in this field
Will yield an inexhaustible harvest

In the three realms.
The Buddha, pure and perfect in discipline,
Rises unsullied from the mundane mire.
He lives in the world as a skillful healer,
Curing and saving sick sentient beings.

In the world, the Buddha is supreme;
He is the king of all Dharmas,
And these men are the Buddha's sons.[5]
Some have attained Arhatship;
Others perform the Bodhisattvas' deeds.

How can the wise avoid them?
Those who perform such wonderful deeds
Deserve the acclaim of the world.
These wise men have long practiced giving.
Brahmacārin, respect them,
And surely all will go well.

Let us praise these men
Who are endowed with a superior appearance.
Pure in mind, they are our excellent fields of blessings.
Brahmacārin, believe my words,
And you will be joyful and free of worry."

The [oldest] brahmacārin said to Pure Giving in verse:

"Do not think like a fool or an idiot!
Shun śramanas when performing sacrificial rites.
A seeker of happiness should not come close
To one who is tonsured and dressed in a monastic robe.
Your parents will not approve of this,
And we, too, feel shame for you.
If you intend to give them things,
That is also not auspicious.
Please, respect not these monks."

Pure Giving said to the brahmacārin in verse:

"Were I to fall to a miserable realm,
My parents, retinue, wealth, jewels,
Or even my own courage and health
Could not save me.

Except for these men of awesome virtue,
Who could rescue me?

To honor the Buddha, Dharma, and Saṁgha,
I will give up life and limb.
There is but one path to follow:
To venerate the Three Jewels."

Then the [elderly] brahmacārin asked Pure Giving, "You have never seen the Buddha or the Saṁgha, nor have you heard the Dharma. How can you have such faith in them?"

Pure Giving replied to the brahmacārin, "Seven days after I was born, as I lay on a gold-legged bed in the lofty palace, I saw five hundred gods flying in the air, praising the countless merits of the Buddha, the Dharma, and the Saṁgha. I heard their every word. Then a god, who had never seen the Buddha or the Saṁgha or heard the Dharma, asked the other gods, 'What is the Buddha like?' Perceiving my own thoughts, and wishing to give joy to the god who had asked the question, the other gods answered in verse:

'The hair of the Buddha is reddish-blue,
Clean, glossy, and curling to the right.
His face, like a full moon, is the color
Of a hundred-petalled lotus flower.

The snow-white single hair between his eyebrows
Spirals to the right;
To all it is delightful to behold.
His brows curve over his eyes,
Like black bees surrounding blue lotus flowers.

His jaws are like those of a lion;
His eyes rove like those of a king of cattle;
His lips are the color of a bright red gourd;
His teeth are white, close, even,
As orderly as a line of flying geese.
His tongue is so broad and long,
It could cover his face.

He speaks with perfect clarity;
His voice gives joy to all who hear it.
It resembles the song of a peacock,
A swan, a lute of lapis lazuli,
A kinnara's bell, a kalaviṅka bird,[6]
A cuckoo, a jīvajīvaka bird,[7]
Or a musical instrument of any kind.

His roar is like that of a lion;
He soundly refutes all arguments

And eradicates all defilements.
His truthful words shatter every wrong view.

Encircled by an assembly,
He can resolve all queries and doubts.
Never erroneous, but gentle and flexible,
He gladdens and convinces the audience.
Steering clear of the two extremes,
Correctly he teaches the middle way.

He speaks in an ever-pleasant voice,
To the delight of all who hear him;
He never flatters or distorts,
And from his speech each hearer
Derives an understanding of his own.
The Buddha's words are adorned with wisdom,
Like a garland woven of wonderful flowers.

His neck is round;
His arms are long and straight;
His palms are flat and clearly marked with wheel-signs;
His fingers, long and slender,
Have copper-colored nails.

The Buddha's body is sturdy,
Balanced, and well-rounded;
His waist is slender,
Incurving like that of a lion;
His navel, deep and round.
His male organ is retracted,
Like that of a stallion.

Like a mountain of gold, his body
Is as robust as that of a dragon or an elephant.
From each pore a hair grows,
Pointing upward and spiraling to the right.

He has even hipbones and calves like a deer's.
His ankles gently curve, with bones firmly joined.
His soles are fully rounded and clearly marked
With wheels of a thousand spokes.'

"Brahmacārin, at that time, the gods in the air praised the Tathāgata thusly. They also said, 'The Tathāgata, the Worthy One, ferries all sentient beings over to the other shore. He protects them with great kindness and compassion, like a great king of healers. He is not affected by aversion or attachment, just as a lotus is not soiled by the mire from which it grows. What we have mentioned is only an insignificant fraction of the merits of the World-Honored One.'

"Brahmacārin, seven days after I was born, I heard of the true merits of the World-Honored One. From that time on, I have not slept, and I have not felt at all the stir of desire, hatred, or annoyance. From that time on, I have not been attached to my parents, brothers, sisters, relatives, wealth, treasures, necklaces, clothes, cities, towns, gardens, or pavilions, or even my own body and life. I have been doing but one deed: remaining mindful of the Buddha. I go to any place where the Tathāgata is teaching the Dharma, and listen attentively.[8] I absorb and remember all he teaches, never missing a single sentence in word or in meaning. Brahmacārin, I see Buddhas, World-Honored Ones, day and night. Brahmacārin, I never get tired of contemplating the Buddha, never feel satiated with hearing the Dharma, and never become weary of making offerings to the Saṁgha."

When Pure Giving had thus praised the Buddha, the Dharma, and the Saṁgha, all the five hundred brāhmins, including the eldest, Brahmā, brought forth supreme bodhicitta.

Then, Pure Giving got down from her carriage and walked toward the Bodhisattvas and Śrāvakas. When she reached them, she bowed with her head at the feet of each one. Then she approached the Virtuous Śāriputra with great respect, and stood before him, saying, "I am a girl; my intelligence is shallow and my afflictions great. I am unrestrained, indulge in mean things, and am dominated by devious thoughts. May the Virtuous Śāriputra, out of compassion, explain the subtle, wonderful Dharma for me, so that after hearing it, I may have benefit in the long night and experience greater peace and happiness."

As she was speaking thus, King Prasenajit came. Hearing Pure Giving's words, the king asked her, "You lack no pleasures; why do you look sad? Why do you not sleep, or enjoy the amusements of the world?"

King Prasenajit then spoke in verse to his daughter:

"You are as fair as a celestial maiden;
After bathing, you anoint yourself,
And put on perfumed clothes;
You have necklaces and every precious ornament.
Why are you so sad you cannot sleep?

Your country is rich and replete with treasures;
Your parents' authority is absolute;
What troubles you, that you do not sleep?

You are beloved by your kin
And adored by the people,
And I am a glorious king.
Why, then, are you not happy?

What have you seen or heard
That makes you so melancholy?
Oh, what is it that you wish?
Please tell me."

Thereupon, Pure Giving answered her father in verse:

"Leading a household life,
Your Majesty, do you not feel
That the aggregates, elements, and sense-organs[9]
Are all fragile?
Mundane existence is like a magic trick;
Life flees past without a moment's pause.

How can one sleep well after taking poison?
How can one be joyful when dying?
How can one expect to live while falling from a cliff?
So it is to dwell in the world of appearance.

If a person lives among serpents,
How can he sleep or lust?
The four elements are like poisonous snakes;
How can one derive pleasure from them?
When surrounded by enemies, and hungry,
How can one be happy?
When surrounded by hostile nations,
How can you, my father, be at ease?

Ever since I saw the World-Honored One,
I resolved to become a Buddha.
Your Majesty, never have I seen or heard
That a Bodhisattva relaxes his efforts for an instant."[10]

II

Then Pure Giving said to Śāriputra, "Virtuous one, I want to ask you one question; may you take pity on me and explain the answer to me. The World-Honored One says that you stand first in wisdom. Is this wisdom conditioned or unconditioned? If it is conditioned, it is illusory and deceptive, not real. If it is an unconditioned dharma, it does not arise, and a dharma which does not arise does not originate. Because it does not originate, Virtuous one, your wisdom does not exist."

Śāriputra was rendered speechless.

The Virtuous Maudgalyāyana asked Śāriputra, "Virtuous one, why do you not answer Pure Giving's question?"

Śāriputra replied to Maudgalyāyana, "This maiden does not ask about conditioned things. She inquires about the ultimate truth.[11] The ultimate truth is beyond speech. Therefore, I cannot answer in words."

Then Pure Giving said to Maudgalyāyana, "Virtuous one, the World-Honored One says that you stand first in the wielding of miraculous powers. Virtuous one, when using your miraculous powers, do you have sentient beings in mind or dharmas in mind? If you have sentient beings in mind, your miraculous powers cannot be real, because sentient beings are unreal. If you have dharmas in mind, consider that dharmas do not change [by their ultimate nature]. Since they do not change, [all dharmas, including your miraculous powers,] are unattainable; being unattainable, they are beyond discriminations."

The Virtuous Maudgalyāyana was also rendered speechless.

Mahākāśyapa asked Maudgalyāyana, "Virtuous one, why do you not answer Pure Giving's question?"

Maudgalyāyana replied, "This maiden's question about miraculous powers is based not on discrimination, but on the Tathāgatas' enlightenment, which defies action and discrimination. It cannot be answered in words."

Then Pure Giving said to Mahākāśyapa, "Virtuous one, the World-Honored One says that you stand first in the practice of austerities. Virtuous one, after attaining the eightfold liberation, if you accept—or for an instant think of accepting—offerings from sentient beings out of compassion for them, how do you intend to repay such favors? Do you repay them with your body, or with your mind? If you [intend to] repay them with your body, you certainly cannot do so, for the body is neutral by nature, and is not different from grasses, trees, walls, tiles, or gravel. If you [intend to] repay them with your mind, you also cannot do so, for the mind changes incessantly from moment to moment. Besides body and mind, there is only the unconditioned. If all that remains is the unconditioned, who repays the favors?"

Mahākāśyapa was also rendered speechless.

The Virtuous Subhūti asked Mahākāśyapa, "Why do you not answer Pure Giving's question?"

Mahākāśyapa replied to Subhūti, "This maiden's question is about the reality of dharmas. It cannot be answered in words."

Then Pure Giving said to Subhūti, "Virtuous one, the World-Honored One says that you stand first among those who do not engage in disputes. Does the practice of nondisputation have the nature of existence or the nature of suchness? If you say it has the nature of suchness, consider that suchness is characterized by neither arising nor cessation. What is characterized by neither arising nor cessation cannot be differentiated.[12] What cannot be differentiated is suchness itself. What is suchness itself is devoid of action. What is devoid of action is beyond speech. What is beyond speech is inconceivable. What is inconceivable transcends expression. If you say nondisputation has the nature of existence, consider that existence is by nature illusory and deceptive. What is illusory and deceptive is not practiced by saints."

The Virtuous Subhūti was also rendered speechless.

Pūrṇamaitrāyaṇīputra asked Subhūti, "Why do you not answer Pure Giving's question?"

Subhūti replied to Pūrṇamaitrāyaṇīputra, "It stands to reason that I should say nothing in reply, because keeping silent is my only delight. Furthermore, this maiden's question is about the Dharma which is apart from play-words. Whatever answer I may give will be wrong. To say nothing about the nature of Dharma is the practice of nondisputation."

Then Pure Giving said to Pūrṇamaitrāyaṇīputra, "Virtuous one, the World-Honored One says that you stand first among the Dharma teachers. When you teach, do you teach the doctrine that there are states and realms, or the doctrine that there are no states or realms? If you teach that there are states and realms, you are the same as an ordinary person. Why? Because only ordinary people teach that there are states and realms. In this regard, you do not go beyond the doctrine of an ordinary person. If [you teach] the absence of states and realms, [you teach that] nothing exists. If nothing exists, how can you be called the first among the Dharma teachers?"

Pūrṇamaitrāyaṇīputra, too, was rendered speechless.

The Virtuous Revata asked Pūrṇamaitrāyaṇīputra, "Why do you not answer Pure Giving's question?"

Pūrṇamaitrāyaṇīputra replied to Revata, "This maiden does not ask about conditioned things, but about the ultimate truth. The ultimate truth is beyond speech. Therefore, there is no way to answer."

Then Pure Giving said to Revata, "Virtuous one, the World-Honored One says that you stand first among those who practice meditation. When you practice meditation, do you rely on your mind or not? If you rely on your mind to enter meditation, then your meditation is unreal, since your mind is unreal, like an illusion. If you enter meditation without relying on your mind, then such external objects as grasses, trees, branches, leaves, flowers, and fruits should also be able to achieve meditation. Why? Because they too have no mind."

The Virtuous Revata was also rendered speechless.

The Virtuous Aniruddha asked Revata, "Virtuous one, why do you not answer Pure Giving's question?"

Revata replied to Aniruddha, "This maiden's question belongs in the Buddha's domain. A Śrāvaka cannot answer her."

Pure Giving said further, "Are the Dharma of Buddhas and the Dharma of Śrāvakas different? If they were different, then the unconditioned would be split into two. All saints and sages practice the unconditioned. An unconditioned dharma does not arise. If it does not arise, it is not dualistic. If it is not dualistic, it is suchness itself, for suchness is not dualistic. Therefore, Virtuous Revata, how can you say that?"

Then Pure Giving said to Aniruddha, "Virtuous one, the World-Honored One says that you stand first among those who have the deva-eye. Virtuous one, is an object seen with the deva-eye existent or nonexistent? If you regard what you see as existent, then you take the view of eternalism. If you regard what you see as nonexistent, then you take the view of nihilism. Apart from the two extremes, you see nothing."

The Virtuous Aniruddha was also rendered speechless.

The Virtuous Ānanda asked Aniruddha, "Virtuous one, why do you not answer Pure Giving's question?"

Aniruddha replied to Ānanda, "This maiden's question is aimed at destroying all arbitrary terms; therefore, it cannot be answered in arbitrary terms."

Then Pure Giving said to Ānanda, "Virtuous one, the World-Honored One says that you stand first among the learned. Is your knowledge that of the real meaning of things, or that of words? If it is knowledge of the real meaning of things, consider that the real meaning is beyond speech. What is beyond speech cannot be known through the auditory consciousness. What cannot be known through the auditory consciousness cannot be expressed by speech. If your knowledge is that of words, [it is meaningless, for] the World-Honored One says that one should rely on the ultimate meaning of a discourse, not on mere words. Therefore, Virtuous Ānanda, you are not learned, nor do you understand the ultimate meaning."

The Virtuous Ānanda, too, was rendered speechless.

Dharma Prince Mañjuśrī asked the Virtuous Ānanda, "Virtuous one, why do you not answer Pure Giving's question?"

Ānanda answered, "This maiden asks about the learning which has nothing to do with words; therefore, it cannot be explained by words. She inquires about equality. Equality is not the mind, because it has nothing to do with mental functions. This doctrine is beyond those in the stage of learning;[13] how can I say anything about it in reply? It is in the domain of the other shore reached by Tathāgatas, the Dharma Kings."

III

Then Pure Giving said to the Dharma Prince Mañjuśrī, "The World-Honored One says that you stand first among the Bodhisattvas of profound understanding. Is your understanding profound because you understand the profundity of the twelve links of dependent origination or because you understand the profundity of the ultimate truth?[14] If it is because you understand the profundity of the twelve links of dependent origination, consider that no sentient being can fathom the profundity of the twelve links of dependent origination.[15] Why? Because the twelve links of dependent origination neither come nor go and cannot be known by the visual, auditory, olfactory, gustatory, tactile, or mental consciousnesses. The twelve links of dependent origination are not active phenomena. If your understanding is profound because you understand the profundity of the ultimate truth, consider that the profundity of the ultimate truth is no profundity, nor is there anyone to apprehend it."

Mañjuśrī said to Pure Giving, "My understanding is [said to be] profound because [I know] the profundity of the beginning point of all things."

Pure Giving said to Mañjuśrī, "The beginning point of all things is not a point; therefore, your knowledge is nonknowledge."

Mañjuśrī said to Pure Giving, "It is because the inapprehensible can be realized by nonknowledge that I can speak of the beginning point of all things."

Pure Giving said to Mañjuśrī, "The inapprehensible defies speech; it transcends the means of speech and nothing can be said about it."

Mañjuśrī said to Pure Giving, "What is said is said in arbitrary words."

Pure Giving said to Mañjuśrī, "The enlightenment of Buddhas transcends words and speech, hence it is inexpressible."

Then Pure Giving said to Bodhisattva No Deluded Views, "Good man, you said, 'When I reach Śrāvastī, I will cause everything seen by the sentient beings in the city who deserve supreme enlightenment to become a Buddha-image, and in this way I will cause them to attain supreme enlightenment without fail.' When you see the Tathāgata, do you see him by his physical body or by his Dharma-body? If you see him by his physical body, then you do not see the Buddha, for the World-Honored One says, 'Those who seek me by form or sound hold wrong views;[16] they do not [really] see me.' If you see the Tathāgata by his Dharma-body, [you do not see him, either, for] the Dharma-body is invisible. Why? The Dharma-body is beyond the reach of vision and hearing, and is intangible; therefore, it cannot be seen or heard."

Bodhisattva No Deluded Views was rendered speechless.

Bodhisattva Precious Form asked Bodhisattva No Deluded Views, "Good man, why do you not answer Pure Giving's question?"

Bodhisattva No Deluded Views replied, "Pure Giving asks about the Dharma apart from entity. The Dharma apart from entity is inexpressible. Therefore, I do not give an answer."

Pure Giving said, "Good man, I do not ask you about the Dharma apart from entity. The Dharma apart from entity cannot be put into a question. When you have completed your learning, you will be able to answer my question without hindrance."[17]

Then Pure Giving said to Bodhisattva Precious Form, "Good man, you said, 'When I reach Śrāvastī, I will cause prodigious quantities of the seven treasures to appear in the houses of all the people in Śrāvastī, regardless of caste.' Is your thought of giving treasures to people defiled with attachment or not? If it is defiled with attachment, you are the same as an ordinary person. Why? Because ordinary people have attachment. If there is no attachment, there is no giving of treasures."

Bodhisattva Precious Form was rendered speechless.

Then, Pure Giving said to Bodhisattva Exempt from Miserable Realms, "Good man, you said, 'When I reach Śrāvastī, I will cause the sentient beings in the city who are destined to fall to the miserable planes of existence [after death] to undergo slight sufferings in their present lives [instead] and be liberated quickly.' Now, the Tathāgata says that karmas are inconceivable. Can inconceivable karmas be eliminated quickly? To say that they can be eliminated contradicts the Tathāgata's words. If they cannot [even] be known, then how can you cause the people to suffer slight pain and have their karmas eliminated quickly? If you could eliminate a karma, you would be the master of a masterless dharma [i.e., karma]; you would also be capable of not eliminating it."[18]

Bodhisattva Exempt from Miserable Realms said to Pure Giving, "By the power of my vow, I can cause the people to suffer less for their karmas and to have their karmas eliminated quickly."

Pure Giving said to Exempt from Miserable Realms, "All dharmas are suchness by nature; they cannot be affected by the power of a vow."

Bodhisattva Exempt from Miserable Realms, too, was rendered speechless.

Then, Pure Giving said to Bodhisattva Free from All Covers, "Good man, you said, 'I will cause the sentient beings in the city of Śrāvastī to completely rid themselves of the five covers.' You think that, after entering dhyāna, you can cause the sentient beings not to be enveloped in the five covers. When you are in dhyāna, is it you or others who achieve freedom? If it is you who achieve freedom, you cannot impart it to others, as no such dharma is accessible to another. Then, how can you remove the five covers of others when you enter dhyāna? If it is others who achieve freedom, then you cannot benefit them at all."

Bodhisattva Free from All Covers said to Pure Giving, "I can do that because I put kindness first."

Pure Giving said to Bodhisattva Free from All Covers, "All Buddhas practice kindness. Good man, is there any Buddha who is not worried about the five covers of sentient beings? However, there still are sentient beings afflicted by the [five] covers in some Buddha-lands."[19]

Bodhisattva Free from All Covers was rendered speechless.

Then Pure Giving said to Bodhisattva Avalokiteśvara, "Good man, you said, 'I will cause the imprisoned sentient beings in the city of Śrāvastī to be freed quickly, those who are about to be killed to be saved, and those who are frightened to become fearless.' Now, concerning fear [and fearlessness, etc.], do you cling to those ideas or not? If you do, [you are not different from] an ordinary person, who also clings to them. Therefore, this cannot be. If you do not cling to these ideas, you cannot give [the people fearlessness]. If you cannot give them fearlessness, how can you remove [fear] from them?"

Bodhisattva Avalokiteśvara was rendered speechless.

Bodhisattva Adorned with Eloquence asked Bodhisattva Avalokiteśvara, "Good man, why do you not answer Pure Giving's question?"

Bodhisattva Avalokiteśvara replied, "This maiden does not ask about things that arise and cease; therefore, I can give no answer."

Pure Giving asked Bodhisattva Avalokiteśvara, "Can one ask about things that neither arise nor cease?"

Bodhisattva Avalokiteśvara replied to Pure Giving, "Concerning what neither arises nor ceases, there is no word or speech."

Pure Giving said to Bodhisattva Avalokiteśvara, "Where there are no words, the wise ones coin arbitrary words without attachment. Just as Dharma-nature is unobstructed, so the wise ones are not obstructed by words."

Then Pure Giving said to Bodhisattva Adorned with Eloquence, "Good man, you said, 'I will cause the sentient beings in the city of Śrāvastī who see me to obtain eloquence so that they can exchange questions and answers in wonderful verses.' Good man, concerning this eloquence you intend to give, does it arise from awareness [or from passion]? If it arises from awareness, it is not quiescent, as all conditioned dharmas arise from awareness and watchfulness. If it arises from passion, then what you give is illusory."

Bodhisattva Adorned with Eloquence said to Pure Giving, "This was my vow when I first brought forth bodhicitta: I wished that all those who saw me would obtain eloquence so that they could exchange questions and answers in marvelous verses."

Pure Giving asked Bodhisattva Adorned with Eloquence, "Good man, do you still have with you the vow that you made when you first brought forth bodhicitta? If you do, you entertain a view of eternalism. If you do not, you cannot give eloquence to people. Therefore, your wish is useless."

Bodhisattva Adorned with Eloquence was rendered speechless.

Then, Pure Giving said to Bodhisattva No Deluded Deeds, "Good man, you said, 'I will cause the sentient beings in Śrāvastī who see me to have no delusive views and to attain supreme enlightenment without fail.' Does this enlightenment exist or not? If it exists, it is a conditioned enlightenment, and you hold an extreme view. If it does not exist, it is illusory, and you hold an extreme view just the same."

Bodhisattva No Deluded Deeds[20] replied to Pure Giving, "The proper name for bodhi is wisdom."

Pure Giving asked Bodhisattva No Deluded Deeds, "Does this wisdom arise or not? If it arises, it is not the product of proper contemplation but a conditioned awareness known to ordinary people. If it does not arise, for that reason it cannot exist; if it does not exist, it cannot be distinguished [as supreme enlightenment]. There are no such distinctions as the bodhi of Bodhisattvas, the bodhi of Śrāvakas, the bodhi of Pratyekabuddhas, and the bodhi of Tathāgatas. Ordinary people discriminate about bodhi, while the wise do not."

Bodhisattva No Deluded Deeds was rendered speechless.

Then, the Virtuous Subhūti said to the other virtuous Śrāvakas and the great Bodhisattvas, "Virtuous ones, we had better go back. We need not go into Śrāvastī to beg for food. Why? What Pure Giving says is the Dharma-food of the wise. Today, we can enjoy Dharma-food and do without a meal."

Pure Giving said to Subhūti, "It is said that all dharmas are devoid of superiority or inferiority. Among such dharmas, for what do you go begging? Virtuous one, the doctrine of transcending play-words is the practice of a monk. Do not delight in play-words. The doctrine of transcending play-words is the doctrine of nonreliance, beyond the domain of those who rely on things. Saints and sages practice it without regression."

Then the eight great Śrāvakas; the eight great Bodhisattvas; the five hundred brāhmins, including the eldest, Brahmā; Pure Giving; King Prasenajit; and others went together to the Buddha. When they arrived, they bowed down with their heads at the Buddha's feet, circumambulated him three times to the right, withdrew to one side, and sat down. Pure Giving made seven more circumambulations, bowed down with her head at the Buddha's feet once again, stood with her palms joined, and asked the Buddha in verse:[21]

"I ask the Peerless, Honored One,
The Worthy One of infinite renown,
The One who bestows the ambrosial joy:
What is the Bodhisattva-path?

Seated under a bodhi-tree,
How can one subdue demons, the torturers? . . .
May the Most Compassionate, Honored One
Explain the practices compatible with bodhi. . . .

How does one cultivate
Pure, wonderful, superior samādhis?
How can one who practices the Dharma
Acquire miraculous powers?
Now I entreat the World-Honored One
To explain to us the right practice. . . .

How can one acquire excellent features, . . .
And be endowed with wealth and wisdom? . . .

How can one learn to recall
The past lives of self and others? . . .

The World-Honored One is omniscient
And knows the past, present, and future.
May the most wise, Honored One of the World
Explain the practices of a Bodhisattva."

IV

Then the World-Honored One praised Pure Giving, saying, "Excellent, excellent! In order to give peace, happiness, and benefit to sentient beings, and extend pity to humans and gods, you ask the Tathāgata questions about the practices of great Bodhisattvas. Listen attentively and think well about what I say. I will explain the various answers to you."

Pure Giving and the whole assembly said in unison, "Yes, we will listen with pleasure."

The World-Honored One then said, "If a Bodhisattva achieves four things, he can conquer demons. What are the four?

(1) Not to resent or envy others' gains;
(2) not to sow discord among people;
(3) to persuade as many sentient beings as possible to plant good roots; and
(4) to be kind to all beings."[22]

To repeat this doctrine, the World-Honored One spoke in verse:

"Be free of resentment and envy;
Sow not discord among others;
Teach many sentient beings
To plant roots of virtue;
Cultivate a heart of great kindness
That extends to all in the ten directions—
One who so practices can subdue demons." . . .

The Buddha continued, "If a Bodhisattva achieves four things, he can acquire samādhis. What are the four?

(1) To abhor saṁsāra;
(2) constantly to delight in solitude;
(3) to strive perpetually for progress; and
(4) to accomplish his undertakings skillfully.

To repeat this doctrine, the World-Honored One spoke in verse:

"To dislike all forms of rebirth;
To live alone, like [the single horn]
Of a rhinoceros;
To be vigorous, as a good person should be;
And to accomplish one's endeavors—
The wise who can achieve these four superb things
Are close to bodhi.

One who seeks the supreme Dharma
And lives with a tranquil mind
Can acquire various samādhis
And realize the supreme bodhi,
Which is in the domain of Buddhas."

The Buddha continued, "Pure Giving, if a Bodhisattva achieves four things, he can acquire the power to perform miracles. What are the four?

(1) To feel lightness in body;
(2) to feel lightness in mind;
(3) to be attached to nothing; and
(4) to regard the four elements as space."

Then the World-Honored One spoke in verse to repeat this doctrine:

"The wise are light in mind
As well as light in body.
They are detached from everything
And regard the four elements as space.

Having achieved these four things,
By their power to be anywhere
At will, instantaneously,
They can appear
In billions of lands in space,
And make offerings to all the Buddhas there."

The Buddha continued, "Pure Giving, if a Bodhisattva achieves four things, he will obtain exquisite features. What are the four?

(1) To eradicate the filth of passions and avoid actions of anger;
(2) to enjoy cleaning the stūpas and temples of Buddhas, and offering them beautiful ornaments;
(3) to maintain a respectable deportment, keep the precepts at all times, and give greetings first; and
(4) not to mock Dharma teachers, but to regard them as World-Honored Ones."

The World-Honored One spoke in verse to repeat this doctrine:

"Be not angry with others,
And renounce impure deeds.
Cleanse the temples of the World-Honored Ones,
And respectfully offer them precious decorations.

Always observe the pure precepts,
And be the first to give greetings.
Hinder not the Dharma teachers,
But respect them as if they were Buddhas.

If you perform these four good actions,
You are called a valiant one,[23]
And will have the most excellent features,
To the delight of all who see you.". . .

The Buddha continued, "Pure Giving, if a Bodhisattva achieves four things, he will acquire great wisdom. What are the four?

(1) Not to begrudge the Dharma to others;
(2) to explain to others how to eliminate faults, so that they may be free of misgivings or regrets;
(3) to persuade those who strive hard for progress not to stop their exertions; and
(4) to delight in practicing the doctrine of emptiness."

Then, to repeat this doctrine, the World-Honored One spoke in verse:

"Be not miserly with the true Dharma;
Teach others, and thus remove
Their misgivings and regrets;
Give constant guidance to sentient beings;
Follow the practices of emptiness
Taught by the Buddhas.

A wise person who enjoys performing these four deeds
Can gain wisdom and renown.
Understanding well the words of Buddhas,
He will soon become an Honored One
Among humans and gods."

The Buddha continued, "Pure Giving, if a Bodhisattva achieves four things, he will be able to recall his own past lives and those of others. What are the four?

(1) To help forgetful people to recall what they have learned and recited;
(2) always to speak in a pleasant voice, giving others joy;
(3) always to give the Dharma, without neglect; and
(4) to enter dhyānas with skill, as the boy Sudhana does,[24] so that one may be liberated from saṁsāra and proceed toward nirvāṇa."

The World-Honored One spoke in verse to repeat this doctrine:

"To cause others to remember what they forget,
To speak always in a pleasant voice,
To be tireless in teaching the Dharma,
And to cultivate dhyānas constantly—
One who accomplishes these four things
Will be able to recall events
Countless kalpas in the past,
And soon apprehend the Buddha's domain.". . .

Then Pure Giving said to the Buddha, "World-Honored One, I shall follow all the Bodhisattvas' practices you have taught. If I fail to follow even one of the practices that the World-Honored One has taught, then I will be deceiving the Buddhas now teaching the Dharma in the ten directions."

Thereupon, the Virtuous Maudgalyāyana said to Pure Giving, "How dare you make a lion's roar in front of the Buddha! Do you not know that the practices of a Bodhisattva are difficult to follow? No one can ever attain supreme enlightenment in a female form."

Pure Giving said to the Virtuous Maudgalyāyana, "Now I will make a sincere declaration in the presence of the Buddha: if I shall unfailingly become a Buddha, a Tathāgata, a Perfectly Enlightened One free of clinging, a World-Honored One, a Teacher of Gods and Humans, then by virtue of my sincere declaration, may the billion-world universe quake in the six ways, without disturbing the sentient beings therein. If all my life I can follow the Bodhisattvas' practices that the World-Honored One has taught, may celestial flowers shower from the sky, may hundreds of thousands of instruments give forth music spontaneously, and may I be changed from a girl into a boy of sixteen, all because of this sincere declaration."

As soon as Pure Giving made this sincere declaration, the billion-world universe quaked in the six ways, celestial flowers showered from the sky, hundreds of thousands of celestial instruments gave forth music spontaneously, and Pure Giving changed from a girl into a boy of sixteen.

Then the Virtuous Maudgalyāyana bared his right shoulder, knelt on his right knee, joined his palms toward the Buddha, and said, "World-Honored One, now I pay homage to all the Buddha's Bodhisattvas, whether they are novices or already at the bodhi-site. How marvelous, World-Honored One, that this maiden can have such awesome merits and miraculous powers to make great declarations and fulfil them right away!"

The Buddha said to Maudgalyāyana, "So it is, so it is, just as you say. All Bodhisattvas, whether they are novices or already at the bodhi-site, are worshipped by gods and humans as the stūpas and temples of the Buddha. Surpassing all Śrāvakas and Pratyekabuddhas, they are the unexcelled fields of blessings for humans and gods."[25]

After that, the World-Honored One smiled graciously and, as all Buddhas do when they smile, emitted from his mouth green, yellow, red, white, violet, and crystalline lights. The lights illuminated innumerable, boundless Buddha-lands, outshining the brilliance of the palaces of gods and demons, and the lights of suns and moons. Then the lights returned and entered the top of the Buddha's head.

Seeing this, the Virtuous Ānanda rose from his seat, adjusted his robe, bared his right shoulder, knelt on his right knee, joined his palms toward the Buddha, and spoke in verse:

"In a voice like that of dragons, gods, or Brahmā;
Like a lion's roar, the song of a kalaviṅka bird,
Or a peal of thunder,
You eradicate desire, hatred, and ignorance,
Giving joy to those who hear.
May the One who has the ten powers
Explain the cause of his smile.

The six quakes have disturbed not a soul,
And the rain of celestial flowers
Brought joy to all who beheld it.
The World-Honored One vanquishes
Followers of the deviant paths,
Just as a lion subdues jackals.
May the World-Honored One tell us
The reason why he smiles.

The brilliance of a trillion suns, moons, and pearls;
The brilliance of gods, dragons, and Brahmā—
All are outshone by the pure lights
Emanating from the mouth of Śākyamuni Buddha.

The [single] curled hair between his eyebrows
Is as soft and impeccable
As a celestial garment,
And shines like a jade-white[26] moon.

The white hair glows with a light
Illuminating countless Buddha-lands.
May the Buddha explain the reason for this light.

The World-Honored One's teeth are spotless, clean,
Even, well-aligned, close, and white as snow.
From the Buddha's mouth emanate lights:
Green, yellow, red, white, violet, and crystalline.

Worlds may decay,
And suns and moons may fall;
Heaven and earth may be filled,
Leaving no space to move;
Fire may change into water,
And water into fire;
And the great ocean may dry up—
But the Tathāgata's words
Will remain forever true.

If all the sentient beings
In the ten directions
Became Pratyekabuddhas at the same instant,
Each with millions of different questions
Accumulated through billions of kalpas;
And if they came together to the Tathāgata
To question him simultaneously,
Each in a different language,
The Tathāgata could resolve
Their innumerable doubts,
And answer all their questions
Immediately, in one voice.

The Supreme, Honored One
Who has achieved wisdom,
Arrived at the other shore,
Adorned himself with all-knowing wisdom,
And acquired the thirty-two auspicious signs
And great, awesome merits—
May he explain why he smiles,
And whose Buddhahood he will prophesy.
This all gods and humans wish to hear.
May the Tathāgata explain why he smiles."

Then the Buddha asked Ānanda, "Did you see Bodhisattva Pure Giving shake the billion-world universe by her sincere declaration?"

Ānanda replied to the Buddha, "Yes, I did."

The Buddha said, "Since she resolved to attain bodhi, Bodhisattva Pure Giving has performed deeds leading to supreme enlightenment for eighty thousand incalculable kalpas. Bodhisattva Pure Giving had been treading the Bodhisattva-path for sixty kalpas when the Dharma Prince Mañjuśrī resolved to become a Bodhisattva. Ānanda, to match the merits and magnificent attributes of Bodhisattva Pure Giving's [future] Buddha-land, it would take all the merits and magnificent attributes of the [future] Buddha-lands of the eighty-six thousand great Bodhisattvas, including Mañjuśrī."[27]

Thereupon, the Virtuous Maudgalyāyana said to Bodhisattva Pure Giving, "Virtuous maiden,[28] you resolved to attain supreme enlightenment long ago. Why do you not change from a female into a male?"

Bodhisattva Pure Giving said to Maudgalyāyana, "The World-Honored One says that you stand first in the achievement of miraculous powers. Why do you not change from a male into a female?"

The Virtuous Maudgalyāyana was rendered speechless.

Bodhisattva Pure Giving said to the Virtuous Maudgalyāyana, "One does not attain supreme enlightenment by means of a female body, nor a male one. Why? Bodhi does not come into being; therefore, it is beyond attainment."[29]

V

Then Mañjuśrī, Prince of the Dharma, said to the Buddha, "How extraordinary, World-Honored One, that Bodhisattva Pure Giving can understand well the extremely profound Dharma and fulfil all her aspirations by the power of her vows!"

The Buddha told Mañjuśrī, "It is so, it is so, just as you say. Bodhisattva Pure Giving has cultivated the samādhi of emptiness[30] under six billion Buddhas, and the Realization of the Nonarising of Dharmas under eight billion Buddhas. She has asked three billion Buddhas about the profound Dharma. She has offered clothing, food, and drink to eight billion Buddhas, and questioned them about the Samādhi of the Seal of Ready Eloquence for Different Occasions.

"Furthermore, Mañjuśrī, suppose a good man or a good women, for the sake of bodhi, gives away precious treasures enough to fill Buddha-lands as numerous as the sands of the Ganges. His or her merits are no match for those of one who accepts, practices, reads, recites, and circulates this sūtra, and explains it widely to others. Even writing down this sūtra will result in the highest, supreme merits, let alone practicing it as taught. Why is this so? Because a person who does so can accept and keep the Bodhisattvas' practices leading to bodhi."

Mañjuśrī asked the Buddha, "World-Honored One, what should we call this sūtra? How shall we uphold it?"

The Buddha told Mañjuśrī, "This sūtra should be called 'A Discourse on Ready Eloquence for Different Occasions,' or 'A Discourse on the Door to Samādhi.' You should uphold it thus."

When the Buddha had spoken this sūtra, eight trillion sentient beings, including gods and humans, resolved to pursue supreme enlightenment without regression.

Then Bodhisattva Adorned with Eloquence asked the Buddha, "World-Honored One, when will Bodhisattva Pure Giving attain supreme enlightenment?"

The Buddha told Bodhisattva Adorned with Eloquence, "Good man, Bodhisattva Pure Giving, after she makes offerings to more Buddhas for several kalpas, will become a Buddha named Tathāgata King of Pure Light, the Worthy One, the Perfectly Enlightened One, the One Perfect in Learning and Conduct, the Well-Gone One, the World-Knower, the Unexcelled One, the Great Tamer, the Teacher of Gods and Humans, the Buddha, the World-Honored One. Her [future] world will be called Immeasurable Merits and Glories. In it there will be no Śrāvakas or Pratyekabuddhas. It will be more splendidly adorned than any celestial palace."

Hearing in person the Tathāgata's prophecy of her attainment of supreme enlightenment, Bodhisattva Pure Giving, her mind pure, was overjoyed. She leaped into the sky to a height of eight billion palm trees one above another, and emitted a great light which illuminated hundreds of thousands of [millions of] billions of Buddha-lands. Over the World-Honored One, the light was transformed into eighty-four thousand precious canopies embellished with various celestial gems. At that moment, by her immeasurable miraculous powers, Bodhisattva Pure Giving paid homage to countless Buddhas in the ten directions and offered the canopies to them. After that, she returned to the Buddha and stood to one side.

After hearing the prophecy of Buddhahood bestowed on Bodhisattva Pure Giving, and seeing her miraculous feat, the five hundred brāhmins, including the eldest, Brahmā, danced with joy and in unison extolled the Buddha in verse:

"One who respects the Buddha
Will gain the greatest benefit in the world.
One who resolves to attain supreme enlightenment
Will become a Buddha, with the highest wisdom.

We did evil in our past lives;
Therefore, we have been born
In families who hold wrong views.
When we saw the Buddha and the Saṁgha,
We uttered abusive words against them.
When we saw the worthy sons of the Buddha,
We said they were an inauspicious sight.
Now, we sincerely repent
Such verbal transgressions.

If we had not seen the Tathāgata,
The Most Honored One among gods and humans,
We would have received the human form in vain
And taken food for humans to no avail.

We, together with Pure Giving,
Went out to offer sacrifice to the shrine.

When she saw the Buddha's sons,
She praised them with veneration.

Hearing her praise them so,
We reproached her as a fool.
Then we questioned her,
'Have you ever seen the Buddha?'
She said in reply,
'Seven days after I was born,
I heard the gods extol the Buddha's name.'

Her praises of the Tathāgata
Did not differ from the truth;
Thus, upon hearing them,
We made the supreme decision
To seek unexcelled bodhi.

Hearing the name of the Buddha,
We were awakened to our past karma.
At once, we came to salute
The Savior of the World
And to seek the supreme Dharma.

After we made homage to the Buddha,
We listened to the unexcelled Dharma.
We see that the Honored Immortal among humans
Has forever parted from all sufferings,
And that the Dharma taught by the Buddha
Can truly deliver worldlings [from saṁsāra].

We will learn the Dharma,
Because it is unexcelled.
We will listen to the practices of a Bodhisattva,
Because we wish to obtain the Buddha-Dharma.
We should also follow these practices,
So that we may realize the Buddha's path.

You have discoursed on the essentials
Of the Bodhisattva-path to emancipation;
We, too, will tread this path
So that we may win
The world's respect and admiration."

Knowing their sincere desire, the Buddha smiled graciously. Thereupon Ānanda said to the Buddha, "Please tell us why you smile."

The Buddha said to Ānanda in verse:

"All these brāhmins, including Brahmā,
Will successively, in the same kalpa,
Attain supreme enlightenment.
In their past lives they have made
Offerings to five hundred Buddhas.
Hereafter, due to their marvelous deeds,
They will see billions of Buddhas.
For eight billion kalpas,
No adversities will befall them.
In each of these kalpas,
They will see billions of Buddhas;
Then they will become
Supreme, Honored Ones among gods and humans.

They will have the same name, 'Pure Light,'
And an identical life span:
Eight billion years.
Their lands, too, will be the same,
Each with a Saṁgha of eight billion beings.

They will deliver countless beings;
Having benefited the worlds thus,
They will enter nirvāṇa,
And realize ultimate quiescence."

When the Buddha had spoken this sūtra, Bodhisattva-Mahāsattva Pure Giving, Brahmā, the brahmacārins, and people in the assembly, the five hundred Bodhisattvas, King Prasenajit, the great Śrāvakas, humans, nonhumans, and the eight divisions of divinities all rejoiced greatly in the Buddha's teaching.

NOTES

1. The five covers (see Numerical Glossary).

2. The Chinese text reads 定. Dissension should be noted concerning Prof. Garma Chang's decision (see Chapter 1, note 16) to translate 定 here as 'dhyāna', because two other Chinese versions (Taishō 338, p.89; 339, p.98) use 三昧, a transliteration of 'samādhi', in the same place. (S.L.M.)

3. A star in the constellation Cancer.

4. Literally, "see."

5. This term usually is reserved for Bodhisattvas, but here it is applied to the group of Śrāvakas and Bodhisattvas.

6. A kalaviṅka bird is a bird described as having a melodious voice, and is found in the valleys of the Himalayas. It is said to sing in the shell before hatching.

7. A jīvajīvaka bird is said to be a bird with two heads and a sweet singing tone.

8. This appears to contradict the earlier statement that Pure Giving has never seen the Buddha. However, she is evidently speaking here in the sense of revelation, or seeing the Buddha in a psychic state, as is indicated below.

9. Literally, "entrances," i.e., the six sense-organs and their six objects. (See Numerical Glossary, "twelve entrances").

10. Alternate translation of this line: "That a Bodhisattva goes astray for an instant."

11. See "The Inexhaustible Wisdom-Stores" (Chapter 9 below), note 13.

12. Literally, "is equal."

13. Among the eight Śrāvakas appearing in this sūtra, Ānanda was the only one who had not attained Arhatship, and so was still in the stage of learning.

14. Generally speaking, the twelve links of dependent origination refer to phenomena, and the ultimate truth to noumena, but since in the ultimate sense they are not different, to penetrate and fully understand one is to fully realize the other. The Prajñāpāramitā literature is full of this kind of dialogue to foster the comprehension of nondistinctions within distinctions, and vice versa, to reveal the deep-rooted clinging to dichotomy within the mind, and to induce devotees to "jump" to a higher plane of unity or nondistinction. (G.C.)

15. Or: "Consider that there are no sentient beings or twelve links of dependent origination which constitute sentient beings." The Tibetan text here is much simpler and more direct: "If it is because the profundity of dependent generation is profound that you are [said to be] profound, [consider that] there is no dependent generation at all!" (G.C.)

16. Literally, "extreme views."

17. Here is a clear statement concerning enlightened beings who can answer any unexpected or abstruse question about emptiness, suchness, or the Dharma-body without the slightest hesitation or hindrance, as may be witnessed in many Zen stories.

18. Alternate translation: "If you could eliminate a karma, you would be the master of the masterless dharmas. If a karma can be eliminated, then it can also not be eliminated."

This paragraph points out the absurdity of eliminating or not eliminating a karma, by quoting the Tathāgata's statement that karmas are inconceivable. No one can be the master of what he does not know. To eliminate or not to eliminate something inconceivable is to take a long, aimless shot in the dark, making no sense at all. (S.L.M.)

19. This sentence is from a different Chinese version (Taishō 339, p. 102), in which the preceding question does not appear.

20. The Chinese here reads "No Deluded Views," which is the name of another Bodhisattva who spoke earlier. We have changed the name in accordance with the preceding paragraph.

21. We have deleted many of the questions in this section. Some were not answered in the full Chinese text; answers to others were deleted in our abridgement process.

22. We have omitted the restatement of the category (e.g., "These four will enable a Bodhisattva to defeat demons") which appears at the end of each paragraph.

23. I.e., a great Bodhisattva.

24. Sudhana is the name of an important character in the *Avataṁsaka Sūtra*. Although this name is the same, it is not clear whether it refers to the same character. (G.C.)

25. The original text reads: "They are the unexcelled fields of blessing for all Śrāvakas

and Pratyekabuddhas." However, following two different versions (Taishō 338, p. 96; 339, p. 106), we have adopted the present translation.

26. Some varieties of jade are pure white.

27. Here the sūtra eulogizes the future Buddha-land of Pure Giving as being superior to many future Buddha-lands, including that of Mañjuśrī. However, in the sūtra "The Prediction of Mañjuśrī's Attainment of Buddhahood" (Chap. 10), Mañjuśrī's Buddha-land is also praised as superlative. This contradiction should be regarded as Oriental hyperbole. It is an example of how one should not treat figures or figurative expressions in Mahāyāna sūtras as precise, but rather as rhetorical or symbolic expressions for a pedagogical purpose. (G.C.)

28. Literally, "Good man." This may be because Pure Giving changed her form into that of a boy, but Maudgalyāyana's question here indicates she has probably returned to her female form.

29. This explanation improves upon the persistent idea in many Mahāyāna sūtras (inspired by Hīnayāna notions) that only a man can attain full Buddhahood and that a woman must change into a male to become fully enlightened. Here it is advanced that Buddha is far beyond such discriminations as male or female; thus, male-oriented descriptions of the Buddha, such as the thirty-two signs, are expedient and not to be misunderstood as describing the Dharma-body of a Buddha, which defies sex or any other characteristic. Furthermore, as the goddess says in the *Vimalakīrti Sūtra*, "While women are not women in reality, they appear in the form of women. With this in mind, the Buddha said, 'In all things, there is neither male nor female.'"

In Tantrism, or Vajrayāna, the male-dominated Buddhist attitude changed further. Tantric yogis follow a set of precepts that prohibit belittling women in any way. Tantric Buddhas, moreover, are very frequently shown in embrace with their consorts, who are fully enlightened female Buddhas. (V.S.B.)

30. The samādhi of emptiness: one of three samādhis. The other two are the samādhi of signlessness and the samādhi of wishlessness (cf. Numerical Glossary, "three doors to liberation").

6 文殊說般若會

Mañjuśrī's Discourse on the Pāramitā of Wisdom

I

Thus have I heard. Once the Buddha was dwelling in the garden of Anāthapiṇḍada, in the Jeta Grove near Śrāvastī, accompanied by one thousand great monks. Also present in the assembly were ten thousand Bodhisattva-Mahāsattvas, all of whom had adorned themselves with great merits and were abiding in the stage of nonregression. Among the great Bodhisattvas were Bodhisattva Maitreya, Bodhisattva Mañjuśrī, Bodhisattva Unhindered Eloquence, and Bodhisattva Never Abandoning Vows.

One day at dawn, Bodhisattva-Mahāsattva Mañjuśrī came from his lodging to the Buddha's dwelling place and stood outside the door. Then Venerable Śāriputra, Venerable Pūrṇamaitrāyaṇīputra, Venerable Mahāmaudgalyāyana, Venerable Mahākāśyapa, Venerable Mahākātyāyana, Venerable Mahākauṣṭhila, and other great Śrāvakas also came from their respective lodgings to the Buddha's dwelling place and stood outside the door.

When the Buddha knew that the entire assembly had gathered, he came out of his dwelling, arranged his seat, and sat down. Then he asked Śāriputra, "Why do you stand outside the door at this early hour?"

Śāriputra replied to the Buddha, "World-Honored One, it was Bodhisattva Mañjuśrī who came and stood outside the door first. I came later."

Then, the World-Honored One asked Mañjuśrī, "Did you really come here first in order to see the Tathāgata?"

Sūtra 46, Taishō 310 pp. 650–657; translated into Chinese by Mandra.

Mañjuśrī replied to the Buddha, "Yes, World-Honored One. I did come here to see the Tathāgata. Why? Because I wish to benefit sentient beings with right contemplation. I contemplate the Tathāgata as characterized by suchness, by nondistinction, by immobility, by nonaction, by neither arising nor ceasing, by neither existing nor not existing, by being located neither in some place nor elsewhere, by being neither in the three phases of time nor otherwise, by being neither dualistic nor nondualistic, and by having neither purity nor impurity. I benefit sentient beings with such right contemplations on the Tathāgata."

The Buddha told Mañjuśrī, "If you can see the Tathāgata in this way, your mind will neither cling nor not cling to anything, and it will neither accumulate nor not accumulate anything."

Then Śāriputra said to Mañjuśrī, "It is very rare for one to be able to see the Tathāgata in such a way as you describe—to see the Tathāgata for the sake of all sentient beings, with one's mind detached from sentient beings. [It is also very rare] to teach all sentient beings to pursue nirvāṇa, with one's own mind detached from the pursuit of nirvāṇa; and to don great adornments[1] for the sake of all sentient beings, with one's own mind detached from the sight of adornments."

Then Bodhisattva-Mahāsattva Mañjuśrī said to Śāriputra, "Yes, indeed, what you say is true. It is very rare for one to don great adornments for the sake of all sentient beings, without ever having the notion of sentient beings in his mind. The realm of sentient beings neither increases nor decreases in spite of his donning great adornments for all sentient beings. Suppose one Buddha dwells in a world for a kalpa or more; and suppose an infinite number of such Buddhas, as innumerable as the sands of the Ganges, succeed one another in dwelling in that Buddha-land, each for a kalpa or more, to teach the Dharma day and night without interruption, and to ferry over to nirvāṇa sentient beings as innumerable as the sands of the Ganges—still, the realm of sentient beings will neither increase nor decrease. It is also true that if the Buddhas in all the Buddha-lands in the ten directions teach the Dharma, and each ferries over to nirvāṇa sentient beings as innumerable as the sands of the Ganges, the realm of sentient beings will still neither increase nor decrease. Why? Because sentient beings are devoid of any definitive entity or form. Therefore, the realm of sentient beings neither increases nor decreases."

Śāriputra asked Mañjuśrī, "If the realm of sentient beings neither increases nor decreases, why do Bodhisattvas, for the sake of sentient beings, seek supreme enlightenment and constantly give discourses on the Dharma?"

Mañjuśrī said to the Buddha, "Since sentient beings are empty in nature, Bodhisattvas do not seek supreme enlightenment or teach sentient beings. Why? Because nothing in the Dharma I teach is apprehensible."

Then the Buddha asked Mañjuśrī, "If no sentient being exists, why is it said that there are sentient beings and the realm of sentient beings?"

Mañjuśrī answered, "The realm of sentient beings is by nature identical with the realm of Buddhas."

Then the Buddha asked, "Does the sentient beings' realm have a scope?"

Mañjuśrī answered, "The sentient beings' realm is identical in scope with the Buddha's realm."

Then the Buddha asked, "Does the scope of the sentient beings' realm have a location?"

Mañjuśrī answered, "The scope of the sentient beings' realm is inconceivable."

Then the Buddha asked, "Does the realm of sentient beings abide anywhere?"

Mañjuśrī answered, "Sentient beings abide nowhere, just like space."

The Buddha asked Mañjuśrī, "If so, how should one abide in the pāramitā of wisdom when cultivating it?"

Mañjuśrī answered, "Abiding in no dharma is abiding in the pāramitā of wisdom."

The Buddha asked Mañjuśrī further, "Why is abiding in no dharma called abiding in the pāramitā of wisdom?"

Mañjuśrī answered, "Because to have no notion of abiding is to abide in the pāramitā of wisdom."

The Buddha asked Mañjuśrī further, "If one thus abides in the pāramitā of wisdom, will his good roots increase or decrease?"

Mañjuśrī answered, "If one thus abides in the pāramitā of wisdom, his good roots will not increase or decrease, nor will any dharma; nor will the pāramitā of wisdom increase or decrease in nature or characteristic.

"World-Honored One, one who thus cultivates the pāramitā of wisdom will not reject the dharmas of ordinary people nor cling to the Dharma of saints and sages. Why? Because in the light of the pāramitā of wisdom, there are no dharmas to cling to or reject.

"Moreover, one who cultivates the pāramitā of wisdom in this way will not delight in nirvāṇa or detest saṁsāra. Why? Because he realizes there is no saṁsāra, let alone rejection of it; and no nirvāṇa, let alone attachment to it.

"One who thus cultivates the pāramitā of wisdom will see neither defilements to reject nor merits to cling to; for him, no dharma increases or decreases. Why? Because such a person realizes there is no increase or decrease in the dharmadhātu. World-Honored One, only one who can do so can be said to cultivate the pāramitā of wisdom.

"World-Honored One, to see that no dharma arises or ceases is to cultivate the pāramitā of wisdom.

"World-Honored One, to see that no dharma increases or decreases is to cultivate the pāramitā of wisdom.

"World-Honored One, to aspire to nothing and to see that nothing can be grasped is to cultivate the pāramitā of wisdom.

"World-Honored One, to see neither beauty nor ugliness, to think of neither superiority nor inferiority, and to practice neither attachment nor renunciation is to cultivate the pāramitā of wisdom. Why? Because no dharma is beautiful or ugly, for all dharmas are devoid of characteristics; no dharma is superior or inferior, for all dharmas are equal in nature; no dharma can be grasped or rejected, for all dharmas abide in reality."

The Buddha asked Mañjuśrī, "Is not the Buddha-Dharma superior?"

Mañjuśrī answered, "I find nothing superior or inferior. The Tathāgata can testify to this, since he himself has already realized the emptiness of all dharmas."

The Buddha said to Mañjuśrī, "So it is, so it is. The Tathāgata, the Supremely Enlightened One, has directly realized the emptiness of dharmas."

Mañjuśrī asked the Buddha, "World-Honored One, in emptiness, is there any superiority or inferiority to be found?"

The Buddha said, "Excellent, excellent! Mañjuśrī, what you say is the true Dharma! The unexcelled is the Buddha-Dharma."

Mañjuśrī said, "Just as the Buddha says, the unexcelled is the Buddha-Dharma. Why? Because the inapprehensibility of dharmas is called the unexcelled."

Mañjuśrī continued, "He who cultivates the pāramitā of wisdom in this way does not think himself able to practice the Buddha-Dharma. If a person does not consider the pāramitā of wisdom as a Dharma with which to enlighten ordinary people, or as the Buddha-Dharma, or as an advanced Dharma, that person is cultivating the pāramitā of wisdom.

"Furthermore, World-Honored One, when cultivating the pāramitā of wisdom, one finds nothing to discriminate or contemplate."

The Buddha asked Mañjuśrī, "Do you not contemplate the Buddha-Dharma?"

Mañjuśrī answered, "No, World-Honored One. If I contemplated it, I would not see it. Furthermore, one should not make such distinctions as 'the dharmas of ordinary people,' 'the Dharma of Śrāvakas,' and 'the Dharma of Pratyekabuddhas.' This is called the unexcelled Buddha-Dharma.

"Furthermore, if a person, when cultivating the pāramitā of wisdom, has no notion of ordinary people, nor a notion of Buddha-Dharma, nor does he perceive a fixed entity in anything, that person is really cultivating the pāramitā of wisdom.

"Furthermore, if a person, when cultivating the pāramitā of wisdom, does not see the Realm of Desire, the Realm of Form, the Realm of Formlessness, or the realm of ultimate quiescence, because he sees no dharma characterized by complete extinction, then that person is really cultivating the pāramitā of wisdom."

"Furthermore, if a person, when cultivating the pāramitā of wisdom, perceives neither the one who does favors nor the one who returns favors, and thus has no discrimination in his mind in dealing with the two, that person is really cultivating the pāramitā of wisdom.

"Furthermore, if a person, when cultivating the pāramitā of wisdom, does not see any pāramitā of wisdom, and finds neither any Buddha-Dharma to grasp nor any dharmas of ordinary people to reject, that person is really cultivating the pāramitā of wisdom.

"Furthermore, if a person, when cultivating the pāramitā of wisdom, sees neither any dharma of ordinary people to be extinguished nor any Buddha-Dharma to be realized, that person is really cultivating the pāramitā of wisdom."

The Buddha told Mañjuśrī, "Excellent! It is excellent that you can explain so well the attributes of the profound pāramitā of wisdom. What you say is a seal of the Dharma learned by Bodhisattva-Mahāsattvas. . . ."

The Buddha told Mañjuśrī further, "A person who is not frightened when he hears this Dharma has not merely planted good roots in the lands of one thousand Buddhas; he has been planting good roots in the lands of hundreds of thousands of [millions of] billions of Buddhas for a long time. . . ."

Mañjuśrī said to the Buddha, "World-Honored One, now I will continue to explain the pāramitā of wisdom."

The Buddha said, "You may proceed."

Mañjuśrī said, "World-Honored One, when cultivating the pāramitā of wisdom, one does not see any dharma in which one should or should not abide, nor does he see any state to cling to or reject. Why? Because, like Tathāgatas, he sees no state of any dharma. He does not see even the states of Buddhas, let alone those of Śrāvakas, Pratyekabuddhas, or ordinary people. He clings neither to the conceivable nor to the inconceivable. He does not see the variety of dharmas. In this manner, he realized by himself the inconceivable emptiness of dharmas. . . ."

The Buddha asked Mañjuśrī, "To how many Buddhas have you given offerings?"

Mañjuśrī answered, "The Buddhas and I are all illusory. I see neither a giver nor a receiver of offerings."

The Buddha asked Mañjuśrī, "Are you not now abiding in the Buddha-vehicle?"

Mañjuśrī answered, "As I think about it, I do not see a single dharma. How could I abide in the Buddha-vehicle?"

The Buddha asked, "Mañjuśrī, have you not attained the Buddha-vehicle?"

Mañjuśrī said, "The so-called Buddha-vehicle is only a name; it cannot be attained or perceived. If so, how can I attain anything?"

The Buddha asked, "Mañjuśrī, have you attained the unobstructed wisdom?"

Mañjuśrī answered, "I *am* the unobstructed. How can the unobstructed attain the unobstructed?"

The Buddha asked, "Mañjuśrī, do you sit on the bodhi-site?"

Mañjuśrī answered, "No Tathāgata sits on the bodhi-site; why should I alone sit on the bodhi-site? Why do I say this? Because by direct perception I know clearly that all dharmas abide in reality."

The Buddha asked, "What is reality?"

Mañjuśrī answered, "Dharmas such as the view of a self[2] are reality."

The Buddha asked, "Why is the view of a self reality?"

Mañjuśrī answered, "As to the reality of the view of a self, it is neither real nor unreal; neither comes nor goes; is both self and nonself. Hence, it is called reality.". . .

Mañjuśrī said to the Buddha, "One who is not afraid, horrified, confused, or regretful at hearing this profound pāramitā of wisdom sees the Buddha.". . .

II

Then Śāriputra said to the Buddha, "World-Honored One, the pāramitā of wisdom spoken by Mañjuśrī is beyond the comprehension of novice Bodhisattvas."

Mañjuśrī said, "It is incomprehensible not only to novice Bodhisattvas, but also to Śrāvakas and Pratyekabuddhas who have already done what they set out to do. No one can comprehend a teaching like this. Why? Because there is really nothing knowable about bodhi, which defies seeing, learning, attaining, thinking, arising, ceasing, speaking, and hearing. Thus, being empty and quiescent by nature and characteristic, beyond realization and comprehension, and devoid of shape or form, how can bodhi be acquired by anyone?"

Śāriputra asked Mañjuśrī, "Does the Buddha not realize supreme enlightenment through the dharmadhātu?"

Mañjuśrī answered, "No, Śāriputra. Why? Because the World-Honored One is the dharmadhātu itself. It is absurd to say that the dharmadhātu realizes the dharmadhātu. Śāriputra, the nature of the dharmadhātu is bodhi. Why? Because, in the dharmadhātu, there is no trace of sentient beings and all dharmas are empty. The emptiness of all dharmas is bodhi, because they are not two and are not different.

"Śāriputra, where there is no discrimination, there is no knower. Where there is no knower, there is no speech. That which is beyond speech is neither existent nor nonexistent; neither knowable nor unknowable. So is it with all dharmas. Why? Because no dharma can be identified, whether by location or by specific nature. . . ."

Then the World-Honored One asked Mañjuśrī, "You call me the Tathāgata. Do you really think I am the Tathāgata?"

Mañjuśrī answered, "No, World-Honored One, I do not think you are the Tathāgata. There is nothing about suchness that distinguishes it as suchness, nor is there a Tathāgata's wisdom capable of knowing suchness. Why? Because the Tathāgata and wisdom are not two. Emptiness is the Tathāgata; therefore the Tathāgata is only an arbitrary name. How, then, can I regard anyone as the Tathāgata?"

The Buddha asked, "Do you doubt the Tathāgata?"

Mañjuśrī answered, "No, World-Honored One, I perceive that the Tathāgata has no definite nature; that he is neither born nor perishes. Therefore, I have no doubt whatsoever."

The Buddha asked Mañjuśrī, "Would you not say that the Tathāgata now appears in the world?"

Mañjuśrī answered, "If the Tathāgata appears in the world, all the dharmadhātu should also appear."

The Buddha asked Mañjuśrī, "Would you say that Buddhas as innumerable as the sands of the Ganges have entered nirvāṇa?"

Mañjuśrī answered, "All Buddhas have one characteristic: inconceivability."

The Buddha said, "So it is, so it is. All Buddhas have one characteristic, that of inconceivability."

Mañjuśrī asked the Buddha, "World-Honored One, does the Buddha stay in the world now?"

The Buddha answered, "It is so, it is so."[3]

Mañjuśrī said, "If the Buddha stays in the world, so should other Buddhas as innumerable as the sands of the Ganges. Why? Because all Buddhas have one identical characteristic: inconceivability. That which is characterized by inconceivability does not arise or cease. If the future Buddhas were to appear in the world, all other Buddhas would appear, too. Why? Because in the inconceivable there is no past, present, or future. However, sentient beings prone to grasping still say that a Buddha appears in the world or that a Buddha enters nirvāṇa."

The Buddha said to Mañjuśrī, "This can be understood by the Tathāgata, Arhats, and nonregressing Bodhisattvas. Why? Because these three kinds of people can hear this profound Dharma without slandering or praising it."

Mañjuśrī said to the Buddha, "World-Honored One, who could slander or praise this inconceivable Dharma?"

The Buddha said to Mañjuśrī, "The Tathāgata is inconceivable, and so are ordinary people."[4]

Mañjuśrī asked the Buddha, "World-Honored One, are ordinary people also inconceivable?"

The Buddha answered, "Yes, they are also inconceivable. Why? Because all minds are inconceivable."

Mañjuśrī said, "If, as you say, both the Tathāgata and ordinary people are inconceivable, then the countless Buddhas who have sought nirvāṇa have worn themselves out for nothing. Why? Because the inconceivable *is* nirvāṇa; they are identical, not different."

Mañjuśrī continued, "Only those good men and good women who have cultivated good roots and associated closely with virtuous friends for a long time can understand that ordinary people, as well as the Buddhas, are inconceivable."

The Buddha asked Mañjuśrī, "Do you wish to treat the Tathāgata as the supreme one among sentient beings?"

Mañjuśrī answered, "I do wish to treat the Tathāgata as foremost among sentient beings, but no attribute of sentient beings is apprehensible."

The Buddha asked, "Do you wish to treat the Tathāgata as the one who has attained the inconceivable Dharma?"

Mañjuśrī answered, "I do wish to treat the Tathāgata as the one who has attained the inconceivable Dharma, but there is no Dharma to be achieved."

The Buddha asked Mañjuśrī, "Do you wish to treat the Tathāgata as a teacher of the Dharma who converts sentient beings?"

Mañjuśrī answered, "I do wish to treat the Tathāgata as a teacher of the Dharma who converts sentient beings, but the Dharma teacher and the listener are both inapprehensible. Why? Because they both abide in the dharmadhātu, and in the dharmadhātu sentient beings are not different from one another.". . .

The Buddha asked. "Do you enter the Samādhi of the Inconceivable?"

Mañjuśrī answered. "No, World-Honored One. I *am* the inconceivable. I do not see any mind capable of conceiving anything; so, how can it be said that I enter the Samādhi of the Inconceivable? When I first brought forth bodhicitta, I did intend to enter that samādhi. However, as I reflect on it now, I see that I enter that samādhi really without thinking about it. Just as, after long practice, one becomes a skillful archer able to hit the target without thinking about it, so, as a result of long practice, I am one with the Samādhi of the Inconceivable at all times without thinking about it, though I had to concentrate my mind on one object when I started to learn that samādhi."

Śāriputra asked Mañjuśrī, "Are there other superior, wonderful samādhis of ultimate quiescence?"

Mañjuśrī answered, "If there were a Samādhi of the Inconceivable, then you might ask whether or not there are other samādhis of ultimate quiescence. However, according to my understanding, even the Samādhi of the Inconceivable is inapprehensible; how could you ask whether or not there are other samādhis of ultimate quiescence?"

Śāriputra asked, "Is the Samādhi of the Inconceivable inapprehensible?"

Mañjuśrī answered, "A samādhi which is conceivable is apprehensible, while a samādhi which is inconceivable is inapprehensible. In fact, all sentient beings have achieved the Samādhi of the Inconceivable. Why? All minds are nonminds, [and to have no mind] is called the Samādhi of the Inconceivable. Therefore, the characteristics of all sentient beings and those of the Samādhi of the Inconceivable are identical and not different."

The Buddha praised Mañjuśrī, saying, "Excellent, excellent! Because you have been planting good roots and cultivating pure conduct in Buddha-lands for a long time, you are able to discourse on the profound samādhi. Now you are abiding securely in the pāramitā of wisdom."

Mañjuśrī said, "If I can give this discourse because I abide in the pāramitā of wisdom, then I have the concept of existence and abide in the concept of a self; if I abide in the concepts of existence and a self, then the pāramitā of wisdom has an abode. However, to think that the pāramitā of wisdom abides in nothingness is also the concept of a self, and [abiding in nothingness] is also called [having] an abode. To steer clear of these two abodes,[5] one should abide in nonabidance as Buddhas do, and dwell securely in ultimate quiescence, the inconceivable state. Only this inconceivable state is called the abode of the pāramitā of wisdom." . . .

Mañjuśrī continued, "The realm of the Tathāgata and the realm of a self are not two. He who cultivates the pāramitā of wisdom with this understanding does not seek bodhi. Why? Because detachment from the notion of bodhi is the pāramitā of wisdom." . . .

Then the Buddha said to Mahākāśyapa, "As an illustration, the budding on a pārijāta tree in the Heaven of the Thirty-Three gives great joy to the gods there, because it is a sure sign that the tree will soon come into bloom. Similarly, the budding of faith and understanding in monks, nuns, laymen, and laywomen who have heard the teaching of the pāramitā of wisdom is a sign that all Buddha-Dharmas will soon blossom forth from these persons.

"If there are monks, nuns, laymen and laywomen in the future who, after hearing the pāramitā of wisdom, accept it with faith and read and recite it without regret or confusion in mind, you should know that they have heard and accepted this sūtra in this assembly, and that they will also be able to elaborate on this sūtra and circulate it among people in cities and villages. You should know that they will be protected and remembered by Buddhas.

"Those good men and good women who believe and delight in this profound pāramitā of wisdom and have no doubt about it, have learned the doctrine long ago from past Buddhas and planted good roots in their lands. For example, if a person who is stringing beads suddenly comes across an unexcelled, real wish-fulfilling pearl and is jubilant, you should know that he must have seen such a pearl before. Similarly, Kāśyapa, if a good man or a good women, while learning other doctrines, suddenly hears the profound pāramitā of wisdom and becomes jubilant, you should know that it is because he or she has heard it before. If there are sentient beings who can faithfully accept and take great delight in the pāramitā of wisdom when they hear it, it is because those persons have associated with countless Buddhas and learned the pāramitā of wisdom from them previously.

"To illustrate further, if a person who has previously seen a city or a village hears another person praising the loveliness and charm of its gardens, ponds, springs, flowers, fruits, trees, and its male and female citizens, he will be greatly delighted. He will then urge the person to relate again the various adornments of its gardens and parks, flowers, ponds, fountains, sweet fruits, various treasures, and other enjoyable things. When the listener hears these things described a second time, he will be exhilarated again. Now, all this is because he has seen that place before. Similarly, if there are good men and good women who, after hearing the pāramitā of wisdom from someone, accept it with faith, take pleasure in it, enjoy hearing it untiringly, and furthermore urge that person to repeat it, you should know that those persons have heard Mañjuśrī explain this profound pāramitā of wisdom before.". . .

Mañjuśrī then said to the Buddha, "World-Honored One, the Buddha says that all dharmas are actionless, signless, and ultimately quiescent. If a good man or a good woman can understand this truth correctly and explain it to others as taught, he or she will be praised by Tathāgatas. What that person says will not conflict with the nature of dharmas, but will be the teaching of the Buddha; it will be the radiance of the pāramitā of wisdom and the radiance of all the Buddha-Dharmas, which result from the penetration of reality, the inconceivable."

The Buddha told Mañjuśrī, "When I was practicing the Bodhisattva-path in the past, I had to [learn the pāramitā of wisdom to] cultivate good roots; I had to learn the pāramitā of wisdom in order to abide in the stage of nonregression and achieve supreme enlightenment. Good men and good women should also learn the pāramitā of wisdom. One who wishes to achieve the thirty-two auspicious signs . . . should learn the pāramitā of wisdom. . . .

"One who wishes to know that all dharmas are equally comprised in the dharmadhātu, and thereby to free his mind from all obstructions, should learn the pāramitā of wisdom. . . .

"One who wishes to extend kindness to all sentient beings without restriction and without entertaining any notion of sentient beings should learn the pāramitā of wisdom. . . .

"One who wishes to know what is right and wrong, to obtain the ten powers and the four fearlessnesses, to abide in the Buddha's wisdom, and to acquire unimpeded eloquence should learn the pāramitā of wisdom."

Then Mañjuśrī said to the Buddha, "World-Honored One, in my opinion, the true Dharma is unconditioned, signless, inapprehensible, not beneficial, nonarising, nonceasing, noncoming, nongoing, and without a knower, a perceiver, or a doer. Neither the pāramitā of wisdom nor its state can be seen, realized, or not realized; the pāramitā of wisdom is devoid of mental constructions and discrimination.[6] Dharmas are neither exhaustible nor inexhaustible; in them there is no Dharma of ordinary people, no Dharma of Śrāvakas, no Dharma of Pratyekabuddhas, and no Dharma of Buddhas; there is neither attainment nor nonattainment, neither the renunciation of saṁsāra nor the realization of nirvāṇa, neither the conceivable nor the inconceivable, neither action nor nonaction. The characteristics of Dharma being such, I do not see why anyone should learn the pāramitā of wisdom.". . .

Mañjuśrī asked the Buddha, "World-Honored One, why is the pāramitā of wisdom so called?"

The Buddha answered, "The pāramitā of wisdom has no bound or border, name or mark; it is beyond thought; it contains no refuge, [like a sea] without an island or a sandbar; in it there is no offense or blessing, light or darkness; it is as indivisible and limitless as the dharmadhātu. That is why it is called the pāramitā of wisdom. It is also called the sphere of action of a great Bodhisattva. [The so-called sphere of action is] neither a sphere of action nor a sphere of nonaction. All that belongs to the One Vehicle is called the sphere of nonaction. Why? Because [in it] there is no thought and no activity."[7]

Mañjuśrī asked the Buddha, "World-Honored One, what should one do to acquire supreme enlightenment quickly?"

The Buddha answered, "If one follows the teaching of the pāramitā of wisdom, one can acquire supreme enlightenment quickly. Furthermore, there is the Single Deed Samādhi: a good man or a good woman who cultivates this samādhi will also quickly acquire supreme enlightenment."

Mañjuśrī asked, "World-Honored One, what is the Single Deed Samādhi?"

The Buddha answered, "To meditate exclusively on the oneness of the dharmadhātu is called the Single Deed Samādhi.[8] Those good men or good women who wish to enter this samādhi should first listen to discourses on the pāramitā of wisdom and cultivate it as taught. Then they can enter this samādhi, which, like the dharmadhātu, is nonregressive, indestructible, inconceivable, unobstructed, and signless.

"Those good men or good women who wish to enter the Single Deed Samādhi should live in seclusion, cast away discursive thoughts, not cling to the appearances of things, concentrate their minds on a Buddha, and recite his name single-mindedly. They should keep their bodies erect and, facing the direction of that Buddha, meditate upon him continuously. If they can maintain mindfulness of the Buddha without interruption from moment to moment, then they will be able to see all the Buddhas of the past, present, and future right in each moment.[9] Why? Because the merits of being mindful of one Buddha are as innumerable and boundless as those of being mindful of countless Buddhas, for the inconceivable teachings of all Buddhas are identical and undifferentiated. All Buddhas achieve supreme enlightenment by the same suchness, and all are endowed with incalculable merits and immeasurable eloquence. Therefore, one who enters the Single Deed Samādhi knows thoroughly that Buddhas as innumerable as the sands of the Ganges are indistinguishable in the dharmadhātu.

"Among all the Śrāvakas who hear the Buddha-Dharma, Ānanda has achieved the highest level of memory, dhāraṇī, eloquence, and wisdom; still, his achievement is limited and measurable. However, one who has attained the Single Deed Samādhi will thoroughly, distinctly, and without any hindrance understand every Dharma-door explained in the sūtras. His wisdom and eloquence will never be exhausted even if he discourses on the Dharma day and night, and Ānanda's erudition and eloquence cannot equal one hundredth, or even one thousandth part of his. A great Bodhisattva should think: 'How shall I attain the Single Deed Samādhi, thus gaining inconceivable merits and immeasurable renown?' "

The Buddha continued, "A great Bodhisattva should keep the Single Deed Samādhi in mind and always strive energetically for it without ever becoming lax or lazy. Thus, learning gradually, he will be able to enter the Single Deed Samādhi, and the inconceivable merits attained thereby will bear witness that he has entered it. However, those who slander or disbelieve the true Dharma and those who are hindered by evil karma or grave offenses will not be able to enter that samādhi.[10]

"Furthermore, Mañjuśrī, as an illustration, suppose a person who has acquired a wish-fulfilling pearl shows it to an expert in pearls. The expert tells him that he has acquired a priceless, real wish-fulfilling pearl. The owner then requests the expert to polish it for him without damaging its luster. After being polished, the pearl shines with full, translucent luster. Similarly, Mañjuśrī, if a good man or a good woman cultivates the Single Deed Samādhi, he or she will penetrate the phenomena of all dharmas without obstruction, and will gain inconceivable merits and immeasurable renown while that samādhi is cultivated.

"Mañjuśrī, just as the sun can illuminate all places without losing its own brilliance, so one who has acquired the Single Deed Samādhi can possess all merits, lacking none, and illuminate the Buddha-Dharma.

"Mañjuśrī, all the Dharmas I teach are of one taste—the taste of detachment, liberation, and ultimate quiescence. What is taught by a good man or a good woman who has acquired the Single Deed Saṃādhi is also of one taste—the taste of detachment, liberation, and ultimate quiescence—and is unerringly consistent with the true Dharma.

"Mañjuśrī, a great Bodhisattva who has acquired the Single Deed Samādhi has fulfilled all the conditions conducive to his swift attainment of supreme enlightenment.

"Furthermore, Mañjuśrī, if a great Bodhisattva sees neither diversity nor unity in the dharmadhātu, he will quickly attain supreme enlightenment. He who knows that the characteristics of supreme enlightenment are inconceivable and that there is no reaching Buddhahood in [the attainment of] bodhi will swiftly attain supreme enlightenment. He who believes and recognizes without fear or doubt that all dharmas are the Buddha-Dharma will swiftly attain supreme enlightenment."

Mañjuśrī asked the Buddha, "World-Honored One, does one attain supreme enlightenment swiftly by such causes?"

The Buddha said, "Supreme enlightenment is achieved neither by a cause nor not by a cause. Why? Because the realm of the inconceivable is acquired neither by a cause nor not by a cause.

"If a good man or a good woman does not relax his or her efforts after hearing this discourse, you should know that he or she has planted good roots in the lands of past Buddhas. Therefore, if a monk or a nun is not frightened after he or she hears this profound pāramitā of wisdom, he or she has really left the household life to follow the Buddha. If a layman or laywoman is not horrified upon hearing this profound pāramitā of wisdom, he or she has found a true refuge.

"Mañjuśrī, if a good man or a good woman does not practice this profound pāramitā of wisdom, he or she is not following the Buddha-vehicle. Just as all medicinal herbs rely on the great earth for growth, Mañjuśrī, so do all the good roots of a great Bodhisattva depend on the pāramitā of wisdom for growth leading to supreme enlightenment."

Then Mañjuśrī asked the Buddha, "World-Honored One, in which city or village of this world should this profound pāramitā of wisdom be taught?"

The Buddha replied to Mañjuśrī, "If anyone in this assembly, after hearing the teaching of the pāramitā of wisdom, vows to conform constantly to the pāramitā of wisdom in future lives, he will in his future lives be able to listen to this sūtra as a result of this faith and understanding. You should know that such a person will not be born with small good roots. He will be able to accept the teaching of this sūtra and rejoice when hearing it. . . ."

Mañjuśrī said to the Buddha, "World-Honored One, if monks, nuns, laymen, or laywomen come to ask me, 'Why does the Tathāgata discourse on the pāramitā of wisdom?', I will answer, 'All the teachings of the Dharma are beyond dispute. The Tathāgata discourses on the pāramitā of wisdom because he does not see any dharma that can conflict with what he teaches, or any sentient beings who can understand the pāramitā of wisdom with their [discriminative mind] or consciousness.'

"Moreover, World-Honored One, I will further explain ultimate reality. Why? Because the phenomena of all dharmas are comprised in reality. An Arhat has no superior Dharma. Why not? Because the Dharma of an Arhat and that of an ordinary person are neither the same nor different. . . ."

Mañjuśrī continued, "If people wish to learn the pāramitā of wisdom, I will tell them, 'You listeners should not think of anything or attach yourselves to anything, nor should you think that you are hearing or acquiring something. You should be as free of discrimination as a magically produced being. This is the true teaching of the Dharma. Therefore, you listeners should not entertain the notion of duality, should not abandon various views to cultivate the Buddha-Dharma, should not grasp the Buddha-Dharma, and should not reject the dharmas of ordinary people. Why? Because the Dharma of the Buddha and the dharmas of ordinary people are both characterized by emptiness, wherein there is nothing to be grasped or rejected.' If people ask me about the pāramitā of wisdom, that is how I will answer; that is how I will console them; that is what I will advocate. Good men and good women should ask me about this and abide by my answer without regression. They should know that I teach the characteristics of dharmas in accordance with the pāramitā of wisdom."

Then the World-Honored One praised Mañjuśrī, saying, "Excellent, excellent! It is just as you say. A good man or a good woman who wishes to see Buddhas should learn this pāramitā of wisdom. One who wishes to associate with Buddhas closely and make offerings to them properly should learn this pāramitā of wisdom.

"One who wishes to say, 'The Tathāgata is our World-Honored One' should learn this pāramitā of wisdom; one who says, 'The Tathāgata is not our World-Honored One' should also learn this pāramitā of wisdom.

"One who wishes to attain supreme enlightenment should learn this pāramitā of wisdom; one who does not wish to attain supreme enlightenment should also learn this pāramitā of wisdom.

"One who wishes to accomplish all samādhis should learn this pāramitā of wisdom; one who does not wish to accomplish any samādhi should also learn this pāramitā of wisdom. Why? Because samādhi is not different in nature from nonaction, and no dharma comes or goes. . . ."

The Buddha said to Mañjuśrī, "If monks, nuns, laymen, and laywomen wish to avoid falling into the miserable planes of existence, they should learn this pāramitā of wisdom. If a good man or a good woman accepts, practices, reads, and recites only a four-line stanza [of this pāramitā of wisdom], and explains it to others in accordance with reality, he or she will without fail attain supreme enlightenment and will live in a Buddha-land.

"The Buddha approves of one who is not afraid or fearful when hearing this pāramitā of wisdom, but instead has faith in it and understands it. The pāramitā of wisdom is the Dharma-seal of the Mahāyāna demonstrated by the Buddha. If a good man or a good woman learns this Dharma-seal, he or she will rise above the miserable planes of existence. Such a person will not follow the paths of Śrāvakas or Pratyekabuddhas, because he or she will have transcended [those paths]."

Then the Thirty-Three Deva Kings, led by Śakra, scattered upon the Tathāgata and Mañjuśrī wonderful celestial flowers, such as blue lotuses, white lotuses, opened white lotuses, and flowers of the coral tree; celestial sandalwood incense, other kinds of powdered incense, and various treasures. The devas also played celestial music, all as offerings to the Tathāgata, to Mañjuśrī, and to the pāramitā of wisdom. After making the offerings, Śakra said, "May I often hear this pāramitā of wisdom, the Dharma-seal! May the good men and good women in this world always have opportunities to hear this sūtra, so that they may surely believe in and understand the Buddha-Dharma; accept, practice, read, recite, and explain it to others; and thus be upheld by all gods."

Then the Buddha told Śakra, "Kauśika, so it is, so it is. Such good men and good women will surely acquire the enlightenment of Buddhas.". . .

When the Buddha had finished teaching this sūtra, the great Bodhisattvas and the four kinds of devotees who had heard this pāramitā of wisdom began to practice it with great joy and veneration.

NOTES

1. That is, virtues which "adorn" a great Bodhisattva.

2. Literally, "the view of a body."

3. The text reads thus, but there may be a textual corruption here. Logically, it seems better to render it as: "The Buddha answered, 'No.'" However, since the Buddha can also be refuted, Mañjuśrī's following statement is appropriate.

4. In this and the following four paragraphs, the Buddha and Mañjuśrī expound the discovery, according to the Mahāyāna tradition, that the Buddha made when he attained enlightenment, viz., all beings have the same nature, which is that of Buddhahood.

5. That is, eternalism and nihilism, usually referred to as the two extremes.

6. Mañjuśrī has here restated the essence of this sūtra.

7. The Tibetan version of this passage reads quite differently from the Chinese, as follows:

Mañjuśrī asked the Bhagavān, "World-Honored One, why is the pāramitā of wisdom so called?"

The Buddha said, "Mañjuśrī, because it neither arises nor ceases, it is called the pāramitā of wisdom. It is quiescent from the beginning without production or action, because there is nothing whatsoever in it. That which is devoid of any existence or being is called the pāramitā of wisdom. All Dharmas are [in the] realm of action; this [fact] itself is the realm of action of a Bodhisattva-Mahāsattva. To act in this manner is to enter the realm of action of a Bodhisattva-Mahāsattva. The nonsphere of action is the sphere of action of all vehicles. This is why it is called the nonsphere of action." (G.C.)

8. Alternate translation: "To meditate with concentration on the one essence of the dharmadhātu is called the Single Deed Samādhi."

The Tibetan text reads: "Mañjuśrī, the so-called Single Deed [Samādhi] is simply a nomenclature of the nonarising [truth]. Those good men and good women who wish to enter the Single Deed Samādhi first should carefully study the pāramitā of wisdom."

9. 一行三昧, here rendered as "the Single Deed Samādhi," is perhaps one of the most important topics of this sūtra. All the major practices of Mahāyāna Buddhism seem to be included in this samādhi practice. However, without a careful reading one is liable to misunderstand the teaching given here. Thus, brief review of the practice of this samādhi may be helpful:

The essence or basic nature of this samādhi is not the recitation of a Buddha's name, as instructed in this paragraph. The recitation of a Buddha's name and the continuous mindfulness of a Buddha's image, as practiced by the Chinese Pure Land School and the Tantra School, are extremely important and necessary as preparatory practices; they cannot, however, substitute for the main practice of the Single Deed Samādhi, because both are still "form-bound," i.e., attached to certain kinds of forms.

The main practice of the Single Deed Samādhi is to meditate on the "one essence of the dharmadhātu," or the "nonarising emptiness," which is beyond all thoughts and discriminations and totally transcendent.

To enter this samādhi, one should first study well the teachings of the Prajñāpāramitā, then recite a Buddha's name singlemindedly. Meditating thus continuously, one will receive the blessing of a Buddha. Combining this blessing with one's insight into Prajñāpāramitā, one can then approach the Single Deed Samādhi without much hazard.

The sequence of practicing the Single Deed Samādhi is therefore as follows:

1. Study and contemplate well the Prajñāpāramitā teaching.
2. Recite a Buddha's name single-mindedly.
3. Meditate on the one essence of the dharmadhātu; i.e., penetratingly observe the emptiness of being, thus causing a great "leap over" to the inconceivable dharmadhātu. (G.C.)

10. When the karmic results for such persons' evil actions or thoughts have been exhausted, those persons will then be able to practice the profound samādhi. (V.S.B.)

7 無畏德菩薩會

The Prophecy of Bodhisattva Fearless Virtue's Attainment of Buddhahood

Thus have I heard. Once the World-Honored One was dwelling on Mount Gṛdhrakūṭa near the city of Rājagṛha, accompanied by five hundred monks. Countless Bodhisattva-Mahāsattvas were also present, and eight thousand of them led the rest. These leaders had all acquired samādhi and dhāraṇī; had penetrated well into emptiness, signlessness, and wishlessness—the three doors to liberation; had acquired a good command of miraculous powers; and had achieved the Realization of the Nonarising of Dharmas. Among them were Bodhisattva Meru,[1] Bodhisattva Great Meru, Bodhisattva Constantly Entering Samādhi, Bodhisattva Ever-Vigorous, Bodhisattva Precious Hand, Bodhisattva Roots of Constant Joy, Bodhisattva Worthy Strength, Bodhisattva Precious Form, Bodhisattva Rāhu,[2] Bodhisattva Śakra God, Bodhisattva Water God, Bodhisattva High Aspiration, Bodhisattva Superior Aspiration, Bodhisattva Intense Aspiration, and so forth.

During the World-Honored One's stay near the city of Rājagṛha, the king, princes, brāhmins, elders, and lay devotees all worshiped, praised, and made offerings to the Buddha.

At that time, the World-Honored One was teaching the Dharma to the incalculable hundreds of thousands of millions of followers who surrounded him respectfully.

One morning, in accordance with the rules, numerous Śrāvakas, including Venerable Śāriputra, Venerable Mahāmaudgalyāyana, Venerable Mahākāśyapa, Venerable Subhūti, Venerable Pūrṇamaitrāyaṇīputra, Venerable Revata, Venerable Aśvajit, Venerable Upāli, Venerable Rāhula, and Venerable Ānanda, all dressed in monastic robes and holding bowls in their hands, went into the city of Rājagṛha

Sūtra 32, Taishō 310 pp. 550–555; translated into Chinese by Buddhaśānta.

for the sole purpose of begging food from house to house. Begging in this way, these Śrāvakas gradually approached the palace where King Ajātaśatru lived. When they arrived there, they stood in silence to one side, without saying whether they wanted food or not.

King Ajātaśatru had a daughter named Fearless Virtue, a maiden incomparable in beauty and grace. She had achieved the most distinctive merits [in the world], although that year she was just twelve. She was sitting with golden, jewelled shoes on her feet in her royal father's hall when she saw the Śrāvakas. She did not stand up to welcome them, but sat in silence, not exchanging greetings with them, saluting them, or asking them to be seated. Seeing Fearless Virtue sitting silently, King Ajātaśatru asked her, "Do you not know that these men are all the foremost disciples of Śākyamuni Tathāgata? Do you not know that they have achieved the great Dharma, and are fields of blessings in the world? It is out of compassion for sentient beings that they beg for food. Now that you have seen them, why do you not stand up to welcome them? Why not salute them, exchange greetings with them, and ask them to be seated? Now, what on earth do you have in mind that keeps you from standing up to welcome them?"

Fearless Virtue asked her royal father, "Has Your Majesty ever seen or heard that a universal monarch stands up to welcome minor kings when he sees them?"

The king answered, "No."

"Has Your Majesty ever seen or heard that a lion, the king of beasts, rises to welcome jackals when it sees them?"

"No."

"Has Your Majesty ever seen or heard that Śakra receives his celestial subjects or that Brahmā salutes his celestial subjects?"

"No."

"Has Your Majesty ever seen or heard that the god of a vast ocean pays homage to gods of rivers and ponds?"

"No."

"Has Your Majesty ever seen or heard that the king of Sumeru, [the unequaled mountain,] pays homage to kings of hills?"

"No."

"Has Your Majesty ever seen or heard that gods of the sun or the moon salute fireflies?"

"No."

The maiden said, "Therefore, Your Majesty, why should a Bodhisattva, who in great kindness and compassion has vowed to pursue supreme enlightenment, pay homage to Śrāvakas of the Hīnayāna, who have neither great kindness nor great compassion? Your Majesty, why should one who follows the path leading to supreme enlightenment, who is like a lion, the king of beasts, salute those who follow the Hīnayāna, who are like jackals?[3]

"Your Majesty, if one is already engaged in a vigorous effort to seek the great, pure path, should he associate with Śrāvakas of small and few good roots?

"Your Majesty, if a person wishes to go to a sea of great wisdom to seek a thorough knowledge of the great Dharma in its entirety, does he bother to turn to Śrāvakas, whose knowledge, based on the Buddha's oral teachings, is as limited as the water in a cow's hoofprint?[4]

"Your Majesty, if one wishes to reach Buddhahood, [the spiritual] Mount Sumeru, and acquire the infinite body of a Tathāgata, should he pay homage to Śrāvakas, who seek only as much samādhi power as could be confined in the space of a tiny mustard seed?

"Your Majesty, [the merits and wisdom of] Śrāvakas may be compared to [the light of] a firefly, because their illumination can only benefit themselves, and their understanding of Dharma comes only through hearing the Buddha's oral teachings. If a person has already learned of the merits and wisdom of Tathāgatas, which may be likened to sunlight and moonlight, should he salute Śrāvakas?

"Your Majesty, I will not pay homage to Śrāvakas even after the Buddha enters nirvāṇa, let alone now, when the World-Honored One still remains in the world. Why?

"Your Majesty, the reason is: one who associates closely with Śrāvakas will vow to attain Śrāvakahood; one who associates closely with Pratyekabuddhas will vow to attain Pratyekabuddhahood; one who associates closely with the supremely enlightened one will vow to attain supreme enlightenment."

After saying this, Fearless Virtue spoke in verse to her father, King Ajātaśatru:

"Like a person who ventures
[To seek a fortune] at sea
And yet returns with one coin only;
So, precisely, do Śrāvakas behave.
Having reached the great ocean of Dharma,
They disregard the treasures of the Mahāyāna,
And engender only the narrow aspiration
To follow the Hīnayāna path.

If a person associates closely with a king,
And enjoys free access to the palace,
But asks that king for only one coin,
His intimacy with the king is in vain.

If one, with a respectful mind,
Keeps close to a universal monarch
And asks him for millions of taels of gold
To help numerous poor people,
His intimacy with the king is indeed fruitful.

To the person who asks for one coin
A Śrāvaka may be compared;
Instead of seeking true liberation,
He pursues only a minor nirvāṇa.

If one engenders a narrow aspiration,
Seeking his own deliverance only, not others',
Then, just like a minor doctor
Who can only cure himself,
He deserves no respect from the wise.

A great skillful healer,
With a kind and compassionate heart,
And a command of all methods of treatment,
Can heal vast numbers of the sick,
Winning respect and a good reputation.
Similarly, those who bring forth bodhicitta
Can cure all beings' afflictions.[5]

Your Majesty, a grove of castor-oil plants
Gives forth no flower's fragrance
And provides no good shade; likewise,
A Śrāvaka does not resolve to save the world.
However, a Bodhisattva can benefit all,
Like a huge tree giving shelter.

Small brooks can be dried up
By the flames of the autumn sun
Before they reach the ocean,
And so cannot nurture myriad beings.[6]
The Śrāvaka-path, like [the water in]
The narrow, lowly hoofprint of a cow,
Cannot eliminate the afflictions of sentient beings.

Upon a small hill
One cannot acquire a golden-hued body;
It is upon Mount Sumeru
That everyone appears golden.[7]
Your Majesty, Bodhisattvas are like Mount Sumeru;
Because they stay in the world,
Beings can be liberated
And have bodies of the same hue.[8]

Bodhisattvas are endowed with all-knowing wisdom,
Which, like productive land,

Can support numberless beings;
But the wisdom of Śrāvakas,
Who do not realize the Dharma,
Is like the morning dew,
Incapable of moistening the world.[9]

A Śrāvaka is like a dewdrop on a flower,
While a Bodhisattva is like a downpour
Or the nurturing water of a vast lake;[10]
All those who associate closely with him
Will attain the great Dharma.

Men and women do not enjoy
The rhododendron,
Which has no scent,
But all enjoy the wonderful fragrance
Of the campaka flower[11]
And the blue lotus.

A Śrāvaka is like a rhododendron flower;
His wisdom cannot help sentient beings.
A Bodhisattva is like a campaka flower;
Out of his compassion,
He can convert numerous beings.

Your Majesty, do you know
Which is more unusual:
One who dwells in the wilderness
Or one who benefits many people?
To provide security to countless beings
And ferry them over [the ocean of saṁsāra],
You should bring forth bodhicitta
And not follow the path of the two vehicles.
Just as a good guide can show
The right way to people lost in the wilderness,
So can Bodhisattvas
[Guide others out of saṁsāra].

Your Majesty, have you ever seen
A small raft sailing across a vast ocean?
Only a huge ship can do so,
Carrying numerous beings.
Your Majesty, while a Śrāvaka is like a raft,
A Bodhisattva is like a huge ship;
After being permeated with the Dharma

While cultivating the path,
He can ferry sentient beings
Over the ocean of hunger and thirst.

Your Majesty, have you ever seen
A man fighting a battle on a donkey?
One can win a battle
Only on an elephant or a horse.
A Śrāvaka is like a donkey,
While a Bodhisattva is like a dragon or an elephant.
He defeats demons under the bodhi-tree
And delivers countless beings [from saṁsāra].

In the nocturnal sky,
All the stars fall into shadow
When the full moon rises
To illuminate every corner of the world.
A Śrāvaka is like a star,
While a Bodhisattva is like the full moon;
Out of compassion for sentient beings,
He shows them the way to nirvāṇa.

The light of a firefly
Cannot help a person work,
But when the sun illuminates the earth
All activities can proceed.
A Śrāvaka, like the glow of a firefly,
Cannot benefit many,
But a Buddha, endowed with the light of liberation,
Has compassion for all beings.

A jackal cannot by its howl
Frighten the king of beasts;
But when the lion roars,
Flying birds fall down with fear.

Your Majesty, Śrāvakas fail
To bring forth bodhicitta;
They eliminate afflictions,
But not to benefit sentient beings.
Seeing this, I do not vow to become a Śrāvaka.
Since I have already engendered the great resolve,
Why should I now make a small vow?

Your Majesty, if one who is fortunate enough
To obtain a human body

Can cherish the unexcelled resolve
To save all beings from saṁsāra,
And give up the Hīnayāna path,
He will have a good human body,
And also good fortune.

It is best, if born in this world,
To bring forth the unexcelled resolve:
To seek the supreme path
And deliver all living beings.

He who can help himself and others
Is well worth extolling;
He will acquire worldly renown
As well as the ultimate truth.

Therefore, I do not salute the Śrāvakas."

Then, King Ajātaśatru reproached Fearless Virtue, saying, "You arrogant girl! How dare you not welcome these Śrāvakas when you see them?"

The maiden said, "Do not say that, Your Majesty. Your Majesty is arrogant, too. Why do you not welcome the poor of the city of Rājagṛha?"

The king answered, "They are not my peers. Why should I welcome them?"

The maiden said, "A novice Bodhisattva is also like that. No Śrāvaka or Pratyekabuddha is his peer."

The king asked his daughter, "Do you not know that Bodhisattvas respect all sentient beings?"

Fearless Virtue answered, "Your Majesty, a Bodhisattva respects them all in order to save arrogant, irate beings and make them turn their minds toward [universal enlightenment]. It is in order to augment sentient beings' good roots that a Bodhisattva extends respect to all. However, Śrāvakas are [already] free of anger and hatred and are unable to increase their good roots. Your Majesty, even though hundreds of thousands of Buddhas explain the wonderful Dharma to them, they will not improve in discipline, meditation, and samādhi.

"Your Majesty, a Śrāvaka is like a piece of lapis lazuli [unable to contain anything], but a Bodhisattva is like a precious container. Your Majesty, a bottle which is full cannot take in even a drop of rain from the sky. In the same way, a Śrāvaka, even after hundreds of thousands of Buddhas, Tathāgatas, explain the wonderful Dharma to him, cannot be helped to improve in discipline, meditation, wisdom, and so forth; nor can he cause sentient beings to aspire to all-knowing wisdom.

"Your Majesty, a vast ocean can receive the water of rivers, rains, and so forth. Why? Because it is an immeasurable container. Your Majesty, when a great Bodhisattva teaches the Dharma, those who listen will be greatly helped and all their good roots will increase. Why? Because the Bodhisattvas are vessels containing infinite kinds of [beneficial] discourses."

Hearing his daughter saying this, King Ajātaśatru sank into silence. At that time, Venerable Śāriputra thought, "Fearless Virtue is so eloquent that she can deliver this boundless discourse. Let me step forward to ask her a few questions; I will find out whether she has realized the truth."

Thereupon, he approached the maiden and asked, "Do you abide in the Śrāvaka-vehicle?"

Fearless Virtue answered, "No."

"Do you abide in the Pratyekabuddha-vehicle?"

"No."

"Do you abide in the Great Vehicle (Mahāyāna)?"

"No."

Śāriputra asked further, "Then, in what vehicle do you abide that you are able to make such a lion's roar?"

The maiden answered Venerable Śāriputra, "If I were abiding in anything now, it would be impossible for me to make a lion's roar. Since I abide in nothing, I can make a lion's roar. However, Śāriputra, you asked: 'In what vehicle do you abide?' Does the Dharma realized and achieved by you, Śāriputra, consist of different vehicles, such as the Śrāvaka-vehicle, the Pratyekabuddha-vehicle, and the Great Vehicle?"

Śāriputra said, "Please listen to me. The Dharma I have realized has no such distinct signs as 'vehicle' or 'non-vehicle,' because it has only one sign, namely, signlessness."

"Venerable Śāriputra, if the Dharma is signless, how can it be sought?"

"Fearless Virtue, what is the difference in excellence between the Dharma of Buddhas and the dharmas of ordinary persons?"

"What is the difference between emptiness and quiescence?"

"There is no difference."

"Śāriputra, just as there is no difference in excellence between emptiness and quiescence, so there is no difference in excellence between the Dharma of Buddhas and the dharmas of ordinary persons. Furthermore, Śāriputra, just as space, while embracing all forms, is not different from them, so the Dharma of Buddhas is not different from the dharmas of ordinary persons, nor can the two be distinguished by signs."

Then Venerable Mahāmaudgalyāyana asked Fearless Virtue, "What difference do you see between a Buddha and a Śrāvaka that prevented you from standing up to welcome these great Śrāvakas, greet them, and yield your seat to them?"

Fearless Virtue replied to Mahāmaudgalyāyana, "Śrāvakas are like stars, which cannot illuminate anything clearly even though they are everywhere throughout a billion-world universe. When Śrāvakas enter dhyāna, they have [enough] wisdom to know something, but when they do not enter dhyāna, they know nothing."

"But it is impossible to know the minds of sentient beings without entering dhyāna!"

"Mahāmaudgalyāyana, a Buddha can, without entering dhyāna, teach the Dharma according to the inclinations of sentient beings and liberate them in worlds as numerous as the sands of the Ganges, because he is proficient in reading sentient beings' minds. This marvelous deed of Buddhas, Tathāgatas, is quite beyond Śrāvakas, who may be likened to the weak lights of stars. Furthermore, Mahāmaudgalyāyana, can Śrāvakas know how many worlds are being formed and how many are being destroyed?"

"No, they cannot."

"Mahāmaudgalyāyana, can Śrāvakas know how many Buddhas have already entered nirvāṇa, how many will enter nirvāṇa, and how many are entering nirvāṇa?"

"No, they cannot."

"Mahāmaudgalyāyana, can Śrāvakas know how many sentient beings are especially prone to desire, hatred, or ignorance, and how many are equally prone to desire, hatred, and ignorance?"

"No, they cannot."

"Mahāmaudgalyāyana, can Śrāvakas know how many sentient beings accept the Śrāvaka-vehicle, how many accept the Pratyekabuddha-vehicle, and how many accept the Buddha-vehicle?"

"No, they cannot."

"Mahāmaudgalyāyana, can Śrāvakas know how many sentient beings can be delivered by Śrāvakas, how many can be delivered by Pratyekabuddhas, and how many can be delivered by Buddhas?"

"No, they cannot."

"Mahāmaudgalyāyana, can Śrāvakas know how many sentient beings have right view and have decided to pursue enlightenment, and how many have decided to pursue heterodox teachings?"

"No, they cannot."

Fearless Virtue said, "Mahāmaudgalyāyana, only the Tathāgata, the Perfectly Enlightened One, understands the realm of sentient beings as it is and can skillfully explain the Dharma to them. This ability is quite beyond the domain of Śrāvakas and Pratyekabuddhas, let alone other people. Mahāmaudgalyāyana, you should know that this unique ability of the Tathāgata results from his all-knowing wisdom, which no Śrāvaka or Pratyekabuddha has."

Then Fearless Virtue continued to Venerable Mahāmaudgalyāyana, "The World-Honored One often says that Mahāmaudgalyāyana stands first in miraculous powers. Mahāmaudgalyāyana, can you, by your miraculous powers, reach the world named Fragrant Elephant and witness that the trees there all exude a most wonderful fragrance, like that of sandalwood?"

Mahāmaudgalyāyana answered, "This is the first time I have heard the name of that world; how can I go there?" Then he asked the maiden, "What is the name of the Buddha who teaches the Dharma in that world?"

The maiden answered, "The Buddha who teaches the Dharma there is named Tathāgata Emitting Fragrance and Light, the Worthy One, the All-Knowing One."

Mahāmaudgalyāyana asked the maiden, "How can one see that Buddha?"

Thereupon, Fearless Virtue, remaining motionless on her seat, made this declaration: "If a mere novice Bodhisattva truly surpasses all Śrāvakas and Pratyekabuddhas, may Tathāgata Emitting Fragrance and Light, because of my declaration, appear here and cause the Śrāvakas and Pratyekabuddhas present to see the world named Fragrant Elephant and to smell the most wonderful fragrance, like that of sandalwood, exuding from the trees there!"

After Fearless Virtue had made this declaration, Tathāgata Emitting Fragrance and Light gave forth a light from his body and, because of that light, all the Śrāvakas [with Fearless Virtue] saw the Fragrant Elephant World. That Buddha was sitting behind a silken net and teaching the Dharma to Bodhisattvas and others who surrounded him. His preaching could be heard clearly by those with Fearless Virtue. By that Buddha's miraculous powers, they also smelled the fragrance of the trees there, which was like that of the most exquisite sandalwood. The Buddha in that world said, "So it is, so it is, just as Fearless Virtue said. Even the initial stage of a Bodhisattva is beyond the domain of Śrāvakas and Pratyekabuddhas."

When this Dharma was being taught, Bodhisattva-Mahāsattva Maitreya, [on Mount Gṛdhrakūṭa,] asked [Śākyamuni] Buddha, "World-Honored One, why is there such a wonderful fragrance of trees?"

The Buddha said, "Maitreya, Fearless Virtue is discussing the Dharma with the Śrāvakas and has made a declaration. Knowing this, the Buddha of the world called Fragrant Elephant, by his miraculous powers, has caused this fragrance to be perceived and has revealed his land. The most wonderful fragrance, like that of sandalwood, issuing from there is now permeating this billion-world universe."

[In the palace,] Fearless Virtue said to Mahāmaudgalyāyana, "If a person sees such an inconceivable, superb deed, and still has the narrow, inferior aspiration of a Śrāvaka, seeking only to deliver himself, then you should know that his good roots are very few and insignificant indeed. Who would not bring forth bodhicitta after seeing a Bodhisattva perform immeasurable meritorious deeds?

"Mahāmaudgalyāyana, do you know how far from here is that Buddha's world?"

Mahāmaudgalyāyana answered, "No, I do not."

Fearless Virtue said, "Mahāmaudgalyāyana, it is absolutely impossible to know and see that Buddha's world with the aid of [ordinary] miraculous powers even in hundreds of thousands of kalpas. The Fragrant Elephant World is located in a place as many Buddha-lands away from here as there are reeds and bushes in all the forests in the world."

Then that Buddha withdrew his light, and as a result, Fragrant Elephant World and its Tathāgata both disappeared suddenly.

Thereupon, Venerable Mahākāśyapa asked Fearless Virtue, "Did you see Fragrant Elephant World and that Tathāgata, the Worthy One, the All-Knowing One?"

The maiden answered, "Mahākāśyapa, can the Tathāgata be seen? The Buddha has said, 'Those who see me by form or seek me by sound are treading the wrong path and can never see the Tathāgata.' Since the Tathāgatas' bodies are no other than the Dharma-body, and the Dharma-body is beyond the reach of vision and hearing, how can the Tathāgata be known or seen? The Buddha will freely manifest any corporeal form to suit every sentient being; this is only his ingenuity.[12]

"However, Mahākāśyapa, you asked me, 'Did you see that world and that Buddha, the Perfectly Enlightened One?' I see that Buddha not with my physical eye, because he is not a form to be seen with the physical eye.[13] I see that Buddha not with the deva-eye, because he is free of feeling. I see that Buddha not with the wisdom-eye, because he is detached from conceptions. I see that Buddha not with the Dharma-eye, because he rises above impulse. I see that Buddha not with the Buddha-eye, because he is beyond consciousness. Mahākāśyapa, I see that Buddha by purging the mind of ignorance, craving, and [all] views, just as Venerable Mahākāśyapa does. Moreover, I see that Buddha [by eliminating] the view of 'I' and 'mine,' just as Venerable Mahākāśyapa does."

Mahākāśyapa asked the maiden, "If no dharma ever exists, how can ignorance, craving, and the 'I' and 'mine' arise, since no sentient being can be seen?"

Fearless Virtue asked in turn, "If no dharma ever exists, how can anything be seen?"

Mahākāśyapa asked, "Is the Buddha-Dharma also ultimately nonexistent so that it, too, cannot be seen?"[14]

Fearless Virtue then asked, "Do you see any growth[15] of the Buddha-Dharma?"

Mahākāśyapa answered, "I do not even know the dharmas of ordinary people, let alone the Buddha-Dharma."

Fearless Virtue said, "So, Venerable Mahākāśyapa, there being no Buddha-Dharma, how can there be an interruption or resumption of it, as seen by those who have not realized [Dharma-nature]? Mahākāśyapa, all dharmas are nonexistent, so they can never appear. If dharmas do not exist in the first place, how can there be a pure dharmadhātu to be seen? Mahākāśyapa, if good men or good women wish to see the pure Tathāgata, they should first purify their own minds."

Then, Mahākāśyapa asked Fearless Virtue, "How can one purify well one's own mind?"

Fearless Virtue answered, "Mahākāśyapa, if one believes that he himself and all dharmas are suchness and are therefore devoid of action or loss,[16] he will see the purity of his own mind."

Mahākāśyapa asked, "What is the substance of one's own mind?"

Fearless Virtue answered, "It is emptiness. If one realizes his mind is empty, he will believe in [the emptiness of] himself; as a result, he will also have faith in the emptiness of suchness, because all dharmas are by nature quiescent."[17]

Then, Venerable Mahākāśyapa asked Fearless Virtue, "From which Buddha did you hear this doctrine, so that you acquired right view? The Buddha says that there are two ways to obtain right view: by hearing the Dharma explained by others, and by thinking within oneself."

The maiden answered, "Mahākāśyapa, I acquired right view by first hearing external discourses and afterwards thinking within myself.

"Mahākāśyapa, without the help of others' verbal teaching, how can a great Bodhisattva abide in ultimate quiescence?"[18]

Mahākāśyapa said, "One reflects within himself according to the Dharma he has heard; this is the practice of contemplation." Then Mahākāśyapa asked the maiden further, "How does a Bodhisattva reflect within himself?"

"Mahākāśyapa, when a Bodhisattva joins other Bodhisattvas in preaching the Dharma and in other Dharma activities, if he does not perceive any form of sentient beings, then he succeeds in internal contemplation. Mahākāśyapa, all dharmas partake of the past, present, and future because all dharmas have suchness as their very substance and are manifested in suchness. He who has this insight is a Bodhisattva who has achieved internal contemplation. This you should know."

"How can one be in harmony with dharmas?"

"Mahākāśyapa, one should view them as suchness, without being attached to them or liberated from them."

"What kind of view is right view?"

"Mahākāśyapa, right view is free from the two extremes, is neither active nor inactive, and therefore is a view and yet not a view. Mahākāśyapa, the Dharma is only a name. It is actually apart from the name, because Dharma [itself] can never be realized."[19]

Then Mahākāśyapa asked the maiden further, "How should one perceive the 'I'?"

Fearless Virtue answered, "Just as Venerable Mahākāśyapa does."

Mahākāśyapa said, "I perceive neither the 'I' nor 'mine.'"

Fearless Virtue said to Venerable Mahākāśyapa, "One should perceive all dharmas in this way, for there is no 'I' or 'mine.'"

When this doctrine was spoken, Venerable Subhūti was overjoyed and said to Fearless Virtue, "You must have attained great insight to achieve such eloquence."[20]

Fearless Virtue said to Venerable Subhūti, "Subhūti, are there such distinctions as 'attainable' and 'unattainable' among dharmas, or is there anything that can be sought? What causes you to tell me that I have well achieved such eloquence? In my opinion, I have eloquence because I perceive nothing, internal or external."

Subhūti at once asked the maiden, "What realization or Dharma enables you to have such ready, wonderful eloquence?"

Fearless Virtue answered, "I do not know by myself or with the help of others the difference between wholesome dharmas and unwholesome ones. Knowing dharmas in this way, I see nothing impure or pure, defiled or undefiled, conditioned or unconditioned, mundane or supramundane. I do not see any dharma as a dharma of ordinary people, because every dharma is the Buddha-Dharma in substance. Because I see no such distinctions, I have acquired the Buddha-Dharma without seeing a Buddha. Subhūti, those who know this and perceive no such distinctions will have such eloquence."[21]

Subhūti asked, "What *is* eloquence?"

Fearless Virtue answered, "Subhūti, it is the elimination of all your attainments."

Fearless Virtue continued to Venerable Subhūti, "Although dharmas are expressed, their substance is neither heard nor attained. So it is with eloquence."

Then Fearless Virtue asked Venerable Subhūti, "Can one abide in the substance of things? Can it increase or decrease? [If not,] how can one have eloquence?"

Subhuti at once answered, "[One can have eloquence] if he realizes that there is no difference between nondefilement and [all] dharmas, and that they are beyond argument and expression, since the substance of dharmas is inexpressible."[22]

Fearless Virtue asked Venerable Subhūti, "All dharmas being so, why did you say, 'You must have gained great insight to achieve such eloquence'?"

Subhūti asked in turn, "[Now, this very question of yours—] is it because you have acquired eloquence that you are able to raise it, or because you have not acquired eloquence?"

Fearless Virtue asked Venerable Subhūti, "Do you believe that all dharmas are like echoes, as the Buddha says?"

Subhūti replied, "I believe it."

Fearless Virtue asked, "Does an echo have eloquence or not?"

Subhūti replied, "It is because there is a sound in the valley that an echo is heard outside."[23]

Fearless Virtue said, "Subhūti, because there is a sound, there is an echo. Does an echo have any entity or form? It has neither. Why? Because that which arises from causes and conditions does not [truly] arise."

Subhūti said, "All dharmas arise from causes and conditions."

Fearless Virtue said, "No dharma arises in substance or by nature."

Subhūti asked, "If all dharmas are ultimately nonexistent in substance and by nature, how can the Tathāgata say, 'Sentient beings as numerous as the sands of the Ganges will attain supreme enlightenment and become Buddhas'?"

Fearless Virtue asked in turn, "Can the dharmadhātu arise?"

Subhūti replied, "No, it cannot."

Fearless Virtue said, "All Buddhas, Tathāgatas, are the nature and form of the dharmadhātu."

Subhūti said, "I do not perceive any dharmadhātu."

Fearless Virtue said, "The Buddha always teaches 'nonarising'[24] in his discourses, yet he says that sentient beings as numerous as the sands of the Ganges will attain supreme enlightenment and become Buddhas. What does this mean? Why does he say so? Actually all his discourses are not discourses, because the dharmadhātu neither arises nor ceases—it is ultimately pure, for it is not an event; it is beyond all words and expressions and apart from [mundane] reality."

Subhūti said, "How extraordinary you are! Although you lead a lay life, you can explain the Dharma very skillfully and have inexhaustible eloquence."

Fearless Virtue said, "Subhūti, a Bodhisattva's eloquence has nothing to do with acquisition or nonacquisition, learning or nonlearning, renouncing the household life or not renouncing it. Why? Because a Bodhisattva's wisdom comes from purity of mind, and along with his wisdom, eloquence appears."

Fearless Virtue said to Venerable Subhūti, "Now, let us discuss the Bodhisattvas' practices."

Subhūti said, "Speak, and I will listen."

Fearless Virtue said, "Subhūti, if a Bodhisattva has achieved eight things, it makes no difference whether he renounces the household life or not. What are the eight?

(1) To acquire purity of body and deep faith in bodhi;
(2) to have great kindness and compassion, and never to forsake any sentient being;
(3) to master all worldly affairs because of great kindness and compassion;
(4) to be able to give up life and limb and achieve ingenuity;
(5) to be able to make infinite vows;
(6) to consummate the practice of the pāramitā of wisdom and be detached from all views;
(7) to have great courage and vigor to cultivate good karmas without satiation; and
(8) to acquire unhindered wisdom as a result of attaining the Realization of the Nonarising of Dharmas.

Subhūti, if a Bodhisattva has achieved these eight things, it makes no difference whether he renounces the household life or not. He can abide in bodhi without hindrance, whether he walks, stands, sits, or lies down."

Then Venerable Rāhula said to Fearless Virtue, "Your discourse is not pure. You wear jewelled shoes and sit on a high couch while discussing the Dharma with these Śrāvakas. Have you not heard that one should not explain the Dharma to those who are not sick while sitting on a high couch?"

Thereupon, Fearless Virtue asked Rāhula, "Do you really know what is pure and what is impure? Venerable Rāhula, is this world pure?"

Rāhula replied, "It is neither pure nor impure, Fearless Virtue,[25] those who accept and practice the precepts set forth by the Tathāgata and then break them can be said to be pure or impure, but those who never break the precepts are neither pure nor impure."

Fearless Virtue said, "Stop! Stop! Do not say so. Those who practice the Dharma as taught and the precepts as set forth can be said to be impure, [whether they later break the precepts or not]. Rāhula, those who have realized the undefiled

Dharma can never break the precepts, and therefore they are neither pure nor impure. Why so? Because such Śrāvakas have transcended the Dharma and the precepts; it is for the Śrāvakas in the three realms who are still in the learning stage that the Tathāgata teaches the Dharma, while those Śrāvakas [who have transcended the Dharma and the precepts] have also transcended the three realms. In this sense, we speak of transcending or not transcending the three realms. Since some people are ignorant of the [true nature of] precepts, purity and impurity are mentioned, [though they, like] empty space, are nothing but expressions. This can only be seen by means of wisdom. It is in this light that purity and impurity can be spoken of."

Rāhula asked, "What is the difference between purity and impurity?"

Fearless Virtue asked in turn, "Is a piece of stainless, real gold used as an ornament different from another piece not used as an ornament?"

Rāhula answered, "No, it is not."

Fearless Virtue said, "Purity and impurity are different in name only, not in other respects. Why? Because by nature, all things are free from filth; they have no contamination or attachment."

Fearless Virtue continued to Venerable Rāhula, "You said that one should not teach the Dharma while sitting on a high, broad couch. A Bodhisattva sitting on a grass seat surpasses those sitting on high couches and Śrāvakas in the Brahmā Heaven."

Rāhula asked, "Why so?"

Fearless Virtue asked in turn, "Rāhula, on what kind of seat does a Bodhisattva attain bodhi?"

Rāhula replied, "On a grass seat."

Fearless Virtue said, "When a Bodhisattva sits on a grass seat, Śakra, Brahmā, the four deva kings who protect the world, and other gods in the billion-world universe, including the gods of Akaniṣṭha Heaven, all come to pay homage to him with their palms joined; they come to him and bow with their heads at his feet."

Rāhula said, "It is so, it is so."

Then, Fearless Virtue asked Rāhula, "[Therefore,] does not such a Bodhisattva, who sits on a grass seat, surpass others sitting on high, spacious couches, and Śrāvakas in the Brahmā Heaven?"

At that time, King Ajātaśatru asked Fearless Virtue, "Do you not know that [Rāhula] is the son of Śākyamuni Tathāgata and that he stands first in discipline?"

Fearless Virtue said to her royal father, "Please, Your Majesty, do not say that Rāhula is the son of the Tathāgata! Your Majesty, have you ever seen or heard that a lion gives birth to a jackal?"

"Never."

"Your Majesty, have you ever seen or heard that a universal monarch pays homage to minor kings?"

"Never."

"Your Majesty, when the Tathāgata, like the king of lions, turns the great Dharma-wheel, Śrāvakas gather around him. Your Majesty, who are the true sons of the Tathāgata? As far as the true Dharma is concerned, the answer should be 'Bodhisattvas.' Therefore, Your Majesty, do not say that the Tathāgata has a son or not. If the Tathāgata has any true son, it is one who brings forth supreme bodhicitta."

When this doctrine was spoken, twenty thousand ladies in the palace of King Ajātaśatru brought forth bodhicitta. Twenty thousand gods who were satisfied with the doctrine [Fearless Virtue taught] also brought forth bodhicitta after hearing her make a lion's roar.

The king said, "These people are the sons of past, present, and future Buddhas. How can those who study the Śrāvaka precepts to free themselves from afflictions be the true sons of the Tathāgata?"

Thereupon, the gods scattered flowers around the Buddha and all over the city of Rājagṛha as an offering to the maiden Fearless Virtue.

Then, Fearless Virtue stepped down from her couch and paid homage to those Śrāvakas.[26] She gave them various kinds of delicious, fragrant food and drink as offerings, all according to the rules. After making offerings, she said, "I do not know why you venerable Śrāvakas left the Tathāgata and came here so early in the morning. You should go out to beg for food only after hearing the Dharma explained. Please go back. I shall be there in a moment."

Thereupon, Fearless Virtue, together with her royal father and mother and surrounded by countless people of Rājagṛha, went to see the Tathāgata that morning. They all bowed with their heads at the Buddha's feet and sat down to one side. The Śrāvakas also returned to the Buddha, bowed with their heads at the Buddha's feet, and sat down to one side.

Then, Venerable Śāriputra said to the Buddha, "World-Honored One, Fearless Virtue is marvelous; she has acquired many blessings and great benefits."

The Buddha told Venerable Śāriputra, "Fearless Virtue has [long ago] brought forth bodhicitta and has planted good roots in the presence of nine billion past Buddhas in order to seek the supreme enlightenment of the Buddha."

Śāriputra asked, "World-Honored One, can she change herself into a man?"

The Buddha said, "Śāriputra, do you consider her as female? Do not take such a view. Why? Because it is by virtue of his vow that this Bodhisattva reveals himself in a female form to win sentient beings over to the Dharma."

Thereupon, Fearless Virtue made this declaration: "If no dharma is masculine or feminine, then, may I now change into a man in full view of all the people here!"

After she said this, her female body changed immediately into a male one. She ascended in midair to a height of seven palm trees one above another, and stayed there.

Then, the World-Honored One asked Venerable Śāriputra, "Śāriputra, do you see Bodhisattva Fearless Virtue staying in midair?"

Śāriputra answered, "Yes, I do, World-Honored One."

The Buddha said, "Śāriputra, Bodhisattva Fearless Virtue will attain supreme enlightenment after seven thousand myriads of kalpas, and will be named Undefiled Tathāgata, the Worthy One, the All-Knowing One. His world will be called Bright, and his life span will be one hundred kalpas. His true Dharma will prevail for ten kalpas [after his parinirvāṇa]. He will have an assembly of thirty thousand monastic Bodhisattvas, all of whom have reached the stage of nonregression. The ground of his world will be made of clear lapis lazuli and adorned by eight rows of magnificent lotus flowers. The names of the miserable planes of existence will be unknown there. His world will be full of gods. Śāriputra, those gods will enjoy wonderful pleasures and the flavor of the supreme Dharma, as do the gods in Tuṣita Heaven."

Bodhisattva Fearless Virtue's mother, named Moonlight, had come to the Buddha with King Ajātaśatru. [After the Buddha had spoken,] she said to him with her palms joined, "World-Honored One, I have gained great benefit: I was pregnant with this child for nine months, and now this good child makes a lion's roar. I now dedicate my good roots to the attainment of supreme enlightenment, so that I may attain supreme enlightenment in the Bright World of Undefiled Tathāgata in the future."

Thereupon, the Buddha asked Venerable Śāriputra, "Śāriputra, do you see this woman now?"

Śāriputra replied, "Yes, I do."

The Buddha said, "Śāriputra, this woman, Moonlight, will be reborn in the Heaven of the Thirty-Three after death and will be named Intense Light. When Bodhisattva Maitreya attains bodhi, this god Intense Light will be the eldest, most prominent son of King Other View. After the prince makes offerings to Maitreya Buddha, he will renounce the household life. He will be able to remember and practice the Dharma taught by Maitreya Buddha from beginning to end. He will see all the Buddhas of the Worthy Kalpa and make offerings to them one by one. Then, when Bodhisattva Fearless Virtue attains supreme enlightenment and becomes Undefiled Tathāgata, the god Intense Light will be an emperor possessing the seven treasures, named Holder of the Earth. After he makes offerings to the Tathāgatas, he will also attain supreme enlightenment and be named Universal Light Tathāgata, the Worthy One, the All-Knowing One. He will establish a Buddha-land exactly like that mentioned before."

Upon hearing this, Queen Moonlight was overwhelmed with joy. She took off her exquisite necklace of precious stones, which cost hundreds of thousands of taels of gold, and offered it to the Buddha. With the king's permission, she received the five hundred precepts [for nuns] and began to lead a pure life.

Then, Bodhisattva Fearless Virtue said to the Tathāgata, "May Bodhisattvas, by virtue of my vow, be reborn by transformation wearing monastic robes when I attain bodhi in the future! May the Tathāgata, because of my vow, now give me the appearance of a young monk ordained for eight years!"

Immediately after Bodhisattva Fearless Virtue uttered these words, she changed into a fully dignified monk dressed in a monastic robe.

Then Bodhisattva Fearless Virtue suddenly changed back to her original appearance and said to her father, King Ajātaśatru, "Your Majesty, all dharmas are like this: they are apart from the forms caused by all discriminations and they defy all misconceptions. Now, Your Majesty, I have revealed myself again in the form of a maiden. Does Your Majesty see me?"

The king answered, "Yes, I do, but I do not [know how to] see you as you physically appear, because I just saw you as a monk, before seeing you now as a maiden again."

The Buddha said to the king, "Your Majesty, which form is the true one? You should learn to abide by right view regarding all dharmas. Sentient beings are burning with afflictions because they do not understand the power of Dharma. Not understanding the power of Dharma, they doubt what should not be doubted. Therefore, you should often keep close to the Tathāgata and the youthful Bodhisattva Mañjuśrī, because the awe-inspiring power of that Bodhisattva's virtue will enable Your Majesty to repent your misdeeds."

Then, the Buddha told Ānanda, "You should accept and practice the Dharma-Door of the Prophecy of Bodhisattva Fearless Virtue's Attainment of Buddhahood. Read and recite it and do not forget it. Ānanda, a good man or a good woman may give to the Buddhas enough of the seven treasures to fill a billion-world universe; however, another person will surpass him in blessing if he can accept and practice even one sentence or stanza of the Dharma-Door of the Prophecy of Bodhisattva Fearless Virtue's Attainment of Buddhahood after hearing it explained—not to mention those who read and recite the entire sūtra, explain it widely to others, and practice it as taught."

When the Tathāgata had spoken the Dharma-Door of the Prophecy of Bodhisattva Fearless Virtue's Attainment of Buddhahood, Queen Moonlight, Fearless Virtue's mother; and all the gods, dragons, asuras, and so forth were jubilant over the Buddha's teaching. They accepted it with faith and began to practice it with veneration.

NOTES

1. Also a name for Mount Sumeru. It has the general meaning of 'lofty'.

2. Also the name of a star, which is believed to cause eclipses of the sun and moon.

3. This paragraph is a free translation. Some apparently irrelevant words in the original text have been deleted. This and many other passages in this sūtra are extremely obscure and difficult to understand. The translators had to resort to somewhat arbitrary interpretations and free translations for the sake of readability.

4. Free translation.

5. The lines in these two stanzas have been altered in sequence for clarity. Also, some redundant words in the original have been deleted.

6. These two lines are freely translated.

7. According to the myth, Mount Sumeru has four sides, each side made of a valuable substance. It is said that one who approaches a side of the mountain will acquire the color of that side; e.g., the body of one who approaches the side made of gold will become golden in color.

8. That is, beings can acquire the "color" of liberation by associating with liberated Bodhisattvas.

9. The sequence in this stanza has been rearranged.

10. Literally, "ocean."

11. A fragrant yellow flower.

12. The original text of this passage is complex and obscure. We have rendered it freely.

13. See Numerical Glossary, "five kinds of eyes." Here each type of eye is associated with one of the five aggregates.

14. Literally, "If all the Buddha-Dharma is ultimately nonexistent, how can it be seen?"

15. This could be interpreted to mean 'change'.

16. This refers to the doctrine that within the dharmadhātu nothing is actually done, no change occurs, and nothing is gained or lost, for all is suchness itself.

17. Alternate translation: "It is emptiness. If one realized emptiness as a result of believing in the quiescent nature of himself and all dharmas, he will believe in the emptiness of suchness."

18. Alternate translation: "Mahākāśyapa, a great Bodhisattva neither depends on others' words, nor on any verbal teaching; how can it be said that he abides in ultimate quiescence?"

19. This is a typical example of the Prajñāpāramitā explanation of "thorough emptiness"; i.e., there is not even such a thing as "Dharma" to be realized.

20. Literally, "You must be skilled at gaining great benefit to achieve such eloquence."

21. These three sentences are freely rendered; the text is confusing.

22. This is a free translation; the text is not clear.

23. Literally, "Because of the inner sound there is an echo outside."

24. Literally, "nondefilement." This may be a misprint in the Chinese text.

25. Text has "Fearless Virtue said," which is probably incorrect, so we have deleted "said."

26. It is noteworthy that this text advises paying homage to Hīnayāna monks, even if one follows the Mahāyāna.

8 文殊師利普門會

The Universal Dharma-Door to the Inconceivable

Thus have I heard. Once the Buddha was dwelling on Mount Gṛdhrakūṭa near Rājagṛha, accompanied by eight hundred great monks and forty-two thousand Bodhisattvas. At that time, Bodhisattva Undefiled Store descended from the sky, surrounded respectfully by ninety-two thousand other Bodhisattvas.

Then the World-Honored One told the assembly, "These Bodhisattvas were urged by Universal Flower Tathāgata, in the world called Every Pure Deed, to come to this Sahā World in order to hear and accept from me the Universal Dharma-Door to the Inconceivable. Other Bodhisattvas will also come to this assembly."

As soon as the World-Honored One had finished saying this, innumerable Bodhisattvas came from this and other worlds and gathered on Mount Gṛdhrakūṭa. After prostrating themselves with their heads at the Buddha's feet, they withdrew and stood to one side.

Then Bodhisattva Undefiled Store approached the Tathāgata, bearing in his hand a thousand-petalled lotus flower made of the seven treasures. He bowed down with his head at the Buddha's feet and said, "World-Honored One, Universal Flower Tathāgata in the world called Every Pure Deed offers you this precious flower and asks me to convey to you his infinite good wishes. He inquires whether you are enjoying good health, freedom from afflictions, and ease and peace in life." After saying this, the Bodhisattva ascended in midair and sat there in the position of meditation.

From among the assembly, Bodhisattva-Mahāsattva Mañjuśrī rose from his

Sūtra 10, Taishō 310, pp. 158–163; translated into Chinese by Bodhiruci.

seat, bared his right shoulder, knelt on his right knee, joined his palms respectfully, and said to the Buddha, "I remember that very long ago I heard Universal Lamp Buddha preach the Universal Dharma-Door to the Inconceivable. Right then, I acquired eight hundred forty billion myriads of samādhis, and could also understand seventy-seven trillion myriads of samādhis. World-Honored One, may you, out of sympathy for the Bodhisattvas, explain this doctrine to them."

Thereupon, the Buddha told Mañjuśrī, "Now, listen attentively and think well about this. I am going to explain it to you."

Mañjuśrī said, "Yes, World-Honored One, we shall gladly listen."

The Buddha said, "If a Bodhisattva wishes to learn this doctrine, he should cultivate these samādhis: the Form-Image Samādhi, the Sound-Image Samādhi, the Scent-Image Samādhi, the Taste-Image Samādhi, the Touch-Image Samādhi, the Mind-Object Samādhi, the Woman-Image Samādhi, the Man-Image Samādhi, . . . the Deva-Image Samādhi, . . . the Animal-Image Samādhi, . . . the Desire-Image Samādhi, the Hatred-Image Samādhi, the Ignorance-Image Samādhi, the Samādhi of Unwholesome Dharmas, the Samādhi of Wholesome Dharmas, the Samādhi of Conditioned Dharmas, and the Samādhi of Unconditioned Dharmas. Mañjuśrī, if a Bodhisattva realizes all these samādhis, he has already learned this doctrine.

"First, Mañjuśrī, what is the Form-Image Samādhi?"

The World-Honored One explained in verse:

"Consider form to be just like foam—
Devoid of substance,
And thus impossible to grasp.
This is called the Form-Image Samādhi."

The Buddha continued, "Mañjuśrī, what is the Sound-Image Samādhi?"

The World-Honored One explained in verse:

"Regard sound as an echo in a valley,
Inapprehensible by nature.
All dharmas are like that,
Free of essence and difference—
To know them all to be quiescent
Is called the Sound-Image Samādhi.

"Furthermore, Mañjuśrī, what is the Scent-Image Samādhi?"

The World-Honored One explained in verse:

"Just as the ocean
Insatiably engulfs all rivers,
So one can smell various scents constantly,
Even for hundreds of thousands of kalpas.

If the scents were real,
One would soon have one's fill.
Yet, because they are mere arbitrary names,
They have no reality to be grasped.

Just as scents cannot be grasped,
The nose, too, has no [true] existence.
To know them all as empty
And quiescent by nature
Is called the Scent-Image Samādhi.

"Moreover, Mañjuśrī, what is the Taste-Image Samādhi?" The World-Honored One explained in verse:

"All that is tasted by the tongue,
Whether salty, sour, or of some other taste,
Arises from dependent generation,
And by nature does not [truly] exist.

To know that flavors arise
From a combination of causes and conditions
Is to know the inconceivable.
This is called the Taste-Image Samādhi."

The Buddha continued, "Mañjuśrī, what is the Touch-Image Samādhi?" The World-Honored One explained in verse:

"Touch is nothing but a name,
Inapprehensible by nature.
Softness, smoothness, and all other textures
Arise from dependent generation.

To comprehend that touch arises
From the combination of causes and conditions
And cannot ultimately be found
Is called the Touch-Image Samādhi.

"Furthermore, Mañjuśrī, what is the Mind-Object Samādhi?" The World-Honored One explained in verse:

"Even if, in the billion-world universe,
All the countless sentient beings assembled
And together sought the objects of the mind,
They could not find them.

Mental objects are not inside or outside,
Nor can they be gathered together.
They are merely varieties of verbal phenomena,
Fabrications of arbitrary names.

They are illusory, like magic;
Ever fleeting, they remain nowhere.
To know that they are empty by nature
Is called the Mind-Object Samādhi.

"Moreover, Mañjuśrī, what is the Woman-Image Samādhi?" The World-Honored One explained in verse:

"A woman has no real existence;
She is a mere assemblage of the four elements.
However, ordinary men, their minds confused,
Believe her to be real.

A woman is illusory, like magic;
This fools cannot understand.
Deceived by the sight of her,
They engender attachment in their hearts.

Like a person magically produced,
A woman has no reality;
Yet, in delusion,
Ignorant men grow desirous of her.

To know perfectly
That women have no self-entity
And are quiescent forms
Is called the Woman-Image Samādhi."

The Buddha continued, "Mañjuśrī, what is the Man-Image Samādhi?" The World-Honored One explained in verse:

"Men consider themselves to be men,
And other humans to be women.
Because of their discrimination,
Lust is aroused within them.

However, from the beginning,
A lustful mind has never been.
No sign of [such a] mind can be found.

By delusive discrimination
One thinks of a physical form as male.
I say it is, in fact, not a man,
But a thing like a mirage.

To know that man is quiescent by nature
Is called the Man-Image Samādhi. . . ."

The Buddha continued, "Mañjuśrī, what is the Deva-Image Samādhi?" The World-Honored One explained in verse:

"Those who have pure faith
And an abundance of good karmas
Will be born with bodies of special beauty
To enjoy superb rewards in heaven.

Precious gems and palaces
Appear without work or effort.
Exquisite flowers of the coral tree
Bloom, though no one plants them.

All such inconceivable events occur
As a result of karmic power,
Just as myriad forms are reflected
In a piece of clear lapis lazuli.

The gods' wonderful bodies,
Palaces, and other things
All arise from delusion.
This [realization]
Is called the Deva-Image Samādhi. . . ."

The Buddha continued, "Mañjuśrī, what is the Animal-Image Samādhi?" The World-Honored One explained in verse:

"Though clouds differ in hue and shape,
They have no substance.
However, they delude and confuse
The ignorant.

Just as the clouds in the sky
Have different colors and shapes,
So sentient beings appear
In various forms as animals.

If one knows that karma is illusory,
He will be free of delusion.
To know that animals are intrinsically quiescent
Is the Animal-Image Samādhi.

"Furthermore, Mañjuśrī, what is the Desire-Image Samādhi?"
The World-Honored One explained in verse:

"Desire is a mere figment of discrimination,
Which cannot be found.
It does not arise, does not appear,
And has no abode.

By nature, desire is like empty space,
Divorced from anything established.
Because of false discrimination, though,
The defilement of desire plagues the ignorant.

The nature of all dharmas is not defiled;
It is pure, like empty space.
Even if one searches for it
Throughout the ten directions,
No trace of it can be found.

One who knows not this emptiness
Is terrified to meet desire.
He fears when there is nothing to fear—
How can he ever secure peace and joy?

A fool may be afraid of empty space
And flee from it in terror.
How can one escape from space
When space is everywhere?

The ignorant, being deluded,
Wrongly discriminate.
Desire is intrinsically unreal,
Yet they try to renounce it.
Their efforts are as vain
As the attempt to elude empty space.[1]

Every dharma, in its nature,
Is unattainable, like nirvāṇa.
Buddhas of the past, present, and future
All realize the natural emptiness of desire.

Secure in this realization,
They never part from [desire].

Although those who fear desire
Rack their brains seeking liberation from it,
It remains forever intrinsically pure.
When I attained enlightenment,
I realized that all things are equal.

Some maintain that desire is real
And that it should be abandoned.
The view that desire should be renounced
Arises from false discrimination.

There is, in truth, no abandoning;
It is only [the function]
Of a discriminative mind.
Desire is inapprehensible by nature,
So it cannot be extinguished or destroyed.

In undifferentiated reality,
There is neither liberation
Nor discrimination.
If one could be liberated from desire,
One could also be liberated from empty space.
Empty space and desire
Are boundless and not different.
If one sees any difference,
I tell him to forsake [discrimination].

In truth, desire never arises;
One perceives it because of delusion.
Desire is empty by nature;
It is but an arbitrary name.
One should not engender attachment
Because of such a name.
To realize that desire is free of impurity
Is to realize ultimate emptiness.

Liberation is not reached
Through the destruction of desire.
Desire and the Buddha-Dharma are equal;
This [realization] is nirvāṇa.

The wise should know:
To enter the realm of utter quiescence

By realizing the quiescence of desire
Is called the Desire-Image Samādhi.

"Moreover, Mañjuśrī, what is the Hatred-Image Samādhi?"
The World-Honored One explained in verse:

"Hatred[2] originates from delusion.
One clings to the 'I'
When there is no 'I'; thus,
When he hears malicious words,[3]
Intense hatred arises,
Which is like a vicious poison.
The malicious words—and hatred, too—
Ultimately cannot be found.

To start a fire by boring wood,
Many conditions must be fulfilled.
No fire can possibly ignite
If these required conditions are not met.

Likewise, speech unpleasant to the ear
Ultimately cannot be found.
If speech is known to be empty by nature,
No hatred will arise again.

Hatred is not in speech,
Nor does it dwell in the body.
It is a product of many causes and conditions,
Without which it can never come to be.

Just as butter and cheese are made
By a combination of milk and other agents,
So hatred, in itself, is unborn,
Though harsh speech [makes it seem to arise].
Fools cannot understand this,
So they ignite with the heat of anger.

This one should know:
Ultimately, nothing can be found.
Hatred is by nature quiescent;
It is but an arbitrary name.

Hatred is reality itself;
Because of suchness it arises.
Knowing hatred to be the dharmadhātu
Is called the Hatred-Image Samādhi."

The Buddha continued, "Mañjuśrī, what is the Ignorance-Image Samādhi?" The World-Honored One explained in verse:

"Ignorance is empty by nature;
It has never by itself arisen.
There is not a single dharma
That can be called ignorance.

Ordinary people
Wrongly conceive of ignorance
While there is no ignorance;
They are attached
While there is nothing to be attached to.
It is as if they try
To tie empty space into a knot.

Strange indeed are those fools!
They do what they should not do.
There are no dharmas,
Yet they discriminate,
And thus engender myriad defilements.

If one attempts to take up [parts of] space
And put them together in a certain place,
He will never complete the task,
Even in millions of kalpas.
For innumerable kalpas since the beginning,
Fools have amassed 'knots of ignorance,'
Yet, [truly,] their ignorance
Has not increased an iota.
Just as one who tries to move empty space
Can never alter its magnitude,
So one can never increase ignorance,
Though he may amass it for many kalpas.

Just as a bellows takes in
Endless amount of air,
So the ignorant attach themselves
Insatiably to sensuous pleasures.
However, ignorance is nowhere,
With neither root nor abode.
Since it has no root,
How can it have an end?
Since it has no end,
Its bounds cannot be found.

For this very reason, I can never finish
Liberating living beings.
Even if, in one day,
I deliver all the beings
In a billion-world universe,
Causing them to realize nirvāṇa;
And for innumerable kalpas
I do the same every day,
The realm of sentient beings
Cannot be exhausted.

The realms of ignorance and of beings
Are both signless
And illusory, like magic,
So they cannot be exhausted.

Ignorance and Buddhahood are not different,
But are equal by nature.
If one discriminates a Buddha,
Then he dwells in delusion.

Ignorance and all-knowing wisdom
Are both empty of self-entity;
Sentient beings and ignorance
Are entirely equal.

Inconceivable are sentient beings;
Inconceivable, too, is ignorance!
Since both are inconceivable,
How can a distinction be made between them?

This mind of thought[4]
Cannot be measured or conceived.
Immeasurable, too, is ignorance,
For it is boundless.

Since it has no bounds,
How can it arise?
It arises not in its self-nature,
And no sign of it can be found.
Realizing that ignorance is signless,
One regards the Buddha in the same way.
It should thus be known
That all dharmas are nondual.

Ignorance is, from the beginning,
Still and quiescent;

It is but an arbitrary name.
When I realized enlightenment,
I understood it as equal [to bodhi].
To be able to contemplate thus
Is called the Ignorance-Image Samādhi.

"Furthermore, Mañjuśrī, what is the Samādhi of Unwholesome Dharmas?" The World-Honored One explained in verse:

"All the manifestations
Of desire, hatred, ignorance,
And the other defilements
Are illusory and unreal.
To have this insight is called
The Samādhi of Unwholesome Dharmas.

"Moreover, Mañjuśrī, what is the Samādhi of Wholesome Dharmas?" The World-Honored One explained in verse:

"All of you should know
That those with good will,
Though different in disposition,
Are the same in deed,
For they are all detached,
And know all dharmas
To be quiescent in nature.
This [insight] is called
The Samādhi of Wholesome Dharmas."

The Buddha continued, "Mañjuśrī, what is the Samādhi of Conditioned Dharmas?"

The World-Honored One explained in verse:

"All of you should know
That no conditioned thing
Is created by anyone,
Or can be measured.

I see that phenomena
By nature cannot accumulate,
And that everything is quiescent.
This [insight] is called
The Samādhi of Conditioned Dharmas.

"Finally, Mañjuśrī, what is the Samādhi of Unconditioned Dharmas?" The World-Honored One explained in verse:

> "Unconditioned things are quiescent by nature;
> One cannot cling to them,
> Nor can one renounce them.[5]
> They are but artificial names
> Uttered for clinging sentient beings.
> To reach such a realization
> Is called the Samādhi of Unconditioned Dharmas.". . .

Then Bodhisattva Mañjuśrī said to the Buddha, "May the World-Honored one teach the Bodhisattvas the names of other samādhis so that:

(1) their sense-organs may become keen and sound;
(2) they may acquire the wisdom to comprehend all dharmas and to become invincible to those with wrong views;
(3) they may realize and achieve the four kinds of unhindered eloquence;
(4) they can master many languages by knowledge of one particular language, and one particular language by knowledge of many languages;
(5) they may teach the essence of the Dharma to sentient beings, and do so skillfully and with boundless eloquence;
(6) they may achieve the realization of the profound Dharma; and
(7) they may understand in an instant all actions, as well as the infinite forms and varieties of each of them."

The Buddha said, "Mañjuśrī, there is a samādhi named Boundless Freedom from Defilements. A Bodhisattva who attains it can appear in all kinds of pure forms.

"There is a samādhi named Awesome Visage. A Bodhisattva who attains it will have an awesome light outshining the sun and moon.

"There is a samādhi named Flaming Light. A Bodhisattva who attains it can outshine the awe-inspiring lights of all indras and brahmās.

"There is a samādhi named Renunciation. A Bodhisattva who attains it can cause sentient beings to rid themselves of desire, hatred, and ignorance.

"There is a samādhi named Unhindered Light. A Bodhisattva who attains it can illuminate all Buddha-lands.

"There is a samādhi named Unforgetting. A Bodhisattva who attains it can hold in mind the teachings of all Buddhas and expound them to others.

"There is a samādhi named Thundering Voice. A Bodhisattva who attains it can speak well in all languages and tones, including those of the Brahmā Heaven.

"There is a samādhi named Joy. A Bodhisattva who attains it can fill sentient beings with joy.

"There is a samādhi named Insatiable Delight. People will not be tired of seeing or hearing a Bodhisattva who attains it.

"There is a samādhi named Inconceivable Merits of Concentration on a Single Object. A Bodhisattva who attains it can perform all miraculous feats.

"There is a samādhi named Understanding the Languages of All Sentient Beings. A Bodhisattva who attains it can speak all languages with proficiency, can express all words in one word, and can understand that all words are one word.

"There is a samādhi named Supreme Dhāraṇī. A Bodhisattva who attains it can thoroughly understand all dhāraṇīs.

"There is a samādhi named Adornments of All Eloquence. A Bodhisattva who attains it will be well versed in all written and spoken languages.

"There is a samādhi named Accumulation of All Wholesome Dharmas. A Bodhisattva who attains it can cause sentient beings to hear the teachings of the Buddha, Dharma, and Saṁgha; of Śrāvakas, Pratyekabuddhas, and Bodhisattvas; or of the pāramitās. When he abides in this samādhi, he can cause sentient beings to hear these teachings continuously."

Then Mañjuśrī said to the Buddha, "World-Honored One, please bless me and help me to obtain unimpeded eloquence to proclaim the superb merits of this Dharma-door."

The Buddha said, "Excellent! Your wish is granted."

Mañjuśrī said to the Buddha, "It should be known that if a Bodhisattva accepts, practices, reads, and recites this Dharma-door without doubt, he will definitely aquire in his present life four kinds of eloquence; namely, ready eloquence, great eloquence, profound eloquence, and inexhaustible eloquence. He will always remember to protect sentient beings, and, by enlightening them, will thwart those who intend to destroy the devotees' Dharma practice."

Thereupon, the World-Honored One praised Bodhisattva Mañjuśrī, saying, "Excellent, excellent! You understand this doctrine very well. Just as those who give will surely gain immense wealth, and as precept-keepers will be reborn in heaven, so those who accept and practice this sūtra will unquestionably achieve eloquence in this life. Just as sunlight can surely dispel all darkness, and as a Bodhisattva will surely attain supreme enlightenment when he sits on the bodhi-seat, so those who accept, practice, read, and recite this sūtra will achieve eloquence in this life without fail. Mañjuśrī, he who wishes to seek eloquence in this life should believe in, rejoice at, accept, practice, read, and recite this sūtra and explain it to others without entertaining any doubts."

Then Bodhisattva Undefiled Store said to the Buddha. "World-Honored One, after the [pari-] nirvāṇa of the Buddha, if any Bodhisattva, free of doubt, accepts, practices, reads, and recites this Dharma-door and explains it to others, I will hold him in my embrace and enhance his eloquence."

At that time, Pāpīyān, the celestial demon, was stricken with worry and grief. With tears in his eyes, he came to the Buddha and said, "When the Tathāgata was attaining supreme enlightenment in the past, I writhed in worry and agony.

Now your preaching of this Dharma-door redoubles my pain, and I feel as if I have been shot by a poisonous arrow. Sentient beings who hear this sūtra will definitely not regress from their pursuit of supreme enlightenment, and will eventually enter parinirvāṇa. This will reduce my kingdom to nought. The Tathāgata, the Worthy One, the Supremely Enlightened One, can give peace and happiness to all living beings in distress. May the Tathāgata be so kind and compassionate as not to bless this sūtra, and thus give me peace and security and eliminate all my worry and pain."

The World-Honored One told Pāpīyān, "Do not worry. I shall not bless this sūtra, nor will sentient beings enter parinirvāṇa."

Hearing this, Pāpīyān, the celestial demon, danced with joy; all his worries and sorrow vanished. He suddenly disappeared from the presence of the Buddha.

Then Bodhisattva Mañjuśrī approached the Buddha and asked, "What was the Tathāgata's implicit intention just now in telling Pāpīyān, 'I shall not bless this Dharma'?"

The Buddha answered, "Mañjuśrī, I bless this Dharma by not blessing it; thus, I told him that. Because all dharmas are equal in reality, return to suchness, are identical with the dharmadhātu, defy speech, and transcend duality, there is no blessing. Because I speak the truth and not falsehood, this sūtra will prevail widely in the world."

After the World-Honored One had said this, he told Ānanda, "This sūtra is named the Universal Dharma-Door to the Inconceivable. Accepting and practicing this sūtra is not different from accepting and practicing the eighty-four thousand Dharma-doors.[6] Why? Because it was only after I became conversant with it that I was able to expound the eighty-four thousand Dharma-doors to all living beings. Therefore, Ānanda, you should carefully protect and uphold this sūtra and read, recite, and circulate it so that it may not be forgotten or lost."

When the Buddha had spoken this sūtra, Bodhisattva Mañjuśrī, Bodhisattva Undefiled Store, Venerable Ānanda, humans, devas, asuras, gandharvas, and others were all jubilant over the Buddha's teaching. They accepted it with faith and began to practice it with veneration.

NOTES

1. This indicates that *true* renunciation of desire can only be attained by realization of emptiness, i.e., both the emptiness of objects of desire, and of desire itself. Other forms of renunciation such as abstinence may be useful, but they are temporary and even discriminatory as the text implies here and below.

In certain advanced yogas, the yogi may even be advised to stir up desire intentionally, and apply the meditation of emptiness to it by thoroughly identifying emptiness with desire and with all else. See Garma C. C. Chang, *Teachings of Tibetan Yoga* (New Hyde Park: University Books, 1963), p. 44. (V.S.B.)

2. The Chinese characters 瞋恚 literally mean 'anger', but may also denote 'hatred', 'resentment', etc. Here we use 'hatred' to be consistent with our rendering of the three poisons.

3. Literally, "sounds."

4. 'The mind of thought' (Ch. 思維心) refers to the mental function of ordinary minds, whereas a Buddha's 'mind' or 'wisdom' has no thought but direct perception, i.e., 現量境.

5. Literally, "There is nothing to be attached to, nor anything to be detached from."

6. A figurative expression denoting all the various Buddhist doctrines.

9 無盡伏藏會

The Inexhaustible Stores of Wisdom

Thus have I heard. Once the Buddha was dwelling on Mount Gṛdhrakūṭa near the city of Rājagṛha, together with one thousand great monks, all of whom had accomplished superb merits and could make the lion's roar; and with five hundred great Bodhisattvas, all of whom had acquired dhāraṇīs, attained unimpeded eloquence, achieved the Realization of the Nonarising of Dharmas, reached the stage of nonregression, acquired samādhis and a free command of miraculous powers, and who knew well the mentalities and inclinations of living beings.

The Bodhisattvas were headed by Bodhisattva-Mahāsattvas Sun Banner, Moon Banner, Universal Light, Moon King, Illuminator of Peaks, Son of the Sun, Lion's Wisdom, Precious Light of Merits, Realization of All Meanings, Fulfillment of Previous Conditions, Accomplishment of Vows and Deeds, Wisdom of Emptiness, Equal Mind, Joy and Love, Fond of Company, Victorious Fighter, Wise Deeds, Lightning Attainment, Superb Eloquence, Lion's Roar, Wonderful Voice, Alert, Deeds of Skillful Conversion, and Deeds of Ultimate Quiescence.

Also in the assembly were Indra; the four deva kings; Brahmā, lord of the Sahā World; and innumerable awe-inspiring, virtuous gods, dragons, yakṣas, gandharvas, asuras, garuḍas, kinnaras, and mahoragas.

At that time, Bodhisattva Lightning Attainment, seeing that all the eminent ones had gathered and that the whole assembly was hushed, rose from his seat, bared his right shoulder, knelt on his right knee, joined his palms, and said to the Buddha, "World-Honored One, I wish to ask you some questions. Please grant me the opportunity."

The World-Honored One said to Lightning Attainment, "The Tathāgata, the Worthy One, the Perfectly Enlightened One, grants your request. Ask whatever questions you wish, and the answers will be explained to you."

Sūtra 20, Taishō 310, pp. 480–486; translated into Chinese by Bodhiruci.

Bodhisattva Lightning Attainment asked the Buddha, "World-Honored One, what should a Bodhisattva accomplish to be able to satisfy sentient beings' desires without being afflicted with defilements; to lead sentient beings skillfully, according to their particular inclinations, and prevent them from falling to the miserable planes of existence after death; to realize without fail the equality [of dharmas]; and to remain undefiled by the world in which he lives, just as a lotus flower is unsoiled [by the muddy water from which it grows]? How can a Bodhisattva travel freely among Buddha-lands without moving at all within the dharmadhātu;[1] be always with the Buddha without seeing him as he physically appears; abide in the three [doors to] liberation without entering the [Hīnayāna] nirvāṇa; adorn and purify a Buddha-land in accordance with the wishes of sentient beings; and attain supreme enlightenment in an instant?"

Then the Bodhisattva-Mahāsattva repeated his questions in verse:

"Unexcelled, Most Honored of Men,
Master of Infinite Knowledge,
You abide in the dharmas common to all.
You benefit the world
And treat living beings with equality.
You are the haven of the world.

You reveal the right path to the heterodox,
So that they may attain ultimate peace and joy.[2]
The supreme merits you have accumulated
Are like a treasure-trove.
May the sun of wisdom in the world,
The Worthy One in the three realms,
Expound the supreme vehicle[3]
For the accomplishment of Bodhisattvahood.

Your countenance is as clear as a full moon;
You are fully proficient in śamatha;
You make manifest the Dharma of tranquillity
Which can extinguish all afflictions.
May you teach the Bodhisattva-path
For the benefit of sentient beings.

Pure are the Buddha's land and life span,
His physical body and retinue,
His actions of body, speech and mind
And all his other attributes.

May the Tathāgata expound now
The pure practices of a Bodhisattva.
How does a Bodhisattva conquer demons?

How does he teach the Dharma?
How does he become ever mindful?
Please explain this to us.

How does the courageous hero[4]
Plunge into saṁsāra again and again,
While abiding securely in nonduality
And remaining unmoved by anything?

How does he associate with Buddhas
And make offerings to them?
How does he observe the Buddha's physical body
While ultimately remaining detached from all forms?

How does he refrain from entering nirvāṇa
Before acquiring all merits,[5]
Though he has realized the three [doors to] liberation
And is as free as a bird in the sky?
How does he know the inclinations
And desires of sentient beings,
Comply with them fearlessly,
And thereby bring those beings to maturity,
While himself remaining undefiled?

How does he first give them mundane delights,
And then persuade them to develop pure minds
To help them achieve supreme wisdom,
And attain supreme enlightenment?
Such doctrines, profound and subtle,
May the Tathāgata explain to us."

Thereupon, the World-Honored One told Bodhisattva-Mahāsattva Lightning Attainment, "Excellent! It is excellent, good man, that you can ask the Buddha such questions in order to give benefit, peace, and happiness to numberless beings, and to win over to the Dharma those gods and humans of the present who will be Bodhisattvas in the future. Therefore, Lightning Attainment, you should listen carefully and think well about what I say. I am going to explain this for you."

Bodhisattva Lightning Attainment said, "Yes, World-Honored One. I am willing and glad to listen."

The Buddha told Lightning Attainment, "A Bodhisattva-Mahāsattva has five stores of wisdom,[6] all of which are great stores of wisdom, inexhaustible stores of wisdom, universally inexhaustible stores of wisdom. Once a Bodhisattva possesses these stores, he will be relieved from poverty forever, achieve the superior virtues you have mentioned, and quickly attain supreme enlightnment with little effort. What are the five? They are: the store of wisdom for the lustful, the store of wisdom for the angry, the store of wisdom for the deluded, the store of wisdom for those afflicted equally by all three defilements, and the store of wisdom of the Dharma.

"Lightning Attainment, what is a Bodhisattva-Mahāsattva's store of wisdom for the lustful? When sentient beings act out of lust, they are bound by wrong views; they make distinctions among all phenomena; they cling to and indulge in forms, sounds, scents, tastes, textures, and dharmas. A Bodhisattva should have true knowledge of their mentalities: what they delight in and wish for, what circumstances aggravate their habitual defilements, what faith and understanding they have achieved, what kinds of good roots they have previously planted, what vehicle's teachings will arouse their aspirations for enlightenment, and how long it will take for their good roots to mature. The Bodhisattva should examine all these carefully and provide the remedy needed to cut off those sentient beings' passions completely and cause them to develop wholesome minds continuously.

"Lightning Attainment, you should know that the various inclinations and activities of sentient beings are difficult to discern. They are not known to any Śrāvaka or Pratyekabuddha, much less to ordinary people and the heterodox. For example, Lightning Attainment, some living beings, *even though they are attached to desires, can nevertheless be brought to maturity and can attain supreme enlightenment. Some can mature and thus attain supreme illumination and liberation as soon as they contact desired objects, or talk about them with a corrupt mind.*[7] Some can be matured and thus attain supreme illumination and liberation through the cessation of passions and deep contemplation on impermanence, which arises from their awareness of the deterioration of the beautiful things they have seen and craved.

"Some men do not have any passion for women at first glance, but when they later recall a woman's charming appearance, they become mentally corrupted and attached to it. Some become lustful and absorbed in desire when they see a beautiful woman in dreams. Some become enchanted with women simply on hearing their voices. Yet, sometimes these men can be brought to maturity and thus attain supreme illumination and liberation merely during a temporary cessation of their craving.

"Therefore, Lightning Attainment, because the Bodhisattva thoroughly knows all diseases derived from lust and their cures, and at the same time sees no duality in the dharmadhātu, he engenders great compassion for all those who are ignorant of the dharmadhātu. Lightning Attainment, since lust, anger, delusion, and the wisdom of the dharmadhātu are all inapprehensible, the Bodhisattva thinks, 'As I see it, these living beings have lust, anger, and delusion regarding composite things, which are devoid of forms, empty in nature, and which exist only as arbitrary names. I will examine this situation realistically and abide in great compassion for these beings who are deluded by lust; I will fulfill my previous vows by bringing them to maturity with effortless wisdom, without becoming perturbed by any dharma.'

"If a man considers a woman to be pure and becomes deeply infatuated with her, the Bodhisattva will transform himself into a woman of great beauty and elegance, adorned with jewels and necklaces, as desirable a celestial maiden as the man has ever seen before, and allow him to lavish on her his passionate love. When the man has indulged his passion to the utmost, the Bodhisattva will, using means commensurate with the man's capacity, pluck out the poisonous arrow of lust in him. Then, by his miraculous power, he will change back from the female form and appear before the man to expound the Dharma for him until he has penetrated the dharmadhātu. After that, he will disappear from sight. In the case of a woman infatuated with a man, the Bodhisattva will do the same—he will appear to her as a man, pluck out the poisonous arrow of lust in her, expound the Dharma to her until she has penetrated the dharmadhātu, and then disappear.

"Lightning Attainment, [though sentient beings are afflicted by] twenty-one thousand actions of desire and other wrong deeds, [totalling] in all eighty-four thousand,[8] a Bodhisattva with effortless wisdom can open up myriads of Dharma-doors to lead them to liberation, without conceiving a notion that he has expounded certain doctrines for living beings or that any being has been liberated.

"Lightning Attainment, for example, the dragon king [of the lake] called No Heat,[9] by the power of his karma, issues forth four great rivers from his palace to cool down the summer heat for sentient beings who live on land or in water; to nourish flowers, fruit trees and grains; and to give living beings peace and happiness. However, he does not conceive the notion that he issues, has issued, or will issue forth the rivers; he spontaneously keeps the four rivers full for sentient beings' use. Similarly, the Bodhisattva fulfills his past vows by expounding the four noble truths with effortless wisdom in order to eliminate all the burning distresses of saṁsāra, and to give the holy bliss of liberation to all gods and humans. However, he does not conceive the notion that he is teaching, has taught, or will teach the Dharma; he spontaneously abides in great compassion, observes sentient beings, and explains the Dharma according to their needs.

"As a further example, Lightning Attainment, Indra can remain unaffected while transforming himself into bodies numerous enough to satisfy separately and simultaneously the sensual desires of his twelve myriad celestial maidens, causing each of them to think that she alone is sporting with Indra. Similarly, the Bodhisattva can remain unaffected while bringing to maturity those beings who are capable of being delivered, in accordance with their wishes.

"Lightning Attainment, to illustrate further: the sun, emerging from behind a mountain, sheds its light all over the world and causes the various colors, such as blue, yellow, red, and white, to appear where it shines, while the sun itself remains one undifferentiated, single-colored light. Similarly, the Bodhisattva, the sun of wisdom, illuminates the entire dharmadhātu in the same manner by rising above the mountainous attachments of sentient beings and teaching them the Dharma according to their needs, while he himself sees no duality in the dharmadhātu.

"Lightning Attainment, this is what is meant by a Bodhisattva-Mahāsattva's store of wisdom for the lustful. Once a Bodhisattva has acquired this store, he can, for a kalpa or more, transform himself into myriad bodies in accordance with sentient beings's wishes and teach the Dharma in various modes of expression without seeing duality in the dharmadhātu.

"Furthermore, Lightning Attainment, as an example, real gold remains the same in nature when an artisan turns it into various necklaces and other ornaments by his craft. In like manner, the Bodhisattva observes the dharmadhātu well, transforms himself into myriad bodies in accordance with sentient beings' wishes, and explains the Dharma to them in many different modes of expression, but he sees no duality in the dharmadhātu. This is [called] constant penetration of the oneness of the dharmadhātu. Having acquired this store of wisdom the Bodhisattva can give various discourses on the Dharma to living beings, who, after hearing them, will be enriched with inexhaustible holy treasures and be freed from the poverty of saṁsāra forever.

"Now, Lightning Attainment, what is meant by a Bodhisattva-Mahāsattva's store of wisdom for the angry? Some living beings are prone to arrogance and conceit; they conceive that the 'I' and 'mine' are real, and cling to discriminations between self and others. Since they never cultivate kindness or patience, their minds are corrupted with anger and other burning defilements; they are not mindful of the Buddha, the Dharma, or the Saṁgha; and, enveloped in wrath, they become confused about things. The Bodhisattva never harms or irritates these ill-tempered people, but thinks instead, 'Strange are these sentient beings! Deluded, confused, and caught in wrong views, they become angry and resentful in spite of the fact that all dharmas are by nature quiescent, detached, undefiled, noncomposite, and beyond contention.' Thinking thus, he will abide in great compassion and sincerely take pity on those beings. In order to subdue their angry actions, he will tolerate such people with steadfast patience even if they dismember his body. If all the innumerable ill-tempered beings were to betray each other and bear grudges, thus dooming themselves to fall to the miserable plane of serpents when that karma ripens, then the Bodhisattva who abides in patience would use his merciful power to convert those beings, causing them not to fall to the miserable planes of existence, but instead to realize equality without fail. Thus does a Bodhisattva with ingenuity eliminate sentient beings' acts of anger.

"Furthermore, Lightning Attainment, when the Bodhisattva sees angry people, he will think: 'All dharmas are pure by nature. Because they do not understand the dharmas' nature, these living beings act according to the appearance of things, vainly make discriminations, and feel anger, in spite of the fact that all dharmas are equal and beyond contention. If they saw the nature of dharmas, they would not bear grudges against each other, but since they do not, they become angry.' The Bodhisattva will then redouble his kindness and abide in great compassion for these beings. He will fulfill his past vows and explain the Dharma to them, revealing various teachings with effortless wisdom to put an end to their angry actions. However, he will not think that he teaches the Dharma to eliminate the sentient beings' anger. Why is this? Because the Bodhisattva has insight into the nature of the dharmadhātu. This is how a Bodhisattva abides securely in the undifferentiated dharmadhātu and eliminates defiled actions.

"Lightning Attainment, for example, the underlying nature of both darkness and light is the same; they are both like undifferentiated empty space. Therefore, darkness is never really dispelled when Light appears, but it cannot be said that it is not dispelled [in the phenomenal sense]. Similarly, a Bodhisattva who relies on the wisdom of nondifferentiation of the dharmadhātu can skillfully elucidate the Dharma to eliminate the various angry actions of sentient beings, and at the same time he makes no distinctions in the dharmadhātu.

"Lightning Attainment, just as sunlight is never separated from the sun wherever it shines, so whatever the Bodhisattva teaches to subdue and destroy sentient beings' angry actions is the Dharma-wheel, [because] he does not differentiate any dharmas in the universe.

"[Though sentient beings are afflicted by] twenty-one thousand angry actions and other wrong deeds, in all eighty-four thousand, a Bodhisattva with effortless wisdom can teach the appropriate Dharmas to cope with their angry actions, without conceiving a notion that he is teaching, has taught, or will teach the Dharma to them. This is what is meant by a great Bodhisattva's store of wisdom for the angry.

"Once a Bodhisattva has acquired this store, he can, for a kalpa or more, teach the Dharma skillfully in various terms to fulfil the wishes of sentient beings. Although sentient beings' angry actions know no bounds, the Bodhisattva's wisdom and eloquence are also inexhaustible. This is how a Bodhisattva who has acquired the store of wisdom for the angry expounds the undifferentiated nature of the dharmadhātu skillfully.

"Now, Lightning Attainment, what is meant by a Bodhisattva-Mahāsattva's store of wisdom for the deluded? Lightning Attainment, it is a very difficult task for Bodhisattvas to cope with the deluded, because such people pursue deluded actions, feel malice toward others, are wrapped up in the shell of ignorance like silkworms wrapped in their own cocoons, are unable to adapt themselves wisely to dharmas, are not keen in observing a proper course of action, cling to the view of a self, follow wrong paths, are slow to progress, and are unable to extricate themselves from saṁsāra.

"For the sake of such deluded beings, the Bodhisattva, soon after he engenders bodhicitta, makes great, intensified efforts untiringly and ceaselessly. He considers how he should teach the Dharma, under what circumstances, and how best to interpret it, all in order to cause deluded persons to follow the Bodhisattva's practices and achieve liberation.

"A Bodhisattva who in the past has gained insight into the dharmadhātu will abide in great compassion by virtue of his effortless wisdom. When he encounters sentient beings who are ignorant of the dharmadhātu, he will subdue them by explaining the Buddha's teachings according to their capacities, yet without conceiving a notion that he is teaching, has taught, or will teach the Dharma. Because of the power of his past vows, he clearly sees the concatention of all events in the universe, and is able to open spontaneously hundreds of thousands of Dharma-doors to prevent sentient beings from performing karmas out of ignorance, and so lead them to liberation.

"Lightning Attainment, consider, for example, a good physician who is proficient at curing diseases. With his great knowledge of medical works, he can diagnose any disease as soon as he sees its symptoms, and then cure it with the right spells or medicines. In the same way, a Bodhisattva who has insight into the dharmadhātu can teach the Dharma with his effortless wisdom for habitually deluded beings in accordance with their various inclinations, causing them to know hundreds of thousands of doctrines.

"Lightning Attainment, this is what is meant by a great Bodhisattva's store of wisdom for the deluded. Once a Bodhisattva has acquired this store, he will have deep insight into the concatenation of all events in the universe, and can, for a kalpa or more, teach the Dharma in many different terms for those deluded beings in accordance with their inclinations and wishes. While their delusions are boundless, his wisdom and eloquence are also inexhaustible. A bodhisattva who has acquired the store of wisdom for the deluded can, in this manner, expound the Dharma skillfully and without making distinctions. In order to eliminate the twenty-one thousand deluded actions and other wrong actions, in all eighty-four thousand, a Bodhisattva teaches hundreds of thousands of doctrines. This is the explanation of the Bodhisattva's store of wisdom for the deluded.

"Now, Lightning Attainment, what is meant by a great Bodhisattva's store of wisdom for those afflicted equally by all three defilements? As an illustration, consider a clean, crystal-clear mirror with four facets. When placed at the crossing of two thoroughfares, it gives a true image of everything around it, but it does not think of itself as being able to produce these images, which are naturally reflected on it when it is well polished. In the same way, when a Bodhisattva has polished the mirror of the dharmadhātu, he abides in effortless samādhi and teaches hundreds of thousands of doctrines in accordance with the different mentalities of sentient beings, so that they may gain a thorough understanding of these doctrines and attain liberation. However, he does not conceive any notions of Dharmas or sentient beings. Why is this? Because the Bodhisattva has insight into the nature of the dharmadhātu. He knows the real situation of sentient beings who are prone to the four defiled states, and teaches them the Dharma according to their inclinations. Yet, in accordance with reality, he views dharmas and sentient beings nondualistically—he clearly sees that there are no differences among them.

"Lightning Attainment, just as one sees in space no distinguishable characteristics or constructions, so a Bodhisattva who observes the dharmadhātu well realizes that all dharmas are one. Due to the power of his past vows, he can explain the Dharma in many ways according to sentient beings' propensities, while he makes no distinctions in the dharmadhātu.

"Lightning Attainment, a Bodhisattva has a clear insight into all the twenty-one thousand actions of those afflicted equally by all three defilements, as well as other wrong actions, in all eighty-four thousand. He can teach the Dharma in different ways by means of his effortless wisdom, just as a good physician can make a proper diagnosis and administer the right medicine for the disease. This is what is meant by a great Bodhisattva's store of wisdom for those afflicted equally by all three defilements.

"Once a Bodhisattva has acquired this store of wisdom, he can, for a kalpa or more, skillfully teach the Dharma to sentient beings in different terms according to their aspirations. Just as sentient beings' wrong actions are boundless, so are a Bodhisattva's wisdom and eloquence. A Bodhisattva who has acquired the store of wisdom for those afflicted equally by all three defilements can, in this manner, skillfully teach nondifferentiation of the nature of the dharmadhātu.

"Furthermore, Lightning Attainment, when a Bodhisattva achieves such wisdom, he will thoroughly know the inclinations and wishes of sentient beings. When he sees sentient beings full of lust, he may, to subdue and cure them, appear as an ordinary person afflicted with desires and possessing a wife, children, property, and necessities of life, but he will remain as undefiled as a lotus flower. Some sentient beings who are deluded and lack wisdom cannot understand such a Bodhisattva's ingenuity, and think, 'How can a wise man be so greedy to fulfil desires that he is indistinguishable from an ordinary person?' Thus they consider that Bodhisattva to be apart from [the pursuit of] enlightenment. Because their minds are impure, they become angry with the Bodhisattva and do not respect him or believe in him. Due to this karma, they will fall to the great hells after death. However, they will be secretly converted by that Bodhisattva, and they without fail will realize the equality [of dharmas] after the retribution for their misdeeds is completed.

"For example, Lightning Attainment, just as a raging fire can burn up all the trees and grasses fed into it, turning them all into fire, so the Bodhisattva's raging wisdom-fire can turn the lust, anger, and delusion of all the sentient beings he encounters into wisdom whether they are good or evil.[10] This is called the unique quality of a Bodhisattva.

"As a further illustration, consider Mount Sumeru, which has unique attributes. Each of its four sides is made of a different kind of jewel, and sentient beings—whether they are blue, yellow, red, or white—all assume the color of lapis lazuli when they draw near the side made of lapis lazuli, the color of gold when they draw near the side of gold, and the color of silver or crystal when they draw near those sides. In the same way, if a Bodhisattva has this unique quality, then sentient beings—whether they are lustful, angry, or deluded; whether they are good or evil—will all acquire the wisdom of the Bodhisattva when they associate with him. Some of these beings, because of their impure minds and evil deeds, may fall to the hells, to the realm of hungry ghosts, to the realm of animals, or to the realm of Yama, yet after the retribution for their misdeeds is completed, they will attain supreme enlightenment without fail, by virtue of the Bodhisattva's unique merits and the power of his vows. . . .

"Lightning Attainment, just as of all mountains Mount Sumeru is the highest, so of all kinds of wisdom the Tathāgata's is supreme. Just as of all bodies of water the sea is the deepest, so of all kinds of wisdom, the Tathāgata's is the most profound. Just as of all monarchs the universal monarch is the most honored, so of all kinds of wisdom the Tathāgata's is the highest.

"Lightning Attainment, because the Tathāgata has achieved this kind of wisdom, he can thoroughly understand the lust, hatred, and delusion of sentient beings and every shift in their minds; he comprehends all these in an instant.

"Lightning Attainment, the Tathāgata, who has achieved all-knowing wisdom, resembles a man who has clear sight: just as such a man can effortlessly see with unquestionable clarity a mango[11] held in his hand, so the Tathāgata can see the mental activities of all beings and give appropriate discourses on the Dharma to assemblies.

"In the immeasurable, countless Buddha-lands, there are sentient beings who are prone to lust, who are inflamed with and pertrubed by lust, who waste their time day and night thinking of methods to gratify their lust, and who create different bodily and verbal karmas because of burning lust. All this the Tathāgata knows and sees.

"There are sentient beings who are smothered with anger and hatred, who bear grudges against one another, and who will fall to the Uninterrupted Hell because of their malice. All this the Tathāgata knows and sees.

"There are sentient beings who are prone to delusion, who are shrouded in ignorance, confused, obdurate, and who delight in following wrong views. All this the Tathāgata knows and sees.

"Some sentient beings are competent, some incompetent; some advance, some regress; some have cultivated good roots for the Tathāgata-vehicle,[12] some for the Śrāvaka-vehicle, some for the Pratyekabuddha-vehicle. All this the Tathāgata knows and sees.

"Because the Tathāgata has achieved this kind of wisdom, he is able to know the different mentalities of sentient beings in an assembly. When it is untimely to preach, he will remain silent and merely think: 'These sentient beings are confused about dharmas and cannot understand my teaching right now.'

"Because the Tathāgata is equipped with supreme power and a skillful sense of timing, he thoroughly knows who can be subdued, who has high aspirations, who is endowed with patience, and who can accept admonitions. Knowing this, he wins people over to the Dharma accordingly, and benefits them. . . .

"When a Bodhisattva sees lustful beings, he should think, 'It is my fault that they are so inflamed with desire.' When he sees sentient beings inflamed with anger or foolish delusions, he should also think 'This is my fault. Why? It is my duty to find medicine and ways to heal sick sentient beings when I see them. I vowed to relieve them from their diseases, but now [they are still sick]. I must have forsaken them, so I am to blame.'

"[Lightning Attainment,] if a Bodhisattva achieves such a mental state, reflecting on his own faults and feeling great kindness toward sentient beings, he will never take revenge on his offenders even if they dismember his body. Lightning Attainment, if a Bodhisattva thus engages in right practice, his past unwholesome karmas will be eradicated completely, and no evil will arise in him in the future.

"Lightning Attainment, numberless, incalculable kalpas ago, before the era of Dīpaṁkara Buddha, there was a Buddha named Tathāgata Born Victorious, the Worthy One, the supremely Enlightened One, the One Perfect in Learning and Conduct, the Well-Gone One, the World-Knower, the Unexcelled One, the Great Tamer, the Teacher of Gods and Humans, the Buddha, the World-Honored One. He was born in a world named Brilliant Light, and lived in a forest near the capital city Secure Peace.

"At that time, there was a ferocious, bloodthirsty, irritable, merciless butcher named Horrible, whose hands were always smeared with blood, making a fearful sight. Once he entered his house to kill a cow tied there. The cow, seeing him, became frightened and dashed out toward the forest where Tathāgata Born Victorious lived, dragging the ropes with it. While the butcher, knife in hand, was chasing it, the cow panicked and fell into a deep pit. Knowing death was near, it moaned and bellowed in agony. At the sight of the cow, the butcher flew into a rage, and immediately jumped into the pit to kill the cow with the knife.

"Just at that time, Tathāgata Born Victorious, surrounded by a huge assembly of numberless hundreds of thousands of devotees, was expounding the doctrine of dependent origination in detail, as follows:

"'On ignorance depend actions; on actions depends consciousness; on consciousness depend name and form; on name and form depend the six sense-organs; on the six sense-organs depends contact; on contact depends feeling; on feeling depends craving; on craving depends grasping; on grasping depends becoming; on becoming depends birth; on birth depend old age, death, worry, sorrow, misery, and distress. Every link of dependent origination is only a great mass of suffering.

"'The adjoining links of the circle, in order from ignorance and actions, to birth, old age, and death, and also in reverse order, do not think of each other, nor are they aware of each other. All these things are inapprehensible by nature; they have no activities, no thought, no "I," and no "mine." Each link is pure in its basic nature and does not know the others. Yet ordinary people, being ignorant of this doctrine, insist that form is the self, that the self has all kinds of form, and that form belongs to the self; and they hold the same view about feeling, conception, impulse, and consciousness.

"'Because they cling to the "I" and "mine," they give rise to the four wrong views—they take impermanence for permanence, suffering for joy, impurities for purities, and egolessness for ego.

"'Because of their wrong views, they are confused by ignorance and fail to think correctly; they allow their minds to be defiled and cannot break through the defilements; they are fettered by their craving for existence, and thus continually circle in saṁsāra. The wise, because they have deep insight into all phenomena, see no self, no others, no sentient beings, no life, birth, old age, illness, or death. They do not see any bondage or killing.'

"Lightning Attainment, when the butcher Horrible heard the voice of the Tathāgata teaching the Dharma from a distance, he was suddenly enlightened, and his intention to kill ceased at once. Casting aside his knife, he came out of the pit, went to the Buddha, and bowed with his head at the Buddha's feet. He withdrew, stood to one side and said, 'World-Honored One, I wish to leave the household life and seek the path through the Buddha-Dharma.'

"The Buddha said, 'Very good! Welcome, monk,' and the butcher immediately became a fully ordained śramaṇa.

"Then Tathāgata Born Victorious, knowing the butcher's mind was gradually coming to maturity, extensively explained the practices of a Bodhisattva for him. After hearing them, Horrible attained the Realization of the Nonarising of Dharmas and never afterwards regressed from the Buddha-Dharma.

"As for the cow, it enjoyed hearing the wonderful voice of the Tathāgata expounding the doctrine of dependent origination. Consequently, after death it was reborn in the Tuṣita Heaven, where it saw Maitreya and attained right faith.

"Lightning Attainment, the activities of sentient beings are very complicated, subtle, and difficult to recognize and understand. Therefore, Lightning Attainment, a Bodhisattva in pursuit of supreme enlightenment should try to know thoroughly the capacities and actions of sentient beings. He should keep an impartial and unobstructed mind toward all beings, and be detached from all dharmas. . . .

"Now, Lightning Attainment; what is a Bodhisattva's store of wisdom of the Dharma? It is this: the Bodhisattva clearly sees all forms as they really are; he knows that they are uncreated from the beginning and pure in self-nature. Because the Bodhisattva has a thorough understanding of forms, he can achieve the four elements of unimpeded eloquence. What are the four? They are: the unhindered understanding of meaning, the unhindered knowledge of dharmas, the unhindered use of language, and the unhindered ability to discourse.

"The unhindered understanding of meaning is the perfect understanding of the meaning of all forms. What is the meaning of forms? It is the same as the ultimate truth.[13] What is the ultimate truth? It is the inapprehensibility of forms. Acquiring an understanding of this ultimate truth is called the unhindered understanding of meaning.

"The unhindered knowledge of dharmas is the thorough knowledge of all forms, which results from accurate observation of them.

"The unhindered use of language is the skillful use of language in presenting forms in all ways, with unobstructed wisdom.

"The unhindered ability to discourse is the ability to reveal and discourse upon all forms to sentient beings according to their propensities without being attached or affected oneself. After achieving this understanding, the Bodhisattva can, with his effortless wisdom, expound the Dharma properly to all the deluded beings who cling to forms. He does this in accordance with their natures and desires, while he himself has no dualistic view of the dharmas. He can also explain the Dharma in the same way to those deluded beings who are attached to sounds, scents, tastes, textures, and dharmas.

"Lightning Attainment, this is what is meant by a great Bodhisattva's store of wisdom of the Dharma. In order to subdue sentient beings deluded by sense-objects, a Bodhisattva who has acquired this store of wisdom can, for a kalpa or more, use various terms to teach the twelve entrances skillfully in accordance with their wishes. While their [attachment to] the twelve entrances is infinite, his wisdom is inexhaustible, because he never deviates from the nondual, undifferentiated dharmadhātu, but always conforms to it. This is a Bodhisattva's skillful exposition of the nondifferentiation of all dharmas.

"Once a Bodhisattva acquires this store of wisdom of the Dharma, he can teach the Dharma to sentient beings properly, causing them to possess fully the inexhaustible Dharma treasures and be free from the poverty of saṁsāra forever.

"Lightning Attainment, these are a Bodhisattva-Mahāsattva's five stores of wisdom, which are great stores of wisdom, inexhaustible stores of wisdom, universally inexhaustible stores of wisdom, and boundless stores of wisdom. If a Bodhisattva acquires these five stores and prefects supreme virtues, he can attain supreme enlightenment quickly and without much effort."

When this doctrine of the stores of wisdom was explained, Bodhisattva Lightning Attainment achieved dhāraṇī, five hundred other Bodhisattvas achieved the Lightning Samādhi, and thirty-six thousand gods brought forth supreme bodhicitta.

At that time, Bodhisattva Moon Banner said to the Buddha, "World-Honored One, you have mentioned effortless wisdom. What does it mean?"

The Buddha said, "If a Bodhisattva, inclined in body and mind to practice wholesome dharmas, clings to one thing after another while performing those [dharmas], that is called effort. A Bodhisattva is said to possess effortless wisdom if he can do the following: remain flexible in body and mind; be free of thought; rely on nothing; manifest no sign of practice; make all kinds of manifestations in thousands of [millions of] billions of Buddha-lands by means of the wisdom resulting from the fulfillment of his past vows, while remaining unmoved in the dharmadhātu; teach the Dharma constantly without entertaining any notion of the Dharma; employ the four inducements to bring sentient beings to maturity without thinking that there are any beings to be liberated; beautify and purify all Buddha-lands without regarding any Buddha-land as impure;[14] be always mindful of Buddhas without seeing them as they physically appear; and traverse all Buddha-lands without moving in the dharmadhātu. By achieving such wisdom, a Bodhisattva can satisfy all the wishes of sentient beings without being attached to what he does." . . .

Then the World-Honored One told Bodhisattva Lightning Attainment, "The Tathāgatas, the Worthy Ones, the Supremely Enlightened Ones of the past revealed and explained this doctrine here, and future Buddhas will also appear here in the world to expound this doctrine. The present Buddhas, Tathāgatas, in the numberless, incalculable worlds are now shedding this great light to celebrate the continuity of this doctrine."

Thereupon Venerable Ānanda rose from his seat, bared his right shoulder, knelt on his right knee, joined his palms, and asked the Buddha, "World-Honored One, what shall this sūtra be named and how should we uphold it?"

The Buddha told Ānanda, "This sūtra is named 'The Inexhaustible Stores of Wisdom' or 'A Discourse on the Nondifferentiation of All Dharmas.' These are the names by which you should uphold it."

When the Buddha had spoken this sūtra, Bodhisattva Lightning Attainment, Venerable Ānanda, the four kinds of devotees, and all the gods, humans, asuras, gandharvas, and other beings of the world were jubilant. They accepted the sūtra with faith and began to practice it with veneration.

NOTES

1. Alternate translations: "While remaining unmoved by dharmas," or "while remaining unaffected in dharmadhātu." 'Dharmadhātu' in this chapter may sometimes be understood simply as 'dharmas'. For example, "to make no distinctions in the dharmadhātu" may be construed to mean "to make no distinctions among dharmas."

2. These two lines may also be translated: "You reveal all paths as right or wrong / So that all may attain ultimate peace and joy." The text is ambiguous.

3. The Great Vehicle, or Mahāyāna.

4. I.e., a great Bodhisattva.

5. Although the text reads this way, it could be misleading. A Bodhisattva who accomplishes all the Buddha's merits will "enter" the nonabiding nirvāṇa 無住涅槃, which means to abide neither in saṁsāra nor nirvāṇa. (G.C.)

6. The term we have translated as 'store of wisdom' literally means simply 'store' or 'treasury'. Because the content of these treasuries is exactly wisdom, we have rendered the term freely.

7. (Italics mine) These two sentences seem to be Tantric in view, implying that a *kleśa,* rendered as 'defilement' or 'passion', is not necessarily something to be eradicated, but instead to be identified with Buddha-nature. According to this view, it is possible for enlightenment and liberation to be attained by association with the *kleśas,* rather than avoidance of them. (G.C.)

8. We believe that these figures are not necessarily precise; they are simply meant to convey numerousness.

9. Anavatapta, literally 'No Burning Afflictions', is the name of a mythical lake located in the center of Jambudvīpa. The four rivers of which it is said to be the source are the Ganges, Indus, Oxus, and Śītā. The lake may be the modern Manasarowar.

10. A somewhat free translation.

11. The original reads "five mangoes."

12. The Tathāgata-vehicle and the Bodhisattva-vehicle are really the same; the vehicle is called the Tathāgata-vehicle when viewed in the aspect of fruit or achievement, and is called the Bodhisattva-vehicle when viewed in the aspect of cause or practice.

13. Chinese 第一義, literally 'the first truth', is a synonym for 勝義諦, 'transcendental truth'. The Tibetan text here also reads *don-dam-pa* ('ultimate truth'). (G.C.)

14. For example, the Buddha-land in which we live, the Sahā World, is said to be an impure one, subject to the five depravities.

10 文殊師利授記會

The Prediction of Mañjuśrī's Attainment of Buddhahood

I

Thus have I heard. Once the Buddha was dwelling on Mount Gṛdhrakūṭa near the city of Rājagṛha. He was accompanied by one thousand great monks; eighty-four thousand Bodhisattvas, led by the Bodhisattvas Mañjuśrī, Avalokiteśvara, and Mahāsthāma. . . .

At that time, in the city of Rājagṛha, the king, his ministers, the four kinds of devotees, gods, dragons, yakṣas, humans, nonhumans, and so forth offered clothing, food and drink, bedding, medicine, and other necessities of life to the Tathāgata with respect and esteem.

One morning, the World-Honored One, dressed in his robe and holding his bowl, walked toward the palace of King Ajātaśatru in the city of Rājagṛha, surrounded by hundreds of thousands of monks and gods. By the awesome miraculous powers of the Buddha, hundreds of thousands of lights of various wonderful colors shone forth; hundreds of thousands of musical instruments sounded together; and exquisite flowers, such as blue lotuses, white lotuses, and giant white lotuses, showered down in profusion. Then, by the awesome miraculous powers of the Tathāgata, precious lotuses, each as big as a cart wheel, sprang forth from the ground on which he walked. The stems of these lotuses were silver, the leaves were real gold, and the pistils were lapis lazuli. On each lotus seat was a magically produced Bodhisattva sitting in the position of meditation. Without rising from

Sūtra 15, Taishō 310, pp. 336–350; translated into Chinese by Śikṣānanda.

their seats, these magically produced Bodhisattvas circled the city of Rājagṛha seven times to the right and spoke [to the citizens] in verse:

"The Worthy One of the Śākya Clan,
Like a great merchant leader,
Benefits and gladdens sentient beings, and makes them secure.
He has great, awesome virtue and a peaceful mind;
Upon him may mankind rely.
Now he will enter the city.

Those who desire freedom
From the sufferings of old age and death,
Those who wish to enjoy heavenly palaces,
And those who want to defeat the demon-hordes
Should keep close to the wonderfully eloquent
Lord of mankind.

Just to hear his name is rare, and now he appears!
He has cultivated [virtuous] practices
For hundreds of thousands of kalpas,
And has appeared in the world out of great compassion.
The Honored One will enter the city.

He has practiced giving
Immeasurably, boundlessly;
Giving even his children, wife, throne,
Head, eyes, ears, nose, hands, and legs,
Let alone clothing, food, and drink.
He has cultivated incalculable merits by giving
And has realized unexcelled all-knowing wisdom.
By giving, he has subdued his mind
And strengthened his virtuous practices.

Greatest of men, he upholds pure discipline
And has achieved innumerable merits by patience.
The ever-calm one will enter the city.

He has practiced with supreme vigor
For millions of kalpas:
Out of vast concern for suffering sentient beings,
He forgets all weariness.
He has perfected immeasurable, peerless meditation;
The one with the pure voice will enter the city.

His wisdom is immeasurable, unrivaled,
And as limitless as space,

As is the discipline
Observed by the Supreme Honored One of humans.

He cultivates all [virtuous] practices with pure wisdom;
He can defeat demon-hordes and rescue sentient beings;
He can abide in the carefree, immovable state;
He, the unequaled Dharma king, turns the Dharma-wheel.
The Lion of the Śākya Clan will enter the city.

Those who wish to become Buddhas,
And to appear in the world
Adorned with the thirty-two signs,
Should engender supreme bodhicitta
And make offerings to the Tathāgata.

Those who wish to abandon
Desire, hatred, and ignorance forever,
And be free from all afflictions
Should at once keep close to the Lion of the Śākya Clan
And make all kinds of offerings to him.

Those who wish to become śakras or brahmās soon,
Attended by a retinue of thousands,
And to enjoy never-ending amusements in heavenly palaces
Should keep close to the Lion of the Śākya Clan.

One who wishes to be a great universal monarch
Ruling over the four continents,
Possessing the seven treasures
To his heart's content,
And having a thousand brave, robust sons,
Should make offerings to the Supreme Honored One.

Those who wish to be elders or rulers of cities,
With immense, even immeasurable wealth,
And household members unrivaled in beauty,
Should make offerings to the Lion of the Śākya Clan.

Because of hearing the Buddha's teaching
On the quiescent Dharma,
[Innumerable] sentient beings have achieved liberation,
And others will do so in the future.
To meet the Supreme One is an opportunity most rare,
So we should hear him teach the nectar-like Dharma,
Which can ease our worries."

After hearing these verses, countless people in the city of Rājagṛha, male and female, young and old, all became enlightened[1] and went to [the outskirts of the city to welcome] the Tathāgata with incense, flowers, precious canopies, banners, and many musical instruments. They paid homage to him with all their hearts, danced for joy [to see him], and respectfully made offerings to him.

When the World-Honored One stepped on the threshold of the city, the earth quaked in six ways, exquisite flowers rained down from the sky, and musical instruments instantly sounded together. The blind regained their sight, the deaf regained their hearing, the lunatics regained their sanity, the naked gained clothes, the hungry gained food, and the poor gained wealth. [The citizens] were no longer oppressed and vexed by desire, hatred, ignorance, and arrogance; they were as kind to one another as a father is to his son. They spoke in verse to the accompaniment of music:

"The greatest man, who has the ten powers,
The Supreme One among humans,
The Lion of the Śākya Clan,
Is entering the capital city
In order to benefit sentient beings
By giving them peace and happiness.

Now, the blind regain their sight,
The deaf regain their hearing,
The lunatics regain their sanity,
The naked gain clothes,
The hungry gain delicious food,
And the poor gain wealth.

In the sky, hundreds of thousands of billions of gods
Play musical instruments as an offering to the Buddha.
The Honored One, endowed with virtues and the ten powers,
Is entering the city now.

In the city, the earth quakes in six ways—
The universal quake and so forth—
But not a single sentient being is afraid;
Rather, all of them are overjoyed.

Now the sentient beings in the city
Are not afflicted by desire,
Hatred, ignorance, avarice, or jealousy;
Their hearts are full of joy,
And they are kind to one another.

May the Buddha enter the city quickly
To give peace and happiness to sentient beings.

As the World-Honored One enters the city,
He emits great lights,

And humans and gods play musical instruments
With cheerful hearts.
Miracles like this are varied and innumerable.
Gods, humans, and asuras all revere the Enlightened One."

At that time, a Bodhisattva named Destroying Vice, the son of an elder, was living in Rājagṛha. Standing in an alley, he saw from a distance the World-Honored One, who possessed the thirty-two wonderful, auspicious signs and the eighty minor ones. The Buddha's face was handsome, and his eyes clear and bright. All his sense-organs were perfectly calm. He was an ever-pleasant sight to those who saw him. He abided in śamatha, holding himself in perfect control. He guarded and protected his sense-organs like a well-tamed elephant. His mindfulness was correct and undisturbed, like a clear deep pool.[2]

When he saw these characteristics of the Tathāgata, Bodhisattva Destroying Vice felt great respect for him and pure faith in him. He went to the Buddha, bowed with his head at the Buddha's feet, circumambulated him three times to the right, and then stood to one side. At the same time, incalculable hundreds of thousands of sentient beings gathered around the Buddha. Gods without number remained in midair, joining their palms and bowing down with veneration.

Then, Bodhisattva Destroying Vice asked the Buddha, "World-Honored One, how can a Bodhisattva attain supreme enlightenment quickly and adorn and purify a Buddha-land as he wishes?"

The World-Honored One, because of his wish to subdue sentient beings and his compassion for Bodhisattva Destroying Vice, then walked to the marketplace and told him in the presence of the crowd, "Good man, if a Bodhisattva achieves one thing, he will attain supreme enlightenment quickly and adorn and purify a Buddha-land as he wishes. Good man, what is that thing? It is to engender bodhicitta with superior aspiration in order to show great compassion for sentient beings.

"What is it to engender bodhicitta with superior aspiration? The answer is: those who engender bodhicitta should not do any evil, not even the slightest amount.

"What evils should they not do? They should keep far away from desire, hatred, and ignorance. If they are lay people, they should maintain dignified deportment and avoid flirtation. If they are monks or nuns, they should not long for fame, profit, or respect, but abide in the practice of those who have left the household life.

"What is that practice? It is to comprehend all dharmas as they really are. . . . By contemplating, for example, that the five aggregates are still and empty, like nonexistent illusions. When one comprehends them in this way, he does not consider himself as comprehending anything, nor does he feel anything or think of anything; all discriminations are extinguished in his mind. If a person comprehends the five aggregates in this way, he comprehends all things. This is the practice of those who have left the household life.

"When a Bodhisattva cultivates this practice, he does not forsake any sentient being. Why? Because the Bodhisattva explains this Dharma to sentient beings according to his own insight, without attachment to the Dharma he explains or to the sentient beings who hear it. Good man, a Bodhisattva who fulfills this will be able to attain supreme enlightenment quickly and to perfect a Buddha-land."

When this doctrine was spoken, Bodhisattva Destroying Vice achieved the Realization of the Nonarising of Dharmas, danced with joy, and ascended in midair to a height of seven palm trees placed one above another. In the assembly, two thousand sentient beings engendered bodhicitta, and fourteen thousand gods and humans freed themselves from defilements and acquired the clear Dharma-eye, capable of penetrating all dharmas. . . .

When the World-Honored One and the monks arrived at the palace of King Ajātaśatru, they arranged their seats and sat down in due order.

The king then personally offered various kinds of food and drink to the World-Honored One and the monks until he had fully provided for them. He also offered the finest garments to the Tathāgata. Then, in front of the Buddha, he took an inferior seat and asked him, "World-Honored One, what is the origin of hatred, anger, and vexation? How can delusion and ignorance be eliminated?"

The Buddha replied to the king, "Hatred, anger, and vexation arise from the 'I' and 'mine.' Those who do not know virtues, faults, and the 'I' and 'mine' have no wisdom. Those who truly know the 'I' and 'mine' are beyond wisdom and non-wisdom. Your Majesty should know that all phenomena come from nowhere and go nowhere. If they neither come nor go, they neither arise nor cease. If they neither arise nor cease, there is neither wisdom nor non-wisdom. Why? Because there is nothing whatsoever which can know arising and nonarising. If one can transcend 'that which knows,' he is said to have true knowledge."

Then, King Ajātaśatru said to the Buddha, "The World-Honored One is most extraordinary! The teaching of the Tathāgata, the Worthy One, the Perfectly Enlightened One, is most wonderful! Now I would rather die in the course of hearing the Dharma explained than continue to live in vain!"

Having instructed and illuminated King Ajātaśatru, and gladdened him, the World-Honored One rose from his seat and returned to Mount Gṛdhrakūṭa. There, the World-Honored One arranged his seat, washed his feet, and sat down to enter samādhi.

Later in the afternoon that day, the Tathāgata emerged from his samādhi in order to preach the Dharma, and the great Bodhisattvas and Śrāvakas also emerged from samādhi. At that time, Mañjuśrī, accompanied by forty-two thousand gods who followed the Bodhisattva-path; Bodhisattva Maitreya, accompanied by five thousand Bodhisattvas; Bodhisattva Lion of Thundering Voice, accompanied by five hundred Bodhisattvas—all these Bodhisattvas, many Śrāvakas, and King Ajātaśatru, all surrounded by their retinues, arrived at the Tathāgata's dwelling place. They bowed down with their heads at the Buddha's feet, and then sat to one side. Also, innumerable hundreds of thousands of other sentient beings went from

Rājagṛha to Mount Gṛdhrakūṭa. When they arrived, they all bowed with their heads at the Buddha's feet, and then sat to one side. . . .

II

Then Bodhisattva Lion of Thundering Voice[3] rose from his seat, bared his right shoulder, knelt on his right knee, joined his palms toward the Buddha, and said, "Bodhisattva Mañjuśrī, the youthful Dharma Prince, is always praised by Buddhas, World-Honored Ones. When will he attain supreme enlightenment? What kind of Buddha-land will he acquire?"

The Buddha said, "Good man, you should ask Mañjuśrī yourself."

Thereupon, Bodhisattva Lion of Thundering Voice asked Bodhisattva Mañjuśrī, "Virtuous One, when will you attain supreme enlightenment?"

Mañjuśrī answered, "Good man, instead of asking me whether I progress toward enlightenment, why do you ask me when I shall attain it? Why do I ask this? Because I do not even progress toward enlightenment; how then can I attain it?"

Bodhisattva Lion of Thundering Voice asked, "Mañjuśrī, Virtuous One, do you not progress toward enlightenment for the benefit of sentient beings?"

Mañjuśrī answered, "No. Why not? Because sentient beings are inapprehensible. If there were sentient beings, I would progress toward enlightenment for their benefit. Since neither a sentient being, nor a life, nor a personal identity exists, I do not progress toward enlightenment, nor do I regress from it."

Bodhisattva Lion of Thundering Voice asked, "Mañjuśrī, Virtuous One, do you progress toward the Buddha-Dharma?"

Mañjuśrī answered, "No, good man. All dharmas progress toward the Buddha-Dharma. Why? Because they are devoid of defilement, bondage, shape, or form. As the Buddha abides in suchness, so do all dharmas.

"Good man, you asked me whether I progress toward the Buddha-Dharma. Now I am going to ask you some questions and you may answer as you like. What do you think? Does form seek enlightenment? Or does the basic nature of form, the thusness of form, the self-entity of form, the emptiness of form, the absence of form, or the Dharma-nature of form seek enlightenment? Good man, what do you think? Does form, the basic nature of form, the thusness of form, the self-entity of form, the emptiness of form, the absence of form, or the Dharma-nature of form attain enlightenment?"

Bodhisattva Lion of Thundering Voice answered, "No, Mañjuśrī. Form does not seek enlightenment, nor does the basic nature of form, the thusness of form, the self-entity of form, the emptiness of form, the absence of form, or the Dharma-nature of form. Form does not attain enlightenment, nor does the basic nature of form, the thusness of form, the self-entity of form, the emptiness of form, the absence of form, or the Dharma-nature of form."

Mañjuśrī asked, "What do you think? Do feeling, conception, impulse, and consciousness [or any of the other categories] up to the Dharma-nature of consciousness seek enlightenment? Do feeling, conception, impulse, and consciousness attain enlightenment? Or does the basic nature of feeling, or any of the other [categories], up to the Dharma-nature of consciousness, attain enlightenment?"

Bodhisattva Lion of Thundering Voice answered, "No, Mañjuśrī. None of them seeks enlightenment and none of them attains enlightenment."

Mañjuśrī asked, "What do you think? Is there an 'I' or 'mine' apart from the five aggregates?"

Bodhisattva Lion of Thundering Voice answered, "No."

Mañjuśrī said, "It is so, it is so, good man. Then, what else can seek and attain enlightenment?

Bodhisattva Lion of Thundering Voice said, "Mañjuśrī, Virtuous One, [usually] your words are sincerely believed by people, but now you say not to seek enlightenment, not to attain enlightenment. Novice Bodhisattvas will certainly be frightened at such statements."

Mañjuśrī said, "Good man, there is nothing to be feared, nor is there fear in reality. It is for those who have no fear that the Tathāgata teaches the Dharma. However, those who fear things will loathe them. Those who loathe things will renounce desire for them. Those who renounce desire for things will be liberated. Those who are liberated do not need enlightenment. Those who do not need enlightenment will not abide in anything. Those who do not abide in anything will not go. Those who do not go will not come. Those who do not come will have no wishes. Those who have no wishes will not regress. Those who do not regress will regress. From what will they regress? They will regress from attachment to a self, a sentient being, a life, a personal identity, nihilism, eternalism, appearance, and discrimination. Those who regress from these will not regress. From what will they not regress? They will not regress from emptiness, signlessness, wishlessness, reality, or the Buddha-Dharma.

"What is the Buddha-Dharma? It is neither detachment nor attachment. It grasps no object, enters nowhere, emerges from nowhere, practices nothing, and defies expression. It is a name only, empty and nonarising. It neither goes nor comes. It is neither defiled nor pure; it is beyond stain and stainlessness. It is egoless and nondiscriminating; it is not composite or clinging. It is equality and noncontradiction.

"Good man, the Buddha-Dharma is neither a dharma nor a nondharma. Why? Because the Buddha-Dharma arises from nowhere. If a novice Bodhisattva hears this statement and becomes frightened, he will eventually attain enlightenment. Observing this, one may think, "I must first bring forth bodhicitta and abide in [deep] realization; then I can attain Buddhahood. Otherwise, if I do not bring forth bodhicitta, I can never attain Buddhahood.' [However, actually one should not even] harbor this kind of discrimination, because both bodhicitta and Buddhahood are inapprehensible. If they are inapprehensible, how can they be observed? If they cannot be observed, the realization will not be possible. Why not? Because without observation, realization would have no [germinating] cause.[4]

"Good man, what do you think? Can empty space attain enlightenment?"

Bodhisattva Lion of Thundering Voice answered, "No."

Mañjuśrī asked, "Good man, has the Tathāgata realized that all dharmas are the same as empty space?"

Bodhisattva Lion of Thundering Voice answered, "Yes, he has."

Mañjuśrī said, "Good man, enlightenment is like empty space and empty space is like enlightenment. Enlightenment and empty space are neither two nor different. If a Bodhisattva knows this equality, then there will be neither that which he knows [and sees] nor that which he does not know or see."

When this doctrine was spoken, fourteen thousand monks ended their defilements and became mentally liberated; twelve myriads of monks were freed from impurity and acquired the clear Dharma-eye which sees all dharmas; ninety-six thousand sentient beings engendered bodhicitta; and fifty-two thousand Bodhisattvas achieved the Realization of the Nonarising of Dharmas.

Then, Bodhisattva Lion of Thundering Voice asked Mañjuśrī, "How long ago did you engender bodhicitta?"

Mañjuśrī answered, "Stop! Good man, do not entertain any delusive thought! In regard to the Dharma, which does not arise, if a person says, 'I engender bodhicitta. I perform the deeds of enlightenment,' he holds a very wrong view. Good man, I do not see any mind which is engendered to seek enlightenment. Because I see neither mind nor enlightenment, I engender nothing."

Bodhisattva Lion of Thundering Voice asked, "Mañjuśrī, what do you mean by 'seeing no mind'?"

Mañjuśrī answered, "Good man, 'seeing no mind' means equality."

Bodhisattva Lion of Thundering Voice asked further, "Why do you say it means equality?"

Mañjuśrī answered, "Good man, it means equality because no nature of any kind exists and all dharmas are of one taste.[5] The 'one taste' means there is no attachment, no contamination, no purity, no nihilism, no eternalism, no arising, no cessation, no grasping, no abandoning, no self, and no sensation. He who explains the Dharma in this way does not consider himself to be explaining anything, nor does he discriminate anything. Good man, to practice Dharma [in the spirit of] this dharma of equality is called equality. Good man, if a Bodhisattva penetrates such equality, he does not see any realm, whether it is the realm of one or the realm of many. He sees no equality in equality and no contradiction in contradiction, because they are both originally pure by nature."

Then Bodhisattva Lion of Thundering Voice said to the Buddha, "World-Honored One, Mañjuśrī will not say how long ago he engendered bodhicitta, but everyone in the assembly is eager to hear it."

The Buddha said, "Good man, Mañjuśrī has achieved the very profound realization of truth. In the very profound realization of truth, neither enlightenment nor mind is to be found. Because both are inapprehensible, he does not say how long ago he engendered bodhicitta. However, good man, now I am going to tell you how long ago Mañjuśrī engendered bodhicitta.

"Good man, in the past, as many kalpas ago as the incalculable sands of seven hundred thousand Ganges Rivers and more, a Buddha named Thunderous Voice Tathāgata, the Worthy One, the Supremely Enlightened One, appeared in the world. At that time, in the east, seventy-two myriads of Buddha-lands away from here, there was a world named Nonarising, where Thunderous Voice Tathāgata taught the Dharma. There were eight billion four hundred million myriads of Śrāvakas there, and twice as many Bodhisattvas.

"Good man, at that time, there was a king named Universal Enfolding. He was a universal monarch who possessed all the seven treasures and ruled the four continents in accordance with the True Dharma. For eighty-four thousand years, he respectfully offered wonderful clothing, food and drink, palaces, towers, pavilions, servants, and services to Thunderous Voice Tathāgata and his Bodhisattvas and Śrāvakas. His empress, royal relatives, maids of honor, princes, and ministers did nothing but make offerings, and never tired of it, though they made offerings for years.

"After that, the king thought alone in a quiet place, 'I have already accumulated many great good roots, but I have not yet decided how I shall dedicate them. Do I seek to be a śakra, a brahmā, a universal monarch,[6] a Śrāvaka, or a Pratyekabuddha?'

"After he thought thus, the gods in the air said to him, 'Your Majesty, do not engender such a narrow, inferior aspiration! Why? Because, having gathered so many blessings and virtues, Your Majesty should engender supreme bodhicitta.'

"When King Universal Enfolding heard those words, he was very glad and thought, 'From now on, I shall most definitely not regress from bodhicitta. Why? Because gods know my mind and come to remind me.'

"Good man, then the king, together with more than eight billion myriads of other sentient beings, went to Thunderous Voice Buddha. On arrival, they all prostrated themselves with their heads at the Buddha's feet, made seven circumambulations to his right, bowed respectfully, and joined their palms toward the Buddha. Then King Universal Enfolding spoke in verse:

'Now I shall ask the Supreme One a question.
May he answer it for me!
How can one become a Supremely Honored One among humans?
To the Refuge of the world
I have made offerings for a long time,
But, wavering in mind, I did not know
How to dedicate my merits.

[Alone, I thought,]
"I have cultivated great blessings and virtues;

How shall I dedicate them?
Do I seek to be a brahmā, a śakra,
Or a universal monarch?
Do I seek to be a Śrāvaka
Or a Pratyekabuddha?"

When I thought in this way,
The gods in the air told me,
"Your Majesty, engender not
A narrow, inferior aspiration
As you dedicate your merits!
For the sake of all living beings,
Your Majesty should make a great vow.
In order to benefit the world
Your Majesty should engender bodhicitta."

Now I beg the World-Honored One,
Who has free command of dharmas,
To tell me how to engender bodhicitta,
So that I shall attain [enlightenment]
As the Muni has.
May the Honored One among gods and humans
Explain this for me!'

"Then Thunderous Voice Tathāgata spoke to King Universal Enfolding in verse:

'Your Majesty, listen attentively.
I am going to explain this to you point by point.
All dharmas result from causes and conditions
And can accord with one's inclinations;
One can acquire the results one wishes.

In my past lives, I also engendered bodhicitta,
Wishing to benefit all sentient beings.
In accordance with my wish and my bodhicitta
Engendered in the past,
I attained enlightenment quickly
And never regressed from it.

Your Majesty should earnestly
Cultivate all [virtuous] deeds;
Then you will attain
The great, supreme enlightenment of Buddhahood.'

"When King Universal Enfolding heard the Buddha's teaching, he rejoiced as he never had before. He made a great lion's roar in the presence of the assembly, speaking in verse:

'Now, in the presence of the entire assembly,
I bring forth bodhicitta
For the sake of all sentient beings.

I vow to involve myself in saṁsāra countless times
To bring great boons to living beings
Until the end of the future.

I shall cultivate all the Bodhisattva's deeds
To save living beings from their sufferings.

From this moment on, if I break my vow
And become greedy, miserly, or resentful,
I shall be deceiving the Buddhas in the ten directions.

From today until the day
I attain enlightenment,
I shall always follow the Buddhas
In cultivating pure conduct;
I shall observe the pure precepts
And commit no misdeeds.

I shall not cherish the idea,
Of attaining Buddhahood in haste,
But until the end of the future,
I shall benefit all living beings,
And adorn and purify incalculable,
Inconceivable Buddha-lands.
My name shall be heard
Throughout the worlds in the ten directions.

Now I prophesy on my own behalf
That I shall without fail become a Buddha.
Because my aspiration is superior and pure,
I have no doubt of my achievement.

I shall purify my words, thoughts, and deeds
And let no trace of evil arise.
In accordance with this sincere vow,
I shall [eventually] become a Buddha,
An Honored One among human beings.

If my vow is truly sincere,
May the six kinds of quakes shake the great earth!
If my words are genuine and not false,
May musical instruments sound spontaneously in the air!
I am free of flattery or resentment;
If this is true,
May flowers of the coral tree rain down!'

"When King Universal Enfolding had spoken this verse, the six kinds of quakes shook billions of Buddha-lands in the ten directions, musical instruments sounded in the air, and flowers of the coral tree rained down, all because His Majesty's vow was sincere. At that time, two billion of the king's attendants rejoiced in ecstasy. They said to themselves with delight, 'We shall attain supreme enlightenment,' and thus followed the king's example by engendering bodhicitta."

The Buddha said to the assembly, "Who was King Universal Enfolding of that time? He was no other than Bodhisattva Mañjuśrī of today. In the past, as many kalpas ago as the incalculable sands of seven hundred thousand Ganges Rivers and more, he engendered bodhicitta for the first time. Then, after kalpas as numerous as the sands of sixty-four Ganges Rivers, he achieved the Realization of the Nonarising of Dharmas, attained all the ten stages of a Bodhisattva, and acquired the ten powers of a Tathāgata. He perfected every Dharma of the Buddha-stage, but he never thought: 'I shall become a Buddha!'

"Good man, the two billion people of that time who attended on the king and engendered bodhicitta in the presence of Thunderous Voice Buddha were all persuaded by Mañjuśrī to practice [the pāramitās of] giving, discipline, patience, vigor, meditation, and wisdom. Now they have all attained supreme enlightenment, turned the great Dharma-wheel, and, after finishing the Buddha-work, have entered parinirvāṇa. Mañjuśrī has made offerings to all those Tathāgatas and protected and upheld their Dharmas. Now only one Buddha [of the two billion] remains, whose name is Mount Earth-Holder. The world of that Buddha is named Earth-Holder, and lies in the lower direction, as many Buddha-lands away from here as the number of the sands of forty Ganges Rivers. There are countless Śrāvakas there. The life span of that Buddha, who is still alive, is immeasurable."

When Mañjuśrī's past was related, seven thousand sentient beings in the assembly engendered supreme bodhicitta.

III

Then Bodhisattva Lion of Thundering Voice asked Mañjuśrī, "Virtuous One, since you have attained the ten stages of a Bodhisattva, fully acquired the ten powers of a Tathāgata, and accomplished all Buddha-Dharmas, why do you not attain supreme enlightenment?"

Mañjuśrī answered, "Good man, no one realizes enlightenment after he has achieved perfection in all[7] Buddha-Dharmas. Why? Because, if one has achieved perfection in all Buddha-Dharmas, he need not realize anything more."

Bodhisattva Lion of Thundering Voice asked, "How can one achieve perfection in all Buddha-Dharmas?"

Mañjuśrī answered, "To achieve perfection in the Buddha-Dharmas is to achieve perfection in suchness. To achieve perfection in suchness is to achieve perfection in empty space. Thus, the Buddha-Dharmas, suchness, and empty space are [all] one and the same. Good man, you ask, 'How can one achieve perfection in all Buddha-Dharmas?' Just as a person can achieve perfection in form, feeling, conception, impulse, and consciousness, so he can achieve perfection in all Buddha-Dharmas."[8]

Bodhisattva Lion of Thundering Voice asked, "What does it mean to achieve perfection in form and other dharmas?"

Mañjuśrī asked in turn, "Good man, what do you think? Is the form you see permanent or impermanent?"

Bodhisattva Lion of Thundering Voice said, "It is neither."

Mañjuśrī asked, "Good man, if something is neither permanent nor impermanent, does it increase or decrease?"

Bodhisattva Lion of Thundering Voice answered, "No."

Mañjuśrī said, "Good man, if you realize that things do not increase or decrease, you are said to achieve perfection in them. Why so? If you do not thoroughly understand things, you will make discriminations among them. If you thoroughly understand things, you will not make discriminations among them. If things are not discriminated, they do not increase or decrease. If they do not increase or decrease, they are equal. Good man, if you see equality in form, you achieve perfection in form. The same is true with feeling, conception, impulse, consciousness, and all other dharmas."

Then, Bodhisattva Lion of Thundering Voice asked Mañjuśrī, "Virtuous One, since you achieved the Realization of the Nonarising of Dharmas, you have never harbored a notion [in your mind] of attaining supreme enlightenment. Why do you now urge others to progress toward enlightenment?"

Mañjuśrī answered, "I really do not urge any sentient beings to progress toward enlightenment. Why? Because sentient beings are nonexistent and devoid of self-entity. If sentient beings were apprehensible, I would cause them to progress toward enlightenment, but since they are inapprehensible, I do not urge them to do so. Why? Because enlightenment and sentient beings are equal and not different from each other. Equality cannot be sought by equality. In equality, nothing originates. Therefore, I often say that one should observe all phenomena as coming from nowhere and going nowhere, which is called equality, that is, emptiness. In emptiness, there is nothing to seek. Good man, you said, 'Since you achieved the Realization of the Nonarising of Dharmas, you have never harbored a notion [in your mind] of attaining supreme enlightenment.' Good man, do you see the mind? Do you rely on the mind to attain enlightenment?"

Bodhisattva Lion of Thundering Voice said, "No, Mañjuśrī. Why not? Because the mind, unlike form, is invisible, and so is enlightenment. They are arbitrary names only. The names 'mind' and 'enlightenment' do not exist."

Mañjuśrī said, "Good man, there is an esoteric implication in your statement that I have never harbored a notion [in my mind] of attaining enlightenment. Why? Because the mind has never come into being. Since the mind has never come into being, what can it apprehend or realize?"

Bodhisattva Lion of Thundering Voice asked, "What does it mean to realize equality?"

Mañjuśrī answered, "To be detached from all dharmas is to realize equality. The so-called realization means the subtle wisdom, which neither arises nor ceases, is identical with suchness, and cannot be discriminated. If a Dharma-cultivator with right view comprehends the truth that in equality there is nothing to be attained, and does not attach himself either to multiplicity or to oneness, then he has realized equality. If a person realizes that all dharmas are signless, comprehends that signlessness is their sign, and does not cling to his body or mind, then he has perfectly realized equality."

Bodhisattva Lion of Thundering Voice asked, "What is 'attainment'?"

Mañjuśrī answered, "'Attainment' is a conventional expression. In fact, what saints attain is inexpressible. Why? Because the Dharma rests upon nothing and is beyond speech. Furthermore, good man, to regard nonattainment as attainment, and as neither attainment nor nonattainment, is called [the true] attainment."[9]

Then, Bodhisattva Lion of Thundering Voice said to the Buddha, "World-Honored One, may you tell us about the Buddha-land which Mañjuśrī will achieve!"

The Buddha said, "Good man, you should ask Mañjuśrī, yourself."

At this, Bodhisattva Lion of Thundering Voice asked Mañjuśrī, "Virtuous One, what kind of merits and adornments will you achieve for your Buddha-land?"

Mañjuśrī, said, "Good man, if I sought enlightenment, you could ask me what kind of Buddha-land I shall achieve."

Bodhisattva Lion of Thundering Voice asked, "Virtuous One, do you not seek enlightenment?"

Mañjuśrī answered, "I do not. Why so? If one seeks anything, he is tainted and attached. If one is tainted, he has craving. If one has craving, he takes birth. If one takes birth, he has [more] craving. If one has craving, he will never be liberated. Therefore, good man, I do not seek enlightenment. Why not? Because enlightenment is unattainable. Because it is unattainable, I do not seek it. Good man, you asked me what kind of Buddha-land I shall achieve, but I cannot tell you. Why not? Because if a Bodhisattva speaks of the merits and magnificence of his future Buddha-land in the presence of the Tathāgata, the All-Knowing One, he is praising his own virtue."

The Buddha told Mañjuśrī, "You may tell them by what kind of vows you will adorn your Buddha-land, so that the Bodhisattvas hearing those vows will resolve to fulfil them also."

Thus instructed by the Tathāgata, Mañjuśrī rose from his seat, bared his right shoulder, knelt on his right knee, joined his palms, and said to the Buddha, "World-Honored One, now, by the miraculous powers vested in me by the Buddha, I am going to speak of my vows. Those who wish to seek great enlightenment should listen attentively, study them according to the truth, and fulfill them after hearing them set forth."

When Mañjuśrī knelt on his right knee, the six kinds of quakes shook Buddha-lands as innumerable as the sands of the Ganges in each of the ten directions.

Mañjuśrī addressed the Buddha, saying, "Hundreds of thousands of [millions of] billions of myriads of kalpas ago, I vowed: 'If all the [future] Tathāgatas[10] in countless Buddha-lands in the ten directions, whom I see with my unhindered deva-eye, are not persuaded by me to engender bodhicitta or taught by me to cultivate giving, discipline, patience, vigor, meditation, and wisdom and to attain supreme enlightenment, I shall not attain bodhi. Only after the fulfillment of this vow shall I attain supreme enlightenment.'"

At that time, the Bodhisattvas in the assembly all thought, "How many Tathāgatas can Mañjuśrī see with his unhindered deva-eye?"

Knowing what all those Bodhisattvas thought, the World-Honored One said to Bodhisattva Lion of Thundering Voice, "Good man, suppose this billion-world universe were broken into tiny dust-motes. What do you think? Could the number of these dust-motes be known through counting?"

Bodhisattva Lion of Thundering Voice answered, "No, World-Honored One."

The Buddha said, "Good man, Mañjuśrī with his unhindered deva-eye sees more Buddhas in the east than the number of such dust-motes. The same is true in the south, in the west, in the north, in each of the four intermediate directions, in the zenith, and in the nadir."

Mañjuśrī then said to the Buddha, "Furthermore, World-Honored One, I have vowed to combine the worlds of Buddhas as innumerable as the sands of the Ganges into a single Buddha-land and to adorn it with incalculable, intermingled, exquisite jewels. If I cannot do this, I shall never attain supreme enlightenment.

"Furthermore, World-Honored One, I have vowed to cause my land to have a bodhi-tree as big as ten billion-world universes; that tree will shed a light all over my Buddha-land.[11]

"Furthermore, World-Honored One, I have vowed not to rise from my seat under the bodhi-tree from the time I sit down upon the seat until I attain supreme enlightenment and enter nirvāṇa, [and during that time] to teach the Dharma by magically produced bodies to sentient beings in incalculable, numberless Buddha-lands in the ten directions.

"Furthermore, World-Honored One, I have vowed to cause my land to lack the name 'woman,' and to be inhabited by numerous Bodhisattvas who are free from the filth of afflictions, who cultivate pure conduct, and who are spontaneously born dressed in monastic robes and seated with crossed legs. [I have vowed to cause my land to] have no Śrāvakas or Pratyekabuddhas, even in name, except those magically produced by the Tathāgata to explain the doctrines of the three vehicles to sentient beings [of other Buddha-lands] in the ten directions."

Then, Bodhisattva Lion of Thundering Voice asked the Buddha, "World-Honored One, what will be Mañjuśrī's name when he becomes a Buddha?"

The Buddha answered, "Good man, when Mañjuśrī becomes a Buddha, he will be named Universal Sight. Why? Because that Tathāgata will make himself visible to all the sentient beings in innumerable hundreds of thousands of billions of myriads of Buddha-lands in the ten directions. The sentient beings who see that Buddha will certainly attain supreme enlightenment. Although [the future] Universal Sight Tathāgata has not yet become a Buddha, all those who hear his name mentioned, either when I still live in the world or after I enter parinirvāṇa, will also attain supreme enlightenment without fail, except those who have already attained the stage of nonrebirth[12] and those who have a narrow, inferior aspiration."

Mañjuśrī said to the Buddha, "Furthermore, World-Honored One, I have vowed that, just as the inhabitants of Amitābha Buddha's land have joy in the Dharma for food, in my land the Bodhisattvas will all have in their right hands a bowl full of delicacies as soon as they think of food. After a moment, they will think, 'Under no circumstances will I eat any of this myself before I have offered it to the Buddhas in the ten directions and given it to poor, suffering sentient beings, such as hungry ghosts, until they are satiated.' After thinking this, they will obtain the five miraculous powers, enabling them to fly in space without hindrance; and then will go to offer the delicacies to the Buddhas, Tathāgatas, and Śrāvakas in numberless Buddha-lands in the ten directions. The Bodhisattvas from my land will give the food to all the poor, distressed sentient beings in all those Buddha-lands and will explain the Dharma to them so as to free them from the thirst of desire. It will take the Bodhisattvas only an instant to accomplish all this and come back to their own land.

"Furthermore, World-Honored One, I have vowed that when they are just born, all the Bodhisattvas in my land will obtain at will in their hands whatever kinds of precious clothes they need, clean and fit for śramaṇas. Then they will think, 'I shall not use these myself until I have offered them to the Buddhas in the ten directions.' Thereupon, they will go to offer their precious clothes to the Buddhas of countless Buddha-lands in the ten directions and then return to their own land, all in a moment. Only after this will they enjoy the clothing themselves.

"Furthermore, World-Honored One, I have vowed that the Bodhisattvas in my land will offer their wealth, treasures, and necessities of life to Buddhas and Śrāvakas[13] before they themselves enjoy them.

"Furthermore, [I have vowed that] my land will be free from the eight adversities, unwholesome dharmas, wrongdoing and prohibition, pain, annoyance, and unhappiness."

Then, Bodhisattva Lion of Thundering Voice asked the Buddha, "What will that Buddha-land be named?"

The Buddha answered, "That Buddha-land will be named Wish-Fulfilling Accumulation of Perfect Purity."

Bodhisattva Lion of Thundering Voice asked, "In what direction will that Buddha-land be located?"

The Buddha answered, "In the south. The Sahā World will also be contained in it."

Mañjuśrī continued speaking to the Buddha, "Furthermore, I have vowed that my Buddha-land will be formed of incalculable amounts of wonderful jewels and adorned with innumerable, interlaced, exquisite pearls. These pearls will be exceptionally rare and difficult to find in the ten directions; their names will be so numerous that no one could finish recounting them, even in millions of years. My land will appear to be made of gold to the Bodhisattvas who wish it to be made of gold, and will appear to be made of silver to the Bodhisattvas who wish it to be made of silver, without affecting its golden appearance to those who wish it to be made of gold. According to the Bodhisattvas' wishes, it will appear to be made of crystal, lapis lazuli, agate, pearls, or any other treasure without affecting its appearance to others. It will also appear to be made of fragrant sandalwood, of fragrant aloewood, of red sandalwood, or of any other kind of wood, all according to the Bodhisattvas' wishes.[14]

"My land will not be illuminated by the brilliance of suns, moons, pearls, stars, fire, and so forth. All the Bodhisattvas there will illuminate hundreds of billions of myriads of Buddha-lands with their own lights. In my land, it will be daytime when flowers open and night when flowers close,[15] and the seasons will change according to the Bodhisattvas' wishes. There will be no cold, heat, old age, illness, or death.

"If they wish, Bodhisattvas in my land may go to any other land to attain [supreme] enlightenment; they will attain it after descending from the Tuṣita Heaven when their lives come to an end there. No one in my Buddha-land will enter nirvāṇa.[16]

"Though they will not appear in the sky, hundreds of thousands of musical instruments will be heard; their music will not be the sounds of greedy desire, but the sounds of the pāramitās, the Buddha, the Dharma, the Saṁgha, and the doctrines of the Bodhisattva canon. The Bodhisattvas will be able to hear the wonderful Dharma in proportion to their understanding. If they wish to see the Buddha, they will see Universal Sight Tathāgata sitting under the bodhi-tree as soon as they think of seeing him, wherever they are, whether walking, sitting, or standing. Bodhisattvas who have doubts about the Dharma will break the net of their doubts and comprehend the import of the Dharma at the sight of that Buddha, without receiving any explanation."

Then, in the assembly, incalculable hundreds of thousands of billions of myriads of Bodhisattvas said in unison, "He who hears the name of Universal Sight Buddha will obtain excellent benefits, let alone those who are born in his land. If a person has an opportunity to hear the doctrine of the Prediction of Mañjuśrī's Attainment of Buddhahood explained and the name of Mañjuśrī mentioned, he is meeting all Buddhas face to face."

The Buddha said to those Bodhisattvas, "It is so, it is so, just as you say. Good men, suppose a person keeps in mind hundreds of thousands of billions of Buddhas' names. And suppose another person keeps in mind the name of Bodhisattva Mañjuśrī. The blessings of the latter outnumber those of the former, let alone the blessings of those who keep in mind the name of Universal Sight Buddha. Why? Because even the benefits which hundreds of thousands of [millions of] billions of myriads of Buddhas give to sentient beings cannot compare with those which Mañjuśrī gives during one kalpa."

Thereupon, in the assembly, innumerable hundreds of thousands of billions of myriads of gods, dragons, yakṣas, gandharvas, asuras, garuḍas, kinnaras, mahoragas, humans, nonhumans, and so forth said in unison, "We take refuge in the youthful Bodhisattva Mañjuśrī. We take refuge in Universal Sight Tathāgata, the Worthy One, the Supremely Enlightened One."

After saying that, eight trillion four hundred billion myriads of sentient beings engendered supreme bodhicitta. Incalculable numbers of sentient beings brought their good roots to maturity and gained nonregression from the three vehicles.[17]

Mañjuśrī again said to the Buddha, "Furthermore, I have vowed to fill my Buddha-land with all the merits and magnificence of the lands of the hundreds of thousands of [millions of] billions of myriads of Buddhas, World-Honored Ones, whom I have seen before. However, my land will lack the two vehicles, the five depravities, and so forth. World-Honored One, if I myself enumerate the merits and magnificence of my Buddha-land, I cannot finish doing so even in kalpas as innumerable as the sands of the Ganges. Only the Buddha knows the scope of my vow."[18]

The Buddha said, "It is so, Mañjuśrī. The Tathāgata can know and see everything in the past, present, and future without limit or hindrance."

Then, in the assembly, some Bodhisattvas thought, "Will the merits and magnificence of the Buddha-land achieved by Mañjuśrī be equal to those of Amitābha's Buddha-land?"

The World-Honored One, knowing these Bodhisattvas' thoughts, immediately told Bodhisattva Lion of Thundering Voice, "Suppose a person splits a hair into one hundred parts and, with one part, takes a droplet of water from a vast ocean. If he compares the droplet of water to the magnificence of Amitābha's Buddha-land, and the remaining water of the vast ocean to the magnificence of Universal Sight Tathāgata's land, the contrast will still not suffice. Why? Because the magnificence of Universal Sight Tathāgata's land is inconceivable."

Bodhisattva Lion of Thundering Voice asked the Buddha, "World-Honored One, is there any Buddha-land as magnificent as that Buddha-land in the past, present, or future?"

The Buddha answered, "There is one, good man. In the east, there is a Buddha-land named Abiding in the Unexcelled Vow, which is so far away that to get there one must pass worlds as innumerable as the sands of ten billion Ganges Rivers. There is a Buddha there named King of Universal, Eternal Light and Meritorious Ocean. The life span of that Buddha is immeasurable and infinite. He always teaches the Dharma to Bodhisattvas. Good man, the merits and magnificence of that Buddha-land are exactly like those of Universal Sight's Buddha-land." . . .

Then, Bodhisattva Lion of Thundering Voice asked the Buddha, "World-Honored One, when will Mañjuśrī attain supreme enlightenment? How long will that Buddha live; how many Bodhisattvas will he have?"

The Buddha answered, "Good man, you should ask Mañjuśrī yourself."

At this, Bodhisattva Lion of Thundering Voice asked Mañjuśrī, "Virtuous One, when will you attain supreme enlightenment?"

Mañjuśrī answered, "Good man, if the realm of space could become a physical body, I could attain supreme enlightenment. If a magically produced person could attain enlightenment, I could attain it. If an undefiled Arhat could be no other than supreme enlightenment, I could attain it. If a dream, an echo, a reflection, or a magically produced being could attain enlightenment, I could attain it. If it could be daytime when the moon shines and nighttime when the sun shines, I could attain supreme enlightenment. Good man, you should ask your question of those who seek enlightenment."

Bodhisattva Lion of Thundering Voice asked, "Virtuous One, do you not seek enlightenment?"

Mañjuśrī answered, "No. Why not? Because Mañjuśrī is no other than enlightenment and vice versa. Why? Because 'Mañjuśrī' is only an arbitrary name and so is 'supreme enlightenment.' Furthermore, the name is nonexistent and cannot act; therefore, it is empty. The nature of emptiness is no other than enlightenment."

Then, the Buddha asked Bodhisattva Lion of Thundering Voice, "Have you ever seen or heard the Śrāvakas and Bodhisattvas in the assembly of Amitābha Tathāgata?"

Bodhisattva Lion of Thundering Voice answered, "Yes, I have."

The Buddha asked, "How many are there?"

Bodhisattva Lion of Thundering Voice answered, "Their number is incalculable and inconceivable."

The Buddha said, "Good man, compare one kernel taken from a bushel of linseed from the kingdom of Magadha to the number of the Śrāvakas and Bodhisattvas in Amitābha Buddha's land, and compare the kernels remaining in the bushel to the number of the Bodhisattvas in Mañjuśrī's assembly when he attains supreme enlightenment—even this contrast is inadequate.[19]

"Good man, if one compares the number of the tiny dust-motes in this billion-world universe to the number of kalpas for which Universal Sight Tathāgata will live, one will find that the former, even multiplied by one hundred thousand billion, or by any amount, numerical or figurative, is still less than the latter. You should know that the life span of Universal Sight Tathāgata is incalculable and limitless.

"Suppose a person breaks a billion-world universe into tiny dust-motes, and another person does the same, and so on [up to ten persons]. Then one of them takes all the tiny dust-motes [from one billion-world universe] and goes toward the east, dropping one dust-mote after he passes through worlds as numerous as all the dust-motes he carries. After he passes again through the same number of worlds, he drops another dust-mote. He does so until he has dropped all the tiny dust-motes. Another person [of the ten] walks toward the south [and does the same]. This continues until the same is done in the west, the north, each of the four intermediate directions, the zenith, and the nadir. Good man, can anyone know the number of these worlds that have been thus traversed?"

Bodhisattva Lion of Thundering Voice answered, "No."

The Buddha asked, "Good man, suppose these ten persons break into tiny dust-motes every world in the ten directions that they pass through, whether they drop a dust-mote there or not. What do you think? Can anyone know the number of these dust-motes through counting?"

Bodhisattva Lion of Thundering Voice answered, "No, World-Honored One. Anyone who tries to count them will become confused and will not be able to know their number."

The Buddha said, "Good man, all Buddhas, Tathāgatas, can know the number of those tiny dust-motes. Even a greater number than this is knowable to the Tathāgatas."

Then Bodhisattva Maitreya said to the Buddha, "World-Honored One, in order to attain such great wisdom, Bodhisattvas should never give up the pursuit of it even if they go through extremely grievous sufferings in vast hells for incalculable billions of kalpas."

The Buddha said, "Maitreya, it is so, it is so, just as you say. For who would not desire and enjoy such great wisdom, except those who are lowly and inferior and those who are lazy and lethargic?"

When this wisdom was explained, ten thousand sentient beings engendered bodhicitta.

Then the Buddha said to Bodhisattva Lion of Thundering Voice, "Good man, what do you think? Mañjuśrī will follow the Bodhisattva-path for kalpas as numerous as the tiny dust-motes in the worlds in the ten directions wherein those ten persons pass. Why? Because inconceivable are Mañjuśrī's great vows, his determination and pursuits; so are his life span and assembly of Bodhisattvas after he attains supreme enlightenment."

Bodhisattva Lion of Thundering Voice said to the Buddha, "World-Honored One, Mañjuśrī's aspiration is very great, and so are the practices he has cultivated. Never has he wearied of them, even for kalpas as numerous as the tiny dust-motes mentioned before."

Mañjuśrī said, "It is so, it is so, good man, just as you say. What do you think? Does the realm of space conceive the idea that it endures for days, nights, months, seasons, years, and kalpas?

Bodhisattva Lion of Thundering Voice answered, "No."

Mañjuśrī said, "It is so, good man. Those who comprehend that all dharmas are [in reality] equal to space have nondiscriminating, subtle wisdom and do not think, 'I endure for days, nights, months, seasons, years, and kalpas.' Why? Because they have no thought of dharmas. Good man, the realm of space never thinks that it feels tired or afflicted. Why? Because, even after kalpas as innumerable as the sands of the Ganges elapse, the realm of space will not arise, nor will it be consumed by fire and ruined; it is indestructible. Why? Because the realm of space does not exist. Therefore, good man, if a Bodhisattva understands that no dharma exists, he will have no burning afflictions and no weariness. Good man, the name 'space' is free from destruction by fire. It is devoid of burning afflictions, and feels no fatigue. It does not move or alter. It neither arises nor ages. It neither comes nor goes. The same is the case with 'Mañjuśrī.' Why? Because a name is devoid of self-nature."

When this doctrine was spoken, the four great deva kings, Śakra, Brahmā, gods of awesome virtue, and others all said in unison, "The sentient beings who hear this doctrine explained will certainly acquire good, great benefits, let alone those who accept, practice, read, and recite it. It should be known that the good roots they achieve will be very extensive and great. World-Honored One, we shall accept, practice, read, recite, propagate, and circulate this profound doctrine, because we want to protect and uphold it."

Then, Bodhisattva Lion of Thundering Voice asked the Buddha, "World-Honored One, suppose a person, after hearing this doctrine explained, accepts, practices, reads, and recites it; ponders upon it; and resolves to adorn a Buddha-land with merits. What degree of blessing will he acquire?"

The Buddha answered, "Good man, the Tathāgata sees many Buddhas and their lands with his unhindered Buddha-eye. Suppose a Bodhisattva offers to each of these Tathāgatas wonderful treasures enough to fill all these Tathāgatas' lands until the end of the future, abides securely in the pure precepts, and treats all sentient beings with impartiality. Suppose another Bodhisattva accepts, practices, reads, and recites the doctrine of [Mañjuśrī's] Adorning a Buddha-Land with Merits, and vows to follow the path Mañjuśrī has trodden, even for as little time as it takes to walk seven steps. The merits of the former, even multiplied by one hundred, or by any amount, numerical or figurative, will still be less than those of the latter."

Then Bodhisattva Maitreya asked the Buddha, "World-Honored One, what should we called this Dharma-door? How should we uphold it?"

The Buddha answered, "This Dharma-door is called 'The Buddhas' Free Command of Miraculous Powers,' or 'The Fulfilment of Vows,' or 'Mañjuśrī's Adorning a Buddha-Land with Merits,' or 'Giving Joy to Bodhisattvas Who Engender Bodhicitta,' or 'The Prediction of Mañjuśrī's Attainment of Buddhahood.' You should accept and uphold it by these names."

In order to make offerings to this doctrine, the Bodhisattvas who had come from the ten directions caused many flowers to rain down, and praised the Buddha, saying, "The World-Honored One is most extraordinary! How fortunate we are to have such an excellent opportunity to hear this inconceivable, magnificent doctrine explained by Mañjuśrī with a lion's roar!" After uttering these words, they returned to their respective lands.

When this doctrine was spoken, Bodhisattvas as innumerable as the sands of the Ganges gained nonregression and the good roots of countless sentient beings came to maturity.

Then Mañjuśrī immediately entered the Samādhi of the Bodhisattva's Emitting Lights to Reveal All Dharmas as Illusory. After he entered the samādhi, he caused the assembly to see all the Tathāgatas in all the incalculable Buddha-lands in the ten directions, and a Mañjuśrī relating the merits and magnificence of his Buddha-land in the presence of each Buddha. After the assembly had seen this, they all believed the sublime, great vows of Mañjuśrī to be extraordinary.

When the Buddha had explained this sūtra, the Bodhisattvas, monks, nuns, laymen, laywomen, gods, dragons, yakṣas, gandharvas, asuras, garuḍas, kinnaras, mahoragas, humans, and nonhumans all rejoiced at the Buddha's teaching, accepted it with faith, and began to practice it with veneration.

NOTES

1. In what sense these people became enlightened is not clear in the text. Does 'enlightenment' here mean the realization of emptiness or suchness, or merely a kind of awakening to certain truths? Did these people all reach the same degree of enlightenment or not? The text does not say. However, it is my opinion that this and the subsequent miracles in this part of the sūtra should be considered to be symbolic. (G.C.)

2. The phrase "His body was adorned with the thirty-two auspicious signs," already stated above, was omitted here in our translation.

3. Literally, "Lion of Darting Thunderbolt."

4. Although this paragraph appears to contradict the preceding statements, they should be understood to be on different levels. The previous statements describe the very nature of the ultimate truth, which is beyond discrimination and observation. On the other hand, from the point of view of Dharma practice, observation is necessary to further one's realization at certain stages. It is said that prior to full realization one must penetratingly observe the emptiness of mind to rid oneself of subject-object dichotomy.

This paragraph is extremely obscure. Three versions (Taishō 310, p. 345, by Śikṣānanda; Taishō 318, p. 896, by Chu Fa Hu; Taishō 319, p. 912, by Amogha) differ widely in their renderings of this paragraph. Alternate translation:

"Good man, the Buddha-Dharma is neither a dharma nor a nondharma. Why? Because the Buddha-Dharma arises from nowhere. If novice Bodhisattvas are horrified at hearing this statement, they will attain enlightenment quickly; if they discriminate, thinking, 'Now I am going to attain enlightenment,' they will engender bodhicitta, aim at immediate realization, and attain enlightenment as a result. If they do not engender bodhicitta, they will never attain enlightenment. Without the above discrimination, enlightenment and bodhicitta are both inapprehensible. What is inapprehensible is beyond discrimination. What is beyond discrimination has nothing to do with immediate realization. Why? Because there is no object of immediate realization."

5. 一味 means literally 'one taste' or 'of the same taste'. In meaning it connotes simply 'the same', 'identical', or 'at-one-ment'.

6. That is, to become a universal monarch again in his next life, as he was in that life.

7. Literally, "is complete with."

8. That is, the aggregates are by nature identical with Buddhahood.

9. Although this sentence is rather cumbersome, we have chosen to render it literally, since it is philosophically important.

10. That is, those who are now ordinary sentient beings, will be Tathāgatas in the future.

11. Another possible rendering: "Furthermore, World-Honored One, I have vowed to cause my land to have as many bodhi-trees as the worlds in ten billion-world universes; those trees will shed a light all over my Buddha-land."

12. This seems to denote Hīnayāna Arhats who have entered parinirvāṇa.

13. This refers to Śrāvakas in other Buddha-lands, as there will be none in Universal Sight Tathāgata's land.

14. These statements suggest the mind-only doctrine; i.e., everything in the exterior world is a mere projection or reflection of one's own mind.

15. This implies that the land will be so brilliantly illuminated by the Bodhisattvas' lights that the opening and closing of flowers will be the only indication of day and night.

16. This is probably the most important "adornment" of Mañjuśrī's future Buddha-land, showing how profound is his intention to save sentient beings before attaining supreme enlightenment himself. (VSB.)

17. Another version, Taishō 319, p. 915, reads: "gained nonregression from supreme bodhi."

18. Here even the eloquence of Bodhisattva Mañjuśrī cannot express the profound wonders of his future Buddha-land.

19. In this sūtra, Mañjuśrī's land is described as incomparably superior in time, space,

merits, etc., to other Buddha-lands, such as that of Amitābha. One should not regard this to be a strict comparative statement about two Buddha-lands, but instead as emphasizing the distinction between the pure land of Nirmāṇakāya and pure land of Saṁbhogakāya. Mañjuśrī's land is that of Saṁbhogakāya, which is eternal and infinite, and is a reflection of emptiness, or the Dharmakāya. See Numerical Glossary, "three bodies of the Buddha."

III

On the Light of the Tathāgata

11 出現光明會

The Manifestation of Lights[1]

I

Thus have I heard. Once the Buddha was dwelling on Mount Gṛdhrakūṭa near Rājagṛha, accompanied by five hundred great monks, all of whom had achieved great freedom; eighty myriad Bodhisattva-Mahāsattvas who were to reach Buddhahood in their next lives, headed by Bodhisattva Maitreya; and forty myriad other great Bodhisattvas, headed by the Dharma Prince Mañjuśrī; and others.

At that time, Moonlight, a boy in the assembly, rose from his seat, bared his right shoulder, knelt on his right knee, bowed down with his head at the Buddha's feet, then joined his palms reverently and said to the Buddha, "World-Honored One, what deeds did the Tathāgata perform to obtain the Absolute Light;[2] the Embracing Light; the Creating Light; the Manifesting Light; the Multicolored Light; the Single-Colored Light; the Narrow Light; the Wide Light; the Pure Light; the Universal Pure Light; the Undefiled Light; the Utterly Undefiled Light; the Stainless Light; the Gradually Increasing Light; the Sparkling Pure Light; the Very Sparkling Pure Light; the Boundless Light; the Utterly Boundless Light; the Immeasurable Light; the Utterly Immeasurable Light; the Infinite Light; the Utterly Infinite Light; the Swift Light; the Very Swift Light; the Nonabiding Light; the Light of No Abode; the Blazing Light; the Illuminating Light; the Light of Delight; the Light of Reaching the Other Shore; the Unimpeded Light; the Immovable Light; the Straightforward Light; the Light of Abiding in the Infinite; the Light of Color and Form; the Light of Various Colors and Forms; the Light of Innumerable Colors and Forms; the Light of Blue, Yellow, Scarlet, and White; the Red-Colored Light; the Crystalline Light; and the Light of the Color of Void

Sūtra 11, Taishō 310, pp. 163–195; translated into Chinese by Bodhiruci.

Space? Each of these lights appears mixed with a light of five colors, and each of the lights of five colors—such as blue, yellow, red, white, and so forth—appears mixed with innumerable kinds of lights of different colors."

In reply, the World-Honored One spoke to Moonlight in verse:

"By inconceivable good karmas,
I have rid myself of delusions
And have achieved various lights.

By all kinds of [virtuous] practices,
I abide securely in the Buddha's path;
By the wisdom of emptiness and nonaction,
I emanate intermingled lights.

Empty, egoless, inactive,
And devoid of thought
Are external things; and yet
They can manifest different forms.

Empty, egoless, and inactive
Is the body, and yet
It can produce various sounds.

In the same way, through the [wisdom of] nonaction,
I can manifest innumerable colored lights
To satisfy the wishes of all sentient beings.

Sometimes one light can produce two colors,
Each radiating three [beams]:
Higher, middle, and lower. . . .

Sometimes one light can produce five colors,
Each radiating three [beams]:
Higher, middle, and lower;
This results from pure karma.

Sometimes one light can produce six colors,
Each radiating three [beams]:
Higher, middle, and lower;
This results from ingenuity. . . .

Sometimes one light[3] can produce fifty colors,
Each radiating three [beams]:
Higher, middle, and lower;
This results from dhyāna.

Sometimes one light can produce sixty colors,
Each radiating three [beams];
Higher, middle, and lower;
This results from wisdom. . . .

Sometimes one light can produce a thousand colors,
Each radiating three [beams]:
Higher, middle, and lower;
This results from a thousand merits.

Sometimes one light can produce ten thousand colors,
Each radiating three [beams]:
Higher, middle, and lower;
This results from the spiritual provision of merits. . . .

Lights of many kinds
Shine from my pores.
I will now tell you
The different names of these lights.

I have a light called The Clouds[4] of Pure Illumination;
It arises from the innumerable good roots
I have accumulated.
In the past, when I saw sentient beings
Afflicted with many kinds of disease,
I gave them medicines out of pity
To restore their health,
And thereby I obtained that light.

Another light, called Pure Eye,
I obtained by offering lamps to Buddhas.

Another light, called Pure Ear,
I obtained by offering music to Buddhas.

Another light, called Pure Nose,
I obtained by offering perfumes to Buddhas.

Another light, called Pure Tongue,
I obtained by offering delicacies to Buddhas.

Another light, called Pure Body,
I obtained by offering clothing to Buddhas.

Another light, called Pure Mind,
I obtained by ever believing
And delighting in Buddhas.

Another light, called Pure Forms,
I obtained by making colored paintings of Buddhas.

Another light, called Pure Sounds,
I obtained by constantly praising the Dharma.

Another light, called Pure Scents,
I obtained by continuously revering the Saṁgha.

Another light, called Pure Tastes,
I obtained by fulfilling sentient beings' needs.

Another light, called Pure Touch,
I obtained by offering perfumed ointments.

Another light, called Pure Phenomena,
I obtained by embracing all dharmas.

Another light, called Pure Earth,
I obtained by cleaning and sweeping the ground
For the Buddha and the Saṁgha. . . .

Another light, called Pure Aggregates,
I obtained by offering my body to Buddhas.

Another light, called Pure Elements,
I obtained by continuously cultivating kindness.[5]

Another light, called Pure Truth,
I obtained by never uttering false words. . . .

Another light, called Revealing the Meaning of the Truth,
I obtained by comprehending emptiness. . . .

Another light, called Understanding Women,
I obtained by remaining detached
From the female appearance.

Another light, called Understanding Men,
I obtained by remaining detached
From the male appearance.

Another light, called The Awesome Power of Vajra,
I obtained by having pure wisdom and pure karma.

Another light, called Unfolding Emptiness,
I obtained by revealing karmic results to the world.[6]

Another light, called Awakening to Reality,
I obtained by parting with wrong views.

Another light, called Elucidating the Buddha's Words,
I obtained by praising the dharmadhātu.[7]

Another light, called Free from Faults,
I obtained by praising superior understanding.

Another light, called Universal Illumination of Adornments,
I obtained by praising the offering of lamps.

Another light, called Forsaking Affection,
I obtained by praising meditation and wisdom.

Another light, called Parting with Habit,
I obtained by praising the knowledge of past [states].

Another light, called Free from Attachment,
I obtained by praising the wisdom
Of the nonarising [of dharmas].

Another light, called Not Falling to Any Plane of Existence,
I obtained by praising the wisdom of nondefilement.

Another light, called The State of Renunciation,
I obtained by praising the knowledge of suffering.

Another light, called The Buddha's Miraculous Feats,
I obtained by praising miraculous powers.

Another light, called Transcending Play-Words,
I obtained by praising all-knowing wisdom.

Another light, called Manifesting Forms,
I obtained by praising
The power to perform miracles.

Another light, called Delight in Spiritual Friends,
I obtained by praising the nature of enlightenment. . . .

Another light, called The Ultimate Exhaustion of the Eye,[8]
I obtained by praising nonexhaustion.

Another light, called Being,
I obtained by praising nonbeing.

Another light, called Indestructible,
I obtained by praising the nature of cessation.[9]

Another light, called Limitless,
I obtained by praising the unlimited.

Another light, called Formless,
I obtained by praising the unconditioned.

Another light, called Unvarying,
I obtained by praising nondifferentiation. . . .

I have a light called Beyond Expression;
It can bring all sentient beings to maturity.

I have a light called
The Basic Nature of Dharmas;
It can shake one million [Buddha-] lands.

I have a light called Subduing Demons;
Its awe-inspiring power can terrorize demons.

I have a light called
The Banner of Blessing;
One who holds its name meets no dangers.

I have a light called Powerful Banner;
One who holds its name
Suffers no bitter antagonism.

I have a light called Tranquil Banner;
One who holds its name has no desire.

I have a light called
The Banner of Dhyāna;
One who holds its name performs no misdeeds. . . .

I have a light called
The Banner of Pure Discipline;
One who holds its name breaks no precepts.

I have a light called
The Banner of Wonderful Fragrance;
One who holds its name
Is free from filth and stench.

I have a light called The Profound Dharma;
One who holds its name harbors no doubts.

I have a light called Nonabiding;
One who holds its name
Is not attached to any form of existence.

I have a light called Free from Discrimination;
One who holds its name clings to nothing.

I have a light called Mount Sumeru;
One who holds its name cannot be swayed.

I have a light called Esoteric Practice;
One who holds its name has no attachments.

I have a light called Acts of Liberation;
One who holds its name is free from bonds.

I have a light called Well Subdued;
One who holds its name
Becomes gentle and tender.

I have a light called Immovable;
One who holds its name
Is not defiled by desire.

I have a light called Well Disciplined;
One who holds its name
Observes the precepts perfectly.

I have a light called All Good Deeds;
One who holds its name is defiled by nothing.

I have a light called Much Benefit;
One who holds its name is free from fault.

I have a light called Superior Knowledge;
One who holds its name is not bewildered.

I have a light called
Seeking to Benefit [Self and Others];
One who holds its name harbors no hatred.

I have a light called Joyful Mind;
One who holds its name
Gains peace and happiness.

I have a light called No Burning Desire;
One who holds its name understands emptiness.

I have a light called Empty of Self-Entity;
One who holds its name
Transcends all play-words.

I have a light called Nonreliance;
One who holds its name remains unshakable.

I have a light called Free from Perplexity;
One who holds its name does not vacillate.

I have a light called No Abode;
One who holds its name is free from ignorance.

I have a light called Weary of the Body;
One who holds its name
Does not take rebirth.

I have a light called No Grasping;
One who holds its name
Is not bound by written words.

I have a light called No Ignorance;
One who holds its name
Is detached from spoken words.

I have a light called Going Nowhere;
One who holds its name forsees the future.

I have light called Reaching all Limits
One who holds its name beholds the past[10]. . . .

I have a light called Free from Stain;
One who holds its name
Is not enveloped in darkness.

I have a light called No Amorous Captivation;
One who holds its name is apart from reliance. . . .

I have a light called The Most Honored One;
One who holds its name gains unimpeded wisdom.

I have a light called Swift;
One who holds its name
Becomes an accomplished monk.

I have a light called Symbolic;
One who holds its name
Comprehends the profound Dharma.[11]

I have a light called Beyond Symbols;
One who holds its name abandons arrogance.[12]

I have a light called Nonarising;
One who holds its name
Attains the nonattainment.

I have a light called Recollecting Buddhas,
Which is exalted by the Tathāgatas.
This light I obtained by cultivating
Right practices in many Buddha-lands.

The lights emanating from the Buddhas' bodies
Are as numerous as the dust-motes
In countless millions of Buddha-lands,
Lands as numerous as the sands of the sea.

Each of these lights,
As numerous as those dust-motes,
And has a retinue [of lights].
All of them
Reach all Buddhaless lands,
Where each is transformed
Into a pure body of a Tathāgata
To expound the subtle, profound Dharma
And to establish sentient beings in patience.

I have a light called Buddha;
It can lead sentient beings
To abide in the Buddha's path.

I have a light called Dharma;
Its radiance is clean and pure,
Without flaws or taints.

I have a light called Saṁgha;
It is always acclaimed by Buddhas, Tathāgatas.

I have a light called Purity;
It is most superb and rare.

I have a light called Blossom;
It can benefit and ripen sentient beings.

I have lights called Brahmā, Śakra,
Deva, Moon, Dragon, Yakṣa,
Asura, Garuḍa,
King, Lady, Girl, and Boy.
Each of these various lights
Can by wholesome dharmas
Convert those beings designated by its name,
Causing infinite millions of sentient beings
To achieve enlightenment.

I have lights called Wisdom, Precepts,
Kindness, Joy, Compassion,
Lamp, Perfume, and Music.
Each of these lights is named for its function
And was achieved by receiving

Innumerable sentient beings
Into my following.

I have a light called Esteem,
Praised by Buddhas, Tathāgatas.
I achieved it as a result
Of ever revering the Buddha's teachings.

Each pore of the Buddha gives forth lights
As numerous as the sentient beings within his sight;
And each of these lights is surrounded
By its own retinue [of lights].

Blessed by these Buddha-lights,
Sentient beings are brought to maturity,
Each in accordance with his inclinations.

If one rejoices and brings forth deep aspiration
Upon hearing these lights described,
He must have heard this sūtra in past lives
In [other] Buddha-lands.

I have a light called Supreme,
With a retinue of eighty million [lights].
This I achieved
By praising a Buddha with one verse.

I have a light called Free from Worry,
With a retinue of eighty myriad [lights].
This I achieved by upholding the Dharma
Expounded by a Tathāgata.

I have a light called Utter Purity,
With a retinue of eighty million [lights].
This I achieved
By cultivating one samādhi.

* * *

In the past appeared a Buddha named Supreme,
Whose life span was immeasurable.
When he attained enlightenment,
There were eighty myriad people
In his first Dharma-assembly.

At that time, in the world,
There was a king named Joyful Voice.
He had five hundred sons,

All handsome, well-formed,
And pleasing to the beholder.

A man of dignity and authority,
The king deeply and joyfully
Believed in the Three Jewels.
He offered to Buddha [Supreme]
All his superb, magnificent gardens. . . .

Out of pity for the king, his sons,
And the others in the assembly,
Buddha Supreme preached this 'Sūtra of Absolute Lights.'

Upon hearing it taught,
The king was overwhelmed with joy.
He chanted countless verses
In praise of that Tathāgata,
And offered to him
Eighty million wonderful, jewelled canopies.
Each canopy was ornamented
With pearls around its net. . . .

The tassels of each canopy were again made
Of eighty million pearls,
Lustrous and luminous,
Shedding lights day and night.
Each light reached a hundred leagues
And outshone the sun and moon. . . .

At that time, all sentient beings,
Even those in the Akaniṣṭha Heaven,
Came to the Tathāgata's dwelling place
To hear this sūtra.

Upon hearing it taught,
Devas, dragons, yakṣas, gandharvas,
Mahoragas, asuras, and others
Were all overwhelmed with joy.
They chanted hundreds of thousands of verses
In praise of the Tathāgata
And brought forth bodhicitta.

The devas, dragons, spirits, and asuras,
With sincere and pure minds,
Showered flowers of the coral tree, pearls,
And various jewels from the sky
As offerings to the Buddha. . . .

You, Moonlight, should know:
King Joyful Voice, who made
Various offerings to that Tathāgata,
Was no other than you [in a previous life].
Since you heard this sūtra in the past,
You now ask me about it once again.

* * *

Only those who have pure faith in my teachings
Can expound this sūtra widely
After my parinirvāṇa, when the Dharma-wheel
Is about to cease its turning.

One who expounds this sūtra in the future
Is the protector of my Dharma,
Just as a good leader of a caravan
Is the guardian of the valuables.

In the coming Last Era,
One who hears this sūtra
And enjoys it at once
Should know he is inspired
By the Buddha's awesome powers
And the blessing of Mañjuśrī.

Merely hearing this sūtra
Is tantamount to meeting many Buddhas,
Who bestow upon the hearer
Secret instructions, and wisdom as well.

One who is gentle and straightforward,
Always makes offerings to Buddhas,
Practices the teaching of no-self,
And is kind and patient
Will delight in this sūtra.

One who bears malice,
Insatiably seeks selfish gains,
And has no aspiration for peace and tranquillity
Will not delight in this sūtra.

One who makes offerings to Tathāgatas,
Comprehends the profound, wonderful Dharma,
And has pure faith in the Buddha's true wisdom
Will delight in this sūtra.

One who is distracted and impure in mind,
Is enslaved by evil passions,
Indulges in killing,
And is hard to subdue
Will not delight in this sūtra.

One who enjoys living alone in a hermitage
With peace of mind,
Detached from worldly gain and kinsfolk,
Will delight in this sūtra.

One who follows bad company,
Corrupts his own and others' wholesome dharmas,
And loses dhyāna and precepts
Or regresses from them
Will not delight in this sūtra.

One who has very pure aspirations,
Often observes dharmas with wisdom,
And is guarded by spiritual friends
Will delight in this sūtra.

One who is attached
To his friends, kinsmen, or household members,
Providing fruits and flowers to please them,
And has a mind not straight, but devious,
Will not delight in this sūtra.

One who always recalls the Buddha's bounty,
Cherishes all wonderful good roots,
And sincerely dedicates them
To the attainment of enlightenment
Will delight in this sūtra.

If one is infatuated with a woman
Who bedecks herself with splendid attire,
And longs to play with her,
He will not delight in this sūtra.

One who is earnest,
Relies on nothing,
Is not defiled by any passions,
And never flatters for the sake of food and drink
Will delight in this sūtra.

One who teaches sentient beings
That carnal desire is not full of faults,

And who slanders the Buddhas
Of the past, present, and future
Will not delight in this sūtra.

One who holds fast to his faith and aspiration,
Seeks the Dharma vigorously,
And is never weary or negligent
Will delight in this sūtra.

One who is enthralled by women,
Always thinks of sex,
And does not cultivate wisdom to benefit others
Will not delight in this sūtra.

One who sits quietly in a mountain grove
Attaining purity by cultivating wisdom,
Without craving for food, clothes, etc.,
Will delight in this sūtra.

One who is bewildered and does not understand
The past and future states of the eye[13]
Is a fool entangled in demons' meshes
And will not delight in this sūtra.

One who clearly understands
The past and future states of the eye
Is freed from demons' meshes
And will delight in this sūtra.

One who is bewildered and does not understand
The existence and nonexistence of the eye
Is a fool entangled in demons' meshes
And will not delight in this sūtra.

One who clearly understands
The existence and nonexistence of the eye
Is freed from demons' meshes
And will delight in this sūtra.

One who is bewildered and does not understand
The formation and destruction of the eye
Is a fool entangled in demons' meshes
And will not delight in this sūtra.

One who clearly understands
The formation and destruction of the eye
Is freed from demons' meshes
And will delight in this sūtra.

As it is with [the eye],
So it is with the ear,
Nose, tongue, body, and mind;
Forms, sounds, scents, tastes,
Textures, and mental objects;
Earth, water, fire, air, substance, and nature;
Events, sentient beings, and suffering;
Aggregates and elements; . . .
Desire, hatred, ignorance,
Conceit, craving, pretense, and arrogance;
Miserliness, jealousy, flattery,
Deceit, and resentment.

One who is bewildered and does not understand
The ultimate exhaustion of the eye,
Falls to the level of ordinary men,
And will not delight in this sūtra.

One who clearly understands, without confusion,
The ultimate exhaustion of the eye
Has risen above the actions of ordinary men,
And will delight in this sūtra. . . .

One who is bewildered and does not understand
The ultimate quiescence of the eye
Falls to the level of ordinary men,
And will not delight in this sūtra.

One who clearly understands, without confusion,
The ultimate quiescence of the eye
Has risen above the actions of ordinary men,
And will delight in this sūtra.

One who is bewildered and does not understand
That the eye does not come or go
Falls to the level of ordinary men,
And will not delight in this sūtra.

One who clearly understands, without confusion,
That the eye does not come or go
Has risen above the actions of ordinary men,
And will delight in this sūtra.

One who is bewildered and does not understand
The nonself of the eye
And the nature of its ultimate exhaustion

Falls to the level of ordinary men,
And will not delight in this sūtra.

One who clearly understands
The nonself of the eye
And the nature of its ultimate exhaustion
Has risen above the actions of ordinary men,
And will delight in this sūtra. . . .

One who is bewildered and does not understand
The nature of the eye's ultimate exhaustion
And the eye's emptiness
Cannot acquire the wisdom of dhāraṇīs
And will not delight in this sūtra. . . .

One who understands
The nature of the eye's ultimate exhaustion
Will achieve the wisdom of dhāraṇīs,
And the peerless, unattached wisdom,
And will therefore delight in this sūtra.

One who does not delight in this sūtra
And is bewildered
By the nature of the eye's ultimate exhaustion
Will suffer regression from dhyānas
Or their loss.
It will be hard for him to realize peerless wisdom.

One who delights in this sūtra
And clearly understands
The nature of the eye's ultimate exhaustion
Will achieve all dhyānas
And easily realize peerless wisdom. . . .

One who diligently ponders, day and night,
The nature of the eye's ultimate exhaustion
Will achieve dhāraṇīs and eloquence
And will always be able to teach this sūtra.

One who meditates on this sūtra
And achieves the wisdom of manifesting lights
Will have the Tathāgatas revealed before him
And realize the emptiness of the eye. . . .

If one makes offerings
For countless millions of kalpas,
To all the sentient beings seen by Buddhas,

Serving them as Tathāgatas,
His merits cannot compare with those of one
Who accepts and practices this sūtra.[14]

If one accepts, upholds, and expounds
Only a four-line verse of this sūtra,
He should be revered [by all]
As a Supreme, Most Compassionate Lord.

For hundreds of thousands of kalpas,
In the three realms of saṁsāric existence.
I made offerings to Buddhas
For the sake of [hearing] this sūtra.

To master it, sometimes I offered
To the Great Teachers
Countless thousands of lamps,
With wicks as long as a league;
Sometimes I offered to Buddhas' stūpas
Various kinds of flowers, . . .
Garlands, banners, and canopies. . . .

I fulfilled the wishes
Of those in need:
I gave them flowers, fruits, gardens, and groves;
I gave them bridges, wells, and drinking water;
I gave them snow-white elephants and unicorns;
I gave them precious steeds and beautiful maidens;
I gave them gold beds and jeweled curtains. . . .
I practiced these kinds of giving untiringly,
Hundreds of thousands of times,
For the sake of [hearing] this sūtra.

II.

"In the past, for the sake of [hearing] this sūtra,
I kept the pure precepts,
Cultivated meditation and wisdom,
And gave charity to sentient beings.

In the past, for the sake of [hearing] this sūtra,
I took pity on
Villains who scolded me
Instead of harming them.

In the past, for the sake of [hearing] this sūtra,
I fulfilled the wishes
Of those who came to ask for favors,
And made them happy. . . .

Moonlight, you should know:
In search of this sūtra,
I have, for innumerable kalpas,
Cultivated so many austerities
That no one could finish counting them,
Even in a hundred thousand kalpas. . . .

If monks and nuns
Feel great emotion and shed tears
Upon hearing this sūtra,
They will meet the Most Honored One;
This I prophesy.

Moonlight, you should know that
The Buddhas, with their miraculuous powers,
Thoroughly know the purity or impurity
Of a person's mind,
And his faith and understanding as well. . . .

You should expound the unexcelled Dharma
With a firm mind,
And transmit this subtle sūtra
To the kindhearted. . . .

This, Moonlight, you should know:
Just as a clever person
Can skillfully handle fire
To cook various dishes
Without being burned by it,
While a clumsy fool
Burns his palm with the fire;
And just as one who becomes stupefied and deranged
After taking poison
Can be cured
By burning out the poison with fire[15]—
So it is with the wise.

By means of the mind,
They realize that the mind is empty,
So they are able to abide in saṁsāra.
By means of the eye,

They realize that the eye is void,
And do not attach themselves to it.
If one knows this truth,
He can use his eyes
Without afflictions.
By realizing the emptiness of the eye,
One can achieve true wisdom,
And thereby can emanate [various] lights.

One who realizes the emptiness of the eye
Can eradicate desires forever;
Free of desire,
He can emanate various lights.

As it is with desire,
So it is with hatred,
Ignorance, clinging to the ego,
Pretense, distress, avarice,
Jealousy, shamelessness, intolerance,
Conceit, pride, arrogance,
Flattery, deceit, self-indulgence,
Fraudulence, and so forth.

One who acquires true wisdom
Will realize the eye's ultimate quiescence,
And will then be able to emanate lights.

One who acquires true wisdom
Will abide in the essence of the Buddha-Dharma,
And will then be able to emanate lights.

One who acquires true wisdom
Will abide in the Buddha's ingenuity,
And will then be able to emanate lights.

Never have I seen anyone
Able to emanate lights
Who has not cultivated true wisdom
And [thereby] freed himself forever
From hindrances and afflictions.

One who cultivates true wisdom with diligence
Will free himself forever
From hindrances and afflictions;
He who complies with this practice
Can emanate lights.

To seek the supreme practice,
One should study this sūtra
And make offerings to Tathāgatas;
Then one will acquire true wisdom and ingenuity. . . .

One who knows not
The ultimate[16] nature of the eye
Cannot know the ultimate [nature]
Of the arising of the eye.
He is not one
Who can emanate lights. . . .

The same is true
With the ear, nose, tongue, body, and mind;
Forms, sounds, scents, tastes,
Textures, and mental objects;
Earth, water, fire, and air. . . ."

At that time, young Moonlight, having heard the Dharma explained, felt great joy. In the presence of the Buddha, he praised the Tathāgata in verse:

"The Tathāgata can display his pure wisdom
Because he realizes the ultimate exhaustion of the eye.
Being able to display pure wisdom,
He is endowed with the Buddha's[17] pure lights.

The Tathāgata can utter pure voices
Because he understands that the eye has no self.
Being able to utter pure voices,
He is endowed with the Buddha's perfect voices.

The Buddha can utter pure speech
Because he has benefited sentient beings.
With the ability to utter pure speech,
He can benefit innumerable worlds.

The Tathāgata can achieve the wisdom of dhāraṇī
Because he realizes that the eye
Is empty by nature.
Being able to achieve the wisdom of dhāraṇī,
He can manifest the Buddha's infinite lights.

The Tathāgata knows the variations of different eyes
And their unlimited, varied names.
Knowing countless names,
He can emit the Buddha's infinite lights.

Knowing the varieties of words and languages,
The Buddha realizes that the eye
Is empty and beyond words.
Therefore, he can emit the Buddha's infinite lights.

If one ponders
That the eye is devoid of self,
He will know that the Buddha speaks the truth;
One who knows that the Buddha speaks the truth
Can manifest the Tathāgata's absolute lights.

Having achieved the supreme miraculous powers,
The Tathāgata realizes the destruction
Of infinite numbers of eyes.
Being able to realize the destruction of eyes,
He can benefit all worlds.

The Supremely Honored One among humans and gods,
The One of great compassion,
Thoroughly realizes the arising
Of infinite numbers of eyes.
May I, too, soon realize the eye's arising,
As the Buddha does.

So may it be with the ear,
Nose, tongue, body, and mind;
Forms, sounds, scents,
Tastes, textures, and mental objects. . . .

The Supremely Honored One among humans and gods,
The One of great compassion,
Has attained the pāramitā of giving.
May I soon attain the pāramitā of giving,
As the Buddha has.

The Supremely Honored One among humans and gods,
The one of great compassion,
Has attained the pāramitā of pure discipline.
May I soon attain the pāramitā of pure discipline,
As the Buddha has.

The Supremely Honored One among humans and gods,
The One of great compassion,
Has attained the pāramitā of patience.
May I soon attain the pāramitā of patience,
As the Buddha has.

The Supremely Honored One among humans and gods,
The one of great compassion,
Has attained the pāramitā of vigor,
May I soon attain the pāramitā of vigor
As the Buddha has.

The Supremely Honored One among humans and gods,
The One of great compassion,
Has attained the pāramitā of dhyāna.
May I soon attain the pāramitā of dhyāna,
As the Buddha has.

The Supremely Honored One among humans and gods,
The One of great compassion,
Has attained the pāramitā of wisdom.
May I soon attain the pāramitā of wisdom,
As the Buddha has.

The Supremely Honored One among humans and gods,
The One of great compassion,
Has attained the perfect Dharma-body.
May I soon attain the perfect Dharma-body,
As the Buddha has.

The Supremely Honored One among humans and gods,
The One of great compassion,
Is endowed with infinite, pure forms.[18]
May I, too, soon acquire pure forms,
As the Buddha has.

The Supremely Honored One among humans and gods,
The One of great compassion,
Has achieved the pure, limitless mind.
May I soon acquire the same pure mind
As the Buddha has. . . .

The Supremely Honored One among humans and gods,
The One of great compassion,
Can utter infinite, pure voices.
May I soon attain the same pure voices
As the Buddha has.

The Supremely Honored One among humans and gods,
The One of great compassion,
Accomplishes infinite, great, miraculous feats.
May I soon accomplish the same feats
As the Buddha does.

The Supremely Honored One among humans and gods,
The One of great compassion,
Dwells in the three realms of existence
In order to convert sentient beings.
May I soon convert sentient beings,
As the Buddha does.

The Supremely Honored One among humans and gods,
The One of great compassion,
Has transcended the countless deeds of saṁsāra.
May I, too, soon transcend those deeds,
As the Buddha has. . . .

Having transcended desire,
The Teacher benefits all worlds.
May I, too, achieve the wisdom
To benefit all worlds,
As the Buddha does.

Having transcended hatred [and ignorance],
The Teacher benefits all worlds.
May I, too, achieve the wisdom
To benefit all worlds,
As the Buddha does. . . .

With surpassing wisdom,
The Tathāgata knows clearly
All karmic results of the world.
May I also achieve such wisdom
To benefit all worlds.

With surpassing wisdom,
The Tathāgata knows clearly
All the particular natures
Of all things in the world.
May I, too, achieve such wisdom
To benefit all worlds.

With surpassing wisdom,
The Tathāgata knows clearly the modes of practice
Leading to various planes of existence.
May I, too, achieve such wisdom
To benefit all worlds. . . .

With surpassing wisdom,
The Tathāgata knows clearly
The various dispositions of all beings.

May I, too, achieve such wisdom
To benefit all worlds.

With surpassing wisdom,
The Tathāgata knows clearly
The practice of meditation.
May I, too, achieve such wisdom
To benefit all worlds.

With surpassing wisdom,
The Tathāgata knows clearly
The practice of liberation.
May I, too, achieve such wisdom
To benefit all worlds. . . .

The Tathāgata realizes that by nature
All dharmas are like illusions, dreams, and mirages.
May I, too, achieve such wisdom
To benefit all worlds.

The Tathāgata thoroughly understands
All conventional words, written and spoken.
May I, too, achieve such wisdom
To benefit all worlds.

With surpassing eloquence,
The Tathāgata reveals the profound, subtle Dharma.
May I, too, achieve such wisdom
To benefit all worlds.

The Tathāgata's body, speech, and mind
Are well subdued;
He acts on wisdom alone,
May I, too, achieve such wisdom
To benefit all worlds.

Knowing well the three phases of time,
The Tathāgata is free
From grasping, attachment, and hindrances.
May I, too, achieve such wisdom
To benefit all worlds. . . .

The Tathāgata knows the whole world thoroughly,
And sees clearly all planes of existence.
May I, too, achieve the wisdom
To know these realms without doubt.

Fully realizing the ultimate exhaustion
Of [the dharmas'] arising,
The Tathāgata is not perplexed at it.
May I, too, achieve the wisdom
To know such truth without doubt.

Fully realizing quiescence,
The Tathāgata is not perplexed at it.
May I, too, achieve the wisdom
To know quiescence without doubt.

Fully realizing the flux of saṁsāra,
The Tathāgata is not perplexed at it.
May I, too, achieve the wisdom
To know the flux of saṁsāra without doubt.

Fully knowing the past and future states,
The Tathāgata has attained self-taught wisdom.
May I, too, achieve the wisdom
To know the past and future states without doubt.

Fully realizing transmigration,
The Tathāgata has attained self-taught wisdom.
May I, too, achieve the wisdom
To know transmigration without doubt.

Fully knowing the past and future states
The Tathāgata does not hold
To a nihilistic or eternalistic [view] of the eye.
May I, too, achieve the wisdom
To know the past and future states without doubt. . . .

If one does not understand
The past and future states,
He is doomed to be fettered by desire.
Since the Tathāgata realizes
The past and future states,
He is not defiled by desire.

If one does not understand being and nonbeing,
He is doomed to be fettered by desire.
Since the Tathāgata realizes them both,
He is not defiled by desire.

If one does not understand
Ultimate exhaustion and nonexhaustion,

He is doomed to be fettered by desire.
Since the Tathāgata realizes them both,
He is not defiled by desire. . . ."

At that time, knowing young Moonlight's earnest thoughts, the World-Honored One smiled graciously and shed a golden light which illuminated innumerable Buddha-lands, and, after rendering benefit to them all, circled the Buddha three times and entered the top of his head. Thereupon, Bodhisattva Maitreya rose from his seat, bared his right shoulder, knelt upon his right knee, bowed with his head at the Buddha's feet, then joined his palms reverently and spoke in verse, praising the Buddha and questioning him:

". . . The Tathāgata will take no further birth;
He embraces all worlds with great compassion.
May the Dharma king,
The Supremely Honored One of men,
Tell us why he smiled.

Now, innumerable great Bodhisattvas
And many awe-inspiring gods
Are all in the air holding wonderful canopies,
While the great earth is shaking.

In the presence of past Tathāgatas,
Who practiced wholesome Dharmas in the long night?
May the impartial, delightful
Lord of great compassion
Tell us why he smiled.

Who in the past made offerings to the Buddhas
And rejoiced at hearing this teaching expounded?
May the Teacher, the Supremely Honored One of men
Tell us why he smiled. . . .

The Supremely Honored One among humans and gods,
The One of great compassion,
Fully knows the wishes of sentient beings.
He has obtained the wonderful, unimpeded eloquence.
May he tell us why he smiled.

The Tathāgata has reached the other shore;
He is endowed
With the three insights[19]
And the six miraculous powers,
And he manifests infinite, pure lights.
May he tell us why he smiled.

The Buddha, for immeasurable kalpas in the past,
Served and made offerings
To hundreds of thousands of World-Honored Ones.
Such deeds do not go unrequited.
May he tell us why he smiled.

The Buddha, for immeasurable kalpas in the past,
Abided in subtle, wonderful samādhis;
And he realizes the arising
And ultimate exhaustion of the eye.
May he tell us why he smiled.

The Great Teacher knows everything
In the past, present, and future;
His pure wisdom is unimpeded and inconceivable.
May he tell us why he smiled."

Thereupon, amid the assembly, the World-Honored One stroked Moonlight's head with his golden-hued hand and then spoke in verse:

"Lad, listen carefully!
I now entrust you
With this teaching of enlightenment,
The Sūtra of the Manifestation of Lights,
So that in the later depraved age,
When the Dharma is about to perish,
You may reveal and expound it to sentient beings. . . .

Numberless kalpas ago,
There was a Buddha named Dīpaṁkara.
I, as the ṛṣi Māṇavaka,
Offered flowers to him.

Thereupon, he prophesied
That I would become a Buddha named Śākyamuni
And would sit at the Dharma-site
To expound this sūtra.

You were then a boy.
Hearing the prophecy about my future,
You felt joy, and became pure in mind.
You vowed with palms joined,
'If Māṇavaka becomes a Buddha,
I will assist him in preaching,
And will protect and uphold his Dharma
After his parinirvāṇa.'

When Dīpaṁkara Buddha explained
The Sūtra of the Manifestation of Lights,
Both Māṇavaka and the boy
Listened, and held it dear.

Once, in the past,
I offered blue lotus flowers to that Buddha.
You were present on that occasion,
And vowed to accept and uphold this sūtra
And preach and circulate it widely
In the Last Era of my Dharma.

One who, upon hearing this doctrine,
Does not feel aversion,
But accepts, upholds, reads, and recites it
Is indeed a man of virtue.
You should in later ages
Uphold this seldom-heard teaching
And elucidate its meaning widely
For all sentient beings. . . ."

When the World-Honored One finished teaching this sūtra, the boy Moonlight and everyone in the assembly, including the gods, humans, asuras, gandharvas, and so forth in the world, were all jubilant over the Buddha's teaching. They accepted it with faith and began to practice it with veneration.

NOTES

1. Among the twenty-two sūtras presented in this volume, "The Manifestation of Lights" is perhaps the most difficult one to comprehend. The central question concerns the meaning of this so-called light. Is it simply a kind of luminous entity such as rays or beams of light, or is it spiritual illumination—the mystical light reported by many meditators? To give an exact answer is difficult. Noticeably, the lights treated in this sūtra appear to denote all the dynamic aspects of Buddhahood, i.e., Saṁbhogakāya and Nirmāṇakāya; all merits and functions of Tathāgatahood are expressed in terms of light. In fact, all the essential principles of Mahāyāna Buddhism seem to be expressed in terms of this light.

In a broad sense, we may associate "mystical light" with the Dharmakāya. However, the lights described in this sūtra are not of the Dharmakāya, but of the Rūpakāya ('body of form'), which is the fruit or dynamic manifestation of Dharmakāya. The "mystical light" can be regarded as preliminary to attainment of Dharmakāya, whereas the light of Rūpakāya is sequent to it. This, however, does not in any sense underrate Dharmakāya, for the dynamic lights of Rupakāya can only be brought forth through the realization of emptiness, as is clearly stated in this sūtra. (G.C.)

2. This may also be translated as 'Decisive Light', or 'Certain Light.'

3. The Chinese text reads 事, 'event'. It is obviously a textual error. 'Light' is meant here.

4. 'Clouds' here does not refer to the clouds in the sky. It is a common term in sūtras to describe profusion, hugeness, bountifulness, multitude, large quantity, gathering, accumulation, and so forth.

5. Since mind and body are interrelated, psychological functions can affect the body and vice versa. Anger can produce bad physical effects; kindness (i.e., to bestow joy upon others) can produce beneficial and purifying effects on the body. Hence, by cultivating kindness it is held that one automatically purifies the mind-body complex. (G.C.)

6. Realization of emptiness and understanding of the law of karma are interdependent. Here, by revealing the karmic principle to the world, it is implied that one's realization of emptiness is enhanced.

7. The Tathāgata utters truthful words, words free of deception, words in accordance with suchness, because his wisdom is no other than realization of the dharmadhātu.

8. The ultimate exhaustion of conditioned dharmas, e.g., the eye, refers to the state of thorough liberation from saṁsāric attachment to dharmas. This is accomplished by cultivating the understanding and realization of the unconditioned dharmas such as emptiness and dependent generation. These unconditioned dharmas constitute not a dead void, nor an annihilation of things, but rather the nonclinging, lacking in self-nature, inexhaustible flow of events in the multidimensional dharmadhātu.

9. Cessation of the cause of suffering; i.e., the state of nirvāṇa.

10. One who goes nowhere and reaches all limits transcends the limits of the three phases of time; therefore, he beholds the past and foresees the future.

11. Buddhist sages were keenly aware of the importance of symbols, through which a major portion of Dharma teaching is understood. This becomes especially evident in the doctrines of Tantrism.

12. One who maintains that there is something attainable in emptiness is arrogant, while one with true realization sees nothing attainable in emptiness and is naturally free from arrogance.

13. Here, as in other places throughout the text, the discussion of the eye is only an example which can also be applied to the ear, nose, etc., and all conditioned dharmas, as explained below.

14. No matter how innumerable are the sentient beings to whom one makes offerings, the merits of such deeds are finite, but those who truly practice this sūtra can realize suchness, and thusly acquire infinite merits.

15. Perhaps refers to moxibustion or cauterization.

16. Literally, "limit."

17. Literally, "Tathāgata's," here and below.

18. Seems to refer to the pure, perfect Saṁbhogakāya, the body of form. See Numerical Glossary, "three bodies of the Buddha."

19. The three insights: first, the insight of past lives, with which one knows the past lives of self and others; second, the insight of birth and death (otherwise called the insight of the deva-eye), with which one knows the conditions of future births and deaths of self and others; third, the insight of nondefilement, with which one knows one's present suffering and knows whether all his defilements are ended.

IV

On Consciousness

12 大乘顯識經

The Elucidation of Consciousness[1]

Thus have I heard. Once the World-Honored One was dwelling in the bamboo grove of Elder Karaṇḍa, in the great city of Rājagṛha, together with twelve hundred fifty great monks who were all Arhats. These monks had ended their defilements and were no longer subject to afflictions. They had acquired ease and achieved liberation from passions and from ignorance. They perceived the past, the present, and the future without hindrance. These great dragons[2] had, in accordance with the Buddha's teaching, done what they had set out to do and abandoned the great burden [of saṁsāra]. They had gained benefit for themselves. They had already freed themselves from the sufferings caused by existence in saṁsāra. By the power of right wisdom, they knew well sentient beings' propensities. These great Śrāvakas were led by Elder Śāriputra.

Also in the assembly were innumerable Bodhisattva-Mahāsattvas.

At that time, at the dwelling place of the World-Honored One, most of the monks felt tired and lethargic. They looked listless and could not deport themselves properly. Thereupon, the face of the World-Honored One beamed like an opened lotus flower. All the monks then became fully awake and straightened themselves up with dignity. They thought, "Now the Buddha, the World-Honored One, emits bright light from his face. What Dharma will he teach to benefit [sentient beings] greatly?"

At that time, Wise Protector, a youth, . . . joined his palms respectfully, bowed down with his head at the Buddha's feet, and said to him, "World-Honored One, you always take pity on all sentient beings and hold them in your embrace and protection. I wish to ask a few questions. May the World-Honored One grant me permission."

Sūtra 39, Taishō 347, pp. 178–186; translated into Chinese by Divākara.

The Buddha said to Wise Protector, "Your request is granted. You may present your doubts and I will answer them with detailed explanations."

Wise Protector asked the Buddha, "World-Honored One, although sentient beings know that consciousness exists, they cannot understand it thoroughly if it is not explained clearly, just as no one knows that there is a treasure if it is locked up in a box. World-Honored One, what form does the consciousness assume? Why is it called consciousness? When sentient beings are dying, they frantically jerk their hands and feet, their eyes change color, they are constricted and cannot move freely, their sense-organs function no more, and their [four] elements disintegrate. After the consciousness leaves the body, where does it go? What is its self-nature? What form does it take on? How does it leave the old body to receive a new body? How can it leave one body here, and, taking all the sense-fields[3] with it, be born again and again in various other bodies to undergo karmic results? World-Honored One, how can sentient beings produce sense organs again after their bodies decay and disintegrate? How can one be rewarded in future lives for meritorious deeds performed in this life? How can a future body enjoy the rewards of meritorious actions performed by the present body? How can the consciousness be nourished and grow in the body? How can the consciousness change and modify itself in accordance with the body?"[4]

The Buddha answered, "Marvelous, marvelous! Wise Protector, your questions are excellent. Listen attentively and think well about this. I will explain it to you."

Wise Protector said to the Buddha, "Yes, World-Honored One, I will accept your teaching with respect."

The Buddha told Wise Protector, "The consciousness moves and turns, transmigrates[5] and expires, and comes and goes like the wind. Wind has no color or shape and is invisible, yet it can [generate and] stir up things and cause them to take on different shapes. It may shake trees so violently that they break or split with a loud crack. It may touch sentient beings' bodies with cold or heat and make them feel pain or pleasure.

"The wind has no hands, no feet, no face, no eyes, and no shape; it is not black, white, yellow, or red. Wise Protector, the same is true of consciousness. Consciousness is without color, shape, or light,[6] and cannot be manifested. It shows its various functions only when [proper] causes and conditions are met. The same is true of the elements of feeling, awareness, and dharmas.[7] These elements, too, are devoid of color and shape and depend on [proper] causes and conditions to display their functions.

"Wise Protector, when a sentient being dies, the elements of feeling, awareness, and dharmas, together with consciousness, all leave the [old] body. Taking the elements of feeling, awareness, and dharmas with it, the consciousness is born again in a new body.

"As an illustration, when the wind passes over exquisite flowers, the flowers remain where they are, while their fragrance spreads far and wide. The substance of the wind does not take in a fragrance of the exquisite flowers. The substances of the fragrance, the wind, and the organ of touch[8] have neither shape nor color, but the fragrance cannot spread far away without the power of the wind. Wise Protector, in the same way, after a sentient being dies, his consciousness will take birth again together with the elements of feeling, awareness, and dharmas. Accompanied by the elements of feeling, awareness, and dharmas, the consciousness is reincarnated through [the union of] its parents, who are the conditions of its rebirth.

"By virtue of [sweet] flowers, the nose smells fragrance; by virtue of the sense of smell, the fragrance is experienced; by virtue of a wind, we see and feel the effect of the wind, whose power spreads the fragrance far and wide. Similarly, from the consciousness comes feeling; from feeling comes awareness; from awareness come dharmas; and as a result, one can tell good from evil. . . .[9]

"Wise Protector, when a sentient being dies at the exhaustion of his karmic results [for that life], his consciousness is still bound by karmic hindrances. [At the moment of death,] the consciousness leaves the body and its elements to take birth in another body, just as the consciousness of an Arhat who has entered the dhyāna of ultimate quiescence disappears from his body. However, by the power of memory, the consciousness knows both the identity of the deceased and all he has done in life, which occur clearly to the dying person and press him mentally and physically.

"Wise Protector, what is the meaning of consciousness? Consciousness is the seed which can bring forth the sprout of various bodily forms as a result of karma. Perception, awareness, conception, and memory are all comprised in the consciousness, so that it can tell joy from pain, good from evil, and wholesome states from unwholesome ones. For this reason, it is called consciousness.

"You ask how the consciousness leaves the body and [takes birth] again to undergo other karmic results. Wise Protector, the consciousness moves into a body as a face appears in a mirror, or as the letters of a seal reveal themselves in the mud. When the sun rises, darkness disappears wherever the sunlight reaches. When the sun sets and there is no light, darkness reappears. Darkness has no form or substance, and is neither permanent nor impermanent; it is nowhere to be found. The same is true of consciousness: it is devoid of form and substance, yet it manifests itself by feelings and conceptions. The consciousness in the body is just like the substance of darkness; it cannot be seen or grasped.

"A mother cannot know whether the baby she has conceived is a boy or a girl; black-, white-, or yellow-skinned; with complete or incomplete organs; with well-formed or deformed organs; or whether its hands, feet, ears, and eyes resemble hers. When the mother eats or drinks something hot, however, her baby moves [in her womb] and she feels pain. Similarly, sentient beings come and go, bend and stretch, look and wink, talk and laugh, carry heavy burdens, and do other things. Through these activities the consciousness manifests itself, but no one can tell exactly where it is except that it is in the body, and no one knows what it looks like.

"Wise Protector, the consciousness, in its self-nature,[10] pervades everywhere [in the body] but is not tainted by any part. Although it dwells in the six sense-organs, the six sense-objects, and the five aggregates which are defiled, it is not stained by any of them; it only functions through them.

"Wise Protector, a wooden puppet strung up somewhere can give a variety of performances, such as walking, prancing, jumping, throwing, playing, and dancing. What do you think? By whose power can the wooden puppet do so?"

Wise Protector said to the Buddha, "I am not intelligent enough to know the answer."

The Buddha told Wise Protector, "You should know that it is by the power of the puppeteer. The puppeteer is out of sight; only the operation of his intelligence can be seen. Similarly, the body does everything by the power of consciousness. Ṛṣis, gandharvas, dragons, gods, humans, asuras, and other beings in the various planes of existence all depend on the power of consciousness to act. The body is exactly like the wooden puppet. Consciousness is devoid of form and substance, but it upholds all in the dharmadhātu;[11] it is fully endowed with the power of wisdom and can even know events of past lives.[12]

"Sunlight impartially illuminates evildoers and such filthy things as stinking corpses without being tainted by their foulness. Similarly, consciousness may reside in a pig, a dog, or a being of another miserable plane who eats dirty food, but is stained by none of them.

"Wise Protector, after leaving the body, the consciousness [takes birth again] with its good and evil karmas to undergo other karmic results. The wind becomes fragrant if it enters a grove of fragrant campaka flowers[13] after coming out of a deep valley. However, if the wind passes through a stinking, dirty place where there are excrement and corpses, it catches an offensive smell. If the wind passes through a place which is permeated with both a fragrant odor and an offensive one, it carries good and bad odors at the same time, but the stronger of the two predominates. The wind is devoid of form or substance. Fragrance and stench, too, have no shape; however, the wind can carry both fragrance and stench far away. The consciousness takes good and evil karmas with it from one body to another to undergo different karmic results.

"Just as a person who is dreaming sees many images and events without knowing that he is lying asleep, so, when a blessed, virtuous person is dying and his consciousness departs, he is peaceful and unaware [of his death]; he passes away fearlessly as if he were dreaming.

"The consciousness does not leave from the throat or any other orifice.[14] No one knows where it departs or how it goes out."

The Elder Wise Protector bowed down with his head at the Buddha's feet and asked him, "World-Honored One, the egg-shell of hen, a goose, or the like is airtight all around when the egg has not hatched. How can the consciousness get into it? If the embryo dies in the egg and the egg-shell does not break, how can the consciousness get out of the egg-shell, which has no opening at all?"

The Buddha answered, "Wise Protector, after being perfumed by campaka flowers, castor[15] beans yield a fragrant oil called campaka oil, which smells much better than ordinary castor oil. By itself, castor oil is not fragrant; it becomes fragrant only because the beans have been perfumed by campaka flowers. The fragrance does not get into or out of the beans by breaking them. Though it is in the oil, the fragrance has no form or substance. It is the power of causes and conditions that moves the fragrance into the oil to make it aromatic. In the same way, the consciousness of a chicken or gosling enters and leaves the egg.

"The consciousness tranmigrates [into a new body] just as the sun sheds light, as a pearl shines, or as wood produces fire. [Transmigration] is also like the sowing of a seed. After a seed undergoes transformation in the soil, sprouts, stems, and leaves emerge. Then come flowers of various colors, such as white or red, manifesting a variety of powers and scents at maturity.

"This same great earth provides nutrients composed of all the four elements to nourish plants, but different seeds will produce different crops. In the same way, from the same consciousness that upholds the entire dharmadhātu come all the saṁsāric beings with bodies of different colors, such as white, black, yellow, and red; and with different dispositions, such as gentleness and irascibility.[16]

"However, Wise Protector, consciousness has no hands, no feet, no members, and no language.

"The power of memory is very strong in the dharmadhātu,[17] so when the consciousness leaves a sentient being's body at his death, it combines with the power of memory to become the seed of his next life. Apart from consciousness, there is no dharmadhātu, and vice versa.

"The consciousness is reincarnated together with the prāṇa-element,[18] and the elements of subtle memory, feeling, and dharmas."

Wise Protector asked the Buddha, "If so, why does the World-Honored One say that consciousness is formless?"

The Buddha answered, "Wise Protector, form is of two kinds: one is internal; the other, external. Visual consciousness is internal, while the eye is external. Similarly, auditory consciousness is internal, while the ear is external; olfactory consciousness is internal, while the nose is external; gustatory consciousness is internal, while the tongue is external; tactile consciousness is internal, while the body is external.

"Wise Protector, suppose a man born blind sees a beautiful woman in a dream.[19] Her hands, feet, and features are all extremely pretty, so in the dream the blind man becomes greatly delighted with her. When he wakes up, there is nothing to be seen. In the daytime, among the crowd, the blind man speaks of the pleasant event in his dream, saying, 'I saw a gorgeous woman in a magnificent garden, together with hundreds of thousands of people, all well-adorned and making merry.

Her skin was lustrous, her shoulders plump, and her arms long and round like the trunk of an elephant. [Seeing these] in the dream, I was filled with joy, comfort, and admiration.'

"Wise Protector, this man, blind from birth, has never seen anything in his life. How can he see those forms in the dream?"

Wise Protector said to the Buddha, "May you explain this to me!"

The Buddha told Wise Protector, "The forms seen in the dream are the internal objects of the eye. It is through the discrimination of intellect, not the physical eye, that the internal objects of the eye are seen. Because of the power of memory, the internal objects of the eye appear for a moment in the dream of the blind man. Also because of the power of memory, the blind man remembers them when he wakes up. Thus do the internal forms relate to the consciousness.

"Furthermore, Wise Protector, when a body dies, the consciousness leaves the body to be reincarnated. As an illustration, consider a seed: after being sown in the soil and supported by the four elements, it will gradually grow into sprouts, stems, branches, and leaves. In like manner, the consciousness leaves the dead body to be reincarnated under the control of four things—memory, feeling, wholesome dharmas, and unwholesome dharmas."

Wise Protector asked the Buddha, "World-Honored One, how do wholesome and unwholesome dharmas control the consciousness?"

The Buddha answered, "Wise Protector, as an illustration, a piece of precious crystal looks white or black according to whether it is put in a white or black place. Similarly, when the consciousness leaves the dead body to be reincarnated and undergo different karmic results, it will become virtuous or nonvirtuous according to whether it is controlled by wholesome or unwholesome dharmas."

Wise Protector further asked the Buddha, "In what way is the body connected with the consciousness?"

The Buddha answered, "Wise Protector, consciousness does not accumulate or grow. As an illustration, there will be no sprout if the seed does not grow or if it rots. It is when the seed changes and undergoes transformation that the sprout emerges. Wise Protector, what do you think? Where does the sprout abide? In the seed, branch, stem, leaf, or the top of the tree?"

Wise Protector answered the Buddha, "World-Honored One, the sprout does not abide in any part of the tree."

[The Buddha said,] "Similarly, Wise Protector, the consciousness does not abide in any part of the body. It abides neither in the eye, nor in the ear, nose, tongue, nor body. The time when the consciousness gains slight awareness may be compared to the time when the seed sprouts; the time when the consciousness acquires feeling may be compared to the time when buds appear; and the time during which the consciousness has a body may be compared to the time during which the flower blossoms and the tree bears fruit.

"From consciousness the body arises, and consciousness covers all the body and its limbs. When we look for consciousness in the body, we cannot find it anywhere; yet without consciousness, the body cannot live.

"The tree bears the seeds of future trees when its fruits are ripe, not when they are unripe. In the same way, when the body dies as the karmic results [of one life] are settled, the consciousness-seed appears. Because there is consciousness, there are sensations. Because there are sensations, there is craving. Because of the bondage of craving, memory occurs and is absorbed by the consciousness. Through the union of the parents, and in accordance with its good and evil karmas, the consciousness takes birth again together with the elements of prāṇa, perceptions, and memory.

"A mirror can reflect a person's face, but if the mirror is not clean and bright, the face will not be reflected. Only when the mirror is bright can the image of the face appear. A person's image in the mirror has no feeling or memory, but it bends, stretches, looks up and down, speaks, comes, goes, advances, stops, and performs other acts just as the person does. Wise Protector, by whose power does the image appear?"

Wise Protector answered the Buddha, "It is by the power of that person: Because there is the face, there is the image of that face. The image and the face are the same in color, and the image is exactly like the face, with or without complete organs."

The Buddha said, "The face is the cause of the image, and the mirror is the condition of it. Through the combination of the cause and condition, the image is produced. Due to the consciousness [serving as the cause of the body], there are feelings, conceptions, impulses, and other mental functions. The parents are the condition [of the body]. Through the combination of the cause and condition, the body is produced.

"The image in the mirror will disappear when the body moves away, yet the body's image may be reflected in water or in other places. In the same way, after leaving the body, the consciousness takes birth again together with good and evil karmas to undergo other karmic results.

"Furthermore, as an illustration, consider the seeds of banyan and udumbara. Though small, these seeds can engender huge trees, which will in turn produce seeds. The new seeds will leave the old trees to produce new trees. In time, the old trees will become weak, sapless, withered, and rotten. Similarly, after leaving its small body, the consciousness of a small sentient being may take on a big body of some kind, according to its karmas.

"Moreover, consider barley, wheat, castor-oil plants, soybeans, green lentils, and so forth: their sprouts, stems, flowers, and fruits grow and ripen because of their seeds. Similarly, because they have a consciousness, sentient beings who are subject to transmigration have awareness. Because they have awareness, they have feelings, and as a result, the consciousness takes on different bodies together with good and evil karmas.

"As a further example, a bee rests on a flower and becomes attached to it. The bee sucks the nectar of the flower to nourish itself, and then leaves the flower to rest on another one. It may fly from a fragrant flower to a stinking one, or from a stinking one to a fragrant one, and it becomes attached to whatever flower it rests upon. Similarly, because of meritorious karmas, the consciousness may acquire the body of a god to enjoy superior bliss. Then the consciousness may lose the body of a god and, because of [previous] evil karmas, be reborn as a hell-dweller to undergo many sufferings. The consciousness is thus born again and again in various bodies.

"The consciousness is like the seed of a tulip, of a red or blue [lotus] flower, or of a giant white lotus flower. The seeds of these flowers are all white. If you break them, you will find no sprout, no flower, and no colors [other than white]. Yet when sown in the soil and moistened with water, the seeds will sprout and, in due time, produce abundant flowers and fruits, which are red, white, or other colors. The colors, sprouts, and so forth are not within the seed, but they cannot be produced if there is no seed. [Similarly,] after the consciouness leaves the body, no features, sense-organs, or sense-fields of the body are to be found within the consciousness. By wonderful vision, wonderful hearing, sound, texture, taste, dharmas, memory, and the sense-fields, the consciousness knows the good and evil karmas it has done and will acquire a [new] body according to those karmas when proper causes and conditions combine.

"Just as a silkworm makes a cocoon in which to wrap itself and then leaves the cocoon behind, so consciousness produces a body to envelop itself and then leaves that body to undergo other karmic results [in a new body].

"Because there is a seed, there are the color, fragrance, and flavor [of a plant]. [Similarly,] after the consciousness leaves the body, the sense-organs, sense-objects, feeling, and the element of dharmas go wherever the consciousness goes.[20]

"Where there is a wish-fulfilling pearl, there are comforts; where there is the sun, there is light. The same is true with the consciousness: feeling, awareness, conception, the element of dharmas, and so forth go wherever the consciousness goes.

"When the consciousness leaves the body, it carries all the body's attributes with it. It assumes an [ethereal] form as its body;[21] it has no body of flesh and bones. Because it has the senses, it has feelings and subtle memory and can tell good from evil.

"The fruits of date, pomegranate, mango, bimba, Persian date,[22] kāpittha, and so on are pungent, bitter, sour, sweet, salty, or astringent. They differ not only in taste, but also in their capacity to quench thirst. After the fruits [ripen and] decay, their flavors go with the seeds no matter where the seeds are sown. In the same way, feeling, memory, and good and evil [karmas] go wherever the consciousness-seed goes. It is called consciousness because it knows that it has left one body to receive another one, knows the good and evil karmas [it has performed], knows that it is accompanied by the karmas, and knows that it will be reincarnated together with the karmas to undergo due karmic results. It is called consciousness because it knows all that the body has done.

"The element air has no form to be grasped and no substance to be held. However, when proper causes and conditions combine, it can manifest its existence in many ways; it can carry cold and heat, waft fragrance and stench, sway trees, and blow violently to destroy things. In the same way, consciousness has no form or substance, and cannot be seen or heard. However, when proper causes and conditions combine, all its attributes appear. Maintained by consciousness, the body feels pain and pleasure, looks healthy, goes and comes, advances and stops, speaks and laughs, experiences joy and sorrow, and performs clearly visible actions. [Seeing these,] one knows there is a consciousness." . . .

The Buddha said to Elder True Moon, ". . . True Moon, in the body born of parents, solid matter is of the element earth, fluid is of the element water, warmth is of the element fire, and motion is of the element air; that which is aware of and remembers sounds, odors, tastes, textures, and so forth is the consciousness."

True Moon asked the Buddha, "World-Honored One, when a sentient being is on the point of death, how can the consciousness leave the body? How can it move into another body? How can it be aware of its own leaving the body?"

The Buddha replied to True Moon, "When a sentient being is rewarded with a body according to his karmas, the consciousness will maintain that body without interruption, like a stream. When the sentient being's life comes to an end and his body dies, the consciousness will leave his body to take birth again together with his karmas.

"As an illustration, consider a mixture of water and milk: when it is boiled over a fire, milk, water, and cream will all separate. Similarly, True Moon, when the life of a sentient being comes to an end, his body, consciousness, sense-organs, and sense-objects will all disperse because the power of karma is exhausted. The consciousness will then become the only reliance [of the ethereal mind-body complex][23] and will contact various objects, make up [all sorts of] notions about them, and be reincarnated, together with the good and evil karmas, to undergo other karmic results.

"True Moon, as an illustration, consider the 'great auspicious butter.'[24] It is prepared by boiling a combination of various good medicines together with the butter. The attributes of ordinary butter all vanish; instead, the butter becomes saturated with the powers of the good medicines and their six flavors: acrid, bitter, sour, salty, astringent, and sweet. It nourishes the body and gives it a sanguine look and a pleasant odor. Similarly, after leaving the [dead] body, the consciousness will take birth again to undergo other karmic results, together with the element of dharmas and good and evil karmas.

"True Moon, the essence of such butter is like the body. Butter combines with the medicines to become the great auspicious butter, just as the sense-organs combine with dharma-objects to produce karmas. Karmas nourish the consciousness in the same way as the medicines flavor butter to make it the great auspicious butter. When nourished with this butter, one beams and becomes full of energy, peaceful, and free from all diseases; similarly, when nourished by good karmas, the consciousness acquires blissful rewards. When fed with improper butter, one turns pale instead of acquiring a rosy complexion; similarly, when nourished by evil karmas, the consciousness suffers painful retributions.

"True Moon, though having no hand, foot, or eye, the precious great auspicious butter can absorb the colors, fragrances, flavors, and powers of good medicines. In a similar manner, after leaving the body and sense-organ complex,[25] the consciousness can take up the element of dharmas, feeling, and good karmas to assume the intermediate existence between death and reincarnation and acquire the wonderful memory of a god.[26] It will see the six heavens of the Realm of Desire and the sixteen hells. It will see itself as having a body with shapely limbs and beautiful sense-organs. When it sees the dead body it has left, it will say, 'This was the body of my previous life.'

"It will also see a celestial palace, which is high, imposing and full of decorations. There are flowers, fruits, plants, and trees entangled with vines which have tendrils as shiny as new gold chains inlaid with various gems. The sight will fill [the consciousness] with exultation. Being very fond of the palace, it will take birth there.

"For a person with good karmas, to give up one body and receive another is comfortable and painless, just like a rider's dismounting from one horse and mounting another. As an illustration, when a brave man skilled in fighting sees enemy troops coming, he will put on strong armor and ride on a brave horse to meet them fearlessly. Similarly, when a person endowed with good roots breathes his last, his consciousness will [happily] leave the [old] body and sense-organ complex[27] and take birth again in the Brahmā Heaven, or even in the Akaniṣṭha Heaven, to enjoy wonderful pleasures."

At that time, Prince Great Medicine rose from his seat in the assembly, joined his palms, and asked the Buddha, "World-Honored One, what form does the consciousness take after leaving the [dead] body?"

The Buddha answered, "Marvelous, marvelous! Great Medicine, what you now ask concerns the great, profound state of the Buddha. No one except the Tathāgata can understand it."

At this, Wise Protector said to the Buddha, "The question raised by Prince Great Medicine is indeed profound. It shows his subtle wisdom and quick mind."

. . .

Seeing that Buddha was benign and that his face was beaming with joy like an autumn lotus flower in full bloom, Prince Great Medicine became jubilant. He joined his palms and said wholeheartedly to the Buddha, "World-Honored One, I love the profound Dharma; I thirst after the profound Dharma. I am in constant fear of the Tathāgata's entering parinirvāṇa, because I will have no chance to hear him explain the true Dharma. I will then be left among the sentient beings of the five depravities, who ceaselessly remain in saṁsāra to undergo sufferings because they are confused and too ignorant to know good from evil, wholesome from unwholesome, or perfect from imperfect." . . .

Prince Great Medicine than asked the Buddha [again], "World-Honored One, what is the form of the consciousness? Please explain it for me."

The Buddha told Prince Great Medicine, "It is like one's image in water. Such an image is ungraspable. It is neither existent nor nonexistent; and it changes shape with the water. . . .

"The 'shape' of good and evil karmas and the form of the consciousness are invisible. Just as a person born blind cannot see sunrise or sunset, day or night, brightness or darkness, so we cannot see the consciousness. There are thirsty desires, feelings, and thoughts within oneself, but these are also invisible. However, all the [four] elements, the [twelve] entrances, and the [five] aggregates which constitute one's self[28] are manifestations of the consciousness. Both the rūpas,[29] such as the eye, ear, nose, tongue, body, form, sound, odor, taste, and texture, and the non-rūpas, such as the experiences of pain and pleasure, are [manifestations of] the consciousness.

"Great Medicine, when a person tastes food with his tongue, he knows the food to be sweet, bitter, acrid, sour, salty, or astringent. The tongue and the food are visible and tangible, while the taste is not. Furthermore, because of bones, marrow, flesh, and blood, a person can be aware of sensations. Bones and so forth are tangible, but sensations are not. The same is true with knowing whether a consciousness is nourished by blessings[30] or not."

Then, bowing with his head at the Buddha's feet, Wise Protector asked the Buddha, "Is it possible to know whether or not a consciousness has blessings?"

The Buddha answered, "Listen attentively! No one can see the consciousness unless he has seen the truth. Unlike a mango in the hand, the consciousness is invisible. It is not within the eye or other sense-organs. If the consciousness were within the eye or other sense-organs, it could be seen if the eye or other sense-organs were dissected. Wise Protector, *I, like all other Buddhas, as numerous as the sands of the Ganges, see that the consciousness has no form. The consciousness cannot be seen by ordinary people; it can be described only through parables. . . .*[31]

"Suppose a god, a ghost, a spirit . . . or other being possesses a person. What do you think? Can we find its entity inside the person's body?"

Wise Protector said to the Buddha, "Certainly not, World-Honored One. When a god, a ghost, or a spirit possesses a person, we cannot see its entity even if we search for it inside and outside the person's body, because it is formless and shapeless."

"Wise Protector," said the Buddha, "if a person is possessed by a great god with superior merits, then fragrant flowers, superior incense, delicious food and drink, and clean quarters must be offered to him, and the offerings must all be magnificent and unsullied. In the same way, a consciousness nourished by blessings will be rewarded with nobility and comfort. It will be reborn as a king, a minister, a nobleman, a very rich man, a chieftain, or a great merchant. It may acquire the body of a god to enjoy wonderful celestial bliss. A person whose consciousness is nourished by blessings acquires blissful rewards, just as a person possessed by a god with superior merits should be given excellent flowers and incense, as well as delicious food and drink, which will make him happy and cure him of his illness when he is sick.[32] Therefore, one should know that those of high standing or great wealth acquire such blissful rewards solely because their consciousnesses are nourished by blessings.

"Wise Protector, when a person is possessed by a lowly, evil ghost or spirit . . . he will be fond of excrement, putrid things, mucus, saliva, and so on; if offered such filthy things for relief, he will be happy and cured of his illness. Owing to the power of the ghost or spirit, the person delights in such impure, stinking things as excrement, just as the ghost or spirit delights in them. Similarly, a consciousness pervaded by sin will be born of poor parents, or in miserable planes of existence, such as the plane of hungry ghosts or the plane of animals which eat dirty food. If one's consciousness is pervaded by sin, he will undergo painful karmic results.

"Wise Protector, the power[33] of a superior god who possesses a person has no substance and no shape, but it can [make the possessed person] obtain fragrant, pure offerings. In the same way, a consciousness nourished by blessings is shapeless, but it can [make the person it resides in] acquire wonderful, blissful rewards. Inferior, evil ghosts . . . cause the people they possess to take impure, bad food. Similarly, a consciousness pervaded by sin will [cause the person it resides in to] undergo painful retributions.

"Wise Protector, this you should know: the consciousness is devoid of form or substance . . . yet, according to whether it is nourished by sin or blessings, it will [make the person it resides in] receive painful or joyous results." . . .

Great Medicine asked the Buddha, "How does the consciousness take on the form of a god or a hell-dweller?"

The Buddha replied to Great Medicine, "The consciousness has subtle vision regarding the element of dharmas. This subtle vision does not depend on the physical eye in order to see. When this subtle vision encounters a blissful realm and sees pleasures and merry-making in celestial palaces, the consciousness becomes delighted and attached to them, thinking, 'I shall go there.' This thought of defiled attachment is the cause of existence [in saṁsāra]. Seeing the dead body forsaken in a cemetary, the consciousness thinks, 'This corpse is my good friend. Because it has hoarded good karmas, I am now rewarded with rebirth in heaven.'"

Great Medicine asked the Buddha, "World-Honored One, since the consciousness still has an attraction to the corpse, why does it not return to the corpse?"

The Buddha asked in turn, "Great Medicine, can hair and beard, though black, lustrous, and fragrant, be inserted into the body to grow there again after being cut and discarded?"

Great Medicine answered the Buddha, "No, World-Honored One. The hair and beard which have been cut and discarded cannot be inserted into the body to grow there again."

The Buddha said, "Similarly, Great Medicine, the consciousness cannot return to the castoff corpse to undergo karmic results."

Great Medicine asked the Buddha, "World-Honored One, consciousness is indeed subtle and abstruse. It has no substance to be grasped and no form to be recognized. How can it maintain the body of a big sentient being like an elephant? How can it get into a strong body as hard as a diamond? How can it maintain the body of a strong man who even can tame nine elephants?"

The Buddha replied, "Great Medicine, take the wind for instance. It is devoid of form or substance, . . . yet it may become fierce enough to blow Mount Sumeru to dust-motes. Great Medicine, what is the form and shape of the wind, which can even destroy Mount Sumeru?"

Great Medicine said to the Buddha, "The wind is subtle and without form or substance."

The Buddha said, "Great Medicine, the wind is [indeed] subtle and without form or substance. The consciousness is also subtle and without form or substance, yet it can maintain any body, whether big or small. It can take on the body of a mosquito, and it can also take on the body of an elephant. As an illustration, consider a lamp with a subtle flame. When put in a room, the lamp can dispel all the darkness of the room, whether the room is large or small. Similarly, the consciousness can maintain a big or a small body according to its karmas."

Great Medicine asked the Buddha, "World-Honored One, what are the characteristics of karmas? What causes and conditions enable them to manifest themselves?"

The Buddha replied, "Great Medicine, it is because of his [good] karmas that [a sentient being] is reborn in heaven, enjoying delicious food, peace, and happiness. Suppose two thirsty persons walk in the wilderness; one finds cool, sweet water, but the other finds nothing and has to suffer from thirst and fatigue. No one gives the former cool water or hinders the latter from obtaining it. They acquire their fruits, blissful or painful, according to their karmas. . . .

"As an illustration, consider a seed which is sown in the soil; afterwards, fruits appear at the top of the tree. However, the seed does not go from branch to branch and finally reach the top of the tree. The seed is not found even if the trunk is dissected. No one puts it into any branch. When the tree grows up and the roots become firm, the seed cannot be found. Similarly, all good and evil karmas rely on the body, but no karma is found when the body is examined. Because of the seed, there are flowers, but within the seed no flower is found; because of flowers, there are fruits, but within the flowers no fruit is found. . . . Similarly, because of the body, there are karmas, and because of karmas, there is the body, but no karmas are found within the body and no body is found within the karmas.

"Fruits do not appear until flowers fall down at maturity. Similarly, the fruit of karma does not ripen until the body dies at life's end. Just as the seed is the cause of the flower and fruit, so the body is the cause of karmas, good and evil.

"Karmas have no form and give no sign of ripening. As an illustration, consider a person's shadow, which is insubstantial, unimpeded, ungraspable, and unattached to the person. It advances, stops, goes, and comes as the person does, yet it is not seen to come out of the body. In the same way, where there is the body, there are karmas, yet karmas are not found within the body or apart from it.

"A dose of good medicine, whether it tastes acrid, astringent, or bitter, can cure a sick person's disease and give him comfort and a good complexion. When people see that person, they immediately know that he has taken fine medicine. The flavor of the medicine can be tasted, but its therapeutic function cannot be seen. Though invisible and ungraspable, [the medicine's potency] can bring a good complexion to the person who takes it. Similarly, though without form or substance, karmas can influence a person. Under the influence of good karmas, a person has abundant, splendid food and drink, clothing, and other internal and external necessities. He has shapely limbs and handsome features. He has sumptuous houses and a hoard of wish-fulfilling pearls, gold, silver, and other treasures. He is peaceful, happy, well-amused, and satisfied. It should be known that all these are the manifestations of good karmas. To be reborn in a lowly, distant, poor region, to lack the necessities of life, to envy others' happiness, to have coarse food or no food, to be shabby and ugly in appearance, to stay in inferior places—all these, you should know, are the manifestations of evil karmas.

"A clear mirror reflects the beauty or ugliness of a face, but the image of the face in the mirror is insubstantial and ungraspable. Similarly, under the influence of good or evil karmas, the consciousness is born in a plane of humans, gods, hell-dwellers, animals, or others. Great Medicine, you should know that karmas stay with the consciousness when it leaves one body for another.". . .

Great Medicine asked. "World-Honored One, how can this soft, subtle consciousness penetrate a hard form?"

The Buddha answered, "Great Medicine, water is extremely soft, yet torrents and cataracts can pierce mountain rocks. What do you think? How soft is water and how hard is a rock?"

Great Medicine said, "World-Honored One, a rock may be as hard as a diamond, while water is soft and pleasant to the touch."

[The Buddha said,] "Great Medicine, the same is true with the consciousness. It is extremely soft and subtle, but it can penetrate into a hard, big body in which to undergo karmic results.". . .

Great Medicine asked the Buddha, "World-Honored One, how can the formless consciousness give birth to a form by virtue of causes and conditions? . . ."

The Buddha replied, "Great Medicine, two pieces of wood rubbed together can produce fire by friction. The fire cannot be found within the wood. However, without the wood, there would be no fire. The fire arises from the combination of causes and conditions; without sufficient causes and conditions, no fire is produced. No one can find the form of the fire within the wood, but the fire which comes from the wood is visible to all.

"In the same way, Great Medicine, the consciousness gives birth to the corporeal body through the union of the parents. However, the consciousness cannot be found either within the corporeal body or apart from it.

"Great Medicine, before the fire is built, no attributes of fire appear, such as warmth and so on. Similarly, Great Medicine, without the body, there would be no appearance of the consciousnesses, feelings, conceptions, or impulses.

"Great Medicine, the sun shines brightly, but ordinary people are unable to know whether the substance of the sun is black, white, yellow, or red, because they have not seen it. However, from the functions of the sun, such as its giving forth light and warmth and its rising and setting, they know that the sun exists. Similarly, *from the functions of the consciousness, it is known that there is a consciousness.*"

Great Medicine asked the Buddha, "What are the functions of the consciousness?"

The Buddha replied, "Great Medicine, feeling, awareness, conception, impulse, thought, grief, sorrow, and distress—all these are functions of the consciousness. The good and evil karmas, which have become seeds sown in the consciousness by pervading it repeatedly, also reveal the consciousness by their functions.". . .

When the Buddhas had explained this sūtra, all those in the assembly, including Elder Wise Protector, Prince Great Medicine, the monks, Bodhisattva-Mahāsattvas, gods, asuras, gandharvas, and so forth, were jubilant over the Buddha's teaching and began to practice it with veneration.

NOTES

1. Buddhism does not usually treat consciousness as an individual unity, but as a group of different consciousnesses. However, in this sūtra the totality of different consciousnesses is viewed as a unity. This consciousness differs from the various component consciousnesses, such as the eye- or visual consciousness, the ear- or auditory consciousness, and so forth.

This sūtra seems to be one of the forerunners or germinal sources of the Mind-Only philosophy of the Yogācāra school. The reader will find that the consciousness discussed here is in many ways similar to the Yogācāra idea of the 'store consciousness' (*ālayavijñāna*). The store consciousness is also called the 'fundamental consciousness', which stores or upholds memory, impressions, and karmic power. Some Buddhists believe that without it, the doctrines of reincarnation, karma, supreme enlightenment of Buddhahood, and, ultimately, the altruistic deeds of a Bodhisattva would not be possible. (G.C.)

2. A term of respect.

3. Literally, "entrances" (*āyatana,* Ch. 入). A special term denoting the six sense-organs and the six sense-objects or sensations, making up twelve entrances to perception.

Here the text reads, "taking all the sense-fields with it." However, we should not interpret this to mean that the consciousness carries the biological sense-organs or their objects with it. Instead, it may be presumed that this refers to the consciousness's carrying with it the impressions and habits of the former life's sense-organ and sense-object complex, thus creating a new, complete, ethereal mind-body complex of the intermediate existence between death and reincarnation (Tib. *bar-do*). (G.C.)

4. These questions and others raised later are not all clearly answered in the text below. However none of the major points of explanation of the consciousness have been omitted in our translation.

5. The text here reads 遷, literally meaning to move from one place to another, which would translate as 'transmigration'.

In certain passages of the text, *The Questions of King Milinda,* the concept of transmigration is severely criticized and refuted; instead of 'transmigration' that sūtra says that 'reincarnation' should be used. However, this may only be a problem of semantics. As long as one does not cling to an eternal, unchanging, indivisible substance of 'self' there will be no conflict with the basic Buddhist no-self (*anātman*) doctrine. Consciousness can transmigrate without being considered as an eternal and indestructible self. Furthermore, the problem of transmigration and reincarnation can be treated on two different levels. On the mundane level, the existence of a consciousness which transmigrates can be admitted. However, on a higher level, even this consciousness is without substance or entity. (G.C.)

6. It should be noted that in other contexts and Buddhist scriptures, pure consciousness is said to have light.

7. Ch. 受覺法界. The second item in the series, 覺, is here translated as 'awareness'. The usage of 覺 here is rather unusual; it is not found in the regular numerical series in Buddhist terminology. 法界 is not used in the usual sense of dharmadātu.

The word 'dharmas' (法) here is also used in an unusual sense (see the Glossary for its ordinary meaning). It probably refers to the impressions and habits left in the consciousness. It is not clear to me whether 法界 (dharma-realm) here refers to the universe or to the realm of entities. (G.C.)

8. Both the Abhidharma and Yogācāra schools seem to believe that within or behind each of the five sense-organs there is a corresponding pure organ of form (淨色根). These organs are invisible to ordinary human beings, and only those with the deva-eye can see them.

Here the text reads, "the organ of touch" (身根), but the other version of this sūtra, translated by Jñānagupta (Taishō 310, chapter 39, p. 610), reads "the olfactory organ," which is more appropriate. (G.C.)

9. Here the text reads, "From consciousness comes feeling. . . ." This seems to mean that from fundamental consciousness—the forerunner of the concept of store consciousness—all feelings, or sensations, can arise. That is to say, without the fundamental consciousness serving as a substratum to uphold the views and impressions impinging upon the sense-organ complex, no feelings could possibly arise.

"From feeling comes awareness" presumably means that from pleasant, unpleasant, or neutral feelings come different kinds of awareness, i.e., pain, pleasure, and so forth.

"From awareness come dharmas" seems to suggest the Yogācāra idea of the 'seed' (種子) or 'habit' (習氣) of consciousness. Memory is only possible when an impression is planted. Impression is not possible without awareness, for impression simply means the awareness of objects (dharmas) being impressed upon the consciousness. This, perhaps, is the significance of the statement "from awareness come dharmas." However, it can also be interpreted to mean that when the consciousness of a person leaves the dead body, it takes along with it the impressions and habits regarding dharmas. These impressions and habits will serve as the seed of his character in the next life. (See also note 7 above.)

Impressions include moral impressions and judgments; thus, "one can tell good from evil." (G.C.)

10. 'Self-nature' (自性) here does not imply the quality of clinging to self-nature (*svabhāva*), but simply denotes the particular nature of consciousness as sentient beings perceive it.

11. See Glossary. In this sūtra it is difficult to identify which meaning (or meanings) of 'dharmadhātu' are intended.

12. Here we clearly see the emergence of the concept of the store consciousness.

13. A kind of fragrant yellow flower.

14. In other scriptures, such as the *Mahāyānasaṁgraha Śāstra,* we do find statements that the consciousness leaves the body through a specific orifice. For instance, if the being is destined to take rebirth in heaven, the consciousness will leave through the "pure orifice" on the head; if the being will fall to hell, the consciousness will leave through the anus or feet, etc. (G.C.)

15. Precise translation of this plant's name is uncertain.

16. In the previous paragraph the consciousness is compared to a seed from which grows a plant; in this paragraph it is compared to the earth which nourishes all plants. This seems to indicate that 'consciousness' as used in the sūtra can mean either the consciousness of a sentient being, or the cosmic consciousness underlying all sentient beings, or both. (G.C.)

17. The text reads, "由法界中念力強大." The Chinese 法界 here seems not to denote the 'element of dharmas' within the eighteen dhātus, but instead it strongly suggests the dharmadhātu of totality which is embraced by and identical with the root-consciousness (根本識). Again, we see a germinal idea of Yogācāra philosophy.

18. The Chinese word 風 may be translated either as 'wind' or 'air'. I presume that here it is the equivalent of 氣 which translates the Sanskrit *prāṇa*. This term can mean vitality, spirit, vital breath, or air. According to tantric doctrine, the consciousness of a sentient being cannot live independently of prāṇa. Mind and prāṇa form a two-in-one unity. Mind is the functional awareness, whereas prāṇa has the function of activity and power. At the time of death, when the consciousness leaves the old body and transmigrates elsewhere, it carries the subtle prāṇa with it. (G.C.)

19. Common sense tells us that a man born blind does not see colors or shapes in dreams. However, this passage may refer to one who can remember his past lives. It is through his memory of past lives that the man born blind can see forms in a dream.

20. This does not mean that the actual sense-organs and sense-objects go with the consciousness. See note 3 above.

21. Literally, "it has the cause of form as its body."

22. The translations 'bimba' and 'Persian date' are uncertain.

23. This refers to a sentient being in the intermediate state (Tib. *bar-do*), in which there is an ethereal body without tangible biological constituents.

24. The translation of 蘇 as 'butter' is uncertain.

25. Literally, "elements."

26. This passage only refers to the consciousness of a sentient being with good karmas, who is destined to be born in heaven.

27. Literally, "elements and entrances."

28. Literally, "the body."

29. 'Rūpa' may be translated either as 'form,' which means the object of vision, or as 'object' or 'matter', which refers to any phenomenal thing. In the former usage, rūpa is one of the six sense-objects. In the latter sense, rūpa contrasts with the mind, as indicated in the Chinese phrase 色心二法 , 'two dharmas of rūpa and mind.'

30. The Chinese word 福 is an abbreviation for either 福報 or 福德 . The Sanskrit equivalent is *puṇya,* which can mean 'merit', 'virtue,' 'luck', 'fortune', 'auspiciousness', 'blessings', etc. Since the meaning is very broad, it is difficult to translate. Although we translate it here as 'blessings', it should not be understood in the theological sense. It has been necessary to translate this word as 'merit' or 'virtue' in other contexts.

31. This passage states one of the central messages of the sūtra, viz., that consciousness has no form, and yet it can manifest all forms; cannot be seen or known by ordinary people; its profundity and wonder are beyond the comprehension of the ordinary mind, and it therefore can be described only by parables.

32. This seems to refer to the sickness resulting from possession.

33. Literally, "entity."

V

On Virtue and Discipline

13 善順菩薩會

Bodhisattva Surata's Discourse

Thus have I heard. Once the Buddha was dwelling in the garden of Anāthapiṇḍada, in the Jeta Grove near Śrāvastī, respectfully surrounded by five hundred Śrāvakas, ten thousand Bodhisattvas, and others.

At that time, a Bodhisattva named Surata was living in Śrāvastī. In his past lives, he had planted good roots of all kinds in the lands of innumerable Buddhas, had served and made offerings to those Buddhas, and had attained nonregression from the pursuit of supreme enlightenment. Dwelling in great kindness, he was free of anger or resentment at heart. Dwelling in great compassion, he never tired of saving others. Dwelling in great joy, he was always in harmony with the dharmadhātu. Dwelling in great equanimity, he saw the equality of misery and happiness.[1] He ate sparingly and at the proper time, had few desires, and was content. Sentient beings were always glad to see him. Out of his compassion for the people in the city, he constantly taught them the five lay precepts and the eight special precepts, and urged them to cultivate [the pāramitās of] giving, discipline, patience, vigor, meditation, and wisdom; also kindness, compassion, joy, and equanimity; and pure conduct.

One day, Bodhisattva Surata, surrounded by an assembly of sentient beings, was about to lead them to see the Buddha and hear the Dharma. Śakra, king of the gods, saw with his clear deva-eye that Surata cultivated austerities and observed the pure precepts, both with remarkable diligence, and that he was firm in his efforts to deliver sentient beings. Śakra thought to himself, "Surata never neglects to cultivate pure conduct. Does he not intend to usurp my throne? Is he not greedy for kingship and pleasures?"

With this in mind, Śakra conjured up four strong men, who went to the Bodhisattva and abused him with all kinds of foul language, beat him with sticks,

Sūtra 27, Taishō 310, pp. 536–540; translated into Chinese by Bodhiruci.

hurt him with knives, and threw tiles and stones at him. However, abiding in the power of kindness and patience, the Bodhisattva endured all this without feeling anger or hatred.

Then Śakra conjured up four more men, who went to the Bodhisattva and said, "Surata, those wicked men scolded and insulted you with evil language, and harmed you with tiles, stones, knives, and sticks, for no reason at all. Why not let us avenge you? We will kill those men for you."

Surata said to them, "Good men, do not say such things! Killing is evil karma. Even if someone should cut me into as many pieces as the leaves of a date tree, I would not think of killing him. Why? Because a killer will fall to the plane of hell-dwellers, hungry ghosts, or animals. Even if he gains a human body, he will always be detested by people, and even his own parents will not love him.

"Good men, all dharmas may generally be grouped into two categories: wholesome and unwholesome. Unwholesome dharmas lead to rebirth in the miserable planes of existence, while wholesome dharmas lead to benefit and blessing."

Then Bodhisattva Surata repeated this in verse:

"As in planting, happiness and misery
Result from the deeds performed.
How can a bitter seed
Yield a sweet fruit?

Seeing this universal truth,
The wise should think:
Evildoing brings painful results,
While good deeds always lead
To peace and happiness."

Hearing this, the men whom Śakra had conjured up realized that they would never be able to cause Surata to kill, and they at once disappeared.

Then Śakra magically produced a huge amount of gold, silver, and other treasures, along with some men, who brought the treasures to the Bodhisattva, saying, "You may take these treasures if you like. They are at your disposal."

At this, Surata told them, "Good men, do not say such things. Why not? Because the karma of stealing can make sentient beings poor, lowly, inferior, and helpless. Even if I were so poor that I could not maintain my life, I would never take anything not belonging[2] to me. You should know that ordinary people are silly, ignorant, and enveloped in desire. How can a wise person take anything not belonging to him?"

Then Bodhisattva Surata spoke in verse:

"One who accumulates billions
And is greedily attached [to his wealth],

Unable to give it away,
Is said by the wise
To be a man ever poor in the world.

A penniless man
Who will readily give whatever he has
Is said by the wise
To be the noblest and richest on earth.

The wise, being free from all evil,
Have forms of perfect magnificence;
But fools, due to their transgressions,
Are ugly from head to foot.

The wise persuade others to do good;
Fools are always for evil.
It is better to be scolded by the wise
Than to be praised by fools."

When they heard this, the men conjured up by Śakra went away disappointed. Then Śakra himself went to test Surata. Taking with him a great amount of gold, he approached the Bodhisattva and said, "I have been in contention with some people in Śrāvastī [in the court of] King Prasenajit. I need someone to give false testimony for me. If you can be my witness, I will give you all this gold."

The Bodhisattva told Śakra, "Virtuous one, you should know that it is evil karma to lie. A liar lies to himself as well as to gods, dragons, yakṣas, gandharvas, asuras, garuḍas, kinnaras and mahoragas. Lying is the origin of all evils; it leads to rebirth in the miserable planes of existence, to breach of the pure precepts, and to corruption of the body. A liar's mouth will often reek, and his words will be scorned and despised."

Then Bodhisattva Surata spoke in verse:

"A liar's mouth will give off a stench.
He will fall to the miserable realms,
Where no one can rescue him.

A liar lies not only
To gods, dragons, mahoragas, and others;
He also lies to himself.

Know that lying
Is the origin of all evils;
It destroys one's pure discipline
And brings one to rebirth
In the three miserable realms.

Even if you gave me enough gold
To fill the entire world,
Never would I tell a lie."

Hearing this, Śakra disappeared at once. Then he ordered the goddesses[3] Śacī, Sūryaprabha, Pañcacūḍa, and others to go to Surata to test him again, by trying to make him break the precepts. Along with five hundred young goddesses, Śacī and the others anointed their bodies with perfumed ointment and adorned themselves with flowers and other beautiful ornaments. They went to the Bodhisattva late at night, saying, "We are lovely women in the prime of life. We wish to share your pillow and bed so that we may enjoy each other."

Looking at those women with his stainless eyes, Surata said to them, "You are relatives and friends of hell-dwellers, animals, beings of the Yama Realm, lunatics, evil-minded people, and atrocious rākṣasas[4] that gorge themselves on stinking, filthy pus and blood and indulge in impure love. You do not belong to the pure family of gods."

Then the Bodhisattva spoke in verse:

"Confused and full of impure thoughts,
Fools are attached to the stinking, filthy body
Filled with pus and blood.
All that they desire, though,
Will quickly perish
And pass into nought.
Then, such fools will fall to hell,
The realm of Yama, and there remain.

Even if all the women in the world
Were transformed into goddesses
As lovely as you,
My mind would remain pristine,
Innocent of even the subtlest desire.
I would regard them all
As dreams or enemies."

Śacī and the other goddesses flirted to the utmost, but the Bodhisattva was not in the least stirred to passion. They returned to the celestial palace and told Śakra, "We found Surata to be resolute. No doubt he will attain supreme enlightenment. Why? Because he is free of even the slightest craving for us. He abhors us all."

Although Śakra heard this, he was still worried and upset and felt as though he had been shot by an arrow. Again and again he thought, "No doubt he will ruin me and deprive me of what is mine. I must now test him once again to determine his true purpose."

With this in mind, Śakra went to Surata. Giving up his conceit and arrogance and prostrating himself with his head at the Bodhisattva's feet, he asked in verse:

"Virtuous one, you are most diligent
In cultivating pure conduct.
What, then, is your aim?
To be a sun-god, a moon-god,
An indra, or a brahmā?
Do you strive for the throne
Of any king in the three realms?"

Bodhisattva Surata answered in verse:

"To me, the rewards of being a sun-god,
A moon-god, an indra, or a brahmā;
Or of being a worldly king
In the three realms
Are all impermanent and insubstantial.
How can the wise seek these?"

Hearing this, Śakra inquired, "If you speak truly, what then do you seek?" The Bodhisattva answered in verse:

"I covet not worldly pleasure,
But seek only that body[5]
Subject to neither birth nor death.
Tirelessly I cultivate ingenuity
To deliver sentient beings,
So that together we may tread
The path to enlightenment."

When he heard this, Śakra felt happy and secure, and was sure at last that Surata did not strive for his throne. Overjoyed, he praised the Bodhisattva in verse:

"You say you wish to save sentient beings.
Great is your ambition—
Indeed, it is unequaled.

May you defeat the demon-hordes
And realize the ambrosial [Dharma],
And thenceforth turn forever
The sublime Dharma-wheel."

After he spoke this verse, Śakra respectfully circumambulated Surata, prostrated himself with his head at the Bodhisattva's feet, and then disappeared in an instant.

The next morning, when Bodhisattva Surata was making his rounds teaching people in the city of Śrāvastī, he found a gold bell made at the beginning of the kalpa, which was worth more than the world itself. The Bodhisattva held the gold bell in his hand and called out at the main crossroads of the city, "Who is the poorest in the city of Śrāvastī? I shall give him this bell."

When the oldest elder of the city heard this, he came running and said to Surata, "I am the poorest in the city. You may give me that bell."

Surata told the elder, "You are not poor. Why do I say so? Because in the city there is a good man who is the poorest of the poor. I shall give him the bell."

The elder asked, "Who is this man?"

Surata answered, "King Prasenajit is the poorest in the city."

The elder said to Surata, "Do not say so. Why? Because King Prasenajit is very rich and noble; his treasury is overflowing with wealth and precious things that will never be exhausted. Why do you say he is the poorest of the poor?"

Surrounded by the assembly [he had been teaching], the Bodhisattva answered in verse:

"If one has a treasury of billions
And yet, due to greed, is still unsatisfied,
He is like a great ocean,
Which never has enough
Of the myriad streams it swallows.
Such a fool is the poorest of the poor.

If such a fool allows his greed
To grow, spread, and perpetuate,
He will always be needy
In his present and future lives."

After speaking this verse, Bodhisattva Surata went with the assembly to see King Prasenajit. At that time, the king, with five hundred elders, was counting and checking the valuables in his treasury. The Bodhisattva approached the king and said, "This morning when I was making my rounds teaching the people in the city, I found a gold bell made at the beginning of the kalpa, which is worth more than the world itself. At that time, I thought to myself, 'I should take the bell and give it to the poorest person in the city.' Then I thought, 'The poorest in the city is His Majesty.' Now I want to offer the bell to Your Majesty. Since Your Majesty is the poorest, please accept it from me."

Having said this, the Bodhisattva spoke further in verse:

"Such a senseless man
Who is monstrously greedy
And amasses riches insatiably
Is called the poorest of all.

Your Majesty, you levy harsh taxes
And punish the innocent for no reason.
Infatuated with your sovereignity,
You never heed
The future effects of your karmas.

While you enjoy power in this world,
You do not protect your subjects,
And have no pity
For the poor and suffering.

You indulge in women's company
Without any fear of falling
To the miserable planes of existence.
You are not even conscious
Of your outrageous wickedness—
Are you not poor?

If one practices mindfulness diligently
And delights in self-control,
He is called rich and noble,
And his wealth of goodness will bring him
Eternal peace and joy.

As a roaring conflagration
Never has enough wood to consume,
So, O King, your avarice
Is never satiated.

As the water can always engulf more clouds,
And the ocean never overflows with water,
So are you, O King,
Never satiated.

As the sun and moon
Incessantly course through space,
So you, O King, will never rest
In all your life.

A wise person, though,
Like roaring flames

Insatiably devouring wood,
Never ceases to do good.

As the water can ever engulf more clouds,
And the ocean never overflows with water,
So a wise man is never satiated
With his ever-increasing goodness.

Although the throne gives power,
It is, after all, impermanent.
All such things are impure;
The wise should abandon them."

When he heard this, King Prasenajit felt shame and remorse, but he said to Surata, "Well said, virtuous one. Although you are very persuasive, I still do not believe you. Is all that you have said merely your own opinion? Can someone else bear witness to its truth?"

The Bodhisattva replied, "The Tathāgata, the Worthy One, the Supremely Enlightened One, who is endowed with all-knowing wisdom, is now dwelling near Śrāvastī in the garden of Anāthapiṇḍada in the Jeta Grove, together with countless gods, humans, gandharvas, asuras, and so forth. Do you not know that? He will bear witness that Your Majesty is a poor man."

The king said, "Virtuous one, if what you say is true, then I will go with you to see the Tathāgata, listen to his teaching, take refuge in him, and make offerings to him."

The Bodhisattva said, "Your Majesty should know that the state of the Tathāgata cannot be fathomed by ignorant, ordinary persons. He is free of all afflictions and arrogance, and has great compassion for sentient beings. He knows the present and the future through his saintly wisdom. He will protect anyone who has good roots and superior aspirations, even if he is far away. If he knows that I wish to convince Your Majesty, he will surely come here and be my witness."

Then, in the presence of the king, Surata bared his right shoulder, kflt on his right knee, respectfully joined his palms, and with this verse invited the Tathāgata to appear:

"The Tathāgata, with true wisdom,
Has compassion for sentient beings.
May he discern the depth of my mind
And be so kind as to be my witness."

The moment the Bodhisattva finished speaking, the ground suddenly quaked and burst open, and the Tathāgata sprang from the chasm, surrounded by five hundred Śrāvakas; ten thousand Bodhisattvas; brahmās, śakras, gods, dragons, spirits, and countless other sentient beings.

Bodhisattva Surata then approached the Buddha with his palms respectfully joined, and said, "World-Honored One, this morning when I was teaching people in the city, I found a gold bell made at the beginning of the kalpa, which is worth more than the entire world itself. I thought, 'I shall give this bell to the poorest person in the city of Śrāvastī.' Then I thought, 'King Prasenajit is the poorest in the city.' Why? Presumptuously resting on his throne, His Majesty has no sympathy for sentient beings. He oppresses, exploits, cheats, and robs them, and harms them unreasonably. He is wrapped in insatiable greed and passion. Therefore, I consider him to be the poorest of men and wish to give him the gold bell.

"His Majesty asked me, 'You say that I am the poorest. Who can prove it to be true?'

"I answered, 'The Tathāgata, the Great Master, the Worthy One, the Supremely Enlightened One, is free of all afflictions, without the slightest trace of hatred, and treats all sentient beings impartially. He will prove the truth of my statement.' May the World-Honored One instruct, benefit, and gladden us!"

Thereupon, wishing to subdue King Prasenajit, the Tathāgata told him, "Your Majesty should know that from one viewpoint, Surata is poor but Your Majesty is rich. From another viewpoint, Your Majesty is poor but Surata is rich. Why? Being enthroned, Your Majesty has worldly power, and your treasury is full of gold, silver, pearsl, sapphires, and corals. In this respect, Surata is poor but Your Majesty rich.

"However, Surata cultivates pure conduct diligently, delights in the pure precepts, has left the household life, has acquired great learning, shuns self-indulgence, and tirelessly delivers large numbers of people by teaching them the five lay precepts and the eight special precepts. Any one of these merits is enough to show that Your Majesty is poor but Surata rich. Your Majesty should know that all the wealth and treasures of the sentient beings in the kingdom of Kosala[6] cannot equal one hundredth, one thousandth, or one millionth of Surata's [treasury of] firmness and purity in keeping the five lay precepts and the eight special precepts."

Hearing for himself the true teaching of the Tathāgata, King Prasenajit abandoned all his conceit and arrogance. Looking up at Surata attentively, he joined his palms and said in verse:

"How wonderful!
You have thwarted my arrogance.
You will acquire
The supreme body of a Tathāgata.
I will abdicate my throne in your favor
And wish to remain forever
Among your enlightened assembly.

I am indeed poor, but you are rich.
Now I know your words are true.

A throne is only a cause of great suffering,
Compelling one to act against good doctrines
And be reborn in the miserable planes of existence."

After speaking this verse, King Prasenajit said to the Buddha, "World-Honored One, I now vow to attain supreme enlightenment. I wish that sentient beings may be secure, happy, and free from the bondage of saṁsāra.

"I will now divide all my wealth and treasures of gold, silver, and so forth into three parts. One portion I will offer to the Tathāgata, the World-Honored One, and to the assembly of monks. Another portion I will give to the poor, distressed, and helpless people in the city of Śrāvastī. The third portion will be reserved for state use. I will offer all my gardens, ponds, flowers, and fruit trees to the Supreme Tathāgata and to the assembly of monks. May the World-Honored One be so kind as to accept them!"

Seeing this occur, five hundred elders of Kosala all engendered supreme bodhicitta.

Then Bodhisattva Surata said to the Buddha, "World-Honored One, may the Tathāgata teach the essence of the Dharma to the assembly so that those who have met the Tathāgata may not have met him in vain!"

The World-Honored One told the assembly, "Good people, there are three provisions of immeasurable merits, merits which cannot be fully enumerated even by Tathāgatas, let alone by Śrāvakas or Pratyekabuddhas. What are the three? To protect and uphold the true Dharma, to bring forth bodhicitta, and to persuade others to make unexcelled vows.

"Furthermore, there are thirty-two Dharmas that good men and good women must practice industriously in order not to have met the Tathāgata in vain:

(1) To have indestructible faith in Tathāgatas;
(2) to protect and uphold the true Dharma so that it may endure;
(3) to esteem the members of the Sagha and never to slight them;
(4) to respect and closely associate with Arhats;
(5) to have an equal mind toward what is lovable or hateful;
(6) always to be fond of hearing the true Dharma and to respect it;
(7) to abide securely in quietude and tranquillity and to shun noise and disturbance;
(8) to teach the Tathāgata-vehicle untiringly;
(9) to teach the Dharma, but not for the sake of fame or profit;
(10) to strive for the truth and practice assiduously in accordance with it;
(11 to practice giving;
(12) to observe discipline;
(13) to have patience;
(14) to strive with vigor;
(15) to cultivate meditation;

(16) to develop true wisdom;
(17) to take good care of sentient beings in accordance with their wishes;
(18) to bring all sentient beings to maturity, so that they may not fall away from the Dharma;
(19) always to subdue oneself well;
(20) to subdue others by skillfully making use of the essence of the Dharma;
(21) not to be contaminated by any defilements;
(22) to delight in leaving the household life;
(23) to live in a forest hermitage;
(24) to rejoice in cultivating the four noble practices;
(25) to practice austerities diligently;
(26) to give up unwholesome dharmas;
(27) to be firm in one's great vows;
(28) to lead the life of a forest-dweller conscientiously;
(29) to plant good roots;
(30) always to abide in self-control;
(31) to abandon the views of the two vehicles; and
(32) to praise the Mahāyāna."

When they heard this doctrine preached, five hundred monks were freed from defilements and achieved the pure Dharma-eye; twelve thousand sentient beings resolved to attain supreme enlightenment.

After benefiting sentient beings by preaching the Dharma, the World-Honored One, together with the monks and others who had appeared [with him in the king's treasury], suddenly disappeared.

Having seen all this, King Prasenajit was jubilant. He gave Bodhisattva Surata two garments, each of which cost one hundred thousand taels of gold, and said, "Wonderful, virtuous one! Please be so kind as to accept these."

Bodhisattva Surata told the king, "Your Majesty should know that I should not take these two garments. Why so? Because I have a patched robe, which I often hang on a branch in lieu of a closet. No one has ever thought of taking it away from me by fraud or by force. Pure are the gifts given by those who are not only free of avarice themselves, but also cause others not to be attached to anything."

At this, King Prasenajit said, "If you do not accept them, please, for my sake, tread upon them to bring me the benefit of peace and happiness in the long night [of saṁsāra]." For the king's sake, Surata trod upon the two garments.

King Prasenajit then told the Bodhisattva, "Now you have personally accepted the garments. What is the use of them to me?"

Bodhisattva Surata told the king, "Take the garments to the poor, distressed people in the city who have no one to depend on."

As instructed by the Bodhisattva, King Prasenajit called the poor people together and gave them the two garments. When they touched the clothes, the lunatics regained their sanity, the deaf regained their hearing, the blind regained their sight, and the deformed were made whole again, all because of Surata's awesome miraculous power.

The people said in unison, "What can we offer Bodhisattva Surata in return for his kindness?"

A voice from the sky told them, "Know that you cannot repay his kindness by offering him flowers, incense, food, or beverage; you can do so only by immediately engendering bodhicitta."

When the five hundred poor people heard this voice from the sky, they all spoke in verse:

"Now we resolve to attain bodhi.
We shall become perfectly enlightened
And teach the superb doctrines,
To give peace and joy to sentient beings.

We delight in bodhi,
For we have obtained the Buddha-Dharma."

Then King Prasenajit said to Surata, "Wonderful, virtuous one. Please tell me when you will go to see the Tathāgata. I shall follow you."

Bodhisattva Surata advised him, "Your Majesty should know that it is very rare to meet a Buddha and hear the true Dharma. Your Majesty should not go alone. Instead, be a good friend to sentient beings and order all the people in the city of Śrāvastī to follow you there. Decree that anyone who disobeys your instructions will be punished according to the royal ordinance. Why? Because just as a Bodhisattva is adorned by the retinue surrounding him, a king should also be thus adorned."

King Prasenajit asked the Bodhisattva, "What is the retinue of a Bodhisattva?"

Surata replied, "To persuade sentient beings to engender bodhicitta is the retinue of a Bodhisattva, because it causes them to be enlightened.

"To persuade sentient beings to see the Tathāgata is the retinue of a Bodhisattva, because they will then not be misled.

"To persuade sentient beings to hear the true Dharma is the retinue of a Bodhisattva, because it causes them to have great learning.

"To persuade sentient beings to see the noble assembly[7] is the retinue of a Bodhisattva, because it enables them to have virtuous friends.

"The four inducements are the retinue of a Bodhisattva, because they attract sentient beings [to the Buddha-Dharma].

"The six pāramitās are the retinue of a Bodhisattva, because they enhance the growth of enlightenment.

"The thirty-seven ways to enlightenment are the retinue of a Bodhisattva, because they lead to the bodhi-site.

"Adorned and guarded by such a retinue, a Bodhisattva can defeat the demon-hordes, make the lion's roar, and ascend to the supreme state."

At this, King Prasenajit and the entire assembly were overjoyed. Nine thousand sentient beings were freed from defilements and obtained the clear [Dharma-] eye.

After the Buddha had spoken this sūtra,[8] Bodhisattva Surata, King Prasenajit, the gods, humans, gandharvas, asuras, and so forth were jubilant over the Buddha's teaching and began to practice it with veneration.

NOTES

1. Kindness, compassion, joy, and equanimity are called the four immeasurables.
2. Literally, "given."
3. I.e., Śakra's consorts.
4. Rākṣasas are demonic, terrifying spirits that are said to devour human beings.
5. This probably refers to the Dharma-body of the Buddha.
6. The city of Śrāvastī was located in the kingdom of northern Kosala (Uttarakosala, the modern Oude), over which King Prasenajit reigned. "Kosala" is sometimes spelled "Kośala" in other texts.
7. I.e., the Saṁgha.
8. Although Surata preached most of this sūtra, the traditional conclusion has been retained. One might say that Surata's preaching was inspired by the Buddha and his teachings.

14 妙慧童女會

Sumati's Questions

Thus have I heard. Once the Buddha was dwelling on Mount Gṛdhrakūṭa near Rājagṛha, accompanied by twelve hundred fifty great monks and ten thousand Bodhisattva-Mahāsattvas.

At that time, an elder's daughter named Sumati, who was only eight years old, was living in the city of Rājagṛha. She had graceful features and was exquisitely beautiful. Because of her beauty and grace, she was adored by everyone who saw her. In her past lives, she had associated closely with innumerable Buddhas, had made offerings to them, and had planted good roots of every kind.

One day this young girl went to visit the Tathāgata. When she arrived, she paid homage to the Buddha by bowing down with her head at his feet and circumambulating him three times to the right. Then, kneeling with her palms joined, she spoke to the Buddha in verse:

"Unexcelled, Perfectly Enlightened One,
Great, brillant light of the world,
Please listen to my questions
About the practices of a Bodhisattva."

The Buddha told Sumati, "Ask whatever questions you wish. I will explain the answers to you and resolve your doubts."

Then Sumati asked the Buddha in verse:

"How does one obtain graceful features,
Or great wealth and nobility?

Sūtra 30, Taishō 310, pp. 547–549; translated into Chinese by Bodhiruci.

What causes one's rebirth
Among harmonious relatives and friends?

By what means may one be born ethereally,
Seated upon a thousand-petaled lotus,
To worship the Buddhas face to face?

How can one obtain a free command
Of superb, miraculous powers,
And thus journey to countless Buddha-lands
To pay homage to myriad Buddhas?

How can one be free from enmity
And cause others to believe one's words?
How may all hindrances to Dharma be removed
And evil deeds forever cast away?

At the end of one's life,
How may one see many Buddhas,
And then, free of pain,
Hear them preach the pure Dharma?

Most Compassionate, Supremely Honored One,
Please tell me all this."

The Buddha said to the young girl Sumati, "Excellent, excellent! It is good that you raise such profound questions. Now, listen carefully and think well about this. I will tell you."

Sumati said, "Yes, World-Honored One, I will listen with pleasure."

The Buddha said, "Sumati, if a Bodhisattva achieves four things, he will be endowed with a graceful appearance. What are the four?

(1) Not to be angry [even] with a bad friend;
(2) to have great kindness;
(3) to rejoice in the true Dharma; and
(4) to make images of Buddhas."

The World-Honored One repeated this in verse:

"Harbor no hatred, which destroys good roots.
Rejoice in the Dharma, be kind,
And make images of Buddhas.
These will give you a well-formed body,
An ever-delightful sight to all."

The Buddha continued, "Furthermore, Sumati, if a Bodhisattva achieves four things, he will be endowed with wealth and nobility. What are the four?

(1) To give timely gifts;
(2) to give without contempt or arrogance;
(3) to give cheerfully; and
(4) to expect no reward."

The World-Honored One repeated this in verse:

"To give timely gifts without contempt or arrogance,
To give gladly without expecting a reward—
One who diligently practices these
Will be reborn with wealth and nobility."

The Buddha continued, "Furthermore, Sumati, if a Bodhisattva achieves four things, he will have harmonious friends and kinsmen. What are the four?

(1) To avoid using words that cause disagreement;
(2) to help those with wrong views to have right view;
(3) to protect the true Dharma from extinction, causing it to endure; and
(4) to teach sentient beings to pursue the Buddha's enlightenment."

The World-Honored One repeated this in verse:

"Sow no discord, help uproot wrong views,
Protect the true Dharma from extinction,
And bring all beings within the secure embrace of bodhi.
For this you will have harmonious friends and kinsmen." . . .

The Buddha continued, "Furthermore, Sumati, if a Bodhisattva achieves four things, he will be able to live among people without enmity. What are the four?

(1) To be close to virtuous friends without using flattery;
(2) not to envy others' superiority;
(3) to rejoice when someone wins a good reputation; and
(4) not to slight or defame the practices of a Bodhisattva."

The World-Honored One repeated this in verse:

"If one does not win friends by flattery,
Is not jealous of others' superiority,
Always rejoices when others gain fame,
And never slanders a Bodhisattva,
He will be free of enmity."

The Buddha continued, "Furthermore, Sumati, a Bodhisattva's words will be trusted if he practices four things. What are the four?

(1) To be consistent in word and deed;
(2) not to conceal one's evil from friends;
(3) never to find fault with the Dharma one hears; and
(4) not to foster malice against a teacher of the Dharma."

The World-Honored One repeated this in verse:

"One who is consistent in word and deed,
And never hides misdeeds from friends,
Nor finds fault with a sūtra or its preacher
Will have his words believed."

The Buddha continued, "Furthermore, Sumati, if a Bodhisattva achieves four things, he will meet no obstacles to [his practice of] the Dharma and will quickly gain purity. What are the four?

(1) To embrace the three rules of conduct[1] with deep joy;
(2) not to disparage profound sūtras when hearing them;
(3) to treat a newly avowed Bodhisattva as an All-Knowing One; and
(4) to be equally kind toward all beings."

The World-Honored One repeated this in verse:

"If one, with deep joy, embraces rules of conduct;
Understands with faith the profound discourses;
Honors a novice as a Buddha;
And is equally kind toward all—
Then such a person's hindrances will vanish."

The Buddha continued, "Furthermore, Sumati, if a Bodhisattva achieves four things, he will be protected from demons. What are the four?

(1) To understand that all dharmas are equal in nature;
(2) to strive vigorously for progress;
(3) to recollect the Buddha continually; and
(4) to dedicate all good roots [to the universal attainment of enlightenment]."

The World-Honored One repeated this in verse:

"If one knows that all dharmas are equal in nature,
Constantly makes energetic progress,
Is ever mindful of the Buddha,
And dedicates all roots of virtue
[To the attainment of Buddhahood by all],
No demon can devise a way to attack him."

The Buddha continued, "Furthermore, Sumati, if a Bodhisattva achieves four things, Buddhas will appear to him at the time of his death. What are the four?

(1) To satisfy those in need of charity;
(2) to understand and deeply believe in virtuous practices;
(3) to provide Bodhisattvas with adornments; and
(4) to make frequent offerings to the Three Jewels."

The World-Honored One repeated this in verse:

"One who fulfills the needs of a seeker,
Understands and believes in the profound Dharma,
Furnishes Bodhisattvas with adornments,
And makes frequent offerings
To the Three Jewels, the fields of blessing,
Will see Buddhas when he dies." . . .

Then Mañjuśrī, the Dharma Prince, asked Sumati, "In what Dharma do you abide, that you are able to make such a sincere vow?"

Sumati replied, "Mañjuśrī, this is not a proper question. Why? Because there is no abiding in the dharmadhātu."

"What is bodhi?"

"Nondiscrimination is bodhi."[2]

"Who is a Bodhisattva?"

"One who knows that all dharmas have the same nature as empty space is a Bodhisattva."

"What are the enlightened deeds [of a Bodhisattva]?"

"Deeds that are like mirages and echoes are the enlightened deeds."

"Upon what esoteric teaching do you base your statement?"

"I do not see anything in this that is esoteric or otherwise."

"If that is the case, every ordinary person should be an Enlightened One."[3]

"Do you think an ordinary person is different from an Enlightened One?[4] Do not take such a view! Why? Because they both share the same nature, that of the dharmadhātu; there is nothing in either to grasp or abandon, to accomplish or destroy."

"How many people can understand this?"

"The illusory beings who understand this are equal in number to the illusory minds and mental functions."[5]

Mañjuśrī said, "Illusions do not exist; how can there be minds and mental functions?"

"They are like the dharmadhātu, which neither exists nor does not exist. The same is true of the Tathāgata." . . .

NOTES

1. The three rules of conduct may refer to the three rules for protecting one from evil, namely, discipline, meditation, and transcendental wisdom. They may also refer to the Bodhisattvas' precepts, which include three branches: the discipline of pure conduct (Prāti-mokṣa), the discipline of altruistic deeds, and the discipline of embracing all virtuous deeds.

2. Literally, "The Dharma of nondiscrimination is bodhi."

3. Literally, "every ordinary person should be bodhi."

4. An Enlightened One: literally, "bodhi."

5. The Chinese term 心所 is here rendered as 'mental functions', but it can also mean the qualities and conditions of mind.

15 優波離會

The Definitive Vinaya

Thus have I heard. Once the Buddha was dwelling in the garden of Anāthapiṇḍada, in the Jeta Grove near Śrāvastī, accompanied by twelve hundred fifty great monks and five hundred thousand Bodhisattva-Mahāsattvas.

The World-Honored One cast his eyes upon the assembly and surveyed it like a king of dragons or elephants. Then he asked the Bodhisattva-Mahāsattvas, "Good men, which one of you can, in the Last Era, protect and uphold the true Dharma? Which one of you can embrace the Dharma leading to supreme enlightenment—the Dharma which took the Tathāgata incalculable hundreds of thousands of [millions of] billions of myriads of kalpas to accumulate—and abide securely in the esoteric [teachings] to bring sentient beings to maturity by various skillful means?"

Then Bodhisattva Maitreya rose from his seat, bared his right shoulder, knelt on his right knee, joined his palms, and said, "World-Honored One, I can, in the Last Era, protect and uphold the Dharma leading to supreme enlightenment—the Dharma which took the Tathāgata incalculable hundreds of thousands of [millions of] billions of myriads of kalpas to accumulate."

Bodhisattva Lion Wisdom said, "I can abide securely in the esoteric [teachings] and bring sentient beings to maturity by various skillful means."

Bodhisattva Infinite Thought said, "I can liberate inexhaustible realms of sentient beings by my great vows."

Bodhisattva Worthy said, "I can cause all sentient beings who hear my name to attain maturity without fail." . . .[1]

Bodhisattva Removing Obstruction said, "I can release sentient beings from the shackles of defilements."

Sūtra 24, Taishō 310, pp. 514–519; translated into Chinese by Bodhiruci.

Bodhisattva Wisdom Banner said, "I can rid sentient beings of the shroud of ignorance." . . .

Bodhisattva Sun Banner said, "I can constantly bring sentient beings to maturity by giving them peace and joy." . . .

Bodhisattva Good Eye said, "I can give sentient beings the peace and happiness that are in their self-nature."

Bodhisattva Avalokiteśvara said, "I can extricate sentient beings from the miserable planes of existence." . . .

Bodhisattva Universal Virtue said, "I can cause sentient beings to liberate themselves by remembering the sufferings they endured in the past." . . .

Bodhisattva Wonderfully Pliant said, "I can bring to maturity the lowly, inferior beings who have little wisdom." . . .

Bodhisattva Great Might said, "I can close the doors to all the miserable planes of existence for sentient beings." . . .

Bodhisattva Moonlight said, "I can give sentient beings ultimate peace and happiness."

Bodhisattva Sunlight said, "I can bring to maturity those sentient beings who have not yet matured."

Bodhisattva Undefiled said, "I can cause sentient beings to fulfil all their aspirations." . . .

Bodhisattva Fearless said, "I can attract sentient beings into the Buddha-Dharma by praising and benefiting them." . . .

Bodhisattva Immeasurable said, "I can show sentient beings the unconditioned truth that underlies all dharmas."

Bodhisattva Fearless said, "I can make whatever kinds of manifestations sentient beings wish." . . .

Bodhisattva Treasure Trove said, "I can deliver sentient beings from all hindrances." . . .

Bodhisattva Diamond said, "I can reveal to sentient beings the right path."

Bodhisattva Blessed Appearance said, "I can liberate sentient beings by pleasing them." . . .

Bodhisattva Undefiled said, "I can love and protect all sentient beings and thereby bring them to maturity." . . .

Bodhisattva Golden Light said, "I can appear in various corporeal forms to bring sentient beings to maturity." . . .

The youthful [Bodhisattva] Net of Light said, "I can manifest light for sentient beings to eliminate their afflictions in the Last Era."

When Śāriputra heard the Bodhisattvas valiantly make these great vows to bring sentient beings to maturity, he marveled at this unprecedented event and said to the Buddha, "Most extraordinary, World-Honored One! These Bodhisattvas are inconceivable. They are filled with great compassion and ingenuity; they adorn themselves with valor and vigor. They cannot be fathomed or corrupted by any being, nor can they be outshone by any brilliance. World-Honored One, I will extol the extraordinary feats of the Bodhisattvas: they can freely give anything they have to anyone who asks for it, including their heads, eyes, ears, noses, bodies, hands, and feet. World-Honored One, I often think that if a Bodhisattva is not afraid or fainthearted even when forced to give up all he has, external and internal, then he must be an inconceivable, liberated Bodhisattva."

The Buddha told Śāriputra, "It is so, it is so, just as you say. No Śrāvaka or Pratyekabuddha can know the state of wisdom, ingenuity, and samādhi in which these Bodhisattvas dwell.

"Śāriputra, these great Bodhisattvas, like Buddhas, can perform miraculous feats to satisfy the desires of sentient beings, while their minds remain unmoved by any dharma.

"If sentient beings are fond of the household life, haughty, and unrestrained, these Bodhisattvas can appear as great laymen of awesome virtue to teach those sentient beings the Dharma, so that they may be brought to maturity.

"If sentient beings with great strength become arrogant, the Bodhisattvas can appear in the form of a gigantic Nārāyaṇa and explain the Dharma to them, so that they may be subdued.

"If sentient beings wish to seek nirvāṇa, these Bodhisattvas can appear as Śrāvakas and explain the Dharma to them, thereby liberating them.

"If sentient beings like to contemplate dependent origination, the Bodhisattvas can appear as Pratyekabuddhas and explain the Dharma to those sentient beings, thereby liberating them.

"If sentient beings wish to attain supreme enlightenment, these Bodhisattvas can appear as Buddhas and lead them into the Buddha-wisdom, thereby liberating them.

"Thus, Śāriputra, these Bodhisattvas employ various skillful means to perfect sentient beings and cause them all to dwell securely in the Buddha-Dharma. Why? Because only the Tathāgata's wisdom can result in liberation and ultimate nirvāṇa; there is no other vehicle that can carry one to salvation. It is for this reason that the Tathāgata is called a Tathāgata. Because the Tathāgata knows thusness as it is, he is called a Tathāgata [a Thus-Come One]. Because he can do anything that sentient beings wish, he is called a Tathāgata. Because he has perfected the root of all wholesome dharmas and cut off the root of all unwholesome dharmas, he is called a Tathāgata. Because he can show sentient beings the path to liberation, he is called a Tathāgata. Because he can cause sentient beings to avoid wrong paths and remain on the right path, he is called a Tathāgata. Because he can explain the true meaning of the emptiness of all dharmas, he is called a Tathāgata.

"Śāriputra, a Bodhisattva knows the various aspirations of sentient beings, and by preaching the Dharma to them accordingly, he liberates them. He reveals true wisdom to ignorant people. He can produce all kinds of illusory splendors without affecting the dharmadhātu, and cause sentient beings to move gradually toward the shore of nirvāṇa.

"Furthermore, Śāriputra, a lay Bodhisattva who dwells in kindness and harmlessness should practice two kinds of giving. What are the two? The first is the giving of Dharma; the second is the giving of material possessions.

"A Bodhisattva who has left the household life should practice four kinds of giving. What are the four?

(1) To give pens [with which to copy sūtras];
(2) to give ink;
(3) to give scriptures; and
(4) to give instruction in the Dharma.

"A Bodhisattva who has achieved the Realization of the Nonarising of Dharmas should always be ready to give in three ways. What are the three? To give his throne; his wife and son; and his head, eyes, and limbs. To give thus is great, most wonderful giving."[2]

Śāriputra asked the Buddha, "World-Honored One, are these Bodhisattvas not afraid of desire, hatred, and ignorance?"

The Buddha answered, "Śāriputra, all Bodhisattvas should guard against two breaches of discipline. What are the two? First, to break the discipline out of hatred; second, to break the discipline out of ignorance. Both are grave breaches.

"Śāriputra, if a breach of discipline is committed out of desire, it is a fine, subtle fault, but hard to eliminate; if out of hatred, it is a gross, serious fault, but easy to eliminate; if out of ignorance, it is a very grave, deep-seated fault and very hard to eliminate.

"Why? Desire is the seed of all kinds of existence; it causes one to be involved in saṁsāra endlessly. For this reason, it is fine and subtle, but hard to sever. One who breaks the precepts out of hatred will fall to the miserable planes of existence, but may quickly get rid [of hatred]. One who breaks the precepts out of ignorance will fall to the eight great hells,[3] and have great difficulty in being released [from ignorance].[4]

"Furthermore, Śāriputra, if a Bodhisattva has committed a pārājika,[5] he should earnestly and sincerely confess his misdeed to ten pure monks (*bhikṣus*). If a Bodhisattva has committed a saṁghāveśeṣa,[6] he should earnestly confess his misdeed to five pure monks. If a Bodhisattva is affected by a woman's passion, or is attracted to her because they have exchanged glances, he should earnestly confess his misdeed to one or two pure monks.

"Śāriputra, if a Bodhisattva has committed one of the five grave offenses, a pārājika, or a saṁghāvaśeṣa; or has done harm to stūpas or monks; or has committed some other crime, he should sincerely repent in solitude day and night before the thirty-five Buddhas, saying:

"'I, so-and-so, take refuge in the Buddha, the Dharma, and the Saṁgha. Namo[7] Śākyamuni Buddha; namo Indestructible Diamond Buddha; namo Jewelled Light Buddha; namo Noble Dragon King Buddha; namo Vigorous Soldier Buddha; namo Joy of Vigor Buddha; namo Precious Flame Buddha; namo Precious Moonlight Buddha; namo Manifesting No Ignorance Buddha; namo Precious Moon

Buddha; namo Stainless Buddha; namo Unsullied Buddha; namo Courageous Giving Buddha; namo Pure Buddha; namo Pure Giving Buddha; namo Sa-Liu-Na[8] Buddha; namo Water Deva Buddha; namo Firm Virtue Buddha; namo Sandalwood Merit Buddha; namo Infinite Quantities of Light Buddha; namo Brilliant Virtue Buddha; namo Confident Virtue Buddha; namo Nārāyaṇa Buddha; namo Flower of Merit Buddha; namo Performing Miracles with Lotus Light Buddha; namo Wealth and Merit Buddha; namo Virtuous Thought Buddha; namo Good Reputation and Merit Buddha; namo King of Red, Flaming Banner Buddha; namo Roaming Well in Merits Buddha; namo Battle-Winning Buddha; namo Good Wayfarer Buddha; namo Surrounded by Glorious Merits Buddha; namo Roaming among Precious Flowers Buddha; namo King Residing Well among Precious Lotuses and Sāla Trees Buddha.

"'May all these and other Buddhas, World-Honored Ones of all the universes, stay in the world forever. May they have compassion on me.

"'I now repent all the transgressions which I have committed by myself, abetted others to commit, or been glad to see others commit, in my present life, in my past lives, and ever since my involvement in beginningless saṁsāra.

"'I repent the crimes of stealing from stūpas, from monks, or from the common possessions of the Saṅgha in the four quarters—crimes which I have committed by myself, abetted others to commit, or been glad to see others commit.

"'I repent the five grave offenses which I have committed by myself, abetted others to commit, or been glad to see others commit.

"'I repent the ten evil deeds which I have committed by myself, abetted others to commit, or been glad to see others commit.

"'I repent the crimes I have committed, which, whether I hide them or not, will cause me to fall to the miserable planes of existence—the planes of hell-dwellers, hungry ghosts, and animals—or cause me to be reborn in the frontiers; as a lowly, inferior being; or in a land of barbarians. May the Buddhas, the World-Honored Ones, be my witnesses and take care of me.

"'In the presence of the Buddhas, the World-Honored Ones, I will further say: if in my present life or other lives I have planted any good roots, such as the good roots of giving, even giving only a handful of food to an animal; of keeping the discipline; of leading a pure life; of helping sentient beings; and of cultivating enlightenment and the unexcelled wisdom—then, I will gather up all these good roots, calculate them, measure them, and dedicate them to [the universal attainment of] supreme enlightenment. I will make the same dedication as that made by all the Buddhas of the present, past, and future.

"'All my transgressions I now repent.
I rejoice in all others' blessings,
And in the virtues of Buddhas.
May I achieve the unexcelled wisdom.

The Buddhas of the past, present, and future
Are supreme among all beings.
I now take refuge in and pay homage to
The Immeasurable Oceans of Virtue.'

"Therefore, Śāriputra, the Bodhisattva should first of all contemplate those thirty-five Buddhas single-mindedly, then pay homage to all Tathāgatas, and thus repent with a pure mind. If his transgressions have been purified, the Buddhas will immediately appear before him.

"Furthermore, in order to deliver sentient beings, Bodhisattvas will, without affecting the dharmadhātu, manifest themselves in different forms to fulfil the various wishes of sentient beings, thereby liberating them.

"Śāriputra, if a Bodhisattva enters the Samādhi of Great Compassion, he can appear in the realms of hells, animals, or Yama to bring sentient beings to maturity. If he enters the Samādhi of Great Magnificence, he can appear as an elder to bring sentient beings to maturity. If he enters the Samādhi of Supremacy, he can appear as a universal monarch to bring sentient beings to maturity. If he enters the Samādhi of Awesome Effulgence, he can appear in the wonderful form of a śakra or a brahmā to bring sentient beings to maturity. If he enters the Samādhi of One Direction, he can appear as a Śrāvaka to bring sentient beings to maturity. If he enters the Samādhi of Purity, he can appear as a Pratyekabuddha to bring sentient beings to maturity. If he enters the Samādhi of Tranquaillity, he can appear as a Buddha to bring sentient beings to maturity. If he enters the Samādhi of the Free Command of All Dharmas, he can manifest all kinds of forms as he wishes to bring sentient beings to maturity.

"A Bodhisattva may appear as a śakra, a brahmā, or a universal monarch in order to bring sentient beings to maturity, but he does not affect the dharmadhātu in doing so. Why? Because although he appears in all forms to comply with [the desires of] sentient beings, he sees no bodily form and no sentient being, for both are inapprehensible.

"Śāriputra, what do you think? Can a small jackal roar like a lion?"

Śāriputra answered, "No, World-honored One."

"Can a donkey bear the same heavy burden borne by a large elephant?"

"No, World-Honored One."

"Can a poor, humble person be as awe-inspiring and free as a śakra or a brahmā?"

"No, World-Honored One."

"Can any small bird soar like a powerful, golden-winged garuḍa, the king of birds?"

"No, World-Honored One."

The Buddha said, "Similarly, Śāriputra, by their wisdom of renunciation, Bodhisattvas who have good roots and courage can purify their transgressions, be free of worry and remorse, and thereby see Buddhas and achieve samādhis. However, ordinary people, Śrāvakas, and Pratyekabuddhas cannot rid themselves of the hindrances caused by their transgressions.

"If a Bodhisattva repeats the names of those Buddhas and does the three things mentioned above[9] day and night, he can eradicate his offenses, be free from worry and remorse, and achieve samādhis."

At that time, Upāli emerged from concentration and went to see the Buddha. After bowing with his head at the Buddha's feet and circumambulating the Buddha three times to his right, he stood to one side and said to him, "World-Honored One, as I was sitting alone in a quiet place meditating, I thought, 'When the World-Honored One was explaining the Prātimokṣa—the pure discipline—to Śrāvakas, Pratyekabuddhas, and Bodhisattvas, he said, "You should rather give up your body and life than break the precepts."' World-Honored One, what should be the Prātimokṣa of Śrāvakas and Pratyekabuddhas, and what should be the Prātimokṣa of Bodhisattvas, while the Buddha stays in the world and after he enters parinirvāṇa? The World-Honored One says I am foremost in precept-keeping. How should I understand the subtle meaning of the Vinaya? If I personally hear it from the Buddha and accept and practice it until I achieve fearlessness, then I can extensively explain it to others. Now that the Bodhisattvas and monks from all places have gathered here, may the Buddha discourse extensively on the definitive Vinaya to resolve our doubts."

Thereupon, the World-Honored One told Upāli, "Now, Upāli, you should know that the pure precepts observed by Bodhisattvas and those observed by Śrāvakas are different both in aim and in practice. Upāli, a pure precept observed by Śrāvakas may be a great breach of discipline for Bodhisattvas. A pure precept observed by Bodhisattvas may be a great breach of discipline for Śrāvakas.

"What is a pure precept for Śrāvakas but a great breach of discipline for Bodhisattvas? For example, Upāli, not to engender a single thought of taking further rebirth is a pure precept for Śrāvakas but a great breach of discipline for Bodhisattvas. What is a pure precept for Bodhisattvas but a great breach of discipline for Śrāvakas? For example, to follow the Mahāyāna doctrine and to tolerate rebirths, without abhorrence, for an incalculable number of kalpas is a pure precept for Bodhisattvas but a great breach of discipline for Śrāvakas.

"For this reason, the Buddha teaches Bodhisattvas precepts which need not be strictly and literally observed, but teaches Śrāvakas precepts which must be strictly and literally observed; he teaches Bodhisattvas precepts which are at once permissive and prohibitive,[10] but teaches Śrāvakas precepts which are only prohibitive; he teaches Bodhisattvas precepts which are for the depth of the mind, but teaches Śrāvakas precepts which guide them step by step.[11]

"Why do the Bodhisattvas' precepts not need to be strictly and literally observed while those for Śrāvakas must be strictly and literally observed? When keeping the pure precepts, Bodhisattvas should comply with sentient beings, but Śrāvakas should not; therefore, the Bodhisattvas' precepts need not be strictly and literally observed while those for Śrāvakas must be strictly and literally observed.

"Why do Bodhisattvas keep precepts which are at once permissive and prohibitive, while Śrāvakas keep precepts which are only prohibitive?

"If a Bodhisattva who has resolved to practice the Mahāyāna breaks a precept in the morning but does not abandon his determination to seek all-knowing wisdom at midday, his discipline-body[12] remains undestroyed. If he breaks a precept at midday but does not abandon his determination to seek all-knowing wisdom in the afternoon, his discipline-body remains undestroyed. If he breaks a precept in the afternoon but does not abandon his determination to seek all-knowing wisdom in the evening, his discipline-body remains undestroyed. If he breaks a precept in the evening but does not abandon his determination to seek all-knowing wisdom at midnight, his discipline-body remains undestroyed. If he breaks a precept at midnight but does not abandon his determination to seek all-knowing wisdom before dawn, his discipline-body remains undestroyed. If he breaks a precept before dawn but does not abandon his determination to seek all-knowing wisdom in the morning, his discipline-body remains undestroyed.

"For this reason, people who follow the Bodhisattva-vehicle keep precepts which are both permissive and prohibitive. If they violate any precept, they should not become dismayed and afflict themselves with unnecessary grief and remorse.

"However, if a Śrāvaka breaks any precept, he destroys his pure discipline. Why? Because Śrāvakas, to eradicate their defilements, must keep the precepts with such intensity as if they were saving their heads from fire. They aspire to nirvāṇa only. For this reason, they keep precepts which are prohibitive only.

"Furthermore, Upāli, why do Bodhisattvas keep precepts for the depth of the mind, while Śrāvakas keep precepts which guide them step by step?

"Even if Bodhisattvas enjoy the five sensuous pleasures with unrestricted freedom for kalpas as numerous as the sands of the Ganges, as long as they do not give up their bodhicitta, they are said not to break the precepts. Why? Because Bodhisattvas are skilled in protecting their bodhicitta, and dwell securely in it; they are not afflicted by any passions, even in dreams. Further, they should gradually root out their defilements instead of exterminating them all in one lifetime.

"In contrast, Śrāvakas ripen their roots of virtue as hurriedly as if they were saving their heads from fire. They do not like to entertain even one thought of taking further rebirth.

"For this reason, followers of the Mahāyāna keep precepts for the depth of the mind, precepts which are both permissive and prohibitive and which need not be strictly and literally observed; while Śrāvakas keep precepts which guide them step by step, which are prohibitive only, and which must be strictly and literally observed.

"Upāli, it is very hard for those who pursue the Mahāyāna to attain supreme enlightenment; they cannot achieve it unless they are equipped with great, magnificent [virtues]. Therefore, Bodhisattvas never feel abhorrence even if they are constantly involved in saṁsāra for an incalculable number of kalpas. This is why the Tathāgata, through his observation, finds that he should not always teach the doctrine of renunciation to followers of the Mahāyāna, nor should he always teach them the way to realize nirvāṇa quickly. Instead, they should be taught the profound, wonderful, undefiled doctrine which is in unison with kindness and joy, the doctrine of detachment and freedom from grief and remorse, the doctrine of unhindered emptiness, so that after hearing it, the Bodhisattvas will not tire of being involved in saṁsāra and will attain supreme enlightenment without fail."

Then Upāli asked the Buddha, "World-Honored One, suppose a Bodhisattva breaks a precept out of desire; another does so out of hatred; and still another does so out of ignorance. World-Honored One, which one of the three offenses is the most serious?"

The World-Honored One answered Upāli, "If, while practicing the Mahāyāna, a Bodhisattva continues to break precepts out of desire for kalpas as numerous as the sands of the Ganges, his offense is still minor. If a Bodhisattva breaks precepts out of hatred, even just once, his offense is very serious. Why? Because a Bodhisattva who breaks precepts out of desire [still] holds sentient beings in his embrace, whereas a Bodhisattva who breaks precepts out of hatred forsakes sentient beings altogether.

"Upāli, a Bodhisattva should not be afraid of the passions which can help him hold sentient beings in his embrace, but he should fear the passions which can cause him to forsake sentient beings.

"Upāli, as the Buddha has said, desire is hard to give up, but is a subtle fault; hatred is easy to give up, but is a serious fault; ignorance is difficult to give up, and is a very serious fault.

"Upāli, when involved in defilements, Bodhisattvas should tolerate the small transgressions which are hard to avoid, but should not tolerate the grave transgressions which are easy to avoid, not even in a dream. For this reason, if a follower of the Mahāyāna breaks precepts out of desire, I say he is not a transgressor; but if he breaks precepts out of hatred, it is a grave offense, a gross fault, a serious, degenerate act, which causes tremendous hindrances to the Buddha-Dharma.

"Upāli, if a Bodhisattva is not thoroughly conversant with the Vinaya, he will be afraid when he transgresses out of desire, but will not be afraid when he transgresses out of hatred. If a Bodhisattva is thoroughly conversant with the Vinaya, he will not be afraid when he transgresses out of desire, but will be afraid when he transgresses out of hatred."

Then, from among the assembly, Mañjuśrī, Prince of the Dharma, asked the Buddha, "World-Honored One, all dharmas are ultimately Vinaya. Why are regulations necessary?"

The Buddha answered Mañjuśrī, "If ordinary people knew that all dharmas are ultimately Vinaya, the Tathāgata would not teach them the regulations, but because they do not know that, the Tathāgata gradually teaches them the rules to enlighten them."

Upāli said to the Buddha, "World-Honored One, the Tathāgata has discoursed on the definitive Vinaya, but Mañjuśrī has not said anything on this subject. May the World-Honored One command Mañjuśrī to explain it breifly."

The Buddha told Mañjuśrī, "Now you should expound the subtle meaning of the Ultimate Vinaya. Upāli will be happy to hear it."

Mañjuśrī, the Dharma Prince, said to Upāli, "All dharmas are ultimately quiescent when the mind is quiescent; this is called the Ultimate Vinaya.

"No dharma is found to have a self-entity when the mind is not defiled or attached; this is called the Vinaya of No Regret.

"All dharmas are pure by nature when the mind is not confused [by wrong views]; this is called the Supreme Vinaya.

"All dharmas are suchness itself when the mind is devoid of all views; this is called the Pure Vinaya.

"No dharma comes or goes when the mind does not discriminate; this is called the Inconceivable Vinaya.

"No dharma abides or clings when the mind ceases from moment to moment; this is called the Vinaya of the Purification of the Planes of Existence.

"All dharmas abide in emptiness when the mind is free of all signs; this is called the Vinaya of Intrinsic Transcendence.

"Dharmas have no past, present, or future, for they are inapprehensible; this is called the Vinaya of the Equality of the Three Phases of Time.

"No dharma can be established when the mind is free from discrimination;[13] this is called the Vinaya of the Permanent Resolution of Doubt.

"Upāli, this is the Ultimate Vinaya of the dharmadhātu, by which Buddhas, World-Honored Ones, have attained Buddhahood. A good man who does not observe this well is far from keeping the pure precepts of the Tathāgata."

Thereupon, Upāli said to the Buddha, "World-Honored One, the doctrines Mañjuśrī expounds are inconceivable."

The World-Honored One told Upāli, "Mañjuśrī expounds the Dharma on the basis of inconceivable, unimpeded liberation. For this reason, whatever doctrine he preaches enables one to be free from mental forms, which is the liberation of mind. He causes the arrogant to give up their arrogance."

Upāli asked the Buddha, "What constitutes the arrogance of a Śrāvaka or a Bodhisattva?"

The Buddha replied to Upāli, "If a monk thinks he has eradicated desire, he is arrogant. If he thinks he has eradicated hatred and ignorance, he is arrogant. If he thinks that desire is different from the Dharma of Buddhas, he is arrogant. If he thinks that hatred is different from the Dharma of Buddhas, he is arrogant. If he thinks that ignorance is different from the Dharma of Buddhas, he is arrogant.[14] If he claims to have gained something, he is arrogant. If he claims to have realized something, he is arrogant. If he claims to have attained liberation, he is arrogant. If he claims to perceive emptiness, signlessness, and wishlessness, he is also arrogant. If he claims to perceive nonarising and nonaction, he is arrogant. If he claims to perceive the existence of dharmas, he is arrogant. If he claims to perceive the impermanence of dharmas, he is arrogant. If he says, 'What is the use of practice, since all dharmas are empty?' he is also arrogant. Upāli, these constitute the arrogance of a Śrāvaka.

"What constitutes the arrogance of a Bodhisattva? If a Bodhisattva thinks he should resolve to seek all-knowing wisdom, he is arrogant. If he thinks he should practice the six pāramitās, he is arrogant. If he says, 'Only the pāramitā of wisdom can be depended upon to achieve liberation; there is no other way out [of the three realms],' then he is arrogant. If he says one doctrine is very profound and another is not, he is again arrogant. If he says one doctrine is pure and another is not, then he is arrogant. If he says, 'This is the doctrine of Buddhas; this is the doctrine of Pratyekabuddhas; this is the doctrine of Śrāvakas,' he is also arrogant. If he says, 'This should be done and that should not,' he is arrogant. If he says, 'This doctrine is profound and that is not,' he is arrogant. If he says one doctrine is close [to enlightenment] and another is not, he is arrogant. If he says, 'This is a right path and that is a wrong one,' he is arrogant. If he asks, 'Can I attain supreme enlightenment quickly or not?' he is arrogant. If he says, 'All dharmas are inconceivable and only I can understand them,' then he is arrogant. If he thinks of the inconceivable supreme enlightenment and becomes greatly attached to it, then he is arrogant. These constitute the arrogance of a Bodhisattva."

Upāli asked the Buddha, "World-Honored One, how can a monk be free from arrogance?"

The Buddha answered Upāli, "If he is not attached to any doctrine, no matter how inconceivable it is, he is completely free from arrogance."

Then, to explain the teaching further, the World-Honored One spoke in verse:

"All play-words arise from the mind;
No discrimination should be made
Between what is dharma and what is not.
He who sees the dharma as inconceivable
Will always dwell happily in the world.

Being deluded, ordinary men
Are turned by their own minds;
For kalpas, they circle and circle
In the various realms of saṁsāra.
It is truly inconceivable
To know that the nature of dharmas
Is no nature.

If a monk stays mindful of the Buddhas,
His thought is not proper
And his mindfulness not right;[15]

Vainly making distinctions about Buddhas,
He sees no truth whatsoever.

One who thinks about the teaching of emptiness
Is a fool, lingering on the wrong path;
Explanations of emptiness are mere words;
Both words and emptiness are inapprehensible.

One who contemplates the teaching of quiescence
Should know the mind is empty and unborn.
The mind's reflections and observations
Are all futile and meaningless.
To have no thought [and make no distinctions]
Is to see all dharmas,
For all dharmas are apart from thought,
And all thoughts and ideas are empty.
One who enjoys contemplation on emptiness
Should transcend even the state without thought.

Dharmas, like grasses and trees, have no awareness;
Apart from the mind they are inapprehensible.
Sentient beings are devoid of self-entity;
So are all dharmas.

The eye can see while there is sunlight,
But it sees nought when night falls.
If the eye could see by itself,
Why should it rely on conditions to act?
It is entirely due to various lights
That the eye can see all colors.
Since sight depends on conditions,
It is obvious that by itself the eye cannot see.

A pleasant sound vanishes as soon as it is heard;
One knows not where it goes.
It is due to discrimination
That the concept of sound arises.

All dharmas are but the sounds of words,
And the words are merely arbitrary fabrications.
Not knowing that these sounds
Are neither dharmas nor nondharmas,
Ordinary persons vainly cling to them.

I praise giving, for the sake of the world,
But giving is intrinsically empty.

I teach, though there is nothing to teach;
Inconceivable indeed is the Buddha-Dharma!

I often praise the observance of pure precepts,
But no being ever breaks any precepts.
Precept-breaking is empty by nature,
And so is precept-keeping.

I say it is superb to be patient,
But patience is apart from views
And by nature does not arise.
There is really nothing to cause anger—
To realize this is called supreme patience.

I say it is unexcelled
To work vigorously day and night,
And to remain alert even in sleep.
Yet, even if one has practiced [vigor]
Diligently for kalpas,
His efforts do not increase or decrease anything.

I teach meditation, liberation, and samādhis
To show the world the door to truth;
Yet, the Dharma-nature is never stirred from the beginning,
And meditation of all kinds is fabricated
Merely to comply [with sentient beings].

That which observes and comprehends is called wisdom;
One who understands all dharmas is called wise.
Yet, dharmas by nature do not exist,
And there is no one who observes or comprehends.

I often praise austere practices
And extol those who delight
In such ways to tranquillity—
But only those who know
That all dharmas are inapprehensible
May really be called pure, contented ones.

I describe the sufferings in the hells,
So that countless people may abhor
Falling to the terrible realms after death;
But, in reality, there are no such miserable places.
No one can produce therein
Knives, cudgels, or similar means of torture;
It is discrimination that causes one to see them
And to suffer immeasurable tortures put to him.

Gardens covered with various lovely flowers
And palaces sparkling with numerous jewels—
These things [of heaven] are created by no one;
They all arise from the discriminating, delusive mind.

The world is deceived by fictitious dharmas
Which confuse one who is attached to them.
However one discriminates among mirages,
Whether accepting or rejecting them,
They are empty just the same.

I say it is supreme to benefit the worlds
By resolving to pursue enlightenment;
But, in truth, enlightenment is inapprehensible,
And there is no one who resolves to attain it.

The mind by nature is ever pure and bright;
Unsullied by falsehood or passion, it is true.
Ordinary persons discriminate
And engender attachment;
Yet, from the beginning,
Their defilements are empty.

All dharmas are always quiescent in their self-nature—
How can there be desire, hatred, or ignorance?
One who sees nowhere
To generate desire or renounce passion,
Is said to have attained nirvāṇa.
Because one's mind is never [truly] defiled,
One is able to achieve great enlightenment.

Striving for various Dharma practices
For countless kalpas,
I have delivered myriad sentient beings,
Yet sentient beings themselves are inapprehensible;
In reality no beings are ever delivered.

If a great magician produces
A magic crowd of a billion beings,
And then destroys them again,
No harm or good is ever done
To these magic creatures.

All beings are illusory, like magic;
No borders or limits can be found.
One who knows this absence of limits
Will never tire of living in the world.

To one who knows the reality of all things,
Constant involvement in saṁsāra is nirvāṇa;[16]
Amidst desires, he is not defiled;
It is only to subdue sentient beings
That he speaks of the renunciation of desires.

The Most Compassionate One benefits all beings,
But there is actually no person or life.
To benefit sentient beings yet see them not—
This is difficult indeed, a great wonder.

One may solace a child with an empty fist,
Saying it contains something for him,
Though the child may cry again
When the hand opens and reveals nothing.

Likewise, the inconceivable Buddhas
Subdue sentient beings skillfully.
While they know dharma-nature is empty,
They fabricate names for the world's sake.

With great kindness and compassion they urge you:
'In my Dharma is supreme happiness.
Leave your households
And abandon your loved ones!
You will then attain the superb fruit
Sought by a śramaṇa.'

After one leaves the household life
And practices the Dharma in earnest,
He attains nirvāṇa at last through his practice.
He then reflects at length
Upon the truth of all dharmas.
To his wonder, he discovers
That no fruit whatsoever is there to attain.

No fruit, and yet realization is achieved!
[Awestruck,] he begins to marvel:
'How wonderful it is
That the Most Compassionate Lion of Men
Is so skillful in teaching the Dharma
In compliance with reality!
All dharmas are like empty space,
But he establishes numerous names, words, and doctrines.

He speaks of meditation and liberation;
He speaks of roots, powers, and enlightenment;

But, from the beginning,
These roots and powers do not arise,
Nor do meditation and enlightenment exist.
Formless, shapeless, and ungraspable, these things
Are only skillful means to illuminate living beings.'

When I speak of the practice that leads to realization,
I mean detachment from all forms.
If one claims to have achieved anything,
He is far from realizing the śramaṇa's fruit.
No dharma has a self-entity;
What is there to realize?
The so-called realization is no attainment at all:
To understand this is called attainment.

Those who have obtained the fruit
Are said to be superior,
But I say all beings are unborn from the beginning.
Since there is no sentient being in the first place,
How can there be anyone achieving the fruit?

If no seed is sown,
How can any sprout come forth,
Even from a fertile field?
Whence can realization come
If there is no sentient being?

All beings are by nature quiescent,
And no one can find their origin.
One who understands this doctrine
Will be in parinirvāṇa forever.

Of the countless Buddhas in the past,
None could deliver sentient beings.
If sentient beings were truly existent,
No one could have achieved nirvāṇa.

All dharmas are quiescent and empty;
Never has a dharma arisen.
He who can see all dharmas in this way
Has already transcended the three realms.

This is the unhindered enlightenment of Buddhas—
Yet, ultimately, nothing exists therein.
If one knows this doctrine,
I say he is free from desires."

When the World-Honored One finished speaking in verse, two hundred arrogant monks ended their defilements permanently and became liberated in mind; and sixty thousand Bodhisattvas attained the Realization of the Nonarising of Dharmas.

Then Upāli asked the Buddha, "What should this sūtra be called? How shall we uphold it?"

The Buddha told Upāli, "This sūtra is called 'The Definitive Vinaya,' or 'The Elimination of the Mind and Consciousness.' You should accept and uphold it by these names."

When the Buddha had taught this sūtra, the venerable Upāli, the monks, Mañjuśrī, the great Bodhisattvas, humans, gods, asuras, and so forth were exceedingly joyful over the Buddha's teaching. They accepted it with faith and began to practice it with veneration.

NOTES

1. For brevity, we have omitted several declarations in this section. Omissions are indicated by ellipses.

2. This passage is relevant to the questions concerning the Bodhisattvas' practices of extreme charity, such as the giving of one's eyes, limbs, kingdom, etc., mentioned in many Buddhist texts. Here, it is stated that only those Bodhisattvas who have attained the Realization of the Nonarising of Dharmas are able to practice extreme charity; for other people, this practice may serve no purpose and even harm themselves and others.

3. The eight great hells are:

(1) the Reviving Hell, where after great suffering, the offender is cooled by a wind and revives, only to be tortured again;
(2) the Black Rope Hell, where the sufferer is bound with black chains and chopped or sawed asunder;
(3) the Converging Hell, where many implements of torture converge upon one;
(4) the Wailing Hell;
(5) the Great Wailing Hell;
(6) the Scorching Hell;
(7) the Great Scorching Hell; and
(8) the Uninterrupted Hell, where suffering is continuous.

4. The soundness of translating 痴 as 'ignorance' here may be seriously questioned. Ignorance of the basic truth or no-self (*anātman*) or emptiness causes one to wander in saṁsāra, including both heaven and hell. However, ignorance (Skt. *avidyā*) alone cannot be the cause of falling to a hell. To be ignorant of a certain truth or law (or simply to lack knowledge of a certain branch of science) cannot be considered a great offense against moral principles, causing one to fall to a hell. Here 痴 probably implies serious wrong views, such as nihilism (*ucchedavāda*) and so forth. Although 'wrong view' is a much better translation here, to

comply with the established formula and sequence, we are forced to translate 痴 as ignorance. The readers are reminded that 'ignorance' here does not mean 'lack of knowledge', but rather 'wrong views' on fundamental moral and religious principles. (G.C.)

5. Pārājika is the most serious type of offense for monastics. For monks, there are four (listed in the Numerical Glossary as the "four heavy transgressions"): sexual intercourse, stealing, manslaughter, and lying.

6. A saṁghāvaśeṣa is an offense second in gravity to a pārājika. If a monk does not purify the offense through repentance and confession, he may be expelled.

7. *Namo* is derived from the Sanskrit *nam,* meaning 'bow to' or 'pay homage to'.

8. The Chinese reads 娑留那 , but the meaning and original Sanskrit are unknown to the translators.

9. The three are: contemplation of the thirty-five Buddhas, paying homage to all Tathāgatas, and repenting with a pure mind.

10. The Bodhisattva precepts prohibit unwholesome actions, but they permit those actions in certain circumstances. In *Yogācārya-Bhūmi-Śāstra,* attributed to Maitreya, we find the following passage (Taishō 1501, p. 1112):

> Those Bodhisattvas who observe the pure Bodhisattva precepts well may, as a skillful means to benefit others, commit some major misdeeds. In doing so, they do not violate the Bodhisattva precepts; instead, they generate many merits.
>
> For example, suppose a Bodhisattva sees that a vicious robber intends to kill many people for the sake of wealth; or intends to harm virtuous Śrāvakas, Pratyekabuddhas, or Bodhisattvas; or intends to do other things that will cause him to fall to the Uninterrupted Hell. When seeing this, the Bodhisattva will think, "If I kill that person, I will fall to the hells; if I do not kill him, he will commit crimes which will lead him to the Uninterrupted Hell, where he will suffer greatly. I would rather kill him and fall to the hells myself than let him undergo great suffering in the Uninterrupted Hell."
>
> Then, deeply regretting the necessity for this action, and with a heart full of compassion, he will kill that person. In doing this, he does not violate the Bodhisattva precepts; instead, he generates many merits.

11. The literal translation reads: "but teaches Śrāvakas the gradual precepts." This appears to contradict the text below, where it is stated that the Hīnayāna followers are in a great hurry to exterminate all their defilements in one lifetime. It may mean that the Bodhisattvas' precepts pertain directly to the mind, while the Śrāvakas' precepts mostly regulate outer actions, leading step by step to mental wholesomeness.

12. According to certain Hīnayāna schools, such as the Sarvāstivādins, when one obtains the *bhikṣu* precepts in formal ordination, he acquires a "discipline-body." This body, though invisible to ordinary people, is said to be visible to those with the deva-eye. The term may also be interpreted to mean simply one's own discipline.

13. Literally, "is equal."

14. Clearly, the Buddha is speaking now on a higher level than his earlier discourse on precepts.

15. Even the concepts of 'Buddha' and 'Buddhahood' are empty, and must be relinquished if one is to attain full enlightenment.

16. An important Mahāyāna concept of nirvāṇa, radically different from Hīnayāna doctrines. See Glossary, "nirvāṇa."

16 寶梁聚會

Abiding in Good and Noble Deportment

I

Thus have I heard. Once the Buddha was dwelling on Mount Gṛdhrakūṭa near the city of Rājagṛha, accompanied by eight thousand great monks. At that time, sixteen thousand Bodhisattva-Mahāsattvas who did not regress from pursuit of supreme enlightenment, and who were destined to become Buddhas in their next lifetimes, came from different Buddha-lands in the ten directions to join the assembly.

That day, Mahākāśyapa asked the Buddha, "The World-Honored One speaks of śramaṇas. What is a śramaṇa?"

The Buddha replied to Kāśyapa, "A śramaṇa is one who can:

attain ultimate quiescence;
keep himself under control;
accept the teachings;
observe the pure precepts;
enter dhyānas;
acquire wisdom;
strive for liberation by understanding the meaning of reality;
have no doubts about the three doors to liberation;
abide securely in the practices of saints;
skillfully cultivate the four mindfulnesses;[1]
avoid all unwholesome dharmas;
securely dwell in the four right efforts;
adeptly cultivate the four bases of miraculous powers;

Sūtra 44, Taishō 310, pp. 638–648; translated into Chinese by Ven. Tao Kung.

achieve the five roots—to have firm faith in the Buddha, the Dharma, and the Saṁgha; not to believe in any doctrine other than the Buddha-Dharma; to strive to eradicate all defilements,[2] avoiding all unwholesome dharmas but cultivating all wholesome ones in accordance with the truth; to know thoroughly the skillful means to acquire right knowledge and right mindfulness, keeping wholesome dharmas in mind exclusively; and to know well the skillful means to attain dhyāna and wisdom;
achieve the five powers so that he is not disturbed by any afflictions;
cultivate well the seven factors of enlightenment [so that] he thoroughly knows the skillful means to perceive the causes and conditions of all dharmas;
know well the skillful means to follow the [eightfold] noble path, which includes right view and right concentration;
obtain the power of the four kinds of [unhindered] eloquence;
disbelieve in heterodox doctrines;
rely on the meaning [of the Dharma] rather than words, on [intuitive] wisdom rather than intellect, on the sūtras which convey the ultimate truth rather than the sūtras which do not, and on the Dharma rather than the person [teaching it];[3]
be apart from the four demons;
thoroughly understand the five aggregates;
uproot all afflictions;
reach the last lifetime [before nirvāṇa];
shun the ways leading to saṁsāra;
be free from all craving;
persevere in comprehending suffering, stopping the arising of suffering, realizing the cessation of suffering, and cultivating the path leading to the cessation of suffering, thus perceiving clearly the four noble truths;
reject all heterodox doctrines after taking refuge in the Buddha-Dharma;
accomplish what he set out to accomplish;
eliminate all defilements;
cultivate the eightfold liberation;
be praised by śakras and brahmās;
from the beginning devote himself to the practice of the path;
delight in living in a secluded forest;
establish himself securely in the noble Dharma;
rejoice in Buddhist rites;
be mentally undisturbed;
avoid close associations, either with monks and nuns or with laypeople;
enjoy being alone, like the single horn of a rhinoceros;
be afraid of bustling crowds;
enjoy living by himself;

always fear the three realms;
achieve the true fruit of a śramaṇa;
have no longing for anything;
shun the eight worldly dharmas[4]—gain, loss, praise, blame, fame, ridicule, pleasure, and pain;
be as steadfast and immovable in mind as the great earth;
guard against any conflict of will between himself and others;
be serene;
cultivate right practices;
achieve a mentality [as pure] as space; and
have a mind which is not tainted by or attached to forms and appearances, just as a hand moving in empty space is not hindered by anything.

Kāśyapa, if a person can accomplish these, he really is a śramaṇa."

Then Mahākāśyapa said to the Buddha, "World-Honored One, the Tathāgata's skillful discourse on the meritorious deeds of a śramaṇa is extraordinary. World-Honored One, if śramaṇas in future ages falsely claim to be true śramaṇas or to practice pure conduct, then they have trespassed on the supreme enlightenment cultivated and perfected by the Tathāgata for countless kalpas."

The Buddha said to Kāśyapa, "The offense of trespassing on the supreme enlightenment of the Tathāgata is so monstrous that no one could ever finish describing it. Kāśyapa, after I enter nirvāṇa, you and my other great disciples will also enter nirvāṇa, and the great Bodhisattvas of this world will go to other Buddha-lands. At that time, in my order, there will be deceitful monks (*bhikṣus*) who will do everything with crooked minds. Kāśyapa, now I am going to explain the corruption of a śramaṇa; that is, the faults and transgressions of a śramaṇa.

"Kāśyapa, in the coming Last Era, there will be monks who will not cultivate morality or discipline, nor will they cultivate their minds or wisdom. They will be as ignorant as children; they will move toward darkness unaware. Because they will not subdue their minds, they will be corrupt śramaṇas. Kāśyapa, what is the corruption of a śramaṇa?

"Kāśyapa, the corruption of a śramaṇa is of thirty-two kinds. One who has renounced the household life should keep them all at a distance. What are the thirty-two?

(1) To feel desire;
(2) to feel hatred;
(3) to feel annoyance;
(4) to praise oneself;
(5) to defame others;
(6) to seek material gains;
(7) to seek profit for its own sake;
(8) to spoil others' blessings resulting from almsgiving;[5]

(9) to conceal one's own misdeeds;
(10) to be intimate with lay people;
(11) to be intimate with monks or nuns;
(12) to take pleasure in noisy crowds;
(13) to seek by devious means material gains not belonging to oneself;
(14) to long for the material gains of others;
(15) not to be content with one's own material possessions;
(16) to envy others' material possessions;
(17) always to find fault with others;
(18) not to see one's own errors;
(19) not to keep strictly the precepts leading to liberation;
(20) not to have a sense of shame and remorse;
(21) not to respect others, but instead to be arrogant, unreliable, and shameless;
(22) to arouse one's passions;
(23) to contradict the twelve links of dependent origination;
(24) to hold extreme views;
(25) not to be tranquil and free of passions;
(26) to delight in saṁsāra, not in nirvāṇa;
(27) to enjoy heterodox scriptures;
(28) to be enveloped in the five covers so that afflictions arise;
(29) to have no faith in karmic results;
(30) to fear the three doors to liberation;
(31) to slander the profound, subtle Dharma instead of cultivating the practices leading to ultimate quiescence; and
(32) to have no respect for the Three Jewels.

All these are corruptions of a śramaṇa. If a śramaṇa can cleanse himself of these kinds of corruption, he is a true śramaṇa.

"Kāśyapa, furthermore, eight things can destroy the [good] deeds of a śramaṇa. What are the eight?

(1) Not to be respectful and obedient to teachers and superiors;
(2) not to esteem the Dharma;
(3) not to have proper thoughts;
(4) to slander the Dharma after hearing it explained for the first time;
(5) to become frightened when hearing the Dharma which teaches the nonexistence of sentient beings, self, life, and personal identity;
(6) to understand only conditioned dharmas, not unconditioned ones, even after hearing that no phenomena ever arise from the beginning;
(7) to fall into the huge, deep pit[6] after hearing the gradual doctrine;[7] and
(8) to be perplexed and confused to hear that no dharma arises, has a self-entity, or goes anywhere.

Kāśyapa, these eight things can destroy the [good]deeds of a śramaṇa. A śramaṇa who has left the household life should shun these eight things.

"Kāśyapa, I do not say that those who shave their heads and dress in monastic robes are śramaṇas; I say that those who are fully endowed with virtues and good deportment are śramaṇas.

"Kāśyapa, a śramaṇa dressed in a monastic robe should keep his mind far away from desire, hatred, and ignorance. Why? Because I allow only those who have no desire, no hatred, and no ignorance to dress in monastic robes.[8] Kāśyapa, śramaṇas who are dressed in monastic robes but have desire, hatred, and ignorance in mind and do not keep the precepts are burning their monastic robes, while those who observe the precepts single-mindedly are not. Why? Because monastic robes should be worn by those who have the attributes of a saint, dwell in ultimate quiescence, practice kindness and compassion, and are free from passions.

"Kāśyapa, now, listen to me. There are twelve signs of a saint. What are the twelve?

(1) To observe the discipline;
(2) to develop meditation;
(3) to cultivate wisdom;
(4) to achieve liberation;
(5) to acquire the knowledge and awareness derived from liberation;
(6) to comprehend the four noble truths;
(7) to comprehend the twelve links of dependent origination;
(8) to fulfill the four immeasurables;
(8) to practice the four dhyānas;
(10) to practice the four dhyānas of the Realm of Formlessness;[9]
(11) to enter right concentration, leading to the four fruits [of the Śrāvaka-vehicle];[10] and
(12) to eliminate all one's defilements.

Kāśyapa, these are the twelve signs of a saint. Kāśyapa, I say the monks who are not fully endowed with the twelve signs of a saint yet dress in monastic robes do not cultivate the Buddha-Dharma or approach nirvāṇa, nor do they proceed toward ultimate quiescence; instead, they perform evil, saṁsāric deeds. They do not cross [the sea of] saṁsāra, but are caught by demons; they do not maintain the true Dharma, but follow wrong doctrines.

"Therefore, Kāśyapa, a monk who has left the household life but has not yet achieved the fruit of a śramaṇa should esteem in eight ways the monastic robe which he wears. What are the eight? When he wears a monastic robe, he should bring forth:

(1) the thought of a stūpa;
(2) the thought of the World-Honored One;
(3) the thought of ultimate quiescence;

(4) the thought of kindness;
(5) the thought of respecting [the robe] as a Buddha;
(6) the thought of shame;
(7) the thought of remorse; and
(8) the thought that the robe will free him of desire, hatred, and ignorance and will cause him to fulfill the right practices of a śramaṇa in future lives.

Kāśyapa, a monk should esteem a monastic robe in these eight ways.

"Kāśyapa, if śramaṇas are not content with the four noble practices, but violate the right practices of a śramaṇa, and do not esteem a monastic robe in these eight ways, they are false śramaṇas and will fall to minor hells. Kāśyapa, false śramaṇas suffer pain in hell: their clothing, bowls, and bodies are all ablaze; the places where they sit or sleep and the things they use burn intensely, like big furnaces. False śramaṇas undergo such sufferings. Why do they fall to such a miserable state? Because they have committed impure deeds, words, and thoughts.

"Kāśyapa, suppose a precept-breaking monk falsely claims to be a true śramaṇa and to practice pure conduct. When meritorious, precept-keeping people make offerings to him and respectfully circumambulate him, he accepts all this without even knowing his own wickedness. That wicked monk will, because of this evil root, reap eight contemptible attributes [in a future life]. What are the eight?

(1) To be foolish;
(2) to be mute;
(3) to be short in stature;
(4) to have such ugly, distorted features that anyone who sees him laughs at him;
(5) to be born female and work as a poor servant;
(6) to be weak, emaciated, and die young;
(7) to be notorious instead of respected; and
(8) not to encounter Buddhas.

Kāśyapa, if a precept-breaking monk allows precept-keeping people to pay homage and make offerings to him, he will have these eight contemptible attributes [in a future life]. Kāśyapa, a precept-breaking monk should, after hearing this explained, not accept the homage and offerings of a precept-keeping monk.

"Kāśyapa, if a precept-breaking monk falsely claims to be a true śramaṇa and to practice pure conduct, he does not deserve a space wide enough for him to spit, let alone a space to raise and lower his feet, to go here and there, to bend down, or to stretch out. Why? Because in the past, great monarchs offered large tracts of land to virtuous precept-keepers to serve as their dwelling-places while they pursued the path. Kāśyapa, a precept-breaking monk is not worthy of any offerings given by faithful donors, not even a space to raise and lower his feet, let alone a place with rooms for resident and visiting monks, or a place to take walking exercise. He is not worthy of any offerings given by faithful donors, such as a house, a bed, a garden, a garment, a bowl, bedding, or medicine.

"Kāśyapa, now I say that if a precept-breaking monk falsely claims to be a true śramaṇa and to practice pure conduct, he cannot requite the kindness of faithful donors, not even with a blessing as tiny as the tip of a hair. Why? Like the vast ocean, noble fields of blessings are supreme and most wonderful. A donor who, out of pure faith, sows a seed of giving in the fields of blessings may think that he has made an immeasurable gift. Kāśyapa, when a wicked, precept-breaking monk accepts from a faithful donor any offering, even as little as one hundredth of a split hair, he will cause his donor to forfeit blissful rewards the size of the vast ocean; such a monk cannot repay at all the kindness of his donor. Kāśyapa, therefore, a monk should have a pure mind when accepting an offering from a faithful donor. Kāśyapa, this you should learn."

At that time, in the assembly, two hundred monks who were pure in deed, had few desires, and were free from [the four] yokes wiped away their tears after they had heard this doctrine explained, and said, "World-Honored One, now we would rather die than accept even one meal from a faithful donor without first having achieved the fruit of a śramaṇa."

The Buddha said, "Excellent, excellent! Good men, since you feel shame and remorse, and your fear of future lives is as strong as adamant, you may be compared in this life to necklaces of precious jewels. Good men, I say now that in the world there are only two kinds of people worthy of offerings given by faithful donors. What are the two? One is those who cultivate [the Dharma] with vigor; the other is those who have achieved liberation."

The Buddha told these monks, "If a monk has achieved liberation, practices wholesome dharmas, strictly keeps the precepts as I have taught, contemplates all phenomena as impermanent and painful and all dharmas as devoid of self, and also contemplates the ultimate quiescence of nirvāṇa with a desire to attain it—then, even if he accepts from faithful donors a pile of offerings the size of Mount Sumeru, he will surely be able to reward the donors with commensurate blessings.

"If such a monk accepts offerings from a faithful donor, he will cause the donor to obtain great benefits and great rewards. Why? Because blessings always result from three things: constant giving of food, building temples and monasteries, and the practice of kindness. Of these three, the practice of kindness results in the supreme blessings."

The Buddha continued. "If a monk enters the immeasurable dhyāna[11] after he accepts clothing, a bowl, bedding, food and drink, or medicine from a donor, he can cause his donor to obtain limitless blissful rewards. Kāśyapa, all the vast oceans in a billion-world universe may dry up, but the blissful rewards which the donor thus acquires cannot be exhausted. Kāśyapa, you should know that a precept-breaking monk damages the blessings of a donor. If a monk performs misdeeds after he accepts offerings from a faithful donor, he will waste the donor's offerings.

"Kāśyapa, therefore I discourse on the corruption of a śramaṇa, the faults and transgressions of a śramaṇa, the deceit and crookedness of a śramaṇa, and the thievery among śramaṇas.

"Kāśyapa, a precept-keeping monk should be single-minded and remain far away from all those unwholesome dharmas. Kāśyapa, a śramaṇa is one who does not let his eyes, ears, nose, tongue, body, or mind be attracted by any objects. One who protects his six sense-organs from being attracted [to objects], comprehends the six miraculous powers, concentrates on the six mindfulnesses,[12] abides securely in the six kinds of reverent harmony in a monastery,[13] and practices the six valuable dharmas[14] is called a śramaṇa."

II

Then the Buddha told Kāśyapa, "One who can destroy his afflictions is called a monk. One who can break up the thoughts of self, a sentient being, a personal identity, a man, or a woman is called a monk. Furthermore, Kāśyapa, one who cultivates discipline and wisdom is called a monk. Furthermore, Kāśyapa, one who is fearless; extricates himself from the three realms and the four currents,[15] sees their faults and distresses, and avoids them all; and situates himself securely on the path of fearlessness is called a monk.

"Kāśyapa, if a monk does not fulfil this or other good doctrines despite his knowledge of them, but gives up all good doctrines and treads different paths, he is not my disciple and I am not his teacher.

"Kāśyapa, there are many wicked monks who do harm to my Dharma. Kāśyapa, it is not the ninety-five kinds of heterodox devotees,[16] nor other kinds of heterodox devotees, but the ignorant persons in my order who can destroy my Dharma. For example, Kāśyapa, after a lion, the king of beasts, dies, no tiger, wolf, bird, or other beast can eat its flesh; [only] the worms living in its body can eat its flesh. Kāśyapa, in my order, there are wicked monks who are greedy for material gains and overwhelmed by avarice. They do not eliminate unwholesome dharmas, do not cultivate wholesome dharmas, and do not cease to tell lies. Kāśyapa, it is these monks who can destroy my Dharma.

"Kāśyapa, a monk who harbors four things is wicked. What are the four?

(1) Desire;
(2) hatred;
(3) ignorance; and
(4) arrogance.[17]

"Furthermore, there are four attributes of a wicked monk. What are the four?

(1) To be conceited;
(2) to be insensitive to shame;

(3) not to feel remorse; and
(4) to be careless in speaking.

"Moreover, there are four deeds of a wicked monk. What are the four?

(1) To be unstable;
(2) to look down on others;
(3) to seek material gains greedily; and
(4) to perform misdeeds frequently.

"Furthermore, there are four [other] deeds of a wicked monk. What are the four?

(1) To be villainous and deceitful;
(2) to delude and confuse others;
(3) to earn a livelihood in an improper way; and
(4) to use abusive language.

"Moreover, there are four [other] deeds of a wicked monk. What are the four?

(1) To accept favors from others without returning favors to them;
(2) to do small favors for others and expect great rewards;
(3) to forget favors previously bestowed by others; and
(4) to do harm to relatives and friends.

"Furthermore, there are four [other] deeds of a wicked monk. What are the four?

(1) Not to requite the kindness of faithful donors with blessings and rewards after accepting their offerings;
(2) not to protect the discipline well;
(3) to despise the precepts one has received; and
(4) not to keep the precepts strictly.

"Moreover, a monk who gives discourses preaching four doctrines is a wicked monk. What are the four?

(1) That there is a self;
(2) that there is a sentient being;
(3) that there is life; and
(4) that there is a personal identity.

"Furthermore, there are four [other] deeds of a wicked monk. What are the four?

(1) Not to respect the Buddha;
(2) not to respect the Dharma;
(3) not to respect the Saṁgha; and
(4) not to respect the discipline.

"Moreover, there are four [other] deeds of a wicked monk. What are the four?

(1) To be unhappy when there is harmony within the Saṁgha;
(2) to dislike living alone;
(3) to enjoy being in crowds; and
(4) to talk of worldly affairs all the time.

"Furthermore, there are four [other] deeds of a wicked monk. What are the four?

(1) To strive for material gains;
(2) to pursue great fame;
(3) to form many acquaintances; and
(4) not to abide in the [four] noble practices.

"Moreover, there are four [other] deeds of a wicked monk. What are the four?

(1) To be bound by demons;
(2) to be perverted by demons;
(3) to indulge in [excessive] sleep; and
(4) not to enjoy practicing virtue.

"Furthermore, there are four [other] deeds of a wicked monk. What are the four?

(1) To cause the Buddha-Dharma to degenerate;
(2) to be a sycophant at heart;
(3) to be harmed by defilements; and
(4) not to pursue the fruit of a śramaṇa.

"Moreover, a monk who burns with four things is a wicked monk. What are the four?

(1) To burn with sexual desire;
(2) to burn with hatred;
(3) to burn with ignorance; and
(4) to burn with any other defilements.

"Furthermore, there are four [other] deeds of a wicked monk. What are the four?

(1) To visit brothels frequently, without knowing the harm it does;
(2) not to be content;
(3) not to be content in spite of having much learning;[18] and
(4) to be always miserly and not to share necessities with others.

"Moreover, there are four [other] deeds of a wicked monk. What are the four?

(1) To go from darkness to [more] darkness and from ignorance to [more] ignorance;
(2) to doubt the four noble truths instead of perceiving them;
(3) to be always bound by saṁsāra; and
(4) to close the door to nirvāṇa.

"Finally, a monk who is deceitful in four ways is a wicked monk. What are the four?

(1) To be deceitful in body;
(2) to be deceitful in speech;
(3) to be deceitful in mind; and
(4) to be deceitful in manner.

"What is it to be deceitful in body? To be deceitful in body is to [pretend to] walk with composure. To be deceitful in body is to [pretend to] look neither to the right nor to the left. To be deceitful in body is to [pretend to] look only a few feet away if one looks right or left. To be deceitful in body is to dress in a monastic robe while relying on improper means of livelihood; to live in a secluded place in order to gain praise, without fulfilling the purpose of living there; to beg for food in order to gain praise, without contemplating the reasons for food-begging; to wear a garment of cast-off rags in order to gain praise, without knowing that it is meant to generate humility; to live in a cave or under a tree in order to gain praise, without studying the twelve links of dependent origination; to take stale, discarded medicine in order to gain praise, without seeking the ambrosial Dharma-medicine. Kāśyapa, all this is called being deceitful in body.

"Kāśyapa, what is it to be deceitful in speech? [It is to say:] 'He knows me'; 'He invites me'; 'I obtain what I seek'; 'I do not seek material gains, but he gives them to me'; 'I have acquired every fine, wonderful offering, and great material gains as well'; 'I often practice wholesome dharmas, so offerings should be made to me'; 'I am good at debating'; 'I know the forms of the dharmas in direct order and in inverted order';[19] 'I know the right and wrong meanings of all dharmas'; 'If he asks me this, I can answer him, convince him, and silence him with my answer'; or 'By speaking, I can please everyone, and I can also make people admire and praise me. I can make them invite me [to their homes], make offerings to me, and ask me to return often after I accept their offerings.' Kāśyapa, if a person does not control his speech and says everything contrary to propriety, he is deceitful in speech. Kāśyapa, this is called being deceitful in speech.

"Kāśyapa, what is it to be deceitful in mind? To be deceitful in mind is to say, 'I do not want such material supports as clothing, bowls, bedding, food and drink, and medicine,' while one's mind is [really] concerned with nothing but the pursuit of these. It is to say falsely that one is content while actually one is seeking many things."

Then the World-Honored One spoke in verse:

"If a person seeks material gains
And pursues them in an improper way,
While claiming he is content,
Then he is forever miserable.

Being falsehearted,
This person is deceitful to all;
His mind is utterly impure.

Gods, dragons, spirits,
Those who have the deva-eye,
And Buddhas, the World-Honored Ones,
All know and see this.

"Kāśyapa, such a wicked monk is apart from wholesome dharmas and behavior, and earns a living in an improper way; he will fall to the three miserable planes of existence."

III

The Buddha told Kāśyapa, "What is the outcaste[20] of śramaṇas? Kāśyapa, an outcaste often goes to a graveyard looking for a corpse, and is glad to see one. He treats sentient beings without kindness or compassion. Similarly, Kāśyapa, the outcaste of śramaṇas has no kindness. He goes to a donor's house with evil intentions, and values highly what he obtains. He does not teach his donors the Buddha-Dharma and discipline after he accepts material offerings from them. He associates closely with laypeople for the sake of material gains, not for the sake of Dharma. He has no kindness and always seeks material possessions. Kāśyapa, this is what is meant by the outcaste of śramaṇas.

"Kāśyapa, all people, including ministers, elders, princes, warriors, brāhmins, and common people, dissociate themselves from an outcaste. Even the most lowly slaves avoid his presence and acquaintance. Similarly, Kāśyapa, all people, including virtuous, respected precept-keepers, monks, nuns, laymen, laywomen, gods, dragons, ghosts, spirits, and gandharvas keep aloof from the outcaste of śramaṇas, because they know that he breaks the precepts and practices evil dharmas. Kāśyapa, this is what is meant by the outcaste of śramaṇas.

"Kāśyapa, an outcaste's clothing, food and drink, and the things he uses are shunned by virtuous people. Similarly, Kāśyapa, the outcaste of śramaṇas procures his monastic robe, bowl, and other necessities of life by breaking the precepts; by performing improper deeds with body, speech, and mind; and by practicing flattery. Precept-keeping śramaṇas and brāhmins shun the things which the outcaste of śramaṇas has procured improperly; they have [only] pity for him. Kāśyapa, this is what is meant by the outcaste of śramaṇas.

"Kāśyapa, an outcaste shamefully begs for food with bowl in hand. Similarly, Kāśyapa, an outcaste of śramaṇas shamefully enters his own room, others' homes, or the presence of people; he goes to the Buddha shamefully; he shamefully pays homage to the stūpa of the Tathāgata; he comes and goes, bends and stretches shamefully; and he walks, stands, sits, and lies down shamefully. To summarize, he does everything shamefully because he conceals his evil dharmas.

"Kāśyapa, an outcaste never goes to a good place, no matter where he goes. Why? Because he practices evil dharmas himself. Similarly, Kāśyapa, the outcaste of śramaṇas does not go to any good plane of existence, no matter where he goes, because he performs many bad deeds and actions leading to rebirth in the miserable planes of existence. Kāśyapa, this is what is meant by the outcaste of śramaṇas.

* * *

"Kāśyapa, what is a corrupt śramaṇa? Kāśyapa, the sediment of wine which remains at the bottom [of a jar] after the good, sweet wine has been taken out is useless and is despised by people. Similarly, Kāśyapa, a corrupt śramaṇa who gives up the flavor of the Dharma and instead clings to the dregs of afflictions is useless and is abhorred by people. He smells the offensive odor of afflictions, not the fragrance of discipline. He can benefit neither himself nor others, no matter where he goes. Kāśyapa, this is what is meant by a corrupt śramaṇa.

"Kāśyapa, corruption may be compared to the transformation of food into dung, which is fetid, impure, and disgusting. Thus, Kāśyapa, a corrupt śramaṇa is like dung, because he is impure in deed, word, and thought. Kāśyapa, this is what is meant by a corrupt śramaṇa.

"Kāśyapa, a spoiled seed sown in the great earth will not sprout or bear fruit. Similarly, Kāśyapa, a corrupt śramaṇa neither plants good roots nor achieves the fruit of a śramaṇa, though he takes refuge in the Buddha-Dharma. Kāśyapa, this is what is meant by a corrupt śramaṇa.

* * *

"Kāśyapa, what is a box-śramaṇa? Kāśyapa, just as an ornate box made by a skillful craftsman may be filled with stinking, dirty things, so, Kāśyapa, a box-śramaṇa outwardly acts as a śramaṇa should act; inwardly he is full of filth and practices evil deeds. Kāśyapa, this is what is meant by a box-śramaṇa

* * *

"Kāśyapa, what is an amaranth-śramaṇa? Kāśyapa, an amaranth is very pretty, but its substance is as hard as wood or stone and its odor as offensive as dung. The wise will not come close to or touch an amaranth, and avoid even the sight of it, while fools who do not know its defects approach and smell it when they see it. Similarly, Kāśyapa, an amaranth-śramaṇa acts like a śramaṇa in appearance, though actually he is rude, indelicate, proud, conceited, filthy, and impure.

He breaks the precepts, deports himself very badly, and does not hold proper views. Kāśyapa, the wise do not associate closely with an amaranth-śramaṇa or respectfully circumambulate him to his right; furthermore, they keep far away from him, because he is an evil man. Kāśyapa, only those as silly as children associate closely with him, make circumambulations to his right to honor him, and accept his words with faith, just as a stupid person goes to pluck an amaranth. Kāśyapa, this is what is meant by an amaranth-śramaṇa.

★ ★ ★

"Kāśyapa, what is a profit-seeking śramaṇa? Kāśyapa, a flattering, deceitful person is always miserly and wrapped in desire. When he sees another person's property, he is so eager to steal it that he does not feel shame or remorse for using a sharp knife or a cudgel to attain his goal. He has no pity, and always harbors harmful intentions. When walking by a desolate marsh, in a forest, or in a village, he is intent on stealing others' property, so he often hides himself.

"Similarly, Kāśyapa, a profit-seeking śramaṇa is always miserly and choked by desire. He is never content with his own gains, but always covets others' property. He goes to a city or a village for the sake of material gains, not for the sake of wholesome dharmas, but he conceals his evil ways. Thinking that good monks know he breaks the precepts and that, when they discourse on discipline, they may act on their knowledge by driving him away from the order, a profit-seeking śramaṇa becomes very fearful of good monks. Inside, he is flattering and deceitful; but outside, he behaves well.

"All gods, dragons, ghosts, spirits, and those who have the deva-eye know this monk for what he is: when he comes, he comes as a thief; when he goes, he goes as a thief; and similarly, as a thief he walks, sits, lies down, rises, takes his robe, puts on his robe, enters a village, leaves a village, eats his meal, drinks, and shaves his hair.

"Kāśyapa, the going, coming, and all other actions of this fool are known and seen by gods, dragons, ghosts, and spirits. They rebuke this evil monk when they see what he does, saying, 'It is such bad men who destroy the Dharma of Śākyamuni Buddha.' When the gods, dragons, ghosts, and spirits see a śramaṇa or brāhmin who keeps the precepts and cultivates pure conduct, they will believe in, honor, and esteem him, saying, 'Such a person deserves material offerings according to the Buddha-Dharma.' Kāśyapa, though a profit-seeking śramaṇa leaves the household life to take refuge in the Buddha-Dharma, he cannot generate even a single thought of ultimate quiescence or a passionless mind, let alone acquire the fruit of a śramaṇa. It is absolutely impossible for him to acquire it. Kāśyapa, this is what is meant by a profit-seeking śramaṇa.

★ ★ ★

"Kāśyapa, what is a darnel-śramaṇa? Kāśyapa, the darnels in a wheat-field look exactly like wheat, so a farmer says that all the plants are good wheat, but later, when the kernels of wheat emerge, he knows that he was wrong to say that.

Kāśyapa, similarly, a darnel-śramaṇa in a group with other śramaṇas seems to be a virtuous precept-keeper, and when a donor sees the group, he says that all of them are śramaṇas. However, actually that fool is not a śramaṇa, though he says he is. He does not cultivate pure conduct, though he says he does. He is corrupt from the outset and does not keep any precepts. He does not belong to the order, either. He lacks the vital wisdom of the Buddha-Dharma and will fall to the miserable planes of existence after death. He is like the darnels among good wheat.

"In the future, when gods, dragons, and those who have the deva-eye see that fool fall to a hell, they will say to each other, 'This fool looked like a śramaṇa in the past, but he performed unwholesome dharmas. Therefore, now he has fallen to a great hell, as he deserves. From now to the far distant future, he will not be able to achieve the virtuous deeds or the fruit of a śramaṇa. He is like darnels among good wheat.' Kāśyapa, this is what is meant by a darnel-śramaṇa.

* * *

"Kāśyapa, what is an undeveloped[21] śramaṇa? Kāśyapa, undeveloped rice plants are so called because they are not mature yet. They are not firm, so they are blown away by the wind. They are not strong or sturdy. They look like rice, but actually they are not yet rice. Kāśyapa, similarly, an undeveloped śramaṇa looks like a śramaṇa in appearance, but no one has taught or corrected him. Because he lacks the power of virtue, he is blown by the wind of demons. He has no vigor and lacks the power of discipline. He learns little and his meditation lacks power. He has no wisdom and cannot destroy the theives of afflictions. Such a śramaṇa is mean, inferior, and powerless, and is bound and controlled by demons. He is submerged in afflictions and blown by the wind of demons, just as undeveloped rice plants are blown by the wind.

"Kāśyapa, just as undeveloped rice plants have no seeds to be scattered in a field and sprout, so undeveloped śramaṇas have no seeds of the path to scatter in the field of the Buddha-Dharma, and cannot liberate themselves from saṁsāra by the doctrines of sages and saints. Kāśyapa, śramaṇas who break the precepts and do evil are called undeveloped śramaṇas.

* * *

"Kāśyapa, what is a false śramaṇa? Kāśyapa, a skillful smith gilds a piece of copper so that it is the color of gold, but the copper article is different from gold in value and people will know by rubbing it that it is not gold. Similarly, a false śramaṇa likes to adorn himself. He bathes often, dresses neatly, and conducts himself strictly in accordance with the rules of a śramaṇa, whether going, coming, bending, or stretching. However, he is always plagued, not only by desire, hatred, and ignorance, but also by greed for material gains, respect, and praise; and by pride, arrogance, and all other defilements. Although he is highly esteemed by people, he in fact is not worthy of esteem at all. He constantly and carefully decks his body with ornaments. He longs for good food and drink. He does not seek the noble Dharma, and has no fear for future lives. He may win temporary honor, but not lasting honor. All he gains is weight. He depends on material supports, not on the Dharma, and is entangled in various bonds. He handles his property assiduously, like a layman. He thinks like a layman, and as a result he reacts like one: he feels pain and pleasure as a layman does, and he is plagued by attachment and aversion. He has no intention to practice the law of a śramaṇa except in rites and manners. He will definitely fall to the miserable planes of hell-dwellers, hungry ghosts, and animals, because he is not a śramaṇa in reality, cannot be qualified as one, and does not deserve the name. Kāśyapa, this is what is meant by a false śramaṇa.

* * *

"Kāśyapa, what is a bloodless śramaṇa? Kāśyapa, a man, woman, boy, or girl whose blood has been sucked by ghosts will become emaciated and weak, because of the loss of blood. Kāśyapa, deprived of blood, he or she cannot be cured by any medicine, spell, knife, or cudgel[22] and will definitely die. Kāśyapa, similarly, a śramaṇa is called a bloodless śramaṇa if he lacks the blood of discipline, meditation, wisdom, liberation, and the knowledge and awareness derived from liberation; the blood of kindness, compassion, joy, and equanimity; the blood of giving, self-control, and the guarding of his bodily, verbal, and mental actions; the blood of abiding securely in the four noble practices; the blood of good deportment; and the blood of pure deeds, words, and thoughts.

"Kāśyapa, though he accepts the Dharma-medicines of the Tathāgata, a bloodless śramaṇa cannot save himself. The Dharma-medicines are:

to contemplate the impurity of the body when one feels carnal desire;
to practice kindness when one feels hatred;
to observe the twelve links of dependent origination when one is deluded;
to ponder afflictions rightly;
to give up fondness for crowds;
to renounce everything one has; and
to take care of three monastic dharmas, namely, to be pure in discipline, to subdue one's mind, and to be concentrated and not distracted.

Kāśyapa, though bloodless śramaṇas take the Dharma-medicines which I prescribe and allow them to take, they cannot save themselves. Kāśyapa, [these Dharma-medicines] are supramundane doctrines:

the contemplation of emptiness, signlessness, and nonaction;
the knowledge of the [five] aggregates, the [eighteen] elements, and the [twelve] entrances;
the four noble truths; and
the twelve links of dependent origination.

Kāśyapa, bloodless śramaṇas cannot save themselves even by taking these [supramundane] Dharma-medicines. Kāśyapa, śramaṇas of this kind are stinking, filthy, and impure. Because they break the precepts and have few blessings, they will be born in the lowliest domains. Because of their arrogance, after death they will surely fall to the great hells, and nowhere else. Just as people who lose their blood will definitely die, so śramaṇas of this kind will certainly fall to the hells after death. Kāśyapa, this is what is meant by a bloodless śramaṇa."

* * *

When these doctrines had been spoken, five hundred monks abandoned the monastic precepts and returned to the lay life. At once, other monks rebuked them, saying, "It is not good or proper for you to regress in the Buddha-Dharma and return to the lay life."

The Buddha told the monks [who blamed the five hundred monks], "Do not say so! Why? Because what they do is in compliance with the Dharma. If monks return to the lay life because they do not wish to accept offerings from faithful donors, they comply with the Dharma. Those monks feel repentant because of their faith in and understanding of the Dharma. When they heard my teachings, they thought: 'We probably did impure deeds, and then accepted offerings from faithful donors. We should feel repentant and return to the lay life.'

"Kāśyapa, now I say that after death those monks will be reborn in the Tuṣita Heaven, where Bodhisattva Maitreya dwells, and when Maitreya Tathāgata appears in the world, they will be among the members of his first assembly."

IV

Then Mahākāśyapa asked the Buddha, "World-Honored One, what kinds of monks may take charge of affairs?"

The Buddha replied to Kāśyapa, "I allow two kinds of monks to take charge of affairs. What are the two? One kind is a monk who can keep the pure precepts, and the other is a monk whose fear of future lives is as strong as adamant. Furthermore, there are two other kinds of monks who may take charge of affairs. What are the two? One kind is a monk who is aware of karmic results and the other is a monk who is repentant and sensitive to shame. Furthermore, there are two other kinds of monks who may take charge of affairs. What are the two? One kind is a monk who has attained Arhatship and the other is a monk who can cultivate the eightfold liberation. Kāśyapa, I permit these kinds of monks to take charge of affairs. Why? Because, Kāśyapa, they are blameless themselves and considerate of others, which is a rare achievement.

"Kāśyapa, there are many kinds of people who have left the household life to take refuge in the Buddha-Dharma. They differ in nature, mentality, liberation, and the eradication of passions. Some are forest-dwellers, some practice begging for food, some like to live in mountain groves, some enjoy staying near a village, some are pure in discipline, some can free themselves from the four yokes, some are diligent in learning much, some debate doctrines, some keep the precepts well, some behave themselves well according to the Vinaya, and some teach the Dharma to people in cities and villages. The administrative monks must well discern the various temperaments of all these kinds of monks.

"Kāśyapa, a monk who dwells in a secluded forest needs to have leisure, so the administrative monk should not assign him any work. If it is a forest-dwelling monk's turn to do a job, the administrative monk should do it for him if he can; otherwise, he should ask another person to do it. He should not order a forest-dwelling monk about, but may give him a small task to do if the monk is not engaged in the practice of the path.

"Kāśyapa, the administrative monk should give good food to those who practice food-begging. He should give monks who can free themselves from the four yokes anything they need, such as clothing, food and drink, bedding, and medicine. He should not shout loudly himself or allow others to shout loudly near the dwelling-places of monks free from the four yokes, in order to protect them. The administrative monk should extend respect to such monks, regard them as World-Honored Ones, and think, 'These monks can be the pillars of the Buddha-Dharma, and I should give them anything they need.'

"Kāśyapa, if there are monks who are diligent in learning much, the administrative monk should encourage them, saying, 'You virtuous ones diligently pursue knowledge, and read and recite so as to have thorough comprehension. I should be at your service. You virtuous, erudite ones are like necklaces of precious stones among the monks. You can ascend to high seats and elaborate on the true Dharma, and also generate wisdom of your own.' The administrative monk should not ask them to work at wrong times but should help them so that they can devote themselves to extensive learning.

"Kāśyapa, the administrative monk should afford everything to a monk who teaches the Dharma, should accompany him to cities and villages and persuade people to hear him explain the Dharma. He should provide a teaching site and make a high, cushioned seat for him. If any monk intends to hurt the Dharma-master by force, the administrative monk should make peace between the two. He should also go frequently to the Dharma-master to offer his praise.

"Kāśyapa, the administrative monk should often visit the monk who keeps the pure precepts well, and who understands the meaning of the Vinaya, saying, 'How should I manage things, so that I may commit no misdeeds and do no harm to myself or others?' The monk who understands the meaning of the Vinaya should observe the mind of the administrative monk and teach him the Dharma in accordance with his managerial duties, advising him how to act.

"The administrative monk should with all his heart have faith in, pay homage to, and make offerings to those who keep the precepts. At the proper times, he should give monks the things they need and are entitled to, and should not conceal those things. When he distributes things, he should not do so with an evil mind, nor in an improper way, nor with a mind full of desire, hatred, ignorance, or fear.

"The administrative monk should act in accordance with the laws of the Saṁgha, not in accordance with the laws of the laity. He should act according to the regulations of the Saṁgha, not according to his own regulations. He should not be free with the things which belong to the Saṁgha. He should consult other monks even on trifling matters and not decide matters arbitrarily by himself.

"As regards the articles used, namely, the resident monks' possessions, the Buddha's possessions, and the visiting monks' possessions, the administrative monk should differentiate them. The resident monks' belongings should not be given to the visiting monks, and vice versa; and the visiting and resident monks' possessions should not be mixed up. The resident and visiting monks' things should not be mixed up with the Buddha's things.

"If the resident monks' belongings are plentiful and the visiting monks need some of them, the administrative monk should summon the resident monks and ask them to give away some of their things. If they agree, then he should give some of their belongings to the visiting monks.

"Kāśyapa, if the stūpa of the Tathāgata needs some repair or is going to ruin, and the resident and visiting monks have many possessions, the administrative monk should summon the monks and ask them to vote whether to give away some of their things, saying, 'The Buddha's stūpa is going to ruin, and needs repair, while the monks' possessions are plentiful. Virtuous monks, it is time for you to consent to my request. If you consent to give away the things you obtained from donors, I shall take and use them, whether they belong to the resident monks or the visiting monks, to repair the Buddha's stūpa.' If the monks vote for it, the administrative monk should use [the proceeds from selling] the monks' possessions to repair the Buddha's stūpa. If the monks vote against it, the administrative monk should persuade lay devotees to contribute money to repair the Buddha's stūpa.

"Kāśyapa, [however,] if the Buddha's things are plentiful, the administrative monk should not distribute them to the resident or visiting monks. Why not? Because he should regard the Buddha's things as the World-Honored One. Everything belonging to the Buddha, even a piece of thread, has been given to the Buddha by faithful donors. Therefore, gods and humans consider even such [trivial] things to be the Buddha's stūpa, let alone precious things. If a garment has been offered to the Buddha's stūpa, it is better to let the garment be blown by the wind, rained upon, and worn out than to exchange it for a precious thing. Why? [First,] because no one can fix a price on anything in the Buddha's stūpa; and second, because the Buddha needs nothing.

"Kāśyapa, a good, pure administrative monk should not mix up the belongings of the Three Jewels. Furthermore, he should be constantly content with what he himself possesses and not think that the belongings of the Three Jewels are his.

"Kāśyapa, if an administrative monk, out of hatred, arbitrarily orders about and employs as servants virtuous precept-keepers, whom people respectfully circumambulate, he will fall to a great hell because of his hatred. If he is born as a human, he will be someone's slave, will be put to hard labor by his master, and will be whipped.

"Furthermore, Kāśyapa, if an administrative monk arbitrarily makes new regulations stricter than the ordinary regulations obeyed by the monks, upbraids and punishes monks [according to his own new regulations], and makes them work at unnecessary times, he will fall to the minor hell of many nails because of this bad root. When he is in this hell, his body will be pierced by hundreds of thousands of nails, and will blaze with fire, emitting great flames like a big furnace.

"If the administrative monk frightens virtuous precept-keepers with serious matters or speaks to them with hatred, he will be born in a hell with a tongue five hundred leagues long. His tongue will be pierced by hundreds of thousands of nails, each of which will give forth great flames.

"Kāśyapa, if the administrative monk begrudges or hides the monks' belongings, or distributes them at the wrong times, unwillingly, bitterly, less than he should, not at all, or to some and not to others, then because of this bad root he will fall to the miserable plane of hungry ghosts after death, and will have only pills made of dung to eat. At that time, other hungry ghosts will show him food without giving it to him. Longing to procure the food, he will gaze at it so intensely that his eyes will not blink at all. He will be hungry and thirsty, but will have nothing to eat or drink for hundreds of thousands of years. After that, he will sometimes obtain food, but the food will soon change into dung or bloody pus. Why? Because he abused his authority by making it difficult for respected precept-keepers to obtain from him their rightful possessions.

"Kāśyapa, the administrative monk will receive a very painful karmic retribution for a kalpa or more if he himself uses without distinction the possessions of the resident monks, the visiting monks, or the Buddha. Why? Because he has encroached on the possessions of the Three Jewels.

"Kāśyapa, if an administrative monk hears such transgressions explained and knows they are transgressions, but is recalcitrant and hates the precept-keepers, I say that he cannot be reformed even by the Buddhas, the World-Honored Ones.

"Kāśyapa, therefore, an administrative monk should guard well his deeds, words, and thoughts after hearing such transgressions explained. He should protect both himself and others.

"Kāśyapa, an administrative monk should prefer to eat his own flesh rather than use without distinction the belongings of the Three Jewels, such as clothing, bowls, food, and drink."

Mahākāśyapa then said to the Buddha, "World-Honored One, extraordinary are these doctrines, which the Tathāgata teaches out of kindness. He speaks of shamelessness to those who are insensitive to shame and speaks of remorse to those who are sensitive to shame."

V

Then Mahākāśyapa asked the Buddha, "World-Honored One, some monks declare themselves to be forest-dwelling monks. World-Honored One, how should a monk act to be called a forest-dwelling monk? How should a monk act to be called a food-begging monk? How should a monk act to be called one who wears a garment of cast-off rags? How should a monk act to be called one who dwells under a tree? How should a monk act to be called one who wanders in a graveyard? How should a monk act to be called one who lives in the open air?"

The Buddha replied to Kāśyapa, "A forest-dwelling monk must delight in a secluded forest and live in it. Kāśyapa, a secluded place is a place where there are no loud noises and no deer, tigers, wolves, flying birds, robbers, cowherds, or shepherds. Such a place is suitable for a śramaṇa's Dharma-practice. Therefore, such a monk should devote himself to Dharma-practice in a secluded place.

"A monk should think of eight things if he wishes to live in a secluded place. What are the eight?

(1) To renounce the body;
(2) to renounce life;
(3) to relinquish material possessions;
(4) to leave all beloved places;
(5) to die on a mountain, like a deer;
(6) to perform the deeds of a forest-dweller when in a secluded place;
(7) to live by the Dharma; and
(8) not to abide in afflictions.

Kāśyapa, a monk who wishes to live in a secluded forest should contemplate these eight things, and then he should go to a secluded place.

"Kāśyapa, after a forest-dwelling monk arrives at a secluded place, he should follow the Dharma of a forest-dweller and perform eight deeds to show kindness for all sentient beings. What are the eight?

(1) To benefit sentient beings;
(2) to gladden sentient beings;
(3) not to hate sentient beings;
(4) to be straightforward;
(5) not to discriminate among sentient beings;
(6) to be compliant with sentient beings;
(7) to contemplate all dharmas; and
(8) to be as pure as space.

Kāśyapa, a forest-dwelling monk should perform these eight deeds to show kindness for all sentient beings.

"Kāśyapa, when a forest-dwelling monk arrives at a secluded place, he should think, 'I have come to this remote place alone, with no companion. No one teaches or rebukes me, whether I practice virtue or nonvirtue.' He should think further, 'However, there are gods, dragons, ghosts, spirits, and Buddhas, the World-Honored Ones, who know that I apply my mind entirely to devotion. They can be my witnesses. Now I am here to practice what a forest-dweller should. If I bear malice, I shall not be free and at ease. Now I am in this remote place all alone; I associate closely with no one and have nothing to call my own. I should now beware of feelings of desire, hatred, annoyance, and so forth. I should not be like those who are fond of crowds or attached to villages. If I am, I shall be deceiving the gods, dragons, ghosts, and spirits; and the Buddhas will not like to see me. If I now follow the right practice of a forest-dweller, the gods, dragons, ghosts, and spirits will not upbraid me, and the Buddhas will be glad to see me.'

"Kāśyapa, when a forest-dwelling monk lives in a secluded place, he should practice the right actions of a forest-dweller:

to persist, with all his heart, in keeping the precepts leading to liberation;
to maintain well the precepts of every category, and purify his own deeds, words, and thoughts;
not to practice flattery or fraud;
to earn his livelihood in a proper way;
to keep his mind inclined to dhyānas;
to memorize the Dharma he has heard;
to cultivate right thought diligently;
to move toward passionless, quiescent, and cessative nirvāṇa;
to be afraid of saṁsāra;
to regard the five aggregates as enemies, the four elements as poisonous snakes, and the six senses as uninhabited villages;
to be adept in devising skillful means;
to contemplate the twelve links of dependent origination in order to part with the views of eternalism and nihilism;
to contemplate the emptiness of a sentient being, of a self, of a personal identity, and of a life;
to understand that the dharmas are devoid of signs, and to practice signlessness;
to decrease his actions gradually and to practice nonaction;
to fear the activities of the three realms;
always to practice the Dharma diligently, as if to save his head from being burned;
always to strive with vigor and never regress;
to contemplate the reality of the body, thinking and contemplating so as to know the origin of suffering, to sever the cause of suffering, to realize the cessation of suffering, and to cultivate assiduously the path leading to the cessation of suffering;

to practice kindness;
to abide securely in the four mindfulnesses;
to avoid unwholesome dharmas and enter the door to wholesome dharmas;
to establish himself in the four right efforts;
to master the four bases of miraculous powers;
to protect the five good roots and to have a command of the five powers;
to be awakened to the seven factors of enlightenment;
to practice the eightfold noble path industriously;
to develop dhyāna and samādhi; and
to discriminate all the forms of dharmas by virtue of wisdom.

"Kāśyapa, a forest-dwelling monk adorns himself with such doctrines. Having adorned himself in this way, he should live in a mountain grove, and diligently cultivate the various practices even in the early and late parts of the night without sleeping then.[23] He should always be eager to attain the supramundane Dharma.

"Kāśyapa, a forest-dwelling monk should constantly cultivate the path wherever he is; he should not decorate his body with fine clothes; he should gather withered grass to cushion his seat; he should not take things from resident or visiting monks. In a secluded place, a forest-dwelling monk should, in order to practice the noble path, be content with any garment which can cover his body.

"Kāśyapa, if a forest-dwelling monk goes to a city or a village to beg for food, he should think, 'I have come to this city or village from my secluded place in order to beg for food; my mind should be neither depressed nor elated, whether I obtain food or not. Indeed, if I am not given food, I should be content and regard it as the karmic retribution [for deeds] in my previous lives, and from now on I should cultivate virtuous deeds industriously.' Furthermore, he should remember that even the Tathāgata did not always acquire food when he begged for it.

"A forest-dwelling monk should adorn himself with the Dharma before he begs for food in a city or a village, and should go to beg only after he has done so. How does he adorn himself with the Dharma? He should not be contaminated with or attached to the sight of pleasant forms, nor be angry at the sight of unpleasant forms, and likewise with pleasant or unpleasant sounds, odors, tastes, textures, and dharmas. He should protect his sense-organs from being attracted, and should gaze no farther than several feet ahead. He should control his mind well and keep in mind the Dharma he has contemplated. He should practice begging for food without defiling his mind with food. He should beg for food from door to door without feeling attachment to a place where he is given food or feeling aversion toward a place where he is not. If he obtains nothing after begging at ten or more houses, he should not be worried, and should think, 'These elders and brāhmins do not give me food for many reasons. They have never even thought of me, not to speak of giving me food.' Kāśyapa, a forest-dwelling monk will not be afraid when begging for food if he can think in this way.

"Kāśyapa, if a forest-dwelling monk sees men, women, boys, girls, or animals when begging for food, he should have kindness and compassion toward them and think, 'I strive with vigor so that I can make the vow that sentient beings who see me and those who give me food will all be reborn in heaven.'

"Kāśyapa, after a forest-dwelling monk obtains food, whether it is coarse or of high quality, he should look for poor people in the city or village and share half the food with them. If he does not see any poor people, he should think, 'I [mentally] give the best of the food I obtain to the sentient beings whom I do not see with my eyes. I am the donor and they are the recipients.'

"Kāśyapa, a forest-dwelling monk should return to his secluded dwelling-place with the food given to him and wash his hands and feet. According to the pure rules of deportment for a śramaṇa, he should arrange a seat with grass he has gathered, sit cross-legged on the seat, and eat without attachment, pride, hatred, or distraction. When he is about to eat, he should think, 'In my body, there are eighty thousand worms which will be secure and happy when they obtain the food I eat. Now I attract these worms to my following with food; but when I attain supreme enlightenment, I shall attract them to my following with the Dharma.'

"Kāśyapa, when a forest-dwelling monk does not have enough to eat, he should think, 'Now that my body is light, I can cultivate patience, purify evils, and have less excrement and urine. My mind is light when my body is light. Therefore, I can sleep little and have no desire.' He should think in this way.

"Kāśyapa, if a forest-dwelling monk is given much food, he should gladly put a handful of it on a clean rock, thinking, 'I give this to the birds and beasts that can eat it. I am the donor and they are the recipients.'

"Kāśyapa, after eating, a forest-dwelling monk should wash and dry his bowl and rinse his hands and mouth. He should put away his patched robe and walk near his secluded place, pondering the forms of dharmas.

"Kāśyapa, a forest-dwelling monk who is still an ordinary man and has not yet achieved the fruit of a śramaṇa may be approached at times by tigers or wolves as he cultivates the practices of a forest-dweller. When he sees these beasts, he should not fear them, but should think, 'Since I came to this secluded place, I have relinquished my body and life; therefore, instead of being afraid, I should cultivate kindness and rid myself of all evils and fears. If tigers or wolves kill me and eat my flesh, I should think that I am greatly benefited, for I shall get rid of my fragile body and gain a stable one.[24] I have no food to give to the tigers or wolves, but they will be comfortable and happy after they eat my flesh.' Kāśyapa, a forest-dwelling monk should relinquish his body and life in this way when he follows the right practice of a forest-dweller.

"Kāśyapa, when a forest-dwelling monk follows the right practice of a forest-dweller, nonhumans may come to his place in either beautiful or ugly forms. Toward such nonhumans, he should generate neither love nor hate.

"Kāśyapa, if the gods who have met the Buddha come to the place of a forest-dwelling monk and bring up many questions, the monk should explain to them as best he can the doctrines which he has studied. If he cannot give an answer to a difficult question which a god puts to him, he should not become arrogant, but should say 'I have not learned much, but do not despise me. From now on I shall cultivate and study the Buddha-Dharma more diligently, so that one day I may be [thoroughly] conversant with the Buddha-Dharma and able to answer all questions.' He should also urge the gods [to preach], saying, 'Please explain the Dharma to me. I shall hear and accept it.' He should also say gratefully, 'May you not refuse my request!'

"Moreover, Kāśyapa, a forest-dwelling monk who follows the right practice of a forest-dweller should cultivate well the thoughts of a forest-dweller: 'Just as grass, trees, tiles, and stones have no [inner] master, self, or owner, so it is with the body. There is no self, no life, no personal identity, no sentient being, no contention. The body arises from the combination of conditions. If I contemplate it well, I shall sever all wrong views.' A forest-dwelling monk should always think of the doctrine of emptiness, signlessness, and nonaction.

"Kāśyapa, when a forest-dwelling monk follows the right practice of a forest-dweller, he will find that fruits, herbs, grass, and trees arise from the combination of conditions and cease with their dispersion. These external things have no master, no 'I' or 'mine,' and no contention; they arise naturally and cease naturally, yet there is no entity that arises or ceases. Kāśyapa, just as grass, trees, tiles, and stones have no [inner] self, master, or owner, so it is with the body. There is no self, no life, no personal identity, no sentient being, no contention. All dharmas arise from the combination of conditions and cease with their dispersion. In reality, no dharma arises or ceases.

"Kāśyapa, a forest-dwelling monk should cultivate this doctrine when he stays in a secluded place. Kāśyapa, a forest-dwelling monk who practices this doctrine will achieve the fruit of a śramaṇa quickly if he follows the Śrāvaka-vehicle. If he is hindered from achieving the fruit of a śramaṇa in this life, he will without fail end all his defilements after seeing one Buddha, or two, or at most three. If he follows the Bodhisattva-vehicle, he will obtain in this life the Realization of the Nonarising of Dharmas and the Dharma of Nonobstruction, see future Buddhas without fail, and attain supreme enlightenment quickly."

When this discourse on the forest-dwelling monk was spoken, five hundred monks eliminated all their defilements and achieved mental liberation.

VI

The Buddha told Kāśyapa, "What is a food-begging monk? Kāśyapa, if a monk abides securely in his past vow to lead a monastic life practicing begging for food, he will be single-minded and will not use flattery or deceit, will decline all invitations to dinner, will accept no food offered to a community of monks, and will adorn himself with dignity.

"A food-begging monk should not think of the flavor of any dishes. When he is given delicacies, he should warn himself, thinking, 'I am like an outcaste. It is my body and mind which should be pure, not my food and beverages. Why? Because all delicious food, when eaten, will change into stinking, filthy, and impure excrement. I should not seek any fine food.'

"Having subdued his mind in this way, a food-begging monk should not think when he begs for food from door to door in a city or a village: 'It is a man, not a woman, who gives me food'; or 'It is a woman, not a man, who gives me food'; or 'It is a boy, not a girl, who gives me food'; or 'It is a girl, not a boy, who gives me food'; or 'I should be given delicacies, not coarse food'; or 'I should be given good food, not bad food'; or 'It is the time to give me food'; or 'It is not the time to give me food'; or 'It should be easy, not difficult, for me to obtain food'; or 'I should be given food quickly, not slowly'; or 'I should be respected and not despised when I enter a village'; or 'I should be given freshly cooked food, not leftover food'; or 'I should acquire food from the rich, not from the poor'; or 'Men and women should welcome me.' Kāśyapa, a food-begging monk should not have these unwholesome ideas.

"Kāśyapa, a food-begging monk should adorn himself with the rules of food-begging: when begging for food, he should not feel sad or joyful, whether he is given food or not; he should not consider whether the food he is given is coarse or of high quality. Why? Because many sentient beings perform evil deeds owing to their attachment to delicacies, and as a result they fall to the miserable planes of hell-dwellers, hungry ghosts, or animals. Those who are content are not greedy for delicacies. Therefore, a food-begging monk should not seek high-quality food but accept coarse food. He should not let his sense of taste become attached to delicacies, but should feel content with any kind of food. Even when he is given the coarsest food, he should be content with it. Thus, he will be reborn in heaven or as a human after death and, if he is reborn in heaven, he will [then] have celestial delicacies.

"Kāśyapa, a food-begging monk should subdue his mind by detachment from delicacies. He should not be unhappy even if he eats nothing but beans for seven days. Why? Because he should eat [only] to live. He is able to cultivate the path after eating; he should eat for this reason.

"Kāśyapa, if a food-begging monk obtains a bowl of food in a proper way, it is a proper material support. The monk should share it with the monks who cultivate pure conduct.

"Kāśyapa, when a food-begging monk is sick and has no food to eat because he has no attendant to beg food for him, he should subdue his mind in this way: 'I am alone without any companion, for I have left the household life. The Dharma is my companion, so I should keep the Dharma in mind. Now I suffer from illness. I should think of the Dharma I have heard before, for the World-Honored One said that monks should keep the Dharma in mind. What should I think of? I should contemplate the body as it is. Having contemplated the body as it is, it is quite possible that a wise person can achieve the first dhyāna if he is single-minded. Those who acquire the joy of dhyāna can live on dhyāna and become cheerful in mind for one day, two days, or even seven days [without food].'

"Kāśyapa, if a food-begging monk does not achieve dhyāna when he practices in this way, he should practice more diligently and abide securely in wholesome dharmas. As many people know, gods, dragons, and spirits will offer food to such a person as a result of his freedom from the yoke [of attachment to food].

"Kāśyapa, when a food-begging monk cannot go out to beg for food because of heavy rains or strong wind and dust, he should live on kindness and adorn himself with it; he should abide securely in and ponder upon the Dharma he practices. If he has nothing to eat for two or three nights, he should think, 'There are many sentient beings who fall to the plane of hungry ghosts because they have performed evil karmas. They are miserable; for a hundred years they do not even have saliva to wet their throats. Now, I abide securely in Dharma-doors. Although physically and mentally I am weak, still I can bear hunger and thirst. I should cultivate the noble path industriously and not regress from it.'

"Kāśyapa, a food-begging monk should not associate closely with laypeople, whether they are men, women, boys, or girls.

"Kāśyapa, if a food-begging monk asks a lay devotee to remove dirt from his food, the monk should teach the Dharma to him while sitting there, until the food is clean and given back to him. Then he should rise from his seat and go away.

"Kāśyapa, a food-begging monk should not be pretentious. How may he be pretentious? He is pretentious if he says to others, 'Today the food I have begged is coarse and inadequate, and yet I am sharing it with many people. Therefore, I have eaten little, and being hungry and thirsty, I will become emaciated and weak.' Kāśyapa, a food-begging monk should avoid such pretension.

"Kāśyapa, a food-begging monk should be detached from all things. He should, without feeling unhappy or glad, accept any food put in his bowl, whether coarse or of high quality, little or much, pure or impure. He should always purify his mind and contemplate the forms of dharmas. He accepts food in order to survive and practice the noble path.

"Kāśyapa, if a food-begging monk is not given any food and leaves with his empty bowl in hand after he begs food from door to door in a city or village, he should think, 'Even the Tathāgata, who has great, awesome virtue, who renounced the throne of a universal monarch and left the household life, and who has eradicated all evils and fulfilled all wholesome dharmas, left a village with his empty bowl in hand after he had begged for food. How can I, who have few virtues and do not plant good roots, not come back with my bowl empty? Therefore, I should not be grieved. Why? Because it is absolutely impossible that the monks who do not plant good roots can obtain food, coarse or of high quality. Now, I am not given any food, probably because demons or their messengers have prevented brāhmins and laymen from giving me food. Therefore, I should be diligent in cultivation so as to stay away from the four demons and eradicate all defilements. If I cultivate the path assiduously, neither Pāpīyān, the king of demons, nor demons' messengers can get in my way.'

"Kāśyapa, a food-begging monk should uphold the noble practices in this way."

VII

The Buddha told Kāśyapa, "A monk who wears a garment of cast-off rags should think when he picks up rags, 'I pick up cast-off rags from garbage because I am sensitive to the shame [of nakedness], not because I want to adorn myself with a garment; because I have to protect myself from the wind, the sun, mosquitos, gnats, and harmful objects; and because I abide securely in the teachings of the Buddha, not because I seek anything pure and fine.'

"He should engender two kinds of thoughts when he is picking up rags. What are the two? One is the thought of contentment and the other is the thought of convenient support.

"Furthermore, he should engender two [other] kinds of thoughts: one is the thought of giving up arrogance and the other is the thought of upholding the noble practices.

"Moreover, he should engender two [other] kinds of thoughts: one is the thought of not adorning the body and the other is the thought of purifying the mind.

"Furthermore, if a monk who wears a garment of cast-off rags stops picking up rags from a rubbish heap when he sees his relatives or friends and thinks, 'Perhaps they will scold me, saying, "You are a dirty person,"' Kāśyapa, I say that this monk is not pure in conduct. Why? Because the mind of a monk who wears a garment of cast-off rags should be as firm as a rock, so that nothing external can penetrate or move it.

"Kāśyapa, a monk who wears a garment of cast-off rags should wash the cast-off rags until they are clean, dye them after they are washed, and then make a patched robe with them. He should patch them up well and wear the patched robe carefully so that it will not burst at the seams.

"Kāśyapa, to free himself from desire, a monk who wears a garment of cast-off rags should wear it with constant contemplation upon the impurity [of the body]. To free himself from hatred, he should wear it with kindness. To free himself from ignorance, he should wear it with contemplation upon the twelve links of dependent origination. To eradicate all afflictions, he should wear it with right thought. To know the [nature of the] six senses, he should wear it while protecting his sense-organs from being attracted. To make gods, dragons, and spirits happy, he should wear it with no flattery or deceit.

"Kāśyapa, why is such a garment called a garment of cast-off rags? Kāśyapa, just as a repugnant corpse that no one wants to own is usually abandoned, so is a garment of cast-off rags. It has nothing to do with [the notions of] 'I' and 'mine.' It is easy to obtain. It was acquired in a proper way, not by begging or currying favor with others. It was discarded as rubbish and does not belong to anyone. Therefore, it is called a garment of cast-off rags.

"Kāśyapa, a garment of cast-off rags symbolizes the Dharma-banner, because it is the sign of the Great Ṛṣi; it symbolizes one's caste, because it is the sign of the caste of saints; it symbolizes one's maintenance of a noble nature, because it is the sign of the noble practices; it symbolizes one's concentrated [right] thought, because it is the sign of wholesome dharmas; it symbolizes one's skillful protection of precepts, because it is the sign of discipline; it symbolizes that one moves toward the doors [of liberation], because it is the sign of dhyāna; it symbolizes that one's mind abides securely, because it is the sign of wisdom; it symbolizes that one's body belongs to nothing, because it is the sign of liberation; it symbolizes one's compliance with the Dharma, because it is the sign of the knowledge and awareness d rived from liberation.

"Kāśyapa, thus, monks who wear garments of cast-off rags achieve great blessings. They do not long for anything. They are not greedy and are attached to nothing. They can free their minds from pride and abandon the heavy burdens [of afflictions].

"Kāśyapa, because of his contentment, gods, dragons, ghosts, and spirits all like to see a monk who wears a garment of cast-off rags.

"Kāśyapa, if a monk who wears a garment of cast-off rags enters dhyāna, then Śakra, Brahmā, and the four deva kings will kneel upright before him, join their palms, and bow with their heads at his feet, let alone other, minor gods.

"Kāśyapa, if an evil monk strives to procure a garment to bedeck himself, outwardly manifesting pure conduct but inwardly being full of desire, hatred, and ignorance, then the gods, dragons, and spirits will not go to his place to pay homage and make offerings to him. Why? Because they know that this monk strives to acquire a garment to bedeck himself instead of [striving to] eliminate the filth of his mind and mental faculties; knowing this, they avoid him.

"Kāśyapa, you saw that Śrāmaṇera Cunda picked up impure, stinking, and dirty cast-off rags [for his garment] and, after having begged for food, went to the Lake of No Burning Afflictions in order to wash the rags there. At that time, gods who lived by the lake came to greet him and bowed with their heads at his feet. Those gods all like to be clean and pure, but they took from Śrāmaṇera Cunda the impure cast-off rags he had picked up and washed out the dirt for him, then bathed with the same water. Those gods knew that Cunda kept the pure precepts, could enter various dhyānas, and had great, awesome virtue; therefore, they came to welcome and salute him.

"Kāśyapa, you saw that when Brahmacārin Virtue desired to go to the Lake of No Burning Afflictions after having begged for food in a pure, clean garment, the gods who lived there stood five miles[25] from the four sides of the lake and prevented him from coming near it, for fear that he might defile the lake with his impure leftover food.

"Kāśyapa, now you have seen these things. Because of his saintly right action and awesome virtue, Śrāmaṇera Cunda received this reward: the gods took his unclean cast-off rags and washed them, then bathed with the same water. However, those same gods stood five miles from the lake to prevent Brahmacārin Virtue from coming close to it. Kāśyapa, who will not cultivate and study the noble Dharma after hearing of these events? Both gods and humans bow with their heads at the feet of the saints and pay homage and make offerings to them. Kāśyapa, it is in order to seek such saintly virtue that monks wear garments of cast-off rags.

"Kāśyapa, a monk who wears a garment of cast-off rags should securely abide in the noble practices and should not be worried. [Seeing] his garment of cast-off rags, he should generate the thought of a stūpa, the thought of the World-Honored One, the thought of the renunciation of the world, and the thought of the nonexistence of 'I' and 'mine.' Only after such contemplation should he wear a garment of cast-off rags and subdue his mind accordingly. Because he is pure in mind, he is pure in body; it is not true that because he is pure in body, he is pure in mind. Kāśyapa, a monk should therefore purify his mind and not decorate his body. Why? In light of the Buddha-Dharma, it is due to mental purity that a monk is said to have cultivated pure conduct.

"Kāśyapa, if a monk who wears a garment of cast-off rags can learn in this way, he is following in my footsteps and yours also.

"Kāśyapa, as you can wear such a coarse garment, you are content with the cultivation of the noble practices.

"Kāśyapa, when you take walking exercise in your upper garment, leaving your patched robe on a couch or a seat, hundreds of thousands of gods pay homage to your patched robe, which, though used to cover the body, is scented by [the fragrance of] discipline, dhyāna, and wisdom. Kāśyapa, you should know that even your robe is so highly esteemed and honored, let alone yourself.

"Kāśyapa, I renounced the throne of a universal monarch and left the household life to follow the path. Before, I wore garments made of the most wonderful silk and cotton, but now I am content with following the noble practices. For the sake of others, I gave up my fine clothes to wear a garment made of rags picked up in graveyards. Future monks should follow my example, when they hear of this deed of mine.

"Kāśyapa, you formerly had a fine, golden, silk garment, and when I asked you for it, you gave it to me. Kāśyapa, it was out of compassion for you that I accepted your garment, not because I coveted your garment or because I wanted to bedeck my body with it.

"Kāśyapa, there are evil monks who follow neither my way nor yours. Engulfed in desire, they collect many monastic robes and bowls, hoard food and drink without giving anything away, and accumulate gold, silver, lapis lazuli, rice, cows, goats, chickens, pigs, donkeys, carriages, and farm tools. They seek and hoard articles which a lay family needs.

"The wise can increase their wholesome dharmas, even if they lead a lay life, but the ignorant can never achieve any wholesome dharmas, even if they leave the household life. How can wise laymen increase their wholesome dharmas? Kāśyapa, some monks put their monastic robes around their necks, do not perform the deeds befitting a śramaṇa, are occupied with many secular things and bound in various ways, and seek fine food and clothing. After they don their monastic robes, lay devotees salute and respect them on sight; give them clothing, food and drink, bedding, and medicine; welcome them when they arrive; and see them off when they leave. Kāśyapa, lay devotees can do such wholesome things, while those monks cannot. Why? Because those monks seek many things they do not need and give nothing to others.

"[However,] Kāśyapa, in the future there will be monks, who own many robes, bowls, and other things and are saluted, esteemed, and praised on sight by lay devotees. Why? Because [in that age] the lay devotees will think, 'The monks have been given many things by others, and they may give me some of them from time to time.'

"Kāśyapa, [in the future] there will [also] be monks who keep the precepts. Seeing the faults and evils of the world, they will cultivate wholesome dharmas assiduously and rid themselves of all defilements as urgently as if to save their heads from being burned; they will be content and seldom engage in worldly activities; they will practice the Dharma diligently for their own benefit and break with all people who are attached to the sources of evil. Nevertheless, not a single lay devotee will go to see those virtuous monks, associate closely with them, salute, esteem, or praise them. Why? Because the lay devotees [then] will be flippant and shallow. They will see only the benefit of this life, not that of future lives. They will think: 'I can get no profit from these virtuous monks. Why should I associate closely with them, or salute, revere, and extol them?' Only poor people, those who have some good roots, and those who are bound to revere them because of a connection in their past lives will associate closely with these monks, salute, revere, and extol them, and consider them as good friends.

"Kāśyapa, two kinds of persons will be pleased with what I have said [in this sūtra]. What are the two? Those who perceive the four noble truths and those who perceive the faults and evils of saṁsāra. Furthermore, there are two [other] kinds: those who strive to free themselves from the four yokes and those who wish to achieve the fruits of a śramaṇa. Moreover, there are two [other] kinds: those who contemplate karmic results wholeheartedly and those who wish to understand the meaning of the forms of dharmas.

"Kāśyapa, now I close the door on all lazy persons; namely, those who are aware neither of karma nor of karmic results; those who have no good deportment; those whose blindness to [consequent] faults and evils in future lives is as immutable as adamant; those who perceive only benefits for this life, not for future lives; and those who have not a single thought to move toward the doors to liberation.

"Kāśyapa, now I say that evil monks should not wish to hear this doctrine explained or to come across it, [because] when they hear it explained, they, knowing their own [evil] deeds, will not understand the profound meaning of it but instead will slander it, saying, 'It is not what the Buddha teaches. It is concocted by a commentator or spoken by demons'; and they will also try to convince others of this. In this way, those evil monks will hurt and defile both themselves and others, and they cannot benefit anyone."

Then Mahākāśyapa said to the Buddha, "World-Honored One, out of compassion as great as that of all Buddhas [combined], the Tathāgata has in this sūtra described how the monks who have devoted themselves to cultivation [of the Dharma] achieve command of all dharmas. World-Honored One, if sentient beings, after hearing this sūtra explained, believe, comprehend, read, and recite it, and are inclined to follow the real Dharma, it should be known that the Buddhas have already accepted them into their following."

Then the Buddha told Ānanda, "If sentient beings can accept and uphold this sūtra, it is because they have already planted good roots in the presence of past Buddhas. Now, if such good men and good women wish to read and recite this sūtra with thorough comprehension in order to achieve liberation, they will surely be able to eradicate all their defilements and attain nirvāṇa by this doctrine, whether they study it as members of the order or as laypeople."

Ānanda said to the Buddha, "World-Honored One, I wish to uphold this sūtra. What should it be named, and how should it be upheld?"

The Buddha told Ānanda, "This sūtra is named 'The Choice of All Dharma-Jewels,' or 'Abiding in Good and Noble Deportment,' or 'Accepting Precept-Keepers into the Order,' or 'An Analysis of Precept-Breakers,' or 'The Precious Bridges,'[26] or 'A Collection of Treasures,' or 'The Treasure-Store,' or 'The Precious Dharma Doors.'"

After Mahākāśyapa finished asking [the Buddha about] "The Sūtra of the Precious Bridges of the Mahāyāna," the monks were overjoyed to hear what the Buddha had taught and began to practice it with veneration.

NOTES

1. This group and those in the following list (up to and including the eightfold noble path) make up the thirty-seven ways to enlightenment.

2. The phrase "cultivate well the seven factors of enlightenment" occurs here, but it is evidently misplaced in this grouping and is repeated later. We have omitted it.

3. These are the four reliances which guide a Buddhist. See Numerical Glossary.

4. Also called the eight worldly winds.

5. As explained at length below, if a religious person accepts offerings from donors but does not observe the precepts, the karmic blessings that would have accrued to the donor (had the recipient kept the precepts) are lost.

6. Probably, the nirvāṇa of the two vehicles.

7. Probably, the teachings of the two vehicles.

8. This is probably a hyperbole.

9. Dhyāna in the state of infinite space, in the state of limitless consciousness, in the state of nothingness, and in the state of neither thinking nor nonthinking.

10. They are: Stream-enterer (*śrotāpanna*), Once-returner (*sakṛdāgāmin*), Nonreturner (*anāgāmin*), and Arhat. See Glossary.

11. This probably means dwelling in the four immeasurable dhyānas.

12. The six thoughts to dwell upon: the Buddha, the Dharma, the Saṁgha, the precepts, giving, and the joys of heaven.

13. The six kinds of reverent unity in a monastery: bodily unity in worship, oral unity in chanting, mental unity in faith, moral unity in observing the precepts, doctrinal unity in view and explanation, and economic unity in the communal goods.

14. Probably the six pāramitās.

15. Also called the four yokes. See Numerical Glossary.

16. Some say ninety-six: allegedly the six founders of heterodox schools, each with fifteen sub-schools. The editor confesses his ignorance of the names and doctrines of the ninety-six schools, as he has never encountered any source providing this information.

17. In this and the following 15 paragraphs, the opening sentence is repeated at the end of the paragraph. In the interest of conciseness, we have eliminated the repetition.

18. This refers to learning which does not further one's wisdom or compassion, or which is not conducive to devotion or enlightenment.

19. This probably refers to the sequential and reverse orders of the twelve links of dependent origination.

20. In this section, the Buddha, whose teachings of equality stridently contradict the prevalent caste system of India, expediently utilizes that very system to make a point about evil śramaṇas. The Buddha welcomed members of all four castes and outcastes into his following, without discrimination.

21. Literally, "new-born."

22. A knife is obviously an instrument which could be used for surgical purposes. The application of a cudgel for medical treatment, though extremely rare, seems also to exist in folk medicine.

23. The night is divided into three periods of three hours each. A forest-dweller, in line with this passage, should sleep only during the middle period.

24. This probably denotes the adamantine Dharma-body.

25. Literally *li*, 里. The Chinese *li* is much shorter than a mile, but lacking an exact equivalent, we have used the word 'mile' here.

26. "Bridges" leading to the other shore, nirvāṇa.

VI

On Pure Land

17 不動如來會

The Dharma-Door of Praising Tathāgata Akṣobhya's Merits

I

Thus have I heard. Once the Buddha was dwelling on Mount Gṛdhrakūṭa near Rājagṛha, together with an assembly of twelve hundred fifty great monks. All these monks were well-known Arhats who had extinguished all defilements and suffered afflictions no more. They were liberated in mind and in wisdom,[1] and were as free and unhindered as great dragons. They had done what should be done and abandoned the heavy burdens. They had benefited themselves and severed all bonds of existence. They were conversant with the true teaching and had reached the other shore. [Among them,] only Ānanda remained in the stage of learning.

At that time, the Venerable Śāriputra rose from his seat, uncovered his right shoulder, knelt on his right knee, joined his palms toward the Buddha, and said, "World-Honored One, how did Bodhisattva-Mahāsattvas of the past resolve to pursue supreme enlightenment, cultivate all pure deeds, and wear the armor of vigor, adorning themselves with merits? How did those Bodhisattva-Mahāsattvas wear the armor of vigor, which enabled them to attain nonregression from the pursuit of supreme enlightenment? May the utterly kind World-Honored One reveal and expound their deeds, their vows, and their engendering of bodhicitta. World-Honored One, those Bodhisattva-Mahāsattvas, for the benefit, peace, and happiness of gods and humans, exerted themselves to cultivate all pure deeds and wore the armor of vigor; thereby they rendered benefit, peace, and happiness to all sentient beings, and illuminated the Buddha-Dharma for Bodhisattvas of the pre-

Sūtra 6, Taishō 310, pp. 101–112; translated into Chinese by Bodhiruci.

sent and future. By praising merits and obtaining good roots, they caused the Bodhisattvas [of the present and future] to learn and cultivate diligently [the insight into] suchness, the Dharma-nature, and to attain supreme enlightenment without fail after hearing the Buddha-Dharma explained."

The Buddha said, "Excellent! It is excellent, Śāriputra, that you can ask me about past[2] Bodhisattva-Mahāsattvas' pure deeds, their illumination, their great armor, and their praising of merits for the sake of embracing Bodhisattva-Mahāsattvas of the future. Now, listen attentively and think in accordance with the truth. I will explain this to you."

Śāriputra said, "Yes, World-Honored One, I am willing and glad to listen."

The Buddha told Śāriputra, "A thousand worlds from here to the east, there is a Buddha-land named Wonderful Joy, where Tathāgata Great Eyes, the Worthy One, the Perfectly Enlightened One, once appeared to expound the subtle, wonderful Dharma to Bodhisattva-Mahāsattvas, beginning with the six pāramitās.

"Śāriputra, at that time, a monk rose from his seat, uncovered his right shoulder, knelt on his right knee, joined his palms toward the Buddha, and said, 'World-Honored One, I am determined to follow the way of the Bodhisattva as taught by the Buddha.'

"That Buddha said, 'Now, good man, you should know that the way of the Bodhisattva is very difficult to follow. Why? Because a Bodhisattva bears no malice against sentient beings.'

"Thereupon, the monk said to the Buddha, 'World-Honored One, I now engender supreme bodhicitta. I will seek all-knowing wisdom by doing away with crookedness and deceit, and by invariably speaking the truth. If I bear malice against sentient beings from now until my attainment of supreme enlightenment, I will be disobeying all the Buddhas, Tathāgatas, who are now expounding the Dharma in numberless, countless, boundless worlds.

"'World-Honored One, now I have resolved to pursue all-knowing wisdom and dedicate myself to this. If, during this pursuit, I feel any inclination to be a Śrāvaka or Pratyekabuddha, I will be deceiving all Buddhas.

"'World-Honored One, now I have resolved to pursue all-knowing wisdom and am dedicated to this. If I generate any desire, hatred, or ignorance toward sentient beings, or am prone to stupor, arrogance, or misdeeds from now until my attainment of supreme enlightenment, I will be deceiving all Buddhas.[3]

"'World-Honored One, now I have resolved to pursue all-knowing wisdom and am firmly dedicated to this goal. If I generate any doubt, any intention to kill or steal, any wrong view or impure deed; or if I am prone to lying, duplicity, or harsh language; or if I hurt others in other ways from now until my attainment of supreme enlightenment, I will be deceiving all Buddhas.'

"Śāriputra, at that time, certain other monks thought, 'After he has first brought forth bodhicitta, this Bodhisattva-Mahāsattva will wear the armor of vigor, and will never be moved by hatred or the like toward any sentient being.' Śāriputra, then, because of their thought, the Bodhisattva was called Akṣobhya[4] of the Land of Wonderful Joy. When Tathāgata Great Eyes, the Worthy One, the Perfectly Enlightened One, saw that this Bodhisattva had obtained the name 'Akṣobhya,' he rejoiced over the name and acclaimed it as excellent. The four deva kings, Śakra, and Brahmā, upon hearing his name, also rejoiced over it.

"Śāriputra, in that Buddha's presence, Bodhisattva-Mahāsattva Akṣobhya continued, 'World-Honored One, now I have resolved to pursue all-knowing wisdom and am dedicated to the attainment of supreme enlightenment. If my practice, from now until my attainment of supreme enlightenment, is ever contrary to these words, then I will be deceiving all the Buddhas, the Tathāgatas, who expound the Dharma in numberless, countless worlds.

"'World-Honored One, now I have made this great decision and have dedicated myself to it. If I say anything that is not in harmony with the recollection of the Buddha or with all-knowing wisdom from now until my attainment of enlightenment, then I will be deceiving all Buddhas.

"'World-Honored One, now I have brought forth this aspiration and am dedicated to it. If I remain in the household life instead of renouncing it in any lifetime from now until my attainment of supreme enlightenment, then I will be disobeying all Buddhas.

"'World-Honored One, now I have resolved to pursue all-knowing wisdom. If I leave the household life in every lifetime, but do not beg for food, take only one meal a day, practice temperance in eating, . . . limit my clothing to the three garments,[5] wear garments of cast-off rags, sit anywhere, practice never lying down, live in a secluded forest, rest under a tree, sit in the open air, or live among graves from now until my attainment of supreme enlightenment, then I will be deceiving all Buddhas.

"'World-Honored One, now I have resolved to pursue great enlightenment and am so dedicated. If I cannot attain unimpeded eloquence to expound the wonderful Dharma from now until my attainment of all-knowing wisdom, then I will be deceiving all Buddhas.

"'World-Honored One, now I have thus resolved. If I do not remain dignified in standing, sitting, and walking from now up to my attainment of supreme enlightenment, then I will be deceiving all the innumerable Buddhas.

"'World-Honored One, now I have thus resolved. If I commit any major offense against sentient beings, or lie, or speak in a worldly or boisterous manner, or have any inclination to defeat others in argument from now until my attainment of all-knowing wisdom, then I will be deceiving all the countless Buddhas.

"'World-Honored One, now I have resolved to pursue all-knowing wisdom and am firmly dedicated to the attainment of supreme enlightenment. If, when expounding the Dharma to women, I do not keep in mind impermanence, suffering, emptiness, or the absence of self, but am attracted by the women's appearance and smile broadly, then I will be deceiving all Buddhas.

"'World-Honored One, I have now resolved to pursue all-knowing wisdom and am firmly dedicated to the attainment of supreme enlightenment. If I look around and gesture frivolously when expounding the Dharma, or do not regard other Bodhisattvas as great masters when I see them, then I will be deceiving numberless Buddhas.

"'World-Honored One, now I have resolved to pursue all-knowing wisdom. From now until my attainment of supreme enlightenment, if I sit down to listen to [heterodox] doctrines or pay homage to heterodox śramaṇas and brāhmins, instead of [listening to the Dharma and paying homage to] Buddhist śramaṇas and devotees, then I will be deceiving all Buddhas.

"'World-Honored One, now I have brought forth this great aspiration. From now until I attain supreme enlightenment, if, when practicing the giving of material things or the giving of the Dharma, I am partial or discriminate among the recipients of my offerings, then I will be deceiving all Buddhas.

"'World-Honored One, now I have resolved to pursue all-knowing wisdom. From now until I attain supreme enlightenment, if, when seeing criminals about to be punished, I do not save them even at the risk of my own life, then I will be deceiving all Buddhas.'[6]

"Śāriputra, from the time when this Bodhisattva began to cultivate such a great practice up to his attainment of supreme enlightenment, not a single sentient being about to be punished for some crime was not rescued by him.

"Śāriputra, at that time, a monk thought, 'The Tathāgata will be the witness for this Dharma-practictioner, as will these gods, humans, asuras, and so forth.'

"Śāriputra, thereupon, perceiving what the monk thought, Tathāgata Great Eyes, the Worthy One, the Perfectly Enlightened One, told him, 'So it is, so it is; the Tathāgata, the Worthy One, the Perfectly Enlightened One, will be his witness, as will these gods, humans, asuras, and so forth. Monk, any Bodhisattva-Mahāsattva who thus wears the armor of great vigor to pursue supreme enlightenment will surely attain it.'

"Śāriputra, after that, the Bodhisattva-Mahāsattva Akṣobhya further said to the Buddha, 'World-Honored One, now I have resolved to pursue all-knowing wisdom. If I mention any offense committed by, or any dissension among, monks, nuns, laymen, or laywomen from now until my attainment of supreme enlightenment, then I will be disobeying all Buddhas, the Tathāgatas. World-Honored One, I will devote myself to the practice of this vow until I attain supreme enlightenment, so as to make my [Buddha-] land vast and pure and the Śrāvakas there all faultless.

"'World-Honored One, from now until my attainment of supreme enlightenment, if I, who have resolved to pursue all-knowing wisdom, have any sensual desire resulting in an ejaculation, even in a dream, then I will be disobeying all Buddhas, the Tathāgatas. World-Honored One, I will follow this practice until I realize supreme enlightenment, so as to make the monastic Bodhisattvas in my land free from ejaculations, even in dreams.[7]

"'World-Honored One, I have resolved to pursue all-knowing wisdom. If, however, when I have attained supreme enlightenment, the women in my Buddha-land have the same female faults as those of women in other lands, then I will relinquish supreme enlightenment. If I do not relinquish it, then I shall be cheating all Buddhas.'. . .

"Śāriputra, at that time, Tathāgata Great Eyes prophesied Bodhisattva Akṣobhya's attainment of supreme enlightenment, saying, 'Good man, in a future life you will become a Buddha named Tathāgata Akṣobhya; the Worthy One, the Perfectly Enlightened One, the One Perfect in Learning and Conduct, the Well-Gone One, the World-Knower, the Unexcelled One, the Great Tamer, the Teacher of Gods and Humans, the Buddha, the World-Honored One.' The prophecy was similar to Dīpaṁkara Buddha's prophecy of my attainment of supreme enlightenment.

"Śāriputra, when Bodhisattva Akṣobhya received the prophecy, there was a great light that illuminated the whole world, and the earth quaked in the six ways, as did the billion-world universe when I realized all-knowing wisdom.

"Furthermore, Śāriputra, at that time all the flowers, trees, and jungles of the billion-world universe leaned toward that Bodhisattva, just as all the grasses and trees leaned toward me when I realized enlightenment.

"Furthermore, Śāriputra, when Bodhisattva Akṣobhya received the prophecy from the Buddha, all the gods, dragons, yakṣas, asuras, garuḍas, kinnaras, and mahoragas of that billion-world universe joined their palms and prostrated themselves with their heads at the Bodhisattva's feet to pay homage to him, just as all the gods, dragons, and so forth of the Sahā World did to me when I realized great enlightenment here.

"Furthermore, Śāriputra, at the moment when Bodhisattva Akṣobhya received the prophecy, all the pregnant women in the world gave birth to their children safely and peacefully, without travail or difficulty; the blind recovered their sight and the deaf restored their hearing, all just as it was when I attained Buddhahood.

"Furthermore, Śāriputra, at the two moments—when the Bodhisattva-Mahāsattva Akṣobhya resolved to pursue supreme enlightenment, and when Tathāgata Great Eyes, the Worthy One, the Perfectly Enlightened One, prophesied his attainment of enlightenment—no sentient being died an unnatural death, just as it was when I realized all-knowing wisdom. . . .

"Śāriputra, when Bodhisattva Akṣobhya received the prophecy, the sentient beings of the Realm of Desire brought superb delicacies to him and played celestial music for him, as offerings.

"Śāriputra, such are the merits achieved by the Bodhisattva-Mahāsattva Akṣobhya after he received the prophecy."

Then the Venerable Śāriputra said to the Buddha, "World-Honored One, most extraordinary is the Tathāgata, the Worthy One, the Perfectly Enlightened One, who is so skillful in explaining the inconceivable states of Buddhas, the inconceivable states of dhyānas, the inconceivable states of dragons, and the inconceivable karmic results. World-Honored One, when the Bodhisattva Akṣobhya abided in the initial generation of bodhicitta, he embraced the before-mentioned merits; when he received the Tathāgata's prophecy, he perfected those great, inconceivable merits."

The Buddha told Śāriputra, "So it is, so it is, as you say."

Then the Venerable Ānanda said to Śāriputra, "Most virtuous one, the World-Honored One has explained only a small portion of that novice Bodhisattva's merits of wearing the armor of vigor, not all of them."

Śāriputra said, "So it is, so it is. The Tathāgata has only touched upon them briefly. Why? Because when that Bodhisattva first brought forth bodhicitta and donned the armor of vigor, he achieved inconceivable, immeasurable merits."

Śāriputra said further to the Buddha, "World-Honored One, now you have praised briefly Bodhisattva Akṣobhya's superb merits of wearing the armor of vigor. May the World-Honored One elaborate upon them for the sake of gathering in Bodhisattvas of the present and future."

The Buddha told Śāriputra, "Inconceivable are the merits of Bodhisattva Akṣobhya when he first brought forth bodhicitta and donned the armor of vigor. Now I will further relate to you a small portion of them. Listen attentively and think well about them."

Śāriputra said, "Yes, World-Honored One. I am willing and glad to listen."

The Buddha said, "The Bodhisattva Akṣobhya once made this vow: 'Even if empty space changes, I shall not withdraw from my great vows.' Because of this vow, Bodhisattva Akṣobhya achieved all merits quickly. Śāriputra, I cannot find any Bodhisattva in the Worthy Kalpa who wears the armor of vigor as Bodhisattva Akṣobhya did. Śāriputra, the practices cultivated by Bodhisattva Precious Banner were less than a small part, or even an infinitesimal part, of those cultivated by Bodhisattva Akṣobhya.

"Śāriputra, in wearing the armor of vigor, Bodhisattva Akṣobhya had no peer among countless thousands of other Bodhisattvas. Śāriputra, with his firm vows, Bodhisattva Akṣobhya has realized supreme enlightenment. Now he is living in the World of Wonderful Joy and is named Tathāgata Akṣobhya, the Worthy One, the Perfectly Enlightened One. . . ."

II

At that time, Śāriputra said to the Buddha, "World-Honored One, the Buddha has explained the merits acquired by Tathāgata Akṣobhya when he was cultivating the Bodhisattva practices. I hope that the World-Honored One will reveal and elaborate upon the merits and magnificence of the present land of Tathāgata Akṣobhya. Why? So that sentient beings who follow the Bodhisattva-path may delight in the merits of that land after hearing them and desire to see, worship, and make offerings to the Buddha there; and so that sentient beings in the Śrāvaka stage who have realized Arhatship may also wish to worship, make offerings to, and serve that Tathāgata after hearing of the merits and magnificence of his land."

The Buddha told Śāriputra, "Well said! It is excellent that you can make a request of such significance. Now listen attentively and think well about this; I will explain it to you in detail."

Śāriputra said, "Yes, World-Honored One, I am willing and glad to listen."

The Buddha told Śāriputra, "When Tathāgata Akṣobhya, the Worthy One, the Perfectly Enlightened One, realized all-knowing wisdom, he emitted a great light over the entire billion-world universe. At the same time, the earth quaked in the six ways. Knowing that Tathāgata Akṣobhya had realized supreme enlightenment, the sentient beings of that world did not think of food, hunger, thirst, fatigue, a resting place, or sleep for seven days and nights; they felt only peace, happiness, joy, love, and kindness. At that time, all sentient beings in that land, including the gods in the Realm of Desire, were rid of sexual desire. Why were those sentient beings able to enjoy such blessings in that lifetime? It was because of the power of that Tathāgata's original vows. Śāriputra, when Tathāgata Akṣobhya, the Worthy One, the Perfectly Enlightened One, realized all-knowing wisdom, all the sentient beings in that land joined their palms with utmost sincerity toward him. Due to this earnest admiration for the Tathāgata, they were able to enjoy such innumerable blessings in that lifetime.

"Furthermore, Śāriputra, that Buddha-land is peerless in merit and magnificence among the innumerable Buddha-lands. Śāriputra, that Tathāgata has achieved a superbly adorned Buddha-land because he made those great vows when following the Bodhisattva path, just as I have now achieved what I originally vowed to achieve.

"Śāriputra, when Tathāgata Akṣobhya, the Worthy One, the Perfectly Enlightened One, realized supreme enlightenment, at that instant, at that very moment, all the sentient beings of that billion-world universe, with or without the deva-eye, could see Tathāgata Akṣobhya. Śāriputra, it was also the fulfillment of that Tathāgata's original vows that caused the sentient beings to attain this blessing.

"Moreover, Śāriputra, when Tathāgata Akṣobhya realized supreme enlightenment while sitting on the bodhi-site, Pāpīyān, the king of demons, did not try to hinder him. Also, innumerable hundreds of thousands of gods made offerings to the Tathāgata with fragrant flowers and celestial music; and each one brought fine, powdered sandalwood to sprinkle over the Buddha. The powdered incense and garlands of flowers formed a canopy in the air. Śāriputra, all this was made possible by the power of Tathāgata Akṣobhya's original vows.

"Furthermore, Śāriputra, when that Buddha attained enlightenment, a great light illuminated the whole billion-world universe, outshining the lights of the sun, moon, and heavens. The appearance of this auspicious sign was also due to the fulfillment of Tathāgata Akṣobhya's past vows."

At that time, Śāriputra said to the Buddha, "World-Honored One, when

Bodhisattva Akṣobhya was following the Bodhisattva path in the past, he wore the great armor of vigor and was therefore able to make those great vows. Because he had cultivated the practices and vows of a Bodhisattva, he could cause innumerable hundreds of thousands of sentient beings to plant good roots leading to supreme enlightenment. He further dedicated those good roots to the attainment of supreme enlightenment and of a pure Buddha-land, which were both fulfilled through the power of such a vow of dedication."[8]

The Buddha told Śāriputra, "Moreover, in that Buddha-land, there is a bodhi-tree made of the seven treasures, one league in height. The trunk of the tree is half a mile[9] in circumference; the shade of its branches and leaves, one league in circumference. Under the tree is a platform, four leagues in circumference, with steps leading down to the ground. That Buddha was seated on the platform when he realized enlightenment. Around the bodhi-tree are rows of palm trees and jasmine trees, which, in the gentle breeze, gave forth a harmonious and elegant sound surpassing all worldly music.

"Furthermore, Śāriputra, that Buddha-land does not have the three miserable planes of existence. What are the three? They are: the plane of hell-dweller, the plane of animals, and the realm of Yama.[10] All sentient beings in that Buddha-land have accomplished the ten good deeds. The ground is as flat as a palm and the color of gold, with no gullies, brambles, or gravel; it is as soft as cotton, sinking as soon as one's foot steps on it and returning to its original state as soon as the foot is lifted.

"Śāriputra, that Buddha-land is free of three kinds of sickness. What are the three? They are: the diseases caused by wind, coldness, and phlegm.[11] Śāriputra, in that Buddha-land, all sentient beings are free from lying, an ugly appearance, a bad odor, and filth. They have little desire, hatred, and ignorance. There are no jails or prisoners.

"Śāriputra, in that Buddha-land, no one learns or follows heterodox doctrines. The trees there are always laden with flowers and fruits, and there is also a special kind of tree named kalpataru, which produces fine garments of five colors. The garments remain bright, beautiful, fresh, clean, and extraordinarily fragrant all the time. Just as celestial flowers give forth various kinds of fragrance, so do the garments. The fragrance issuing from the bodies of those who wear these garments is exactly the same as that issuing from the garments. The sentient beings in that land, like people in this world who are rich and happy, have plenty of wonderful garments to wear as they please.

"Śāriputra, the sentient beings in that land, like those in the Heaven of the Thirty-Three, obtain the food and drink they need whenever they wish; and they do not discharge excrement, filth, or anything impure.

"Śāriputra, the palaces and towers of that land are all decorated with the seven treasures and surrounded by many ponds filled with the water of eight meritorious qualities, to be enjoyed at will. There are also many gardens and pavilions, all pure and clean. The sentient beings there all live with joy in the Dharma.

"Śāriputra, in that land, there is no jealousy among human beings. Every woman is better than the best in this world, and has achieved celestial merits of which earthly merits are less than one hundredth, one thousandth, one hundred thousandth, one of a hundred thousand million myriad parts, one of any number of parts, numerical or figurative, down to one infinitesimal part.

"Śāriputra, the people of that land possess lavishly decorated couches made of the seven treasures, in accordance with their karmic results. When they sleep or rest, they use pillows made of cotton floss. All these splendid things are achieved by virtue of Tathāgata Akṣobhya's past vows.

"Śāriputra, the food and drink of the people in that land are the same as those of the gods in color, fragrance, and taste. Just as the people of Uttarakuru[12] have only one king, so the people of the Land of Wonderful Joy have only Tathāgata Akṣobhya as their Dharma-Lord; and just as the gods of the Heaven of the Thirty-Three attend on Śakra, so the people of the Land of Wonderful Joy all attend on Tathāgata Akṣobhya.

"Śāriputra, you should know the merits and magnificence of Akṣobhya Buddha's land. Śāriputra, none of the sentient beings of that land are mentally unrestrained. Why? It is also because of the power of Tathāgata Akṣobhya's original vows."

At that time, hearing the Buddha praise the merits of the Buddha-land of Tathāgata Akṣobhya, a monk became greedily attached to it and said to the Buddha, "World-Honored One, now I wish to be born in Akṣobhya Buddha's land."

The Buddha told the monk, "With your foolishness and delusion, how can you be born there? Why? Because one with any passion or attachment cannot be born in that Buddha-land. Only those who have planted good roots and cultivated pure conduct can be born there."

Then he addressed Śāriputra again, "Furthermore, Śāriputra, in that land, if the sentient beings wish it, a clean pond will appear at their thought, filled with the water of eight meritorious qualities, fit for drinking, rinsing the mouth, washing, and bathing. If anyone dislikes it, it will immediately disappear.

"Śāriputra, in that Buddha-land, there is a fragrant breeze, gentle, agreeable, and pleasant to everyone's mind. The fragrant breeze carries fragrance to all gods and humans who like it, but not to those who do not like it. Śāriputra, all these merits and splendors are brought about by the power of Tathāgata Akṣobhya's original vows. . . .

"Furthermore, in that land, mother and child are safe and unsullied, from conception to birth. How can this be? All this is due to the power of Tathāgata Akṣobhya's original vows. Śāriputra, in that Buddha-land, there is such peace and bliss.

"Śāriputra, in the land of Tathāgata Akṣobhya, the Worthy One, the Perfectly Enlightened One, there is neither trade nor trader, neither farms nor farming; there is happiness at all times.

"Śāriputra, in that Buddha-land, singing and playing do not involve sexual desire. The sentient beings there derive their joy exclusively from the Dharma.

"Śāriputra, in that Buddha-land, there are rows of jasmine trees and palm trees, which, when stirred by a gentle breeze, will give forth a harmonious and elegant sound that surpasses even the celestial music played by gods.

"Śāriputra, any Bodhisattva-Mahāsattva who intends to acquire a Buddha-land should accumulate such merits, adornments, and purity for his Buddha-land as Tathāgata Akṣobhya did for his when he was following the Bodhisattva practices.

"Śāriputra, there is no darkness in that Buddha-land. It has suns and moons, but they do not give out light. Why? Because Tathāgata Akṣobhya has an ever-shining light which illuminates the entire Buddha-land.

"Śāriputra, if a wish-fulfilling pearl is put in the center of a high, large tower with its windows and doors closed tightly, the sentient beings therein will see a brilliant light day and night. In the same manner, the sentient beings of that Buddha-land always see the radiance of the Tathāgata. Śāriputra, the large tower stands for the World of Wonderful Joy; the wish-fulfilling pearl stands for Tathāgata Akṣobhya; the light of the wish-fulfilling pearl, the light of that Buddha; and the sentient beings within the tower, the sentient beings in the World of Wonderful Joy.

"Śāriputra, wherever Tathāgata Akṣobhya walks or stands, a thousand-petaled lotus appears spontaneously to support his feet. The flower is golden in color; there is nothing like it in this world. Śāriputra, this is also achieved by the superb power of the vows of Tathāgata Akṣobhya, the Worthy One, the Perfectly Enlightened One."

Thereupon, Śāriputra asked the Buddha, "World-Honored One, when Tathāgata Akṣobhya enters a room, will a golden lotus support his feet or not?"

The Buddha told Śāriputra, "Why do you bother to ask such a trivial question? When that Buddha, the World-Honored One, enters a village or a house, a thousand-petaled lotus appears with him. If any good man or good women thinks, 'When the Tathāgata condescends to enter this room, may the lotus beneath his feet close its petals,' the flower will do so immediately. If anyone wishes the lotus to stay in the air, the flower will also do so immediately. All this is due to that Tathāgata's awesome power.

"Śāriputra, the lotus which holds the feet [of the Tathāgata] will then be given to the people, and they will build a stūpa for it and make offerings to it.

"Śāriputra, that Buddha, the World-Honored One, travels through the whole billion-world universe to expound the Dharma; and wherever he goes, a flower appears with him. Moreover, in whatever land that Tathāgata manifests himself, in that land golden lotuses also appear. By the awesome power of that Buddha, his entire billion-world universe is adorned with thousand-petaled golden lotuses."

III

"Furthermore, Śāriputra, when Tathāgata Akṣobhya expounds the Dharma, he can skillfully subdue countless sentient beings, making them all attain Arhatship; numerous are those who will dwell in the meditation of the eightfold liberation.

"Śāriputra, Tathāgata Akṣobhya, the Worthy One, the Perfectly Enlightened One, has a host of Śrāvakas incalculable in number. I cannot find any arithmetician or any arithmetician's disciple able to compute how many hundreds of thousands of millions of billions of trillions of Śrāvakas there are in the host. Śāriputra, no one can ascertain the total number of the Śrāvakas in terms of those figures. Śāriputra, just as the number of good men who have attained the fruit of a Stream-enterer, the fruit of a Once-returner, or the fruit of a Nonreturner in my land is difficult to ascertain, so is the number of good men who have attained the fruit of an Arhat in that land.

"Śāriputra, [in my land,] indolent people can attain the fruit of a Stream-enterer. They will be born as humans seven more times and be further taught the Dharma before they can attain the superior fruit [of an Arhat]; therefore, I call them 'people of seven rebirths.' Śāriputra, [in the land of Tathāgata Akṣobhya,] indolent people can attain the fruit of a Stream-enterer at Tathāgata Akṣobhya's first discourse on the Dharma, the fruit of a Once-returner at the second discourse, the fruit of a Nonreturner at the third discourse, and the fruit of an Arhat at the fourth discourse. They are said to be indolent because they fail to end all their defilements at one sitting.

"Śāriputra, in that Buddha-land, those who have attained the fruit of a Stream-enterer will be cleansed of all defilements in one lifetime, unlike the Stream-enterers of this world, who have to go through seven more births. Those who have attained the fruit of a Once-returner will be freed from all suffering in one lifetime, unlike those called Once-returners in this world, who have to go through one more birth. Those who have attained the fruit of a Nonreturner will become Arhats in one lifetime, unlike those called Nonreturners in this world, who have to be born in the upper realms [before they are liberated], though they will not return to this earth. . . .[13]

"Furthermore, Śāriputra, in that Buddha-land, there are steps made of three precious materials—gold, silver, and lapis lazuli—extending from Jambudvîpa to the Heaven of the Thirty-Three. Śāriputra, when the gods of the Heaven of the Thirty-Three desire to see Tathāgata Akṣobhya, to worship and make offerings to him, they can descend the precious steps to the Buddha's place. When they find that the people of [that] Jambudvîpa are rich, prosperous, and have everything they need, they will become desirous and say, 'We gods have the good fortune of gods, and the people of Jambudvîpa have the good fortune of human beings. Now I see that their fortune is as excellent as ours. What is more, the people of Jambudvîpa have a good fortune even surpassing ours: Tathāgata Akṣobhya is expounding of the true Dharma there. This is why we gods always prefer the human world.'

"Śāriputra, the people of that Jambudvīpa have no desire at all to be born in the heavens. Why? Because [they think,] 'In the human world, Tathāgata Akṣobhya constantly expounds the true Dharma to benefit us, and our good fortune is not different from that of the gods. The gods of the Heaven of the Thirty-Three are no match for us.'

"Śāriputra, in that land, by the Buddha's divine power, gods and humans can see each other. Just as the people of this Jambudvīpa see the moon and stars, so, Śāriputra, the people there can look upward and see the palaces of the gods above. Śāriputra, this is also achieved by the power of the original vows which Tathāgata Akṣobhya made when he was cultivating the Bodhisattva practices.

"Śāriputra, the voice of the Buddha expounding the Dharma spreads over the entire billion-world universe, and is heard everywhere by the four kinds of devotees.

"Śāriputra, the Śrāvakas there wish for no other food than Dharma-food. When listening to the Dharma, they are single-minded and calm; they do not feel tired physically or mentally, whether sitting or standing. Śāriputra, Tathāgata Akṣobhya stays in midair when expounding the Dharma to the assembly. The Śrāvakas, whether or not they themselves have miraculous power, all stay in midair by the awesome power of the Buddha when they listen to the essence of the Dharma, bearing themselves with dignity in the three deportments. What are the three? Walking, standing, and sitting.

"When these Śrāvakas intend to enter parinirvāṇa, they sit cross-legged and then immediately enter it. At that moment, the earth quakes. After their parinirvāṇa, all gods and humans come to make offerings to them.

"When the Arhats are ready for parinirvāṇa, they produce fire from their bodies to cremate themselves; or become extinct spontaneously, leaving no relics behind; or roam in the sky like clouds of five colors, and then disappear in an instant, without leaving a trace; or stand in the sky and then vanish like rain falling to the ground.

"Śāriputra, this is also because, while cultivating the Bodhisattva practices in the past, Tathāgata Akṣobhya, the Worthy One, the Perfectly Enlightened One, made this vow: 'If I realize supreme enlightenment, the Śrāvakas [in my land] will enter parinirvāṇa with dignity in the three deportments.'

"Furthermore, Śāriputra, many Śrāvakas of that Buddha-land have attained the four fearlessnesses, and even more have attained the four bases of miraculous powers. Śāriputra, the Śrāvakas of that land have accomplished these complete merits."

At that time, Śāriputra said to the Buddha, "World-Honored One, illustrious, great, and vast indeed are the merits accomplished by the Śrāvakas of Tathāgata Akṣobhya, the Worthy One, the Perfectly Enlightened One."

IV

At that time, the Venerable Śāriputra thought, "The World-Honored One has just now discussed the merits of the Śrāvakas. May the Tathāgata also expound the complete merits of the Bodhisattvas. Why? Because all other merits come from them."

Then, knowing Śāriputra's thought, the Buddha told him, "In that Buddha-land, innumerable hundreds of thousands of [millions of] billions of Bodhisattvas attend the assembly, and, by the divine power of the Buddha, all the Bodhisattvas who have left the household life can understand, accept, uphold, read, and recite what they have heard.

"Śāriputra, the Dharma which I have expounded in this world is a very small part—less than one hundredth, one thousandth, one hundred thousandth, one hundred billionth, one of any number of parts, one minute part, or even one infinitesimal part—of the Dharma-treasure expounded by Tathāgata Akṣobhya.

"Śāriputra, this is all because Tathāgata Akṣobhya, the Worthy One, the Perfectly Enlightened One, made this vow when cultivating the Bodhisattva practices: 'When I attain Buddhahood, may all the Bodhisattvas in my land, by my awesome power, be able to understand, accept, uphold, read, and recite whatever they hear [from the Buddha].' Śāriputra, by the divine power of the original vow made by that Tathāgata, those Bodhisattvas are able to understand, accept, uphold, read, and recite with facility all that they have heard from the Buddha.

"Furthermore, Śāriputra, if those Bodhisattvas want to go to another Buddha-land, they arrive there as soon as they think of that land, wearing the native costume, speaking the local language with no accent, and acting in harmony with the customs of that land. They pay homage and make offerings to the Tathāgata of that land, listen to the true Dharma, and ask pertinent questions. When they have done all they can, they return to Akṣobhya Buddha.

"Śāriputra, nine hundred ninety-six Buddhas will appear in this world during this Worthy Kalpa.[14] A Bodhisattva who wishes to see these Tathāgatas should make a vow to be born in Akṣobhya Buddha's land.

"Śāriputra, if good men or good women [who follow the Bodhisattva-path], after their death in this Buddha-land or another Buddha-land, have been born, are being born, or will be born in the Buddha-land of Tathāgata Akṣobhya, they will not believe or abide in the stage of Śrāvakas. Why? Because those who follow the Buddha-path will always meet the Tathāgata, and give the celestial demon Pāpīyān no opportunity to hinder them. They will give up the two vehicles forever, and attain supreme enlightenment without fail. They will always participate in that Tathāgata's great assemblies.

"Śāriputra, you should know that those sentient beings who dwell in the pure Buddha-land of Tathāgata Akṣobhya will never be subject to degeneration, seduction, or regression; they will abide in the pursuit of supreme enlightenment, have great power, be immovable, and never regress.

"Śāriputra, if good men or good women are born in that land after their death in this world or other worlds, they will, at the time of their birth, have this thought: 'I have entered the Tathāgata's room and have taken up my abode in the city of fearlessness.'

"Śāriputra, those Bodhisattvas will comply with the pāramitā of wisdom in whatever they say, and they will respect one another and regard one another as teachers.

"Furthermore, Śāriputra, of the Bodhisattvas in that Buddha-land, few are householders; many are monks. By the Buddha's divine power, they can understand, accept, uphold, read, and recite whatever they have heard [from the Buddha]. Śāriputra, the lay Bodhisattva-Mahāsattvas who are unable to participate in the assembly[15] can by the Buddha's miraculous power hear, understand, accept, uphold, read, and recite with facility the Dharma expounded, wherever they are, whether sitting or standing. The Bodhisattvas who have left the household life and are not in the assembly can do the same. Also, these Bodhisattvas, in the course of decease and rebirth, never forget the sūtras they have heard, and can be born in any Buddha-land they wish. Śāriputra, this is also achieved through the merits of Tathāgata Akṣobhya's original vows.

"Śāriputra, if a Bodhisattva wishes to see numerous hundreds of thousands of [millions of] billions of myriads of Buddhas in one lifetime, he should vow to be born in the land of Tathāgata Akṣobhya. After his birth there, he will see innumerable Buddhas and plant all kinds of good roots; he can also expound the essence of the Dharma to numerous hundreds of thousands of sentient beings to increase their good roots.

"Śāriputra, if Bodhisattvas, after their death in this world or other worlds, have been born, are being born, or will be born in the Buddha-land of Tathāgata Akṣobhya, they will all attain the stage of nonregression. Why? Because in that Buddha-land, one is not obstructed by the celestial demon Pāpīyān or disturbed by demonic influences.

"Śāriputra, a venomous snake subjugated by a magic spell cannot hurt anyone, and insects or worms will not be worried or afraid upon seeing it. Yet, harmless as it is, it is still called a venomous snake because it has received the form of a snake as a result of its previous karmas. Śāriputra, the same is true with the celestial demon Pāpīyān. When Tathāgata Akṣobhya was following the Bodhisattva practices in the past, he vowed to dedicate his good roots thus: 'When I realize supreme enlightenment, I will subjugate all demons so that they will not cause hindrances or troubles. They will not hinder or trouble the Bodhisattvas, Śrāvakas, ordinary people, or others in the whole billion-world universe.' [Subjugated as they are,] the demons remain in demons' forms because of their previous karmas. They regret this in the heaven where they are born, and blame themselves for being incarnated as beings called 'demons' owning to their previous karmas performed from beginningless time. In spite of the power they enjoy, they loathe their state. When that Tathāgata expounds the Dharma, the demons and their retinues are often among the listeners. After hearing the Dharma, they become pure in mind and yearn to be Śrāvakas, thinking, 'How can we, too, abide in tranquillity, have few desires, and be content?' Because those demons have a constant desire to leave the household life and have no intention of hindering others, the Śrāvakas, Bodhisattvas, and ordinary people in that land can all abide in peace and happiness. This is also due to the awesome power of that Buddha's previous vigor and great vows. Śāriputra, this is also a superb adornment of Akṣobhya Buddha's land. . . .

"Śāriputra, those Bodhisattvas who have received my prophecy and attained nonregression will be born in Akṣobhya Buddha's land. However, Śāriputra, this does not mean that I forsake the Bodhisattvas born in that Buddha-land. If an anointed kṣatriya king learns that the army of a hostile nation is coming to steal his wealth and throne, he will think, 'My queen, concubines, and beloved children are not strong enough to resist the enemy. I will keep them, together with my treasures, in the palace, out of harm's way.' Then he will overcome his enemy, so that his country is blessed with peace and freed from danger, and there is no longer any fear of disaster. Śāriputra, just as the king does not abandon his treasures, beloved children, queen, and concubines, so I do not forsake the Bodhisattvas, and those who follow the Bodhisattva practices should know this. Like the palace, that Buddha-land is free from fear; like the leader of the enemies, the celestial demon Pāpīyān [in my land] tries in every way to hinder those who follow the Bodhisattva practices; and like the great king who is not disturbed by the invading enemies, the Tathāgata is not harassed by the celestial demons.

"Śāriputra, suppose a man, afraid of his creditor, runs far away to the frontier. He will be spared persecution at the hands of the creditor and others concerned. Why? Because the creditor and his family cannot reach him, due to the great distance and danger involved. In the same way, the Bodhisattvas born in the Land of Wonderful Joy are beyond the reach of Pāpīyān, who is kept away by the insurmountable difficulty of the journey.[16]

"Śāriputra, in this billion-world universe, the celestial demon Pāpīyān hinders Bodhisattvas and Śrāvakas in every way. In the Land of Wonderful Joy, the celestial demons do not do devilish deeds. The Bodhisattvas born there in the past, present, and future are free from fear forever. Why? Because when that Tathāgata was following the Bodhisattva-path, he dedicated all his good roots thus: 'When I realize supreme enlightenment, the celestial demons will not hinder anyone or do any devilish deeds.' Śāriputra, just as poison loses its toxicity and becomes food for a strong man who can take it skillfully and digest it, so the celestial demons of that land, instead of doing harm, are always beneficial.

"Śāriputra, innumerable such merits are achieved in that Buddha-land."

At that time, Śāriputra thought, "Now I wish to see Tathāgata Akṣobhya, the Worthy One, the Perfectly Enlightened One, and the Śrāvakas of that Buddha-land." Thereupon, perceiving what was in Śāriputra's mind, the World-Honored One, by his divine power and without rising from his seat, caused Śāriputra to see all of them.

The Buddha asked Śāriputra, "Have you seen them now?"

Śāriputra answered, "Yes, I have."

The Buddha asked Śāriputra, "Do you see any difference, such as superiority or inferiority, among those gods and humans?"

Śāriputra answered, "No, I do not. Why? Because I see that the clothing, food and drink, and valuable objects enjoyed by the humans of the Land of Wonderful Joy are gods' implements of pleasure. Tathāgata Akṣobhya, expounding the Dharma to the assembly, is like a gold mountain, shining brilliantly. There are innumerable, limitless Śrāvakas. Just as the horizons in the four directions are boundless in the eyes of one sailing upon the great ocean, so the Śrāvakas there are limitless in number to the beholder. When those Śrāvakas are listening to the Dharma, they keep their bodies and minds as still as if they had entered dhyāna, unlike the people in this world, who sway and stir, sometimes even in meditation." . . .

At that time, a thought occurred to Ānanda: "Now I should test the power of Venerable Subhūti's eloquence." With this in mind, he said to Subhūti, "We should have a look at Tathāgata Akṣobhya, his disciples, and his Buddha-land."

Subhūti told Ānanda, "If you want to see that Tathāgata, you should look upwards."

After Ānanda had looked upwards, he said to Subhūti, "I have looked upwards as far as I could, but I saw nothing except emptiness and stillness."

Subhūti said, "Tathāgata Akṣobhya, his disciples, and his Buddha-land are similar to what you saw when you looked upwards."

Then Śāriputra said to the Buddha, "World-Honored One, as the Buddha has said, the Bodhisattvas in this world whose attainment of Buddhahood has been prophesied are not different from the Bodhisattvas born in that land. World-Honored One, now I do not know why they are equal."

The Buddha told Śāriputra, "Because of the equality of the dharmadhātu, there is no difference between them."

V

At that time, the Venerable Śāriputra thought further, "The World-Honored One has spoken of the infinite merits of Tathāgata Akṣobhya, the Worthy One, the Perfectly Enlightened One, in following the Bodhisattva-path. He has also spoken of the vast, great adornments of that land and the excellent, virtuous deeds of the Śrāvakas and Bodhisattvas there. I hope that the World-Honored One will further tell us about that Buddha's parinirvāṇa and his deeds of deliverance thereafter."

Then, knowing Śāriputra's thought, the World-Honored One told him, "Śāriputra, on the day of Tathāgata Akṣobhya's parinirvāṇa, his magically produced bodies will appear throughout all the worlds, including the hells, and will expound the wonderful Dharma. He will subdue with the Dharma numerous sentient beings, all of whom will attain Arhatship. As a result, there will be more people who have attained the stage beyond learning than there were before that Buddha's parinirvāṇa.

"On that day, he will also predict Bodhisattva Fragrant Elephant's attainment of Buddhahood, saying, 'After my parinirvāṇa, you will become a Buddha, named Tathāgata Golden Lotus, the Worthy One, the Perfectly Enlightened One.' Furthermore, Śāriputra, the merits of Tathāgata Golden Lotus's Buddha-land and the number of his disciples will be the same as those of Tathāgata Akṣobhya.

"Furthermore, Śāriputra, when Tathāgata Akṣobhya enters parinirvāṇa, the great earth will quake all over, and the whole billion-world universe will roar in the quake. The sound will reach up to the Akaniṣṭha Heaven. When the gods hear the sound, they will know that the Buddha has entered parinirvāṇa.

"Moreover, Śāriputra, the forests and herbs of that Buddha-land will all incline toward the place where Tathāgata Akṣobhya is entering parinirvāṇa. At that time, the gods and humans will all scatter over the Buddha garlands of flowers, many kinds of incense, and clothing. The scattered fragrant flowers will pile up around the Buddha to a height of one league.

"Furthermore, Śāriputra, when Tathāgata Akṣobhya is entering parinirvāṇa, all the gods, dragons, yakṣas, gandharvas, asuras, garuḍas, kinnaras, and mahoragas of the billion-world universe will join their palms to salute him; also, by the divine power of the Buddha, the gods in other lands will be able to see that Buddha enter parinirvāṇa. For seven days and nights, these gods will be overwhelmed with grief, will desist from the amusements of gods and humans, and will feel no desire. They will say to one another, 'Tathāgata Akṣobhya has been the light of the world and the eye of sentient beings. Alas, why does he enter parinirvāṇa so soon?'. . .

"Furthermore, Śāriputra, Tathāgata Akṣobhya, the Worthy One, the Perfectly Enlightened One, will issue fire from his own body to cremate himself. All his relics will be golden in color. Just as the timira tree reveals a swastika sign[17] in its cross-section wherever it is cut, so will the relics of that Tathāgata.

"Moreover, Śāriputra, every relic of Tathāgata Akṣobhya will be round, with the auspicious swastika sign both inside and outside. Śāriputra, just as the pulaka tree reveals the auspicious swastika sign both inside and outside wherever it is cut across, so will the relics of that Buddha.

"Śāriputra, the sentient beings of that land will build stūpas out of the seven treasures for the relics all over that billion-world universe, and will offer to the stūpas thousand-petaled golden lotus flowers. These stūpas and lotus flowers will then serve as splendid adornments of that billion-world universe. . . .

"Furthermore, Śāriputra, after Tathāgata Akṣobhya has entered great nirvāṇa, the true Dharma will endure in his world for a hundred thousand kalpas."

Thereupon, Śāriputra asked the Buddha, "World-Honored One, for [a hundred thousand] kalpas of what kind will the true Dharma of Tathāgata Akṣobhya endure in the world?"

The Buddha told Śāriputra, "Twenty small kalpas make one kalpa,[18] and the true Dharma will endure for a hundred thousand such kalpas.

"Śāriputra, after the extinction of the true Dharma, there will be a great light illuminating all the worlds in the ten directions, and all the earths will quake, making a great sound. However, [you should know that] the true Dharma cannot be destroyed by the celestial demons, nor will the Tathāgata and his disciples pass into oblivion of their own accord. It is because people of that time will lack interest in learning the Dharma that those who can expound the Dharma will go away from them. Hearing little of the true Dharma, the people will become more incredulous, and as a result, they will not strive to practice the Dharma. Seeing the indifference of the people, monks well-versed in the Dharma will naturally withdraw into seclusion and preach the Dharma no more. In this way, the subtle, profound teaching of the Buddha will gradually disappear."

VI

At that time, the Venerable Śāriputra asked the Buddha, "World-Honored One, what causes and good roots enable Bodhisattva-Mahāsattvas to be born in that Buddha-land?"

The Buddha told Śāriputra, "Bodhisattva-Mahāsattvas who wish to be born in the World of Wonderful Joy should follow the Bodhisattva practices cultivated by Tathāgata Akṣobhya in the past, and make a great vow to be born in that land. These practices and this vow will enable them to be born in that Buddha-land.

"Furthermore, Śāriputra, if Bodhisattva-Mahāsattvas, when practicing the pāramitā of giving, dedicate the ensuing good roots to the attainment of supreme enlightenment and wish to meet Tathāgata Akṣobhya, then they will consequently be born in that Buddha-land. The same is true if they do likewise when practicing the pāramitā of discipline, and so on up to the pāramitā of wisdom.

"Moreover, Śāriputra, the light of Tathāgata Akṣobhya shines over the whole billion-world Buddha-land. One should vow to realize supreme enlightenment in a future life as a result of seeing this light, so that, after attaining great enlightenment in that way, he will in turn emanate a light from his own body to illuminate the whole world. Śāriputra, a Bodhisattva who so vows will be born in that land.

"Furthermore, Śāriputra, Tathāgata Akṣobhya, the Worthy One, the Perfectly Enlightened One, has a limitless number of Śrāvakas. One should vow to see them and, afterwards, to perform deeds leading to the attainment of the Buddha's enlightenment. This will enable one to have the same limitless number of

Śrāvakas after he realizes enlightenment. Śāriputra, a Bodhisattva-Mahāsattva who so vows can be born in that Buddha-land.

"Furthermore, Śāriputra, in that Buddha-land, there are innumerable Bodhisattva-Mahāsattvas. One should wish to see these Bodhisattvas, to learn from them the practice of meditation, to be with them at all times, to study with them the same vehicle, and to attain the ultimate goal together with them. One should wish to meet those who pursue perfect, great kindness and compassion, who seek enlightenment and śramaṇahood, who forgo the intention to follow the two vehicles, who abide in the real emptiness, and who are constantly mindful of the name of the All-Knowing Buddha, the Tathāgata, and the names of the Dharma and the Saṁgha.

"Śāriputra, even those good men and good women who have heard the names of such Bodhisattvas will be born in that Buddha-land, let alone those who plant good roots in harmony with the pāramitā of wisdom and dedicate them to Tathāgata Akṣobhya, the Worthy One, the Perfectly Enlightened One. Śāriputra, these are causes and conditions which enable one to be born in that Buddha-land without fail.

"Furthermore, Śāriputra, Bodhisattva-Mahāsattvas who wish to be born in that Buddha-land should often visualize the Buddhas, the Tathāgatas, expounding the subtle, wonderful Dharma in the innumerable eastern worlds, together with their disciples. They should vow: 'I will realize enlightenment, expound the subtle, wonderful Dharma, and have [a limitless number of] disciples, just as those Buddhas do.'

"Śāriputra, these Bodhisattvas should cultivate the good roots of the three kinds of recollection;[19] they should wish to practice recollection together with all sentient beings equally, and dedicate these good roots to the attainment of supreme enlightenment.

"Śāriputra, the Bodhisattvas' good roots thus dedicated are limitless. Suppose all sentient beings, each holding a container with the same capacity as that of [all] space, said [to one of the Bodhisattvas], 'Great man, please give me some of your good roots.' Śāriputra, these good roots, supposing they were material and given to the sentient beings, would fill all their containers and the containers would be taken away without exhausting the good roots. [Why?] Because these good roots are dedicated to the attainment of supreme enlightenment, and so are infinite and unchangeable.

"Śāriputra, because of these good roots, which are achieved through these three kinds of recollection and are dedicated to all-knowing wisdom, one will be followed [and protected] by the Three Jewels wherever he goes. Śāriputra, you should know that if a Bodhisattva has achieved these good roots, he will not fall to any miserable plane of existence, he will be able to subjugate Pāpīyān and other demons, and he will be born as he wishes in any Buddha-land in the east, south, west, north, northeast, northwest, southeast, southwest, the zenith, or the nadir. Therefore, a Bodhisattva-Mahāsattva should accumulate the good roots of such recollection, and, having accumulated them, dedicate them to Tathāgata Akṣobhya. In this way he can be born in that Buddha-land.

"Furthermore, Śāriputra, the merits and vast adornments of the Buddha-land of Tathāgata Akṣobhya cannot be found in any other of the countless Buddha-lands. A Bodhisattva-Mahāsattva, therefore, should resolve thus: 'By virtue of these good roots, I wish to see that land, acquire its adornments, and see the Bodhisattvas there.' By doing this, Śāriputra, the Bodhisattva will be born in that Buddha-land.

"Śāriputra, Bodhisattva-Mahāsattvas who wish to be born in that Buddha-land should generate an intense aspiration for it. Śāriputra, if good men or good women have generated such intense aspiration, I will predict their birth in that Buddha-land.

"Śāriputra, a city is not magnificent without such embellishments as towers, gardens, groves, ponds, and places for elephants and horses to roam, though its ruler may have power to maintain peace and order. Similarly, Śāriputra, since my Buddha-land does not have the same merits [as Tathāgata Akṣobhya's], it is not as magnificently adorned. . . .

"Śāriputra, Tathāgata Akṣobhya leads the Bodhisattvas and followers of other vehicles in other lands as well as in the World of Wonderful Joy. Śāriputra, if good men and good women, after hearing the Dharma-door of Tathāgata Akṣobhya's merits, are well able to accept, uphold, read, recite, and comprehend it, and wish to be born in that land, then Tathāgata Akṣobhya will always protect and remember them until the time of their death, and will keep demons and demons' retinues from causing them to regress from their determination.

"Śāriputra, you should know that right up to their attainment of supreme enlightenment, these good men and good women will be free from the fear of regression; free from harm by water, fire, knives, cudgels, ferocious beasts, and poisonous insects; and free from the terror of [evil] humans or nonhumans. Why? Because they are always protected and remembered by Tathāgata Akṣobhya, and will be born in his Buddha-land.

"Śāriputra, just as the sun, though far away, gives light to the sentient beings of this world, so Tathāgata Akṣobhya, though far away, illuminates the Bodhisattvas of other worlds.

"Śāriputra, just as a monk who has the deva-eye can see different things[20] in the distance, so Tathāgata Akṣobhya, while remaining in his own land, can see the forms of all kinds of Bodhisattvas in other worlds.

"Śāriputra, furthermore, just as a monk who has acquired the perfect command of the power of [knowing others'] thoughts can read the minds of sentient beings even if he is remote from them, so Tathāgata Akṣobhya can perceive the minds of the Bodhisattvas in other worlds.

"Śāriputra, just as a monk who has attained the deva-ear can hear any sound at a distance, so Tathāgata Akṣobhya can hear the sentient beings living in other worlds say, 'I wish to be born in that land.' Śāriputra, Tathāgata Akṣobhya knows the names of all such good men and good women; he knows, protects, and remembers all those who accept, uphold, read, recite, and comprehend this Dharma-door of merits."

Śāriputra then said to the Buddha, "It is most extraordinary, World-Honored One, that that Buddha, the World-Honored One, protects and remembers those Bodhisattva-Mahāsattvas."

After Śāriputra said this, the Buddha told him, "So it is, so it is. As you say, Tathāgata Akṣobhya protects and remembers those Bodhisattva-Mahāsattvas. Why? Because, by protecting and remembering Bodhisattvas, he protects and remembers all sentient beings.

"Śāriputra, an anointed kṣatriya king who has many barns full of grain and beans will strictly command the keeper to guard them well. Why? Because he will then be able to relieve [the hunger of] sentient beings when famine occurs. Similarly, Śāriputra, the Tathāgata renders good protection to those Bodhisattvas so that, after his parinirvāṇa, they will realize supreme enlightenment and serve as an abundant harvest during the famine of the true Dharma.

"Śāriputra, in this world, there are Bodhisattvas who, after hearing the Dharma-door of Tathāgata Akṣobhya's merits, can accept, uphold, read, recite, and comprehend it, and wish to be born in that Buddha-land. You should know that these people have attained nonregression. . . .

"Śāriputra, good men and good women with pure faith should expound this merit-praising Dharma-door to others at all times. Those who do so will be cleansed of all defilements in their present lifetimes, or [at most] in two lifetimes.

"Furthermore, Śāriputra, this Dharma-door of praising Tathāgata Akṣobhya's merits cannot be accepted by foolish, shallow people. It can be accepted and upheld only by those with profound, vast wisdom. Śāriputra, those good men and good women [with such wisdom] will see Buddhas and will certainly obtain this merit-praising Dharma-door in their present lifetimes.

"Śāriputra, suppose there are priceless pearls taken from the sea. Who do you think will be the first to obtain these priceless treasures?"

Śāriputra said to the Buddha, "World-Honored One, kings, princes, and ministers will be the first to obtain them."

The Buddha told Śāriputra, "In the same way, Bodhisattvas will be the first to acquire the Dharma-door of that Buddha's merits, and those Bodhisattvas will attain the stage of nonregression. They will surely be able to accept, uphold, read, recite, and comprehend this Dharma after hearing it; they will diligently study the nature of suchness for the purpose of attaining supreme enlightenment."

Śāriputra said to the Buddha, "World-Honored One, if Bodhisattvas wish to abide in the stage of nonregression, they should accept, uphold, read, recite, and comprehend this merit-praising Dharma-door after hearing it. Why? Because Bodhisattva-Mahāsattvas who abide in this Dharma-door will not regress from [their realization of] the Dharma-nature."

The Buddha told Śāriputra, "If a man, in order to hear this Dharma, gave away enough gold to fill the entire world, he might still be unable to hear it. Why? Because this meritorious Dharma cannot be upheld by sentient beings with meager blessings.

"Furthermore, Śāriputra, if followers of the Śrāvaka-vehicle accept, uphold, read, and recite this meritorious Dharma-door after hearing it, and practice it diligently in order to conform to supreme enlightenment and suchness, they will attain realization[21] in their next lifetimes; they will attain candidacy for Buddhahood in two lifetimes; they will attain supreme enlightenment in no more than three lifetimes. . . .

"Furthermore, Śāriputra, if, in pursuit of this Dharma-door, good men and good women listen to, accept, uphold, read, recite, and circulate it in a village or town, and for this purpose live in the houses of laypeople though they themselves are monks or nuns, I will say they are faultless and will allow them to stay in such places. Why? Because these good men and good women are trying to keep this Dharma from falling into oblivion after their death. Śāriputra, even if the village or town is far away, these Bodhisattvas still should go and stay there to accept, uphold, read, and recite this Dharma-door, and reveal and expound it to others.

"Śāriputra, good men and good women should make this vow: 'I should not think of regressing from the pursuit of supreme enlightenment, for I have heard the name of the Dharma-door[22] of Tathāgata Akṣobhya." . . .

Śāriputra said to the Buddha, "World-Honored One, this Dharma-door can bring vast merits."

The Buddha told Śāriputra, "So it is, so it is, as you have said. Śāriputra, if a country is assailed by hailstorms, untimely thunder, or other terrible things, good men and good women should concentrate their minds on Tathāgata Akṣobhya and invoke his name;[23] this will put an end to all the disasters. [Why?] Because in the past, that Tathāgata helped hundreds of thousands of dragons out of their sufferings.[24] Because his compassionate original vows are genuine and sincere, and because he wishes to fulfil the dedication of his good roots without fail, all those who invoke his name will have their sorrow and distress relieved spontaneously, except those sentient beings whose previous [evil] karmas have ripened."

Śāriputra said to the Buddha, "World-Honored One, Bodhisattvas who wish to realize supreme enlightenment in this life should act as Tathāgata Akṣobhya acted when he was fulfilling his vows."

The Buddha told Śāriputra, "So it is, so it is. . . ."

At that time, the gods of the Realm of Desire and the gods of the Brahmā Heaven all joined their palms toward [Akṣobhya] Buddha, prostrated themselves to pay homage to him, and chanted three times: "We pay homage to Tathāgata Akṣobhya, the Worthy One, the Perfectly Enlightened One, who is most extraordinary; and we take refuge in Tathāgata Śākyamuni, the Worthy One, the Perfectly Enlightened One of this world, who is so skillful in expounding this merit-praising Dharma-door."

Then the gods of the Realm of Desire strewed flowers of the coral tree and celestial incense over the Buddha. In the air, the incense and flowers fused and formed a canopy. Furthermore, the gods scattered the celestial flowers and incense toward Akṣobhya Buddha as offerings from afar. . . .

When the Buddha had expounded this Dharma-door, five hundred monks acquired mental liberation concerning the undefiled Dharma; five thousand Bodhisattvas, six thousand nuns, eight thousand laymen, ten thousand laywomen, and numerous gods of the Realm of Desire all wished to be born in that Buddha-land. Thereupon, the Tathāgata predicted that they would all be born in that Buddha-land. . . .

When the Buddha finished expounding this sūtra, Śāriputra, the gods, humans, asuras, gandharvas, garuḍas, kinnaras, and mahoragas were all jubilant over the Buddha's Teaching. They accepted it with faith and began to practice it with veneration.

NOTES

1. To be liberated in wisdom means the complete eradication of subtle ignorance or innate ego-clinging, which is the obstruction to wisdom. To be liberated in mind implies the liberation from passions and defilements which are the obstructions to meditation.

2. The text reads "past and future," but this was not the question asked. Also, it is inappropriate here, for the entire sūtra is an account of Akṣobhya who is a past Bodhisattva. Therefore we have deleted "and future."

3. This vow and many others in this sūtra are sublime and exalted. They seem to be of superhuman nature, beyond the reach of ordinary human beings. However, this can also be interpreted as meaning that it was because of Akṣobhya Buddha's superhuman effort that he was able to create such an extraordinary pure land, thus enabling the sentient beings there to practice Dharma easily in peace and joy. (G.C.)

4. Akṣobhya means 'the Immovable One'.

5. Bhikṣus should have no more than three sets of robes. Most of the items in this list are among the twelve ascetic practices allowed by the Buddha.

6. If Akṣobhya lived in our Sahā World, I doubt if he would have time for anything else. (G.C.)

7. To the best of my knowledge, neither in Hīnayāna, Mahāyāna, nor Tantric teachings is a "wet dream" or sexual desire in a dream considered to be a violation of precepts, because a purely physical, involuntary action cannot be construed as an offense. (G.C.)

8. Alternate translation: ". . . he could cause innumerable hundreds of thousands of sentient beings to plant good roots leading to supreme enlightenment, and to dedicate those good roots to the attainment of supreme enlightenment and of a pure Buddha-land. Through the power of his dedication his vows were all fulfilled."

9. The text reads "half a krośa." A krośa is the distance that the lowing of an ox can be heard.

10. The three miserable planes of existence are usually listed as the planes of hell-dwellers, hungry ghosts, and animals.

11. Instead of "coldness" (寒), the text reads "yellowness" (黃), which we think may be a misprint. (See 增一阿含經, Taishō 2122, p. 986). We do not know exactly what kinds of diseases the three are. (W.H.)

12. One of the four continents in Buddhist cosmology.

13. A Nonreturner will not return to this world, the Realm of Desire, before he is liberated, but he will be born in either the Realm of Form or the Realm of Formlessness.

14. This refers to the tradition that in the Worthy Kalpa, a total of one thousand Buddhas will appear. Since Śākyamuni Buddha was the fourth, 996 more will appear.

15. Literally, "who are not thinking of the assembly."

16. This sentence is a free translation. The text literally reads: "Similarly, [concerning] those Bodhisattvas born in the Land of Wonderful Joy, Pāpīyān's road is ended."

17. A swastika is an auspicious symbol in Buddhism.

18. Such a kalpa is called a "medium kalpa." See Glossary, "kalpa."

19. The three kinds of recollection are probably the recollection of the Buddha, the Dharma, and the Saṁgha.

20. Literally, "good and bad forms."

21. Literally, "reach achievement."

22. Here we see the power of the name of the Dharma-Door of Praising Tathāgata Akṣobhya's Merits. As far as the practice of the Pure Land teaching is concerned, however, it is most important to recollect and repeat the Buddha's name constantly. One should also recollect the Buddha's original vows, his merits, purity, land, etc. Since we treat this sūtra as a Pure Land discourse, it seems appropriate to stress the importance of recollecting Tathāgata Akṣobhya's name.

23. This is an example of the power of repeating the Buddha's name.

24. According to Buddhist mythology, dragons cause some natural disasters such as floods, thunder, and hailstorms. Because he helped the dragons in the past, Tathāgata Akṣobhya has the power to influence them to stop causing such disasters.

18 無量壽如來會

The Land of Utmost Bliss

I

Thus have I heard. Once the Buddha was dwelling on Mount Gṛdhrakūṭa near the city of Rājagṛha, accompanied by twelve thousand great monks, who were great Śrāvakas well known to everyone. Among them, the foremost were the Venerable . . . Mahākāśyapa, Śāriputra, Mahāmaudgalyāyana, . . . Rāhula, and Ānanda.

Surrounding the Buddha were also such leading Bodhisattva-Mahāsattvas as Bodhisattva Samantabhadra, Bodhisattva Mañjuśrī, Bodhisattva Maitreya, and other Bodhisattva-Mahāsattvas of the Worthy Kalpa. . . .

All these Bodhisattvas followed the path of Samantabhadra. They had fulfilled all the practices and vows of a Bodhisattva. They abided securely in all meritorious dharmas, and had reached the ultimate other shore of Buddha-Dharmas. They aspired to attain supreme enlightenment in all the worlds. . . .

At that time, the Venerable Ānanda rose from his seat, adjusted his robe, bared his right shoulder, knelt on his right knee, joined his palms toward the Buddha, and said, "Most virtuous World-Honored One, your body and organs are completely pure, shedding an awesome light as bright as that of a pile of gold, and shining like a clear mirror. I have never seen such a sight before. I am filled with joy to have this rare chance to gaze at them. World-Honored One, you have perfected the deeds of a Tathāgata and have skillfully established the deeds of a Great Man. Now, entering the great, tranquil dhyāna, you are thinking about past, present, and future Buddhas. World-Honored One, why do you have such a thought in mind?"

Thereupon, the Buddha asked Ānanda, "How can you know this? Is it

Sūtra 5, Taishō 310, pp. 91–101; translated into Chinese by Bodhiruci.

because some gods have come to tell you? Or because you see me and know it by yourself?"

Ānanda answered the Buddha, "World-Honored One, this idea occurs to me because I see the extraordinary, auspicious light of the Tathāgata, not because the gods have told me."

The Buddha told Ānanda, "Excellent, excellent! You have asked a very good question. It is because you are very observant and wonderfully eloquent that you can ask the Tathāgata such a question. You have brought up this question so that in this world may appear all Tathāgatas, the Worthy Ones, the Perfectly Enlightened Ones, and the great Bodhisattvas as well, for they all abide securely in great compassion to benefit sentient beings, and their appearance in the world is as rare as the blossoming of an uḍumbara flower. It is also because you take pity on sentient beings and wish to benefit and gladden them that you ask the Tathāgata this question.

"Ānanda, the Tathāgata, the Worthy One, the Perfectly Enlightened One, is skilled in revealing immeasurable knowledge and views. Why? Because the Tathāgata is unhindered in his knowledge and views." . . .

Then the Buddha told Ānanda, "An innumerable, incalculable number of great kalpas ago, there was a Buddha . . . named Freest in the World, the Tathāgata, the Worthy One, the Perfectly Enlightened One, the One Perfect in Learning and Conduct, the Well-Gone One, the World-Knower, the Unexcelled One, the Great Tamer, the Teacher of Gods and Humans, the Buddha, the World-Honored One.

"Ānanda, in the era of that Buddha, there was a monk named Dharmākara. He was a man of superior deeds and vows, and had strong powers of mindfulness and wisdom. He was firm and immovable in mind. He had great blessings and knowledge and his features were handsome.

"Ānanda, [one day], Monk Dharmākara went to the Tathāgata Freest in the World, bared his right shoulder, bowed down with his head at the Buddha's feet, joined his palms toward the Buddha, and praised him in verse. . . .

"Ānanda, after Monk Dharmākara had praised the Buddha's merits, he said, 'World-Honored One, now I am determined to pursue supreme enlightenment. May the Tathāgata expound to me the doctrines that will cause me to attain the great enlightenment unequaled in the world, and to develop a pure, magnificent Buddha-land!"

"That Buddha told the monk, 'You should develop a pure Buddha-land by yourself.'

"Dharmākara said to that Buddha, 'World-Honored One, I have no power to develop one. May the Tathāgata relate the purity and magnificence of other Buddha-lands! I swear to endow [my Buddha-land with those pure, magnificent qualities] after hearing them revealed.'

"Thereupon, that World-Honored One told him in detail the perfect adornments of two billion one hundred million pure Buddha-lands. It took that Buddha a hundred million years to do this.

"Ānanda, Monk Dharmākara assimilated all the pure, magnificent qualities of these two billion one hundred million Buddha-lands. Then he engaged in contemplation and practice of [fulfilling] them for five complete kalpas."

Ānanda asked the Buddha, "World-Honored One, how long did Tathāgata Freest in the World live?"

The World-Honored One answered, "That Buddha lived for forty kalpas. Ānanda, the Buddha-land which Monk Dharmākara would develop surpasses any of the two billion one hundred million Buddha-lands mentioned above. After he had assimilated [all the practices for developing a Buddha-land], he went to Tathāgata Freest in the World, bowed down with his head at that Buddha's feet, circumambulated him seven times to the right, stood to one side, and said, 'World-Honored One, I have assimilated [all the practices to develop] a pure, magnificent Buddha-land with full merits.'

"That Buddha said, 'It is time for you to reveal the practices completely, so that you can make the assembly joyful, and also enable them to develop perfect Buddha-lands.'

"Dharmākara said, 'May the World-Honored One be so kind as to listen. Now I am going to proclaim my great vows:

(1) I shall not attain supreme enlightenment if there would still be the planes of hell-dwellers, hungry ghosts, and animals in my land.[1]

(2) I shall not attain supreme enlightenment if any sentient being from my land would fall to the three miserable planes of existence [in other lands].

(3) I shall not attain supreme enlightenment if the sentient beings in my land would not all be endowed with a complexion of genuine gold.

(4) I shall not attain supreme enlightenement if there would be such distinctions as good and ugly appearances among the sentient beings in my land.

(5) I shall not attain supreme enlightenment if any sentient being in my land would fail to achieve the power to remember the past lives of himself [and others]—even events that happened hundreds of thousands of [millions of] billions of myriads of kalpas ago.

(6) I shall not attain supreme enlightenment if any sentient being in my land would not be endowed with the deva-eye, enabling him to see hundreds of thousands of [millions of] billions of myriads of Buddha-lands.

(7) I shall not attain supreme enlightenment if any sentient being in my land would fail to obtain the deva-ear, enabling him to hear the Dharma expounded by another Buddha hundreds of thousands of [millions of] billions of myriads of leagues away.

(8) I shall not attain supreme enlightenment if any sentient being in my land would not be endowed with the power of knowing others' minds, so that he would not know the mentalities of the sentient beings in hundreds of thousands of [millions of] billions of myriads of other Buddha-lands.

(9) I shall not attain supreme enlightenment if any sentient being in my land would fail to achieve the perfect mastery of the power to appear anywhere at will,[2] so that he would not be able to traverse hundreds of thousands of [millions of] billions of myriads of Buddha-lands in a flash of thought.

(10) I shall not attain supreme enlightenment if any sentient being in my land would entertain even an iota of the notion of 'I' and 'mine.'

(11) I shall not attain supreme enlightenment if any sentient being in my land would not certainly achieve supreme enlightenment and realize great nirvāṇa.

(12) I shall not attain supreme enlightenment if my light would be so limited as to be unable to illuminate hundreds of thousands of [millions of] billions of myriads—or any number—of Buddha-lands.

(13) I shall not attain supreme enlightenment if my life span would be limited to even hundreds of thousands of [millions of] billions of myriads of kalpas, or any countable number of kalpas.

(14) I shall not attain supreme enlightenment if anyone would be able to know the number of Śrāvakas in my land. Even if all the sentient beings and Pratyekabuddhas in a billion-world universe exercised their utmost counting power to count together for hundreds of thousands of years, they would not be able to know it.

(15) I shall not attain supreme enlightenment if any sentient being in my land would have a limited life span, except those who are born due to their vows.

(16) I shall not attain supreme enlightenment if any sentient being in my land would have a bad reputation.

(17) I shall not attain supreme enlightenment if my land would not be praised and acclaimed by innumerable Buddhas in countless Buddha-lands.

(18) When I realize supreme enlightenment, there will be sentient beings in other Buddha-lands who, after hearing my name, dedicate their good roots to birth in my land in thought after thought. Even if they have only ten such thoughts, they will be born in my land, except for those who have performed karmas leading to the Uninterrupted Hell and those who speak ill of the true Dharma or saints. If this would not be the case, I shall not attain enlightenment.

(19) When I become a Buddha, I shall appear with an assembly of monks at the deathbeds of sentient beings of other Buddha-lands who have brought forth bodhicitta, who think of my land with a pure mind, and who

dedicate their good roots to birth in the Land of Utmost Bliss.[3] I shall not attain supreme enlightenment if I would fail to do so.

(20) When I become a Buddha, all the sentient beings in countless Buddha-lands, who, having heard my name and dedicated their good roots to birth in the Land of Utmost Bliss, will be born there. Otherwise, I shall not attain supreme enlightenment.

(21) I shall not attain supreme enlightenment if any Bodhisattva in my land would fail to achieve the thirty-two auspicious signs.

(22) I shall not attain supreme enlightenment if any Bodhisattvas in my land on their way to great bodhi would fail to reach the stage of being only one lifetime away from Buddhahood. This excludes those Bodhisattvas with great vows who wear the armor of vigor for the sake of sentient beings; who strive to do beneficial deeds and cultivate great nirvāṇa; who perform the deeds of a Bodhisattva throughout all Buddha-lands and make offerings to all Buddhas, the Tathāgatas; and who establish as many sentient beings as the sands of the Ganges in supreme enlightenment. [This also excludes] those who seek liberation by following the path of Samantabhadra, devoting themselves to [Bodhisattvas'] practices even more than those [who have attained the stage of being only one liftime away from Buddhahood].

(23) I shall not attain supreme enlightenment if the Bodhisattvas in my land would not, by the awesome power of the Buddha, be able to make offerings to countless hundreds of thousands of [millions of] billions of myriads of Buddhas in other Buddha-lands every morning and return to their own land before mealtime.

(24) I shall not attain supreme enlightenment if the Bodhisattvas in my land would not possess every variety of offering they need to plant good roots in various Buddha-lands.

(25) I shall not attain supreme enlightenment if the Bodhisattvas in my land would not be skilled in expounding the essence of the Dharma in harmony with all-knowing wisdom.

(26) I shall not attain supreme enlightenment if the Bodhisattvas in my land would not have the enormous strength of a Nārāyaṇa.

(27) When I become a Buddha, no one will be able to describe completely the articles of adornment in my land; even one with the deva-eye will not be able to know all their varieties of shape, color, and brilliance. If anyone could know and describe them all, I shall not attain supreme enlightenment.

(28) I shall not attain supreme enlightenment if in my land there would be Bodhisattvas with inferior roots of virtue who could not know the numerous kinds of trees, one hundred thousand leagues high, which will abound in my land.

(29) I shall not attain supreme enlightenment if those sentient beings in my

land who read and recite sūtras and explain them to others would not acquire superb eloquence.

(30) I shall not attain supreme enlightenment if any Bodhisattva in my land would be unable to achieve limitless eloquence.

(31) When I become a Buddha, my land will be unequaled in brightness and purity; it will clearly illuminate countless, numberless Buddha-lands—inconceivable in number—just as a clear mirror reveals one's features. If this would not be so, I shall not attain supreme enlightenment.

(32) When I become a Buddha, there will be innumerable kinds of incense on land and in the air within the borders of my land, and there will be hundreds of thousands of [millions of] billions of myriads of precious censers, from which will rise the fragrance of the incense, permeating all of space. The incense will be superior to the most cherished incense of humans and gods, and will be used as an offering to Tathāgatas and Bodhisattvas. If this would not be the case, I shall not attain supreme enlightenment.

(33) When I become a Buddha, sentient beings in countless realms—inconceivable and unequaled in number—throughout the ten directions who are touched by the awesome light of the Buddha will feel more secure and joyful in body and mind than other humans or gods. Otherwise, I shall not attain supreme enlightenment.

(34) I shall not attain supreme enlightenment if Bodhisattvas in countless Buddha-lands—inconceivable and unequaled in number—would not realize [the truth of] nonarising and acquire dhāraṇīs after they hear my name.

(35) When I become a Buddha, all the women in numberless Buddha-lands—inconceivable and unequaled in number—who, after hearing my name, acquire pure faith, bring forth bodhicitta, and are tired of the female body, will rid themselves of the female body in their future lives. If this would not be the case, I shall not attain supreme enlightenment.

(36) I shall not attain supreme enlightenment if Bodhisattvas in countless Buddha-lands—inconceivable and unequaled in number—who attain the doctrine of nonarising[4] after hearing my name would fail to cultivate superb, pure conduct until they attain great bodhi.

(37) I shall not attain supreme enlightenment if, when I become a Buddha, humans and gods would not pay homage to all the Bodhisattvas of numberless Buddha-lands who, after hearing my name, prostrate themselves [in obeisance to me] and cultivate the deeds of a Bodhisattva with a pure mind.

(38) When I become a Buddha, sentient beings in my land will obtain the clothing they need as soon as they think of it, just as a man will be spontaneously clad in a monastic robe when the Buddha says, "Wel-

come, monk!" If this would not be the case, I shall not attain supreme enlightenment.

(39) I shall not attain supreme enlightenment if any sentient being in my land would not at birth obtain the necessities of life and become secure, pure, and blissful in mind, like a monk who has ended all defilements.

(40) When I become a Buddha, if sentient beings in my land wish to see other superbly adorned, pure Buddha-lands, these lands will immediately appear to them among the precious trees, just as one's face appears in a clear mirror. If this would not be the case, I shall not attain supreme enlightenment.

(41) I shall not attain supreme enlightenment if any sentient being in any other Buddha-land, after hearing my name and before attaining bodhi, would be [born] with incomplete organs or organs restricted in function.

(42) When I become a Buddha, any Bodhisattva in any other Buddha-land, after hearing my name, will be able to know distinctly the names of superb samādhis. While in remaining in samādhi, they will be able to make offerings to countless, numberless Buddhas—inconceivable and unequaled in number—in a moment, and will be able to realize great samādhis[5] instantly. If this would not be the case, I shall not attain supreme enlightenment.

(43) I shall not attain supreme enlightenment if, when I become a Buddha, any Bodhisattva in any other Buddha-land who has heard my name would not be born in a noble family after death.

(44) I shall not attain supreme enlightenment if, when I become a Buddha, any Bodhisattva in any other Buddha-land would not immediately cultivate the Bodhisattva practices, become purified and joyful, abide in equality, and possess all good roots after he hears my name.

(45) When I become a Buddha, Bodhisattvas in other Buddha-lands will achieve the Samādhi of Equality after hearing my name and will, without regression, abide in this samādhi and make constant offerings to an innumerable, unequaled number of Buddhas until those Bodhisattvas attain bodhi. If this would not be the case, I shall not attain supreme enlightenment.

(46) I shall not attain supreme enlightenment if Bodhisattvas in my land would not hear at will the Dharma they wished to hear.

(47) I shall not attain supreme enlightenment if, when I become a Buddha, any Bodhisattva in any other Buddha-land would regress from the path to supreme enlightenment after he hears my name.

(48) I shall not attain supreme enlightenment if, when I become a Buddha, any Bodhisattva in any other Buddha-land would not acquire the first, the second, or the third realization[6] as soon as he heard my name, or would not instantly attain nonregression with regard to Buddha-Dharmas.'"

Then the Buddha told Ānanda, "Having made these vows in the presence of Tathāgata Freest in the World, Monk Dharmākara, by the awesome power of the Buddha, spoke in verse:

"'I now make great oaths
In the presence of the Tathāgata:
If I have not fulfilled these lofty vows
The day when I would realize supreme bodhi,
I shall not become an unequaled Honored One
Possessing the ten powers.

If I cannot always give abundantly
To relieve the poor and suffering,
And to benefit worldlings with peace and joy,
I shall not become
A world-delivering Dharma King.

If, when I would realize enlightenment
On the bodhi-site,
My name is not known throughout the ten directions
In countless, boundless Buddha-lands,
I shall not become a World-Honored One
With the ten powers.

If I lack wisdom, mindfulness, and pure conduct
When moving toward supreme bodhi
And renouncing the household life
To be free from desire,
I shall not become the Tamer,
The Teacher of Gods and Humans.

I vow to acquire the immeasurable light
Of a Tathāgata, illuminating
All Buddha-lands in the ten directions;
I vow to eradicate
All desire, hatred, and ignorance,
And to eliminate the miserable realms of the world.

I vow to open the clear wisdom-eye,
[Gaining] the light to dispel darkness
In all realms of existence.
I vow to eliminate
All adversities completely,
And to become the Great, Awesome One
Among gods and humans.

When I have cultivated the original practices[7]
To the stage of purity,
I shall acquire the limitless, superb, awesome light
Which can outshine the brilliance
Of suns, moons, gods, pearls,
Or any other source of light.

After the Supreme Man has cultivated those practices,
He will be a hidden treasure to the poor.
Unequaled, perfect in wholesome Dharmas,
He will make the lion's roar
Among the crowd.

In the past, for many kalpas,
I made offerings to those with spontaneous wisdom,
And persevered in practicing austerities
To seek the supreme store of wisdom,
Fulfil my original vows,
And become an Honored One among gods and humans.

A Tathāgata is unhindered in knowledge and views;
He can understand everything in the world.[8]
May I become an Unequaled One,
A Supreme Knower, a True Teacher!

If I can truly fulfill these great vows,
And realize great enlightenment,
May the billion-world universe quake
And the gods shower flowers from the sky!'

"Thereupon, the great earth began to quake, celestial flowers and the sounds of drums and music filled the sky, and a drizzle of fine powdered sandalwood began to fall. A voice proclaimed, 'You will become a Buddha in the future!'. . ."[9]

Then Ānanda asked the Buddha, "World-Honored One, when does Bodhisattva Dharmākara attain enlightenment? Has he done so in the past, will he do so in the future, or does he do so now in another world?"

The Buddha said to Ānanda, "In the west, ten trillion Buddha-lands away from here, there is a world called Utmost Bliss. Monk Dharmākara has become a Buddha there named Amitāyus.[10] Right now, surrounded respectfully by countless Bodhisattvas and Śrāvakas, he is preaching the Dharma.

"Ānanda, the light of that Buddha is illuminating all Buddha-lands, incalculable and inconceivable in number. Now I will speak about this briefly. His light illuminates Buddha-lands in the east as numerous as the sands of the Ganges, and equally numerous Buddha-lands in the south, the west, the north, in each of the four intermediate directions, the zenith, and the nadir, except for places illuminated by other Buddhas with their own lights, through the power of their original vows. The lights of Amitāyus Buddha may reach as far as several feet, one league, and so on, up to hundreds of thousands of [millions of] billions of myriads of leagues; some may even shine over all Buddha-lands. Ānanda, for this reason, Amitāyus Buddha has other names, such as Infinite Light, Boundless Light, Detached Light, Unhindered Light, King of Illumination, Magnificent Light, Loving Light, Joyful Light, Pleasant Light, Inconceivable Light, Unequaled Light, Immeasurable Light, Light Outshining the Sun, Light Outshining the Moon, and Light Outshining Suns and Moons. His light, pure and immense, makes all sentient beings [in his land] feel joyful in body and mind. It also gives joy to gods, dragons, yakṣas, asuras, and other beings in all other Buddha-lands. Ānanda, if from this moment I began to describe the light of that Buddha, I would not be able to finish describing it even in an entire kalpa.

"Furthermore, Ānanda, the number of Tathāgata Amitāyus's assembly of Śrāvakas cannot be known by counting. Suppose there were hundreds of thousands of [millions of] billions of myriads of monks, all of whom enjoyed the same mastery of miraculous powers as Mahāmaudgalyāyana, and who could in the morning traverse a billion-world universe and return to their own abodes in an instant. Furthermore, suppose all these monks gathered together and spent hundreds of thousands of [millions of] billions of myriads of years, exercising their miraculous powers to the utmost until they entered nirvāṇa, in calculating the number of Śrāvakas in the first assembly held by Amitāyus Buddha. They would still be unable to know one hundredth, one thousandth, one hundred thousandth, and so on, down to one infinitesimal part of its number. . . . The same is true of the number of Bodhisattva-Mahāsattvas in his land, which cannot be known by counting.

"Ānanda, the life span of that Buddha is immeasurable and limitless; it is impossible for anyone to know how many kalpas he will live. The same is true of the Śrāvakas, Bodhisattvas, gods, and humans [in his land]."

Ānanda asked the Buddha, "World-Honored One, how long has it been since that Buddha, who can enjoy such an immeasurable life, appeared in the world?"

The Buddha told Ānanda, "It has been ten kalpas since that Buddha was born.

"Furthermore, Ānanda, the Land of Utmost Bliss abounds in countless merits and adornments. It is a rich land. Gods and humans thrive there; they are congenial, peaceful, and always feel secure. There are no planes of hell-dwellers or animals, nor the domain of Yama. The land is pervaded by the fragrance of all kinds of incense and spread with various wonderful flowers. Banners bedecked with the seven treasures stand in rows everywhere. Over the jewelled banners are set canopies, from which precious bells of hundreds of thousands of wonderful colors are suspended.

"Ānanda, there are many precious trees in that Tathāgata's land: gold trees, silver trees, lapis lazuli trees, crystal trees, red pearl trees, agate trees, and jade trees. Some of them are made purely of one treasure, not mixed with other treasures. Some are adorned with two, three, and so on, up to seven treasures. . . .

"Also, all over that Buddha-land, there are numberless trees adorned with pearls or other treasures. The brilliance of these precious trees is incomparable in the world. They are covered with nets made of the seven treasures, as soft as cotton.

"Moreover, Ānanda, in Amitāyus Buddha's land, there is a bodhi-tree sixteen hundred million leagues high, with branches and leaves spreading out over an area eight hundred million leagues [in radius]. Its roots above the ground are five thousand leagues high. . . . The bodhi-tree is adorned all around with gold chains from which hang jeweled tassels made of various gems,[11] red, white, and green pearls, and so forth. The jeweled columns [of the bodhi-tree] are decorated with chains made of 'lion-cloud-gathering' gems. The chains are covered with a net, to which are attached bells made of pure gold, pearls, and various other gems. On the net, crystal swastikas,[12] half-moon jewels, and so forth reflect one another. When a breeze stirs, many kinds of sounds are given forth, which cause the sentient beings in that billion-world universe to attain [various degrees of] the Realization of Nonarising with regard to the profound Dharma, according to their respective inclinations. Ānanda, after hearing the sounds, some sentient beings in that billion-world universe will not further regress from the path to supreme enlightenment, and innumerable others will achieve the Realization of the Nonarising of Dharmas.

"Furthermore, Ānanda, if a sentient being sees the bodhi-tree, hears its sounds, smells its fragrance, tastes the flavor of its fruit, touches its brilliance and shade, or thinks of its merits, he will have no ailments of his five sense-organs, will not be distracted in mind, and will not regress from his progress toward supreme enlightenment until he enters nirvāṇa. Moreover, because he sees the bodhi-tree, he will acquire three kinds of realization. What are the three? First, the realization derived from sound; second, the realization of pliancy;[13] third, the Realization of the Nonarising of Dharmas. All this is possible because Amitāyus Buddha has vested [in the bodhi-tree] the divine power of his original vows. . . ."

II

The Buddha told Ānanda, "In the Land of Utmost Bliss, there are no seas, but there are rivers. The narrowest river is ten leagues wide and the shallowest water twelve leagues deep. Some rivers are twenty, thirty, and so on, even a hundred leagues in depth or width. The deepest and the widest ones measure up to one thousand leagues. The water is clear and cool and has the eight meritorious qualities. The deep currents flow rapidly, giving forth a wonderful sound, which is like the sound of hundreds of thousands of musical instruments played by gods; it is heard all over the Land of Utmost Bliss. Beautiful flowers float downstream on the water. A gentle breeze wafts fragrance of all kinds. On the two banks of the rivers, there are many sandalwood trees with long branches and dense foliage interlaced into canopies over the rivers. They produce beautiful, fragrant flowers and bear lovely, shiny fruit. People come there to roam about and enjoy themselves as they like. Some wade through the water, washing their feet in the streams and making merry. The celestial water in the streams is agreeable to all and alters its depth and temperature at any time to suit the people in it.

"Ānanda, the bottom of the great rivers is covered with gold sand. The rivers give forth a celestial fragrance spread by the wind, with which nothing worldly can compare. The sweet-smelling water flows along, strewed with celestial flowers of the coral tree, blue lotus flowers, red lotus flowers, white lotus flowers, and giant white lotus flowers. Furthermore, Ānanda, when people in that Buddha-land go together on an excursion to the riverside, those who do not wish to hear the sound of the rapids will not hear it at all, even if they have acquired the deva-ear. Those who wish to hear it will immediately hear hundreds of thousands of pleasant sounds, such as the sounds of the Buddha, the Dharma and the Saṁgha; the sounds of cessation; the sounds of no essence, the sounds of the pāramitās; the sounds of the ten powers and the four fearlessnesses; the sounds of miraculous powers; the sounds of nonaction; the sounds of nonarising and noncessation; the sounds of quiescence, universal[14] quiescence, and utter quiescence; the sounds of great kindness and great compassion; the sounds of the Realization of the Nonarising of Dharmas; and the sounds of anointment and enthronement. After hearing these various sounds, the listeners will be overwhelmed by feelings of great joy and delight, and become responsive to [the teachings on] contemplation, renunciation, destruction [of defilements], quiescence, universal quiescence, utter quiescence, the taste of the doctrine, the Buddha, the Dharma, the Saṁgha, the ten powers, the four fearlessnesses, the miraculous powers, cessation, enlightenment, Śrāvakahood, and nirvāṇa.

"Furthermore, Ānanda, in the Land of Utmost Bliss, the names of the miserable planes of existence are not heard. There are no such terms as hindrance, or enshrouding defilements; nor such terms as hell, Yama, or animal. There are no such terms as the eight adversities, nor terms for painful or neutral feelings. There is not even the concept of suffering, let alone real suffering. This is why that Buddha-land is called Utmost Bliss. Ānanda, now I can speak only briefly of this blissful land. If I spoke of it in detail, I would not be able to finish even if I spent an entire kalpa.

"Moreover, Ānanda, all the sentient beings of the Land of Utmost Bliss, whether they have been, are being, or will be born there, have exquisite bodily forms and handsome features. They have free command of miraculous powers and a full complement of merits. They enjoy all kinds of palaces, gardens, groves, garments, food and drink, incense, flowers, and necklaces. Whatever they want appears to them spontaneously, as it is with the gods of the Paranirmita-Vaśavartin Heaven.

"Furthermore, Ānanda, in that Buddha-land there is a kind of subtle food which sentient beings eat without using their mouths; they feel they are eating the food as soon as they think about it, as it is with the gods in the Sixth Heaven. The food nourishes the body but produces no excrement.

"Moreover, there are unlimited quantities of the most agreeable incense, perfumed ointment, and powdered incense, the fragrance of which permeates all that Buddha-land. Also found everywhere are banners and scattered flowers. Those who wish to smell the fragrance will smell it at will, while those who do not wish to will smell nothing. . . .

"If sentient beings want palaces, storied buildings, or pavilions—whether high or low, long or short, wide or narrow, square or round—or if they want beds or couches with wonderful coverings, decorated with various gems, these things will appear before them spontaneously according to their respective wishes, so that everyone will think he is living in a palace of his own.

"Furthermore, Ānanda, the sentient beings in the Land of Utmost Bliss are not different from one another in appearance; however, to conform to the conventions of other lands, they assume the names of gods or humans. . . . Ānanda, you should know that the sentient beings in that land are all like the king of the Paranirmita-Vaśavartin Heaven.

"Ānanda, every morning, a gentle breeze blows all over the blissful land, which causes no reverse or disturbing winds and carries the fragrance of various flowers to every corner of that Buddha-land. All sentient beings, when touched by the breeze, feel as peaceful and comfortable as a monk who has achieved the Dhyāna of Complete Cessation of Feeling and Conception.[15] When the trees made of the seven treasures are blown by the breeze, their blossoms fall and form piles as tall as seven persons, and the entire Buddha-land is illuminated by their multicolored lights. The flowers are evenly mixed and spread out according to their different colors, as if someone had spread them over the ground and leveled them with his hands. They are exquisite flowers, large, and as soft as cotton. When the sentient beings tread on the piles, their feet sink as much as four fingers deep, but when they lift their feet, the ground returns to its original condition. When the morning is over, the flowers spontaneously sink into the ground. As the old flowers disappear, the great earth becomes refreshingly clean, and then a rain of new flowers entirely covers the ground again. The same thing happens [six times a day]: in the early, middle, and last part of the day, and in the early, middle, and last part of the night.[16]

"Ānanda, all the rarest treasures are found in the Land of Utmost Bliss. Ānanda, in that Buddha-land, there are lotus flowers made of the seven treasures, and each of the lotus flowers has countless hundreds of thousands of [millions of] billions of petals in numerous hundreds of thousands of rare colors. Each lotus is adorned with hundreds of thousands of wonderful wish-fulfilling pearls and covered with precious nets, all of them mutually reflecting. Ānanda, a lotus flower there has a diameter of half a league, or one, two, three, four, even one hundred or one thousand leagues, and each emits three billion six hundred million myriads of lights.[17] In each light appear three billion six hundred million myriads of Buddhas. These Buddhas are golden in complexion and superbly adorned with the thirty-two auspicious signs and the eighty minor ones. They emit hundreds of thousands of lights to illuminate every corner of the world. They go to the east to preach the Dharma to the people and establish countless sentient beings in the Buddha-Dharma. For the same purpose, they also go to the south, the west, the north, the four intermediate directions, the zenith, and the nadir.

"Furthermore, Ānanda, in the Land of Utmost Bliss, there is no darkness or gloom, nor the light of fire. There is no name for spring, pond, or lake. There is no name for residence, home, grove, or garden. There is no kind of symbol of expression to denote children. There is no sun or moon, day or night. There is no designation or name anywhere except those which are blessed by the Tathāgata.

"Ānanda, all the sentient beings in that Buddha-land are among those who will eventually attain supreme enlightenment and reach nirvāṇa. Why? Because those who support heterodox views and those who are undecided cannot know how to establish the cause for being born there.[18]

"Ānanda, in the east, there are as many Buddha-lands as the sands of the Ganges; the Buddhas in those lands all praise the countless merits of Amitāyus Buddha. The same is the case with the Buddhas in the south, the west, the north, the four intermediate directions, the zenith, and the nadir. Why? Except those who commit the five grave offences and those who slander the true Dharma and defame saints, any sentient being in any other Buddha-land can do the following:[19] after hearing the name of Tathāgata Amitāyus, if they have even one thought of pure faith, joy, and aspiration and dedicate all their good roots to birth in that Buddha-land, they will be born there as they wish, and will achieve nonregression from the path to supreme enlightenment.[20]

"Ānanda, if a sentient being in another Buddha-land engenders bodhicitta, single-mindedly thinks of Amitāyus Buddha, constantly plants roots of virtue and dedicates them to birth in that Buddha-land, then, when he is about to die, Amitāyus Buddha, surrounded by a host of monks, will appear before him. The dying person will immediately follow the Tathāgata to be born in that land, attain nonregression, and be destined to realize supreme enlightenment. Therefore, Ānanda, if good men and good women wish to be born in the Land of Utmost Bliss and see Amitāyus Buddha, they should engender supreme bodhicitta, concentrate their thoughts on the Land of Utmost Bliss, accumulate good roots, and dedicate them as taught. Thereby, they will see that Buddha, be born in his land, and attain nonregression from the path to supreme enlightenment.

"Ānanda, suppose a sentient being in another Buddha-land engenders bodhicitta and dedicates his merits to birth in Amitāyus Buddha's land, but does not concentrate his mind on Amitāyus Buddha or constantly plant numerous good roots. When he is about to die, Amitāyus Buddha will send a magically produced Buddha to him, surrounded by a host of monks. The magically produced Buddha, who is exactly the same as the real Buddha in brilliance and auspicious signs, will appear before the dying person to receive and guide him, and that person will immediately follow the Buddha to be born in that land and attain nonregression from the path to supreme enlightenment.

"Ānanda, if a sentient being who abides in the Mahāyāna feels pure-minded devotion for Tathāgata Amitāyus for only ten consecutive thoughts, wishing to be born in his land; or if he believes and understands this profound teaching as soon as he hears it expounded, with no doubt in his mind, and thereby thinks of Amitāyus Buddha for even one pure thought, then, when he is about to die, he will see Amitāyus Buddha as if in a dream. The dying person will without fail be born in that Buddha-land to achieve nonregression from the path to supreme enlightenment.

"Ānanda, it is because of these benefits that all the Buddhas, Tathāgatas, in countless worlds—inconceivable, unequaled, and limitless in number—extol the merits of Amitāyus Buddha. . . .

"Moreover, Ānanda, all the Śrāvakas in that Buddha-land have haloes several feet in radius; the Bodhisattvas' haloes reach as far as hundreds of thousands of feet in radius. There are two Bodhisattvas whose lights constantly illuminate the whole billion-world universe."

Ānanda asked the Buddha, "World-Honored One, who are the two Bodhisattvas?"

The Buddha told Ānanda, "Now, listen carefully. One of the two Bodhisattvas is called Avalokiteśvara; the other, Mahāsthāmaprāpta. Ānanda, these two Bodhisattvas were born in that Buddha-land after their lifetimes came to an end in the Sahā World.

"Ānanda, all the Bodhisattvas born in the Land of Utmost Bliss have the thirty-two auspicious signs. They are supple physically, keen in senses, and endowed with wisdom and ingenuity. They know all diversified phenomena, and have a free command of dhyāna and miraculous powers. None of them has little virtue or an inadequate capacity. An incalculable number of those Bodhisattvas have achieved the first or the second realization;[21] some have attained the Realization of the Nonarising of Dharmas.

"Ānanda, the Bodhisattvas in that Buddha-land will not fall to the miserable planes of existence on their way to attainment of supreme enlightenment. They will remember all their previous lives wherever they are born, except when they appear in the world of five depravities.

"Ānanda, every morning, the Bodhisattvas in that Buddha-land make offerings to countless hundreds of thousands of Buddhas in other Buddha-lands. Due to the divine power of Amitāyus Buddha, garlands, perfumed ointment, powdered incense, banners, canopies, and musical instruments of all kinds appear in their hands as they wish, to be offered to the Buddhas. Such offerings are immense, countless, and inconceivable. When the Bodhisattvas wish it, various rare blossoms resplendent with incalculable hundreds of thousands of lights and colors will appear in their hands to be scattered on the Buddhas as an offering. Ānanda, the flowers they scatter will immediately change into flower canopies in the sky, the smallest of which measures ten leagues [in diameter]. The flowers first scattered will not fall from the air unless new flowers are scattered. Ānanda, some of these canopies measure twenty leagues, thirty, forty, and so on, up to one thousand leagues [in diameter]. Some are large enough to cover the four continents; some are large enough to cover a thousand-world, a million-world, or even a billion-world universe. Thus, the Bodhisattvas engender minds full of wonder and hearts full of great joy.

"Every morning, these Bodhisattvas attend on, make offerings to, show respect for, and praise incalculable hundreds of thousands [of millions] of billions of myriads of Buddhas. After they have thus planted good roots, they return to their land in the same morning. All this is made possible because Amitāyus Buddha vests in them the power of his original vows, which he thoroughly cultivated, maintained, and fulfilled, and because of his good roots in making uninterrupted and perfect offerings to Tathāgatas in the past.

"Furthermore, Ānanda, whatever the Bodhisattvas in the Land of Utmost Bliss say is in consonance with all-knowing wisdom. They do not take possession of anything they enjoy. They travel to all Buddha-lands without attachment or aversion, expectation or nonexpectation; they have no thought of a self, defilement, the 'I,' disputation, discord, hatred, or anger. Why? Because these Bodhisattvas have the great mind of kindness, compassion, and beneficence toward all sentient beings. They have the mind which is supple, unobstructed, free of filth and resentment, impartial, regulated, quiet, patient, subdued by patience, equable, clear, without distraction, free of coverings, pure, extremely pure, illuminating, unsoiled, awe-inspiring, virtuous, vast, incomparable, profound, fond of the Dharma, exultant over the Dharma, well-intentioned, free from all attachments, and [able to] rid sentient beings of all defilements and to eliminate the miserable planes of existence.

"They have cultivated the practices of wisdom, and achieved immeasurable merits. They are able not only to discourse on meditation and the other factors of enlightenment, but also to have a free command of them. They diligently cultivate supreme enlightenment and explain it to others. They can discern things well with their physical eyes, see various Buddha-lands with their deva-eyes, free themselves from attachment with their clear Dharma-eyes, reach the other shore with their penetrating wisdom-eyes, and realize the Dharma-nature with their Buddha-eyes.[22] They engender unimpeded wisdom with which they can teach the Dharma extensively to others. . . ."

The World-Honored One then told Ānanda, "Such is Amitāyus Buddha's Land of Utmost Bliss. You should rise from your seat, join your palms respectfully, and prostrate yourself full-length on the ground to pay homage to that Buddha. That Buddha's name is known throughout the ten directions; in each direction, there are Buddhas as numerous as the sands of the Ganges who praise him incessantly and without reservation."

Thereupon, Ānanda rose from his seat, bared his right shoulder, joined his palms toward the west, prostrated himself full-length on the ground, and said to the Buddha, "World-Honored One, now I wish to see Amitāyus Buddha in the Land of Utmost Bliss and to make offerings to and serve countless hundreds of thousands of [millions of] billions of myriads of Buddhas and Bodhisattvas, in order to plant good roots."

Right then, Amitāyus Buddha emitted from his palm a great light which illuminated hundreds of thousands of millions of myriads of Buddha-lands. In those lands, all the mountains, small and large, such as Black Mountain, Treasure Mountain, Mount Sumeru, Mount Meru, Mount Mahāmeru, Mount Mucilinda, Mount Mahāmucilinda, Mount Iron Circle, and Mount Great Iron Circle; . . . and all the gods, humans, and so forth were revealed by the light of that Buddha. Just as a person with the pure deva-eye can see everything clearly within a distance of several feet, and just as a person can see everything clearly when the sun comes out, so the monks, nuns, laymen, and laywomen in other Buddha-lands all saw Tathāgata Amitāyus. He, like Mount Sumeru, the king of mountains, illuminated his Buddha-land and revealed it as clearly as if it had been only a few feet away. Because the wonderful light of Tathāgata Amitāyus was extremely pure and clear, they saw his high throne, and his assemblies of Śrāvakas, Bodhisattvas, and so forth. It is just like when a flood submerges all trees, mountains, and rivers, there is nothing to be seen on the great earth except the great flood. Likewise, in that Buddha-land, where there were no heterodox believers or beings other than great Śrāvakas, with haloes several feet in radius; and Bodhisattva-Mahāsattvas, with haloes hundreds of thousands of leagues in radius, the light of Tathāgata Amitāyus, the Worthy One, the Perfectly Enlightened One, outshone the lights of all the Śrāvakas and Bodhisattvas and enabled all the sentient beings to see him.

At the same time, the Bodhisattvas, Śrāvakas, humans, and gods in the Land of Utmost Bliss all saw Tathāgata Śākyamuni of the Sahā World preaching the Dharma, surrounded by an assembly of monks.

Then the Buddha asked Bodhisattva Maitreya, "Did you see the magnificent Buddha-land, which is perfectly pure and full of awesome merits? . . . Did you see myriads of flowers scattered as adornments in the sky over the earth and in the heavens up to the Akaniṣṭha Heaven? Did you see the birds in the sky, which are not real creatures but magical creations, uttering various sounds which, like the voice of the Buddha, are heard all over that world?"

Maitreya answered the Buddha, "Yes, I did."

The Buddha further asked Bodhisattva Maitreya, "Did you see the sentient beings who, after entering palaces a hundred to a thousand leagues across, traveled in space, unattached and unhindered, to all Buddha-lands to make offerings to the Buddhas? Did you see those sentient beings who think of the Buddha continuously day and night?"

Maitreya answered, "Yes, I did."

The Buddha asked further, "Did you see any difference between the things used by people in the Land of Utmost Bliss and those used by gods in the Paranirmita-Vaśavartin Heaven?"

Maitreya answered, "I did not see any difference between them."

The Buddha asked Maitreya, "Did you see any being in the Land of Utmost Bliss conceived in a womb?"[23]

Maitreya answered, "World-Honored One, gods in the Heaven of the Thirty-Three and the Yama Heaven and so forth play and make merry in palaces one hundred to five hundred leagues wide. I saw that when people in the Land of Utmost Bliss are conceived in a womb, they feel just like those gods living in palaces. I also saw sentient beings who were seated cross-legged in lotus flowers and then born ethereally all of a sudden."

The Bodhisattva Maitreya asked the Buddha, "World-Honored One, why are some beings in that Buddha-land born from the womb and others born ethereally?"[24]

The Buddha told Maitreya, "If a sentient being is full of doubt and regret when he accumulates good roots and seeks Buddha-wisdom, universal wisdom, inconceivable wisdom, unequaled wisdom, great wisdom, and the wisdom of awesome merits, then, because he has no faith in his own good roots, he has to stay in the palace [-like womb] for five hundred years without seeing a Buddha, a Bodhisattva, or a Śrāvaka, or hearing the Dharma expounded. If a sentient being is completely free of doubt and regret when he accumulates good roots and seeks Buddha-wisdom, then, because he believes in his own good roots, he will be seated cross-legged in a lotus flower and be born ethereally all of a sudden, emerging from it in an instant. Just as people have come here from other countries, so such a Bodhisattva, due to his vow, has been born in the Land of Utmost Bliss to see, serve, and make offerings to Amitāyus Buddha and the assembly of Bodhisattvas and Śrāvakas.

"Ajita, you see, those superior, intelligent beings, due to their immense wisdom, are born ethereally from the louts flowers in which they sit cross-legged. As for the inferior ones, they [are born from the womb, and,] for five hundred years, see no Buddhas, Śrāvakas, or Bodhisattvas, hear no Dharma, and know no rules for a Bodhisattva's conduct. Because they cannot cultivate merits [in the womb], they find no chance to serve Amitāyus Buddha. All this is a result of their doubt and regret in the past.

"As an illustration, consider a kṣatriya king's son who breaks the law and consequently is imprisoned in an inner palace. He lives among gardens, storied buildings, and halls that are exquisitely furnished with rare treasures, precious curtains, and gold couches with thick, soft mattresses. The floor is covered with rare flowers, the most precious incense is burned, and all necessary articles are abundantly provided. However, his feet are fettered with a chain of Jambu-river gold."

The Buddha asked Maitreya, "What do you think? Does that prince enjoy all this?"

Maitreya answered, "No, World-Honored One. When he is imprisoned, he will try to be set free, asking relatives, friends, respectable people, ministers, elders, and courtiers for help. However, although the prince is anxious to be released, his wish will not be fulfilled until the king willingly agrees to it."

The Buddha said to Maitreya, "So it is, so it is. Similarly, if one is full of doubt and regret when he plants good roots and seeks the Buddha-wisdom, the great wisdom, then, though he will be born in that land due to his engendering of faith in the Buddha at hearing his name, he will remain in the [womb of a] lotus flower after birth and be unable to come out, all because he has no faith in his own good roots.

"Such a sentient being, living in the flower womb, will think of it as a palace with gardens. Why? Because the lotus womb is clean and free of filth, and nothing in it is unpleasant. Nevertheless, the sentient being will for five hundred years see no Buddhas, Bodhisattvas, or Śrāvakas, and hear no Dharma; he cannot make offerings to or serve the Buddhas; he cannot inquire about the Bodhisattva canon; he is far apart from all superb roots of virtue. He does not enjoy living in the flower womb, for he cannot come out of it to practice wholesome dharmas until all his faults committed in the past are exhausted. When he comes out, he will lose all sense of direction, not knowing the zenith, the nadir, or the four cardinal directions. Not until all his doubts disappear during those five hundred years will he be able to make offerings to countless hundreds of thousands of millions of myriads of Buddhas and plant incalculable, limitless roots of virtue. Ajita, you should know that doubt does great harm to Bodhisattvas."

Then Bodhisattva Maitreya asked the Buddha, "World-Honored One, how many nonregressing Bodhisattvas in this Buddha-land will be born in the Land of Utmost Bliss?"

The Buddha told Maitreya, "In this Buddha-land, seven billion two hundred million Bodhisattvas, who have planted good roots in incalculable hundreds of thousands of [millions of] billions of myriads of Buddha-lands and have become nonregressing, will be born in that Buddha-land. The Bodhisattvas who will be born in that Buddha-land because of fewer roots of virtue are countless. . . .

"Ajita, if I enumerate the names of the Bodhisattvas in other lands who have been, are being, and will be born in the Land of Ultimate Bliss to make offerings to, pay homage to, and worship Amitāyus Buddha, I will not be able to finish doing so even if I spend an entire kalpa.

"Ajita, you see how highly those Bodhisattva-Mahāsattvas benefit. If one can generate a single thought of joy after hearing that Buddha's name, he will obtain the merits mentioned above, he will feel neither inferior nor superior, and all the good roots he has achieved will be enhanced. Therefore, Ajita, I tell you and gods, humans, and asuras: I now entrust you with this Dharma-door. You should take pleasure in practicing it. You should accept, retain, read, and recite it, even day and night. You should aspire for this sūtra, explain it to others, and have people write it and preserve it. You should regard this sūtra as a teacher.

"Ajita, if Bodhisattva-Mahāsattvas wish to cause numerous sentient beings to be rapidly and securely established in nonregression from [pursuit of] supreme enlightenment, and wish to see the magnificent adornments of that superb Buddha-land and to embrace its perfect merits, then they should strive vigorously to learn this Dharma-door. They should not back away or become pretentious in seeking the Dharma, even if they have to go through a raging fire that fills a whole billion-world universe. They should read, recite, accept, retain, and copy this sūtra, and make use of every moment to explain it to others and persuade them to listen to it without worry or annoyance. Even if they are thrown into a fire for doing so, they should entertain no doubt or regret. Why? Countless billions of Bodhisattvas seek, esteem, learn, and obey this subtle teaching. Therefore, all of you should seek this teaching, too. Ajita, those sentient beings will obtain great, high benefits. In the future, even at the time of the true Dharma's decline, some sentient beings will plant good roots. These are the sentient beings who have made offerings to innumerable Buddhas and who, being blessed by those Tathāgatas, are able to acquire this great Dharma-door, which is praised and approved by all Tathāgatas. If one accepts and upholds this Dharma-door, he will acquire the vast all-knowing wisdom and plant good roots as he pleases. Good men and good women who have a superior understanding of this teaching will be able to obtain great joy from hearing it; they will accept, uphold, read, and recite it, explain it to others, and always delight in practicing it.

"Ajita, innumerable billions of Bodhisattvas have sought this teaching untiringly. You good men and good women will benefit greatly if you are able to seek this teaching in your present or future lives. Ajita, the Tathāgata has already done what he should do. You should be firm and free of doubt in planting good roots; you should constantly study and practice anything that can remove your doubt, lest you be imprisoned [in a palace-like womb] made of various treasures.

"Ajita, there are one hundred million Bodhisattvas of great, awesome virtue who can propound numerous other doctrines of the Buddha-Dharma, but have regressed in [the pursuit of] supreme enlightenment because they have not heard this teaching.

"Ajita, it is difficult to find a Buddha appearing in the world. It is also difficult to have a body free from the eight adversities. Even an eloquent Dharma-teacher finds it difficult to explain the Buddhas' unexcelled Dharmas, such as the very profound Dharmas of the ten powers, the four fearlessnesses, unimpededness, and detachment, and the Bodhisattva doctrines such as the pāramitās, and so on. Ajita, it is not easy to meet a person who is adept in preaching the Dharma. It is also rare to encounter one of firm and deep faith. Now I have taught this discourse in accordance with the truth, and you should all practice it as I have taught.

"Ajita, I entrust to you this teaching and the Dharma of all Buddhas. You [all] should practice it and not let it perish. This great, subtle Dharma-door is praised by all Buddhas. Do not abandon it in defiance of the Buddha's instructions; otherwise, you will encounter hindrances—you will be engulfed in the long night to go through all dangers and sufferings. Therefore, I now solemnly bid you to do everything to cause this doctrine to last long. You should practice this teaching diligently as I have taught.". . .

When the Buddha had spoken this sūtra, Bodhisattva Maitreya, Venerable Ānanda, and everyone in the assembly were jubilant over what the Buddha had taught.

NOTES

1. A more literal translation of these forty-eight vows follows this formula: "[When] I become a Buddha, if, in my land, there are still the planes of hell-dwellers, hungry ghosts, or animals, I will not ultimately take up supreme enlightenment."

2. "The power to appear anywhere at will" may also be called "the power of performing miracles." It can include such miraculous powers as remaining under water without drowning, touching fire without being burned, or transforming oneself into any kind of creature or object. However, in some contexts, "the power to appear anywhere at will" seems to be a more appropriate translation, as in this paragraph.

3. Monk Dharmakāra's land when he becomes Amitāyus Buddha.

4. Or, "the doctrine concerning freedom from saṁsāra." In Taishō 360, p.268, this reads, ". . . who hear my name would fail to cultivate pure conduct after death and before achieving Buddhahood." A third version, Taishō 363, p.320, does not mention "the doctrine concerning freedom from saṁsāra" and "after death." It may make more sense and be less misleading to ignore these two phrases altogether.

5. The Chinese text reads "six samādhis." Perhaps 'six' (六) is a misprint for 'great' (大).

6. The realization derived from sound, the realization of pliancy, and the Realization of the Nonarising of Dharmas.

7. Original practices: the practices that a Buddha cultivated when he was still following the Bodhisattva-path. The fundamental practices for achieving Buddhahood.

8. Literally, "He can understand all conditioned (*saṁskṛta*) dharmas."

9. This paragraph forms the last part of the above verse in the Chinese text.

10. Amitāyus means 'Infinite Life'. As related below, his life span is immeasurable. His other name, more frequently used, is Amitābha, or 'Infinite Light'.

11. The Chinese text reads 盧遮迦寶 and 未瑳寶 . The identities of these two gems are unknown to us.

12. An ancient Aryan auspicious symbol, used by Hindus and Buddhists.

13. With this realization, there is engendered a pliant, flexible mind of wisdom to comply with the Dharma and to accommodate sentient beings.

14. The Chinese reads 邊, meaning 'border' or 'side'. Perhaps it is a misprint of 遍, meaning 'universal'.

15. Dhyāna that leads one to nirvāṇa.

16. Actually there are no such distinctions as day and night in that land; it is to

conform to the convention of other lands that the day there is divided into six parts. See two paragraphs below.

17. Literally, "three billion six hundred million myriads of hundreds of thousands of lights." The next sentence reads similarly.

18. These three kinds of people are the three groups. See Numerical Glossary.

19. This paragraph describes the general karmic reward for faith in Amitāyus Buddha. The next paragraph describes the highest reward, followed by paragraphs describing the middle and lowest rewards, respectively.

20. According to the Chinese Pure Land School, the Buddha's teachings fall into two categories: those which teach people to reach salvation and liberation by faith, i.e., by the Buddha's power (the Pure Land school belongs to this category); and those which teach salvation and liberation by one's own strength. This passage is an example of the first category. (W.H.)

21. See note 6 above.

22. The original is very obscure here. Freely translated, it could be as follows: "Having achieved Buddha-eyes, they can enlighten [others by] revealing [to them the truth]." The translation given in the text is based on another version (Taishō 360, p. 274). Moreover, it is a doubtful point whether or not a Bodhisattva can be endowed with the Buddha-eye, which is generally understood as a unique quality of the Buddhas.

23. A lotus flower womb. See below.

24. In Buddhist tradition there are four modes of birth: (1) birth from a womb, as with mammalia; (2) birth from an egg, as with birds; (3) birth from moisture or water, as with worms and fishes; and (4) birth by transformation (alternate translation: ethereal birth), as with hell-dwellers, devas, the first beings in newly evolved worlds, and superior beings who are born in a pure Buddha-land such as the Land of Utmost Bliss.

VII

On General Mahāyāna Doctrine

19 勝鬘夫人會

The True Lion's Roar of Queen Śrīmālā

Thus have I heard. Once the Buddha was dwelling in the garden of Anāthapiṇḍada, in the Jeta Grove, near Śrāvastī. At that time, King Prasenajit and Queen Mallikā of Kosala had just had an initial realization of the Dharma. They said to each other, "Our daughter, Śrīmālā, is kind, intelligent, learned, and wise. If she could see the Tathāgata, she would be quick to understand the profound Dharma and would have no doubt about it whatsoever. We should now send an eloquent messenger to her to arouse her sincere faith."[1]

Immediately upon this decision, the king and queen wrote Queen Śrīmālā a letter extolling the true merits of the Tathāgata, and sent a messenger, Chandra, to deliver it to her at Ayodhyā. Queen Śrīmālā received the letter with reverence and joy. After she opened and read it, she felt how unusual its message was and spoke to the messenger in verse:

> "It is said that the Tathāgata's voice
> Is difficult to encounter in this world.
> If this saying is true,[2]
> I shall reward you with apparel.
> If the Buddha, the World-Honored One,
> Has manifested himself to benefit this world,
> His compassion will certainly extend to me,
> That I may see his true appearance."

As soon as she had so spoken, the Buddha appeared in the air in an inconceivable form, emitting a brilliant light. Queen Śrīmālā and her retinue gathered

Sūtra 48, Taishō 310, pp. 672–678; translated into Chinese by Bodhiruci.

together. With palms joined, they bowed respectfully to him, and the queen, looking up in adoration, praised the great teacher:

"The wondrous form of the Tathāgata
Is unequaled in this world;
It is incomparable and inconceivable;
Therefore I pay homage to him.

The form of the Tathāgata knows no bounds,
And boundless, too, is his wisdom.
All aspects [of his nature] abide eternally;[3]
Therefore I take refuge in him.

He has skillfully subdued all mental faults,
As well as the four vices of the body;[4]
He has reached the inconceivable stage;
Therefore I pay homage to him.

He knows everything that can be known,
For his wisdom-body meets no obstacles;
He forgets nothing;
Therefore I pay homage to him.

I bow down to the One who is infinite;
I bow down to the One who is peerless;
I bow down to the One
Who has free command of all dharmas;
I bow down to the One
Who is beyond thought.

May his compassion shelter me
And cause the seeds of the Dharma
To grow [within me],
So that I may always be with the Tathāgata
Until my last existence [in saṁsāra].

I have practiced all meritorious deeds
In this life and in all other lives.
May the Buddha always take me,
With all my roots of virtue,
Into his following."

When Queen Śrīmālā had spoken these verses, she and her entire retinue prostrated themselves at the Buddha's feet. Then the World-Honored One spoke to Śrīmālā in verse:

"In your former lives I taught you
And revealed to you the path of enlightenment.
Now once again you meet me here;
We shall also meet in future lives."

After speaking this verse, the Buddha prophesied to the assembly that Queen Śrīmālā would attain supreme enlightenment, saying, "You now praise the superb merits of the Tathāgata. Because of this good root, you will be a sovereign among gods and humans for incalculable kalpas. All your needs will be fulfilled. Wherever you are born, you will be able to meet me and praise me face to face, just as you do now. You will also make offerings to innumerable, countless other Buddhas, World-Honored Ones. After twenty thousand incalculable kalpas, you, too, will become a Buddha, named Universal Light Tathāgata, the Worthy One, the Perfectly Enlightened One.

"In your Buddha-land, there will be no miserable planes of existence, no suffering of aging or sickness, and no evil deeds, not even their names. The sentient beings there will appear in magnificent forms, and will solely experience the five exquisite [sensuous] pleasures, enjoying them even more than do the gods in the Paranirmita-Vaśavartin Heaven and other heavens. All these sentient beings will follow the Mahāyāna teachings. Others who have correctly learned the Mahāyāna [elsewhere] may be born in that land."

After Queen Śrīmālā had received the prophecy, innumerable gods and humans were jubilant, and they all wished to be born in that Buddha-land. The World-Honored One then prophesied that they would all be born in that land.

After having heard the Buddha's prophecy, Queen Śrīmālā stood before the Tathāgata with her palms joined, and made ten great vows, saying:

(1) "World-Honored One, from now until my attainment of enlightenment, I will never think of breaking the precepts I have received.
(2) "World-Honored One, from now until my attainment of enlightenment, I will never be arrogant toward teachers or my superiors.
(3) "World-Honored One, from now until my attainment of enlightenment, I will never feel ill will toward any sentient being.
(4) "World-Honored One, from now until my attainment of enlightenment, I will never be jealous of my superiors or those whose possessions are superior to mine.
(5) "World-Honored One, from now until my attainment of enlightenment, I will never be reluctant to give, even if I have only a little food.
(6) "World-Honored One, from now until my attainment of enlightenment, I will not accept money or accumulate property for my own sake, but only for the sake of relieving the poverty and sufferings of sentient beings.

(7) "World-Honored One, from now until my attainment of enlightenment, I will practice the four inducements without expecting rewards. I will embrace sentient beings with a mind that never covets profit, is never weary, and is free of hindrances.

(8) "World-Honored One, from now until my attainment of enlightenment, if I see any sentient being bereft of parents or children, imprisoned, sick, distressed, or suffering from any kind of danger or misfortune, I will not forsake him. Instead, I will give him peace and security, help him properly, and relieve him of all sufferings.

(9) "World-Honored One, from now until my attainment of enlightenment, if I see anyone pursuing evil ways or violating the pure precepts of the Tathāgata, [I will not forsake him]. In the cities, towns, and villages under my influence, I will subdue whoever should be subdued and embrace whoever should be embraced. Why? Only by subduing and embracing [sentient beings] will the true Dharma[5] endure. When the true Dharma endures, gods and humans will thrive, the miserable planes of existence will diminish, and the Tathāgata's Dharma-wheel will turn perpetually.

(10) "World-Honored One, from now until my attainment of enlightenment, I will never forget the true Dharma I have embraced. Why? To forget the true Dharma is to forget the Mahāyāna; to forget the Mahāyāna is to forget the pāramitās; to forget the pāramitās is to abandon the Mahāyāna. If a Bodhisattva wavers in regard to the Mahāyāna, then he will not be firm in embracing the true Dharma, and consequently will not be able to transcend the state of an ordinary person, causing a great loss. World-Honored One, the Bodhisattvas who embrace the true Dharma now or in the future will receive unlimited, great benefits.

"World-Honored One, Noble Master, although you have witnessed the pronouncement of these great vows, sentient beings with meager roots of virtue may very well doubt the ten great vows, for they are most difficult to accomplish. These sentient beings may habitually perform unwholesome actions in the long night and be afflicted by all kinds of suffering. It is to benefit these sentient beings that I now make this sincere declaration before the Buddha: World-Honored One, if the ten great vows are true and not false, may celestial flowers rain down over this assembly and may a celestial voice be heard."

As soon as Queen Śrīmālā had said this to the Buddha, the sky began to rain down celestial flowers, and a celestial voice exclaimed, "Excellent, Queen Śrīmālā! What you have said is true indeed."

After the assembly saw the auspice, they were freed from every doubt and were overjoyed. They proclaimed in unison their desire to be born wherever Queen Śrīmālā would be born, to make the same vows she had made, and to perform the same deeds she would perform. Thereupon, the Buddha, the World-Honored One, prophesied that all their wishes would be fulfilled.

Then Queen Śrīmālā made three more great vows before the Buddha, saying, "I will benefit an infinite number of sentient beings through the power of these vows: first, I will, by my good roots, attain the wisdom of the true Dharma in all my lifetimes; second, after I have attained the true wisdom, wherever I may be born I will explain it untiringly to all sentient beings; third, in whatever form I may be born, I will not spare life or limb in embracing, protecting, and upholding the true Dharma."

When the World-Honored One heard these vows, he told Śrīmālā, "Just as all forms are contained in the realm of space, so all the Bodhisattva's vows, as numerous as the sands of the Ganges, are contained in these vows. These three vows are truly vast."

Then Queen Śrīmālā said to the Buddha, "World-Honored One, through the eloquence vested in me by the Buddha's miraculous power, I would like to explain the great vow. Please grant me permission to speak."

The Buddha said, "Śrīmālā, speak as you wish."

Śrīmālā said, "The Bodhisattva's vows, as numerous as the sands of the Ganges, are all contained in one great vow. This one great vow is called the embracing of the Tathāgata's True Dharma. This embracing of the true Dharma is truly great and vast."

The Buddha said, "Well said, Śrīmālā! You have practiced the Dharma for a long time; your wisdom and ingenuity are subtle and profound. Anyone who can understand your words must have planted many good roots in the long night. You speak of the embracing of the true Dharma; it is the teaching of the Buddhas of the past, present, and future. Now that I have attained supreme enlightenment, I, too, often teach the embracing of the true Dharma in various ways. The merits derived from praising the embracing of the true Dharma are limitless, just as the wisdom of the Tathāgata is limitless. Why? Because it is most meritorious and beneficial to embrace the true Dharma."

Queen Śrīmālā then said to the Buddha, "World-Honored One, by the Buddha's divine power, I wish to explain the broad meaning of the embracing of the true Dharma."

The Buddha said, "Speak as you wish."

Śrīmālā said, "To embrace the true Dharma, broadly speaking, means to attain all the infinite Buddha-Dharmas, including the eighty thousand practices.

"Just as the multicolored clouds at the beginning of a kalpa rain down myriad gems, so the cloud of the good root of embracing the true Dharma rains down immeasurable blessings.

"World-Honored One, to illustrate further, the great flood at the beginning of a kalpa contains the cause of the billion-world universe, including the forty billion different continents.[6] In the same way, the embracing of the true Dharma contains the cause of the immeasurable realm of the Mahāyāna, and also the miraculous powers of the Bodhisattvas, the various Dharma-doors, and the perfection of the mundane and supramundane joy never before experienced by any god or human.

"To illustrate further, the great earth bears four burdens. What are the four? The oceans, the mountain ranges, the grasses and trees, and the sentient beings. The good men and women who embrace the true Dharma can bear four burdens heavier than those borne by the earth. What are the four?

(1) To teach [cultivation of] the good roots of gods and humans to the sentient beings who are apart from virtuous friends, lack learning, and are sinful, thus bringing those beings to maturity;
(2) to teach the Śrāvaka-vehicle to those who seek to be Śrāvakas;
(3) to teach the Pratyekabuddha-vehicle to those who seek to be Pratyekabuddhas; and
(4) to teach the Mahāyāna to those who seek the Mahāyāna.

These are the four burdens, heavier than those borne by the earth, borne by the good men and women who embrace the true Dharma.

"World-Honored One, the good men and women who embrace the true Dharma are able to establish [themselves like] the great earth to bear these four heavy burdens. They become the friends of all sentient beings universally, without need of an invitation. They are the Dharma-mothers of the world, who benefit sentient beings out of pity and great compassion.

"To illustrate further, the great earth is the source of the four categories of gems. What are the four? The invaluable gems, those of high value, those of medium value, and those of low value. Similarly, the good men and women who embrace the true Dharma and establish [themselves like] the great earth can cause the sentient beings who meet them to obtain the four great treasures, which are the best of all precious things. What are the four? When sentient beings meet such virtuous friends, they will obtain the good roots leading to birth as humans or gods, to Śrāvakahood, to Pratyekabuddhahood, or to realization of the Unexcelled Vehicle. Sentient beings will obtain these four great treasures after meeting the good men and women who embrace the true Dharma and establish [themselves like] the great earth.

"World-Honored One, that which yields the [four] great treasures is the real embracing of the true Dharma.

"World-Honored One, regarding the embracing of the true Dharma, I do not mean that the true Dharma and the embracing of the true Dharma are different. The true Dharma *is* to embrace the true Dharma.

"World-Honored One, the embracing of the true Dharma is no other than the pāramitās, and the pāramitās are no other than the embracing of the true Dharma. Why?

"For those sentient beings who can best be matured through giving, the good men and women who embrace the true Dharma practice charity, giving even their own lives and limbs. In this way, they bring those sentient beings to maturity in accordance with their inclinations, to establish them firmly in the true Dharma. This is called the pāramitā of giving.

"For those sentient beings who can best be matured by discipline, [those who embrace the true Dharma] guard their own six senses; purify their own verbal, bodily, and mental actions; and conduct themselves with dignity. In this way, they bring those sentient beings to maturity in accordance with their inclinations, to establish them firmly in the true Dharma. This is called the pāramitā of discipline.

"For those sentient beings who can best be matured by patience, [those who embrace the true Dharma] are free of ill will; intend only to benefit; and bear rebukes, scoldings, insults, outrage, slander, libel, annoyance, and harassment with the utmost patience, even without their faces changing color in the slightest. In this way, they bring those sentient beings to maturity in accordance with their inclinations, to establish them firmly in the true Dharma. This is called the pāramitā of patience.

"For those sentient beings who can best be matured by vigor, [those who embrace the true Dharma] do not have an indolent or negative mentality, but show great aspiration and supreme vigor, whether walking, standing, sitting, or lying down. In this way, they bring those sentient beings to maturity in accordance with their inclinations, to establish them firmly in the true Dharma. This is called the pāramitā of vigor.

"For those sentient beings who can best be matured by meditation, [those who embrace the true Dharma] are not distracted, and achieve right mindfulness and remembrance. In this way, they bring those sentient beings to maturity in accordance with their inclinations, to establish them firmly in the true Dharma. This is called the pāramitā of meditation.

"For those sentient beings who can best be matured by wisdom and who ask questions about the Dharma in order to benefit from it, [those who embrace the true Dharma] untiringly explain all doctrines, all sciences, and all techniques, until those sentient beings fully comprehend what is ultimate. In this way, they bring those sentient beings to maturity in accordance with their inclinations, to establish them firmly in the true Dharma. This is called the pāramitā of wisdom.

"Therefore, World-Honored One, the embracing of the true Dharma is not different from the pāramitās; the embracing of the true Dharma *is* the pāramitās."

The Queen Śrīmālā continued, "World-Honored One, through the eloquence vested in me by the Buddha's divine power, I wish to elaborate on the great meaning [of the embracing of the true Dharma]."

The Buddha said, "What is the great meaning?"

"World-Honored One, in referring to those who embrace the true Dharma,

I do not mean that they constitute an entity that differs from the embracing of the true Dharma.[7] The good men and women who embrace the true Dharma *are* the embracing of the true Dharma. Why?

"The good men and women who embrace the true Dharma give their bodies, lives, and possessions for the sake of the true Dharma. By giving their bodies, these people will realize that which transcends the limits of saṁsāra, will be free from old age and sickness, and will attain the Tathāgata's Dharma-body, which is indestructible, eternal, changeless, ultimately tranquil, and inconceivable. By giving their lives, they will realize that which transcends the limits of saṁsāra, will be forever released from death, will attain eternity, will acquire the inconceivable merits, and will securely abide in all the Buddha-Dharmas and miraculous powers. By giving their possessions, they will realize that which transcends the limits of saṁsāra, and will go far beyond the realm of sentient beings. They will attain inexhaustible, undiminishing, perfect accomplishments; will acquire inconceivable merits and magnificent attributes; and will be honored and served by other sentient beings.[8]

"World-Honored one, the good men and women who give their bodies, lives, and possessions in order to embrace the true Dharma will receive the Tathāgata's prophecy [of their attainment of Buddhahood].

"World-Honored One, when the true Dharma is on the verge of extinction, the monks, nuns, laymen, and laywomen will gather in groups, form factions, and dispute with one another. At that time, the good men and women who, without crookedness or deceit, cherish and embrace the true Dharma will associate with the good faction;[9] those who associate with the good faction will definitely receive the Buddha's prophecy [of their attainment of enlightenment].

"World-Honored One, I see that to embrace the true Dharma has this tremendous power. The Tathāgata regards this [doctrine] as the eye [of the Dharma], the basis of the Dharma, the guide of the Dharma, and the understanding of the Dharma."

Then the World-Honored One, having heard Queen Śrīmālā explain the great power of embracing the true Dharma, exclaimed, "So it is, so it is! Excellent, Śrīmālā! Just as you say, to embrace the true Dharma has tremendous, awesome power. A person will feel great pain or even become severely ill when one of his vulnerable spots[10] is touched even slightly by a strong man. In the same way, Śrīmālā, the demon Pāpīyān feels excruciating pain, worry, and distress, and howls and moans with woe when someone embraces even a small portion of the true Dharma. Śrīmālā, I have never seen any way to cause that demon worry and distress as effective as embracing the true Dharma, even a small portion of it.

"Śrīmālā, just as the king of cattle is more beautiful in form and color and larger in size than other cattle, so, Śrīmālā, one who practices the Mahāyāna, even if he embraces only a small portion of the true Dharma, is superior to the Śrāvakas and Pratyekabuddhas with all their wholesome dharmas.

"Śrīmālā, Mount Sumeru, the king of mountains, surpasses all other mountains in height, breadth, and beauty. In the same way, Śrīmālā, a novice in the Mahāyāna who, in order to benefit others, embraces the true Dharma without regard for his life or limb is superior to a person who has long been abiding in the Mahāyāna, but who is always concerned with his body and life, in spite of all his good roots.

"Therefore, Śrīmālā, you should reveal, demonstrate, and teach the embracing of the true Dharma to all sentient beings.

"Thus, Śrīmālā, to embrace the true Dharma yields great blessings, benefits, and karmic fruits. Śrīmālā, although for innumerable, incalculable kalpas I have praised the merits of embracing the true Dharma, I have not exhausted them. Therefore, to embrace the true Dharma brings about infinite merits."

The Buddha told Śrīmālā, "You should now explain further the embracing of the true Dharma, which I have taught, and which is cherished by all Buddhas alike."

Śrīmālā said, "Very well, World-Honored One. The embracing of the true Dharma is called the Mahāyāna. Why? Because the Mahāyāna gives birth to all Śrāvakas and Pratyekabuddhas, and all mundane and supramundane wholesome dharmas. Just as Lake Anavatapta is the source of the eight rivers,[11] so the Mahāyāna produces all Śrāvakas and Pratyekabuddhas, and all mundane and supramundane wholesome dharmas.

"World-Honored One, just as all seeds, grasses, trees, and forests depend upon the great earth in order to grow, so all Śrāvakas and Pratyekabuddhas, and all mundane and supramundane wholesome dharmas, depend upon the Mahāyāna in order to grow. Therefore, World-Honored One, to abide in and embrace the Mahāyāna is to abide in and embrace [the vehicles of] the Śrāvakas and the Pratyekabuddhas, and all mundane and supramundane wholesome dharmas.

"The Buddha, the World-Honored One, has discoursed on six subjects, namely, the abiding of the true Dharma, the extinction of the true Dharma, the Prātimokṣa, the Vinaya, true renunciation of the household life, and full monastic ordination. It is for the sake of the Mahāyāna that these six subjects are taught. Why? The abiding of the true Dharma is taught for the sake of the Mahāyāna because the abiding of the Mahāyāna is the abiding of the true Dharma. The extinction of the true Dharma is taught for the sake of the Mahāyāna because the extinction of the Mahāyāna is the extinction of the true Dharma. As for the Prātimokṣa and the Vinaya, these two Dharmas differ in name, but mean the same. Vinaya is instruction for the Mahāyāna. Why? It is for the sake of Buddhahood, [which is the aim of the Mahāyāna,] that one leaves the household life and receives full monastic ordination. Therefore, the Vinaya, true renunciation of the household life, and full monastic ordination are all Mahāyāna disciplines.

"World-Honored One, the Arhats do not [truly] leave the household life or receive full monastic ordination. Why? Because it is not for the sake of Tathāgatahood that they leave the household life or receive full monastic ordination.

"The Arhats take refuge in the Tathāgata out of fear. Why? The Arhats are constantly afraid of all phenomena, as if someone sought to harm them with a sword in hand. Therefore, they do not actually accomplish the deeds of renunciation, nor do they attain the ultimate bliss. World-Honored One, [he who does not need] a refuge does not seek a refuge. Just as sentient beings without refuge are afraid of this and that and seek refuge for the sake of security and peace, so, World-Honored One, the Arhats take refuge in the Tathāgata out of fear.

"Thus, the Arhats and the Pratyekabuddhas have not ended their rebirths, have not sufficiently cultivated pure conduct, have not accomplished what should be accomplished, and have not completely eradicated what should be eradicated; they are still far from nirvāṇa. Why? Only the Tathāgata, the Worthy One, the Perfectly Enlightened One, has attained nirvāṇa; has achieved all the infinite, inconceivable merits; has eradicated all that should be eradicated; is ultimately pure; is adored by all sentient beings; and has transcended the states of the two vehicles and of the Bodhisattvas. The Arhats and so forth have not done so. It is only as skillful means that the Buddha speaks of them as having attained nirvāṇa. Therefore, they are still far from nirvāṇa.

"World-Honored One, when the Tathāgata says that the Arhats and Pratyekabuddhas have an insight into liberation, thoroughly possess the four knowledges,[12] and have attained ultimate relief and rest, he is speaking of the expedient truth in order to accommodate others' inclinations. Why? There are two kinds of [birth and] death. What are the two? They are the recurring [birth and] death and the transformational [birth and] death. The recurring [birth and] death are the [birth and death of] sentient beings who continue [to exist in saṁsāra]. The transformational [birth and] death are [the birth and death of] the mind-created bodies[13] of Arhats, Pratyekabuddhas, and liberated Bodhisattvas,[14] which they retain until they attain bodhi. Now, of the two kinds of [birth and] death, it is with regard to the recurring [birth and] death that the Arhats and Pratyekabuddhas are said to know they have exhausted their rebirths. Because they have realized the incomplete fruit, they are said to know they have fully cultivated pure conduct. Because they have thoroughly eradicated the continuous defilements[15]—which cannot be accomplished by any ordinary people or by the seven grades of learners[16]—they are said to know they have accomplished what should be accomplished.

"World-Honored One, to say that the Arhats and Pratyekabuddhas know they are no more subject to future existence does not mean that they have eradicated all defilements or that they know all their rebirths. Why? The Arhats and Pratyekabuddhas still have some residual defilements not yet eradicated; therefore, they cannot know all their rebirths.

"There are two kinds of defilements: underlying defilements and active defilements.[17] The underlying defilements are four in number. What are they? Attachment to a particular viewpoint, attachment to desire, attachment to form, and craving for existence. World-Honored One, these four underlying defilements can produce all active defilements. The active defilements arise from moment to moment in concomitance with the mind. World-Honored One, the underlying defilement of ignorance never arises in concomitance with the mind from beginningless time.[18]

"World-Honored One, the four underlying defilements are powerful; they can breed all the active defilements. Yet, in comparison with them, the underlying defilement of ignorance is so much more powerful that the difference is inexpressible either by figures or analogies. Thus, World-Honored One, the underlying defilement of ignorance is more powerful than the craving for existence. Just as the form, power, authority, and retinue of the demon king overshadow those of the gods of the Paranirmita-Vaśavartin Heaven, so the underlying defilement of ignorance overshadows the other four underlying defilements. All other defilements, which are more numerous than the sands of the Ganges, depend on the underlying defilement of ignorance. It also causes the other four underlying defilements to endure. It can be eradicated only by the wisdom of the Tathāgata, not by the wisdom of the Śrāvakas or the Pratyekabuddhas. This being the case, World-Honored One, the underlying defilement of ignorance is the most powerful of all.

"World-Honored One, with grasping as the condition and defiled karmas as the cause, the three realms are produced. Likewise, with the underlying defilement of ignorance as the condition and undefiled karmas as the cause, the mind-created bodies of Arhats, Pratyekabuddhas, and powerful Bodhisattvas are produced. These three kinds of mind-created bodies and the undefiled karmas all depend on the underlying defilement of ignorance, being conditioned as well as conditioning. Therefore, World-Honored One, the three kinds of mind-created bodies and undefiled karmas all have the underlying defilement of ignorance as their condition, just as the craving for existence [also depends on the underlying defilement of ignorance as its condition].

"World-Honored One, the underlying craving for existence functions differently from the underlying defilement of ignorance. The underlying defilement of ignorance is different from the other four underlying defilements, and for this reason it can be eradicated only by the Buddha. Why? Because, though the Arhats and Pratyekabuddhas have eradicated the four underlying defilements, they have not fully mastered the power of utter exhaustion of defilements. They have not realized that state. Why? World-Honored One, to say that their defilements have been exhausted is an exaggeration. Being clouded by the underlying defilement of ignorance, the Arhats, Pratyekabuddhas, and Bodhisattvas in their last [saṁsāric] existences do not know and perceive all dharmas. Because they do not know and perceive all dharmas, they have left uneradicated what should be eradicated, and left unfinished what should be finished. Because they have not eradicated and finished all that should be eradicated and finished, they have attained incomplete liberation, not complete liberation; incomplete purity, not complete purity; incomplete merits, not complete merits. World-Honored One, because they have only attained incomplete liberation, not thorough liberation, and only incomplete merits, not all merits, their knowledge of suffering is incomplete, their eradication of the cause of suffering is incomplete, their realization of the cessation of suffering is incomplete, and their following of the path is incomplete."

Queen Śrīmālā continued, "World-Honored One, if one knows suffering only in part, eradicates the cause of suffering only in part, realizes the cessation of suffering only in part, and follows the path only in part, he is said to have realized partial nirvāṇa. One who has realized partial nirvāṇa is only advancing toward the realm of nirvāṇa.

"However, if one knows suffering completely, eradicates all causes of suffering completely, realizes the complete cessation of all suffering, and follows the path in its entirety, then he will realize the permanent, quiet, cool nirvāṇa within an impermanent, decaying, corrupt world. World-Honored One, such a person can be a protector and refuge in a world where there is no protector or refuge. Why? One who sees high and low in things cannot realize nirvāṇa. Only one who perceives equality in wisdom, equality in liberation, and equality in purity can realize nirvāṇa; therefore, nirvāṇa is called the uniform, one taste. What is the one taste? It is the taste of liberation.

"World-Honored One, one cannot attain nirvāṇa, the one taste, the uniform taste, if he does not completely eradicate and exhaust the underlying defilement of ignorance. Why? Because if he does not do so, he cannot completely wipe out all the faults that should be wiped out, which are more numerous than the sands of the Ganges. If he does not wipe out all faults, which are more numerous than the sands of the Ganges, he cannot realize all merits, which are equally numerous.

"This being the case, the underlying defilement of ignorance is the breeding ground of all defilements that should be eradicated. From it arise all the defilements causing hindrances to the mind: hindrances to tranquillity, contemplation, meditation, samāpatti, intensive effort, wisdom, fruition, realization, power, and fearlessness. [From it arise] all the defilements, more numerous than the sands of the Ganges, that can be eradicated only by the Tathāgata's enlightenment and the Buddha's diamondlike wisdom. All active defilements depend on the underlying defilement of ignorance, for ignorance is their cause and condition.

"World-Honored One, these active defilements arise from moment to moment in concomitance with the mind. However, World-Honored One, the underlying defilement of ignorance never arises in concomitance with the mind from beginningless time.

"World-Honored One, all the defilements, more numerous than the sands of the Ganges,[19] which should be eradicated by the Tathāgata's enlightenment and the Buddha's diamondlike wisdom, depend on and are established by the underlying defilement of ignorance. As an illustration, consider seeds, plants, and forests, all of which germinate and grow from the great earth. If the earth were destroyed, they would also be destroyed. Similarly, all the defilements, more numerous than the sands of the Ganges, which should be eradicated by the Tathāgata's enlightenment and the Buddha's diamondlike wisdom, depend on the underlying defilement of ignorance for their existence and growth. Once the underlying defilement of ignorance is cut off, all these defilements[20] will simultaneously be cut off.

"When all things—the [underlying] defilements and active defilements, more numerous than the sands of the Ganges—which should be cut off have been cut off, one will be able to realize the inconceivable Buddha-Dharmas, which are [also] more numerous than the sands of the Ganges. He will penetrate all dharmas without obstruction,[21] become all-knowing and all-seeing, be free from all faults, achieve all merits, and become a great Dharma king who has gained mastery of all dharmas and who has realized the state of free command of all dharmas. He will be able to make the true lion's roar: 'I have ended my rebirths; I have fully cultivated pure conduct; I have done what should be done; and I am no more subject to [saṁsāric] existence.' This is why the World-Honored One constantly makes his firm proclamation in a lion's roar based on the ultimate truth.

"World-Honored One, the knowledge of being no more subject to [saṁsāric] existence is of two kinds. What are the two? The first [knowledge] belongs to the Tathāgatas. The Tathāgatas have vanquished, with their harnessing and subduing power, the four demons; have transcended all worlds and are esteemed by all sentient beings; have realized the inconceivable, pure Dharma-body; have attained mastery in all fields of knowledge; are unexcelled and supremely magnificent; have nothing more to do and see no further stage to realize; are endowed with the ten powers; have ascended to the supreme stage of fearlessness; and observe all dharmas without hindrance. Therefore, they can make the true lion's roar, proclaiming that they are no more subject to [saṁsāric] existence.

"The second [knowledge of being no more subject to saṁsāric existence] belongs to the Arhats and Pratyekabuddhas. They have been released from the fear of countless births and deaths and are enjoying the bliss of liberation; therefore, they think, 'I have left the frightful saṁsāra behind and will suffer no more pain.'

"World-Honored One, by making this observation, the Arhats and Pratyekabuddhas also claim that they are no more subject to [saṁsāric] existence. However, they have not realized the highest state of relief and rest—nirvāṇa. On the other hand, if they are not deluded by the Dharma they have realized, they will be able to understand [that there are] states they have not realized, [saying to themselves,] 'Now I have only realized an incomplete state'; and they will definitely attain supreme enlightenment. Why? Because [the vehicles of] the Śrāvakas and the Pratyekabuddhas are both included in the Mahāyāna, and the Mahāyāna is the Buddha-vehicle. This being the case, the three vehicles are the One Vehicle.

"One who realizes the One Vehicle attains supreme enlightenment. Supreme enlightenment is nirvāṇa. Nirvāṇa is the pure Dharma-body of the Tathāgata. To realize the Dharma-body is the One Vehicle. The Tathāgata is not different from the Dharma-body; the Tathāgata *is* the Dharma-body. The realization of the ultimate Dharma-body is the ultimate One Vehicle.

"The ultimate One Vehicle is that which is apart from [ordinary] continuity.

Why? World-Honored One, if one says that the abiding time of the Tathāgata is immeasurable, equal to the boundless future, and that the Tathāgata can benefit the world with limitless compassion and limitless vows, he is said to speak well. If one says that the Tathāgata is permanent, is an unending Dharma, and is the ultimate refuge of all sentient beings, he is also said to speak well. Therefore, the Tathāgata, the Worthy One, the Supremely Enlightened One, is an inexhaustible refuge, an ever-abiding refuge, and an ultimate refuge, for an infinite length of time stretching into the future, in a world without [any other] protection or refuge.

"The Dharma is the path of the One Vehicle. The Saṁgha is the assembly of the three vehicles. However, the Dharma and the Saṁgha are partial refuges, not ultimate refuges. Why? Although the path of the One Vehicle is taught, it is no longer mentioned after one has attained the ultimate Dharma-body. Because they have fear, those in the assembly of the three vehicles take refuge in the Tathāgata and learn and practice the Dharma; they are still in the active process of working toward supreme enlightenment themselves. Therefore, the two refuges are only limited refuges, not ultimate ones.

"When sentient beings are subdued by the Tathāgata and take refuge in the Tathāgata, their thirst is relieved by the nectar of Dharma, and they generate faith and joy; [consequently] they take refuge also in the Dharma and the Saṁgha. These two refuges are [conceived as] refuges because of sentient beings' faith generated through the quenching of their thirst by the nectar of Dharma. The Tathāgata is not such a refuge; the Tathāgata is a true refuge. Nevertheless, in terms of the ultimate truth, to take refuge in the Dharma and the Saṁgha *is* to take ultimate refuge in the Tathāgata. Why? The Tathāgata is not different from these two refuges; the Tathāgata *is* the three refuges.

"Why is the path of the One Vehicle taught? The Tathāgata, the Supreme One, is endowed with the four fearlessnesses and is able to make the true lion's roar. If the Tathāgatas, in accordance with sentient beings' needs, teach the two vehicles as skillful means, [then the two vehicles they teach] are no other than the Great Vehicle, because in the highest truth there are no two vehicles. The two vehicles both merge into the One Vehicle, and the One Vehicle is the vehicle of supreme truth.

"World-Honored One, when Śrāvakas and Pratyekabuddhas reach the initial realization of the four noble truths, it is not with the one [supreme] knowledge that they eradicate the underlying defilements, realize the merits of complete knowledge of the four noble truths, or understand the essence of the four truths. World-Honored One, they lack the supramundane knowledge, so the four knowledges [of the four truths] come to them gradually, each conditioning the next. World-Honored One, the supramundane knowledge, like a diamond [which cuts things at one stroke], is not gradual in nature.

"World-Honored One, the Śrāvakas and Pratyekabuddhas eradicate the underlying defilements by knowing the noble truths in many ways, but they do not possess the supreme, supramundane knowledge. Only the Tathāgata, the Worthy

One, the All-Knowing One, can break up the shells of all defilements by his inconceivable knowledge of emptiness; it is beyond the domain of the Śrāvakas and Pratyekabuddhas.

"World-Honored One, the ultimate knowledge which shatters the shells of defilements is called the supreme, supramundane knowledge. The initial knowledge of the noble truths is not the ultimate knowledge; it is knowledge only *leading* to supreme enlightenment.

"World-Honored One, the true meaning of the word 'noble' does not apply to [those who follow] the two vehicles. Why? The Śrāvakas and Pratyekabuddhas are said to be noble merely because they can attain a small part of the merits [of a Tathāgata]. World-Honored One, the [real] noble truths are not truths belonging to Śrāvakas or Pratyekabuddhas, and are not merits belonging to them. The [real] noble truths are realized only by a Tathāgata, a Worthy One, a Perfectly Enlightened One, and afterwards revealed, demonstrated, and explained to sentient beings in the world who are confined in shells of ignorance. Hence the name 'noble truths.'

"World-Honored One, the [real] noble truths are very profound, subtle, difficult to perceive, hard to understand, and not to be discriminated; they are beyond the realm of thought and speculation, and they transcend the credence of all the world. They are known only to Tathāgatas, Worthy Ones, Perfectly Enlightened Ones. Why? These truths explain the very profound Tathāgata-embryo.[22] The Tathāgata-embryo belongs in the realm of the Buddha and is beyond the domain of the Śrāvakas and Pratyekabuddhas. Since the noble truths are explained on the basis of the Tathāgata-embryo, and since the Tathāgata-embryo is profound and subtle, the noble truths are also profound and subtle, difficult to perceive, hard to understand, and not to be discriminated; they are beyond the realm of thought and speculation, and transcend the credence of all the world. They can be known only by a Tathāgata, a Worthy One, a Perfectly Enlightened One.

"If one has no doubt about the Tathāgata-embryo, which [in ordinary beings] is wrapped in an incalculable number of defilements, he will also have no doubt about the Dharma-body of the Tathāgata, which is beyond all defilement.

"World-Honored One, if one can have true faith in the Tathāgata-embryo and the Buddha's Dharma-body—the inconceivable, esoteric realm of the Buddha—he will then be able to believe in and understand well the two meanings of the noble truths.

"What are the two meanings of the noble truths? They are the active and the nonactive. The active noble truths are the four noble truths in an incomplete sense. Why? When one has to rely on others for protection, he cannot completely know suffering, eradicate all causes of suffering, realize the complete cessation of suffering, or follow in its entirety the path leading to the cessation of suffering. Therefore, he cannot know conditioned things, unconditioned things, or nirvāṇa.

"World-Honored One, the nonactive noble truths refer to the four noble truths in the complete sense. Why? Because, when one can rely on himself for protection, he can completely know suffering, eradicate all causes of suffering, realize the complete cessation of suffering, and follow in its entirety the path leading to the cessation of suffering.

"Thus, there are in all eight noble truths mentioned; however, the Buddha teaches them only [in terms of] four noble truths. The meaning of the nonactive four noble truths is perfectly realized only by Tathāgatas, Worthy Ones, Perfectly Enlightened Ones, and is beyond the capacity of Arhats and Pratyekabuddhas. Why? Because nirvāṇa is not to be realized by any dharma, whether superior or inferior, whether low, middle, or high.

"What does it mean that the Tathāgatas perfectly realize the nonactive truths? The Tathāgatas, the Worthy Ones, the Supremely Enlightened Ones, completely know suffering; have eradicated all causes of suffering, which are the defilements; have realized the complete cessation of all suffering, [even that] derived from the aggregates of a mind-created body; and have followed in its entirety the path leading to the cessation of suffering.

"World-Honored One, the term 'cessation of suffering' does not imply the destruction of anything. Why? Because the cessation of suffering has no beginning, no action, no origination, and no end; it is ever-abiding, immovable, intrinsically pure, and free from the shell of defilements.[23]

"World-Honored One, the Tathāgata has achieved inconceivable Dharmas more numerous than the sands of the Ganges, Dharmas which embody the wisdom of liberation and which are referred to as the Dharma-body. World-Honored One, when this Dharma-body is not apart from defilements, it is called the Tathāgata-embryo.[24]

"World-Honored One, the Tathāgata-embryo is the Tathāgata's knowledge[25] of emptiness. The Tathāgata-embryo has never been seen or realized by any Śrāvaka or Pratyekabuddha. It is perceived and witnessed only by the Buddhas.

"World-Honored One, the knowledge of emptiness of the Tathāgata-embryo is of two kinds. What are the two? The first is the knowledge that *the Tathāgata-embryo is empty*: that it is apart from all defilements and apart from knowledge which does not lead to liberation. The second is the knowledge that *the Tathāgata-embryo is not empty*: that it contains inconceivable Dharmas more numerous than the sands of the Ganges, which embody the Buddhas' wisdom of liberation.

"World-Honored One, the advanced Śrāvakas can, through faith, gain access to these two knowledges of emptiness. World-Honored One, the knowledge of emptiness possessed by the Śrāvakas and Pratyekabuddhas is connected with and revolves around the four wrong views. Therefore, no Śrāvaka or Pratyekabuddha has ever perceived or realized the complete cessation of suffering. Only the Buddha has realized it directly; he has eradicated all defilements and followed in its entirety the path leading to the cessation of suffering.

"World-Honored One, of the four noble truths, three truths are impermanent, and one truth is permanent. Why? The three noble truths [of suffering, the cause of suffering, and the path leading to the cessation of suffering] belong to the realm of conditioned dharmas. What is conditioned is impermanent, and what is impermanent is destructible. What is destructible is not true, not permanent, and not a refuge. Therefore, in the ultimate sense, the three noble truths are not true, not permanent, and not a refuge.

"World-Honored One, the noble truth of the cessation of suffering is beyond the realm of conditioned dharmas. What is beyond the realm of conditioned dharmas is ever-abiding by nature. What is ever-abiding by nature is indestructible. What is indestructible is true, permanent, and a refuge. For this reason, World-Honored One, the noble truth of the cessation of suffering is in the ultimate sense true, permanent, and a refuge.

"World-Honored One, this noble truth of the cessation of suffering is inconceivable. It is beyond the realm of all sentient beings' mind and consciousness; it is also beyond the domain of all Arhats' and Pratyekabuddhas' knowledge. Just as the myriad colors cannot be seen by a man born blind, or as the sun cannot be seen by a seven-day-old infant, so the noble truth of the cessation of suffering cannot be an object of ordinary people's mind and consciousness, nor is it in the domain of any Śrāvakas' or Pratyekabuddhas' knowledge.

"The consciousness of ordinary people refers to the two extreme views. The knowledge of Śrāvakas and Pratyekabuddhas means their *pure* knowledge.

"Extreme views mean [the views which arise when] one clings to the five aggregates as the self and makes various discriminations. There are two extreme views. What are the two? The eternalistic view and the nihilistic view.

"World-Honored One, if one sees saṁsāra as impermanent and nirvāṇa as permanent, his view is neither nihilistic nor eternalistic, but is the right view.[26] Why? When deluded people see that bodies, sense-organs, and that which thinks and feels all perish in this life, but do not understand the continuation of existence, then, being blind and without the eye of wisdom, they conceive a nihilistic view. When they see the continuity of the mind but fail to see the aspect of its momentary perishing, then being ignorant of the [true] state of consciousness, they conceive an eternalistic view.[27]

"World-Honored One, the before-mentioned truth is beyond all discrimination and beyond inferior understanding. Because fools have delusive thoughts and cling to misconceived ideas, they believe either nihilism or eternalism.

"World-Honored One, concerning the five aggregates, deluded sentient beings consider the impermanent to be permanent, suffering to be joy, nonself to be self, and the impure to be pure. The Śrāvakas and Pratyekabuddhas, with all their pure wisdom, never glimpse the Buddha's Dharma-body or the state of the Tathāgata.

"If a sentient being, out of faith in the Tathāgata, regards the Tathāgata as permanent, joyous, pure, and possessing a self, he does not see [the Tathāgata] wrongly; he sees him correctly. Why? Because the Dharma-body of the Tathāgata is the perfection[28] of permanence, the perfection of joy, the perfection of self, and the perfection of purity. Those sentient beings who assume such a view are said to have the right view. Those who assume the right view are called the true sons of the Buddha, born from the Buddha's mouth, born from the true Dharma, born from the Dharma miraculously,[29] and heirs to the Buddha-Dharma.

"World-Honored One, the so-called pure knowledge is the perfection of knowledge of all Arhats and Pratyekabuddhas. Even this pure knowledge, pure as it is said to be, cannot embrace the realm of the noble truth of the cessation of suffering, let alone the knowledge of [those who practice] the four reliances. Why, then, does the World-Honored One teach the four reliances? In order that the novices of the three vehicles may not be ignorant of the Dharma and may eventually realize its meaning.

"World-Honored One, these four reliances are mundane dharmas. World-Honored One, there is one reliance which is the highest of all reliances, which is the supramundane, supreme, and ultimate reliance—namely, [nirvāṇa,] the noble truth of the cessation of suffering.[30]

"World-Honored One, the cycle of birth and death [saṁsāra] is based on the Tathāgata-embryo. Because of the Tathāgata-embryo, the beginning [of saṁsāra] cannot be known. World-Honored One, if one says that because there is the Tathāgata-embryo there is saṁsāra, he speaks well.

"World-Honored One, the cycle of birth and death means the cessation of the sense faculties and the immediate arising of new sense faculties. World-Honored One, the two dharmas, birth and death, are the Tathāgata-embryo itself; they are called birth and death from the conventional viewpoint. World-Honored One, death means the cessation of sense faculties, and birth means the arising of sense faculties. The Tathāgata-embryo, however, neither arises nor ceases to be, neither emerges nor vanishes; it is beyond the realm of conditioned [dharmas].

"World-Honored One, the Tathāgata-embryo is permanent and indestructible. Therefore, World-Honored One, the Tathāgata-embryo is the base, the support, and the foundation of the wisdom of liberation. It is also the base, the support, and the foundation of all conditioned dharmas.

"World-Honored One, if there were no Tathāgata-embryo, there would be no abhorrence of suffering and no longing for nirvāṇa.[31] Why? The seven dharmas—the six consciousnesses and their objects—are momentary and nonabiding, and therefore cannot retain the experience of suffering. Hence, they are unable to abhor suffering or aspire to nirvāṇa. The Tathāgata-embryo has no beginning, neither arises nor ceases, and can retain the experience of suffering. It is the cause of [sentient beings'] renunciation of suffering and aspiration for nirvāṇa.

"World-Honored One, the Tathāgata-embryo is not a self, a personal identity, a being, or a life. The Tathāgata-embryo is not in the domain of sentient beings who believe in a real self, whose thinking is confused, or who cling to the view of emptiness.

"World-Honored One, the Tathāgata-embryo is the store of the dharmadhātu, the store of the Dharma-body, the store of the supramundane, and the store of intrinsic purity.

"This intrinsically pure Tathāgata-embryo, as I understand it, is always the inconceivable state of the Tathāgata even if contaminated by defilements, the adventitious dust. Why? World-Honored One, the mind, whether virtuous or nonvirtuous, changes from moment to moment, and it cannot be contaminated by defilements, the adventitious dust. Why? Defilements are not in contact with the mind; the mind is not in contact with defilements. How can anything that is not in contact with the mind contaminate the mind? Yet, World-Honored One, because there are defilements there is a defiled mind. It is extremely difficult to know and understand contamination by defilements. Only the Buddha, the World-Honored One, who is the eye, the wisdom, the root of the Dharma, the guide, and the foundation of the true Dharma, can know and see it as it is."

Then the Buddha praised Queen Śrīmālā, saying, "Splendid, splendid! Just as you say, it is difficult to know and understand how the intrinsically pure mind can be contaminated by defilements.

"Śrīmālā, there are two things difficult to understand. What are the two? First, the intrinsically pure mind; second, the contamination of this mind by defilements. Only you and those Bodhisattvas who have already accomplished the great Dharma can accept these two things upon hearing of them. The Śrāvakas can understand them only through faith.

"Śrīmālā, if my disciples strengthen their faith and comply with the Dharma-wisdom, then they will reach the utmost [understanding] of this Dharma. Compliance with the Dharma-wisdom means: contemplation of the sense-organs, the consciousnesses, and their objects; contemplation of karmas and their results; contemplation of the dormant defilements of the Arhats; contemplation of the joy of a liberated mind and the bliss of meditation; and contemplation of the noble, miraculous powers of the Śrāvakas and Pratyekabuddhas. By accomplishing these five skillful contemplations, my present and future Śrāvaka followers will, because of their strengthened faith and their compliance with the Dharma-wisdom, be able to understand the intrinsically pure mind and how it becomes contaminated by defilements. They will reach the utmost [understanding of this Dharma]. Śrīmālā, the utmost [understanding] is the cause of the Mahāyāna.

"Now you should know that he who has faith in the Tathāgata does not slander the profound Dharma."

Then Queen Śrīmālā said to the Buddha, "World-Honored One, there are still other doctrines that will be of great benefit. By the awesome, divine power of the Buddha I will explain them."

The Buddha said, "Excellent! Now speak all you wish."

Queen Śrīmālā said, "There are three kinds of good men and women who can, with regard to the profound Dharma, avoid harming themselves, generate numerous merits, and enter the path of the Mahāyāna. What are the three? They are: the good men and women who have by themselves attained the wisdom of the profound Dharma; those who succeed in complying with the Dharma-wisdom; and those who cannot understand the profound Dharma but fully rely on the Tathāgata, saying, 'This is only known to the Buddha; it is not in my domain.'

"Aside from these three kinds of good men and women, other sentient beings may take from the profound Dharma only what they like, cling to mistaken interpretations, defy the true Dharma, or learn heterodox doctrines. Wherever these rotten seeds [i.e., wrong beliefs,] are, we should go there and eliminate them. All gods and humans should combine their efforts to destroy these rotten seeds."

After Queen Śrīmālā had thus spoken, she and her retinue bowed down at the feet of the Buddha.

The Buddha then praised Queen Śrīmālā, saying, "It is wonderful, Śrīmālā, that you can skillfully protect the profound Dharma and properly vanquish its enemies. Because you have already associated intimately with hundreds of thousands of millions of Buddhas, Tathāgatas, you are able to explain this doctrine."

Then the World-Honored One emanated a magnificent light illuminating the entire assembly, and elevated himself into midair to the height of seven palm trees. Using his miraculous powers, he walked in the air and returned to the city of Śrāvastī. Meanwhile, without taking their eyes off the World-Honored One for an instant, Queen Śrīmālā and her retinue gazed at him with adoration until he passed out of sight. Then they all danced with joy and exchanged praises of the virtues of the Tathāgata. Recollecting the Buddha single-mindedly, they returned to Ayodhyā.

[When she had returned to the city, Śrīmālā] persuaded King Mitrakīrti[32] to establish the Mahāyāna [as the state religion]. She taught the Mahāyāna to all females of the city over seven years of age, and King Mitrakīrti taught the Mahāyāna to males over seven; as a result, all the citizens of the country, without exception, learned the Mahāyāna.

When the World-Honored One entered the Jeta Grove, he called the Venerable Ānanda. He also summoned the king of devas by thinking about him. In response to the Buddha's summoning thought, Śakra, the king of devas, and his retinue instantly appeared before the Buddha.

Then the World-Honored One told Śakra the deva king, "Kauśika, you should accept and uphold this sūtra, explain it, and reveal it for the sake of the peace and happiness of those who dwell in the Heaven of the Thirty-Three."

He then told Ānanda, "You, too, should accept and uphold this sūtra and explain it in detail to the four kinds of devotees."

Śakra, king of devas, said to the Buddha, "World-Honored One, what should we call this sūtra? How should we uphold it?"

The Buddha told the king of devas, "This sūtra has limitless merits. It is beyond the power of all Śrāvakas and Pratyekabuddhas, let alone other sentient beings. Kauśika, you should understand that this sūtra is very profound and subtle and is a great amassment of merits. I shall now tell you briefly its names. Listen carefully! Listen carefully and think well about it."

Thereupon, Śakra, king of devas, and the Venerable Ānanda said to the Buddha, "Yes, World-Honored One. We shall accept your teaching."

The Buddha said, "This sūtra is called 'Acclamation of the Tathāgata's True Virtues,' and should be upheld accordingly.

"It is also called 'A Discourse on the Ten Inconceivable Vows,' and should be upheld accordingly.

"It is also called 'A Discourse on the One Great Vow That Comprises All Vows,' and should be upheld accordingly.

"It is also called 'A Discourse on the Inconceivable Embracing of the True Dharma,' and should be upheld accordingly.

"It is also called 'A Discourse on the Entry into the One Vehicle,' and should be upheld accordingly.

"It is also called 'A Discourse on the Boundless Truth,' and should be upheld accordingly.

"It is also called 'A Discourse on the Tathāgata-embryo,' and should be upheld accordingly.

"It is also called 'A Discourse on the Buddha's Dharma-body,' and should be upheld accordingly.

"It is also called 'A Discourse on the Hidden Reality in the Doctrine of Emptiness,' and should be upheld accordingly.

"It is also called 'A Discourse on the One Truth,' and should be upheld accordingly.

"It is also called 'A Discourse on the One, Ever-abiding, Immovable, and Quiet Refuge,' and should be upheld accordingly.

"It is also called 'A Discourse on Inversion and Reality,' and should be upheld accordingly.

"It is also called 'A Discourse on the Intrinsically Pure Mind Wrapped in Defilements,' and should be upheld accordingly.

"It is also called 'A Discourse on the True Sons of the Tathāgata,' and should be upheld accordingly.

"It is also called 'A Discourse on the True Lion's Roar of Queen Śrīmālā,' and should be upheld accordingly.

"Moreover, Kauśika, this sūtra's teaching resolves all doubts; it is the definitive, ultimate teaching, the way to the One Vehicle. Kauśika, I now entrust you with this 'Sūtra of the Lion's Roar of Queen Śrīmālā.' Reveal and explain it to the beings in the ten directions as long as the Dharma endures."

Śakra, the king of devas, said, "Yes, World-Honored One. We will follow your instructions."

Then, hearing what the Buddha had said, Śakra, the king of devas, the Venerable Ānanda, and all the gods, humans, asuras, gandharvas, and others in the assembly were jubilant. They accepted the sūtra with faith and began to practice it with veneration.

NOTES

1. The other extant Chinese version of this sūtra, translated from the Sanskrit by Guṇabhadra (Taishō 353, p. 217), reads: "We should promptly send her a letter to arouse her thought of bodhi." Since it is the letter which is eloquent, not the messenger, this reading may be preferable.

2. This line can also be translated as: "If what is said [in the letter] is true. . . ."

3. Literally, "All dharmas eternally abide." According to *The Record of a Discourse on the Śrīmālā Sūtra* (勝鬘夫人經講記), by Ven. Yin Shun (Taipei, 1970), p. 36, this refers to all the physical and mental attributes of the Tathāgata, which are an accumulation of merits.

4. Killing, stealing, sexual misconduct, and lying. Here the vices of the body are interpreted in a broad sense, and include the vice of speech, i.e. lying. In a more detailed classification, the vice of speech is separated from the vices of the body and expanded into four items: lying, slander, harsh speech, and frivolous chatter. These four, combined with the unwholesome actions of mind and body, form the ten evil deeds. See Numerical Glossary.

5. See Glossary, "true Dharma."

6. Ancient Buddhist cosmology holds that in a billion-world universe there are ten billion Mount Sumerus, each surrounded by four continents. Hence "the forty billion continents."

7. Here the text is obscure. This is a free, extremely interpretive translation.

8. An alternative translation based on Guṇabhadra's version (Taishō 353, p. 219). reads:

> By [continually] giving their bodies until the end of saṁsāra, these people will be free from old age and sickness, and will attain the Tathāgata's Dharma-body, which is indestructible, permanent, changeless, ultimately tranquil, and inconceivable. By [continually] giving their lives until the end of saṁsāra, they will be forever released from death; will attain infinite, eternal, inconceivable merits; and will securely abide in all the Buddha-Dharmas and miraculous powers. By [continually] giving their possessions until the end of saṁsāra, they will attain endless, undiminishing, perfect karmic results; will acquire inconceivable merits and splendors surpassing those of others; and will be honored and served by other sentient beings.

9. Guṇabhadra's version reads "the faction of the Dharma," instead of "the good faction."

10. Skt. *marman*. A marman is a spot on the body, a slight touch on which may cause great pain or result in death. According to different sources, there are either 64 or 120 such spots; M. Monier-Williams, *Sanskrit-English Dictionary*, (Oxford, 1899) p. 791, gives their number as 107.

11. Lake Anavatapta is a lake in Buddhist and Hindu cosmology, north of the Snow Mountain and south of the Fragrant Mountain. The eight rivers are: Ganges, Indus, Oxus, Śītā, Jumna, Saravastī(?), Hiranyavatī or Ajiravatī, and Mahī(?). Sometimes only the first four are mentioned.

12. I.e., knowledge of the four noble truths.

13. The mind-created body refers to those who have been released from ordinary birth and death, and can appear in any form at will without being subject to the limitations of time and space.

14. Bodhisattvas of the seventh or eighth stage, who have attained the Realization of the Nonarising of Dharmas. There are other interpretations. See Ven. Yin Shun, *op. cit.*, pp. 152–3.

15. The four underlying defilements mentioned below.

16. The seven grades of learners are: those who are approaching the fruit of a stream-enterer, and those who have obtained it; those who are approaching the fruit of a once-returner, and those who have obtained it; those who are approaching the fruit of a non-returner, and those who have obtained it; and those who are approaching the fruit of one beyond learning, i.e., an Arhat.

17. The active defilements are the unwholesome mental functions such as lust, anger, etc., which arise when the mind stirs.

18. We are conscious of the active defilements arising from moment to moment, whereas underlying ignorance, which serves as a "store" or basis for other defilements, is very subtle and deeply inherent, so the ordinary mind is not aware of its existence. This is presumably the meaning here. The text reads "the underlying defilement of ignorance never arises in concomitance with the mind from beginningless time." This implies that since beginningless time, when the mind arises, ignorance is latent, not active; therefore, a sentient being is not conscious of it.

19. In the text, "more numerous than the sands of the Ganges" seems to modify 'enlightenment', not 'defilements'.

20. The text reads in full: "all the defilements, more numerous than the sands of the Ganges, which should be cut off by the Tathāgata's enlightenment and the Buddha's diamondlike wisdom. . . ."

21. Literally, "He will realize the unobstructed miraculous powers with regard to all dharmas."

22. See Glossary, "Tathāgata-embryo."

23. Alternative translation: "Because the cessation of suffering means the emergence of the pure original nature from the shell of defilements. This nature has no beginning, no action, no origination, no end, and is ever-abiding and immovable."

24. Tathāgata-embryo is sometimes translated as the 'womb of the Tathāgata', or 'treasure of the Tathāgata'; that is to say, there is a complete, perfect Buddha-nature within every sentient being. It cannot manifest itself due to the covering of defilements. When one attains supreme enlightenment, the Tathāgata-embryo is no more. It manifests in full Tathāgatahood.

25. 'Knowledge', here, and in other passages, can also be rendered 'wisdom'. In many cases, 'wisdom' is a better translation. However, in order to make the translation uniform, we use 'knowledge' here.

26. Guṇabhadra's version (Taishō 353, p. 222) seems to be better and deeper. It reads: "If one sees all phenomena as impermanent, his is a nihilistic view, not the right view. If one sees nirvāṇa as permanent, his is an eternalistic view, not the right view."

27. This sentence is a free translation; the text is obscure.

28. 'Perfection' here translates pāramitā.

29. We usually translate 化生 as 'ethereally born' when it refers to an actual birth in a heaven, a Pure Land, etc. However, here it is used allegorically, so we use 'born miraculously'.

30. For these two paragraphs we follow entirely the reading of Guṇabhadra's version (Taishō 353, p. 222); the original text is extremely obscure.

31. Here is an important statement indicating that within every human being there is Buddha-nature, which gives rise to religious aspiration, i.e., the quest for perfection and ultimate meaning in life. This Buddha-nature is called here the 'Tathāgata-embryo'.

32. Presumably Queen Śrīmālā's husband.

20 普明菩薩會

The Sūtra of Assembled Treasures

Thus have I heard. Once the Buddha was dwelling on Mount Gṛdhrakūṭa near Rājagṛha, accompanied by eight thousand great monks. Also in the assembly were sixteen thousand Bodhisattva-Mahāsattvas from various Buddha-lands, all of whom had attained the stage of nonregression and were destined for supreme enlightenment in their next lives.

That day, the World-Honored One told Mahākāśyapa, "Four things cause a Bodhisattva's wisdom to decrease or be lost. What are the four?

(1) To disrespect the Dharma or Dharma-masters;
(2) to withhold the profound Dharma he has acquired instead of disclosing it fully;
(3) to hinder those who rejoice in the Dharma by giving them reasons to despair; and
(4) to be arrogant and conceited, and to disdain others.[1]

Furthermore, Kāśyapa, four things cause a Bodhisattva to gain great wisdom. What are the four?

(1) Always to respect the Dharma and revere Dharma-masters;
(2) to preach widely whatever Dharma he has learned, with a pure mind not in pursuit of fame or profit;
(3) to know that wisdom arises from much learning, and to pursue learning with such constant, urgent effort as if to save his head from fire; and
(4) to recite the sūtras he has learned, and practice cheerfully as instructed, without becoming entangled in words.

Sūtra 43, Taishō 310, pp. 631–638; translated into Chinese by an anonymous translator.

"Furthermore, Kāśyapa, four things cause a Bodhisattva to lose his bodhicitta. What are the four?

(1) To deceive his teacher and pay no respect to the sūtras he has been taught;
(2) to cause unwarranted doubt or regret in others;
(3) to revile and slander those who seek the Mahāyāna, thus defaming them far and wide; and
(4) to be fawning and crooked in dealing with people.

"Furthermore, Kāśyapa, four things enable a Bodhisattva to retain his bodhicitta from one lifetime to another, so that it will always be naturally present in him until his attainment of Buddhahood. What are the four?

(1) Not to lie even when his life is at stake, much less in jest;
(2) always to deal with people sincerely and honestly, without flattery or crookedness;
(3) to think of Bodhisattvas as World-Honored Ones, and to extol their names in all the four directions; and
(4) not to enjoy the Hīnayāna doctrines, but [instead] to cause all who believe in the Dharma to pursue supreme bodhi.

"Furthermore, Kāśyapa, four things cause the wholesome practices cultivated by a Bodhisattva to stop increasing or to cease. What are the four?

(1) To read, recite, and study the secular scriptures out of arrogance;
(2) to approach a donor with a mind lusting for material gains;
(3) to resent and slander other Bodhisattvas; and
(4) to discredit and contradict sūtras which he has not heard before.

"Furthermore, Kāśyapa, four things cause the wholesome practices cultivated by a Bodhisattva to grow instead of ceasing. What are the four?

(1) The Bodhisattva rejects heterodox doctrines and seeks the orthodox scriptures—such as those on the six pāramitās, which constitute the Bodhisattva's canon—and when doing so, casts away arrogance and remains humble toward all sentient beings.
(2) He receives offerings in accordance with the Dharma, is content with what he obtains, does not earn a livelihood in improper ways, and abides in the four noble practices.
(3) He does not expose others' wrongdoings, whether they are true or not, and does not look for people's shortcomings.
(4) When he finds some [Buddhist] doctrines incomprehensible, he thinks, 'The Buddha-Dharma has infinite varieties, for it is preached according to the inclinations of sentient beings. It is known to the Buddha only, not to me. I should defer to the Buddha as the certifying authority and not harbor disobedience or opposition.'

"Furthermore, Kāśyapa, a Bodhisattva must shun four wrong mentalities.[2] What are the four?

(1) To harbor doubts about the Buddha-Dharma or to regret [having accepted it];
(2) to be resentful and arrogant toward sentient beings;
(3) to be jealous of others for their gains and good living; and
(4) to [wish to] revile other Bodhisattvas and defame them far and wide.

"Furthermore, Kāśyapa, four signs indicate a Bodhisattva's right mentality.[3] What are the four?

(1) The Bodhisattva does not hide his transgressions, but exposes them to others so that his mind is free from covers and bonds.
(2) He never speaks false words even if he loses his own body, life, country, or kingdom.
(3) When he encounters misfortunes, being scolded, beaten, slandered, bound, or otherwise injured, he blames himself only; resigning himself to karmic retribution, he does not hate others.[4]
(4) He maintains his faith firmly; when he hears the Buddha-Dharma which is profound and difficult to believe, his pure mind can accept and uphold it entirely.

"Furthermore, Kāśyapa, four signs indicate a Bodhisattva's corruption. What are the four?

(1) After reading a scripture, a corrupted Bodhisattva indulges in play-words, instead of practicing in accordance with the Dharma.
(2) He does not obey, respect, or gladden his masters.
(3) He wastes devotees' offerings by accepting them even when he has broken his former vows.
(4) He is contemptuous and disrespectful toward virtuous Bodhisattvas.

"Furthermore, Kāśyapa, four signs indicate a Bodhisattva's willing compliance. What are the four?

(1) The Bodhisattva faithfully accepts a sūtra the first time he hears it, and practices it as taught, relying on the doctrine rather than on the words.
(2) He follows his master's instructions, knows his intention, and speaks with him openly; everything he does is in harmony with virtue and his master's intention.
(3) He never regresses in discipline or dhyāna, and accepts offerings with a mind well subdued.
(4) When he sees a virtuous Bodhisattva, he respects him, admires him, and emulates his virtuous deeds.

"Furthermore, Kāśyapa, there are four mistakes that a Bodhisattva may make. What are the four?

(1) To comply with an untrustworthy person;
(2) to preach a profound doctrine to a sentient being who is incapable of accepting it;
(3) to praise the Hīnayāna among those who rejoice in the Mahāyāna; and
(4) to give only to virtuous precept-keepers, not to wicked people.

"Furthermore, Kāśyapa, there are four right paths for a Bodhisattva. What are the four?

(1) To treat all sentient beings impartially;
(2) to teach all sentient beings impartially [on the basis of the] Buddha's wisdom;
(3) to preach the Dharma to all sentient beings without discrimination; and
(4) to cause all sentient beings to abide in right action equally.

"Furthermore, Kāśyapa, there are four kinds of people who are not good friends or companions for a Bodhisattva. What are the four?

(1) Śrāvakas, who desire only to benefit themselves;
(2) Pratyekabuddhas, who enjoy having few things to attend to;
(3) the worldly scholars, who study heterodox scriptures and indulge in flowery literature; and
(4) associates who can only increase his worldly acquisitions, not his acquisition of the Dharma.

"Furthermore, Kāśyapa, there are four kinds of people who are good friends and companions for a Bodhisattva. What are the four?

(1) Those who call upon a Bodhisattva for help are his good friends, because they cause him to walk upon the Buddha's path.
(2) Those who can expound the Dharma are his good friends, because they spread wisdom.
(3) Those who can persuade others to renounce the household life are his good friends, because they can increase [others'] virtues.
(4) All the Buddhas, the World-Honored Ones, are his good friends, because they cause all Buddha-Dharmas to grow and thrive.

"Furthermore, Kāśyapa, there are four kinds of people who may appear to be Bodhisattvas but actually are not. What are the four?

(1) Those who lust for material gains instead of seeking the Dharma;
(2) those who wish to acquire fame instead of virtues;
(3) those who seek their own happiness and do not show other sentient beings the path to the cessation of suffering; and
(4) those who enjoy the company of many disciples and dislike detachment and seclusion.

"Furthermore, Kāśyapa, there are four kinds of true Bodhisattvas. What are the four?

(1) Those who not only understand and believe in emptiness, but also believe in karmic retribution;[5]
(2) those who know that all dharmas are devoid of self-entity, but who still have great compassion for sentient beings;[6]
(3) those who deeply cherish nirvāṇa, but continue to roam in saṁsāra; and
(4) those who practice giving for the benefit of sentient beings, without seeking any reward.

"Furthermore, Kāśyapa, a Bodhisattva has four great treasures. What are the four?

(1) Encountering Buddhas;
(2) hearing the six pāramitās and the elucidation of their meaning;
(3) regarding a Dharma-master with an unobstructed mind; and
(4) being inclined to the unremitting practice of renunciation.

"Furthermore, Kāśyapa, four things enable a Bodhisattva to transcend devilish hindrances.[7] What are the four?

(1) Never to be apart from bodhicitta;
(2) to harbor no ill feelings against sentient beings;
(3) to be aware of every kind of knowledge and view; and
(4) never to despise or belittle any sentient being.

"Furthermore, Kāśyapa, four things enable a Bodhisattva to accumulate good roots. What are the four?

(1) To avoid a wrong mentality when in solitude;
(2) to practice the four inducements among sentient beings without expecting any reward;
(3) to pursue the Dharma vigorously, even at the cost of his life; and
(4) to cultivate numerous good roots without satiety.

"Furthermore, Kāśyapa, a Bodhisattva has four adornments [causing] immeasurable blessings.[8] What are the four?

(1) To teach the Dharma with a pure mind;
(2) to have great compassion for those who break the precepts;
(3) to extol bodhicitta among sentient beings; and
(4) to practice patience when insulted by the lowly and inferior.

"Furthermore, Kāśyapa, a [true] Bodhisattva is not a Bodhisattva in name only. One who can practice wholesome dharmas and has a mind of equality is called a Bodhisattva. Briefly speaking, one who accomplishes thirty-two things is called a Bodhisattva. What are the thirty-two?

(1) To aspire to bring sentient beings peace and happiness;
(2) to enable all sentient beings to abide in all-knowing wisdom;
(3) not to resent others' wisdom;
(4) to shatter one's own haughtiness and arrogance;
(5) to take deep pleasure in the Buddha's path;
(6) to love and respect all sentient beings sincerely;
(7) to remain thoroughly kind to friends and foes alike up to one's attainment of nirvāṇa;
(8) always to speak with a smile and be the first to offer greetings;
(9) never to stop halfway through in performing a task;
(10) to extend great compassion equally to all sentient beings;
(11) to seek extensive learning untiringly and insatiably;
(12) to look for one's own faults, but not to speak of others' shortcomings;
(13) to be inspired by bodhicitta in every aspect of one's behavior;
(14) to practice giving without expecting anything in return;[9]
(15) to observe the discipline, but not for the purpose of a higher rebirth;
(16) to practice patience with an unimpeded mind among sentient beings;
(17) to strive with vigor to cultivate all good roots;
(18) to practice meditation without aspiring to rebirth in the realm of formlessness;
(19) to apply the wisdom of skillful means;
(20) to practice the four inducements;
(21) to be equally kind to both good and evil sentient beings;
(22) to listen to the Dharma single-mindedly;
(23) to remain detached in mind;
(24) not to indulge in worldly affairs;
(25) not to enjoy the Hīnayāna, but always to see great benefit in the Mahāyāna;
(26) to avoid bad friends and associate with good ones;
(27) to accomplish the four immeasurables and achieve total command of the five miraculous powers;
(28) always to rely on the true wisdom;
(29) not to forsake any sentient beings, whether their actions are right or wrong;
(30) always to discourse with decisiveness;
(31) to value the true Dharma; and
(32) to dedicate all one's deeds to bodhi.

Kāśyapa, if a person fulfills these thirty-two things, he is called a Bodhisattva.

"Furthermore, Kāśyapa, the virtues of a Bodhisattva are innumerable and boundless; they can only be illustrated by parables and similes.

"Kāśyapa, just as the great earth, used by all sentient beings, does not discriminate or seek rewards, so a Bodhisattva benefits all sentient beings from the time he engenders bodhicitta until the time he attains Buddhahood, but does not discriminate or seek rewards.

"Kāśyapa, just as the element water causes all kinds of grains, medicinal herbs, and trees to grow, so a Bodhisattva, because his mind is pure, extends his kindness and compassion to all sentient beings and causes all wholesome dharmas to grow.

"Kāśyapa, just as the element fire ripens all grains and fruits, so a Bodhisattva's wisdom ripens all wholesome dharmas.

"Kāśyapa, just as the element air causes the formation of all the worlds, so a Bodhisattva's ingenuity causes the formation of all the Buddha-Dharmas.

"Kāśyapa, just as the brilliance and size of a new moon increase from day to day, so all the wholesome dharmas in a Bodhisattva's pure mind grow from day to day.

"Kāśyapa, just as the light of the rising sun simultaneously illuminates all sentient beings, so a Bodhisattva's light of wisdom simultaneously illuminates all sentient beings.

"Kāśyapa, just as the lion, the king of beasts, is fearless wherever it goes, so a Bodhisattva, being flawless in keeping the precepts and endowed with true wisdom, is fearless wherever he dwells.

"Kāśyapa, just as a well-trained, huge elephant can perform great feats without tiring, so a Bodhisattva, due to his well-subdued mind, can yield great benefits to sentient beings without feeling weary at heart.

"Kāśyapa, just as the lotus grows in muddy water but is not soiled by the mud, so a Bodhisattva lives in the world, but is unsullied by worldly things.

"Kāśyapa, after a tree is felled, its stump will continue to grow as long as its root remains. In the same way, after a Bodhisattva has severed the knots of defilement, he still takes rebirth in the three realms by the power of his ingenuity, because he retains his intrinsic love [for sentient beings].

"Kāśyapa, just as the streams flowing from all directions assume a uniform taste when they join the ocean, so the numerous good roots accumulated in different ways by a Bodhisattva become uniform in taste[10] when they are dedicated to the attainment of supreme enlightenment.

"Kāśyapa, just as Mount Sumeru, the king of mountains, is the dwelling-place of the gods of the Heaven of the Thirty-Three and the Heaven of the Four Deva Kings, so the Bodhisattva's bodhicitta is the basis of all-knowing wisdom.

"Kāśyapa, just as the king of a large country can administer state affairs with the assistance of his ministers, so a Bodhisattva's wisdom can accomplish all the Buddha's undertakings with the power of ingenuity.

"Kāśyapa, just as a sunny sky without a speck of cloud is a sure sign that there will be no rain, so a Bodhisattva who has learned little will show no sign of a Dharma-rain.

"Kāśyapa, just as a dark, cloudy sky will inevitably produce rain to fulfill the needs of sentient beings, so a Bodhisattva produces a heavy Dharma-rain from the cloud of great compassion, for the benefit of sentient beings.[11]

"Kāśyapa, just as the seven treasures appear wherever a universal monarch appears, so the thirty-seven ways to enlightenment appear in the world whenever a Bodhisattva appears.

"Kāśyapa, just as there is an infinite quantity of gold, silver, and precious gems wherever a wish-fulfilling pearl is found, so there are infinite numbers of Śrāvakas and Pratyekabuddhas wherever a Bodhisattva appears.

"Kāśyapa, when the gods of the Heaven of the Thirty-Three enter the Garden of Equality, all the things they use are the same; similarly, a Bodhisattva, with his truly pure mind, teaches all sentient beings equally.

"Kāśyapa, just as poisons can be rendered harmless by charms and antidotes, so the poison of defilements is rendered harmless to a Bodhisattva by the power of his wisdom, and does not cause him to fall to the miserable planes of existence.

"Kāśyapa, just as the excrement and garbage discarded by the people living in big cities will yield benefits when placed in vineyards and sugarcane fields, so the residual defilements of a Bodhisattva will yield benefits because they are conducive to all-knowing wisdom.[12]

"Moreover, Kāśyapa, a Bodhisattva who wishes to learn this Sūtra of Assembled Treasures should constantly cultivate the right insight into all dharmas. What is the right insight? It is to think of all dharmas as they really are. The true, right insight means not to see a self, a personal identity, a sentient being, or a life. This is called the middle way,[13] the true, right insight.

"Furthermore, Kāśyapa, true insight means to regard forms as neither permanent nor impermanent; to regard feelings, conceptions, impulses, and consciousness as neither permanent nor impermanent. This is called the middle way, the true, right insight.

"Furthermore, Kāśyapa, true insight means to regard the element earth as neither permanent nor impermanent, and to regard the elements water, fire, and air as neither permanent nor impermanent. This is called the middle way, the true, right insight.

"Why? Permanence is one extreme, impermanence is the other, and [the two-in-one of] permanence-impermanence is the middle, which is formless, shapeless, incognizable, and unknowable. [To realize] it is called the middle way, the true insight into all dharmas.

"Ego is one extreme, egolessness is the other, and [the two-in-one of] ego-egolessness is the middle, which is formless, shapeless, incognizable, and unknowable. [To realize] it is called the middle way, the true insight into all dharmas.

"Furthermore, Kāśyapa, [to regard] the mind as real is one extreme; [to regard] it as unreal is the other. [To realize] that there is no mind or mental function is called the middle way, the true insight into all dharmas.

"The same is true of the dharmas which are wholesome and unwholesome, mundane and supramundane, sinful and not sinful, afflictive and nonafflictive, conditioned and unconditioned, defiled and undefiled. That which is apart from the two extremes cannot be felt[14] or expressed. [To realize] it is called the middle way, the true insight into all dharmas.

"Furthermore, Kāśyapa, existence is one extreme, nonexistence is the other, and that which falls on neither extreme is formless, shapeless, incognizable, and unknowable. [To realize] it is called the middle way, the true insight into all dharmas.

"Next, Kāśyapa, there is a doctrine I have expounded, namely, the twelve links of dependent origination: on ignorance depend actions; on actions depends consciousness; on consciousness depend name and form; on name and form depend the six senses; on the six senses depends contact; on contact depends feeling; on feeling depends craving; on craving depends grasping; on grasping depends becoming; on becoming depends birth; on birth depend old age, death, worry, sorrow, misery, and distress. These links of dependent origination are nothing but a great mass of suffering. If ignorance ceases, actions cease; if actions cease, consciousness ceases; if consciousness ceases, name and form cease; if name and form cease, the six senses cease; if the six senses cease, contact ceases; if contact ceases, feeling ceases; if feeling ceases, craving ceases, if craving ceases, grasping ceases; if grasping ceases, becoming ceases; if becoming ceases, birth ceases; if birth ceases, then old age, death, worry, sorrow, distress, and the whole mass of suffering altogether cease.

"[Concerning the twelve links of dependent origination,] ignorance, [or not knowing], and wisdom, [or knowing], are one and the same. To understand this is called the middle way, the true insight into all dharmas. In like manner, actions and nonactions, consciousness and the objects of consciousness, the perceptible and the imperceptible aspects of name and form, the six senses and the six miraculous powers, contact and objects of contact, feeling and its cessation, craving and its cessation, grasping and its cessation, becoming and its cessation, birth and its cessation, old age and death and their cessation—all these are one and the same. To understand this is called the middle way, the true insight into all dharmas.

"Next, Kāśyapa, to one who has the true insight, things are empty, not because one contemplates them as empty; they are empty by nature. Things are signless, not because one contemplates them as signless; they are signless in themselves. Things are unsought,[15] not because one contemplates them as unsought; they are unsought in themselves. Things are devoid of origination, arising, entity, and self-nature; they are impossible to grasp, not because one contemplates them as such; they are so in themselves. This understanding is called the true insight.

"Furthermore, Kāśyapa, personal identity is empty, not because one thinks there is no personal identity; it is empty in itself. It was empty in the past; it will be empty in the future; and it is empty at present. Therefore, one should rely on emptiness, not on personal identity.

"However, if one thinks that he has realized emptiness and becomes attached to emptiness, then he regresses in the pursuit of the Buddha-Dharma. Thus, Kāśyapa, it is better for one to take a view of the self as massive as Mount Sumeru than to take a view of emptiness and become arrogant. Why? Because all views can be eliminated by emptiness, but if one gives rise to the view of emptiness, there is no way to do away with it.[16]

"Kāśyapa, if a physician gives his patient some medicine to purge an illness, but the medicine stays in the body instead of being discharged, what do you think? Will the patient get better?"

"No, World-Honored One. The patient's illness will become worse if the medicine is not discharged."

"In like manner, Kāśyapa, all views can be eliminated by emptiness, but the view of emptiness cannot be eradicated.

"Suppose a person is afraid of empty space and wails in grief and pounds his chest, saying, 'I want to escape from empty space!' What do you think? Can one escape from empty space?"

"No, World-Honored One."

"Similarly, Kāśyapa, if a person is afraid of the doctrine of emptiness, I say he is crazy and has lost his mind. Why do I say so? Because he is always in emptiness, and yet is afraid of it.

"Just as a painter paints a picture of demons and then faints at the sight of his own creation, so ordinary people fabricate forms, sounds, odors, tastes, and textures, and then wander in saṁsāra afflicting themselves with all kinds of suffering without knowing it.

"Just as a magician produces an illusory being and then is devoured by it, so a monk who follows the path engenders the view that all dharmas are empty, still, and insubstantial; and then he, the viewer, is also voided [by this view].[17]

"Kāśyapa, just as fire produced by rubbing two pieces of wood together will burn up wood, so, Kāśyapa, the sacred wisdom born of true insight will burn up true insight.

"When a lamp is lit, the darkness completely vanishes. The darkness goes nowhere, just as it comes from nowhere—it does not go to or come from the east, the south, the west, the north, the four intermediate directions, the zenith, or the nadir. Furthermore, the lamplight does not think. "I can dispel darkness,' though it is because of the light that the darkness vanished. Both light and darkness are empty, inert, and impossible to grasp. Similarly, Kāśyapa, once true wisdom arises, ignorance ends. Both wisdom and ignorance are empty, inert, and impossible to grasp.

"Kāśyapa, suppose a room has been totally dark for a thousand years and then a lamp is lit therein. Do you suppose the darkness will think to itself, 'I have lived here for a long time and do not want to go'?"

"No, World-Honored One. When the lamp is lit, the darkness will be powerless. Even if it should refuse to go, it would surely be dispelled."

"In the same way, Kāśyapa, with one true insight, all the defilements and karmas accumulated through hundreds of thousands of millions of kalpas can be eradicated. The lamplight stands for the sacred wisdom; the darkness stands for the defilements and karmas.

"To illustrate, Kāśyapa, it is absolutely impossible for a seed to grow in midair. Likewise, it is impossible for a Bodhisattva to develop the Buddha-Dharma if he clings to his realization [of emptiness]. Kāśyapa, just as a seed sprouts when sown in a fertile field, so, Kāśyapa, the Buddha-Dharma grows when a Bodhisattva dwells among defilements and involves himself in worldly things.[18]

"Kāśyapa, just as a lotus flower cannot grow in high, dry land, so the Buddha-Dharma cannot grow in a Bodhisattva who stays in [the realm of] the unconditioned. Kāśyapa, just as a lotus flower grows in a low, wet, muddy land, so the Buddha-Dharma grows only when a Bodhisattva stays in the mire of saṁsāra among those in the group convinced by heterodox teachings.[19]

"Kāśyapa, the quantity of a Bodhisattva's conditioned good roots is like the quantity of cream sufficient to fill the four great oceans, while the quantity of a Śrāvaka's good roots is like a tiny droplet from that ocean suspended from a hundredth part of a hair.

"Kāśyapa, a Śrāvaka's conditioned wisdom is like the space inside a tiny mustard seed. Kāśyapa, a Bodhisattva's conditioned wisdom[20] is like the immeasurable, boundless space throughout the ten directions, and its power is infinite.

"Kāśyapa, suppose the wife of a kṣatriya ruler bears the child of a poor, lowly man. What do you think? Will the child be a prince?"

"No, World-Honored One."

"In the same way, Kāśyapa, although my Śrāvaka disciples [and the Bodhisattvas] both realize the Dharma-nature and are born of it, Śrāvakas are not called the true sons of the Tathāgata.

"Kāśyapa, if a kṣatriya ruler has a child with his maidservant of low caste, the child may be called a prince. Similarly, though a novice Bodhisattva is not fully equipped with merits or wisdom, wanders in saṁsāra, and can only benefit sentient beings within the limits of his [meager] power, he is still called a true son of the Tathāgata.

"Kāśyapa, if a universal monarch has a thousand sons, but not one of them bears the characteristics of a universal monarch, the monarch will not consider any of them as heir to the throne. Similarly, if a Tathāgata is surrounded by hundreds of thousands of millions of Śrāvakas, but no Bodhisattvas, he will not consider any of them as his true son.

"Kāśyapa, suppose the wife of a universal monarch is pregnant for seven days with a son who is already endowed with all the characteristics of a universal monarch. This son will be respected by gods more than other, grown sons [who lack those characteristics]. Why? Because this embryo prince will someday inherit the throne and perpetuate the lineage of the universal monarch. Similarly, Kāśyapa, though a novice Bodhisattva does not yet fully possess the qualities of a

Bodhisattva, he will, as in the case of the embryo prince, be more deeply honored by gods and spirits than great Arhats who have achieved the eightfold liberation. Why? Because such a Bodhisattva is heir to the supreme throne [of the Tathāgata] and will perpetuate the Buddha-lineage.

"Kāśyapa, just as one bead of lapis lazuli is worth more than ordinary crystal beads piled as high as Mount Sumeru, so a Bodhisattva, even when he first brings forth bodhicitta, surpasses all Śrāvakas and Pratyekabuddhas combined.

"Kāśyapa, when a prince is newly born, all the chieftains and ministers come to pay their respects to him. Similarly, when a Bodhisattva first brings forth bodhicitta, all gods and humans should pay homage to him.

"Kāśyapa, just as the herbs growing in the Himalayas belong to no one and will cure any person of his illness without discrimination, so the medicine of wisdom acquired by a Bodhisattva can deliver all sentient beings equally, without discrimination.

"Kāśyapa, just as people adore a new moon more than a full moon, so those who believe my words adore a Bodhisattva more than they adore a Tathāgata. Why? Because Tathāgatas are born of Bodhisattvas.[21]

"Kāśyapa, a fool may worship stars instead of the moon, but a wise man will never pay homage to Śrāvakas instead of Bodhisattvas.

"Kāśyapa, no matter how skillful a god or human may be in making artificial gems, he cannot turn an ordinary bead into a precious bead of lapis lazuli. Similarly, for all their accomplishments in discipline and meditation, those who seek Śrāvakahood can never sit at the bodhi-site to realize supreme bodhi.

"Kāśyapa, when a bead of lapis lazuli is formed, myriads of gems will appear with it. Similarly, when a Bodhisattva is taught and develops, he will yield myriads of Śrāvakas and Pratyekabuddhas."

Then the World-Honored One told Mahākāśyapa further, "A Bodhisattva should always try to benefit sentient beings. He should correctly cultivate all meritorious deeds and good roots and dedicate them to all sentient beings equally. He should administer to sentient beings everywhere in the ten directions the medicines of wisdom he has acquired, and thus cure them thoroughly.

"What are the genuine medicines of wisdom?[22] Contemplation on [bodily] impurities cures lust. Contemplation on kindness cures anger and hatred. Contemplation on dependent origination cures ignorance.[23]

"Contemplation on the emptiness of phenomena cures all deluded views. Contemplation on signlessness cures memories, discriminations, and wandering thoughts. Contemplation on wishlessness cures the desire to escape from the three realms.

"Contemplation on the four right views cures the four wrong views; contemplation on the impermanence of all conditioned dharmas cures the wrong view of regarding the impermanent as permanent; contemplation on the sufferings caused by conditioned dharmas cures the wrong view of regarding suffering as pleasure; contemplation on the absence of self-entity in dharmas cures the wrong view of regarding that which has no self as having a self; and contemplation on the tranquillity of nirvāṇa cures the wrong view of regarding the impure as pure.

"The four mindfulnesses[24] cure clinging to body, feelings, mind, and dharmas. One who practices the Dharma and contemplates the body as it really is will not be trapped by the view of a real self. One who contemplates feelings as they really are will not be trapped by the view of a real self. One who contemplates the mind as it really is will not be trapped by the view of a real self. One who contemplates dharmas as they really are will not be trapped by the view of a real self. These four mindfulnesses, therefore, cause one to abhor the body, feelings, mind, and all dharmas, and thereby open the door to nirvāṇa.

"By the four right efforts one can put an end to present unwholesome dharmas, prevent new unwholesome dharmas from arising, bring new wholesome dharmas into existence, and at the same time cultivate all virtues and good roots. . . . When such a Bodhisattva has acquired the medicine of wisdom, he will proceed in all the ten directions to cure sentient beings thoroughly [of their afflictions].

"What is a Bodhisattva's medicine of supramundane wisdom? It is to know that all dharmas arise from combinations of causes and conditions. It is to believe that all dharmas are devoid of self-entity, personal identity, being, or life; that there is no knower, seer, doer, or receiver.[25] It is to believe in and penetrate this truth [that] there is no 'I' or 'mine.'

"A Bodhisattva should not be afraid of or terrified by this Dharma of emptiness, in which nothing is apprehensible. He should further exert himself to probe the characteristics of the mind.

"A Bodhisattva probes the mind by thinking: 'What is the mind? Is it desire? Is it hatred? Is it ignorance? Does it belong to the past, the present, or the future?' If it belongs to the past, the past is gone. If it belongs to the future, the future has not yet come. If it belongs to the present, the present never stands still. The mind is not inside or outside [the body], nor in between. It is formless, shapeless, incognizable, and unknowable; it relies on nothing and has no location. Such a mind was not, is not, and will not be seen by any of the Buddhas of the ten directions and the three phases of time. If it is not seen by any of the past, present, or future Buddhas, how can it exist? It is due to wrong thinking that the mind arises, and along with it all the different dharmas. The mind is illusory, but through thought, fantasy, and discrimination, it gives rise to all kinds of karmas and consequently causes one to receive various bodily forms [as karmic results].

"Furthermore, Mahākāśyapa, the mind is like the wind blowing, which no one can catch. It is like flowing water, continually arising and ceasing. It is like the flame of a lamp, caused by various factors. It is like lightning, for it perishes from moment to moment. It is like the air, for it is polluted by the dust of external objects. It is like a monkey, for it clings to the six desires one after another. It is like a painter, for it is able to create numerous karmic causes and conditions.

"The mind is not fixed, for it runs after various defilements. It is like a mighty ruler, for all dharmas are governed by it. It acts alone, without companion, for two minds cannot exist simultaneously. It is a bitter enemy, for it causes all sufferings. It can ruin all good roots, just as a mad elephant may trample mud huts under its feet. It behaves like [a fish] swallowing a hook, considering suffering to be pleasure. It is like a dream, giving rise to the idea of an 'I' where there is no 'I.' It is like a fly, considering impurities to be pure.

"The mind is like a rogue, for it can torture one in every way. It is like a demon, always looking for opportunities to attack. It constantly swings between high and low, for it is spoiled by greed and anger. It is like a bandit, for it can rob one of all good roots. It lusts for forms, just as a moth plunges into fire. It yearns for sounds, just as a veteran soldier yearns to hear drumbeats signaling victory. It is always greedy for fragrances, just as a hog enjoys wallowing in filth. It always pursues flavors, just as a young girl indulges in delicacies. It always craves pleasant textures, just as a fly clings to oil.

"Thus, Kāśyapa, [a Bodhisattva] probes the characteristics of the mind but finds the mind to be inapprehensible. If it is inapprehensible, it has nothing to do with the past, present, or future. If it has nothing to do with the past, present, or future, it transcends the three phases of time. If it transcends the three phases of time, it is neither existent nor nonexistent. If it is neither existent nor nonexistent, it is birthless. If it is birthless, it has no self-nature. If it has no self-nature, it does not arise. If it does not arise, it does not cease. If it does not cease, it parts with nothing. If it parts with nothing, then it neither comes nor goes, and neither gains nor loses anything. If it neither comes nor goes, and neither gains nor loses anything, then it performs no actions. If it performs no actions, then it is unconditioned.

"Since it is unconditioned, it is the root from which all saints develop. In the unconditioned, there is no keeping or breaking of precepts. If there is no keeping or breaking of precepts, then there is no action or inaction. If there is no action or inaction, then there is no mind or mental function. If there is no mind or mental function, then there is no karma or karmic result. If there is no karma or karmic result, then there is no joy or suffering. What is free from joy and suffering is the holy nature; in it, there is no karma or creator of karma; no bodily karma, no verbal karma, and no mental karma; nor any such distinctions as high, middle, or low.

"The holy nature is equal throughout, for it is like empty space. It is beyond distinction, for all dharmas are of one taste. It is detachment, for it is detached from all phenomena of body and mind. It is apart from all dharmas, for it accords with nirvāṇa. It is purity, for it is free from all defilements. It has no 'I,' for it is devoid of the 'I' and 'mine.' It has no high or low, for it is born of equality.

"The holy nature is the real truth, for it is the ultimate truth. It never ends, for it ultimately does not come into being. It always abides, for all dharmas forever remain the same. It is bliss, for nirvāṇa is the highest [bliss]. It is pure, for it is apart from all phenomena. It has no 'I,' for the 'I' is inapprehensible. The holy nature is true purity, for it is ultimately pure from the beginning.

"Furthermore, Mahākāśyapa, all of you should contemplate inwardly. Do not let your minds gallop outside.

"Now, Mahākāśyapa, some monks in the future will behave like a dog chasing clods of earth. What does this mean? If a person throws clods of earth at a dog, the dog will chase the clods instead of the person. In the same way, Kāśyapa, a śramaṇa or brāhmin may fear the bondage of pleasant forms, sounds, scents, tastes, and textures, and live completely alone in a secluded place, far away from the bustling multitude; but, while his body is separated from the objects of the five sensuous desires, his mind has not renounced them. Such a person will at times think about pleasant forms, sounds, scents, tastes, and textures, and yearn to enjoy them instead of contemplating inwardly. He does not know how to detach himself from forms, sounds, scents, tastes, and textures. Because he does not know this, when he enters a city, town, or village and mingles with the crowd, he will still be attached to the pleasant forms, sounds, scents, tastes, and textures. Because he has observed the mundane rules of conduct in a secluded place, he can be reborn in heaven after death. However, he will then be bound again by the five sensuous pleasures in heaven; and when his life there ends, he will still be unable to escape falling to the four miserable planes of existence, namely, those of hell-dwellers, hungry ghosts, animals, and asuras. Such a monk may be likened to a dog chasing clods of earth.[26]

"Furthermore, Kāśyapa, how can a monk not be like a dog chasing clods of earth? Suppose a monk does not return a scolding for a scolding, nor does he retaliate for beatings, injuries, hatred, or slander; instead, he only reflects inwardly, seeking to subdue his own mind, and thinks, 'Who is the scolder? Who is the scolded? Who is the beater, the injurer, the hater, or the slanderer?' Such a monk is not like a dog chasing clods of earth.

"Kāśyapa, just as a good horse trainer can immediately tame a rampageous, unruly horse, so one who practices the Dharma can instantly arrest his mind whenever it wanders, not allowing it to go astray.

"Kāśyapa, just as a throttling disease can cut short one's life immediately, so, Kāśyapa, among all views, the view of an 'I' can cut short the life of wisdom instantly.

"Just as a person seeks to release himself from whatever bonds restrict him, so, Kāśyapa, one should seek to release himself from whatever his mind is attached to.

"Furthermore, Kāśyapa, one who has left the household life may have two impurities of the mind. What are the two? First, to read heterodox scriptures, such as those of the materialists; second, to collect fine robes and bowls.

"Furthermore, Kāśyapa, one who has left the household life may suffer from two strong fetters. What are the two? First, the fetter of wrong views; second, the fetter of material gains.

"Furthermore, one who has left the household life may meet two obstacles. What are the two? First, to be intimate with laypeople; second, to resent virtuous persons.

"Furthermore, one who has left the household life may have two blemishes. What are the two? First, to tolerate defilements [in himself]; second, to be attached to donors.

"Furthermore, one who has left the household life may be afflicted by two hailstorms that will ruin his good roots. What are the two? First, to rebel against and to corrupt the true Dharma; second, to accept offerings from devotees after having broken the precepts.

"Furthermore, one who has left the household life may suffer from two abcesses. What are the two? First, to find fault with others; second, to hide his own faults.

"Furthermore, one who has left the household life may be afflicted with two fevers. What are the two? First, to be defiled in mind while wearing a monastic robe; second, to accept offerings from virtuous people who keep the precepts, [while violating the precepts himself].

"Furthermore, one who has left the household life may suffer from two illnesses. What are the two? First, to be arrogant and refuse to be humble; second, to ruin others' aspirations for the Mahāyāna.

"Moreover, Mahākāśyapa, there are four kinds of śramaṇas. What are the four?

(1) Śramaṇas in appearance and attire [only];
(2) śramaṇas who are deceptively dignified in conduct;
(3) śramaṇas who lust for fame; and
(4) śramaṇas who really practice the Dharma.

"What is a śramaṇa in appearance and attire [only]? Suppose a śramaṇa is fully dressed in a monastic robe, has cleanly shaven hair and beard, and an alms-bowl in hand, yet he performs impure actions of body, speech, and mind. Instead of properly guarding himself from evil, he is miserly, jealous, idle, and lazy; he violates the precepts and engages in vile pursuits. Such a śramaṇa is one in appearance and attire [only].

"What is a śramaṇa who is deceptively dignified in conduct? Suppose a śramaṇa displays full dignity in walking, standing, sitting, and lying down. He is composed and serene; does not take delicacies; follows the four noble practices; avoids the bustling crowd, even a group of monks; and speaks softly. However, he does all this deceitfully, not for the sake of true purity. Or, he thinks there is something to be attained in emptiness, and is afraid of the doctrine of nonattainment, just as one is afraid of an abyss; he regards as enemies or bandits those monks who preach that all dharmas are ultimately empty. Such a śramaṇa is one who is deceptively dignified in conduct.

"What is a śramaṇa who lusts for fame? Suppose a śramaṇa observes the precepts only because he wants to be known and to achieve certain goals in his present life. He reads and recites the sūtras on his own because he wants people to know that he is learned; and he lives alone in a secluded spot because he wants people to know that he is a recluse who has few desires, is content, and practices detachment. In short, he does everything for the sole purpose of fame, not out of renunciation, nor to achieve true tranquillity, nor to realize the truth, nor to attain the fruit of a śramaṇa or brāhmin, nor to achieve nirvāṇa. Such a śramaṇa is one who lusts for fame.

"Finally, Kāśyapa, what is a śramaṇa who really practices the Dharma? Suppose a śramaṇa does not even crave for physical existence, much less for material gains. When he hears that all dharmas are empty, signless, and unsought, he understands this doctrine thoroughly, conforms to it, and practices it as taught. He does not cultivate pure conduct in order to achieve nirvāṇa, much less to [be reborn in] the three realms. He does not cherish the idea of emptiness, or the idea that there is no 'I,' let alone the idea of an 'I,' a being, or a personal identity.

"He parts with reliance in seeking release from all defilements; seeing that all dharmas are originally undefiled and ultimately pure, he relies on himself instead of others. Realizing the true Dharma-body, he does not even see the Buddha, much less [his physical] form. Through realizing emptiness, he has become detached, and does not even perceive the Dharma; much less does he crave for the sounds and words [describing it]. Realizing the unconditioned, he does not even see the Saṁgha, much less the existence of a harmonious assembly. He does not eradicate anything or cultivate anything; he does not abide in saṁsāra or attach himself to nirvāṇa.[27] Knowing that all dharmas are from the beginning ultimately quiescent, he perceives no bondage and seeks no liberation. Such a śramaṇa is one who really practices the Dharma.

"Thus, Kāśyapa, you should imitate the śramaṇa who really practices the Dharma. Do not be ruined by names. Kāśyapa, suppose a poor, lowly man assumed the name of a rich, noble person. Do you think the name would fit him?"

"No, World-Honored One."

"In the same way, Kāśyapa, if one is called a śramaṇa or brāhmin but does not perform the real meritorious deeds of a śramaṇa or brāhmin, he will be ruined by the name.

"For example, a person swept away by a flood may die of thirst and fatigue. Similarly, Kāśyapa, if a śramaṇa reads many sūtras but cannot quench his thirst of desire, hatred, and ignorance, he will be swept away by the Dharma-flood, die of the thirst of defilements, and fall to the miserable planes of existence.

"For example, a physician who always carries a medicine pouch may be unable to cure his own illness. The same is true of a learned person afflicted with the illness of defilements; although he has much learning, he cannot benefit himself unless he puts an end to his defilements.

"A person who takes a king's expensive medicine may be unable to adjust himself to it and be hurt by it. The same is true of a learned person afflicted with the illness of defilements: although he has obtained the good medicine of the Dharma, he will hurt his own root of wisdom if he does not cultivate virtues.

"Kāśyapa, just as a wish-fulfilling pearl that has just fallen into filth cannot be worn, so a learned person who covets material gains cannot benefit humans or gods.

"Just as a corpse may wear gold ornaments, so a learned monk who breaks the precepts may [improperly] wear monastic robes and accept offerings from people.

"If an elder's son trims his nails, bathes, rubs himself with red sandalwood incense, puts a garland around his neck, and wears new, white clothing, then his appearance befits his social status. Similarly, Kāśyapa, a learned monk who observes the precepts is worthy to wear a monastic robe and accept offerings from people.

"Next, Mahākāśyapa, there are four kinds of monks who break the precepts but appear to keep the precepts well. What are the four?

"Some monks observe the precepts completely. They are always afraid of committing any transgression, whether major or minor, and obey all the rules of discipline they have learned. They are pure in action, word, and thought, and adopt a pure, right means of livelihood. However, they uphold the doctrine which claims that there is a real 'self.'[28] These people constitute the first kind of monk who breaks the precepts but appears to keep the precepts well.

"Furthermore, Kāśyapa, some monks recite the code of discipline and practice its teachings. However, they continue to hold the view of a real body. They constitute the second kind of monk who breaks the precepts but appears to keep the precepts well.

"Furthermore, Kāśyapa, some monks observe the precepts completely. However, in practicing kindness they become attached to sentient beings, and when they hear that no dharma ever arises, they are terrified. They constitute the third kind of monk who breaks the precepts but seems to keep the precepts well.

"Finally, Kāśyapa, some monks practice all twelve austerities,[29] but see something attainable in doing so. They constitute the fourth kind of monk who breaks the precepts but seems to keep the precepts well.

"Next, Kāśyapa, one who observes the precepts well sees no 'I.' or 'mine'; no doing or nondoing, no deed or doer, no action or inaction, no name or form, no signs or nonsigns, no cessation or continuation, no clinging or abandoning, nothing to grasp and nothing to give up, no sentient being and no term 'sentient being,' no mind and no term 'mind,' no world or nonworld, and no reliance or nonreliance. Such a person does not pride himself on keeping the precepts, nor does he look down upon the way others observe the precepts, nor does he think or discriminate about the precepts. He is called one who observes the discipline of all saints; he is free from defilements and bondage, not caught in the three realms, and beyond all doctrines of reliance."

Thereupon, to clarify this point, the World-Honored One spoke in verse:

> "One who observes the precepts purely
> Is free from any blemish;
> He is free from everything.

In keeping the precepts,
He is not arrogant,
And relies upon nothing.
In keeping the precepts,
He is not deluded,
And is free from all bonds.

In keeping the precepts,
He is untainted,
And does nothing amiss.
In keeping the precepts,
His mind is pliant and gentle,
And he always dwells in ultimate quiescence.

Such a person is far apart
From all thoughts and discriminations;
He is liberated from every stirring
Of the mind.
This is the pure observance
Of the Buddha's precepts.

If one is not attached to his [present] life,
Nor craves for any [future] birth,
But performs only right actions,
And abides securely in the noble path—
He is one who purely, and in truth,
Observes the Buddha's precepts.

One who keeps the precepts
Is not defiled by the world,
Nor does he rely
On anything mundane.
Once he attains the light of wisdom,
All darkness vanishes and nothing remains;
Without a notion of self or others,
He knows and sees all phenomena.
He is one who purely, and in truth,
Observes the Buddha's precepts.

There is no this or other shore,
Nor anything in between.
Be not attached [to them], nor
To the absence of the three.
To be free from bondage, defilements, and deceit
Is called the true, pure observance
Of the Buddha's precepts.

If one is not attached to name or form
And has no notion of 'I' or 'mine,'
He is said to securely abide
In the true, pure observance
Of the precepts.

Although one may observe all precepts,
His arrogance should not increase,
Nor should he regard
The discipline as supreme.
He should transcend it,
And seek the holy path.
To do this is a sign
Of the true, pure observance
Of the precepts.

Do not regard the discipline as supreme,
Nor overvalue samādhi.
If one can transcend both discipline and samādhi,
But cultivate wisdom,
He will realize emptiness, still and void,
Which is the very nature shared
By all saints and sages.
To do this is the true, pure
Observance of the precepts,
Extolled by all Buddhas.

Release the mind from the view of a self,
Eliminate the 'I' and 'mine,'
Believe in and understand
The teaching of quiescence and emptiness,
Which all Buddhas practice;
He who so observes the holy discipline
Is indeed peerless.

One depends on discipline to achieve samādhi,
And on samādhi to cultivate insight.
Relying on the insight thus cultivated,
One achieves the pure wisdom:
He who achieves the pure wisdom
Is able to keep the pure precepts."

When this was spoken, five hundred monks became detached from all dharmas and achieved mental liberation;[30] thirty-two thousand persons left mundane filth behind and attained the clear Dharma-eye.[31] However, five hundred monks did not understand or believe in the profound Dharma they had heard, and they rose from their seats and walked away.

Seeing this, Mahākāśyapa said to the Buddha, "World-Honored One, these five hundred monks have all attained dhyāna; however, because they cannot understand or have faith in the profound Dharma, they have risen and gone away."

The Buddha said to Kāśyapa, "These monks all have arrogance; therefore, when they hear of the pure, flawless discipline, they cannot understand it or have faith in it. The meaning of the verses spoken by the Buddha is profound. Why? Because the enlightenment of Buddhas is profound. If a person has not planted good roots abundantly, or associates with evil friends, he will lack the power of faith and understanding, and it will be difficult for him to accept and believe in [this doctrine].

"Furthermore, Mahākāśyapa, at the time of Kāśyapa Buddha, these five hundred monks were disciples of heterodox masters. Once they visited Kāśyapa Buddha in order to find fault with him; however, after they heard that Buddha expound the Dharma, they acquired a little faith and thought, 'This Buddha is unusual; how wonderfully he speaks!' Because of this virtuous thought, they were born in the Heaven of the Thirty-Three after death. When their lives ended there, they were born in this world, and here they renounced the household life for the Dharma.

"These monks are strongly attached to various views; therefore, they cannot believe in, conform to, or thoroughly understand the profound Dharma they hear expounded. Although they do not thoroughly understand the profound Dharma, they will obtain great benefit merely because they have heard it. They will not be reborn in the miserable planes of existence, but will realize nirvāṇa in this very life."

Then the Buddha told Subhūti, "Go bring those monks back."

Subhūti said, "World-Honored One, these people do not even believe the Buddha; much less will they believe Subhūti."

Thereupon the Buddha magically produced two monks to follow the five hundred monks. When the [real] monks saw the two magically produced ones, they asked them, "Where are you going?"

The magically produced monks answered, "We are going to some secluded spot to enjoy the practice of meditation. Why? Because we cannot understand or believe in what the Buddha said."

The other monks said, "Elders, we cannot understand or believe in what the Buddha said, either. We, too, are going to a secluded spot to practice meditation."

Then the magically produced monks said to the others, "We should give up arrogance, defiance, and contention, and try to understand and believe in what the Buddha taught. Why? Because to have no arrogance or contention is the law of śramaṇas. Nirvāṇa means cessation. What ceases? In the body, is there an 'I,' a personal identity, a doer, a receiver, or a life to cease?"

The other monks said, "In the body, there is no 'I,' no personal identity, no doer, no receiver, and no life that ceases. It is the cessation of desire, hatred, and ignorance that is called nirvāṇa."

The magically produced monks asked, "Do the desire, hatred, and ignorance you mentioned have definite forms to be totally extinguished?"

The other monks answered, "Desire, hatred, and ignorance are neither inside nor outside the body, nor anywhere in between. When one does not stir his mind, they do not arise."[32]

The magically produced monks said, "In that case, you should not stir your minds. If you do not stir your minds or make distinctions about dharmas, then you will be neither defiled by nor detached from anything. To be neither defiled by nor detached from anything is called ultimate quiescence. Discipline does not come or go or perish; meditation, wisdom, liberation, and the knowledge and awareness derived from liberation[33] also do not come or go or perish. It is in light of this doctrine that we speak of nirvāṇa. This truth is empty [in itself], detached from all things, and cannot be grasped. You should abandon even the thought of nirvāṇa. Do not follow any thought[34] or nonthought. Do not rid yourselves of a thought by another thought. Do not contemplate a thought by another thought. If you rid yourselves of a thought by using a thought, you are still bound by thought. You should not discriminate anything concerning the Dhyāna of Cessation of Feeling and Conception, because all dharmas are beyond discrimination. If a monk eliminates all feelings and conception and attains this dhyāna, then he fulfills himself to the utmost."

When the magically produced monks had spoken thus, the five hundred [real] monks became detached from all dharmas and liberated in mind. They returned to the Buddha, bowed with their heads at his feet, and stood to one side.

Subhūti asked the monks, "Where did you go and where do you come from?"

The monks said, "The Dharma expounded by the Buddha comes from nowhere and goes nowhere."

"Who is your teacher?"

"He who has never been born and will never die is our teacher."

"Where do you learn the Dharma?"

"We learn the Dharma in the place where the five aggregates, the twelve entrances, and the eighteen elements do not exist."

"Why do you learn the Dharma?"

"Not for the sake of bondage or for the sake of liberation."

"What doctrine do you practice?"

"We do not try to attain anything or to eliminate anything."

"Who subdued you?"

"We are subdued by [one whose] body has no definite nature and [whose] mind does not act."[35]

"What action leads to the liberation of the mind?"

"Neither the eradication of ignorance nor the generation of wisdom."

"Whose disciples are you?"

"We are disciples of one who attains nothing and knows nothing."

"You have attained [the ultimate liberation]; when will you enter nirvāṇa?"

"When a person magically produced by the Tathāgata enters nirvāṇa, we will do so, too."[36]

"Have you obtained benefit for yourselves?"

"Self-benefit is inapprehensible."

"Have you accomplished what you set out to do?"

"Deeds are inapprehensible."

"Have you cultivated pure conduct?"

"We cultivate nothing in the three realms, nor do we not cultivate anything; this is our pure conduct."

"Have you exhausted your defilements?"

"Ultimately, nothing can be exhausted."

"Have you vanquished the demons?"

"The demons of the aggregates are inapprehensible."

"Do you serve the Tathāgata?"

"Not with body or mind."

"Do you abide in the fields of blessings?"

"We do not abide in anything."

"Have you cut off circling in saṁsāra?"

"There is neither permanence nor severance."

"Do you conform to the Dharma?"

"We are liberated from every obstruction."[37]

"What is your ultimate destination?"

"Wherever a person magically produced by the Tathāgata goes, we will go."

While Subhūti was questioning the monks, five hundred other monks became detached from all dharmas and liberated in mind; thirty-two thousand people parted from mundane defilements and attained the clear Dharma-eye.

Then a Bodhisattva in the assembly named Universal Light asked the Buddha, "World-Honored One, if a Bodhisattva wishes to learn this Sūtra of Assembled Treasures, what should he abide in and how should he learn it?"

The Buddha answered, "A Bodhisattva learning this sūtra should know that what I have said has no definite nature, and he should not be attached to it or cling to it. If he follows this instruction in his practice, he will benefit greatly.

"Universal Light, suppose a person tries to cross the Ganges in a poorly built boat. With what vigor should he row the boat?"

Bodhisattva Universal Light replied, "World-Honored One, he should row it with great vigor. Why? Because it may collapse in midstream."

The Buddha said, "Universal Light, a Bodhisattva who wishes to cultivate the Buddha-Dharma should exert himself twice as hard. Why? Because the body is impermanent and uncertain, a decaying form which cannot long remain and will eventually wear out and perish; it may disintegrate before one benefits from the Dharma.

"[A Bodhisattva should think,] 'I will learn to navigate the Dharma boat in this stream [of saṁsāra], so that I may ferry sentient beings across the four currents. I will ply this Dharma boat back and forth in saṁsāra to deliver sentient beings.'

"The Dharma boat which a Bodhisattva should use is made for the purpose of saving all sentient beings equally. Its strong, thick planks are the immeasurable merits resulting from the practice of pure discipline; its embellishments are the practice and the fruit of giving; its beams are the pure faith in the Buddha-path; its strong riggings are all kinds of virtues; its nails are patience, tenderness, and thoughtfulness. The raw wood is the various ways to enlightenment, cultivated with vigor, taken from the forest of the supreme, wonderful Dharma.

"Its builders are the infinite, inconceivable dhyānas and the tranquil, well-subdued mind resulting from one's meritorious deeds. Ever-enduring compassion and the four inducements are the means to attract immense numbers of sentient beings aboard to ferry them over the great distance. The power of wisdom guards the boat from robbers. Ingenuity of all kinds and the four immeasurables are its splendid adornments. The four right mindfulnesses form its golden bridge. The four right efforts and the four bases of miraculous powers are the swift winds [that propel the boat].

"The five roots are the able navigator who steers the boat away from the dangerous waters. The five powers are its strong buoyancy. The seven factors of enlightenment serve to discover and vanquish devilish pirates. By sailing [on the course of] the eightfold noble path, the boat will arrive at its destination on the other shore, away from the landings of heterodox teachings.

"Concentration serves as the helmsman, while insight brings the true benefit. The boat steers clear of [the reefs of] the two extremes and sails safely by the law of dependent generation. The follower of the vast Mahāyāna has inexhaustible eloquence, and his name spreads far and wide. Being able to deliver sentient beings in the ten directions, he proclaims, 'Come aboard this Dharma boat! It sails on a safe course to nirvāṇa. It ferries you from the shore of all wrong views, including that of a real self, to the shore of Buddhahood.'

"Thus, Universal Light, a Bodhisattva-Mahāsattva should learn everything about this Dharma boat. For hundreds of thousands of millions of billions of incalculable kalpas, he should use this Dharma boat to rescue those sentient beings who are drifting and drowning in the vast stream of saṁsāra."

The Buddha then said to Universal Light, "Moreover, there are other Dharma instructions that can cause a Bodhisattva to achieve Buddhahood quickly. They are:

Be sincere in every endeavor and cultivate an abundance of virtue.
Keep a pure, deeply [compassionate] mind and never cease to be vigorous.

Take delight in approaching enlightenment and cultivate all good roots.
Always maintain right thought and enjoy wholesome dharmas.
Learn the Dharma insatiably in order to be filled with wisdom.
Shatter your conceit and arrogance in order to increase your knowledge.
Rid yourself of play-words in order to accomplish meritorious deeds.
Take pleasure in solitude in order to be detached in body and mind.
Stay away from noisy crowds in order to avoid wicked people.
Probe the depth of the Dharma in accordance with the ultimate truth.
Seek the wisdom that penetrates reality.
Seek the real truth to attain the indestructible Dharma.
Seek the doctrine of emptiness so that your practice may be right.
Seek detachment in order to attain ultimate quiescence.

In this way, Universal Light, a Bodhisattva may quickly achieve Buddhahood."

When this sūtra had been spoken, Bodhisattva Universal Light, Mahākāśyapa, and all the gods, asuras, and humans were jubilant. With great veneration, they began to practice the sūtra as taught.

NOTES

1. After each series of four, the category is repeated (e.g., "These four cause a Bodhisattva's wisdom to decrease.") We have omitted this repetition for brevity.

2. Literally, "crooked minds."

3. Literally, "straight mind."

4. That is, he considers all adversity as retribution for his own negative karma committed in a previous life.

5. This is a recurring quandary for people who are interested in Buddhist doctrine: If there is no 'I', no 'mine', and all dharmas are utterly empty, how can the law of karma prevail? The answer is: it is precisely because everything *is* empty and there is no self or 'I', that everything *can* exist and the principle of karma *can* prevail. If things were truly existent, i.e., with a definite, enduring substance or entity, then *no* change or flow would be possible. Because nothing has a self-nature (*svabhāva*), everything is possible. The Buddhist way of thinking is unique in this aspect. To understand this point more clearly, the reader is referred to the Mādhyamika and Prajñāpāramitā literature, such as T.R.V. Murti, *The Central Philosophy of Buddhism* (London: Allen & Unwin, 1955) ch. 1, 2, and 3; and Garma Chang, *The Buddhist Teaching of Totality*, (University Park: Pennsylvania State University Press, 1971) Part 2, sec. 1. (G.C.)

6. A similar quandary. If sentient beings, like all dharmas in the universe, are utterly empty and do not exist, on whom is compassion bestowed?

I think this problem is much more difficult to explain than that in note 5. I personally do not know any completely satisfactory answer, for it is not only an ontological problem, but also an ethical one; hence, it involves a much broader spectrum of questions than the preceding one. The traditional Buddhist answers to this problem are as follows:

A. When a Bodhisattva sees the illusory sentient beings undergo the illusory sufferings caused by their illusory karma, he generates an illusory compassion toward the illusory sentient beings and delivers them from their delusions. The Bodhisattva is illusory and empty, for he has no concept of 'self'; the sentient beings and their sufferings are also illusory and empty because they have no self-entities; the compassion of the Bodhisattva and the sufferings of sentient beings are also illusory, because they are inapprehensible or unobtainable, like dreams or magic. Everything in saṁsāra is illusory (*māyā*), like magic. However, an illusory or magic-like Buddhist game—the Bodhisattva's compassion and his altruistic deeds—can still take place without there being attachment to man's innate view that self and beings are all real (*satkāyadṛṣṭi*).

B. On the mundane level, sentient beings and their sufferings, Bodhisattvas and their vows, etc., are all 'real' and do appear to exist, but on the transcendental level they are all empty or nonexistent. However, these two levels (the two truths system) are not separate realms or entities; they are actually one. There is a mutually penetrating and mutually identical all-merging totality, in which the arising of compassion and the emptiness of sentient beings are not contradictory but interdependent and mutually supplementary. The complete merging of the mundane and the transcendental is expressed here as the coexistence of the arising of the Bodhisattvas' compassion and the emptiness of sentient beings. Compassion and emptiness seem to be irreconcilable and contradictory by definition. However, this is only from the limited human viewpoint; in the great merging totality (圓融法界) the contradictions all become harmonious noncontradictions. As long as there is the appearance of a dichotomy of saṁsāra and nirvāṇa, these contradictions are unavoidable, because the *svabhāva* way of thinking preconditions men to think in this manner. In the totalistic way of thinking no such problem exists. See Chang, *The Buddhist Teaching of Totality*, Part 2, sec. 2.

7. The literal translation of *mo shih* (魔事) could be 'devilish matters'. Its meaning is very broad; it can include acts of demons affecting the Bodhisattva, as well as any devilish tendencies he may have himself.

8. Literally, "four immeasurable virtuous adornments" (四無量福德莊嚴).

9. This and the five following lines refer to the practice of the six pāramitās.

10. 一味 is translated here as 'uniform in taste'. 'Taste' here means 'nature'. 一味 has been translated by different scholars as 'one taste', 'one nature' or 'at-one-ment'.

11. These two similes taken together indicate the two main themes of the Mahāyāna: wisdom and compassion.

12. This perhaps is suggestive of the Tantric view that enlightenment can be found directly in defilements themselves, as when the Bodhisattva identifies his defilements with bodhi.

13. 'The middle way', as it is translated here, may also be interpreted as an adjective modifying 'insight', and meaning 'not favoring one extreme or another'. (Y.C.H.)

14. Although the Chinese text reads 受 ('felt'), I believe that this could be a mistranslation, and that it should be rendered as 'apprehended'. That which is apart from the two extremes cannot be apprehended or expressed, but it can be "felt" or "experienced" by enlightened beings. (G.C.)

15. 'Unsought' indicates that things cannot be wished for. Since 'wishless' and 'beyond wishing' are ambiguous terms—though corresponding to the third door to liberation called wishlessness—we use 'unsought'.

16. The tendency to cling to emptiness is very common, especially for advanced yogis. Many Zen koans bear witness to this fact. (G.C.)

17. Alternate translation: "Just as beings magically produced by a magician may destroy each other and finally all comes to nought, so dharmas contemplated by a monk who follows the path are empty, still, and insubstantial, and even his contemplation of them is also empty."

18. Literally, "he is apart from worldly things," but the Chinese word 離 ('apart from') does not fit the context. It may be a misprint for 雜 ('become involved'). Shih Hu's translation, Taishō 352, p. 208, comes close to our interpretation here.

19. One of the three groups. See Numerical Glossary.

20. This and the preceding sentences all use the word 'conditioned' (有爲). It could be a corruption of the text; Shih Hu's translation has no modifying word 'conditioned', and it reads more smoothly and clearly. Of course, Shih Hu's text is obviously a different version, probably of a much later date. See Taishō 325, pp. 208–209. (G.C.)

21. A novice Bodhisattva, with all his immaturity and imperfections, strives for Buddhahood and practices the Bodhisattva's deeds. In his undertaking of the Bodhisattva's acts, he often appears more attractive and appealing to man, because he speaks our language, understands our problems, and shares our feelings. He is one of us. As in the parable of the new moon and the full moon, imperfection is sometimes more beautiful than perfection. (G.C.)

There may be a different interpretation. Those who believe the Buddha's words (as opposed to people in general) "adore a Bodhisattva more than they adore a Tathāgata" simply because they accept the Buddha's statement that "Tathāgatas are born of Bodhisattvas." To "adore a new moon more than a full moon" may be just a custom in India, marking the beginning of a bright future, and thus a handy illustration in this case; it may have nothing to do with beauty. (S.L.M.)

22. Or, "the Bodhisattva's ultimate medicines of wisdom."

23. In this way, the three poisons or defilements are counteracted.

24. This and the subsequent six paragraphs apply the thirty-seven ways to enlightenment.

25. All these eight terms are different names for the 'I', which non-Buddhists think of as that which knows and sees, performs actions, and receives karmic results.

26. This parable is not clear in the text, but we presume it means this: the person who throws the clods of earth at the dog represents the inner desires, while the clods he throws represent sensuous pleasures. The person is the root of the dog's problem; as long as the person is there, the clods of earth will keep coming. Therefore, to free itself from the attack, the dog should chase the person instead of the clods of earth. Similarly, a śramaṇa should conquer the desires within instead of trying to live in a secluded place devoid of sensuous pleasures in order to cure his defilements.

27. See Glossary, "nirvāṇa." This is the nonabiding nirvāṇa.

28. *Ātma-vāda*, Ch. 有我論. This is the doctrine which claims that 'self' (*ātman*), which also may be translated as 'soul' or 'substance', is real, permanent, eternal, unchanging, and irreducible.

29. The twelve are:

1) living in a secluded forest;
2) begging for food;

3) taking turns at begging for food;
4) eating only one meal a day;
5) eating only a small amount of food;
6) taking no food, and no drinks made with fruit or honey, after midday;
7) wearing garments of cast-off rags;
8) having only three garments;
9) dwelling among graves;
10) staying under a tree;
11) sitting on bare ground; and
12) never lying down.

30. To become detached from all dharmas and achieve mental liberation is tantamount to attaining Arhatship, the fourth and ultimate fruit of a Śrāvaka.

31. To leave mundane filth behind and attain the clear Dharma-eye is to achieve the fruit of a Stream-enterer, the first fruit of a Śrāvaka.

32. Literally, "When one does not remember and think, they do not arise."

33. Discipline, meditation, wisdom, liberation, and the knowledge and awareness derived from liberation are called 'the five factors and the Dharma-body'.

34. The Chinese word *hsiang* (想) is here rendered as 'thought', which is not an altogether satisfactory translation. Other renderings have difficulties, too, however. *Hsiang* seems to contain many meanings; here, in this context, it denotes thoughts, concepts, notions, ideas, etc., a broad range of mental activities.

35. Alternate translation: "We are subdued because we realize that the body has no definite nature and the mind does not act." (W.H.)

36. Shih Hu's translation reads:

> "When will you enter nirvāṇa?"
>
> The monks said, "When the Tathāgata enters nirvāṇa, we will then enter nirvāṇa." (Taishō 352, p. 215)

37. This can also be translated, "We are unimpededly liberated." (Y.T.L.)

21 無盡慧菩薩會

Dialogue With Bodhisattva Infinite Wisdom

Thus have I heard. Once the Buddha was dwelling near Rājagṛha on Mount Gṛdhrakūṭa, together with an assembly of twelve hundred fifty monks. There were also ten thousand Bodhisattva-Mahāsattvas present, among whom were Bodhisattva Wisdom Banner, Bodhisattva Dharma Banner, Bodhisattva Moon Banner, Bodhisattva Sun Banner, and Bodhisattva Boundless Banner; sixteen lay Bodhisattvas, with Bhadrapāla foremost; sixty Bodhisattva-Mahāsattvas of incomparable mind, with Mañjuśrī foremost; all the Bodhisattva-Mahāsattvas of the Worthy Kalpa, with Bodhisattva Maitreya foremost; and sixty thousand other Bodhisattva-Mahāsattvas, with Bodhisattva Infinite Wisdom foremost.

At that time, Bodhisattva Infinite Wisdom rose from his seat, uncovered his right shoulder, knelt upon his right knee, faced the Buddha with palms joined, and paid homage to him by bowing down with his head at the Buddha's feet. He then scattered precious flowers around the Buddha as an offering and said, "The World-Honored One speaks of bodhi-mind [*bodhicitta*]. By what principle do you speak of it? What are the ways in which a Bodhisattva achieves bodhi-mind? What is bodhi-mind? In bodhi, the mind is inapprehensible; in the mind, bodhi is also inapprehensible. Apart from bodhi, the mind is inapprehensible; apart from the mind, bodhi is also inapprehensible. Bodhi is formless, signless, and inexpressible; the mind is also formless, signless, and not demonstrable; thus, too, are sentient beings. None of the three is apprehensible. World-Honored One, since all dharmas are such, by what principle should we cultivate ourselves?"

The Buddha said, "Good man, listen to me attentively. The bodhi I speak of has intrinsically no name or description. Why? Because in bodhi, name and description are inapprehensible. The same is true of the mind and sentient beings. Such an understanding is called bodhi-mind.

Sūtra 45, Taishō 310, pp. 648–650; translated into Chinese by Bodhiruci.

"Bodhi has nothing to do with the past, present, or future. The mind and sentient beings also have nothing to do with the past, present, or future. He who understands this is called a Bodhisattva. However, in Bodhisattvahood, too, there is nothing apprehensible.

"One who realizes that all dharmas are inapprehensible is said to have attained bodhi-mind. An Arhat who has attained Arhatship has actually attained nothing; it is only to follow convention that he is said to have attained Arhatship.

"All dharmas are inapprehensible, and bodhi-mind is no exception. To guide novice Bodhisattvas, bodhi-mind is mentioned, but there is neither mind nor the term 'mind' in all this, neither bodhi nor the term 'bodhi,' neither sentient beings nor the term 'sentient beings,' neither Śrāvakas nor the term 'Śrāvakas,' neither Pratyekabuddhas nor the term 'Pratyekabuddhas,' neither Bodhisattvas nor the term 'Bodhisattvas,' neither Tathāgatas nor the term 'Tathāgatas,' neither the conditioned nor the term 'the conditioned,' neither the unconditioned nor the term 'the unconditioned,' neither attainment at present nor attainment in the future.

"Nevertheless, good man, I will use words as a means of expression and explain to you [the ten ways to generate bodhi-mind]:

"First is the vow to be foremost in the cultivation of extensive good roots, just as Mount Sumeru towers above everything else. This is the basis of the pāramitā of giving.

"Second is the vow to establish all one's undertakings firmly, just as the great earth anchors all things. This is the basis of the pāramitā of discipline.

"Third is the vow to have a strong will to bear all afflictions with courage and ease, just as an awesome lion fearlessly subdues all beasts. This is the basis of the pāramitā of patience.

"Fourth is the vow to have overwhelming power to conquer defilements, just as Nārāyaṇa vanquishes his opponents. This is the basis of the pāramitā of vigor.

"Fifth is the vow to cultivate virtues and develop all kinds of good roots, which will blossom like flowering pārijāta and kovidāra trees. This is the basis of the pāramitā of meditation.

"Sixth is the vow to eradicate ignorance and delusion, just as the boundless light of the sun dispels darkness. This is the basis of the pāramitā of wisdom.

"Seventh is the vow to consummate all meritorious aspirations and all glories, so that one can deliver people from dangers and disasters, like a wealthy, [benevolent] merchant who uses his resources skillfully. This is the basis of the pāramitā of ingenuity.

"Eighth is the vow to overcome all obstacles, and thus acquire a mind as perfectly peaceful and pure as a clear, full moon. This is the basis of the pāramitā of power.

"Ninth is the vow to adorn and purify all beings and all Buddha-lands, to perform all wholesome deeds, and to succeed in whatever one does, just as a poor man who acquires inexhaustible treasures can fulfil all his wishes. This is the basis of the pāramitā of volition.

"Tenth is the vow to acquire blessings and knowledge as boundless as space, and to master all dharmas, like an anointed universal monarch [who is master of the world]. This is the basis of the pāramitā of knowledge.

"Good man, one who succeeds in cultivating these ten ways to generate bodhi-mind is called a Bodhisattva, a pre-eminent being, a being free of hindrance, not an inferior being. Yet, since the reality of things is inapprehensible, there is actually neither sentient being nor mind nor bodhi in all this.

"Furthermore, good man, a Bodhisattva who practices the pāramitā of giving regards ten things as foremost:

(1) the root of faith;[1]
(2) the power of faith;
(3) aspiration;
(4) ever-increasing aspiration;
(5) benefiting sentient beings;
(6) great kindness;
(7) great compassion;
(8) the practice of the four inducements;
(9) love for the Buddha-Dharma; and
(10) the quest for all-knowing wisdom.

These are the ten.

"Good man, a Bodhisattva who practices the pāramitā of discipline regards ten things as foremost:

(1) keeping his bodily actions pure and clean;
(2) keeping his verbal actions pure and clean;
(3) keeping his mental actions pure and clean;
(4) not bearing grudges or ill will;
(5) purification and abolition of the miserable planes of existence;
(6) avoiding the eight adversities;
(7) transcending the stages of Śrāvakas and Pratyekabuddhas;
(8) abiding securely in the Buddha's merits;
(9) fulfillment of all wishes; and
(10) fulfillment of his great vows.

These are the ten.

"Good man, a Bodhisattva who practices the pāramitā of patience regards ten things as foremost:

(1) abandoning hatred;
(2) disregarding his own body;
(3) disregarding his own life;
(4) belief in and understanding of [the Dharma];
(5) bringing sentient beings to maturity;
(6) the power of kindness;

(7) the realization of compliance with the Dharma;
(8) the realization of the profound Dharma;
(9) the vast, supreme patience; and
(10) dispelling the darkness of ignorance.

These are the ten.

"Good man, a Bodhisattva who practices the pāramitā of vigor regards ten things as foremost:

(1) acting in conformity with sentient beings;
(2) always rejoicing over others' [meritorious] actions, words, and thoughts;
(3) never being indolent;
(4) devoting himself to progress;
(5) cultivating right effort;
(6) cultivating the [four] mindfulnesses;
(7) destroying afflictions, the enemies;
(8) observing all dharmas;
(9) bringing sentient beings to maturity; and
(10) pursuing all-knowing wisdom.

These are the ten.

"Good man, a Bodhisattva who practices the pāramitā of meditation regards ten things as foremost:

(1) abiding securely in wholesome dharmas;
(2) fixing the mind on one object;
(3) attaining poise by fixing the mind on one object;
(4) right concentration;
(5) liberation through dhyāna;
(6) the root of concentration;[2]
(7) the power of concentration;
(8) the destruction of afflictions, the enemies;
(9) the perfection of all dhyānas;[3]
(10) the samādhi that protects the Dharma.

These are the ten.

"Good man, a Bodhisattva who practices the pāramitā of wisdom regards ten things as foremost:

(1) skillful observation of the [five] aggregates;
(2) skillful observation of the [eighteen] elements and [twelve] entrances;
(3) right view;
(4) right mindfulness;
(5) thoroughly understanding the [four] noble truths;
(6) abandoning wrong views;
(7) the root of wisdom;

(8) the Realization of the Nonarising of Dharmas;
(9) the power of wisdom; and
(10) unimpeded knowledge.

These are the ten.

"Good man, a Bodhisattva who practices the pāramitā of ingenuity regards ten things as foremost:

(1) penetrating the mentalities and desires of sentient beings;
(2) strengthening sentient beings with his powers;
(3) great kindness and great compassion;
(4) untiringly bringing sentient beings to maturity;
(5) rejecting the states of the Śrāvaka and Pratyekabuddha;
(6) superior knowledge and views;
(7) cultivating all the pāramitās;
(8) seeing all dharmas as they really are;
(9) acquiring the inconceivable powers; and
(10) [attaining] the state of nonregression.

These are the ten.

"Good man, a Bodhisattva who practices the pāramitā of power regards ten things as foremost:

(1) knowing the jungle of all beings' mentalities;
(2) knowing the jungle of all beings' defiled activities;
(3) knowing the jungle of all beings' activities of aspiration and superior understanding;
(4) knowing the jungle of all beings' sensuous activities;
(5) knowing the jungle of all beings' activities of the [eighteen] elements;
(6) knowing the jungle of the secondary defiled activities[4] of all beings;
(7) knowing the jungle of all beings' activities in saṁsāra;
(8) knowing the jungle of all beings' karmic results from activities in the past, present, and future;
(9) knowing the jungle of all beings' defiled habits; and
(10) tirelessly bringing to maturity sentient beings with their jungle-like capacities.[5]

These are the ten.

"Good man, a Bodhisattva who practices the pāramitā of volition regards ten things as foremost:

(1) knowing that no dharma arises;
(2) knowing that all dharmas are formless;
(3) knowing that no dharma ceases;
(4) knowing that there are no dharmas;
(5) being attached to nothing;

(6) knowing that no dharma comes [into being];
(7) knowing that no dharma goes [into extinction];
(8) knowing that all dharmas are devoid of self-nature;
(9) knowing that all dharmas are equal, without a beginning, middle, or end; and
(10) not differentiating the beginning, middle, or end of any dharma.

These are the ten.

"Good man, a Bodhisattva who practices the pāramitā of knowledge regards ten things as foremost:

(1) skillful understanding and analysis of all dharmas;
(2) skillful perfection of white [i.e., wholesome] dharmas;
(3) accumulating the numerous spiritual provisions of a Bodhisattva;
(4) gathering an abundant provision of blessed deeds and knowledge;
(5) perfecting great compassion;
(6) entering all different worlds;
(7) understanding the defiled activities of all sentient beings;
(8) exerting himself to enter the Tathāgata's state;
(9) seeking to enter the excellent states of possessing the ten powers, the [four] fearlessnesses, and the [eighteen] unique qualities of a Buddha; and
(10) ascending to the throne of an Anointed One[6] and achieving the supreme qualities of an All-Knowing One.

These are the ten.

"Good man, when Bodhisattva-Mahāsattvas practice the ten pāramitās, they regard the ten things in each category as foremost.

"Furthermore, good man, what are the meanings [and functions] of the pāramitās? [They are to cause one:]

to recognize clearly the practices that surpass those of Śrāvakas and Pratyekabuddhas;
to recognize clearly the vast, perfect wisdom of the Tathāgatas;
to be detached from both conditioned and unconditioned dharmas;
to understand the undesirability of saṁsāra as it really is;
to enlighten those who are not yet enlightened;
to acquire the inexhaustible Dharma-treasury of the Tathāgata;
to obtain unhindered liberation;
to save sentient beings by giving;
to fulfill his original vows by discipline;
to obtain all the majestic auspicious signs through patience;
to fathom the ultimate depth of all the Buddha's teachings by vigor;
to generate the four immeasurables by meditation;
to eradicate all afflictions by wisdom;
to accumulate the Buddha's teachings by ingenuity;

to fulfill the Buddha's teachings by volition;
to awaken sentient beings' pure faith by power;
to obtain the all-knowing wisdom of the Tathāgata by knowledge;
to acquire the Realization of the Nonarising of Dharmas;
to attain the state of nonregression;
to purify a Buddha-land;
to bring sentient beings to maturity;
to consummate at the bodhi-site the wisdom of all Tathāgatas;
to vanquish all demons;
to gain command of the four bases of miraculous powers;
to abide neither in saṁsāra nor in nirvāṇa;
to transcend all the virtues of Śrāvakas, Pratyekabuddhas, and Bodhisattvas;
to overcome all heterodox doctrines;
to achieve the ten powers, the four fearlessnesses, and the [eighteen] unique qualities of the Buddha;
to realize supreme enlightenment; and
to turn the twelve kinds of Dharma wheels.[7]

All these are the meanings [and functions] of the pāramitās.

"Furthermore, good man, when a Bodhisattva-Mahāsattva is about to abide in the Stage of Great Joy—the first stage of Bodhisattva development—he will first have a vision of all the hundreds of thousands of millions of myriads of hidden treasures in the billion-world universe.

"When a Bodhisattva is about to abide in the Stage of Stainless Purity—the second stage—he will first have a vision of a billion-world universe with its ground as flat as one's palm and with pure adornments of innumerable hundreds of thousands of millions of myriads of precious lotus flowers.

"When a Bodhisattva is about to abide in the Stage of Illumination—the third stage—he will first have a vision of himself clad in armor and brandishing a cudgel, repressing enemies dauntlessly and resolutely.

"When a Bodhisattva is about to abide in the Stage of Radiant Flames—the fourth stage—he will first have a vision of all kinds of rare flowers being scattered over the ground by the wind from the four quarters.

"When a Bodhisattva is about to abide in the Stage of Invincible Strength—the fifth stage—he will first have a vision of women with garlands of atimuktaka, vārṣika, and campaka flowers on their heads and various adornments on their bodies.

"When a Bodhisattva is about to abide in the Stage of Direct Presence—the sixth stage—he will first have a vision of a beautiful pond filled with pure, lucid water having eight merits. Gold sand will form the bottom of the pond, four jewelled flights of steps will be on its sides, and it will be adorned with blue, red, white, and variously colored lotus flowers. He will see himself playing in this pond.

"When a Bodhisattva is about to abide in the Far-Reaching Stage—the seventh stage—he will first have a vision of hells to his left and right, and will see himself passing through them unharmed.

"When a Bodhisattva is about to abide in the Stage of Immovable Steadfastness—the eighth stage—he will first have a vision of himself bearing the signs of a lion king on his shoulders, frightening all beasts.

"When a Bodhisattva is about to abide in the Stage of Meritorious Wisdom—the ninth stage—he will first have a vision of himself as a universal monarch teaching the true Dharma, surrounded by innumerable hundreds of thousands of millions of myriads of kings, and shaded by various clean, white, jewelled canopies.

"When a Bodhisattva is about to abide in the Stage of the Dharma-Cloud—the tenth stage—he will first have a vision of himself [with a body] the color of genuine gold, complete with all the thirty-two auspicious signs of a Tathāgata, and haloed with a circle of light several feet in radius.[8] He will be seated comfortably on a broad, high lion-throne, and surrounded by innumerable hundreds of thousands of millions of myriads of gods from the Brahmā Heaven, who will respectfully make offerings to him and listen to his preaching of the Dharma.

"Good man, due to the power of samādhi, a Bodhisattva-Mahāsattva will have each of these visions respectively prior to his attainment of each of the ten stages.

"Furthermore, good man, a Bodhisattva:

in the first stage perfects the pāramitā of giving;
in the second stage, the pāramitā of discipline;
in the third stage, the pāramitā of patience;
in the fourth stage, the pāramitā of vigor;
in the fifth stage, the pāramitā of meditation;
in the sixth stage, the pāramitā of wisdom;
in the seventh stage, the pāramitā of ingenuity;
in the eighth stage, the pāramitā of power;
in the ninth stage, the pāramitā of volition; and
in the tenth stage, the pāramitā of knowledge.

"Furthermore, good man, a Bodhisattva who brings forth:

the first vow [in generating bodhi-mind] will attain the Treasure-Revealing Samādhi;
the second vow, the Well-Abiding Samādhi;
the third vow, the Immovable Samādhi;
the fourth vow, the Nonregressing Samādhi;
the fifth vow, the Precious Flower Samādhi;
the sixth vow, the Sunlight Samādhi;
the seventh vow, the Samādhi of the Realization of All Meanings;
the eighth vow, the Samādhi of the Torch of Wisdom;

the ninth vow, the Samādhi of Direct Realization of the Buddha-Dharma; and
the tenth vow, the Śūraṁgama Samādhi.[9]

"Furthermore, good man, a Bodhisattva attains:

the Dhāraṇī of Superior Blessings in the first stage;
the Unsurpassable Dhāraṇī in the second stage;
the Well-Abiding Dhāraṇī in the third stage;
the Indestructible Dhāraṇī in the fourth stage;
the Stainless Dhāraṇī in the fifth stage;
the Dhāraṇī of the Wheel of Wisdom-Light in the sixth stage;
the Superb Deed Dhāraṇī in the seventh stage;
the Pure Discernment Dhāraṇī in the eighth stage;
the Dhāraṇī of the Manifestation of Boundless Doctrines in the ninth stage; and
the Inexhaustible Dharma Store Dhāraṇī in the tenth stage."

At that time, in the assembly, a god named Lion Banner of Unimpeded Light rose from his seat, bared his right shoulder, knelt upon his right knee, faced the Buddha with palms joined, and said, "How wonderful, World-Honored One! How wonderful, Well-Gone One! This doctrine is so profound and extensive that it comprises all the teachings of the Buddhas."

Thereupon, the Buddha told Lion Banner of Unimpeded Light, "So it is, so it is, as you have said. Good man, if a Bodhisattva can listen to and accept this doctrine, even temporarily, he or she will never regress from the pursuit of supreme enlightenment. Why? That good man or good woman has planted and matured various roots of virtue; therefore, he or she is impressed by the sūtra upon hearing it.

"Good man, if men or women hear this sūtra, all the good roots they have planted will be purified, and consequently they will not fail to see the Buddha, listen to the Dharma, make offerings to the Saṁgha, and bring sentient beings to maturity. They will not be separated from:

the Dhāraṇī of the Ocean Seal;
the Dhāraṇī of Boundless Manifestations;
the Dhāraṇī of Penetrating the Desires and Mentalities of Sentient Beings;
the Dhāraṇī of the Banner of Pure Sunlight;
the Dhāraṇī of the Banner of Stainless Moonlight;
the Dhāraṇī of Breaking All Bonds;
the Dhāraṇī of Destroying Boundless Afflictions as Adamant as a Diamond Mountain;
the Dhāraṇī of Understanding Words Expressing the Equality of the Dharma-Nature;
the Dhāraṇī of Understanding the Language and Voice of Reality;

the Dhāraṇī Imprinted by the Seal of Boundless Purity as Revealed by Emptiness; and
the Dhāraṇī of Achieving and Manifesting the Boundless Buddha-Body.

"Good man, if a Bodhisattva achieves these dhāraṇīs, he will then be able to transform himself into Buddha-forms to teach sentient beings in all the lands of the ten directions. However, in light of the Dharma-nature, he neither comes nor goes, nor does he teach any sentient beings. He does not cling to the words he uses to teach the Dharma. He is impartial and steadfast. Although he manifests a body that lives and dies, in reality nothing ever arises or ceases; not a single dharma comes or goes. He realizes that all phenomena are originally quiescent, and thus abides securely in the Buddha-Dharma. Why? Because he makes no distinctions among dharmas."

During the preaching of this doctrine, thirty thousand Bodhisattvas in the assembly achieved the Realization of the Nonarising of Dharmas; innumerable Bodhisattvas attained the state of nonregression from the pursuit of supreme enlightenment; innumerable sentient beings resolved to seek enlightenment; and innumerable monks attained the clear Dharma-eye.

When the Buddha finished teaching this sūtra, Bodhisattva Infinite Wisdom and the monks, gods, humans, asuras, gandharvas, and so on were all jubilant. They accepted it with faith, and began to practice it with veneration.

NOTES

1. The root of faith is one of the five roots. See Numerical Glossary.

2. The root of concentration is another of the five roots.

3. We render the Chinese characters 定聚 as 'all dhyānas'. 定聚 usually means 'the group of people decided on enlightenment', but this does not suit the context.

4. The activities resulting from the secondary defilements. Desire, hatred, ignorance, arrogance, doubt, and wrong views are the primary defilements. All other unwholesome mentalities, such as jealousy, vexation, and miserliness, are secondary defilements.

5. Literally, "tirelessly ripening the jungle-like capacities of sentient beings."

6. One who has reached the tenth stage of Bodhisattvahood, and is about to attain Buddhahood.

7. We are not sure of the identity of the twelve kinds of Dharma wheels; they may refer to the threefold formula of the four noble truths.

8. The Chinese text reads 圓光一尋. 尋 is a measure of eight Chinese feet. The original Sanskrit for this phrase is not known to us. It is also ambiguous whether the halo is eight feet in diameter or in radius. We expediently translate it as 'several feet'.

9. Śūraṁgama means 'heroic', 'durable', or 'all things completed'. This samādhi is attained by a Buddha or advanced Bodhisattva.

VIII

On Skillful Means

22 大乘方便會

On the Pāramitā of Ingenuity

I

Thus have I heard. Once the Buddha was dwelling near Śrāvastī, in the Garden of Anāthapiṇḍada in the Jeta Grove, accompanied by eight thousand monks, all of whom were great Śrāvakas in the learning stage or in the stage beyond learning; and by twelve thousand Bodhisattva-Mahāsattvas known to all, who had achieved miraculous powers, dhāraṇīs, unhindered eloquence, the realization of dharmas, and countless merits.

At that time, the Tathāgata emerged from samādhi and was ready to teach the Dharma to the incalculable hundreds of thousands of [millions of] billions of sentient beings who surrounded him respectfully. Then, in the assembly, a Bodhisattva-Mahāsattva named Superior Wisdom rose from his seat, bared his right shoulder, knelt on his right knee, joined his palms toward the Buddha, and said, "World-Honored One, I wish to ask a question. May you be so kind as to allow me to do so. I dare not bring up my question without the permission of the Buddha."

The Buddha told Bodhisattva Superior Wisdom, "Good man, you may inquire as you like. I will answer you and resolve all your doubts."

Then Bodhisattva Superior Wisdom asked the Buddha, "World-Honored One, regarding ingenuity, what is the ingenuity of a Bodhisattva? World-Honored One, how does a Bodhisattva-Mahāsattva practice ingenuity?"

After Bodhisattva Superior Wisdom had asked his question, the Buddha praised him, saying, "Excellent! It is excellent, good man, that for the sake of Bodhisattva-Mahāsattvas, you ask about the meaning of ingenuity. This will bene-

Sūtra 38, Taishō 310, pp. 594–607; translated into Chinese by Nandi.

fit, comfort, and gladden many sentient beings. Good man, in order to show compassion for gods and humans, to bring them peace, happiness, and benefit, and to help them obtain the wisdom of the future Bodhisattvas and the Buddha-Dharmas of the past, present, and future, I will now explain this to you. Listen attentively and think carefully about it."

Bodhisattva Superior Wisdom obeyed and listened.

The Buddha said, "Good man, a Bodhisattva who practices ingenuity can use even a handful of food as alms for all sentient beings.[1] Why? When a Bodhisattva who practices ingenuity gives a handful of food to any single sentient being, even an animal, he does so with an aspiration for all-knowing wisdom, and vows to share the merit of this giving with all sentient beings by dedicating it to the [universal] attainment of supreme enlightenment. Because of these two—his seeking all-knowing wisdom and his skillful vow—he attracts sentient beings into his following. Good man, this is the ingenuity practiced by a Bodhisattva-Mahāsattva.

"Furthermore, good man, when a Bodhisattva-Mahāsattva who practices ingenuity sees others practice giving, he rejoices and wishes to share with all sentient beings this merit[2] of sympathetic joy by dedicating it to the [universal] attainment of supreme enlightenment. He also hopes that givers and recipients will not be apart from the aspiration for all-knowing wisdom,[3] even if the recipients are Śrāvakas or Pratyekabuddhas. This is the ingenuity practiced by a Bodhisattva-Mahāsattva.

"Moreover, good man, when a Bodhisattva-Mahāsattva who practices ingenuity sees flowers, trees, or any kind of incense which do not belong to anyone in any of the worlds of the ten directions, he will gather them up and offer them to Buddhas. When he sees flowers, trees, or any kind of incense which once belonged to someone but now have been blown away by the wind, he will gather them up and offer them to the Buddhas in the worlds of the ten directions. He cultivates these good roots in order to cause himself and all other sentient beings to have the aspiration for all-knowing wisdom. Because of this good root, he will achieve immeasurable discipline, meditation, wisdom, liberation, and the knowledge and awareness derived from liberation.[4] This is the ingenuity practiced by a Bodhisattva-Mahāsattva.

"Furthermore, good man, when a Bodhisattva-Mahāsattva who practices ingenuity sees sentient beings in any of the worlds in the ten directions enjoy blissful karmic results, he will think: 'May all sentient beings attain the bliss of all-knowing wisdom!' When he sees sentient beings in any of the worlds of the ten directions suffer from painful karmic results, he will repent their transgressions on their behalf and adorn himself with this great vow: 'I will undergo all the sentient beings' sufferings in their stead, and make them happy.' By this good root, he hopes to achieve all-knowing wisdom and to relieve the afflictions of all sentient beings. Because of this, [he and all those sentient beings] will be completely free from all suffering and can enjoy pure bliss. This is the ingenuity practiced by a Bodhisattva-Mahāsattva.

"Moreover, good man, when a Bodhisattva-Mahāsattva who practices ingenuity pays homage to one Buddha, respects him, makes offerings to him, honors him, or praises him, the Bodhisattva-Mahāsattva will think: 'All Tathāgatas share the same dharmadhātu and Dharma-body; they share the same discipline, meditation, wisdom, liberation, and the knowledge and awareness derived from liberation.' With this in mind, he will know that to pay homage to one Buddha, respect him, make offerings to him, honor him, or praise him is to do so to all Buddhas. For this reason, he can make offerings[5] in this way to all the Buddhas in the worlds of the ten directions. This is the ingenuity practiced by a Bodhisattva-Mahāsattva.

"Furthermore, good man, a Bodhisattva-Mahāsattva who practices ingenuity should not feel inferior if he is slow to learn. Even if he is conversant with only a four-line stanza, he should think: 'If one understands the meaning of one four-line stanza, he understands all Buddha-Dharmas, because all Buddha-Dharmas are comprised in the meaning of this stanza.' When he thoroughly knows this, he will spare no effort to explain the stanza to others widely, out of kindness and compassion, whether he is in a city or in a village. He does so without seeking material gains, reputation, or praise. He will vow: 'I will cause others to hear this four-line stanza.' By this good root and skillful vow, he will cause all sentient beings to be as well-learned as Ānanda and to acquire the eloquence of a Tathāgata. This is the ingenuity practiced by a Bodhisattva-Mahāsattva.

"Furthermore, good man, if a Bodhisattva-Mahāsattva who practices ingenuity is born in such a poor family that he has to beg for food, and if he obtains only a handful of food and gives it to a monk, he will not be ashamed of this. Instead, he will think: 'Just as the Buddha says, "To develop a great mind is better than to give material gifts." Although I give so little, I give it with an aspiration for all-knowing wisdom, hoping that I shall, by this good root, achieve all-knowing wisdom and cause all sentient beings to acquire precious hands like the Tathāgata's.' For this reason, he is fully endowed with the blessings of giving, discipline, and meditation. This is the ingenuity practiced by a Bodhisattva-Mahāsattva.

"Furthermore, good man, when a Bodhisattva-Mahāsattva who practices ingenuity sees Śrāvakas and Pratyekabuddhas obtain many offerings and much profit, respect, and praise, he will console himself with this thought: 'Because there are Bodhisattvas there are Tathāgatas, and because there are Tathāgatas there are Śrāvakas and Pratyekabuddhas.[6] Although Śrāvakas and Pratyekabuddhas acquire profit and offerings, I am still superior to them. What they eat belongs to my father;[7] why should I covet it?' This is the ingenuity practiced by a Bodhisattva-Mahāsattva.

"Furthermore, good man, a Bodhisattva-Mahāsattva who practices ingenuity can cultivate all the six pāramitās while practicing [the pāramitā of] giving. How? Good man, a Bodhisattva who practices ingenuity will not be miserly but will be generous when he sees a beggar. This is the pāramitā of giving.

"He himself keeps the precepts and makes offerings to those who keep the precepts; he persuades those who have broken the precepts to observe the precepts, and then bestows offerings upon them. This is the pāramitā of discipline.[8]

"He rids himself of hatred, practices kindness and compassion, and, with an undefiled mind, benefits sentient beings by impartially giving them alms. This is the pāramitā of patience.

"While giving food and drink and medicine, he is full of vigor in mind and body, whether he is going or coming, advancing or stopping, bending or stretching, looking up or looking down. This is the pāramitā of vigor.

"After he has practiced giving, his mind becomes tranquil, cheerful, and undistracted. This is the pāramitā of meditation.

"After giving, he analyzes these matters: Who is the giver? Who is the recipient? Who is the one who receives the karmic results? After contemplating these, he finds that there is no giver, no recipient, and no one who will receive the karmic results. This is the pāramitā of wisdom.

"Good man, a Bodhisattva-Mahāsattva who cultivates ingenuity can in this way fulfill the six pāramitās when he practices giving."

Then, Bodhisattva Superior Wisdom said to the Buddha, "Marvelous, World-Honored One! A Bodhisattva-Mahāsattva who practices giving with ingenuity is able to acquire all Buddha-Dharmas and attract all sentient beings into his following by his giving."

The Buddha told Bodhisattva Superior Wisdom, "Good man, it is just as you say. Even when a Bodhisattva-Mahāsattva who practices ingenuity gives only a little, he obtains immeasurable, countless blessings and merits by virtue of his ingenuity."

The Buddha told Bodhisattva Superior Wisdom further, "Good man, even when a Bodhisattva-Mahāsattva has reached the stage of nonregression, he still practices giving skillfully. This is the ingenuity practiced by a Bodhisattva.

"Good man, sometimes bad people may urge a Bodhisattva [to forsake sentient beings], saying, 'Why do you stay in saṁsāra for such a long time? You may enter nirvāṇa early, in this life.' The Bodhisattva should leave them as soon as he hears this, thinking, 'I have adorned myself with the great vow to teach and convert all sentient beings, and these people are trying to stop me. If I do not stay in saṁsāra, how can I teach and convert incalculable numbers of sentient beings?"

Bodhisattva Superior Wisdom asked the Buddha, "World-Honored One, what if a sentient being commits the four heavy transgressions[9] because of erroneous thoughts?"

The Buddha told Bodhisattva Superior Wisdom, "Good man, if a Bodhisattva who is a monk commits the four heavy transgressions because of erroneous thoughts, [another] Bodhisattva well versed in ingenuity can purge him of all his sins. I also say that [actually] no one commits transgressions or receives karmic results."[10]

Bodhisattva Superior Wisdom asked the Buddha, "World-Honored One, when does a Bodhisattva commit transgressions?"

The Buddha replied to Bodhisattva Superior Wisdom, "Good man, if a Bodhisattva harbors the view of the Dharma held by Śrāvakas and Pratyekabuddhas, then he commits heavy transgressions, even if he keeps the Prātimokṣa precepts, has eaten only fruits and grass for hundreds of thousands of kalpas,[11] and is able to tolerate the good and bad words uttered by sentient beings. Good man, just as Śrāvakas cannot enter nirvāṇa in this life if they commit heavy transgressions, so Bodhisattvas cannot attain supreme enlightenment if they continue, without repentance, to harbor the view of Dharma held by Śrāvakas and Pratyekabuddhas. [As long as they think thus,] it is absolutely impossible for such Bodhisattvas to acquire the Buddha-Dharma."

Then the Venerable Ānanda said to the Buddha, "World-Honored One, this morning when I begged for food from door to door in Śrāvastī, I saw Bodhisattva King Honored by All sit on the same couch with a woman."

As soon as Ānanda uttered these words, quakes of six kinds shook the great earth. From the assembly Bodhisattva King Honored by All ascended in midair to the height of seven palm trees one above another and asked Ānanda, "Venerable one, how can an offender stay in midair? Ānanda, you may ask the World-Honored One this: 'What is a transgression, and what is not a transgression?'"

Then, Ānanda, kneeling on his right knee and clasping the Buddha's feet with his hands, said woefully, "World-Honored One, now I repent my fault: I slandered such a great giant,[12] saying he was an offender; I found fault with this great Bodhisattva. World-Honored One, now I repent my wrongdoing. May the World-Honored One accept my sincere repentance!"

The Buddha told Ānanda, "You should not find fault with great Bodhisattvas of the Mahāyāna. Ānanda, you Śrāvakas practice in a secluded place the meditation leading to ultimate quiescence and cut off all passions without hindrance. However, Ānanda, a Bodhisattva who practices ingenuity has achieved a mind so inclined to all-knowing wisdom that, though he may even amuse himself with maids of honor in a palace, he will not be affected by demons' influences and various hindrances, and he will attain supreme enlightenment. Why? Because, Ānanda, when enjoying pleasures with sentient beings, the Bodhisattvas who practice ingenuity, without exception, all persuade them to pursue supreme enlightenment through the Three Jewels. Ānanda, as long as good men and good women who learn the Mahāyāna are not apart from the aspiration for all-knowing wisdom, they can amuse themselves with the five delightful sensuous pleasures when they encounter them.[13] Ānanda, you should think: 'Such Bodhisattvas [cultivate] the root that leads to Tathāgatahood.'"

The Buddha said to Ānanda further, "Now, listen attentively. Why did Bodhisattva-Mahāsattva King Honored by All sit on a couch with that woman? Ānanda, that woman has been the wife of Bodhisattva King Honored by All for five hundred lifetimes. Because of past habit, she was attached to Bodhisattva King Honored by All and could not tear herself away from him whenever she saw him. Bodhisattva King Honored by All has awesome virtues and handsome features because of the power of his discipline. At the sight of him, that woman was overwhelmed with joy. Alone, in a secluded place, she thought, 'If Bodhisattva King Honored by All can sit on the same couch with me, I shall bring forth bodhicitta.'

"Ānanda, at that time, Bodhisattva King Honored by All read that woman's mind. On the following morning, clad in a monastic robe and holding a bowl in his hands, he begged for food from door to door in Śrāvastī. When he arrived at that woman's house, he entered it, thinking at once: 'The inner earth-element and the outer earth-element are one and the same.'[14] He took the woman's hand and sat together with her on the couch with a mind [as steady] as the earth. Seated on the couch, Bodhisattva King Honored by All spoke in verse:

'The Tathāgata disapproves of
Indulgence in desires.
One who is free from desires and lust
Can become a Teacher of Gods and Humans.'"

The Buddha said to Ānanda, "Hearing the verse, that woman was overwhelmed with joy. Immediately, she rose from her seat, prostrated herself with her head at the feet of Bodhisattva King Honored by All, and spoke in verse:

'I will uproot my lust and desires,
Which the Buddhas decry;
For one who is free from desires and lust
Can become a Teacher of Gods and Humans.'

"Having spoken this verse, she said: 'I should repent having had an improper desire.' Right then, she engendered a proper desire: she brought forth bodhicitta for the benefit of all sentient beings."

The Buddha told Ānanda, "After Bodhisattva King Honored by All had influenced that woman to bring forth bodhicitta, he rose from his seat and left. Ānanda, see what blissful results that woman will receive from her devotion: I, as an All-Knowing One, predict that the woman will change from a female into a male when her present life ends, and that she will make offerings to incalculable hundreds of thousands of Buddhas for ninety-nine kalpas. After perfecting all Buddha-Dharmas, she will become a Buddha named Tathāgata Free of Stain and Defilement, the Worthy One, the All-Knowing One. When that Buddha attains the path,[15] not a single person [in his world] will cherish nonvirtuous intentions. Ānanda, you should know that when a Bodhisattva who practices ingenuity attracts people into his following, they will never fall to the three miserable planes of existence."

Thereupon, Bodhisattva King Honored by All descended from midair, bowed down with his head at the Buddha's feet, and said to the Buddha, "World-Honored One, suppose, out of great compassion for a person and in order to cause him to accumulate wholesome dharmas, a Bodhisattva who practices ingenuity apparently or actually commits misdeeds serious enough for him to fall to the great hells and remain there for hundreds of thousands of kalpas. Then, his virtuous vow not to forsake a single person would enable him to bear all the evils and sufferings of the hells."

Then the World-Honored One praised Bodhisattva King Honored by All, saying, "Excellent, excellent! Good man, a Bodhisattva who has achieved such a compassionate mind commits no heavy transgressions, even if he enjoys the five sensuous pleasures. He is free from all transgressions and from all karmas leading to the miserable planes of existence.

"Good man, I remember that in the past, countless kalpas ago and more, there was a brahmacārin named Constellation. He cultivated pure conduct in a secluded forest for four billion two hundred million years. When he came out of the forest, he entered the city called Ultimate Bliss, and encountered a woman there. At the sight of this handsome brahmacārin, the woman's passion was aroused. She went to him immediately, clasped his feet with her hands, and prostrated herself on the ground.

"Good man, then the brahmacārin asked the woman, 'What do you want, sister?'

"The woman answered, 'I want you, brahmacārin.'

"The brahmacārin said, 'I do not indulge in desire, sister.'

"The woman said, 'If you do not consent to my demand, I shall die.'

"Good man, at that time, the brahmacārin Constellation thought: 'That is not proper for me to do, especially at this time. I have cultivated pure conduct for four billion two hundred million years. How can I destroy it now?'

"Thus, the brahmacārin forced himself to leave her, but after he had walked seven steps away, he felt pity for her and thought, 'I can endure the pain of the hells if I fall to them because of breaking the precepts, but I cannot bear to see this woman suffer so much. I will not let her die for me.'

"Good man, with this thought in mind, the brahmacārin went back to the woman. He took her with his right hand and said, 'Stand up, please. You may do as you like.'

"Good man, the brahmacārin was married to her for twelve years. After that, he left the household life and immediately regained the four immeasurables. He was reborn in the Brahmā Heaven after death.

"Good man, have no doubt. The brahmacārin of that time was no other than myself [in a former life]. That woman was Gopā[16] of today.

"Good man, because at that time I took compassion on that woman who was engulfed in desire, I skipped the suffering of one million aeons of saṁsāra.

"Good man, you see, sentient beings fall to the hells because of their lust and desires, but a Bodhisattva who practices ingenuity is reborn in the Brahmā Heaven [even if he indulges in lust and desire]. This is the ingenuity practiced by a Bodhisattva."

The Buddha told Bodhisattva Superior Wisdom further, "Good man, if

Śāriputra and Mahāmaudgalyāyana had practiced ingenuity, they would not have let [Monk] Untimely fall to the hells.[17] Why? Good man, I remember that in the Era of Krakucchanda Buddha, there was a monk named Undefiled who stayed in a cave in a secluded forest, not far from where five ṛṣis lived. One day, dense clouds suddenly gathered and soon it rained heavily. At that time, a poor girl was caught walking in the heavy rain. Cold, poorly dressed, and frightened, she entered the cave where Monk Undefiled lived. When the rain stopped, Monk Undefiled came out of the cave together with the girl. When the five ṛṣis saw this, their minds became perverted and they said to one another, 'Monk Undefiled is deceptive and crooked. He has committed an impure deed.'

"At that time, knowing the thoughts of the five ṛṣis, Monk Undefiled ascended in midair to the height of seven palm trees one above another. When the five ṛṣis saw Monk Undefiled ascend in midair, they said to one another, 'According to the books and scriptures we have read, a person cannot ascend in midair if he has committed impure deeds, but he can if he has cultivated pure deeds.'

"Then the five ṛṣis threw themselves full-length on the ground before Monk Undefiled, joined their palms, and repented their misdeeds, not daring to hide them."

The Buddha continued to Bodhisattva Superior Wisdom, "Good man, if Monk Undefiled had not resorted to the skillful means of ascending in midair at that time, the five ṛṣis would have fallen bodily to the hells right then. Good man, who was Monk Undefiled? He was no other than Bodhisattva Maitreya [in a former life].

"Good man, now you should know, if Śāriputra and Mahāmaudgalyāyana had resorted to skillful means such as ascending in midair, Monk Untimely would not have fallen to the hells. Good man, now you should know that Śrāvakas and Pratyekabuddhas do not have the ingenuity practiced by Bodhisattva-Mahāsattvas.

"Good man, as an illustration, consider a prostitute. She has sixty-four seductive wiles; for example, to obtain wealth and treasures, she may coax a man into generously giving her his valuables by pretending that she is going to marry him, and then she drives him away without regret when she has obtained the precious objects. Similarly, good man, a Bodhisattva who practices ingenuity can use his skill according to [particular] circumstances; he teaches and converts all sentient beings by manifesting himself in forms they like and by freely giving them everything they need, even his body. For the sake of sentient beings, he delights in creating roots of virtue without expecting any blissful karmic results. As soon as he knows that the sentient beings [he teaches] are cultivating good roots and will not regress, he abandons without the least attachment the five sensuous pleasures which he pretended to enjoy.

"Good man, as an illustration, consider a black bee. Although it enjoys the fragrances of all flowers, it does not think of taking up an abode in or becoming attached to any flower, nor does it take away the petals, stalk, or scent of any flower when it leaves. In like manner, good man, a Bodhisattva-Mahāsattva who practices ingenuity plunges himself into the five sensuous pleasures in order to convert sentient beings, but, seeing that dharmas are impermanent, he does not think the five sensuous pleasures are permanent, and so has no love for them.[18] He hurts neither himself nor others.

"Good man, as an illustration, consider a small seed. When it produces sprouts, it does not lose its original qualities[19] and produce something alien to its nature. Similarly, good man, though a Bodhisattva may have defilements and amuse himself with the five sensuous pleasures, still, because he has the wisdom-seed of emptiness, signlessness, nonaction, and nonself within him, he will not fall to the miserable planes of existence, lose the qualities of his good roots, or regress [from the pursuit of supreme enlightenment].

"Good man, as an illustration, consider a fisherman. He rubs his net with bait and casts it into a deep river; when his wishes are fulfilled, he hauls it out. In the same way, good man, a Bodhisattva who practices ingenuity cultivates his mind with the wisdom of emptiness, signlessness, nonaction, and nonself. He knits a net of this wisdom, rubs it with the bait of aspiration for all-knowing wisdom, and casts it into the filthy mire of the five desires. When his wishes are fulfilled, he hauls it out of the Realm of Desire. At the end of his life he is reborn in the Brahmā Heaven.

"Good man, as an illustration, consider a man well-versed in spells. If he is caught by an official and bound with five cords, he will, by the power of his incantation, soon break the cords and go away at will. In the same way, good man, though a Bodhisattva-Mahāsattva who practices ingenuity joins sentient beings and amuses himself with the five sensuous pleasures, he does so in order to deliver those beings. When his object is attained, he will, by the spell of all-knowing wisdom, break the bondage of the five sensuous pleasures and be reborn in the Brahmā Heaven.

"Good man, as an illustration, consider a fighter, who hides the sharp knife he carries and escorts a group of travellers. None of the travellers know this man's secret stratagem. They despise and pity him, showing no respect, and say to one another, 'He has no weapon and no partner, and is not even strong or powerful. He cannot save even himself from danger; how can he help others? It is absolutely impossible for him to defeat any robber. He will certainly run into trouble.' When a pack of robbers suddenly appears from an uninhabited marsh, the fighter stands ground firmly and at once draws out the hidden knife. With one stroke, he kills all the robbers, and then he again hides the knife he carries. In like manner, good man, a Bodhisattva who practices ingenuity hides well his knife of wisdom and joins sentient beings, amusing himself with the five sensuous pleasures as a skillful means to convert those beings. When people who do not know this to be a skillful means see the Bodhisattva amuse himself with the pleasures, they become defiled in mind, pity him, and think him to be dissipated, saying, 'Such a person cannot save even himself from saṁsāra, let alone all sentient beings. It is absolutely impossible for him to defeat demons.' However, the Bodhisattva is skilled at using ingenuity and the knife of wisdom. When he has attained his object [of converting sentient beings], he will, by the knife of wisdom, eradicate all afflictions and reach a pure Buddha-land where there are no women and no thoughts of desire."

At the time [the Buddha was preaching,] a Bodhisattva named Loving Deed was begging for food from door to door in Śrāvastī, gradually approaching the home of an elder. The elder had a daughter named Increasing Virtue, who lived in a high tower. The maiden took some food and went out toward Bodhisattva Loving Deed as soon as she heard his voice. When she saw the Bodhisattva, she became attached to his handsome appearance and fine voice, and her passion was at once aroused. Burning with desire, she died on the spot, and her bones disintegrated.

Bodhisattva Loving Deed also had sensual craving for Increasing Virtue when he saw her. However, at that very moment, he thought, "What is that? That is attachment. What is that eye [of hers]? What is this eye [of mine]? The eye is insensible by nature and is nothing but a lump of flesh. It neither loves nor knows, neither thinks nor feels, discriminates nothing, and is empty by nature. The same is true of the ear, nose, tongue, body, and mind." He contemplated membranes, skin, blood, flesh, fat, hair, pores, nails, teeth, bones, marrow, sinews, and veins. He contemplated everything from head to foot and found that no [part of the body], internal or external, is worthy of craving, attachment, aversion, or delusion. When he had correctly observed all these dharmas, he was freed from desire and achieved the Realization of the Nonarising of Dharmas.[20] Overwhelmed with joy, he ascended in midair to the height of a palm tree, and circled Śrāvastī seven times.

When the World-Honored One saw Bodhisattva Loving Deed fly unhindered in the air like a king of swans, he asked Ānanda, "Ānanda, do you see Bodhisattva Loving Deed fly unhindered in the air like a king of swans?"

Ānanda answered, "Yes, I do."

The Buddha told Ānanda, "Bodhisattva Loving Deed contemplated the dharmas when his carnal desire was aroused, and at that moment defeated demons. He will turn the Dharma-wheel."

Increasing Virtue was immediately reborn after death as a male in the Heaven of the Thirty-Three. Suddenly, he found himself living in a palace made of the seven treasures, twelve leagues square. He was attended by fourteen thousand celestial maidens. Knowing his previous life, Devaputra Increasing Virtue investigated his past karma, asking himself, "What karma caused my rebirth in this place?" Then he remembered that he had been the daughter of an elder in Śrāvastī, whose carnal desire had been aroused by seeing Bodhisattva Loving Deed. With her desire raging, she had died immediately and changed from a female into a male. Because of this event, she acquired vast miraculous powers.[21]

Then Devaputra Increasing Virtue thought: "I received this result because of my carnal desire [for Bodhisattva Loving Deed]. Now, I should respect him and make offerings to him with a pure mind. It is not fitting for me to enjoy the five [heavenly] sensuous pleasures here first."

With this resolution, he decided to go to see the Tathāgata and Bodhisattva Loving Deed, in order to pay homage and make offerings to them. Therefore, at nightfall he and his retinue came to the place where the Buddha was staying, bearing celestial, fragrant flowers, perfumed ointment, and powdered incense. Illuminating the Jeta Grove with their own lights, they approached the World-Honored One and Bodhisattva Loving Deed. They offered the Buddha the celestial flowers, perfumed ointment, and powdered incense; bowed down with their heads at the Buddha's feet; made three circumambulations to the right of the Buddha, Bodhisattva Loving Deed, and the assembly; and joined their palms toward the Buddha. Then Devaputra Increasing Virtue spoke in verse:

"Inconceivable is the Honored One among gods and humans;
Inconceivable are the Bodhisattva's deeds.
The Dharma of the Tathāgata is inconceivable,
As is the Renowned One himself.

In my previous life, in Śrāvastī,
I was an elder's daughter
Named Increasing Virtue.

I was young and pretty then,
Cherished and protected by my parents.
We never jested at the Tathāgata, the World-Honored One.

One day, the Buddha's son[22] Loving Deed,
Who had great, awesome virtue,
Approached my father's house
While begging for food in Śrāvastī.

I was filled with great joy
When I heard his fine voice.
At once, I took some food
And went out toward Bodhisattva Loving Deed,
Son of the Tathāgata
And cultivator of the great mind.

When I found the Bodhisattva so handsome and elegant,[23]
My mind was defiled with desire for him.
I thought, 'If my desire is not fulfilled,
I shall die instantly.'

I could not utter a word then,
Nor could I give him the food I held in my hand,

For the depths of my heart were burning
With aroused carnal desire.

My body was inflamed with heat,
And thereupon I died.

Within the span of a flash of thought
After my death, I was born
In the Heaven of the Thirty-Three,
Changed from a lowly girl
Into a male god praised by mankind.

A superb, wonderful palace spontaneously appeared,
Full of marvelous, precious treasures.
Fourteen thousand beautiful women
Became my retinue.

This event prompted me
To examine my past lives at once
By contemplation [in solitude].

Then, I knew the reason [for my rebirth]:
It was the result
Of my carnal desire—
Because I had gazed at Bodhisattva Loving Deed
With a passionate mind.

Because I saw the Bodhisattva,
I obtained the light of joy;
The bright flames now radiating from my body
Are caused by that karma.

Even carnal desire [for a Bodhisattva]
Can produce such a [blissful] result,
Let alone making offerings to him
With a virtuous mind.

I do not wish to seek the two vehicles;
What I want, only the Buddha can tell.

Now, in the presence of the World-Honored One,
I vow to seek all-knowing wisdom.
I will not regress in pursuing Buddha-wisdom
Even if I must practice for kalpas
As numerous as the sands of the Ganges.

I have met a good friend, Bodhisattva Loving Deed;
Now I want to make true offerings to him.

Only one offering is true:
To bring forth bodhicitta.
To cultivate bodhi
Is the supreme, most venerated deed.

I will never look at women with lust,
And wish to be [forever] free
From a female body thereby.
I say this to the Buddha
Who has the four fearlessnesses.

When my parents found me dead and rotten,
They wept with much grief, and said
That it was due to Monk Loving Deed.
Complaining and crying, they scolded the monk."

Then[24] the Buddha, by his miraculous power, caused the god to go to upbraid his [former] parents and admonish them not to blame the monk, lest they should undergo sufferings in the long night.

The god [did so], saying, "Your daughter Increasing Virtue has been reborn in the Heaven of the Thirty-Three, and has changed from a female into a male. He has the body of a god, with a light shining far and wide. Now you, his [former] parents, should go to the World-Honored One and repent your maliciousness. Except for the Tathāgata, the Buddha, the World-Honored One, there is no one in whom you can take refuge." The god thus admonished his [former] parents with a fearless mind. As soon as they heard the name of Śākyamuni Buddha, they went together to see him. When they arrived, they bowed down with their heads at the Buddha's feet and said, "Honored One among gods and humans, now we repent the hatred we harbored, and pay our respect to the Honored One among humans.

"The Tathāgata knows the questions in our minds. How should we make offerings to the Buddha, the Dharma, and the Saṁgha? How should we perform and cultivate good deeds? May the Buddha tell us! We will practice single-mindedly according to your instruction."

Knowing that they were determined, the Teacher of Gods and Humans said, "If one wishes to make offerings to all Buddhas, he should firmly bring forth bodhicitta."

Hearing the Teacher of Gods and Humans say this, Increasing Virtue, his [former] parents, and his retinue, five hundred in number, all brought forth bodhicitta and made great vows.

The Buddha then told the Venerable Ānanda, "Now, heed my words. The Bodhisattva acts I speak of are inconceivable. With unexcelled wisdom and ingenuity, Bodhisattva Loving Deed often makes this vow: 'If a woman is seized with lust when she sees me, she shall change into a male at once and win others' respect.'

"Ānanda, you see how wonderful is the power of his virtue. If an ordinary person performs a misdeed, he will fall to the miserable planes of existence; but if a courageous one [i.e., a Bodhisattva] does it, he can defeat demons thereby and cause others to be born in heaven as gods.

"Now Devaputra Increasing Virtue makes offerings to me respectfully. He is proceeding toward bodhi. After making offerings to countless World-Honored Ones, he will become a Buddha named Good View in a future life. The five hundred persons here who are moving toward bodhi will also become Buddhas, Teachers of Gods and Humans. Buddhas have great merits; who would not make offerings to them?

"Those who have deep faith in Bodhisattva Loving Deed will acquire immeasurable joy. It is not one woman, or two or three, but incalculable hundreds of thousands of millions of billions of women who are seized with carnal desire when they see Bodhisattva Loving Deed, and die immediately, to be reborn as males; they will become great healers with wide renown. Who does not esteem such a Bodhisattva? Even one who has carnal desire for such a Bodhisattva can acquire joy, let alone one who venerates him."

II

Then the Venerable Ānanda said to the Buddha, "World-Honored One, just as different colors take on the color of gold when they are beside Mount Sumeru,[25] so sentient beings, whether they are wrathful, pure, or mentally defiled with desire, take on the color of all-knowing wisdom when they stand beside a Bodhisattva. World-Honored One, from now on I will hold Bodhisattvas in as great esteem as I do Mount Sumeru.

"World-Honored One, there is a medicine named 'All-Seeing' which is an antidote for all poisons; it will cure all those who take it, whether they are wrathful or pure in mind. In the same way, a Bodhisattva can cure those who come to him of any disease of desire, hatred, or ignorance, whether they are wrathful or pure in mind."

Then the World-Honored One praised Ānanda, saying, "Excellent, excellent! It is just as you say."

Mahākāśyapa then said to the Buddha, "Marvelous, World-Honored One! Bodhisattva-Mahāsattvas are the supreme, most venerable beings. Bodhisattva-Mahāsattvas cultivate all dhyānas and samādhis, but, after such cultivation, they again enter the Realm of Desire to teach and convert sentient beings. Although they practice emptiness, signlessness, and nonaction[26] to convert sentient beings and to cause them to become Śrāvakas or Pratyekabuddhas, still, out of great kindness and compassion, they are never apart from the mind of all-knowing wisdom.

"World-Honored One, inconceivable is the ingenuity which Bodhisattva-

Mahāsattvas practice. They are not attached to forms, sounds, scents, tastes, or textures, though they may be involved in them.

"World-Honored One, with great delight, I will enumerate a few merits of the Bodhisattva."

The Buddha said to Kāśyapa, "You may do as you wish."

Kāśyapa said, "World-Honored One, suppose there is a vast marsh, whose inhabitants are afflicted with a grievous famine. Surrounding it is a wall high enough to reach the Realm of Formlessness. Leading out of the marsh, in which many sentient beings live, there is only one gate. Not far from the marsh, suppose there is a large city, which is rich, happy, prosperous, beautiful, and grand. The sentient beings who enter that city do not suffer from old age, sickness, or death. The only path from the marsh to that city is one foot wide and very straight.

"Among the people in the marsh, there is a wise person, who suddenly, out of great kindness and compassion, decides to give benefit, peace, and joy to all the sentient beings there. He announced loudly in the center of the marsh, 'Know that, not far from here, there is a large city where many gods live, which is rich, happy, prosperous, beautiful, and grand. The sentient beings who enter that city will not suffer from old age, sickness, or death, and will be able to teach others the way to avoid old age, sickness, and death. You may go there with me. I shall be your guide.'

"In the marsh, there are lowly and inferior sentient beings who wish to acquire liberation but say, 'We will accept your teaching if you can enable us to live on in the marsh; we will not accept it if you wish us to move from here.'

"The superior sentient beings there say: 'We will go with you to that place.' However, after hearing the wise person's words, other sentient beings in the marsh who are less fortunate do not believe him and refuse to follow him.

"World-Honored One, when the wise person emerges from the marsh, he looks around and sees the narrow path, only one foot wide. To the left and right of the path, there are large pits, hundreds of thousands of feet deep. After the wise person fences both sides of the path with boards, his followers crawl forward without looking left or right; they do not look back even when malicious robbers pursue them and frighten them. Brave and fearless, they proceed gradually along the road. Finally, they see the city, and then feel assured. After entering the city, they suffer no more from old age, sickness, or death; furthermore, they can now benefit countless other sentient beings by teaching them the way to avoid old age, sickness, and death.

"World-Honored One, the vast marsh afflicted with a grievous famine is the marsh of saṁsāra; the thick, high wall reaching to the Realm of Formlessness is ignorance and the craving for existence; the many sentient beings in the marsh stand for all the ordinary persons involved in saṁsāra; the only road to that city, the foot-wide path, is the One Path. The wise person in the marsh is a Bodhisattva-Mahāsattva; the lowly and inferior sentient beings who wish to acquire liberation but remain in the marsh are Śrāvakas and Pratyekabuddhas; the superior sentient beings who say, 'We will go with you to that place' are other Bodhisattvas; the unfortunate sentient beings who hear the wise person's words but do not believe him are the heterodox masters and their disciples. Those who escape from the marsh are those who diligently cultivate the mind of all-knowing wisdom; the only gate[27] leading out of the marsh is the gate of the Dharma-nature; the huge pits on the left and right of the path, which are hundreds of thousands of feet deep, are the Śrāvaka-vehicle and the Pratyekabuddha-vehicle; to fence both sides of the path with boards is skillful means born of wisdom. Those who crawl forward are sentient beings attracted to the Buddha-Dharma by Bodhisattvas using the four inducements;[28] the malicious robbers who pursue and frighten them are the king of demons and his subjects, the sentient beings who stubbornly hold the sixty-two [wrong] views, and those who despise and slander Bodhisattvas. Not to look back is to be fully absorbed in the pāramitā of patience; not to look left or right is not to praise the Śrāvaka-vehicle or the Pratyekabuddha-vehicle; the large city is the mind of all-knowing wisdom. Those who, having proceeded gradually along the road, finally see that city and feel assured are Bodhisattvas who, having seen Buddhas and their deeds, respect the Buddhas' wisdom and awesome virtue with all their hearts, learn well the pāramitā of wisdom, and gradually acquire the skill to approach all sentient beings with propriety and without misgivings. Those who suffer no more from old age, sickness, and death after entering that city are Bodhisattvas who benefit countless sentient beings [by teaching them the way to] avoid old age, sickness, and death; this way is [the Dharma] taught by Tathāgatas, the Worthy Ones, the All-Knowing Ones. World-Honored One, now I pay homage to all Bodhisattvas."

After Mahākāśyapa had said this, ten thousand gods and humans brought forth bodhicitta.

Then the World-Honored One praised Mahākāśyapa, saying, "Excellent, excellent! You encourage many Bodhisattva-Mahāsattvas and achieve incalculable merits. A Bodhisattva-Mahāsattva will never perform any deed harmful to himself or others, nor will he utter any word harmful to himself or others."

Then Bodhisattva-Mahāsattva Increasing Virtue asked the Buddha, "World-Honored One, you say that no Bodhisattva will perform any deed or utter any word harmful to himself or others. Then, World-Honored One, when you were a great brahmacārin named Constellation treading the Bodhisattva-path in the era of Kāśyapa Buddha, with Buddhahood only one life away from you, why did you say 'It is very hard to attain the bodhi-path. How can a bald-head [Kāśyapa Buddha] attain it? I do not wish to see him'? World-Honored One, what is the meaning of the words you spoke at that time?"[29]

The Buddha replied to Bodhisattva Increasing Virtue, "Good man, do not doubt Tathāgatas or Bodhisattvas. Why? Because Buddhas and Bodhisattvas have achieved inconceivable ingenuity, and they abide in all kinds of ingenuity to teach and convert sentient beings. Good man, heed my words and think well about them. There is a sūtra named The Pāramitā of Ingenuity, which I shall explain to you. I also shall reveal to you a few of the skillful means which the Bodhisattva[30] has devised gradually since the era of Dīpaṁkara Buddha.

"Good man, the Bodhisattva-Mahāsattva acquired the Realization of the Nonarising of Dharmas as soon as he saw Dīpaṁkara Buddha. From then on he has never made a mistake; been frivolous, unmindful, or distracted; or become less wise.

"Good man, seven days after the Bodhisattva fulfilled a past vow by attaining the Realization of the Nonarising of Dharmas, he could have attained supreme enlightenment, and if he had so desired, he could also have attained it one hundred kalpas later. For the sake of sentient beings, the Bodhisattva-Mahāsattva was reborn many times and, wherever he was, fulfilled all sentient beings' wishes by the power of his wisdom. Only after that did he attain supreme enlightenment.

"Good man, by the power of his ingenuity, the Bodhisattva-Mahāsattva has dwelled in the world for countless billions of kalpas without worry or repugnance. This was the ingenuity practiced by the Bodhisattva-Mahāsattva.

"Furthermore, good man, if a Śrāvaka entered one of the dhyānas or samādhis of the Bodhisattva-Mahāsattva, he would become unmoved in body and mind, and think that he had already entered nirvāṇa. However, when the Bodhisattva entered any dhyāna or samādhi, he became vigorous in body and mind instead of indolent. He attracted sentient beings into his following by the four inducements. Out of great kindness and compassion, he taught and converted sentient beings by means of the six pāramitās. This was the ingenuity practiced by the Bodhisattva-Mahāsattva.

"Moreover, good man, when the Bodhisattva fulfilled a past vow by residing in the palace of the Tuṣita Heaven, he could have attained supreme enlightenment and turned the Dharma-wheel then. However, he thought, while in the Tuṣita Heaven: 'People in the world cannot ascend to this heaven to hear the Dharma explained, while gods in the Tuṣita Heaven can descend to the world to hear the Dharma taught.' Therefore, he left the Tuṣita Heaven and attained supreme enlightenment in this world. This was the ingenuity practiced by the Bodhisattva-Mahāsattva.

"Furthermore, good man, after the Bodhisattva fulfilled a past vow by coming here from the Tuṣita Heaven, he could have attained supreme enlightenment without entering his mother's womb. However, if he had not entered his mother's womb, sentient beings would have had doubts, saying, 'Where does the Bodhisattva come from? Is he a god, a dragon, a ghost, a spirit, a gandharva, or a being produced by magic?' If they had had such doubts, they could not have heard the Dharma explained or devoted themselves to Dharma practice to eradicate their afflictions. Therefore, the Bodhisattva-Mahāsattva did not attain supreme enlightenment before entering his mother's womb. This was the ingenuity practiced by the Bodhisattva-Mahāsattva.

"Good man, do not say that the Bodhisattva really stayed in the womb of his mother. Do not think so. Why? Because the Bodhisattva-Mahāsattva actually did not enter his mother's womb. Why? Because the Bodhisattva had entered the Undefiled Dhyāna in the Tuṣita Heaven; he remained in that dhyāna when he descended from the heaven, until the time when he sat under the bodhi-tree. The gods in the Tuṣita Heaven thought that the Bodhisattva's life had come to an end and he would not again return to that heaven, but actually he remained unmoved in that heaven all that time. He appeared to enter the womb of his mother, enjoy the five sensuous pleasures, leave the household life, and practice austerities. All sentient beings took these deeds for real, but to the Bodhisattva, these were just a magical display. The Bodhisattva entered the womb of his mother, amused himself with sensuous pleasures, left the household life, and practiced austerities; but all these were a magical display. Why? The Bodhisattva was pure in conduct. He did not enter the womb, and so on, because he had renounced all these [worldly actions] long ago. This was the ingenuity practiced by the Bodhisattva-Mahāsattva.

"Why did the Bodhisattva appear to enter his mother's womb in the form of a white elephant?[31] Good man, in the billion-world universe, the Bodhisattva was the most venerable. Having achieved white, pure dharmas, he appeared to enter the womb in the form of a white elephant. No god, human, ghost, or spirit could enter a womb in this way. This was the ingenuity practiced by the Bodhisattva-Mahāsattva.

"Why did the Bodhisattva stay in his mother's womb for a full ten [lunar] months before he was born? Good man, some sentient beings might think: 'If the child does not stay in his mother's womb for a full ten months, his body may not be fully developed.' Therefore, the Bodhisattva appeared to stay in his mother's womb for a full ten months. During this period, gods often came close to the mother to show respect for the Bodhisattva and make circumambulations around him. Once, the gods saw the Bodhisattva living in a high tower, surpassing even those of the gods, beautifully adorned with the seven treasures; seeing this auspicious sign, twenty-four thousand gods brought forth bodhicitta. This was the ingenuity practiced by the Bodhisattva-Mahāsattva.

"Why did the Bodhisattva enter the womb of his mother through her right side? Good man, some sentient beings might doubt and say, 'The Bodhisattva is born of the combination of his father's sperm and his mother's egg-cell'; in order to resolve their doubt and to manifest his miraculous birth, the Bodhisattva entered the womb of his mother through her right side. Though he entered [her body] through the side, he [really] entered no place at all. Queen Māyā experienced then a physical and mental joy that she had never experienced before. This was the ingenuity practiced by the Bodhisattva-Mahāsattva.

"Why was the Bodhisattva born in a secluded place, not at home in the city? Good man, the Bodhisattva always delighted in solitude; he praised lonely, solitary spots in a mountain forest as good places to cultivate ultimate quiescence. If the Bodhisattva had been born at home in the city, no god, dragon, ghost, spirit, or gandharva would have come to offer him fragrant flowers, powdered incense, perfumed ointment, and countless hundreds of thousands of kinds of music. All the people in Kapila at that time were intemperate, unrestrained, and arrogant; they could not make offerings to the Bodhisattva. Therefore, he was born in a secluded place, not at home in the city. This was the ingenuity practiced by the Bodhisattva-Mahāsattva.

"Why did the Bodhisattva's mother reach up and hold a branch of a tree when she gave birth to him? Good man, sentient beings might suspect that Queen Māyā went through travail when she gave birth to the Bodhisattva, just as other women do [when they give birth]. In order to show them that she was joyful, she reached up and held the branch when she gave birth to the Bodhisattva. This was the ingenuity practiced by the Bodhisattva-Mahāsattva.

"Why did the Bodhisattva come into the world with right mindfulness through the right side of his mother, not through any other part of her body? Good man, the pure deeds of the Bodhisattva were supreme, the most venerable in the great billion-world universe; he did not enter the female organ, or come out of it. Only a Bodhisattva who will become a Buddha in his next life can perform such a feat, not any other cultivator of pure conduct. Hence, the Bodhisattva came into the world through his mother's right side. Though he was born thus, he [really] came from nowhere, just as [he entered no place] in his pure conception described before. This was the ingenuity practiced by the Bodhisattva-Mahāsattva.

"Why was it Śakra, not any other god, who received the Bodhisattva with a precious garment when he was born? Because, good man, Śakra made this vow in the past: 'When the Bodhisattva is born, I will receive him with a precious garment because of his wonderful good roots. This will cause other gods to have more faith in the Bodhisattva, more respect for him, and to make more offerings to him.' This was the ingenuity practiced by the Bodhisattva-Mahāsattva.

"Why did the Bodhisattva walk seven steps, not six or eight, immediately after he was born? Good man, the Bodhisattva doubtless had great miraculous powers, vigor, and the auspicious signs of a great man, and he wished to show sentient beings a manifestation that no one else could make. If it had been more beneficial to sentient beings to walk six steps than to walk seven steps, the Bodhisattva would have walked six steps. If it had been more beneficial to sentient beings to walk eight steps than to walk seven steps, the Bodhisattva would have walked eight steps. Since it was most beneficial to sentient beings to walk seven steps, he walked seven steps, not six or eight, with no one supporting him.[32] This was the ingenuity practiced by the Bodhisattva-Mahāsattva.

"Why did the Bodhisattva say after he had walked seven steps, 'I am supreme, the most venerable in the world; I am free from old age, sickness, and death'? Good man, at that time, in the assembly [which beheld his birth], Śakra, Brahmā, and other gods were very proud and had claimed, 'I am the most venerable in the world.' Since they were arrogant and conceited, they had no respect for anyone. At that time, the Bodhisattva thought: 'The gods are arrogant; because of this, they will fall to the three miserable planes of existence in the long night.' Consequently, he said, 'I am supreme, the most venerable in the world. I am free from old age, sickness, and death.' When he said that, his voice was heard in the entire billion-world universe. Those gods who had not come [to see him] at the time of his birth all came when they heard this voice. Then the gods of the Realm of Desire and the Realm of Form joined their palms respectfully and paid homage to the Bodhisattva. They said to one another, 'How marvelous!' This is why the Bodhisattva spoke truthfully after he walked seven steps, saying, 'I am supreme, the most venerable in the world. I am free from old age, sickness, and death.' This was the ingenuity practiced by the Bodhisattva-Mahāsattva.

"Why did the Bodhisattva laugh loudly after he had walked seven steps? Good man, he laughed not because of desire, arrogance, or frivolity. At that time, the Bodhisattva thought: 'Now these sentient beings [who have come to see me] have desire, hatred, ignorance, and other afflictions, as they have had in their past lives. I previously persuaded them to bring forth bodhicitta. Now I have already reached accomplishment, but they are still in saṁsāra, the ocean of suffering, with their afflictions unsevered, because they have been idle and negligent. These sentient beings and I brought forth bodhicitta at the same time. Now I have already attained enlightenment,[33] but they are still in saṁsāra, the ocean of suffering, because they have been idle and negligent. These inferior sentient beings, out of desire for material gains, neglected to make vigorous efforts to pursue all-knowing wisdom. Now they are still in a position of paying homage and making offerings to me. In the past, I took great compassion on them [and vowed to attain enlightenment to deliver them]; now I have fulfilled my vow.' It was for this reason that the Bodhisattva laughed loudly. This was the ingenuity practiced by the Bodhisattva-Mahāsattva.

"When the Bodhisattva was born, his body was immaculate; why did Śakra and Brahmā bathe him? Good man, because the Bodhisattva wished to cause the heavenly subjects of Śakra and Brahmā to make offerings, and because convention demands that a newborn baby be bathed, he caused Śakra and Brahmā to wash his body, though it was immaculate. This was the ingenuity practiced by the Bodhisattva-Mahāsattva.

"Why did the Bodhisattva go to the palace after he was born in the secluded place, instead of going immediately to the bodhi-site? Good man, in order to let his organs fully develop, he appeared to live in the palace and amuse himself with the five sensuous pleasures; then he appeared to give up the four continents and leave the household life.[34] Also, in order to convert other people so that they may abandon the five sensuous pleasures, shave their beards and hair, don monastic robes, and leave the household life, the Bodhisattva went home instead of going immediately to the bodhi-site after he was born in the secluded place.[35] This was the ingenuity practiced by the Bodhisattva-Mahāsattva.

"Why did Queen Māyā die seven days after the Bodhisattva was born? Good man, Queen Māyā died simply because her life had come to an end; it was not the Bodhisattva's fault. Good man, when the Bodhisattva was still in the Tuṣita Heaven, he saw with his deva-eye that Queen Māyā had only ten months and seven days to live in the world. It was then that he descended from the Tuṣita Heaven to be reborn here, knowing already by his ingenuity that Queen Māyā would soon die.[36] Therefore, it was not his fault. This was the ingenuity practiced by the Bodhisattva-Mahāsattva.

"Why did the Bodhisattva thoroughly learn reading, debating, chess, archery, chariot-driving, strategy, planning, and various arts and techniques? Because, good man, he wanted to follow mundane conventions. There was nothing in the billion-world universe which the Bodhisattva did not know. When he was born, he was already conversant with all such things as poetry, speech, debate, incantation, drama, singing, dancing, music, and craftsmanship. This was the ingenuity practiced by the Bodhisattva-Mahāsattva.

"Why did the Bodhisattva take a wife and concubines? Good man, the Bodhisattva did not do so out of desire. Why? Because he was a man free of desire. If he had not appeared to have a wife and concubines at that time, sentient beings might have said, 'The Bodhisattva is not a man.' If they had had such suspicion, they would have committed a very great transgression. Therefore, in order to forestall their suspicion, the Bodhisattva appeared to marry a woman of the Śākya clan and beget Rāhula. If a person says that Rāhula was born of the union between his father and mother, [he is wrong;] he should not view the event in this way. The fact is that as soon as his life in heaven ended, Rāhula came down from heaven and entered the womb of his mother. He was not born of the union between his father and mother.[37] Besides, Rāhula had previously made a vow to be the son of a Bodhisattva who would attain Buddhahood in that lifetime.

"In the era of Dīpaṁkara Buddha, Gopā[38] said, 'I hope that from now on, this brahmacārin will be my husband and I will be his wife, even in the lifetime in which he will attain Buddhahood.' At that time, the Bodhisattva, after receiving seven blue lotus flowers [from her], said, 'Though I do not want to accept this gift, I will now gratify the wishes of this good woman.' After he said that, she was never apart from the good root of having offered the seven flowers. Hence, the Bodhisattva took that woman for his wife.

"Furthermore, the Bodhisattva, who would attain Buddhahood in that lifetime, appeared to stay with the ladies in the palace. At that time, the Bodhisattva had a wonderful body and the gods made offerings to him, but he finally left the household life. Seeing all these things clearly, the woman of the Śākya clan[39] brought forth bodhicitta and made this vow sincerely: 'May I [also] achieve such things!' Hence, it was in order to cause Gopā to bring forth bodhicitta that the Bodhisattva took her for his wife.

"Moreover, there are great-minded sentient beings who lead the life of laymen and enjoy the five sensuous pleasures, wealth, treasures, the service of attendants, and the company of household members. In order to cause these beings to give up the lay life, the five sensuous pleasures, and so on, and to leave the household life, the Bodhisattva first appeared to stay at home enjoying the five sensuous pleasures, wealth, treasures, the service of attendants, and the company of household members, and then appeared to give up all these and leave the household life. After seeing this, the sentient beings think: 'The five sensuous pleasures which the Bodhisattva enjoyed were the most wonderful; they were unrivaled. If he can give them up and leave the household life, why can we not do the same?'

"Furthermore, the Bodhisattva's wife and his male and female household members were people whom the Bodhisattva had converted through wholesome dharmas when he trod the Bodhisattva-path in the past. These sentient beings had also vowed to be his wife or household members until the lifetime in which the Bodhisattva would attain Buddhahood. In order to increase the white, pure dharmas of these people, the Bodhisattva appeared to stay with his wife and household members.

"Moreover, in order to teach and convert the forty-two thousand ladies, to make them bring forth bodhicitta, and to cause others not to fall to the miserable planes of existence, the Bodhisattva appeared to stay with his wife and household members in the palace.

"Furthermore, all women who were burning with the fire of carnal desire parted with their desire when they saw the Bodhisattva.

"Moreover, the Bodhisattva produced by magic many Bodhisattvas who were exactly like himself in features and bodily form. The women who amused themselves with the magically produced Bodhisattvas said to themselves that they amused themselves with the real Bodhisattva. Actually, all the time the Bodhisattva remained in meditation and cultivated practices causing peace and joy. Just as the magically produced Bodhisattvas had no thoughts of desire when enjoying the five sensuous pleasures, so the real Bodhisattva was free from carnal desire from the era of Dīpaṁkara Buddha until the lifetime in which he would attain Buddhahood.[40] This was the ingenuity practiced by the Bodhisattva-Mahāsattva.

"Why was the Bodhisattva absorbed in thought under the rose-apple tree? Good man, the Bodhisattva wished to teach and convert the seven hundred million gods; he wished to cause his parents to know that he would surely shave his beard and hair, don a monastic robe, and leave the household life; he wished to show that he added to his wisdom when he took shade under the rose-apple tree; and he wished to cause sentient beings to increase their good roots. This is why he sat in meditation under the rose-apple tree. This was the ingenuity practiced by the Bodhisattva-Mahāsattva.

"Why did the Bodhisattva go forth from the city to observe things instead of amusing himself with the five sensuous pleasures?[41] Good man, because he wished to show that he saw an old person, a sick one, and a dead one, he went forth from the city. He wished his relatives to know that he left the household life from fear of old age, sickness, and death, not out of arrogance; that he left the household life in order to benefit his relatives, not to harm them; that he left the household life because he saw the faults of household life. In order to show all sentient beings the sufferings of old age, sickness, and death, the Bodhisattva went forth from the city to observe things instead of amusing himself with the five sensuous pleasures. This was the ingenuity practiced by the Bodhisattva-Mahāsattva.

"Why did the Bodhisattva appear to leave home at midnight? Good man, it was because the Bodhisattva wished to show what is beneficial for sentient beings' good roots, for he improved sentient beings' good roots wherever he was. Good man, it was also because the Bodhisattva wanted to abandon the five sensuous pleasures for the sake of white, pure dharmas. In order to part with pleasures, not white, pure dharmas, he renounced the household life; and in order not to let his relatives know, he left home at midnight. This was the ingenuity practiced by the Bodhisattva-Mahāsattva.

"Why did the Bodhisattva make his attendants sleep before he left home? Because, good man, he wished to make the gods responsible for his leaving home. Some of his relatives would become angry when they were informed that the Bodhisattva had left the household life. The Bodhisattva thought, 'If they harbor malice against me, they will suffer very much in the long night and fall to the miserable planes of existence. However, if they think that it is gods who have cheated the attendants into sleep, opened the door for me, led the way, and then ascended in the sky and flown away, and that it is not my fault, they will have more faith in me and distrust the gods.'[42] With this in mind, the Bodhisattva made his attendants sleep before he left home. This was the ingenuity practiced by the Bodhisattva-Mahāsattva.

"Why did the Bodhisattva send [his charioteer] Chandaka back with the Bodhisattva's white horse, precious clothes, and necklaces? Because, good man, he wished to let his relatives know that he was not greedy for the fine clothes and precious necklaces of a layman. Besides, the Bodhisattva thought, 'My doing this will cause others to follow my example in giving up everything and leaving the household life for the sake of the Buddha-Dharma. After people imitate me in parting with all they love, they will cultivate the four noble practices. Nevertheless, they should not [follow my example and] leave the household life without the permission of their parents.[43] This was the ingenuity practiced by the Bodhisattva-Mahāsattva.

"Why did the Bodhisattva himself shave his hair with a knife? Good man, in the billion-world universe, no god, dragon, ghost, spirit, gandharva, human, or nonhuman could go near the Bodhisattva, who had awesome virtue; how could any one shave his hair? Furthermore, the Bodhisattva appeared to shave his hair with a knife in order to cause sentient beings to believe that he deeply wished to leave the household life. Moreover, the Bodhisattva did so for the sake of [his father] King Śuddhodana. When [the Bodhisattva left home], King Śuddhodana harbored malice and, presuming upon his own power, said arrogantly, 'I will kill the person who shaves my son's hair.' When he heard that the Bodhisattva himself had shaved his own hair with a knife, his malice vanished. This was the ingenuity practiced by the Bodhisattva-Mahāsattva.

"Good man, heed my words. Why did the Bodhisattva practice austerities for six years? Good man, it was not due to the results of his past karmas that the Bodhisattva endured the sufferings. It was because he wished to cause all sentient beings to be afraid of all miserable karmic results and turn to the Bodhisattva.

"Furthermore, good man, in the era of Kāśyapa Buddha, the Bodhisattva once said, 'I do not want to see that bald recluse [Kāśyapa Buddha]. How can a bald-head attain bodhi? The bodhi-path is very profound and hard to attain.' This was also the ingenuity practiced by the Bodhisattva. You should know the meaning of what he said. Why did the Bodhisattva utter such rude words?

"Good man, when Kāśyapa Buddha appeared in the world, there was a brāhmin's son named Constellation.[44] He had five close friends, all of whom were sons of great brāhmins and had studied the Mahāyāna before [in their previous lives]. At that time, the five had lost bodhicitta because they had associated closely with bad friends for a long time. Good man, in the era of Kāśyapa Buddha, these five men, who had no faith in the Buddha-Dharma, served heterodox masters. They understood the words of the heterodox masters, not the words of [Kāśyapa] Buddha. They comprehended the doctrines of heterodox masters, not the Buddha-Dharma. These five men were then following a heterodox master, who said, 'I am the Buddha, the World-Honored One, the All-Knowing One. I have also attained the bodhi-path.'

"At that time, Brahmacārin Constellation devised a skillful means to induce the five men to practice the Dharma again and to break their wrong faith in the heterodox master. Using ingenuity, he went to see a potter and said, 'Now I want to see that bald recluse. How can a bald-head attain bodhi? The bodhi-path is very profound and hard to attain.'

"Good man, not long after he had uttered these words, Brahmacārin Constellation was with the five men in a secluded place. At that time, the potter went to see them and spoke to Brahmacārin Constellation, praising Kāśyapa Buddha, the Tathāgata, the Worthy One, the All-Knowing One. He also said to Brahmacārin Constellation, 'You may go with me to the Buddha.'

"Good man, at that time, Brahmacārin Constellation thought, 'The good roots of these five men have not yet come to maturity. They will be skeptical if I praise Kāśyapa Buddha instead of their heterodox teacher. It will be impossible for them to go with me to the Buddha.' Therefore, in order to keep his original vow and practice the skillful means resulting from the pāramitā of wisdom, he said, 'I do not want to see that bald recluse. How can a bald-head attain bodhi? The bodhi-path is very profound and hard to attain.'

"What is the result of the pāramitā of wisdom? The Bodhisattva who practices the pāramitā of wisdom has no thought of bodhi or Buddha. At that time, Constellation saw neither Buddha nor bodhi; he did not see bodhi [in any location,] inside, outside, or in between. Thus, he comprehended thoroughly that bodhi is empty and nonexistent. Knowing that all dharmas are nonexistent, as a skillfull means Constellation said, 'I do not want to see that bald recluse. How can a bald-head attain bodhi? The bodhi-path is very profound and hard to attain.'

"Later, good man, Brahmacārin Constellation and the five persons went to the bank of a river. In order to convert the five men, the potter, invested with miraculous power by the Buddha, again came to see them and said to Brahmacārin Constellation, 'You may go with me to the Buddha and pay homage, make offerings, show respect, and accord praise to him. The appearance of a Buddha, a World-Honored One, in the world is a very rare occasion.'

"Hearing what the potter had said, Brahmacārin Constellation purposely refused to go. Then the potter approached the brahmacārin, seized him by the hair, and pulled him by force to the Buddha. The five men followed on the heels of Brahmacārin Constellation and consequently arrived at the place where the Buddha was.

"According to the law of the country at that time, a person who seized another by the hair had to die, if he were accused before an official. When the five men saw the potter seize Brahmacārin Constellation by the hair and pull him by force to the place where the Buddha was, they followed on the heels of the brahmacārin with this thought in mind: 'What merits does the Dharma of the Tathāgata have that this potter, risking the death penalty, seized Constellation by the hair and is pulling him to pay homage, make offerings, show respect, and accord praise to that Buddha?'

"When the five men arrived at the place where Kāśyapa Buddha was staying and saw the Buddha, they again brought forth their original vows [generated in past lives] and believed in and respected the Buddha. After that, they reproached Constellation before the Buddha, saying, 'The World-Honored One has such awesome virtue! If you had heard about this before, why did you not respect and believe in him?'

"Good man, when the five men had seen the awesome virtue of Kāśyapa Buddha and heard his eloquence, they again brought forth supreme bodhicitta.

"Seeing that the five men were devoted to bodhi, Kāśyapa Buddha explained to them first the Diamondlike Sentences of the Nonregressive Dhāraṇī of the Bodhisattva Canon, and then the Realization of the Nonarising of Dharmas. The five men immediately achieved the Realization of the Nonarising of Dharmas.

"Good man, now I have fully attained Buddha-wisdom. I know that if, at that time, Brahmacārin Constellation had praised Kāśyapa Buddha instead of their heterodox teacher, the five men would not have gone to see the Buddha, and certainly would not have believed in or respected the Buddha.

"Good man, in order to induce the five men to learn the Bodhisattva-vehicle, Brahmacārin Constellation devised a skillful means by his accomplishment of the pāramitā of wisdom and said, 'I do not want to see that bald recluse. How can a bald-head attain bodhi? The bodhi-path is very profound and hard to attain.' Good man, the Bodhisattva, who never regressed [from the path], had no doubt about the Buddha, bodhi, or the Buddha-Dharma. This was the ingenuity practiced by the Bodhisattva-Mahāsattva.

"Furthermore, in order to teach and convert the five men and to exemplify karmic retribution, the Bodhisattva appeared to be hindered by the karma [of having slandered Kāśyapa Buddha], and he endured six years of austerities as an apparent result. It is an entirely different case if sentient beings, for lack of knowledge and perception, speak ill of precept-keeping śramaṇas or brāhmins, calling the learned unlearned and the liberated unliberated; they will really undergo suffering in the long night without gaining any benefit, and fall to the miserable planes of existence. It was for the sake of such sentient beings that the Bodhisattva appeared to receive the retribution from the apparent karma, though he was actually free from all obstructive karmic results. The same is true of [all] Tathāgatas. Some sentient beings were afflicted with worry and distress and could not acquire liberation or the fruit of the path because they had slandered precept-keeping śramaṇas or brāhmins. In order to free these sentient beings from worry and distress, the Bodhisattva appeared to undergo that karmic result, and thus those sentient beings thought, 'Even the Bodhisattva, who achieved Buddhahood in this life, can obtain liberation, in spite of the fact that he slandered Kāśyapa Buddha. As for us, we have uttered abusive language only from ignorance. Now we should repent our own transgressions and never again perform any evil karma.'

"Good man, it was also in order to subdue the heterodox devotees [of asceticism] that the Bodhisattva practiced austerities for six years, not due to any real karmic hindrances. Why? Some śramaṇas and brāhmins in the world ate a grain of sesame or rice a day and said that they could achieve purity and liberation thereby. In order to subdue them, the Bodhisattva appeared to eat a grain of sesame or rice a day, to show them that, by taking [such small amounts of] coarse food, the Bodhisattva could not attain the noble path, let alone purity and liberation.[45] The Bodhisattva [deliberately] had said, 'I do not want to see that bald recluse. How can a bald-head attain bodhi? The bodhi-path is very profound and hard to attain,' and appeared to suffer for it by enduring austerities[46] for six years, for the purpose of subduing the ascetics, including five million two hundred thousand gods, some heterodox ṛṣis, and some Bodhisattvas. This was the ingenuity practiced by the Bodhisattva-Mahāsattva.

III

"Why did the Bodhisattva reach the bodhi-tree when he had eaten[47] and was full of energy, not when he was emaciated and weak? Good man, the Bodhisattva could have attained supreme enlightenment even if he had eaten and drunk nothing and so had become feeble, let alone when he had taken a grain of sesame or rice [daily]. At that time, out of pity for sentient beings of the future, the Bodhisattva ate the wonderful food [offered to him]. Why? Because if sentient beings who wish to seek the path when their good roots are still immature suffer hunger and thirst as a result of eating and drinking nothing, they cannot obtain wisdom; but if they practice [the Dharma] peacefully and happily, they can obtain wisdom. In order to make it clear that the Dharma does not demand austerities, the Bodhisattva showed sentient beings that he obtained wisdom by practicing [the Dharma] peacefully and happily. Also, out of pity for the future sentient beings, the Bodhisattva wished to cause them to take good food, as he had; therefore, he [appeared to] achieve the thirty-seven ways to bodhi and to attain supreme enlightenment only after having eaten the food given to him by the woman Sujātā. This woman also achieved the [thirty-seven] ways to bodhi. Furthermore, the Bodhisattva was blissful even when in the first dhyāna, and could abide in it without taking food for hundreds of thousands of kalpas. This was the ingenuity practiced by the Bodhisattva-Mahāsattva.

"Why did the Bodhisattva ask the god Auspiciously Peaceful for grass to cover his seat? Good man, it was because former Buddhas did not cover the seat of liberation with fine silken fabric, and also because the Bodhisattva wished to help the god Auspiciously Peaceful achieve the thirty-seven ways to bodhi. After he gave grass to the Bodhisattva, Auspiciously Peaceful brought forth bodhicitta. Good man, I now predict that the god Auspiciously Peaceful will, in a future life, become a Buddha named Pure Tathāgata, the Worthy One, the Supremely Enlightened One. This was the ingenuity practiced by the Bodhisattva-Māhasattva.

"When the Bodhisattva sat under the bodhi-tree, why did he cause Pāpīyān, the demon king, to attempt to prevent his attainment of supreme enlightenment? Good man, the demon king could not approach the bodhi-tree [by his own power]. It would have been absolutely impossible for him to do so if the Bodhisattva had not summoned him. Good man, the Bodhisattva thought when sitting under the bodhi-tree, 'Who is supreme, the most honored one in the four continents? To whom do the four continents belong?' Immediately, the Bodhisattva knew that Pāpīyān, the demon king, was the most honored one in the Realm of Desire. He thought: 'Now, if I battle with the demon king and he loses, it will prove that he and all the sentient beings in the Realm of Desire are inferior to me. At that time, a multitude of gods will come together to the bodhi-tree and engender faith [in the Three Jewels] when they arrive. Gods, demons, dragons, ghosts, spirits, gandharvas, asuras, garuḍas, kinnaras, and mahoragas will then encircle the bodhi-tree; some of them will bring forth supreme bodhicitta, some will aspire to be Bodhisattvas, and some will engender faith [in the Three Jewels] when they see me [perform] the lion's sport; some will even achieve liberation just because they see me.'

"Good man, with this thought in mind, the Bodhisattva emitted from the white curl between his brows a light which overshone the palace of Pāpīyān. At that time, every corner of the billion-world universe became very bright because of the brilliance of the light. From the light came this voice: 'The offspring of the Śākya Clan, who has left the household life to learn the path, will now attain supreme enlightenment. He will transcend the realm of demons, overcome demons, and decrease the number of future demons. Now he is fighting with Pāpīyān, the demon king.'

"Good man, having heard the voice, Pāpīyān became extremely worried, and felt as if an arrow had been shot into his heart. Then he ordered his four kinds of soldiers,[48] marching in a file thirty-six leagues long, to come besiege the bodhi-tree in order to cause the Bodhisattva trouble. At that time, the Bodhisattva abided in great kindness, great compassion, and great wisdom. By virtue of his wisdom he beat the ground with his golden-hued hand, and soon the demons were dispersed. After the demons had been dispersed, eight trillion four hundred billion gods, dragons, ghosts, spirits, gandharvas, asuras, garuḍas, kinnaras, mahoragas, kumbhāṇḍas, and so forth brought forth supreme bodhicitta, because they saw the awesome virtue, exquisite body, handsome features, and dauntless strength of the Bodhisattva. This was the ingenuity practiced by the Bodhisattva-Mahāsattva.

"Why did the Tathāgata remain sitting cross-legged, looking up at the bodhi-tree without blinking, for seven days and seven nights? Good man, at that time, some gods in the Realm of Form were cultivating ultimate quiescence. They were very glad to see the Tathāgata sitting cross-legged, and thought, 'Now, let us try to find out what Śramaṇa Gautama's mind rests on.' The gods could not locate a single thought in the Tathāgata's mind after seven days and seven nights of searching, so they became doubly joyful. Thirty-two thousand of them brought forth supreme bodhicitta and made this vow: 'We will in a future life achieve such quiescence that we can look up at a bodhi-tree [in the same way.]' Hence, after the Tathāgata had attained the path, he remained sitting cross-legged, looking up at the bodhi-tree without blinking, for seven days and seven nights. This was the Tathāgata's ingenuity.

"Since the Tathāgata cultivated countless deeds and vows to give all sentient beings the joy of liberation when he trod the Bodhisattva-path, why did he teach the Dharma only after Brahmā had asked him to do so? Good man, the Tathāgata knew that many gods and humans took refuge in Brahmā and held him in esteem, because they thought that Brahmā had created them, that he was the most venerable being in the world, and that no one except him could create the world. Good man, at that moment, knowing this, the Tathāgata thought, 'Now, I should wait for Brahmā to ask me to teach the Dharma. If Brahmā bows to me, then the sentient beings who take refuge in him will all take refuge in me and say to one another, "Brahmā asked the Tathāgata to teach the Dharma. He truly did so."'

"Good man, because the Tathāgata had great, awesome virtue, Brahmā came to him and asked him to teach the Dharma and turn the Dharma-wheel. Good man, if I had not through my miraculous power caused Brahmā to ask me, he would not have come to ask, because he had no intention of doing so. Good man, in order to cause the sentient beings who took refuge in Brahmā to part with him, it was necessary for the Buddha to wait for Brahmā to make his request;

Brahmā's action proved the excellence of the Buddha. Good man, when Brahmā asked the Tathāgata to turn the Dharma-wheel, six million eight hundred thousand gods of the Brahmā Heaven brought forth supreme bodhicitta and said, 'He is really a Buddha. He is supreme, the most venerable of sentient beings.' They made this vow: 'I will in some future life achieve the same wisdom and awesome virtue the Buddha has achieved.' This was the Tathāgata's ingenuity.

"Good man, I have just spoken about the causes and conditions of manifesting the ten deeds[49] to sentient beings. In performing these ten deeds, the Bodhisattva, the Tathāgata, manifested ingenuity. The wise alone can understand this. Good man, you should not think that the Bodhisattva must have committed some transgressions, even the slightest ones. It would have been absolutely impossible for the Bodhisattva to sit on the bodhi-site and attain supreme enlightenment if he had done any unwholesome things, even the slightest ones. Why? Because, good man, the Tathāgata has achieved all wholesome dharmas and severed all unwholesome ones. He is free from saṁsāra, karmic results, and force of habit; it is absolutely impossible that he has not yet eradicated any of them, let alone that he is hindered by karmic retributions. Good man, for the sake of sentient beings who said there was no karmic retribution and did not believe in it, the Tathāgata appeared to create causes and conditions for 'karmic retributions.' He actually had no karmic retributions, but manifested them to sentient beings, so that they could think, 'Even he, the King of Dharma, was subject to karmic results, let alone other sentient beings.'[50]

"Good man, the Tathāgata does not have any karmic hindrances. As an illustration, suppose a well-learned teacher of children reads to them some chapters of a book. He does so not because he does not understand the book, but because he thinks that the children will follow his example and read. In like manner, good man, the Tathāgata, who has learned all dharmas well, says certain words and makes certain manifestations [not because he still has karmic hindrances, but] because he wants to cause other sentient beings to perform pure deeds.

"Good man, as an illustration, consider a great doctor who can cure all diseases. He may take some bitter medicine in the presence of his patients though he himself is not ill, so that, having seen this, the patients may also take the medicine and be healed of their diseases. Similarly, good man, the Tathāgata has cured himself of all the diseases of defilements, and is not [karmically] obstructed at all. However, he can manifest anything, and so may appear to undergo certain retributions for certain 'evil karmas' in order to cause sentient beings to perform pure deeds and to be free from all bodily, verbal, and mental karmic hindrances.

"Good man, as an illustration, consider the wet nurse of an elder's son. For the sake of the baby committed to her care because of his parents' love for him, she may take bitter medicine without having any illness. She drinks the bitter medicine because she wishes to make her milk pure. In like manner, good man, the Tathāgata, Father of All the Worlds, does not fall ill, but may appear to be ill in order to teach the sentient beings who do not know karmic results; he may appear to receive particular results of particular karmas, so that, after hearing of this, sentient beings may be frightened and not do any more evil deeds."

The Buddha told Bodhisattva Superior Wisdom further, "Good man, in the era of Dīpaṁkara Buddha, there were five hundred traders who went to the ocean to seek precious treasures. Good man, with the five hundred traders, there was a wicked man who was treacherous and often did evil things remorselessly. He was skilled at devising strategies. This robber constantly deprived others of their possessions, though he looked like a trader. When he was in the same ship with the other traders, he thought, 'These traders have acquired many precious treasures. I should kill them and return alone to Jambudvīpa with the loot.' With this thought in mind, he decided to kill them. Good man, at that time, there was a man named Great Compassion, who was the leader of those traders. In a dream, a sea-god appeared to him, saying, 'Among your people, there is a wicked man with a certain appearance who is a robber and often steals from others. Now he has the evil intention to kill these five hundred men and return alone to Jambudvīpa with the precious treasures. If this wicked man carries out his intention to kill these five hundred men, he will perform an extremely evil karma. Why? Because all these five hundred men are Bodhisattvas who do not regress from their advance toward supreme enlightenment. If this wicked man kills the Bodhisattvas, for this grave offense he will remain in hell for as long as the period of time from the moment these Bodhisattvas brought forth bodhicitta to the moment they will attain supreme enlightenment. You are their leader. You may devise a skillful means to prevent this wicked man from falling to the hells, and also to save the lives of these five hundred Bodhisattvas.'

"Good man, Great Compassion, the leader, then thought, 'What skillful means should I devise to prevent that wicked man from falling to the hells and save the lives of the five hundred Bodhisattvas?' Though he thought in this way, he told nobody about it.

"At that time, they were waiting for the wind, which was expected to come in seven days to bring them back to Jambudvīpa. After seven days had passed, he thought, 'There is no way to save the lives of these five hundred persons except to put this wicked man to death.' Then he thought further, 'If I tell these five hundred people about him, they will hate this wicked man and kill him themselves, and then they will fall to the miserable planes of existence.'

"Good man, Great Compassion, the leader, then thought, 'I should kill him myself. Though I may fall to the miserable plane of hell and undergo sufferings for hundreds of thousands of kalpas because of killing him, I am willing to bear those sufferings, but I will not let this wicked man kill these five hundred Bodhisattvas and suffer in hell for that evil karma.'

"Good man, at that time, the leader Great Compassion took pity on that wicked man and devised a skillful means. Thinking to himself, 'I will kill this wicked man because I want to protect these five hundred people,' he killed the wicked man with a spear. In the end, the traders returned to Jambudvīpa safe and sound.

"Good man, you should not harbor any doubt. The leader at that time was no other than myself, and the five hundred traders were the five hundred Bodhisattvas of the Worthy Kalpa who will attain supreme enlightenment during this kalpa.

"Good man, because I used ingenuity out of great compassion at that time, I was able to avoid the suffering of one hundred thousand kalpas of saṁsāra, and that wicked man was reborn in heaven, a good plane of existence, after death.

"Good man, now you should know this was only a display of the power of the Bodhisattva's ingenuity. Do not think that the Bodhisattva could receive obstructive karmic retributions and yet avoid the suffering of hundreds and thousands of kalpas of saṁsāra.

"Good man, for the sake of all sentient beings, the Tathāgata as a skillful means appeared to be pierced by the thorn of a khadira tree [as an apparent retribution for killing the man with a spear]. Good man, once a khadira thorn pierced the foot of the Tathāgata, and you should know, good man, that it was the Buddha's miraculous power causing the thorn to pierce his foot. Why? Because the Tathāgata's adamantine body cannot be in any way damaged.

"Good man, once in the past, in Śrāvastī, there were twenty persons who had come to their last existence in saṁsāra. Each of the twenty persons had one enemy, and each enemy thought: 'Pretending to be his close friend, I will go to his house and kill him, without telling anyone about it.'

"Good man, at that time, because of the Buddha's miraculous powers, the twenty persons who had come to their last existence in saṁsāra, along with their twenty enemies, came to the place where the Buddha was staying.

"Good man, in order to subdue these forty persons, the Tathāgata said to Mahāmaudgalyāyana in the presence of the assembly, 'A khadira thorn will now emerge from the ground and pierce my right foot.'

"Thereupon, the thorn came out of the ground to a length of one foot. Before it reached the Buddha's foot, Mahāmaudgalyāyana said to the Buddha, 'World-Honored One, let me pull this thorn out of the ground and throw it to another world.'

"The Buddha told Mahāmaudgalyāyana, 'This is beyond your power. The khadira thorn is here, but you cannot pull it up.'

"Then, Mahāmaudgalyāyana took the thorn and pulled it with all his divine strength. The whole billion-world universe shook violently and all the worlds were lifted up, but the thorn did not move a hair's breadth.

"Good man, at that time, by his miraculous power, the Tathāgata ascended to the Heaven of the Four [Deva Kings], but the khadira thorn went with him. Then the Tathāgata went up to the Heaven of the Thirty-Three, the Yama Heaven, the Tuṣita Heaven, the Nirmāṇarati Heaven, and the Paranirmita-Vaśavartin Heaven, but the thorn went with him to those places, too; it was the same even when he ascended to the Brahmā Heaven. Then, the Tathāgata returned from the Brahmā Heaven to his seat in Śrāvastī, but the thorn came back with him, jutting toward him. Then, the Tathāgata seized the khadira thorn with his right hand and, placing his left hand on the ground, trod upon it with his right foot. Thereupon, the whole billion-world universe shook violently. Seeing this, the Venerable Ānanda rose from his seat, bared his right shoulder, and paid homage to the Buddha; then he joined his palms toward the Buddha, and asked, 'World-Honored One, what karma did you perform in your past lives that you receive this retribution now?'

"The Buddha replied to Ānanda, 'In one of my past lives, on an ocean voyage, I pierced a man to death with a spear. Ānanda, because of that karma, I received this retribution.'

"Good man, after I had explained this karma, the twenty enemies who wished to kill the twenty persons thought, 'Even the Tathāgata, the King of Dharma, has to receive such a retribution for his negative karma; how can we be exempt from karmic results?'

"The twenty enemies rose from their seats instantly, bowed down with their heads at the Buddha's feet, and said, 'Now, in the presence of the Buddha, we repent our fault and dare not hide it. World-Honored One, we maliciously intended to kill twenty persons. Now, we repent it in earnest and dare not hide it.'

"Then, for the sake of these twenty enemies, the Honored One discoursed on the conditions of the performance of karmas and the exhaustion of karmas. Having heard this doctrine, the twenty enemies acquired a right understanding of the Dharma, as did forty thousand others. This was the reason why the Tathāgata appeared to have his foot hurt by a khadira thorn. This was the Tathāgata's ingenuity.

"Why did the Tathāgata once ask the doctor Life-Giving for a blue lotus flower,[51] smell it, and swallow it, though he was not ill? Good man, not long after the Tathāgata composed the precepts for liberation, there were five hundred monks who had come to their last existence in saṁsāra and who had often cultivated the path in secluded forests. These monks were afflicted with a disease which could not be cured with the stale medicine they had, but they did not seek or take other medicine, because they kept the Buddha's precepts with respect and care.

"Good man, at that time, the Tathāgata thought, 'What skillful means should I devise to give them permission to take other medicine?' If the Tathāgata gave them permission, those monks would seek and take another medicine [which could cure them]. If the Tathāgata did not give them permission, future monks would break the noble law [when they take good medicines]. Hence, the Tathāgata as a skillful means asked the doctor Life-Giving for a blue lotus flower, smelled it, and swallowed it.

"Then, a god of the Pure-Abode Heaven[52] went to those monks and said, 'Virtuous ones, you may seek another medicine. Do not die of sickness.'

"Those monks said, 'We dare not disobey the instructions of the World-Honored One. If we disobey his instructions, we will feel terrible. We would rather die than disobey the instructions of the Buddha. We will not seek a life-prolonging good medicine.'

"After they had said so, that god said, 'Virtuous ones, the Tathāgata, the King of Dharma, has himself sought a good medicine, rejecting stale ones. Virtuous ones, you may seek another medicine [which will cure you].

"Having heard these words, the monks no longer hesitated to seek and take the good medicine, and thus they were healed of their disease. Less than seven days after they had recovered from their illness, they realized Arhatship. Good man, if the Tathāgata had not taken other medicine, the monks would not have done so, either. If they had not taken other medicine, it would have been impossible for them to get rid of their disease, sever their defilements, and realize Arhatship. This was the Tathāgata's ingenuity.

"Why did the Tathāgata once enter the city to beg for food and then come out with his bowl empty? Good man, the Tathāgata is free from karmic hindrance. At that time, the Tathāgata had pity on future monks. Those monks who enter a city or a village to beg for food but are given nothing because they lack blessings and merits will think: 'Even the Tathāgata, the World-Honored One, who had achieved [all] merits, once entered the city to beg for food but came out with his bowl empty; not to speak of us, who have few good roots. We should not become worried or annoyed just because when we beg for food we are not given any.' This is why the Tathāgata appeared to enter the city to beg for food and appeared to come out with his bowl empty.

"Good man, if you say that it is because the demon king Pāpīyān [by himself] confused the minds of the elders and brāhmins in the city, so that they did not give the Tathāgata even a handful of food, good man, do not think so! Why? Because the demon king Pāpīyān could not have prevented the Tathāgata from receiving food. At that time, the Buddha by his miraculous power caused the demon king Pāpīyān to confuse the minds of the people in the city. The demon king could not have done this by his own power.

"At that time, I was completely free from karmic hindrances. In order to teach sentient beings, I appeared to come out of the city with my bowl empty. When I and my assembly of monks were not given any food, the demons and gods all thought, 'Do the Buddha and the monks become worried when they acquire no food?' That night, when they saw the Buddha and monks, they found that they were not worried or annoyed at all, and that they were neither elated nor depressed, feeling just as they had felt before [they had begged in vain]. Good man, seeing this, seven thousand gods began to respect and have faith in the Tathāgata, whereupon I explained the Dharma to them. As a result, they obtained the clear Dharma-eye regarding all things.

"Good man, a little later, some of the brāhmins and elders heard that the World-Honored One had great, awesome virtue; so, filled with sincere admiration, they went to see the Buddha, bowed down with their heads at the Buddha's feet, and repented their faults. The Tathāgata then taught them the four noble truths. As soon as he explained the Dharma, twenty thousand persons acquired the clear Dharma-eye regarding all things. This is why the Tathāgata entered the city to beg for food but came out with his bowl empty. This was the Tathāgata's ingenuity.

"Why did Ciñcā-Māṇavikā, a brāhmin woman, tie a piece of wood to her belly and slander the Tathāgata, saying, 'It is Śramaṇa Gautama who has made me pregnant. He should supply me with clothing, bedding, food, and drink'? Good man, the Tathāgata had not the least karmic hindrance regarding this event; if he had had karmic hindrance [in the form of that brāhmin woman], he could have thrown her to a place as many worlds away from here as the sands of the Ganges. However, as a skillful means, the Tathāgata manifested this karmic hindrance to teach ignorant sentient beings. Why? In the future, there will be monks who take refuge in my Dharma and leave the household life to learn the path. Some of them may be slandered. Because of this, they might feel ashamed, dislike the Buddha-Dharma, give up discipline, and return to the lay life. However, now, when slandered, these monks will think of the Tathāgata: 'Even the Tathāgata, who has achieved all wholesome dharmas and possesses great, awesome virtue, was slandered; how can we avoid being slandered?' Thinking thus, they will not feel ashamed, and will be able to cultivate wonderful, pure conduct.

"Good man, being always wrapped in evil karma, the brāhmin woman Ciñcā-Māṇavikā was faithless in character; and not being subdued by the Buddha-Dharma, she was wrapped in evil karma even more. She slandered others even in her dreams and felt happy because of it when she woke up. This woman would have fallen to the hells after death. Good man, by special ingenuity, I was able to be the woman's savior, ridding her of her evil karma and delivering her from saṁsāra. Good man, do not think that the Tathāgata will not save certain persons. Why? Because the Tathāgata treats all sentient beings impartially. This was the Tathāgata's ingenuity.

"Why did some brāhmins kill Sundarī,[53] the brāhmin woman, and bury her in a moat of the Jeta Grove? Good man, at that time, the Tathāgata knew all about this but did not say a word. The Tathāgata has achieved the mind of all-knowing wisdom and is obstructed by nothing. By his miraculous power, he could have caused the knife not to run into the woman's body, but he knew that the life of Sundarī would come to its end anyway and [her karma] would cause her to be killed by others for certain. So as a skillful means, he let this happen [and did not intervene]. As a result, the evildoings of those heretics were displayed and the evildoers all fell to inferior places. Only the Buddha knew this event [and all its implications] in advance. He let the event run its own course and did not intervene, so that more sentient beings could generate pure faith and increase their good roots.

"At that time, the Tathāgata did not enter Śrāvastī for seven days. During this time, he subdued six billion gods. After seven days had passed, gods and humans came together to his place, and the Tathāgata explained the Dharma to the four kinds of devotees. Having heard the Dharma, eighty-four thousand people acquired the clear Dharma-eye regarding all things. This was the Tathāgata's ingenuity.

"Why did the Tathāgata and the monks eat horses' wheat for three months in the village where Brāhmin Verañja lived? Good man, from the outset, I knew that this brāhmin would certainly give up his original intention of inviting the Buddha and the monks and would offer them neither food nor drink, but I accepted his invitation and went to his place on purpose. Why? I did this for the sake of five hundred horses. The five hundred horses had already learned the Bodhisattva-vehicle and had made offerings to past Buddhas, but because they had associated closely with bad friends and performed evil deeds, they were born as animals. With the five hundred horses, there was a large one named Sun-Store, who was [actually] a great Bodhisattva. In his past lives, when he was a man, Bodhisattva Sun-Store had already persuaded the five hundred horses to bring forth bodhicitta. In order to deliver them from saṁsāra, he appeared to be born as a horse. Because of the awesome virtue of the large horse, the five hundred horses remembered their previous lives and regained their lost aspirations for bodhi. Good man, out of pity for the five hundred Bodhisattvas who were born as horses, and to enable them to be liberated from the plane of animals, the Tathāgata accepted the invitation given by the brāhmin, though he already knew that he would meet with bad treatment.

"Good man, at that time, the five hundred horses ate half of their wheat and gave the other half to the monks, and the large horse offered the Tathāgata half of his wheat. For the large horse had explained the Dharma to the five hundred horses in a horse's voice; he had also taught them to repent their own misdeeds and to pay homage to the Buddha and the monks, and had said, 'You should offer half of your food to the monks.'

"After they had repented their misdeeds, the five hundred horses engendered pure faith in the Buddha and the Saṁgha. Three months later, the five hundred horses died and were reborn [as gods] in the Tuṣita Heaven. Soon after that, the five hundred gods descended from the heaven to the Buddha's dwelling-place to make offerings to the Tathāgata. Right then, the Tathāgata explained the Dharma to them. Having [again] heard the Dharma, they subdued their minds well. In their future lives, they will first achieve Pratyekabuddhahood, and then without fail will attain supreme enlightenment. In his future lives, the large horse Sun-Store will make offerings to countless Buddhas and achieve the thirty-seven ways to bodhi. After that, he will become a Buddha named Skillful Subduer Tathāgata, the Worthy One, the Supremely Enlightened One.

"Good man, there is no delicacy in the world which the Tathāgata does not enjoy. Good man, even if the Tathāgata ate grass, a piece of wood, a clod of earth, or a broken tile, no dish in the billion-world universe would be as delicious as the grass, the piece of wood, the clod of earth, or the broken tile eaten by the Tathāgata. Why? Good man, because the Tathāgata, the Great Man, has attained the supreme taste among all tastes. Even when the Tathāgata eats the coarsest food, it tastes better than any celestial ambrosia. Good man, therefore, you should know that the Tathāgata's food is the best and the most wonderful.

"Good man, at that time, Ānanda felt grief-stricken because the Tathāgata, who belonged to the royal caste and had left the household life to follow the path, ate horses' wheat just like lowly people. I perceived what Ānanda had on his mind. Thereupon, I gave a grain of wheat to him and said, 'Try this grain of wheat and see how it tastes.'

When Ānanda tried it, he found it marvelous and said to the Buddha, 'World-Honored One, I was born and brought up in a royal family, but I have never before experienced such a good taste.' For seven days and seven nights after he ate that grain of wheat, Ānanda did not eat or drink anything and was free of hunger and thirst. Therefore, good man, you should know that this was the ingenuity of the Tathāgata, not his karmic hindrance.

"Good man, some precept-keeping śramaṇas and brāhmins may accept a person's invitation as I did, but, after learning that their misled and confused host will not give them anything, they may refuse to go to his house. Lest they should do this,[54] the Tathāgata demonstrated that he would definitely go to a patron's place once he had accepted his invitation. He did so also because he wished to manifest the existence of karmic results. Good man, it should be known that, as a rule, even if the Tathāgata is offered nothing to eat when he is invited, he will not let the host fall to the miserable planes of existence.

"Good man, of the five hundred monks who, together with the Tathāgata, ate horses' wheat during that summer retreat, four hundred had engendered carnal desire because they had seen many attractive[55] [women]; if they had eaten fine food, that would only have added to their desire. Since they only ate coarse food, they were not overcome with desire. Three months later those monks were released from carnal desire and realized Arhatship. Good man, in order to subdue the four hundred monks and save the five hundred Bodhisattvas from the plane of animals, the Tathāgata, by the power of ingenuity, ate horses' wheat for three months. This was not the Tathāgata's karmic retribution, but his ingenuity.

"Why did the Tathāgata say to the elder Kāśyapa, 'My back is aching; you discourse [on my behalf] on the seven factors of enlightenment,' when he was explaining discipline on the fifteenth day of a month? Good man, at that time, sitting in the assembly were eight thousand gods who subdued themselves with the Śrāvaka doctrines. Good man, these gods had been taught by Mahākāśyapa in their past lives. They took refuge in the Buddha, the Dharma, and the Saṁgha, and did not lose self-control. They had often heard Monk Kāśyapa explain the seven factors of enlightenment. Good man, except for Monk Kāśyapa, no one could have made those gods understand the doctrine, not even hundreds of thousands of Buddhas. At that time, Kāśyapa explained the seven factors of enlightenment in detail to the gods. After they had heard the doctrine explained by Monk Kāśyapa, they acquired the clear Dharma-eye.

"Good man, if diseased sentient beings cannot go to the place where the Dharma is taught to listen respectfully to it, they should think, 'The Buddha is the King of Dharma. Even he was cured of his sickness by hearing the seven factors of enlightenment; how can we not go to hear the Dharma and show respect for it?'

"Good man, in order to subdue the gods, to rid people of their sufferings, and to manifest respect for the Dharma, the Tathāgata said, 'Kāśyapa, my back is aching. You discourse on the seven factors of enlightenment.' Why? Because the Dharma should be revered. The Tathāgata does not have a coarse, weighty body made of the four elements; how can he be afflicted with a disease? This was the Tathāgata's ingenuity.

"Why did the Tathāgata say, 'My head is aching,' when the Śākya clan was defeated? Good man, some sentient beings said, 'The World-Honored One cannot benefit his clan; he does not take pity on them or wish to give them security. Since he left the household life, he has had no feeling for his clan and no desire to save and protect them.' These sentient beings said so because they did not know the facts. Good man, the Tathāgata had transcended all suffering. However, knowing those sentient beings' thoughts, he sat under a withered tree and said that his head was aching. Good man, when I said to Ānanda that my head was aching, there were three thousand gods present in the assembly who held the view of nihilism, as well as numberless sentient beings who were inclined to kill. In order to manifest the existence of karmic hindrances to those gods who held the view of nihilism and those beings who delighted in killing, the Tathāgata said, 'Because I [once] enjoyed seeing a person kill, now I suffer from a headache.' After I said this, seven thousand humans and gods were subdued. This was the Tathāgata's ingenuity.

"Why did the Tathāgata remain patient when the brāhmin Keen Mind reviled him with five hundred kinds of abusive words? Good man, by his miraculous power, the Tathāgata could have thrown this brāhmin to another world; he also could have made this brāhmin unable to utter a single abusive word. Good man, at that time there were many gods and humans in the assembly. They saw that the Tathāgata could put up with this bitter abuse without saying anything in retort, and that the Tathāgata felt just as he had felt before he was reviled, with a mind of equanimity, beneficence, and patience. Thereupon, four thousand persons brought forth bodhicitta. All this was perceived by the Tathāgata. Furthermore, good man, when the brāhmin Keen Mind had reviled the Buddha with five hundred kinds of abusive words and found that the World-Honored One remained equanimous, the brāhmin's mind became filled with faith and respect. He took refuge in the Buddha, the Dharma, and the Saṁgha and planted the root of liberation. This was the Tathāgata's ingenuity.

"Good man, Devadatta[56] and the Bodhisattva have been born in the same place in every lifetime. This is also a skillful means of the Bodhisattva. Why? Because of Devadatta, I have fulfilled the six pāramitās and benefited countless sentient beings. How can this be understood? Good man, in a past age, [when the Bodhisattva was a king,] there were sentient beings who enjoyed themselves heartily, but did not know how to give or to whom to give, and the Bodhisattva wished to teach them to practice giving. Devadatta, who became jealous of the Bodhisattva, went to see him and asked for his capital city, wife, children, head, eyes, hands, and feet. The Bodhisattva gave him all these gladly. At that time, incalculable numbers of sentient beings became cheerful, and believed in and understood giving when they saw the Bodhisattva give in this way. They said, 'I will practice giving just as the Bodhisattva does, so that I may attain bodhi.'

"Good man, once, knowing that the Bodhisattva kept the precepts purely, Devadatta tried to cause the Bodhisattva to break them, but the Bodhisattva did not violate any of them. When countless sentient beings saw the Bodhisattva keep the precepts they followed his example and did so themselves. The Bodhisattva, who kept the precepts, harbored no malice when he was despised, slandered, or reviled by others; at such times he fulfilled the pāramitā of patience. Seeing the Bodhisattva subdue his mind with patience, innumerable sentient beings followed his example and practiced patience. Good man, you should know that Devadatta has benefited the Bodhisattva greatly.[57]

"Good man, recently Devadatta, trying to kill the Buddha, released a huge drunken elephant. He also pushed down a large boulder from the peak of Mount Gṛdhrakūṭa for the same purpose. All these were manifestations of the Tathāgata's ingenuity, not his karmic retributions. Why? Because these skillful means would benefit numberless sentient beings.

"Good man, the Tathāgata has explained the causes and conditions of these ten events,[58] which were all manifestations of his ingenuity, not karmic retributions. Why? Sentient beings did not know that karma brings about results. For their sake, the Tathāgata manifested these karmic results and said, 'If you have done this karma, you will get this result; if you have done that karma, you will get that result. Such and such a karma brings about such and such a result.' After hearing this, sentient beings would perform certain karmas and refrain from others; they would avoid evil karmas and cultivate good ones.

"Good man, now I have finished explaining and revealing my ingenuity. You should keep this a secret and not speak of it to lowly, inferior people who have few good roots. Why? Because, even Śrāvakas and Pratyekabuddhas cannot comprehend this sūtra, much less can lowly, inferior, ordinary persons believe or understand it. Ordinary people cannot learn ingenuity, and so the Sūtra of Ingenuity is of no use to them; not a single ordinary person can accept or practice it.

"Only Bodhisattvas can learn and teach the doctrine of ingenuity. Good man, just as one can see everything in a room when a large lamp is lit at night, so a Bodhisattva can, after hearing about ingenuity, see the path that all Bodhisattvas tread and know what he should learn. For those who are skilled in following the Bodhisattva-path, it is not difficult to perform the deeds of all Tathāgatas and Bodhisattvas who have already reached the other shore.

"Good man, I now say: if those good men and good women who wish to attain the wholesome dharmas of the bodhi-path hear that the Sūtra of Ingenuity is taught hundreds of thousands of leagues away from their homes, then they should go and listen to it. Why? Because, if a Bodhisattva has heard this Sūtra of Ingenuity, he will achieve illumination and have no doubt about any dharmas."

When this sūtra was spoken, the four kinds of devotees and other humans and gods who were able to practice this Dharma heard and understood it. However, those who were unable to practice this Dharma did not hear or understand it, though they were present in the assembly. Since they did not even hear this sūtra with their ears, how could they explain it to others with their speech? Because they were unable to practice this Dharma and because they were not blessed by the Buddha with miraculous power, they did not hear or understand this Dharma when the Tathāgata explained it to the assembly.

When this sūtra had been spoken, seventy-two thousand persons brought forth supreme bodhicitta.

Then, the Venerable Ānanda asked the Buddha, "World-Honored One, what is this sūtra called? How shall we uphold it?"

The Buddha replied to Ānanda, "This sūtra is called 'The Pāramitā of Ingenuity,' 'The Application of Ingenuity,' or 'The Discourse on Subduing by Ingenuity.' You should uphold it by these names."

When the Buddha had said this, Bodhisattva Superior Wisdom was jubilant, and all the followers of the Śrāvaka-vehicle, the Pratyekabuddha-vehicle, and the Bodhisattva-vehicle; monks, nuns, laymen, laywomen, gods, dragons, ghosts, spirits, gandharvas, asuras, garuḍas, kinnaras, mahoragas, and nonhumans applauded, [saying], "Excellent, excellent!"

Here ends the explanation of the Sūtra of the Ingenuity of the Mahāyāna.

NOTES

1. Alternate translation (based on the Tibetan): ". . . when a Bodhisattva who practices ingenuity intends to give even a handful of food as charity, he gives it to all sentient beings." (G.C.)

2. Literally, "good root."

3. I.e., bodhicitta.

4. Chinese 解脱知見 : Here, 'awareness' implies the Buddha's transcendental wisdom.

5. Offerings are of three kinds: (1) incense, flowers, food, etc,; (2) praise and reverence; (3) right conduct.

6. Literally, "He will console himself with two thoughts. What are the two? One is that there are Tathāgatas because there are Bodhisattvas; the other is that there are Śrāvakas and Pratyekabuddhas because there are Tathāgatas."

7. This refers to the Buddha.

8. Since the pāramitā of giving is applied to all six pāramitās, the definition of the pāramitā of discipline given here extends beyond keeping the precepts oneself.

9. Killing, stealing, adultery, and lying.

10. The Buddha here momentarily escalates the dialogue to the higher level of emptiness, which is the ultimate solution for purifying all transgressions.

11. This indicates not only vegetarianism, but also ascetic practice.

12. Literally, "dragon," or "dragon elephant;" a term of respect applied to a Bodhisattva, as here, or to a saint or Buddha.

13. Here we see the great difference between the doctrine of the Hīnayāna and that of the Mahāyāna. The latter stresses the importance of the Bodhisattva's compassionate and altruistic involvement with living beings in saṁsāra. He is allowed to enjoy the five sensuous pleasures as long as he does not lose his bodhicitta. The greatest sin a Bodhisattva can commit is to harbor the Śrāvakas' intention; i.e., the wish to enter parinirvāṇa even at the cost of abandoning sentient beings. (G.C.)

14. This probably means that the Bodhisattva contemplated the earth-element of his own body ("inner") and the earth-element of the woman's body ("outer") as identical, and thus he penetrated the apparent differences between man and woman and perceived their essential sameness (S.L.M.)

15. Meaning his supreme enlightenment and acquisition of a Buddha-land.

16. She is usually called Yaśodharā, the wife of Prince Siddhārtha (who became Śākyamuni Buddha).

17. This refers to the following story:

Śāriputra and Mahāmaudgalyāyana lodged in a potter's house overnight because of rain, not knowing that there was a woman in the place. The woman took a bath the following morning, after having had a female nocturnal emission. Monk Untimely saw her bathing, and accused the two venerable disciples of having had an affair with her. For his wrong accusation, he was reprimanded three times by the Buddha, but he did not repent. He suffered much the rest of his life and fell to hell after his death. (Based primarily on *The Sūtra of Miscellaneous Treasures*, III, Taishō 203, p. 461.)

18. Note the emphasis here on the Bodhisattva's utter lack of attachment to the pleasures he enjoys in the practice of ingenuity for the sake of other beings. In actuality, this is perhaps rather difficult before one has attained a thorough realization of emptiness.

19. Literally, "color," as also below.

20. The sūtra describes the Bodhisattva's contemplation in detail. However, judging from the sequence of the events, his insight might be instantaneous, inclusive of all details in one moment.

21. The reason for this is a vow made by Bodhisattva Loving Deed, explained below.

22. "The Buddha's son" indicates Loving Deed is a Bodhisattva.

23. Literally, "purely elegant."

24. The rest of this section was originally in verse form, but since the narrative resumes at this point, and since the verse is prosaic in tone, we present it as prose.

25. As noted elsewhere, the four sides of Mount Sumeru are each said to be made of a different precious substance. Mythology has it that when anyone nears one of the sides, he takes on the color of that side. One side is gold.

26. The three doors to liberation are usually given as emptiness, signlessness, and wishlessness.

27. The Chinese text reads here: "the foot-wide path," but that has already been interpreted as 'the One Path'. Probably 'gate' is meant here.

28. These sentient beings were identified above as being Bodhisattvas themselves.

29. This question is answered below, p. 450.

30. Here and in the following discussion, "the Bodhisattva" refers to Śākyamuni

Buddha when he was engaged in Bodhisattva practice for countless kalpas before his supreme enlightenment.

31. Tradition has it that at the time of the Bodhisattva's conception, his consciousness entered the womb of his mother through her right side, and at that moment she dreamed that an albino elephant entered her body. The following birth stories are self-explanatory.

32. This paragraph has been rearranged slightly to make sense. Seven steps were best, presumably because seven is an auspicious and mystical number in many religions.

33. Literally, "supreme enlightenment," but this appears to be a corruption of the text.

34. It is said that the Bodhisattva's father, King Śuddhodana, received a prediction from the seer Asita shortly after the Bodhisattva's birth. The seer noticed the wheel-signs on the prince's feet, the webbing between his fingers and toes, the white curled hair between his eyebrows, and the infant's great vigor. The seer predicted that if the Bodhisattva could be isolated from the sight of suffering, he would become a universal monarch and rule the four continents. Otherwise, Asita prophesied, the prince would renounce the household life and become the Teacher of the world. The king wished his son to become the great monarch, so he saw to it that the palace was inhabited only by young, beautiful, and happy people.

35. That is, the Bodhisattva went through the normal events of a noble lay life, and then renounced the palace to become a śramaṇa, afterwards attaining full Buddhahood. In this way, he set an example of renunciation for others to follow. This point is emphasized below.

36. The traditional explanation of this is that if his mother had not died after his birth, it could have hindered the Buddha's going forth from the palace, since people might have considered the prince heartless for leaving his mother. After her death, it is said that Queen Māyā went to the Tuṣita Heaven, and no longer had to suffer in this world. Some sūtras state that the Buddha went to that heaven to preach the Dharma for his mother after his full enlightenment.

37. It is quite understandable that certain monastically oriented people of later Buddhism tried to deify the Buddha and propound the view that he was completely free of sexual conduct. Some people of our age feel that Gautama's sexual activity with his wife before he renounced the household life was not a blemish; rather, it was a normal thing for a married lay Bodhisattva to do, though the prince may have been free of attachment to it. (G.C.)

38. See note 16 above.

39. Yaśodharā.

40. The following sentence appears here in the text: "The courtier Chandaka and the steed Kaṇṭhaka were also caused by the Bodhisattva's previous vows." It is out of context here. Chandaka was the charioteer who helped Prince Siddhārtha escape from the palace, and the horse Kaṇṭhaka drew the chariot. See note 41.

41. This story is almost too well known to bear repeating. The sheltered future Buddha instructed his charioteer to take him out of the palace grounds. The prince saw a sick man, an old man, and a dead man; thus he learned of the suffering in life. The fourth sight was of a wandering ascetic. Some traditions hold that all four visions were magically produced by the gods, in order to induce the Bodhisattva to leave the household life.

42. The Bodhisattva had misgivings about the heavy karmic retribution his relatives would have incurred if they had felt ill-will toward the future Buddha. Therefore, he caused them to blame the gods instead.

43. This sentence is obscure and strange, and does not appear in the Tibetan text. In the Vinaya, Buddha established the rule that one cannot become a monk or nun without the permission of one's parents. However, Buddha himself renounced the household life against

his father's strong opposition, showing that if one is truly determined, he can renounce the world even without his parents' consent.

44. This brahmacārin, mentioned in Part I, was Śākyamuni Buddha, in a former life.

45. The story goes that the Bodhisattva attained supreme enlightenment only after he gave up the ascetic practice of self-starvation. (See note 47.)

46. The Chinese words 粗行, literally "rough practices," have here been interpreted to mean ascetic practices. The Tibetan text does not have this sentence at all.

47. After the Bodhisattva had endured six years of austerities without attaining supreme enlightenment, he resolved to resume normal eating habits. As he sat under a tree, a woman named Sujātā approached the place, carrying a bowl of milk-porridge which she intended to offer to the tree-spirit. When she saw the Bodhisattva seated there, she was moved by his holy appearance and offered the food to him. After he had eaten the nourishing meal, the Bodhisattva went to the bodhi-tree and attained supreme enlightenment.

48. Soldiers mounted on elephants, cavalry, charioteers, and infantry.

49. The ten deeds of the Buddha are:

(1) descent from Tuṣita Heaven;
(2) pure conception in a vision of a white elephant;
(3) remaining in his mother's womb;
(4) birth from the right side;
(5) renunciation of the household life;
(6) six years of austerities;
(7) conquering all demons at the bodhi-site;
(8) attaining supreme enlightenment;
(9) turning the Dharma-wheel and enduring the ten distresses; and
(10) entering parinirvāṇa.

50. This is a central theme in this sūtra. The Buddha was exempt from karmic retribution because he was incapable of creating bad karma. Any apparent "misdeeds" committed by him were in fact ingenious methods to help other sentient beings, and were not evil karma at all. However, by his power, he caused events to occur that *appeared* to be his karmic retributions. He did so, the text states, in order to prevent sentient beings from doubting the law of karma. (V.S.B.)

51. Used as a medicine.

52. This refers to the five Pure-Abode Heavens of the fourth dhyāna heaven. It is said that those who have eradicated defilements, the "ārya saints," can be born and reside there.

53. Referred to above as Ciñcā-Māṇavikā, the woman who accused the Buddha of fornication with her.

54. If they declined the patron's invitation, they would prevent him from acquiring any merit at all. Also, they would be breaking a promise.

55. Literally, "pure."

56. The Buddha's cousin, who often sought to harm the Buddha out of spite.

57. That is, Devadatta, by his very malice, gave the Buddha many opportunities to practice the pāramitās, and to set an example of virtuous patience and compassion. In Buddhism, enemies are considered to be greatly beneficial to one's Dharma-practice.

58. This refers to the ten apparent afflictions, or distresses, which the Buddha faced after his enlightenment, all of which have been related above.

Glossary

ācārya. A teacher or guru, especially the teacher who imparts the precepts to monks or nuns during ordination.

afflictions. *See* "defilements."

aggregates. (*See also* Numerical Glossary, "five aggregates.") The primary goal of Buddhism is to attain liberation. That which hinders liberation is the clinging to ego or self, that is, to an entity which is indivisible, unchanging, definite, and eternal. In order to eliminate this deep-rooted clinging, three major practices are given: adherence to precepts, practice of meditation, and prajñā or nonself (*anātman*) training.

By applying the nonself observation in deep samādhi, the deeply entrenched clinging to self can be broken and liberation obtained.

In order to practice nonself observation, a yogi should first have a thorough, rational understanding of how the erroneous concept of self arises, and how it can be eliminated. For this purpose, the very tedious and awkward Buddhist formulas, such as the five aggregates, the twelve entrances, and the eighteen elements, were developed.

First, since the self is considered to be an eternal, definite, and indivisible unity, the antidote to this idea is to emphasize that there is no such entity, but instead there are only aggregates. For instance, when we analyze the so-called self, we find only a momentary, ever-changing, flowing, psycho-physical complex of aggregates (components). Hence, we have first the aggregate of form, which includes all the bodily organs, such as the eye, ear, brain, etc. Going one step further, we examine the mental aspects, in which we cannot find a definite, indivisible entity. Instead, we find conceptions, feelings, impulses, and mental awareness.

Another approach to analyze the so-called self is to regard it as an illusion created by the impact of sense-objects upon sense-organs. One such analysis is the formula of the twelve *āyatanas*, literally translated as 'entrances', which are composed of the six sense-organs and the six sense-objects. (The six sense-organs should not be treated merely as biological organs. They refer to the sense-organs–consciousness complex). For example, the "form" of an object impresses itself upon ("enters") the eye and generates sight, and so forth with the other senses. This also includes the mind, which has dharmas, or things in general, for its objects. The fact that the sense data, impinging upon the sense-organs, generate mental awareness indicates that there is no entity called "self" who perceives objects. Rather, there is a continuous, fluctuating *process of seeing* caused by the combination of various factors.

Another device is the less confusing group of eighteen elements: the six organs, the six objects, and the six consciousnesses.

The reader should bear in mind that the entrances and elements do not differ in content, but simply in the method of analysis. Above all, it should be stressed that these three major devices (the aggregates, entrances, and elements) are for the purpose of nonself observation leading to spiritual liberation. (G.C.)

Ajātaśatru. Son of King Bimbisāra of Magadha. Abetted by the rebellious Devadatta, he usurped the throne, imprisoned his parents, and starved them to death. After he had conquered and annexed neighboring states, laying the foundation for the unification of India, he became afflicted with a skin disease. Remorseful, he went to the Buddha to repent his sin and take refuge in him. After the Buddha's parinirvāṇa, King Ajātaśatru sponsored the five hundred Arhats to collect the Buddha's teaching. Indian Buddhism is greatly indebted to the converted King Ajātaśatru for its prevalence and prosperity.

Ajita. 'The Invincible One'; an epithet of Maitreya.

Akaniṣṭha Heaven. The highest heaven in the Realm of Form.

ālayavijñāna. *See* "store consciousness."

all-knowing wisdom (Skt. *sarvajña*). The Buddha's wisdom of omniscience. Because the Buddha is the embodiment of perfection, his wisdom is also perfect. It is of two types: vertical and horizontal. The former is penetrative wisdom, knowing the underlying truth, or suchness, of all things. The latter is all-embracing wisdom, knowing the forms and characteristics of all dharmas.

Amitābha Buddha. The "Buddha of Infinite Light," also called Amitāyus. See Chapter 18.

Ānanda. A cousin, and long-time attendant, of Śākyamuni Buddha. Ānanda was noted for his great learning and was present at most of the Buddha's preachings. He was said to remember all the sūtras, and to have recited them at the time of their compilation.

Anāthapiṇḍada, Garden of. A garden in the Jeta Grove near Śrāvastī, where Śākyamuni Buddha gave numerous sermons. So named because it was donated to the Buddha by the elder Anāthapiṇḍada. *See* "Jeta Grove."

Arhat. A saint who has fully realized the truth of nonself and eradicated all passions and desires. One who has reached the highest stage of enlightenment in Hīnayāna Buddhism.

arising (Skt. *utpatti* or *utpāda*). This word appears frequently in Mahāyāna texts, often in the negative form. It denotes the appearance, production, or coming into being of a thing or event. According to the emptiness (*śūnyatā*) view, that which arises from dependent generation is by nature empty, hence all arising things are illusory (*māyā*).

asura. A demi-god often grouped with the devas (gods) in the five planes of existence. Asuras, though they have great good fortune, are known for their quarrelsomeness and jealousy toward the devas. Female asuras are beautiful and male ones ugly.

Avalokiteśvara (Ch. 觀自在菩薩). A Bodhisattva who will come to the aid of anyone who invokes his name. This Bodhisattva is the embodiment of the compassion of all Buddhas. He appears in many sūtras and tantras, and plays an important role in most Mahāyāna activities. Avalokiteśvara is worshipped in either a male or a female form in the various Buddhist countries.

Ayodhyā. The capital of Kosala.

bardo (Skt. *antarābhāva*, Tib. *bar-do*). The intermediate stage between death and rebirth.

bhikṣu. *See* "monk."

bhikṣuṇī. *See* "nun."

bhūmi. *See* Numerical Glossary, "ten stages of a Bodhisattva."

birth by transformation. When a being is suddenly born with all the sense-organs and limbs of a complete body, without depending on anything such as an egg or a womb, he is said to be born by transformation, or born ethereally. All hell-dwellers, devas, and beings in the bardo; some dragons, garuḍas, and hungry ghosts; and humans born at the very beginning of a kalpa are born in this manner.

The Chinese for this term is 化生; it is difficult to find an exact equivalent in English for it. Some scholars use 'birth by transformation', 'metamorphic birth', or 'miraculous birth', but none of these are completely accurate. Since the major portion of sentient beings are 化生, it cannot be considered "miraculous" at all, or even magical—it is a common phenomenon in the cosmos. We use the term 'birth by transformation' or 'ethereal birth'.

blessings. The Chinese term 福德, a translation of the Sanskrit word *puṇya*, has a variety of meanings and usages, as do karma, dharma, bodhicitta, etc., and it is impossible to translate it correctly into English. We translate it as virtue, merit, fortune, blessing, blessed deed, meritorious deed, and so forth in different contexts. However, the reader should bear in mind that none of these translations is a completely satisfactory one.

When translated as 'blessing', it should not be understood in the theological sense, i.e., as that which is bestowed by the grace of God. The blessings or fortunes in the Buddhist sense are caused by one's own karma or previous actions.

bodhi. *See* "enlightenment."

bodhicitta. The thought of, or spirit of, enlightenment (also: thought on, or in, enlightenment). Generally, it refers to the initial motivation of a Mahāyāna Buddhist who aspires to the attainment of Buddhahood for the benefit of all sentient beings. As soon as one arouses this aspiration, and makes a formal vow to carry out the Bodhisattva's acts, one is considered to be a Bodhisattva, a 'being for enlightenment'. This initial aspiration and determination may be called the "thought of enlightenment." When one reaches the first stage of enlightenment, he no longer stays in saṁsāra, but is fully absorbed in the actualization of enlightenment. Hence, like all other Bodhisattvas who have reached any of the ten stages (*bhūmis*), he can be said to possess "mind in enlightenment." Bodhicitta seems to have many degrees of profundity and application, but the Sanskrit word by itself does not suggest these distinctions.

bodhi-mind. The same as "bodhicitta."

Bodhisattva. One who aspires to the attainment of Buddhahood and devotes himself to altruistic deeds, especially deeds that cause others to attain enlightenment. *See also* "bodhicitta."

Bodhisattva in his last existence. A Bodhisattva who will achieve Buddhahood in this very lifetime. An example would be Śākyamuni Buddha after he was born as Prince Siddhārtha and before he achieved Buddhahood under the bodhi-tree.

A Bodhisattva in his last existence is different from a Bodhisattva who has attained the candidacy for Buddhahood in that the latter will achieve Buddhahood in his *next* lifetime. An example of the latter would be Śākyamuni Buddha when he was in the Tuṣita Heaven, awaiting his birth to Queen Māyā.

Bodhisattva-Mahāsattva. A Bodhisattva who has reached the advanced stages of enlightenment.

bodhi-seat. The seat upon which the Buddha sat during his enlightenment, under the bodhi-tree. All Buddhas are enlightened upon a bodhi-seat, according to tradition.

bodhi-site. The place where a Buddha is enlightened.

bodhi-tree. The tree under which a Buddha sits during his enlightenment. Sometimes it symbolizes Buddhahood.

Brahmā. The god who, in the Hindu view, created the world. In Buddhism, one of the major gods. When uncapitalized, the word indicates the corresponding god of any particular world, not only the Brahmā of this world.

brahmacārin. A brāhmin who practices spiritually pure acts, such as celibacy, diligent study, refraining from taking intoxicants, and so on. A person who is undergoing the training of the first of the four stages of a brāhmin.

Brahmā Heaven. A dhyāna heaven in the Realm of Form where the god Brahmā dwells, according to Buddhist (not Hindu) tradition.

brāhmin. A Hindu priest and scholar. Brāhmins have the highest social rank in the fourfold caste system in Hindu tradition.

Buddha. A Supremely Enlightened One, or 'Awakened One'. According to Mahāyāna tradition, Buddha Śākyamuni is the present one in a series of Buddhas, past and future.

Buddha-Dharma. The all-encompassing principle about reality as expounded by the Buddha. *See* "Dharma."

Buddha-land. A universe in which a particular Buddha dwells and teaches.

Buddha-nature. The basic, quintessential nature of sentient beings, which is identical with the nature of Buddha, without any differentiation whatsoever. Sentient beings wander in saṁsāra because they do not realize their Buddha-nature. The complete unfoldment of Buddha-nature is supreme enlightenment itself. Thus, Buddha-nature is also the seed of Buddhahood.

Buddha-vehicle. The Great Vehicle, or Mahāyāna.

candidacy for Buddhahood. A Bodhisattva is said to be a candidate for Buddhahood when he achieves the stage from which Buddhahood is only one lifetime away; that is, he will take only one more birth before he achieves Buddhahood.

For example, Bodhisattva Maitreya, who will succeed Śākyamuni Buddha as the Buddha of our world, has attained candidacy for Buddhahood.

Another term, 'a Bodhisattva who will achieve Buddhahood in his next lifetime', is an equivalent of 'a Bodhisattva who has attained candidacy for Buddhahood'. *See also* "Bodhisattva in his last existence."

causation. *See* "dependent generation."

clear Dharma-eye. The enlightened vision which clearly sees the four noble truths (for Hīnayāna), or the truth of the nonarising of dharmas (for Mahāyāna). In the *Mahāratnakūṭa Sūtra*, this term mainly applies to Hīnayāna. *See* "Stream-enterer."

compassion. Sympathy for people who suffer, and the will to end their sufferings. Mahāyāna Buddhism greatly emphasized compassion, along with wisdom. These two form the outstanding Mahāyāna virtues, sometimes called the "two-in-one" (compassion-wisdom). The infinite compassion of the Buddhas and Bodhisattvas is reflected in their constant attempt to succor sentient beings.

conditioned dharmas (Skt. *saṁskṛta*). Phenomena which appear to arise due to causes and conditions; things which are transient and changeable.

concentration. *See* "śamatha."

craving (Skt. *rāga* or *kāma*). Also 'desire', one of the major defilements. The basic worldly instinct of grasping, especially manifested in lust, avarice, and greed.

defilements (Skt. *kleśa*). The passions and ignorance that cause one to wander in saṁsāra and hinder one from reaching enlightenment. Sometimes called "afflictions," which emphasizes the effects of defilements. One list of the basic defilements names six: desire, hatred (or anger), ignorance (or delusion), arrogance, doubt, and wrong views. *See also* Numerical Glossary, "three poisons."

delusion (Skt. *moha*). Also translated as 'ignorance' or 'blindness'.

demon (Skt. *māra*). The personification of any defilement or negative tendency which hinders one from practicing the Dharma. The beings in the Paranirmita-Vaśavartin Heaven are also called "demons," or "celestial demons," for they are supposed to hinder practioners of the Dharma. *See* Numerical Glossary, "four demons."

dependent generation. Since all things in the phenomenal world are brought into being by the combination of various causes and conditions, they are relative and without substantiality or self-entity. From the transcendental viewpoint, this absence of self-entity is called emptiness; from the phenomenal viewpoint, it is called dependent generation, and is the central doctrine of Buddhism that denies the existence of any form of eternal or substantial being. When applied to sentient beings' endless lives in saṁsāra, it becomes the twelve links of dependent origination (q.v.).

In the *Mahāratnakūṭa Sūtra*, we often find passages connecting emptiness with dependent generation, or causation; however, no clear explanation is provided, for the author of the sūtra assumes that the emptiness-causation relationship is understood by the readers. For those to whom it is not obvious, the following may be helpful:

1. All things in the phenomenal world are found to consist of and to depend on other things. For example, a book consists of paper, ink, and binding. Apart from these parts, there is nothing to be called "book." The paper, ink, and binding, too, can be dissected into molecules and other particles. Everything in the world is divisible, so there are no real entities. Therefore, objects are merely name conglomerates of dependent parts with imputed, not real, existence. In this sense, all products of dependent generation are empty.
2. All entities of dependent generation are perceived to exist in time. The classic justification for calling them empty from this viewpoint is that the present does not remain, the past has gone, and the future has not yet come.
3. All things are in continual flux, and momentarily changing, perishing as soon as they arise. Since things are momentary, they have no duration, and that which is without duration cannot be said to be truly existent.
4. From the functional viewpoint, a thing may also change. (For example, if we use a chair to feed a fire, it is no longer a "chair," but "fuel.") Thus there is nothing with real existence to be termed "chair."
5. From different viewpoints, a thing may be regarded in a totally different manner. For example, what is H_2O to the chemist is something to drink for one who is thirsty, and a place to dwell for a fish. Therefore, "water" is not a definite thing, as we would think. It is relative to the viewpoint or sphere from which it is regarded.

For these reasons, all products of dependent generation are said to be empty. (G.C.)

dependent origination. *See* Numerical Glossary, "twelve links of dependent origination."

deva. A celestial being, or god. Gods are on the highest of the five planes of existence in saṁsāra, and enjoy long life and celestial pleasure. When the rewards for their previous virtuous karmas end, however, they must fall from the heavens to be reborn in other realms. Therefore, they also suffer greatly. Buddhists are urged not to strive for temporary heavenly bliss, but for permanent liberation or enlightenment.

Devadatta. Cousin of Śākyamuni Buddha, whom he rivaled and attempted to thwart. For his wicked designs on the Buddha he is said to have been swallowed up alive in hell; nevertheless, he is predicted to become a Buddha as Devarāja.

deva-ear. One of six miraculous powers. Supernatural hearing is the ability to hear the sounds of humans and nonhumans, distant and near sounds, and so on. The degree of this power differs according to one's karmic reward or yogic achievement.

deva-eye. *See* Numerical Glossary, "six miraculous powers," and "five kinds of eyes."

devaputra. Literally, "son of the gods," but seems generally to denote a celestial being who resides in a particular heaven.

dhāraṇī. 1. A synonym for mantra, spell, or incantation; 2. the capability of holding in mind the vast amount of the Buddha's teachings; 3. extraordinary memory and comprehension.

Dharma. The teaching given by the Buddha; the moral principles; the truth; the all-encompassing principle that governs all manifestations of things and events; transcendental reality. (It is capitalized to distinguish it from 'dharma', which refers to any thing or phenomenon.)

dharma. A thing, phenomenon, event, attribute, being—a general term for anything regarded as an event or "entity." Some Buddhist scholars disagree that 'dharma' means a thing in general, and hold that the term denotes one of the 75 particular dharmas mentioned in the Abhidharma literature. In Mahāyāna texts, however, 'dharma' clearly denotes a thing or phenomenon of any kind.

Dharma-body. *See* Numerical Glossary, "three bodies of the Buddha."

dharmadhātu. Literally, "the realm of dharmas." However, in Buddhist texts it has four meanings:

1. The nature or essence of dharmas (the same as tathatā), which is the unifying, underlying reality regarded as the ground of all things, both noumenal and phenomenal.
2. Infinity; the all-embracing totality of the infinite universes as revealed before the Buddha's eyes.
3. In certain sūtras, denotes one of the eighteen elements: the dharma-element; that is, the mental objects (dharmas).
4. The infinite universe per se.

The reader should bear in mind that 'dharmadhātu' may have any of the above four meanings.

Dharma-door. A figurative term for a specific doctrine, implying that it is an entry-way to understanding of the Dharma.

Dharma-eye. *See* Numerical Glossary, "five kinds of eyes."

Dharmakāya. *See* Numerical Glossary "three bodies of the Buddha."

Dharma-nature. The quintessence, or true nature, of all things. Same as 'emptiness', 'suchness', 'reality', or 'dharmadhātu'; in some schools, 'Buddha-nature'.

dharma-nature. The apparent nature of phenomena, or the nature of a particular thing.

Dharma-realm. *See* "dharmadhātu."

Dharma-wheel. "Turning the Dharma-wheel" is a figurative expression for preaching the Dharma. An eight-spoked wheel is the symbol of the Dharma.

dhyāna (Ch. 定 or 禪定). An equivalent of samādhi in Buddhism. We find that, in many Mahāyāna sūtras, these two words are used interchangeably. Some Buddhist scholars are of the opinion that 定 is exactly samādhi. The difference lies perhaps in the fact that dhyāna stresses the unifying aspect. Samādhi is considered the highest state of yogic achievement in Hinduism. However, in Buddhism there are innumerable kinds of samādhis. In reading Buddhist scriptures, one should bear in mind that the usage of the word samādhi is quite different from that of the Hindu tradition. *See also* "meditation" and Numerical Glossary, "four dhyānas."

dhyāna heavens. This refers to the four dhyāna heavens of the Realm of Form and the four dhyāna heavens of the Realm of Formlessness. Each of the first four contains four heavens; together with the four formless dhyāna heavens, they total 20. According to tradition, one who attains certain kinds of meditation will be reborn in the dhyāna heavens, but he will not stay there eternally. The dhyāna heavens are still in the realms of saṁsāra.

Dhyāna of the Cessation of Feelings and Thoughts. A state of pure concentration in which one's mind and mental functions stop arising. It is achieved by parting with the defilements of the formless dhyānas. The saints who abhor the fatigue of the distracted, fluctuating mind in saṁsāra can temporarily enter this dhyāna, and thereby immediately dwell in a state similar to that of nirvāṇa. This should not be confused with the dhyāna of no thought, which belongs in the fourth dhyāna heaven of the Form Realm.

Dīpaṁkara Buddha. The Buddha who prophesied Śākyamuni's attainment of enlightenment. According to legend, in a past life when Śākyamuni Buddha was still treading the Bodhisattva-path, he brought some lotus flowers to offer to Dīpaṁkara Buddha, and spread his hair over a puddle so the ancient Buddha could pass it unsoiled. Upon doing that, he attained the Realization of the Nonarising of Dharmas and received the prophecy of his attainment of Buddhahood.

discrimination (Skt. *vikalpa*). The fundamental cause of saṁsāra: the mental function of distinguishing things. In reality, all phenomena are one and empty. The phenomenal world appears to exist as a result of discrimination. Transcendental wisdom goes beyond discrimination, reaching the realm of equality and nondifferentiation.

dragon (Skt. *nāga*). A mythical snakelike being, usually said to be living in the oceans. Dragons are believed to have miraculous powers and to cause rain to fall in the world.

elements (Skt. *dhātu*, Ch. 界). *See* "aggregates"; *See also* Numerical Glossary, "eighteen elements," and, in other contexts, "four elements."

emptiness (Skt. *śūnyatā*). The void or insubstantial nature of everything; the central teaching of Buddhism. Through realization of emptiness one attains liberation and the perfections of Buddhahood. Emptiness is not a nihilistic void, but a wondrous state wherein dynamic events and dramas can take place. True realization of emptiness is a state free of all types of clinging, a state encompassing all and unifying all.

enlightenment (Skt. *bodhi*). In the Mahāyāna sense, enlightenment is the awakening to the primordial, fundamental truth of suchness (*tathatā*) and to the innate Buddha-nature in all beings. To be enlightened is to dwell in the constant, living realization of one's own Buddha-nature, as well as that of other beings. *See also* "supreme enlightenment."

entrances (Skt. *āyatana* Ch. 入). *See* "aggregates," and Numerical Glossary, "twelve entrances."

equality. A "characteristic" of the reality of all dharmas, which are one, nondual, undifferentiated, and not to be discriminated. Equality is often illustrated by empty space.

eternalism. *See* Numerical Glossary, "two extreme views."

ethereal birth. This refers to all 化生 , or metamorphic births, such as those of devas, asuras, hungry ghosts, and inhabitants of hell, the Pure Land, and the bardo. *See* "birth by transformation."

field of blessings. A figurative term for someone who is worthy of offerings. Just as a field can yield crops, so people will obtain blessed karmic results if they make offerings to one who deserves them. There are many kinds of "fields of blessings": monks, enlightened beings, parents, the poor, etc., including animals.

gandharva. A mythical spirit that feeds on fragrance and gives forth a fragrant odor. Gandharvas are Indra's musicians.

garuḍa. A mythical bird with strong, large wings. It feeds on dragons.

gāthā. A stanza, a set of verses.

giving. *See* Numerical Glossary, "six pāramitās."

god. *See* "deva."

good planes of existence. The states of gods, asuras, and humans are the three "good planes of existence." These beings are not subject to as much suffering as are animals, hungry ghosts, and hell-dwellers. In the three good planes, one has the opportunity to practice the Dharma; one cannot do so in the lower states.

good roots (Skt. *kuśalamūla*). Virtuous deeds accumulated in past or present lives which contribute to one's practice and realization of the Dharma.

Great Vehicle. *See* "Mahāyāna."

Heaven of the Thirty-Three. A heaven in the Realm of Desire, with thirty-two deva kings presided over by Indra, thus totaling thirty-three; located at the summit of Mt. Sumeru.

hell. Hell in Buddhism is actually a purgatory. It is not a hell in the Christian sense, because it is not permanent. Although the duration of life in hell may be long, depending on the gravity of one's karmic offenses, eventually it will be terminated, and the hell-dweller will once more be born in higher planes of existence.

Hīnayāna. "Small Vehicle" or "Lesser Vehicle"; the early Buddhism. A term coined by Mahāyānists to distinguish this school of Buddhism from Mahāyāna. It is so called because the teaching of this school puts emphasis on one's own Liberation, whereas the teaching of Mahāyāna stresses the attainment of Buddhahood for all sentient beings. Hīnayāna is now prevalent in southeast Asia, while Mahāyāna has spread over the northern area from Nepal to Japan.

hungry ghost (Skt. *preta*). A denizen of one of the miserable planes of existence. Some hungry ghosts have huge stomachs which always burn with hunger, but tiny throats through which food cannot pass. One may be reborn in this state if he has extreme greed or avarice.

ignorance. *See* Numerical Glossary, "three poisons."

illusion (Skt. *māyā*). Things in the phenomenal world are not real or substantial, as ordinary people regard them to be. They are transient, momentary, indefinite, insubstantial, and subject to constant alteration. In reality they are like phantoms or hallucinations.

inapprehensible. The English word "apprehend" means "to seize, to perceive, to grasp mentally," and so forth. The Chinese phrase 不可得 does not exactly mean "inapprehensible," although it is close. 不可得 literally should be translated as "unobtainable" or "unattainable," which could apply both to the subjective perceiver or to the object which is perceived or grasped. Since we are unable to find a better word, we use "inapprehensible" throughout to translate 不可得. However, the reader is reminded that wherever "inapprehensible" appears, he should know that this denotes the complete absence of either the subject, i.e., the perceiver, or the perceived object, or both.

incantation (Skt. *mantra* or *dhāraṇī*). Sacred or holy sounds blessed by a Buddha or a Bodhisattva. By reciting mantras one may receive blessings and spiritual guidance, and obtain miraculous powers.

Indra. *See* "Śakra."

ingenuity (Skt. *upāya*). The ingenious, expedient, and even roundabout methods by which a compassionate Buddha or Bodhisattva teaches sentient beings and brings them to maturity. Also may be translated as 'skillful means.'

Jambudvīpa. The 'Continent of the Jambu Tree', so called because it is overlooked by a gigantic Jambu tree growing on the summit of Mount Sumeru. Jambudvīpa is the southernmost of the four continents, supposedly the world in which we humans live. It is said to be wide in the north and narrow in the south, shaped almost like a triangle. We now think it probably denotes the sub-continent of India.

Jeta Grove. A grove near Śrāvastī in India, originally owned by a Prince Jeta and donated to Śākyamuni Buddha. Site of a monastery, frequently the location of Dharma-preachings by the Buddha.

Jīva (or Jīvaka). A contemporary of the Buddha and an influential sponsor and protector of Buddhism. Son of King Bimbisāra by a concubine. On his birth he is said to have seized the acupuncture needle and bag. He became famous for his medical skill and was honored as the king of healers. 'Jīva' can be rendered as 'Life-Giving'.

kalpa. According to Hinduism, a kalpa is one day for Brahmā, and consists of 1,000 yugas (1 yuga = 4,320,000 years), altogether 4,320,000,000 years for mortals. However, in Buddhism, a kalpa generally indicates the length of time between the creation and recreation of a world or universe, spanning the period of a world's formation, existence, destruction, and nonexistence. There are different interpretations of measurement of a kalpa in Buddhism. It often simply denotes a very long period of time, similar to an aeon. There are small, medium, great, and incalculable kalpas.

karma. Literally, "action" or "deed." It also means the effect of a deed or deeds that survives death and contributes to the formation of one's next life. The "law of karma" asserts that virtuous or evil deeds of body, speech, and mind will inevitably bring corresponding results to the doer, in this or a future life. A group of people, such as a nation, may create a common karmic power that determines their fate or destiny; the whole cosmos and all sentient beings, by implication, are driven on and on in an endless circle by this mystical power.

karmic result. The natural reward or retribution for a deed, brought about by the law of karma. *See* "karma."

Kāśyapa. *See* "Mahākāśyapa."

Kāśyapa Buddha. One of the Buddhas who have appeared in this kalpa.

Kauśika. An epithet of Śakra.

kinnara (*kiṁnara*) A kind of mythical celestial musician. It has a horse-like head with one horn, and a body like that of a human. The males sing, and the females dance.

Kosala. A region in ancient India divided into Northern Kosala (the modern Oude) and Southern Kosala (the modern Central Provinces).

kṣatriya. One of the four Indian castes; the warrior and ruling class.

kumbhāṇḍa. A ghost shaped like a gourd or pot; or with a scrotum shaped thus. It devours the vitality of men.

Last Era. The third and final era of the presence of the Dharma in the world, when genuine Buddhism almost disappears. The first era is the period immediately following the Buddha's parinirvāṇa, when people teach and practice the true Dharma, and many can achieve various stages of genuine enlightenment. The second era begins when the

Dharma is taught and practiced in a "diluted" manner, but certain samādhis and realizations are still possible. In the third era, only the appearance of the Dharma remains, few care to practice it, and realization is extremely difficult to attain.

Lesser Vehicle. *See* "Hīnayāna."

liberation. Freedom from the suffering and entanglement of saṁsāra.

lion's roar. A figurative expression to denote the preaching of the Buddha or an advanced Bodhisattva. Such preaching can overcome all erroneous doctrines, just as a lion's roar can subdue all the beasts of the jungle.

lion-throne. A glorified throne adorned by lions, on which the Buddha may sit to preach. It is often depicted in Mahāyāna art.

long night. A figure of speech denoting the perdurable suffering and darkness of saṁsāra.

Mādhyamika. The "Middle Way" School of Buddhism, founded by Nāgārjuna and his followers. Its tenets are mainly based upon the Prajñāpāramitā Sūtra group, stressing the teaching of emptiness (*śūnyatā*).

Magadha. An ancient kingdom in central India, the center of Buddhism up to about A.D. 400. Rājagṛha was its capital city.

magical production. A miraculous feat such as the creation of forms out of nothing. Some gods and even humans can also effect magical productions. Therefore, such power is not evidence of enlightenment.

magically produced being. A being temporarily created for a specific purpose by the miraculous power of a Buddha or high Bodhisattva. Also, an illusory being conjured up by a magician.

magically produced Buddha (Ch. 化佛). An illusory Buddha-form produced with miraculous powers. This is different from the incarnated Buddha (Skt. *nirmāṇakāya*, Ch. 化身)—*see* Numerical Glossary, "three bodies of the Buddha." A magically produced Buddha or Bodhisattva is identical in form with an actual Buddha or Bodhisattva and can interact with sentient beings.

Mahākāśyapa. A chief disciple of Śākyamuni Buddha, foremost in the practice of austerities.

Mahāmaudgalyāyana. One of the Buddha's main disciples, who was noted for his powers to perform miraculous feats.

Mahāratnakūṭa Sūtra. Literally, "The Great Jewelled Pinnacle Sūtra," or "Jewelled Heap Sūtra," indicating that this sūtra is like a jewelled summit or a treasury of jewels.

Mahāyāna. The "Great Vehicle" of Buddhism, whose followers vow to attain enlightenment for the sake of delivering all other sentient beings from suffering. The spiritual hero of the Mahāyāna is the Bodhisattva (q.v.), in whom the virtues of wisdom and compassion are stressed and balanced.

mahoraga. A mythical being with a head shaped like a python, and a man-like body.

Maitreya. Literally, "the kind one"; a great Bodhisattva. The future Buddha after Śākyamuni, who will come to this world to teach the Dharma.

Mañjuśrī. The youthful Bodhisattva who is the embodiment of the wisdom of all Buddhas.

Māra. The chief demon, who usually creates hindrances to Dharma practice. Also called Pāpīyān.

māyā. *See* "illusion."

meditation (*dhyāna*). A state of pure concentration, in which the meditator and the object meditated upon are unified. Also, a general term for serene contemplation. There are numerous ways to meditate, but all of them are methods to purge unwholesome thoughts and desires, and to cause one to reach insight or realization of the highest wisdom.

We have translated 'dhyāna' as 'meditation' where the term is used in a general sense. When the more technical meaning is intended, we have retained the Sanskrit word. *See also* "dhyāna," "samādhi," and Numerical Glossary, "four dhyānas."

middle way. The "way" that falls on neither side of such extremes as nihilism and eternalism, asceticism and hedonism, being and nonbeing, saṁsāra and nirvāṇa, etc.

mindfulness (Skt. *smṛti*). 1. In Hīnayāna, it is a meditational device for practicing the nonself (*anātman*) doctrine; 2. in Mahāyāna, refers generally to the practice of holding to correct thought or a right mental state.

miserable planes of existence. The three lower states of saṁsāra: hell-dweller, hungry ghost, and animal. To be born in a miserable state is the result of evil karma committed in a past life. When the retribution for that karma is completed, one will again be born in a higher state.

monk. Usually refers to a fully ordained monk (Skt. *bhikṣu*).

Mount Gṛdhrakūṭa. "Vulture Peak," a mountain where the Buddha often preached, located near Rājagṛha in Central India.

Mount Sumeru. Also called Mount Meru. The mythical mountain of ancient Indian cosmology, located at the center of each world.

Muni. In Sanskrit this means a 'seer' or a 'sage'; from the Chinese it translates as 'He who is capable of doing virtuous things'. When used as a proper noun, it refers to the Buddha (cf. "Śākyamuni Buddha").

Nārāyaṇa. In Indian mythology, Nārāyaṇa is somewhat like an Indian version of Hercules. He is an immensely strong being.

nihilism. *See* Numerical Glossary, "two extreme views."

Nirmāṇakāya. *See* Numerical Glossary, "three bodies of the Buddha."

Nirmāṇarati Heaven. The heaven of "transformational delight." One of the heavens of the Realm of Desire, located above Mount Sumeru.

nirvāṇa. Originally meant total extinction of desire and suffering. Refers to the state of liberation through full enlightenment. In Mahāyāna, nirvāṇa is classified into four categories:

1. nirvāṇa with residue, the state of a person who has realized the nature of nirvāṇa, but has not yet eliminated the five aggregates;
2. nirvāṇa without residue, wherein the aggregates have been eliminated;
3. svabhāva nirvāṇa (Ch.自性涅槃), the primeval nirvāṇa which is always present, whether we realize it or not; and
4. nonabiding nirvāṇa, in which one abides neither in saṁsāra nor in ultimate quiescence. This is the nirvāṇa of the Buddhas and the highest Bodhisattvas.

nonarising (Skt. *anutpāda*). Never coming into being; not truly existing. *See* "arising."

nonregression. One who has reached realization of emptiness or Buddha-nature will never regress from the Bodhisattva-path. Nonregression sometimes simply denotes an advanced stage of aspiration and practice from which one will never retreat. Some sources say nonregression is not reached until the eighth of the ten stages of a Bodhisattva (q.v., Numerical Glossary).

Nonreturner (Skt. *anāgāmin*). An enlightened being in the third stage of the four classes of Hīnayāna enlightenment, who will no more return to the Realm of Desire, but will be born in a heaven in the Realm of Form or Formlessness and attain Arhatship there.

nun. Usually refers to a fully ordained nun (Skt. *bhikṣunī*).

Once-returner (Skt. *sakṛdāgāmin*). An enlightened being in the second stage of the Hīnayāna path, who has realized the four noble truths and has eradicated a great portion of defilements. He will return to the human world for only one more rebirth before he reaches full realization of Arhatship.

outflow. Another name for defilement (q.v.).

Pāpīyān. *See* "Māra."

pāramitā. This can be translated as 'the perfection of . . .' or 'reaching the other shore by means of . . .'. It may have both meanings in Mahāyāna sūtras. 'Perfection' implies the positive aspect, whereas 'reaching the other shore' refers to the transcending aspect.

Pāramitā is the central practice of a Bodhisattva. It is sometimes divided into six or ten, making the six (or ten) pāramitās (q.v.).

Pāramitā practice is the cultivation of one's potential intelligence, love, and will. When all these three potential capacities, or "Buddha-seeds," are cultivated to perfection, pāramitā practice is completed.

Paranirmita-Vaśavartin Heaven. The dwelling place of Pāpīyān the Māra. The heaven of the "enjoyments of delights created by others." The sixth of the six heavens in the Realm of Desire.

parinirvāṇa. According to the Hīnayāna concept, one who realizes nirvāṇa in his lifetime will enter parinirvāṇa at death, and will not be reborn. For the Mahāyāna view, *see* "nirvāṇa."

path (Skt. *marga*). The way along which a Dharma practitioner proceeds toward liberation and enlightenment.

patience. *See* Numerical Glossary, "six pāramitās."

passions. *See* "defilements."

play-words. Words derived from delusive thinking and discrimination, which have no real value or serve no practical purpose for religious awakening. Thus, in the Buddhist sense, all metaphysical speculations and all forms of "isms" are play-words, for they are not only useless in one's search for truth, but are also not conducive to liberation or realization. Play-words, in "emptiness literature," often refer to any form of clinging to extremes, such as the doctrines of nihilism, eternalism, monism, dualism, and so forth. Any views that imply 'self-nature' (*svabhāva*) clinging, and are expressed in words, are play-words.

power of knowing others' minds. Also rendered as "power of reading thoughts." One of the six miraculous powers.

Prajñāpāramitā. The pāramitā (or perfection) of wisdom. Also refers to an important and voluminous sūtra group in which the doctrine of emptiness (*śūnyatā*) is taught.

Prajñā is translated as intuitive wisdom, in contrast to the mundane wisdom of conceptual knowledge. Prajñā wisdom is a transcendental, mystical, immediate, and direct "seeing" or realization of the ultimate truth. This "seeing" or realization, however, has many degrees of profundity and thoroughness.

That which the prajñā wisdom knows or sees is the omnipresent suchness (*tathatā*), which is sometimes called the prajñāpāramitā of reality. The intuitive wisdom is sometimes called the prajñāpāramitā of observation; that is; the intuitive or transcendental seeing by the subject. Third is the prajñāpāramitā of words, the expression of the other two through symbols. Thus, the Prajñāpāramitā literature is merely the prajñāpāramitā of words.

Prātimokṣa. The rules of conduct for guarding against evil bodily and verbal actions, thereby freeing one from the bondage of defilements. It is slightly different from the Vinaya in that it refers to a specific set of rules practiced by both monks and laymen, while the Vinaya deals only with the discipline prescribed for ordained monks.

Pratyekabuddha. In Hīnayāna, a self-enlightened being who has contemplated dependent origination and thus attained realization of truth without a teacher.

precepts. Vows of moral conduct taken by lay and ordained Buddhists. There are five vows for lay Buddhists, and 250 for fully ordained monks. *See also* Numerical Glossary, "five lay precepts."

Rājagṛha. An ancient city in Central India, located near the present-day town of Rājgir. The capital of the ancient domain of Magadha.

rākṣasa. A terrifying ghost or demon with a black body, red hair, and green eyes. Rākṣasas are reputed to be devourers of humans.

reality. Can refer to the eternal, unchanging, all-embracing truth, which is no other than suchness, dharmadhātu or the Dharma-body; in other contexts it refers to "reality" in the ordinary sense.

realization. Immediate, direct "seeing" or "perception" of reality, in contrast with mere conceptual understanding, which is indirect and secondary.

Realization of Compliance with the Dharma-Truth. The word 'realization' is here a rendering of the Skt. *kṣānti*, Ch. 忍, which literally means 'patience' or 'tolerance', but in extension also means 'acceptance', 'recognition', or 'realization'. In the process of practicing the Buddha's teaching, there is a stage where one recognizes, accepts, and complies with the truth that there is no self-substance in any dharma, even though one may not yet have fully realized the prajñā truth. The actual acceptance of and compliance with this truth is called the Realization of Compliance with the Dharma-Truth. When one goes a step further and realizes fully this truth of suchness, he is said to attain the Realization of the Nonarising of Dharmas.

Realization of the Nonarising of Dharma (Skt. *anutpāda-dharma-kṣānti*). 'Realization' here is a free translation of *kṣānti*, which literally means 'patience', or 'patient acceptance'. An enlightened Bodhisattva of the eighth stage (some say the first) has fully realized the nonarising nature of all things. Therefore, he is said to have truly achieved the Realization of the Nonarising of Dharmas.

realization of the profound Dharma. The direct, immediate realization of the profundity and emptiness of dependent generation. It is of several kinds, including "the Realization of Compliance with the Dharma-Truth" (q.v.).

Realm of Desire. *See* Numerical Glossary, "three realms."

Realm of Form. *See* Numerical Glossary, "three realms."

Realm of Formlessness. *See* Numerical Glossary, "three realms."

refuge. The Buddha, the Dharma, and the Saṁgha are the three refuges in which Buddhists put their trust and reliance.

relics (Skt. *śarīra*). When an enlightened being dies and his body is cremated, certain incombustible particles are found in the ashes. This phenomenon is believed to be due to the enlightened being's accomplishments. Such relics are said to have been left by innumerable saints and Bodhisattvas. Naturally, true relics of the Buddha are most treasured.

renunciation. According to Buddhist teaching, the first step toward serious Dharma-practice is to renounce all worldly ties and desires.

right action (also, right concentration, effort, livelihood, mindfulness, speech, thought, and view). *See* Numerical Glossary, "eightfold noble path."

ṛṣi. A yogi or saint who dwells in a hermitage.

Sahā World. This world, in Buddhist cosmology. 'Sahā' means 'to bear'; thus, sentient beings of this world, like the earth which bears all burdens, must bear misery, defilement, and contention.

Śakra. The chief god of the Heaven of the Thirty-Three. A protector of Buddhism. An epithet of Indra. When uncapitalized, 'śakra' indicates the equivalent god of any world, not Śakra of the Sahā World. In a billion-world universe there are one billion Heavens of the Thirty-Three and one billion śakras.

Śākya Clan. One of the important clans of the kṣatriya caste in Northern India, of which Gautama Buddha was a member.

Śākyamuni Buddha. Śākyamuni literally means 'Sage of the Śākya Clan'. The name of the Buddha of this age, also called Gautama.

samādhi. It usually denotes the particular, final stage of pure concentration. In Mahāyāna Buddhism, however, samādhi is defined more generally: there are innumerable samādhis, not only of static, serene nature, but also with the dynamic and powerful functions of those who abide in spiritual realization. *See also* "dhyāna."

Samantabhadra. A well-known Bodhisattva whose particular eminence is the adherence to profound vows of great compassion. He is also the embodiment of all Buddhas' vows (or bodhicitta) and practices.

samāpatti. This word literally means 'coming together', 'meeting', or 'completion'. It is practically a synonym of dhyāna.

Chinese Buddhologists interpret samāpatti as 等至 : "through the effort of equilibrium, the state of samādhi is reached." 'Equilibrium' here implies overcoming both distraction and drowsiness in meditation practice, thus reaching the state of perfect absorption, or samādhi.

śamatha. A meditational technique to calm the mind to a state of tranquility and concentration. It is practically an equivalent of dhyāna.

Saṁbhogakāya. *See* Numerical Glossary, "three bodies of the Buddha."

Saṁgha. *See* Numerical Glossary, "Three Jewels."

saṁsāra. The relentless cycle of repeated birth and death in which ordinary, unenlightened sentient beings are deeply entangled. The cause of saṁsāra is the presence of defilements, particularly desire, hatred, and ignorance.

Śāriputra. One of the principal disciples of the Buddha, sometimes said to be the wisest among them.

Satori. The Japanese pronunciation of the Chinese word "Wu" (q.v.).

self. Sentient beings consider the five aggregates (q.v.) to constitute a unitary self or ego (*ātman*). This wrong idea derives from deep-rooted clinging.

self-entity. *See* "self-nature."

self-nature (Skt. *svabhāva*). Things in the phenomenal world are transient, momentary, and without duration; hence they have no self-nature (self-entity) or individual substantiality. However, ordinary beings cling to the idea of existence or being (*bhāva*). This clinging is called clinging to self-nature or self-entity. However, in some contexts, 'self-nature' is used in an approbative sense to denote the Buddha-nature within one's mind. This usage is particularly common in Zen literature.

sentient being. Any living being who has a consciousness.

Sixth Heaven. The Paranirmita-Vaśavartin Heaven (q.v.), highest of the heavens of the Desire Realm.

skillful means. *See* "ingenuity."

spirit of enlightenment. *See* "bodhicitta."

spiritual provisions. Provisions for the journey toward Buddhahood. They are twofold: provisions of wisdom (right understanding of the Dharma) and provisions of merit (virtuous deeds).

śramaṇa. A religious devotee, often a forest-dwelling ascetic, who attempts to purify his defilements; also, a monk.

Śrāvaka. Literally "hearer." One who has heard the Buddha's teaching. Generally denotes a follower of the Hīnayāna path. Śrāvaka is also translated as 'disciple'.

Śrāvaka-vehicle. *See* Numerical Glossary, "three vehicles."

Śrāvastī. A city and ancient kingdom in India, now called Rapetmapet. The Jeta Grove, where Śākyamuni Buddha often preached, is near Śrāvastī.

stage beyond learning. The highest stage of Hīnayāna development, that of Arhatship. From the viewpoint of the Hīnayāna, no more learning or striving for religious achievement is needed when one reaches this stage.

stage of learning. One who has attained one of the first three stages of Hīnayāna enlightenment before Arhatship—the stages of a Stream-enterer, a Once-returner, and a Non-returner—is said to be in the stage of learning. According to Mahāyāna, although such a person has reached some enlightenment, it is not complete; there is still more to be learned and a fuller realization to be gained.

stage of nonregression. A stage of spiritual achievement in which a Bodhisattva will never fall away from the stage of a Bodhisattva and become a Śrāvaka, Pratyekabuddha, or ordinary person. There are different opinions concerning in which stage a Bodhisattva attains the stage of nonregression. Generally, however, it refers to the time when one acquires the enlightened vision which *sees* the truth of nonarising (the first stage), or when one attains the Realization of the Nonarising of Dharmas (the first or the eighth stage).

stages of a Bodhisattva. *See* Numerical Glossary, "ten stages of a Bodhisattva."

stillness. He who realizes suchness perceives that all dharmas never arise or come into being, and are "still" or peaceful through and through without disturbance.

store consciousness (Skt. *ālayavijñāna*). The fundamental consciousness that underlies all other consciousnesses; it holds all memories, forms a personality, sustains the efficacy of karma, and makes religious progress and enlightenment possible. It is the seed of the Dharma-body, the foundation of both saṁsāra and nirvāṇa. One of the most important doctrines of the Yogācāra school.

Stream-enterer (Skt. *śrota-āpanna*). One who has reached the first Hīnayāna stage, so called because he has entered the "stream," the undefiled noble path. Alternate translation of this term is "one who goes against the stream," in which case the stream represents the current of saṁsāra. Upon acquiring the enlightened vision which clearly sees the four noble truths, one eradicates all the delusive views of the three realms, such as the view of a real self. *See* "clear Dharma-eye."

stūpa. A monument built over relics (q.v.) of Buddhas, Bodhisattvas, or saints.

subdue. To subdue a sentient being is to cause him or her to abandon passions and other hindrances to enlightenment. Subdue here does not mean to vanquish by force, but to convert by skillful persuasion, training, or the like.

Subhūti. One of the Buddha's chief disciples, known best for his ability to expound the doctrine of emptiness, and for his achievement of non-contention.

suchness (Skt. *tathatā*). Also, 'thusness'. Refers to Buddha-nature, Dharma-body, reality, dharmadhātu, Dharma-nature. Reality is beyond all words and descriptions, so in referring to it, Buddhists often use the term 'suchness'. A frequent synonym is *bhūtatathatā*, 'reality-suchness'.

suffering. *See* Numerical Glossary, "four noble truths."

śūnyatā. *See* "emptiness."

supreme enlightenment (Skt. *anuttara-samyak-saṁbodhi*). Same as supreme Buddhahood. The Sanskrit means 'unexcelled perfect enlightenment'; i.e., the perfect wisdom which comprehends truth that is attained only by a Buddha, in contrast to the different grades of enlightenment attained by Bodhisattvas and saints.

sūtra. A preaching of the Buddha as recorded in documents. In the early stages of Buddhist history, sūtras were memorized, and only in later times were they written down.

svabhāva. *See* "self-nature."

Tathāgata. Literally, "the Thus-Come One." A title of the Buddha. It may mean he who has come and gone as have former Buddhas—that is, he imparts the same truth and follows the same path to the same goal. The Mahāyāna interprets Tathāgata differently, as one who has attained full realization of suchness (*tathatā*), and who thus neither comes from anywhere, nor goes anywhere.

Tathāgata-embryo (Skt. *tathāgata-garbha*). 1. The innate Buddha-nature (suchness) obscured temporarily by defilements; 2. the "storehouse" of the Buddha's teaching.

Tathāgata-vehicle. Synonymous with the Bohisattva-vehicle and the Mahāyāna ('Great Vehicle'). 'Bodhisattva-vehicle' is used when referring to the cause and practice, while 'Tathāgata-vehicle' is used when referring to the result. *See also* Numerical Glossary, "three vehicles."

Theravāda Buddhism. The 'sect of the elders'. The sole survivor of the eighteen sects of the original Hīnayāna school. Sometimes called the Southern School, as it is prevalent in Southeast Asia. *See* "Hīnayāna."

thusness. *See* "suchness."

true Dharma. The equivalent of the Chinese 正法; here 'true' is *dam* in Tibetan and *sat* in Sanskrit. The Tibetan word *dam* can be translated in a number of ways: 'true', 'eminent', 'outstanding', 'holy', 'right', etc.

truth. In these texts, usually denotes transcendental truth, or emptiness (*śūnyatā*); also, Buddha-nature, or suchness.

Tuṣita Heaven. The heaven in the Realm of Desire from which each Buddha descends to earth. The 'heaven of contentment'. The present dwelling-place of Maitreya, the next Buddha of our world.

uḍumbara flower. An uḍumbara tree is said usually to bear fruit without flowers. Once in a very long period of time it is said to bloom; hence, the uḍumbara flower is a symbol of the rare appearance of a Buddha.

ultimate quiescence (Ch. 寂滅). This term, as it appears in the *Mahāratnakūṭa Sūtra,* has a variety of meanings. Often it denotes the absolute, quiescent, still, and undisturbed

Dharma-nature, which is the pure transcendency above the distrubances of saṁsāra. Secondly, it can refer to the realization of the above-mentioned Dharma-nature. Also, in some cases it refers to the stage of the Dhyāna of the Cessation of Feelings and Thoughts. Furthermore, it refers to the nature of nirvāṇa, which is no other than the nature of all dharmas.

ultimate truth (Skt. *paramārtha*). Also may be translated as 'first truth'. Connotes the supreme truth, in contrast to mundane or expedient truth.

unconditioned dharmas (Skt. *asaṁskṛta*). Those dharmas which do not arise or cease, and are not transient. Examples: nirvāṇa, the Dharma-body, and the ancient philosophical concept of space.

Unexcelled Vehicle. The highest vehicle to Buddhahood; in these texts, the Mahāyāna.

Uninterrupted Hell (Skt. *avīci*). The worst of the hot hells, in which suffering, death, and painful rebirth are continuous until the retribution for the suffer's evil karma is exhausted, at which time he or she will be reborn in a higher plane of existence.

universal monarch (Skt. *cakravartin*). In the Indian mythological history of the world, a universal monarch occasionally appears who is supposed to be a most powerful and meritorious king capable of ruling the entire world.

Upāli. A leading disciple of Śākyamuni Buddha, famous for his knowledge of Vinaya and his observance of it. He was a member of the śūdras, the lowest Indian caste.

upāya. *See* "ingenuity."

vajra. Literally "a diamond." Usually a symbol of the indestructible nature of Buddha's wisdom. A weapon to conquer demons and protect Buddhism.

vehicle (Skt. *yāna*). *See* Numerical Glossary, "three vehicles."

vigor. *See* Numerical Glossary, "six pāramitās."

Vinaya. The precepts for monks and nuns, designed to help them eliminate defilements. One of the major sections of the Buddhist canon.

vipaśyanā. The intuitive observation on the prajñā truth practiced in Mahāyāna meditations.

wisdom. *See* Numerical Glossary, "six pāramitās."

Worthy Kalpa (Skt. *bhadrakalpa*). A kalpa is the period of time between the creation and recreation of a world or universe. In Mahāyāna tradition, the present kalpa is called "Worthy" because during its span, 1,000 Buddhas will appear to save sentient beings.

wrong views. Usually, views belonging either to nihilism or eternalism. May also mean wrong ideas about religious teachings. *See also* Numerical Glossary, "four wrong views."

Wu. The Chinese word *Wu* (悟) can be translated as awakening, cognition, realization, or enlightenment. It is widely used by the Zen Buddhists to denote the intuitive realization of the Buddha-nature within one's own mind.

yakṣa. A swift, powerful kind of ghost or demon, which is usually harmful, but in some cases is a protector of the Dharma. Some yakṣas, according to Buddhist mythology, live in the air, and some on land.

Yama Heaven. One of the heavens in the Realm of Desire, the 'heaven of constant joy' is located above the Heaven of the Thirty-Three.

Yama Realm. A dismal place where the dead are judged.

Yogācāra. The name of a Buddhist school, founded probably in the fourth century by the brothers Asaṅga and Vasubandhu. It advocates the doctrine of "mind only"; i.e., all dharmas of saṁsāra and nirvāṇa are projections of one's own mind; hence everything in the external world is merely an illusion.

Zen Buddhism. 'Zen' is the Japanese mispronunciation of the Chinese name *Ch'an*, which in turn derives from the Sanskrit *dhyāna*. A school of Mahāyāna Buddhism in China founded by Bodhidharma. This school stresses the cultivation of intuitive wisdom. An extremely influential Buddhist sect in China and Japan.

Numerical Glossary

One Vehicle (Skt. *Ekayāna*). According to Mahāyāna Buddhism, the true teaching of the Buddha is provided only in one vehicle—the Mahāyāna. Other vehicles, such as those of the Śrāvaka and Pratyekabuddha, are only expedient teachings for the unprepared. The One Vehicle is also called the Buddha-vehicle.

two extreme views.

1. Nihilism: considering that things do not exist in any sense, even the delusory manifestations of the world; also, the tenet that nothing continues after death, i.e., the denial of the doctrine of reincarnation.
2. Eternalism: believing that there is true existence of real being in objects, or that there is some entity that exists forever.

two vehicles. The Śrāvaka-vehicle and the Pratyekabuddha-vehicle, which together constitute what is called Hīnayāna.

three bodies of the Buddha (Skt. *trikāya*).

1. Dharmakāya: The Dharma-body, or the 'body of reality', which is formless, unchanging, transcendental, and inconceivable. Synonymous with suchness, or emptiness.
2. Saṁbhogakāya: the 'body of enjoyment', the celestial body of the Buddha. Personification of eternal perfection in its ultimate sense. It "resides" in the Pure Land, and never manifests itself in the mundane world, but only in the celestial spheres, accompanied by enlightened Bodhisattvas. Example: Vairocana in the *Avataṁsaka Sūtra*.
3. Nirmāṇakāya: the 'incarnated body' of the Buddha. In order to benefit certain sentient beings, a Buddha incarnates himself into an appropriate visible body, such as that of Śākyamuni Buddha.

   The incarnated body of the Buddha should not be confused with a magically produced Buddha. The former is a real, tangible human body which has a definite life span. The latter is an illusory Buddha-form which is produced with miraculous powers and can be withdrawn with miraculous powers. Both types of bodies are translated in Chinese as 化身; whereas in Tibetan texts, the distinction is rather clear: Nirmāṇakāya is translated as *sprul-sku*, and a magically produced being as *sprul-pa*.

three doors to liberation. Liberation is possible only through these three realizations:
1. All things are devoid of a self (emptiness).
2. There are no objects to be perceived by sense-organs (signlessness).
3. No wish of any kind whatsoever remains in the yogi's mind, for he no longer needs to strive for anything (wishlessness).

three groups. People are divided into three groups according to their inclinations and views (or achievement) *in the present life*. They are: first, the group decided to pursue bodhi; second, the group decided to pursue other faiths; and third, the undecided group.

According to Buddhism, in the ultimate sense every being will pursue bodhi sooner or later, in this life or in the future, and eventually will achieve supreme enlightenment. Therefore, people now belonging to the group decided to pursue other faiths or the undecided group will be in the first group in their future lives.

Three Jewels.
1. The Buddha—the supremely enlightened being.
2. The Dharma—the teaching imparted by Buddha.
3. The Saṁgha—the congregation of monks and nuns, or of genuine Dharma followers.

These three are said to be jewels because they can protect one, impart truth, and fulfill one's good wishes. They are also the refuges of Buddhist followers. Note: A Buddhist should take refuge in the "jewel-like" Saṁgha; i.e., the enlightened beings, not ordinary monks and nuns, though they should also be respected.

three periods of time. The past, present, and future.

three poisons. The major causes of saṁsāric suffering:
1. Desire (Skt. *kāma, rāga*, or *tṛṣṇā*): lust or greed. Broadly, to try to "get hold of" something, and to have more and more of it. In its most specific sense, *tṛṣṇā* refers to sexual craving. Desire can also mean avarice or any kind of attachment.
2. Hatred or anger (Skt. *dveṣa*): animosity, aversion, rejection of what displeases one or infringes upon one's ego.
3. Ignorance or delusion (Skt. *avidyā, moha*): In Hīnayāna, ignorance implies holding wrong views—clinging to nonself as self, etc. In Mahāyāna, there are two aspects: first, wrong knowledge; and second, lack of knowledge. Wrong knowledge is the same as the Hīnayāna concept. Lack of knowledge means all the hindrances to attaining the all-knowing wisdom of Buddhahood. Therefore, eradication of ignorance or delusion in Mahāyāna requires, on the one hand, elimination of wrong views, and on the other hand, the positive acquisition of all-knowing wisdom.

three realms (of saṁsāra). The Realm of Desire, the Realm of Form, and the Realm of Formlessness.

Sentient beings living in the Realm of Desire possess lust, hatred, jealousy, infatuation, and other passions. Within this realm there are six different planes of existence: gods, asuras, humans, animals, hungry ghosts, and hell-dwellers.

The Realm of Form contains sixteen heavens inhabited by various celestial beings who have certain accomplishments in one of the four dhyānas of form.

The Realm of Formlessness has four heavens, inhabited by those with different accomplishments in one of the four dhyānas of formlessness. The heavens both in the Realm of Form and in that of Formlessness are classified according to the depth of dhyāna attained in their former lives by the celestial beings who dwell there.

three vehicles. The three paths to enlightenment: the Śrāvaka-vehicle, the Pratyekabuddha-vehicle, and the Bodhisattva-vehicle (also called the Tathāgata-vehicle).

three wheels. Three components or spheres of an action: the actor, the object of the action, and the person who is affected by the action. For example, the three wheels of the action "giving" are: the giver, the gift, and the recipient. All three, the Buddha teaches, should be known as empty, devoid of self-nature. 'Wheels' suggests something that may destroy as well as move: when performing an action, one should crush attachment to these three spheres and at the same time, by riding on the emptiness of the three wheels, move towards perfection.

four bases of miraculous powers. 1. Strong aspiration; 2. vigor; 3. intense concentration; and 4. intense contemplation.

four continents. The four land areas centered around Mount Sumeru, according to ancient Buddhist cosmology: Jambudvīpa in the south, Pūrvavideha in the east, Aparagodāna in the west, and Uttarakuru in the north.

four currents. 1. Desire; 2. saṁsāric existence; 3. [wrong] views; and 4. ignorance. These are the defilements that sweep away the wholesome dharmas and cause sentient beings to drift and drown in the "torrential stream" of saṁsāra.

four demons (*māra*). 1. Defilements; 2. the aggregates; 3. death; and 4. the Māra of the Paranirmita-Vaśavartin Heaven (the sixth heaven in the Realm of Desire). These four are called demons because they bring suffering and impede one's Dharma-practice and liberation.

four deva kings. The rulers in the four directions of the lowest of the heavens in the Realm of Desire. Their names are: Vaiśravaṇa (in the north), Dhṛtarāṣṭra (in the east), Virūḍhaka (in the south), and Virūpāksa (in the west).

four dhyānas. Four stages of meditation that correspond with the dhyāna heavens (q.v.):
1. The first stage, in which one experiences joy and pleasure due to the relinquishment of desire and unwholesome thoughts.
2. The second stage, in which one feels joy and pleasure due to concentration (one-pointedness of mind), with all thoughts overcome.
3. The third stage, in which one dwells in subtle bliss due to the relinquishment of joy.
4. The fourth stage, in which one experiences equanimity and pure awareness, and all feelings of joy and bliss are absent.

four elements. The four basic constituents of matter: 1. earth (solid matter), 2. water (liquid), 3. fire (heat), and 4. air (energy or motion).

four fearlessnesses. There are two groups, one for Buddhas and one for Bodhisattvas.

For a Buddha:
1. fearlessly realizing all things;
2. fearlessly extinguishing all defilements;
3. fearlessly expounding all obstructions to liberation; and
4. fearlessly asserting the true path to liberation.

For a Bodhisattva:
1. fearlessly teaching the Dharma as he has learned it;
2. fearlessly teaching the Dharma according to sentient beings' different inclinations and spiritual ills;
3. fearlessly dealing with all arguments in teaching; and
4. fearlessly resolving sentient beings' doubts.

four fruits. These are the four stages of enlightenment in the Hīnayāna path, namely, the stage of the Stream-enterer, the Once-returner, the Nonreturner, and the Arhat (qq. v.).

four great oceans. In Buddhist cosmology, the four oceans on each of the four sides of Mt. Sumeru. In each ocean there is a continent (see "four continents").

four heavy transgressions (for a monk). 1. Killing, 2. stealing, 3. sexual misconduct, and 4. lying.

four immeasurables. 1. Kindness (*maitrī*), 2. compassion (*karuṇā*), 3. joy (*muditā*), and 4. equanimity (*upekṣā*).

four inducements. The four methods by which a Bodhisattva attracts people to the Dharma: 1. giving unsparingly; 2. using pleasant words; 3. always helping others; 4. comaradeship and accommodation.

four kinds of devotees. The four categories of Buddhist followers: 1. monks (*bhikṣus*); 2. nuns (*bhikṣunīs*); 3. laymen (*upāsakas*); and 4. laywomen (*upāsikās*).

four kinds of unhindered eloquence. 1. Unhindered eloquence in expressing the Dharma; 2. unhindered eloquence in explaining the meaning of the Dharma; 3. unhindered command of language; and 4. unhindered pleasure in preaching and debating the Dharma.

four kinds of unimpeded understanding. The same as the four kinds of unhindered eloquence, but taken from the viewpoint of the Bodhisattva's understanding.

four mindfulnesses. 1. Mindfulness of the body as impure; 2. mindfulness of feeling as suffering; 3. mindfulness of the mind as impermanent; and 4. mindfulness of dharmas as dependent, without self-entity.

four noble practices. To be content with: 1. simple clothing; 2. simple sustenance; 3. simple sleeping facilities; and 4. cultivation of virtues and severing of defilements.

four noble truths. The four fundamental truths taught by Buddha:

1. Life is suffering.
   a. This is so, first, because any pleasure or happiness has an ending; thus pleasure or joy is a prelude to eventual suffering. During the experience of pleasure, one is afraid of losing it, causing attachment and suffering.
   b. Most pleasures enjoyed by individuals involve suffering for other beings.
   c. In comparison with the ecstasy of samādhi and nirvāṇic joy, all saṁsāric pleasures are various forms of suffering. Therefore, from the viewpoint of enlightened beings, all saṁsāra is a raging fire, including whatever "pleasure" exists therein. (Cf. the Buddha's famous *Fire Sermon*.)
2. Defilements are the cause of suffering.
   a. When desire, the instinct to have and to possess, is fulfilled, it merely leads to further desire. Thus desire is bound to follow a pattern in which craving and greed expand continuously.
   b. Hatred, animosity, anger, jealousy, etc., are all instincts which exclude others instead of including them. This increases clinging to ego and aversion to others.
   c. Ignorance is the innate wrong view concerning the self and things: for example regarding the impermanent as permanent, what is really suffering as joy, what is not a self as a self, and what is impure as pure. Therefore, ignorance is the root cause of all suffering in saṁsāra.
3. There is a state in which all suffering is ended. All enlightened beings in Buddhism testify that there is a state called nirvāṇa, which is forever free from all sufferings and entanglements in saṁsāra. It is a state beyond words and descriptions, yet it can approximately be said to be filled with peace, joy, and ultimate meaning.
4. There is a correct path that leads to the cessation of suffering.
   a. Discipline, or keeping the precepts, results in the avoidance of thoughts and actions which hinder one's spiritual progress.
   b. Through meditation (*dhyāna*), ever-flowing discursive thoughts and passion-desires can be controlled. The ordinary state of mind is transformed into a

lucid, reflective, pure awareness. By the practice of meditation, great yogic joy, both physical and mental, is produced. One's intelligence, insight, compassion, and spiritual awakening are enhanced and elevated in all aspects.

c. Through intuitive wisdom; all precepts and dhyānas are the foundation for the nondiscursive, penetrating wisdom to observe the truth of no-self (*anātman*). In Mahāyāna, the penetrating intuitive wisdom is applied not only to no-self, but also to the Buddha-nature within and the totality of the dharmadhātu without. Thus, by eliminating innate, inborn ignorance, one reaches enlightenment.

four reliances. 1. Relying on the true meaning or spirit of a Dharma statement in a sūtra, not merely on the words of that statement; 2. relying on the teaching, not on any person; 3. relying on intuitive wisdom, not on intellectual understanding; and 4. relying on sūtras that give ultimate teachings, not on those which preach expedient teachings.

four right efforts. 1. Ending existing evil; 2. preventing new evil; 3. causing new virtue; and 4. increasing existing virtue.

four wrong views. 1. Considering what is really impermanent to be permanent; 2. considering what is really suffering to be joy; 3. considering what is not a self to be a self; and 4. considering what is impure to be pure.

four yokes. An equivalent of the "four currents" (q.v.); namely, desires, saṁsāric existence, [wrong] views, and ignorance.

five aggregates. The aggregates of which a human being is composed are: form, feeling, conception, impulse, and consciousness. The physical body is made of various materials with color, shape, and so forth; it belongs to the category of form. Pain, joy, etc. belong to the aggregate of feeling. Conceptions are the notions or abstract ideas formulated by the mind. Impulses are the mental drives, which include the will and all kinds of emotions. Consciousness is the faculty of awareness; for example, the eye-consciousness is the faculty of awareness of forms; the ear-consciousness, of sounds; the nose-consciousness, of smells; the tongue-consciousness, of tastes, and the mind-consciousness, of dharmas. *See also* main Glossary, "aggregates."

five covers. Five dharmas that can "cover" the mind and prevent wholesome dharmas from arising. They are: 1. desire; 2. anger; 3. drowsiness; 4. excitability and remorse; and 5. doubt.

five depravities (or five filths). Some historical periods, such as the present era, are times of chaos and degeneration. The five are: 1. the filth of kalpa, when the historical cycle is in a period of degeneration; 2. the filth of views, when all sorts of wrong views prevail; 3. the filth of passions, when desire, hatred, and other defilements are predominant; 4. the filth of human condition, when people are more often miserable than happy; and 5. the filth of life span, when the human life span diminishes, or, we may say, when the leisure and opportunity to practice the Dharma become more rare.

five desires. *See* "five sensuous pleasures."

five grave offenses. 1. Patricide; 2. matricide; 3. killing an Arhat; 4. maliciously causing the Buddha to bleed; and 5. causing disharmony in the Saṁgha. Such offenses are said to lead to birth in the Uninterrupted Hell.

five kinds of eyes. 1. The physical eye; 2. the deva-eye of celestial beings, which can be developed by humans through meditation and which can see even in darkness, at great distances, and through obstacles; 3. the wisdom-eye, which sees the emptiness of all things, is possessed by all enlightened beings, including Śrāvakas and Pratyekabuddhas; 4. the Dharma-eye of Bodhisattvas, which sees the truth of the Buddha's teaching and all Dharma-doors; and 5. the Buddha-eye, which nondualistically sees everything in its real nature, and which is possessed only by Buddhas.

five lay precepts. The vows taken by lay Buddhists, prohibiting: 1. killing; 2. stealing; 3. lying; 4. sexual misconduct; and 5. intoxication.

five miraculous powers. The first five of the six miraculous powers (q.v.).

five planes of existence (in saṁsāra). Usually six: the states of being a god, an asura, a human, an animal, a hungry ghost, and a hell-dweller. In the sequence of five, gods and asuras are grouped together. Sentient beings in saṁsāra circle within these planes of existence according to their karma. To be liberated is to be freed from destined rebirth in these planes.

five powers. Powers arising from the five roots (q.v.).

five roots. 1. Faith; 2. vigor; 3. mindfulness; 4. concentration; and 5. wisdom. They are called "roots" because they can give rise to other wholesome dharmas.

five sensuous pleasures. Saṁsāric delights of the senses: forms, sounds, scents, tastes, and textures. The awakened ones see them as impure and painful by nature, but ordinary sentient beings consider them to be pleasurable.

six consciousnesses. The consciousnesses associated with the eye, ear, nose, tongue, body, and mind.

six kinds of quakes. Three of movement: shaking, rising, and surging; and three of sound: banging, roaring, and crackling.

six miraculous powers. 1. The deva-eye, supernatural vision capable of seeing things even in darkness, at great distances, and through obstacles; 2. the deva-ear, supernatural hearing; 3. the power to know others' thoughts; 4. the power to know the past lives of oneself and others; 5. the power to perform miracles, such as appearing anywhere at will; and 6. the power to totally eradicate defilements.

six pāramitās. *Pāramitā* (q.v. in Glossary) means 'reaching the other shore', 'perfection', or 'consummation'. There are usually six, and sometimes ten, pāramitās. The six (explained in many places in the text) are the pāramitās of giving, discipline (precepts), patience, vigor, meditation (*dhyāna*), and wisdom (*prajñā*).

In the case of ten pāramitās, four more are added to these six, in order to correspond with the ten stages of a Bodhisattva. The four are the pāramitās of ingenuity, vows, power, and knowledge (*jñāna*).

six periods. The six divisions of a day, three for daytime and three for nighttime: the first, middle, and last parts of the day (morning, midday, and afternoon); and the first, middle, and last parts of the night.

six sense-objects. Forms, sounds, smells, tastes, textures, and mental objects.

six sense-organs. The eye, ear, nose, tongue, body, and mind.

six ways to foster harmony in a monastery. The cultivators of pure living in a monastery will dwell in mutual respect and harmony if they do the following: 1. engage in the same bodily deeds; 2. engage in the same verbal deeds; 3. engage in the same mental deeds; 4. keep the same precepts; 5. share material offerings; and 6. hold the same views. The very word for the monastic community (Saṁgha) implies harmony.

seven factors of enlightenment. 1. Mindfulness; 2. discriminative investigation of Dharma; 3. vigor; 4. joy; 5. ease of body and mind; 6. concentration; and 7. equanimity.

seven treasures. Gold, silver, lapis lazuli, crystal, agate, red pearl, and carnelian.

For a universal monarch, the seven treasures are: the golden wheel; white elephants; dark steeds; beautiful pearls; fine women; able ministers; and loyal generals.

eight adversities. The eight conditions which prevent one from seeing the Buddha or hearing the Dharma: 1. rebirth in hell; 2. rebirth as a hungry ghost; 3. rebirth as an animal; 4. rebirth in Uttarakuru (the continent where life is easy, so that one who lives there is not motivated to seek Dharma); 5. rebirth in the long-life heavens (where one is also not motivated to seek Dharma); 6. rebirth with impaired faculties; 7. rebirth as a worldly philosopher clever at sophistry; and 8. rebirth in a world where there is no Buddha.

eight divisions of divinities. 1. Gods (devas), 2. dragons (nāgas), 3. yakṣas, 4. gandharvas, 5. asuras, 6. garuḍas, 7. kinnaras, and 8. mahoragas. (For descriptions of each of these beings, see main Glossary.)

eightfold liberation. Liberation from attachment to forms and desires through eight kinds of meditation:

1. Because of having an internal sensual desire for pleasant forms, the yogi meditates on external impure forms.
2. Having no internal desire for forms, the yogi meditates on external forms in order to stablize the vision of impurities.
3. Since there is no impurity remaining, the yogi meditates on pure light of different colors.
4. The yogi meditates on endless space.
5. The yogi meditates on infinite consciousness.
6. The yogi meditates on nothing whatsoever.
7. The yogi meditates on neither conception nor nonconception.
8. The yogi experiences the cessation of conception and feeling.

eightfold noble path. The fundamental teaching of Śākyamuni Buddha; the path to liberation:

1. Right view: understanding the four noble truths (q.v.) and having penetrative insight into reality (emptiness).
2. Right thought: having only thoughts which are unselfish, loving, and nonviolent.
3. Right speech: abstention from lying, slander, harsh or abusive language, and idle chatter.
4. Right action: conducting oneself in moral, peaceful, and honorable ways, and keeping the basic precepts.
5. Right livelihood: living honorably by a profession which is in no way harmful to sentient beings, and avoiding such livelihoods as trading in weapons, intoxicants, or poisons.
6. Right effort: following the four right efforts (q.v.).
7. Right mindfulness: practicing the four mindfulnesses (q.v.).
8. Right concentration: developing one's meditation according to the four dhyānas (q.v.).

These eight are sometimes classified in three groups: ethical conduct (right speech, action, and livelihood); mental discipline (right effort, mindfulness, and concentration); and wisdom (right view and thought).

eight merits (said of water). 1. Clarity and cleanliness; 2. coolness; 3. sweetness; 4. lightness; 5. moistening power; 6. ability to give comfort; 7. ability to quench thirst; and 8. ability to improve health.

eight special precepts. Vows which may be taken by lay Buddhists for a day's span or longer: 1. not killing; 2. not stealing; 3. not engaging in sexual activity; 4. not lying; 5. not taking intoxicants; 6. not singing, dancing, or wearing ornaments; 7. not sitting or sleeping on a high bed; and 8. not eating after noon.

eight worldly winds. Four pairs of influences which hinder one's Dharma-practice: praise and blame, gain and loss, happiness and suffering, and fame and ridicule.

ten directions. The eight points of the compass (north, south, east, west, northeast, southeast, northwest, and southwest), plus the zenith and nadir. "In the ten directions" is a figurative term meaning "in all space."

ten evil deeds. 1. Killing, 2. stealing, 3. sexual misconduct, 4. lying, 5. harsh speech, 6. words causing rifts, 7. frivolous chatter, 8. covetousness, 9. ill will and 10. holding wrong views.

ten good deeds. Abstaining from each of the ten evil deeds (q.v.).

ten pāramitās. The six pāramitās (q.v.) plus: ingenuity, vows, power, and knowledge.

ten powers. There are two groups, one for Bodhisattvas and one for Buddhas.

For Bodhisattvas, the ten are: 1. the power of profound aspiration; 2. the power of ever-increasing profound aspiration; 3. the power of ingenuity; 4. the power of wisdom; 5. the power of vows; 6. the power of vehicle; 7. the power of practice; 8. the power of miraculous feats; 9. the power of enlightenment; and 10. the power of turning the Dharma-wheel.

For a Buddha:

1. He knows wisely, as it really is, the possible to be possible, and the impossible to be impossible.
2. He knows wisely, as they really are, the karmic results of past, future, and present actions, and of the undertaking of actions with regard to place and cause.
3. He knows wisely, as they really are, the various elements in the world.
4. He knows wisely, as they really are, the various dispositions of other beings and persons.
5. He knows wisely, as they really are, the higher and lower faculties of other beings and persons.
6. He knows wisely, as it really is, the way that leads everywhere.
7. He knows wisely, as they really are, the trances, deliverances, concentrations, and meditational attainments, as well as their defilements, purifications, and the conditions in which they are well established in purity.
8. He recollects his various previous lives.
9. With his deva-eye, he knows the decease and rebirth of beings as they really are.
10. Through extinction of the outflows, he dwells in the attainment of the liberation of his heart and wisdom, which is without outflows, and which has, in this very life, been well known and realized by himself.

Another source gives the following list for the ten powers of a Buddha:

1. He knows wisely, as it really is, what is right or wrong.
2. He knows wisely, as they really are, the cause and effect of the karmic results of past, present, and future.
3. He knows wisely, as they really are, the order and grades of all dhyānas, liberations, samādhis, and other meditational attainments.
4. He knows wisely, as they really are, the higher and lower faculties of sentient beings.
5. He knows wisely, as they really are, the various understandings and aspirations of sentient beings.
6. He knows wisely, as they really are, the various conditions and circumstances of sentient beings.
7. He knows wisely, as they really are, which ways and practices lead to which destinations and consequences (rebirth as a human, a god, etc., or attainment of sainthood), and also the cause and effect of such courses.
8. He remembers, as they really are, past lives.
9. With his deva-eye, he knows wisely, as it really is, the decease and rebirth of sentient beings, and the maturity of good and evil karma in future lives.
10. He knows wisely, as it really is, the present extinction of defilements by himself and others.

ten stages of a Bodhisattva. These ten stages (Skt. *bhūmi*) are the ten levels of Bodhisattva enlightment: 1. the Stage of Great Joy; 2. the Stage of Stainless Purity; 3. the Stage of Illumination; 4. the Stage of Intense Wisdom; 5. the Stage of Invincible Strength; 6. the Stage of Direct Presence; 7. the Far-Reaching Stage; 8. the Stage of Immovable Steadfastness; 9. the Stage of Meritorious Wisdom; and 10. the Stage of the Dharma Cloud.

twelve entrances. The six sense-organs (eye, ear, nose, tongue, body, and mind) and their corresponding objects (forms, sounds, scents, tastes, textures, and mental objects). *See also* main Glossary, "aggregates."

twelve links of dependent origination (Skt. *dvādaśāṅga-pratītya-samutpāda*). Interlinked factors of saṁsāra: ignorance, action, consciousness, name and form, the six sense-organs, contact, feeling, craving, grasping, becoming, birth, and old age and death.

eighteen elements—Usually translated as 'eighteen realms', but this translation is misleading. The eighteen are: a. the six sense-organs (eye, ear, nose, tongue, body, and mind); b. the six sense-objects (forms, sounds, scents, tastes, textures, and mental objects); and c. the six consciousnesses (associated with the six organs).

Actually, there are *six* "realms," each composed of an organ, an object, and a consciousness (for example, the eye, form, and the eye-consciousness constitute one realm). Since there are six such realms, each composed of three elements, a better translation of the term for the entire group is 'eighteen elements', rather than 'eighteen realms'.

The eighteen elements should not be confused with the four elements of matter, i.e., earth, water, fire, and air. *See also* main Glossary, "aggregates."

eighteen unique qualities of a Buddha. These eighteen virtues are exhibited exclusively by a fully enlightened Buddha: 1. unerring bodily actions; 2. unerring verbal actions; 3. unerring mental actions; 4. impartiality; 5. never losing concentration; 6. remaining equanimous in spite of his awareness of all dharmas; 7. unfailing zeal; 8. unfailing diligence; 9. unfailing mindfulness; 10. unfailing wisdom; 11. unfailing liberation; 12. unfailing knowledge and awareness derived from liberation; 13. all bodily deeds guided by wisdom; 14. all verbal deeds guided by wisdom; 15. all mental deeds guided by wisdom; 16. unimpeded knowledge of the past; 17. unimpeded knowledge of the present; 18. unimpeded knowledge of the future.

thirty-two auspicious signs. The major signs adorning the visible body of a Buddha or that of a universal monarch. Some examples are: a protuberance on the crown; a curling, white hair between the eyebrows; a golden complexion; a long, broad tongue; a halo ten feet in radius; even, close, white teeth; an excellent voice, etc.

thirty-seven ways to bodhi. These are: a. the four mindfulnesses; b. the four right efforts; c. the four bases of miraculous powers; d. the five roots; e. the five powers; f. the seven factors of enlightenment; and g. the eightfold noble path. (See definitions of each group, listed separately.)

sixty-two [wrong] views. A group of doctrines based on the view of a self.

eighty minor signs. Bodily attributes of a Buddha, more subtle than the thirty-two auspicious signs. Examples: copper-colored nails, thin and lustrous; long, slender fingers;

youthful complexion; a soft body; lips colored like a red, bright gourd; face like a full, clear moon; emitting fragrance from the pores and mouth; deportment as awesome as that of a lion; graceful and steady gait, etc.,

billion-world universe.

a. One of the innumerable systems in Buddhist cosmology, containing a billion worlds or solar systems. Each world has its sun and moon, Mount Sumeru, eight concentric rings of mountains separated by eight concentric rings of oceans, and four inhabited continents. A world reaches up to the first dhyāna heaven in the Realm of Form.

b. A thousand worlds constitute a thousand-world universe, which reaches up to the second dhyāna heaven. A thousand thousand-world universes constitute a million-world universe, which reaches up to the third dhyāna heaven. A thousand million-world universes constitute a billion-world universe, which reaches up to the fourth dhyāna heaven, the highest heaven in the Realm of Form.

DATE DUE

APR 23 '87			
MAY 9 '87			